VOLUME 1: TO 1650

Connections

A World History

Third Edition

Edward H. Judge
Le Moyne College

John W. Langdon
Le Moyne College

PEARSON

Boston   Columbus   Indianapolis   New York   San Francisco   Amsterdam
Cape Town   Dubai   London   Madrid   Milan   Munich   Paris   Montréal   Toronto
Delhi   Mexico City   São Paulo   Sydney   Hong Kong   Seoul   Singapore   Taipei   Tokyo

Editorial Director: Craig Campanella
Editor-in-Chief: Dickson Musslewhite
Executive Editor: Brita Nordin
Program Manager: Deb Hartwell
Managing Editor: Denise Forlow
Project Manager: Gail Cocker
Editorial Assistant: Veronica Grupico
Team Lead, Program Management: Maureen Richardson
Team Lead, Project Management: Denise Forlow
Senior Manufacturing and Operations Manager:
  Mary Fischer
Operations Specialist: Mary Ann Gloriande
Executive Field Marketing Manager: Wendy Albert

Director of Field Marketing: Jonathan Cottrell
VP Marketing, Business & Arts: Maggie Moylan
Product Marketing Manager: Jeremy Intal
Marketing Assistant: Frank Alarcon
Digital Product & Project Manager: Liz Roden Hall
Senior Art Director: Maria Lange
Cover Design: Pentagram
Cartographer: Maps.com
Full-Service Project Management and Composition:
  Lumina Datamatics, Inc.
Printer/Binder: R.R. Donnelley/Owensville
Cover Printer: Lehigh-Phoenix Color/Hagerstown
Text Font: 9.5/13 Palatino LT Pro

Cover images: The Saint Elizabeth's Day Flood, Master of the St Elizabeth Panels, Anonymous, c. 1490–c. 1495, oil on panel, h 127.5 cm × w 110.5 cm. Purchased with the support of the Vereniging Rembrandt, Public Domain/Rijksmuseum.

Credits and acknowledgments borrowed from other sources and reproduced, with permission, in this textbook appear on appropriate page within text and on page 396–398.

Library of Congress Cataloging-in-Publication Data
Judge, Edward H.
   Connections: a world history / Edward H. Judge, Le Moyne College John W.
Langdon, Le Moyne College. — Third edition.
      pages cm
   Includes index.
   ISBN 978-0-13-384274-6 (combined)
   ISBN 978-0-13-384144-2 (volume 1)
   ISBN 978-0-13-384139-8 (volume 2)
   ISBN 0-13-384274-6 (combined)
   ISBN 0-13-384144-8 (volume 1)
   ISBN 0-13-384139-1 (volume 2)
   1. World history.   I. Langdon, John W.   II. Title.
   D21.J73 2012
   909—dc23
                                                         2014036623

10 9 8 7 6 5 4 3 2 1

Combined Volume:
ISBN 10: 0-13-384274-6
ISBN 13: 978-0-13-384274-6
Instructor's Review Copy:
ISBN 10: 0-13-386030-2
ISBN 13: 978-0-13-386030-6
Volume 1:
ISBN 10: 0-13-384144-8
ISBN 13: 978-0-13-384144-2

Books a la carte Volume 1:
ISBN 10: 0-13-384960-0
ISBN 13: 978-0-13-384960-8
Volume 2:
ISBN 10: 0-13-384139-1
ISBN 13: 978-0-13-384139-8
Books a la carte Volume 2:
ISBN 10: 0-13-384953-8
ISBN 13: 978-0-13-384953-0

PEARSON

Brief Contents

Contents

Connecting with World History Students: Why We Wrote This Book

We are two professors who love teaching world history. For the past quarter century, at our middle-sized college, we have team-taught a two-semester world history course that first-year students take to fulfill a college-wide requirement. Our students have very diverse backgrounds and interests. Most take world history only because it is required, and many find it very challenging. Helping them to understand it and infecting them with our enthusiasm for it are our main purposes and passions.

This is an exciting time to be teaching world history. In an age of growing global interconnectedness, an understanding of diverse world cultures and their histories has never been more essential. Indeed, it is increasingly apparent that students who lack this understanding will be poorly prepared to function in modern society or even to comprehend the daily news.

At the same time, the teaching of world history has never seemed more challenging. As the amount of material and its complexity increase, students can get bogged down in details and inundated with information, losing sight of the overall scope and significance of the human experience. Conveying world history to college students in a comprehensible and appealing way, without leaving them confused and overwhelmed, is one of the toughest challenges we face.

To help meet this challenge and better connect with our students, we have written a compact, affordable world history text that is tailored to meet their needs. In developing this text, we pursued several main goals:

First, because students often find it difficult to read and process lengthy, detailed chapters, we sought to write a text that is *concise and engaging*, with short, interesting chapters that focus on major trends and developments.

Second, since students often see history as a bewildering array of details, dates, and events, we chose a unifying theme—connections among world societies—and grouped our chapters to reflect the growth of such connections from regional to global.

Third, having seen many students struggle because they lack a good sense of geography, we included more than 200 maps—far more than most other texts—and provided a number of other features designed to help readers better understand and process the material.

A Concise and Readable Text

Since even the best text does little good if students do not read it, we endeavored above all to produce one that is concise and readable. We addressed ourselves to first-year college students, using a simple, straightforward narrative that tells the compelling story of the peoples and societies that preceded us and how they shaped the world. To avoid drowning our readers in a welter of details, we chose to take an introductory approach rather than an encyclopedic one. With this text, students will become familiar with the most important trends, developments, and issues in world history, and they will gain an appreciation for the vast diversity of human societies and endeavors.

To make our book less overwhelming and more accessible to students, we have limited most chapters to about 10,000 words and divided each chapter into short topical subsections. By writing concise chapters, we have enabled average students to read them in an hour or so. By keeping subsections short, we have partitioned the text into manageable segments, so that readers can process material before they move on. By furnishing learning objectives at the start of each chapter and a review section at the end, with focus questions and prompts for journaling and shared discussion throughout, we have highlighted major issues and themes while keeping in sight the overall trends and developments..

Connections in World History

In our teaching we have found that many students find world history confusing and overwhelming, in part because they have no overall framework for understanding it. To help them sort things out, we have focused our text on a central theme of connections among world societies. By stressing this theme, we have sought to maintain a sense of coherence and purpose, and to give our readers a framework that will help them to make sense of history.

Rather than divide our text into ancient, medieval, and modern eras, an arrangement that works for Europe but has limited value elsewhere, we have instead grouped our chapters into two overlapping ages: an Age of Regional Connections, lasting until about 1650 C.E., and an Age of Global Connections, dating from roughly 1500 to the present. Each age is then subdivided into three eras, reflecting the expansion of connections from regional to global levels. This framework, summarized in our Introductory Overview ("Making Sense of World History") and in our table of contents, is designed to give students the "big picture" of world history that they often lack.

Within each era are chapters that provide both regional and global perspectives, stressing not only each culture's distinct features but also its connections with other regions and cultures. Readers thus can readily appreciate both the diversity and the interconnectedness of human societies.

Within each chapter, on almost every page, are focus questions and journaling prompts that highlight major issues and our connections theme. Readers thus can delve into details while also keeping sight of the overall context.

An Extensive and Consistent Map Program

Many students approach world history with only a rudimentary understanding of world geography, and maps are a crucial tool in understanding world history. Our text contains an abundance of carefully crafted maps, designed within each chapter to build one upon another. With more than 200 maps throughout the book, *Connections* offers one of the most extensive map programs of any world history survey textbook.

We have worked very hard to make the maps clear and to place them where readers can refer to them without turning pages. As much as possible, the maps use colors, fonts, labels, and other markers consistently, so that students will find these features familiar from one map to the next. And in the digital version of our text, many of the maps are dynamic and interactive, with features that animate changes over time and enable readers to focus specifically on each major element in turn.

Finally, the map captions were carefully written to clarify the maps, to connect them with surrounding text, and to guide the students' attention to the most important elements in that map. Each map caption includes a question to help students consider critical issues.

Features

We have incorporated in our text a carefully selected set of features, each chosen with this basic guideline in mind: Will it help students to better envision, understand, and process the material they are reading?

VISUALS   We provide an ample array of photos and other visuals, selected to illustrate developments explicitly discussed in the text. To ensure that students will connect the text with the images, we have placed them in the margins near the passages that they illustrate, and in the digital text we have provided photo galleries with multiple images and caption.

PRONUNCIATION GUIDES   Since students often struggle to pronounce unfamiliar names and places, we have placed parenthetical pronunciation guides immediately following first use of such names and places in the text.

CHAPTER-OPENING VIDEOS AND VIGNETTES   Each chapter opens with a vignette designed to capture the reader's interest and introduce the chapter's main themes. In the digital text these vignettes are part of a chapter-opening video titled **Introduction: What to Look for in This Chapter**, which also highlights key themes and learning objectives.

PRIMARY SOURCE DOCUMENT EXCERPTS   To acquaint students with primary sources and illuminate materials covered in our text, we have provided concise excerpts from selected historical sources, in feature boxes placed where the document is discussed in the text, with marginal links to additional documents in the digital version.

CHAPTER REVIEW SECTIONS   Each chapter has a comprehensive end-of-chapter review section that incorporates the following features:

- **Consequences and Connections.** This feature, furnished via video in the digital version, provides a concise overview of the chapter's main themes, highlights key connections, and puts them in historical perspective.

- **Key Concepts.** Key concepts are highlighted in boldface in the text and listed at the end of each chapter with page references to facilitate review. In the digital version, readers can click on any key concept in the Chapter Review to be taken to the section of the text that discusses that concept in depth.

- **Ask Yourself.** A set of questions at the end of every chapter encourages further reflection and analysis of topics, issues, and connections considered in the chapter.

- **Key Dates and Developments.** Each chapter contains a comprehensive chronology that lists the key dates and developments, helping students to see at a glance the sequence of important events. In the digital text, this feature is delivered with an interactive timeline.

A Student-Centered Textbook

For a number of years, we and our colleagues have used our text, with highly encouraging results. Since the book is affordable and readily accessible, especially in its digital version, students can easily access it in the classroom or almost anywhere else. Since chapters are concise and engaging, we find that students actually read them before coming to class and thus are better prepared to understand and discuss key issues. Students who completed questionnaires or wrote reviews of our chapters said they found them clear and compelling. By pointing out passages they found dry or confusing, these students also helped make the book more readable. We went to great lengths to create a text that is useful, accessible, and attractive to our students. For they, after all, are the reasons we wrote this book.

Ed Judge
judge@lemoyne.edu
John Langdon
langdon@lemoyne.edu

New to This Edition

- Learning objectives are provided at the outset of each chapter and at the start of every major section within.

- Focus questions are supplied throughout every chapter, with jounaling prompts also furnished in the digital version.

- Shared writing prompts, designed to encourage student collaboration, are furnished at the end of each chapter in the digital text.

- Many photos and illustrations have been added, with multiple photo galleries and numerous new images added to the digital text.

- The coverage of various topics, including early migrations to the western hemisphere and recent historical developments, has been updated and enhanced.

- Chapter-opening videos, entitled **Introduction: What to Look for in This Chapter**, have been added to each chapter in the digital version, each of them featuring compelling vignettes and stressing key themes and objectives.

- Videos that feature prominent scholars discussing major themes and important issues have been inserted throughout the text to enhance explanations and analyses.

- End-of-chapter videos, entitled **Consequences and Connections**, designed to emphasize key outcomes and reinforce our connections theme, have been added to each chapter review section in the digital version.

- Maps have been revised to make them easier to use and placed right by the sections that they illustrate, with animations and interactive features added to the maps in the digital version.

- Our **Key Concepts** feature has been revised and enhanced to facilitate in-depth explanation and discussion of important issues, ideas, conceptions, and developments.

- Interactive timelines and review exams have been added to chapter review sections in the digital text.

REVEL™

Educational technology designed for the way today's students read, think, and learn

When students are engaged deeply, they learn more effectively and perform better in their courses. This simple fact inspired the creation of REVEL: an immersive learning experience designed for the way today's students read, think, and learn. Built in collaboration with educators and students nationwide, REVEL is the newest, fully digital way to deliver respected Pearson content.

REVEL enlivens course content with media interactives and assessments—integrated directly within the author's narrative—that provide opportunities for students to read about and practice course material in tandem. This immersive educational technology boosts student engagement, which leads to better understanding of concepts and improved performance throughout the course.

Learn more about REVEL

http://www.pearsonhighered.com/revel/

Acknowledgments

In conceiving, composing, and bringing out this book, we are deeply grateful to the many people who helped us along the way. Our senior colleagues Bill Telesca and Fr. Bill Bosch, with whom we first taught world history, shared with us their many decades of experience as teachers and scholars. Our current colleagues, Doug Egerton, Bruce Erickson, Godriver Odhiambo, Holly Rine, Yamin Xu, Bob Zens, Tom Magnarelli, and Joshua Canale, have class-tested our book and provided us with feedback from their students and insights from their expertise in Atlantic World, Latin American, African, Amerind, East Asian, and Islamic history. Yamin Xu has also been particularly helpful with the spelling and pronunciation of East Asian names. Bill Zogby and Stacey McCall at Mohawk Valley Community College, along with Connie Brand and her colleagues at Meridian Community College, have likewise class-tested our book and supplied us with valuable input.

We also thank the many scholars and teachers whose thoughtful and often detailed comments helped improve our book. Whatever errors remain are, of course, our own.

Numerous others have contributed immensely to this work. Kathryn Buturla, Greg Croft, Gwen Morgan, Dan Nieciecki, Adam Zaremba, and the late Marc Ball assisted us with various aspects of our research and writing. Jaime Wadowiec, Vicky Green, and Jenna Finne each read our work at various stages and supplied us with a student's perspective on its clarity, structure, coherence, and appeal to readers. James Kellaher helped us with our maps. Erika Gutierrez, Lisa Pinto, and Janet Lanphier challenged us, believed in us, supported us, and pushed us to expand our vision and our goals. Joshua Johnson and his assistant Paul Sauline did a superbly professional job of filming, editing, and enhancing our chapter-opening and chapter-closing videos. Our various editors and collaborators, including Phil Herbst, David Kear, Charles Cavaliere, Rob DeGeorge, Jeff Lasser, Billy Grieco, Renee Eckhoff, Emily Tamburri, Gale Cocker, Deb Hartwell, and Clark Baxter, have poured their hearts into supporting our workcorrecting our mistakes, improving our style, sharpening our insights, enlivening our narrative, clarifying our explanations, enhancing our maps and images, and pressing us to excel.

Our biggest debt of gratitude is the one that we owe to our wives. Sue Judge and Jan Langdon sustained, encouraged, and supported us, especially when the going got tough, enduring numerous sacrifices as they shared both our burdens and our joys. We owe them far more than words can express or than we can ever repay. This book is rightfully theirs as much as it is ours.

A Note on Dates and Spellings

In labeling dates, like many other world history teachers, we use the initials B.C.E. (Before the Common Era) and C.E. (Common Era), which correspond respectively to the labels B.C. (Before Christ) and A.D. (*Anno Domini*, "The Year of the Lord"), long used in Western societies. In spelling Chinese names, we use the Pinyin system, internationally adopted in 1979, but we sometimes also give other spellings that were widely used before then. (In Chapters 3 and 35, for example, Chinese Nationalist leader Jiang Jieshi is also identified as Chiang Kaishek.) Our spelling of names and terms from other languages follows standard usage, with alternative versions given where appropriate. (Chapter 17, for example, notes that Central Asian warrior Timur Lenk was also called Tamerlane in Europe.)

About the Authors

EDWARD H. JUDGE
JOHN W. LANGDON
Edward H. Judge and John W. Langdon are professors of history at Le Moyne College, where they team-teach a two-semester world history course for first-year students and courses on modern global history for upper-level students. Ed earned his doctorate at the University of Michigan and spent a year in the USSR as an IREX scholar. John earned his doctorate at Syracuse University's Maxwell School of Public Affairs, where he was a National Defense Fellow. Ed has taught at Le Moyne since 1978, was the College's Scholar of the Year in 1994, and was awarded the J. C. Georg Endowed Professorship in 1997. John has taught at Le Moyne since 1971, directed its Honors Program, and was awarded the O'Connell Distinguished Teaching Professorship in 1996. Each has been named the College's Teacher of the Year and has chaired its Department of History. They have written or edited eight books: three in collaboration with each other, three as individuals, and two in collaboration with other scholars. They love teaching world history, especially to students of diverse backgrounds and interests, and they derive great joy from infecting their students with a passion and enthusiasm for the study of the human past.

Making Sense of World History: An Introductory Overview for Students

The study of world history is exciting, filled with fascinating insights, exploits, ventures, tragedies, and triumphs. But it can also be daunting. Faced with countless details, dates, and events, how can we possibly make sense of it all?

One way is to organize the past around a theme that applies the world over. Our central theme in this book is *connections*: the ways that people and societies interact with each other over time. We focus not only on actions and achievements of people in diverse societies, but also on how they learned from, traded with, and conflicted with each other.

To put these connections in global context and illustrate the "big picture," we divide the past into two main *ages* and six overlapping *eras*, reflecting the expansion of connections from regional to global levels, with the six main parts in our table of contents each covering an era. This structure is artificial, imposed by us on the past, but it furnishes a useful framework for making sense of world history.

I. An Age of Regional Connections, to 1650 C.E. (Chapters 1–19)

In our first age, connections were regional, and people survived mainly by finding or raising food. After foraging for food in small nomadic bands for tens of thousands of years, people increasingly took up farming and lived in more permanent settlements, typically villages surrounded by fields on which they grew crops or grazed animals. In regions unsuited for farming, people hunted and/or herded animals, moving periodically to find fresh grazing grounds. In regions where farming supplied surplus food, some people came to live in towns and cities, specializing in such pursuits as governance, warfare, religion, crafting goods, and trading with other regions. As populations grew, some societies formed states, territories run by a central government, often headed by a powerful ruler. Eventually some states conquered others to create large empires, expanding regional and transregional connections.

ERA ONE. EMERGENCE AND EXPANSION OF REGIONAL SOCIETIES, TO 300 C.E. (CHAPTERS 1–8) During this lengthy era, as foraging gave way to farming in some regions, food production and population increased. People formed regional states—groups of villages, towns, and cities ruled by a single government—first in northeastern Africa and West Asia, and later in India, China, the Americas, and elsewhere. States connected and conflicted with each other, eventually creating transregional empires—large expanses with various lands and cultures under a single government—such as those established by Persians, Macedonians and Greeks, Indians, Chinese, and Romans. By the era's end, many regions were also connected by land and sea trade routes and by belief systems such as Buddhism, Hinduism, Zoroastrianism, Confucianism, Daoism, Judaism, and Christianity.

ERA TWO. TRANSREGIONAL CONFLICTS AND RELIGIOUS CONNECTIONS, 200–1200 C.E. (CHAPTERS 9–14) During this thousand-year era, connections among diverse regions were often created by expansive religions offering hope of salvation, and by states that espoused and spread these religions. Christianity, originating in Palestine in the first century C.E., spread across West Asia, Europe, and North Africa, until challenged by Islam, a new faith that soon linked much of Africa and Eurasia religiously, culturally, and commercially. Buddhism, after taking hold in India by the first century C.E., divided into branches and spread through much of Asia, until challenged by resurgent Hinduism and Confucianism.

ERA THREE. CROSS-CULTURAL CONFLICTS AND COMMERCIAL CONNECTIONS, 1000–1650 (CHAPTERS 15–19) Our third era was marked by the formation of vast new political and commercial empires. Some were land based, created by Central Eurasian Turks and Mongols and by Aztecs and Inca in the Americas. Others were sea based, forged by Portuguese and Spanish sailors and soldiers. Their conquests brought mass devastation but also fostered new connections among distant and diverse cultures, laying foundations for the emergence of a global economy.

II. An Age of Global Connections, 1500–Present (Chapters 20–37)

Our second age has been marked by the growth of global connections and commerce. Instead of raising their own food, people increasingly worked in commercial pursuits, selling goods and services for money to buy food and goods. More and more people came to live in urban areas, engaged in enterprises using technologies to provide goods and services, and connected by global networks supplying resources, products, fuels, and information. Conflicts, too, became global, as nations vied for resources and markets as well as for lands and beliefs, and revolutionary ideals fueled upheavals the world over.

ERA FOUR. THE SHIFT FROM REGIONAL TO GLOBAL CONNECTIONS, 1500–1800 (CHAPTERS 20–25) In this era, wealth and power shifted from East to West. Seeking direct commercial access to India, China, and Indonesia,

Europeans wrested Indian Ocean trade from the Muslims (who connected much of Eurasia and Africa) and also developed American colonies sustained by an Atlantic slave trade. As global commerce expanded, Western nations such as Spain, France, and Britain grew to rival in power and wealth the Chinese and Islamic empires. Russia, too, became a world power, expanding to the east, west, and south to create a Eurasian empire.

ERA FIVE. REVOLUTION, INDUSTRY, IDEOLOGY, AND EMPIRE, 1750–1914 (CHAPTERS 26–30)   During our fifth era, revolutionary forces reshaped the West and eventually much of the world. Political revolutions in North America, Europe, and Latin America spread ideas of liberty and equality. An industrial revolution, beginning in Britain, spread across Europe and North America, radically altering societies. These upheavals bred new ideologies, including liberalism, socialism, and nationalism, fueling new revolts. As European nations industrialized, they forged new connections through imperialism, using new weapons and technologies to dominate Africa and Asia. Africans and Asians, their cultures threatened by Western domination, began adapting the new ideas and technologies to fit their own cultures and needs.

ERA SIX. GLOBAL UPHEAVALS AND GLOBAL INTEGRATION, 1900–PRESENT (CHAPTERS 31–37)   By the 20th century, Western nations had connected much of the world under their economic and political sway, while competing among themselves for resources and power. Their competition spawned two world wars, destroying much of Europe and millions of people, followed by a long cold war, dividing Europe and encompassing the globe. Africans and Asians, capitalizing on these conflicts while selectively adapting Western ways, freed themselves from Western domination and sought to modernize their economies. By the 21st century, the world was divided politically into numerous nations, but connected commercially by an increasingly integrated global economy.

Ask Yourself

1. Why and how did humans transition from foraging to farming and organize themselves into settlements and states?

2. What roles did empires, religions, commerce, and technologies play in expanding connections among cultures?

3. What were the advantages and disadvantages of increased connections among cultures? Why and how were such connections often accompanied by conflict, exploitation, and suffering?

4. Why and how did societies transition from economies based on subsistence farming to economies based on commerce and technology? What impacts did these transitions have on the lives of ordinary people?

5. Why is it important for modern people to learn and understand world history?

Chapter 1
The Emergence of Human Societies, to 3000 B.C.E.

EARLY HUMAN CAVE ART Fossils and cultural artifacts, such as these dramatic paintings on cave walls in southern France, provide us with insights into the lives and societies of early humans.

After reading this chapter, you should be able to:

1.1 Describe what we know about prehistoric hominids and explain how we know it.

1.2 Trace the course and assess the importance of the Neolithic Agricultural Revolution.

1.3 Account for and explain the emergence of complex societies.

Early Farming and Herding Areas

In August 2005, at a site near Dmanisi in the Republic of Georgia, a team of scientists made a remarkable discovery. In a den where giant sabre-toothed cats apparently consumed their prey a few million years ago, the team came upon the intact and well-preserved fossilized skull of a **hominid** (*HAH-mih-nid*)—a term that scientists apply to humans and their two-legged prehuman predecessors. Later testing showed that the skull was 1.8 million years old—the oldest fully intact hominid skull yet discovered. In 2013, after eight years of study, the Georgian scientists reported that their finding, compared with other remains at the site, showed that human evolution may have been much simpler, involving fewer species, than previously supposed.

Their findings and claims illustrate the challenge of studying the distant past. Although hominids have existed for millions of years, humans have left behind written records only for about 5000 years. The preceding ages, encompassing all human existence before the emergence of writing, are often called the prehistoric era, despite the probability that people who lived then kept track of their history by passing on oral accounts. Since these early people left no surviving written records, however, modern scholars must rely mainly on analysis of fossils and artifacts, augmented by enlightened speculation subject to scholarly debate. And indeed some scholars, while acknowledging the importance of the Dmanisi discovery, challenged the claims made by the Georgian scientists, asserting that more evidence was needed to substantiate their interpretation.

Despite such disputes, the general outlines of our ancestry are reasonably clear. Hominids first emerged in Africa at least 5 million years ago, and for millions of years most likely survived by eating wild plants. Over many generations, they learned to communicate by spoken language, form small nomadic groups for cooperation and protection, fashion stone tools, hunt wild animals, and use fire, passing on their knowledge and skills to their young. In their quest for food, some hominid groups migrated from Africa to parts of Eurasia (including what is now the Republic of Georgia). Over time, most early hominid species died out, but one branch of the hominid family survived, evolving within the past half million years into modern humans like ourselves.

Equipped with greater intelligence and communication skills than their hominid forerunners, humans formed larger communities, devised better tools and weapons, learned to hunt more effectively, and occasionally fought with other groups vying for food. Some communities, seeking new food sources, migrated to Australia and the Americas. Some eventually figured out how to raise food, by growing crops and domesticating certain animals. Farming and herding made possible even larger communities, such as cities and states, which established commercial, cultural, and political connections, inaugurating the historical era.

Our Earliest Ancestors

1.1 Describe what we know about prehistoric hominids and explain how we know it.

Since no historical records survive from before 5000 years ago, most of what we know of the prehistoric era is based on the work of archeologists and anthropologists, who study early hominids through fossils, cultural artifacts, and genetic comparisons with other animals. Using such sources, scholars surmise that humans are descended from hominids who lived in eastern Central Africa millions of years ago (and hence that we all have African ancestry). By modern standards, early hominids were small, only 3 or 4 feet tall, with brains that were smaller and less complex than ours. But hominids had larger brains than other animals, and voice boxes that could make more complex sounds, enabling them to better communicate what they learned with each other and their offspring. And hominids walked on two feet rather than four, enabling them to use their arms and hands for creative purposes, such as fashioning and using tools and weapons.

About 2 million years ago, as hominids grew in dexterity and brainpower, some began to chip and shape pieces of stone into rough-hewn tools. Modern researchers have characterized this activity—the first indication of conscious cultural behavior—as the onset of the Old Stone Age or **Paleolithic** (*pā-lē-ō-LITH-ik*) **period**, the earliest and longest stage of cultural development, lasting from approximately 2,000,000 B.C.E. until about 10,000 B.C.E. During this extended period, hominids vastly improved their social and communicative skills, learned to hunt in groups that pursued prey from one region to another, and migrated to diverse regions, including northern Africa and parts of Eurasia. In the process they developed diverse ways of life.

Early hominid tools.

What is cultural adaptation, and why was it important in hominid development?

Hominids and Cultural Adaptation

Beginning in the Paleolithic period, hominids diverged from other animals in a significant way. Rather than adjusting to their environment mainly through biological evolution, as most other organisms did, hominids also developed through **cultural adaptation**, using their intellectual and social skills to adjust to their surroundings and improve their chances for survival. Organized into small kinship groups that traveled from place to place, they developed new techniques that they shared with each other and their young, thus transmitting their knowledge and skills to future generations.

With their growing intellectual capacities, hominids increasingly found better ways to adapt to their environment. From long and sometimes bitter experience, for example, they learned which plants were digestible, which could be harmful or lethal, and which had certain medicinal or intoxicative properties. In time some hominids learned how to hunt with crude stone axes, which they used to hurl at their prey and then to strip away the hides for clothing and the meat for food. Later, they learned to use fire for cooking meats and plants to make them more digestible, for warding off wild animals, and for providing nighttime warmth and light.

Furthermore, as their memory and speech improved, hominids transmitted their discoveries to each other and their offspring. A hominid woman who learned to build a fire, for example, could share this knowledge with the rest of her group and also teach it to her children. A hominid band returning from the hunt could sit around the fire, cook their meat, share their experiences, and pass on wisdom and practices from earlier generations. One result was that hominids could build upon their knowledge from one generation to the next and thus adapt more quickly than other animals. Another result was that separate societies eventually developed their own **cultures**: unique combinations of customs, beliefs, and practices—including languages, arts, rituals, institutions, and technologies—that distinguished societies from each other.

Foraging, Family, and Gender

How might gender roles have developed in early hominid groups?

Early hominids apparently were scavengers, living in small nomadic groups that survived mainly by gathering wild nuts and berries, feeding occasionally on carcasses of dead animals, and then moving on after exhausting the area's readily accessible food resources. As they learned to hunt, they increased their consumption of meat but also killed or drove away their prey, so they still moved periodically to find new sources of game. Since these groups survived by searching and scouring for food, they are

Depiction of hominid foragers.

often called **foragers**—those who subsist by gathering wild plant foods and hunting wild animals.

Having no written records of early **foraging societies**, modern scholars study them by examining archeological remains, comparing what they learn with the practices of the few foraging cultures that still exist today in Siberia, South Africa, Australia, and the Americas. These sources suggest that Paleolithic peoples traveled in foraging bands, mobile communities of perhaps 30 to 60 people connected by kinship. While large enough to provide their members with sustenance and protection, groups of this size, unencumbered by material possessions, were small enough to easily pack up and relocate to find new food sources and adjust to changing seasons. As members of the same **kinship group**—an extended family comprising grandparents, parents, siblings, aunts, uncles, cousins, and other relatives—they were also connected by familial obligations and affections.

Compared with many other large mammals, which grow to maturity within a few years, human children remain physically immature, and thus dependent on older caregivers, for a dozen years or more. They therefore require a high level of protection, nurturing, and supervision, usually provided by their parents and other relatives. Furthermore, unlike many other animals, adult humans frequently form an enduring emotional bond with a specific sexual companion. These traits help explain why human parents often stay together to care for their children, and why the central institution of most human societies has been the family.

Family concerns may also help explain why our ancestors probably developed **gender roles**. Evidence suggests that in foraging societies men usually did the hunting and fighting, while women were more likely to gather plant food, tend the campsite, and care for the young. This division of labor was not rigid: women at times helped with the hunting or defense, while men at times assisted in tending the hearth and taking care of the children. Nor did the gender roles imply that women were valued less than men. On the contrary, since a group's survival depended on women to bear children, and since gathering plant food supplied a more reliable source of nutrition than hunting wild game, the functions of the women may have been considered more important than those of the men. A community, after all, could endure the loss of several adult males, but women and children were essential to its long-term survival. Since the men thus were more expendable, it made sense for them to perform the dangerous duties of hunting wild animals and defending the camp against predators and outsiders, and for women to handle the safer yet more essential tasks of minding the campfire, foraging for plant food, and nurturing the young.

Since the foraging band was relatively small and its members were mostly related, its structure was probably simple. Some members might have greater influence due to intellect, experience, or personality, but there was no real need for government officials or class divisions such as those that later arose in larger, more diverse societies.

The absence of rank in foraging bands did not mean everyone was equal, but rather that the adults in the group could collaborate in making decisions, securing the campsite, procuring food, raising the young, and moving to new places. Societies whose members cooperated—supporting one another, sharing the burdens, and passing on their knowledge to their young—tended to be stable and enduring. Some were also able, when the need arose, to migrate substantial distances to ensure their survival or improve their way of life.

Ice Age Migrations and *Homo Sapiens*

How did the Great Ice Age influence hominid migrations?

The Paleolithic period corresponded roughly with what geologists call the Pleistocene (*PLĪ-stuh-sēn*) epoch, also called the **Great Ice Age**, an immense stretch of time (roughly 2,000,000 B.C.E. to 10,000 B.C.E.) marked by frigid glacial stages when enormous ice masses called glaciers spread across much of the globe (Map 1.1). These prolonged "ice ages," each lasting tens of thousands of years, alternated with shorter intervals of relative warmth. Although tropical regions did not experience glaciers, their climates fluctuated considerably, bringing major changes in vegetation and animal life.

Induced perhaps by growing populations or environmental changes that threatened their food supply, many mammals migrated during the Pleistocene epoch to new habitats. Among these mammals were foraging hominid bands, some of which left Africa and traveled to Asia, possibly following herds of wild animals, by about 1.8 million years ago. Much later, by about 800,000 years ago, other hominid groups made their way to Europe. These hominid migrants used their cultural skills to adapt

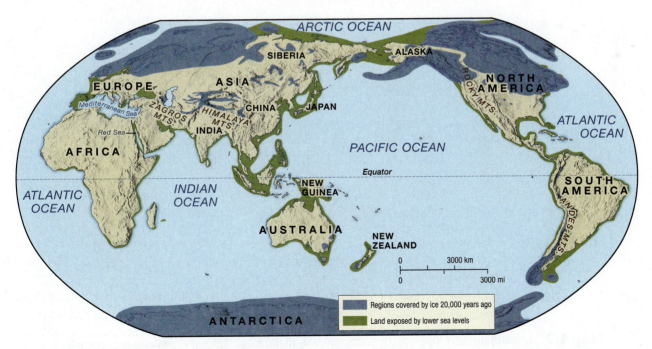

Map 1.1   THE GREAT ICE AGE, 2,000,000–10,000 B.C.E. In the Great Ice Age, or Pleistocene epoch (2,000,000–10,000 B.C.E.), ice covered much of the earth's land surface during prolonged glacial stages, commonly called ice ages. Notice that the areas in green, which are now under water, were exposed as dry land as sea levels dropped during the last ice age. How might this development have aided human migrations?

to their new surroundings, employing local materials such as wood, bamboo, and rock to make shelters, hatchets, and hunting axes.

Then, by about 150,000 to 200,000 years ago, as hominid development and migrations continued, there emerged a new species now called *Homo sapiens* (*HŌ-mō SĀ-pē-enz*). This term, which means "wise human," designates the species that includes all modern people and distinguishes us from other types of hominids that no longer exist.

The complex processes by which our species developed, and the reasons why it prevailed while other hominids died out, are not fully understood. Humans, it is clear, have larger skulls, housing larger brains, than earlier hominid species. But so did the people modern scholars call **Neanderthals**, a group of large-brained hominids whose remains were first discovered in 1856 in Germany's Neander Valley, who existed from roughly 200,000 to 30,000 years ago.

Even the basic outlines of what happened have been subject to dispute. Some experts, for example, formerly asserted that distinct groups of *Homo sapiens* developed independently in separate parts of Africa and Eurasia, evolving from earlier hominids already there. But most experts now think *Homo sapiens* first appeared only in Africa, migrating later to Eurasia and thence to the rest of the world (Map 1.2). Along the way, according to genetic evidence, some may have mated with Neanderthals, so many modern humans may well have a little Neanderthal ancestry.

In any case, *Homo sapiens* eventually developed greater intellectual and linguistic skills than other hominids and thus could more effectively reason, communicate, and cooperate. Early humans thereby developed more effective tools and weapons, including needles and fishhooks carved from antlers and tusks, and spears to hurl at large animals from a safe distance. Using sturdy plant fibers, humans also fashioned ropes and lines that were tied to hooks and harpoons, used to make nets and traps, and eventually strung onto bows from which to shoot arrows at prey.

These innovations helped early humans hunt more effectively, and thus acquire warmer clothes and larger amounts of meat, fish, and fowl. Modern scholars speculate

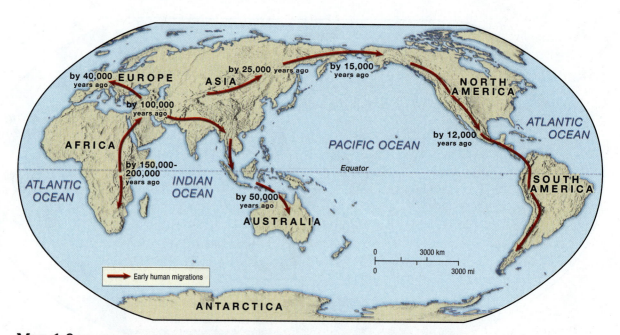

Map 1.2 **HUMANS INHABIT THE CONTINENTS, 200,000–10,000 B.C.E.** Although prehuman hominids migrated from Africa to Asia over a million years ago, most scholars think that human beings (*Homo sapiens*) first emerged in Africa about 150,000–200,000 years ago. Note that more than 100,000 years ago humans began to migrate out of Africa, and that by about 12,000 years ago (10,000 B.C.E.)—and perhaps much earlier—they inhabited all of the continents except Antarctica. What factors prompted early humans to move to distant places?

that, with access to more and better food, people could live longer and support more children. Increasing population probably brought growing competition for food, inducing some groups to migrate to new regions searching for new food sources. As their hunting skills improved, human societies spread across Africa and Eurasia, depleting the numbers of bears, deer, and lions and destroying the herds of fur-covered mammoths that once roamed Eurasia.

In their search for sustenance, some societies migrated even farther. By 50,000 B.C.E., according to archeological evidence, people made their way from Southeast Asia to Australia, an impressive feat that meant traveling in boats on the open seas. Others apparently migrated from northeast Asia to the Americas during the last ice age (which ended about 12,000 years ago), when the huge glaciers absorbed so much water that sea levels dropped hundreds of feet, exposing a broad land bridge that connected Siberia with Alaska (Map 1.1). From Alaska, the migrants spread throughout the Americas, where they found pristine lands still teeming with mammoths, bears, and deer. By the end of the Paleolithic period, in almost every region of the globe fit for human habitation, there were human societies.

Physical and Cultural Diversity

As humans moved to various lands and latitudes, their bodies adjusted to differing climates and conditions. Over time this adaptation apparently produced some modest physical differences. People who lived in northern regions, for example, eventually developed lighter skin, which was better able to produce nutrients from the scarcer sunlight, and sometimes hairier bodies to protect them from the cold. Those in hotter regions typically had darker pigmentation, which could better protect them from the sun's harmful rays.

Despite such outward differences, however, all humans belong to the same species (*Homo sapiens*) and can readily mate and produce healthy offspring with those of different skin color and other features. Thus, the concept of **race**, which divides human beings into categories based on external characteristics, relies on relatively insignificant distinctions. Indeed, in mapping the human genome, modern scientists have found that genetic variability among humans is remarkably small, providing no scientific basis for racial categorization.

Far more important than physical diversity has been **cultural diversity**, resulting from the variety of ways in which separate human societies have adapted to their separate conditions. In a number of ingenious ways, people have adjusted their habits and lifestyles to take advantage of the terrain, vegetation, climate, and wildlife of the regions they inhabit.

Even in Paleolithic times, differences emerged among cultures in various parts of the world. People who lived on warm prairies, including Africa's great grasslands, wore lightweight clothes made from skins and fibers and dwelt in easily assembled structures made of grasses or skins. Those in colder regions, such as northern Eurasia and North America, needing more protection from the elements, wore rugged hides and furs and resided in warmer, sturdier shelters. Where terrain was rocky or mountainous, people lived in stone structures and caves; where it was wooded, they built lodgings from branches, boughs, and bones. Those who lived near lakes or rivers teeming with fish, having little need to travel far for food, built durable dwellings made of wood and stone.

These early distinctions gradually developed into different ways of life, with societies diverging not only in clothing and shelter, but also in customs, institutions, languages, and beliefs. Consequently, the great diversity among humans has not been physical but cultural. The study of world history thus focuses mainly on the development of diverse cultures, their similarities and differences, and on the connections among them.

How would you compare and contrast the significance of physical diversity and cultural diversity?

In what ways did Paleolithic peoples express their ideas about life and death?

Venus figurine.

What types of connections developed among early human societies during the Paleolithic period?

Paleolithic Cultural and Spiritual Perspectives

As Paleolithic peoples pondered their world and thought about life and death, they developed new forms of expression. Paintings, carvings, and burial sites surviving from the Stone Age display the arts and rituals of early peoples, doubtless seeking to understand and influence the forces shaping their lives.

In southern Africa, for example, researchers have found rocks adorned with geometric symbols, suggesting that more than 100,000 years ago humans may have used symbols to express ideas. Other discoveries, on inner walls of caves in Africa, Australia, Europe, and South America, include illustrations dating from between 40,000 and 10,000 years ago. Using charred sticks, brushes made of ferns, furs, or feathers, and natural pigments from the soil mixed with animal fats, prehistoric artists created life-sized paintings of large animals in motion (see page 1). Dramatic images of horses, reindeer, bulls, and buffaloes, many of them galloping or gamboling, leave little doubt that the artists who drew them were creative and contemplative people who could communicate and conceptualize. Perhaps they were simply decorating their caves by portraying scenes from their world. Or perhaps, as some scholars suggest, they were engaged in magic or religious rituals that sought to capture or command the spirits of the animals portrayed, hoping thus to ensure the success of the hunt.

Other artwork from this era includes sketches of humans adorned with paints and animal hides, discovered on cave walls in southern France, and little statues of women with enlarged breasts and reproductive organs, found throughout Central Europe. The former may depict people engaged in community rituals or celebrations. The latter, labeled Venus figurines, possibly played a role in ancient fertility rites. These and other artifacts suggest that early humans believed in spiritual forces and sought to influence them, employing arts and rituals in efforts to make hunting, gathering, and procreation more fruitful.

Burial practices provide further insights into Paleolithic outlooks. Archeological evidence suggests that people have buried their dead for at least 100,000 years. At many prehistoric grave sites, found in central and Southwest Asia and Central Europe, human remains are accompanied by tools, clothing, and other ornaments. The burial of such objects with the deceased might simply show respect for the dead. Or, more intriguingly, it might indicate that early humans believed in some form of life after death and were equipping departed loved ones for an eternal journey.

Intercultural Connections

Although separate societies created distinctive cultures, they typically did not develop in isolation from each other. At various times and places, in moving about or expanding their domains, some human groups came into contact with others. Scholars believe most foraging groups developed contacts with neighboring societies, thus creating intercultural connections.

At times these connections were no doubt practical, based on agreements to divide or share lands and other resources. At times the links may have been familial, marked by intermarriage between members of separate communities, forming family ties and mutual interests that bound the communities together. At times connections involved exchanges of goods and information, sometimes over vast areas: in southwest Australia, for example, researchers have found prehistoric artifacts produced in that continent's northwest regions, several thousand miles away. These early connections foreshadowed more elaborate arrangements, including formal trade and diplomatic relations, which emerged later as societies grew larger.

Connections at times also resulted in conflicts, especially when sharing or trading arrangements failed to meet the needs of all involved. If hunting depleted a region's wild game, for example, groups that had earlier shared hunting grounds might clash, compelling the losers to move elsewhere, where they might forge connections or conflict with other groups. With resources scarce and survival at stake, human societies had to protect their habitats and hunting grounds against outside intrusions, or move to a new region if the outsiders proved stronger. People thus often feared outsiders as potentially dangerous foes.

Because the Paleolithic period covered most of the duration of human existence, behavior patterns evolving in that era influenced later societies. Hence, throughout history humans have identified with their own cultures, connected with societies having similar interests, united with others facing common threats, and struggled for resources such as land and food against competing societies. Connections among cultures have thus been central to the human experience.

The Origins and Impact of Agriculture

1.2   Trace the course and assess the importance of the Neolithic Agricultural Revolution.

By the end of the last ice age, about 10,000 B.C.E., people in some regions, prompted perhaps by environmental changes, were turning from nomadic foraging toward a more settled life. Especially in West Asia, as the warming climate expanded the area covered by grasses and grains, people developed new techniques to gather and process them for food. They made sickles out of flint stone to cut grain, for example, and grinding stones to pulverize the kernels. Archeologists who first found evidence of such tools dating from this era called it the New Stone Age. But something far more important was happening than the use of new stone tools. People were beginning to grow their own food.

In the New Stone Age, or **Neolithic** (*nē-ō-LITH-ik*) **period**, lasting roughly from 10,000 to 3000 B.C.E., people not only developed better tools but also domesticated plants and animals, cultivated crops, herded livestock, and established permanent settlements. This transition from foraging to farming, one of history's most momentous developments, has been called the **Neolithic Agricultural Revolution**. Although it took several thousand years, when compared with the many millennia of foraging that preceded it, and when measured by its immense long-range impact, agriculture's onset was revolutionary indeed.

The Origins of Farming and Herding

How did farming and herding develop in West Asia?

Based on archeological evidence, including the remains of early farm settlements and tools, scholars have surmised that farming first began in West Asia, between 9000 and 8000 B.C.E., in a crescent-shaped region (sometimes called the "Fertile Crescent") that today encompasses Israel, Syria, and Iraq (Map 1.3). Although experts disagree about specific dates and events, they have provided a general outline of what probably took place.

Scholars believe that by 10,000 B.C.E., as the last ice age ended, a warming climate and melting glaciers had left much of this region—today mostly desert—covered with forests and grasslands. Over the next few millennia, some people there began subsisting mainly by harvesting wild wheat and barley grains that grew in abundance in the grasslands. No longer having to move about in search of wild game and plant food, these people often settled in a single place for many years. Unlike nomads, whose need to move precluded having too many children and possessions, the West Asian settlers had little need to limit their families or belongings. With less need to move and more food to feed their offspring, these settlers could sustain larger families, build more permanent shelters, and accumulate a wider variety of tools, clothes, and other belongings. Their numbers thus began to grow as their mobility declined.

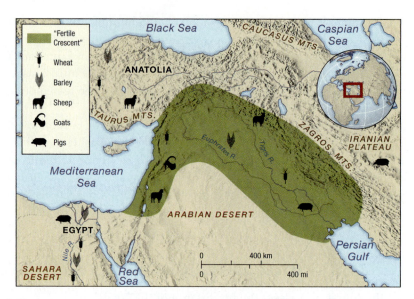

Map 1.3 AGRICULTURE EMERGES IN WEST ASIA, 9000–8000 B.C.E. Scholars believe that humans first developed agriculture between 9000 and 8000 B.C.E. in a region of West Asia sometimes called the "Fertile Crescent." Observe that this region, extending from the Mediterranean Sea to the Zagros Mountains, included the valleys of the Tigris and Euphrates rivers. What factors may have aided the rise of farming and herding in this region?

Eventually, however, as the region's population increased, and perhaps as drier weather reduced the abundance of wild wheat and barley, the supply of wild plant food was no longer sufficient to feed all the inhabitants. Some no doubt responded to this challenge by resuming their nomadic ways. But others, encumbered by large families and numerous possessions, opted instead to stay put.

Those who stayed put, in order to survive, found ways to produce more food. They learned to enhance the yield of wild grains by pulling out the weeds that grew among them. They discovered that if they took seeds from productive plants and sprinkled them in bare spots elsewhere, new plants would eventually grow there. In time some people found they could save the seeds and sow them the next year, enabling them to plant and raise their own crops. These first farmers were probably women, as they were the usual plant food gatherers. Although they could scarcely have foreseen the immense long-term impact of their efforts, the resourceful people who first developed farming rank among history's most influential innovators.

West Asian hunters developed an equally momentous food production process. They discovered that certain game animals, such as wild sheep and goats, could be captured and kept alive in captivity rather than killed in the hunt. At first this practice merely provided a useful standby food source: by keeping a few live animals, a family or community could kill them and eat their meat when other food ran out. Eventually, however, people learned that sheep and goats—as well as cattle, pigs, and horses—would mate and reproduce in captivity. These animals thus were domesticable: they could be bred and adapted by people to meet human needs. People could raise their own herds and produce their own meat.

Eventually other uses were found for domesticable animals. Their fleeces and hides, for example, were used to make blankets and clothes. Their manure served to fertilize the soil and prolong its productivity. The milk of cows, mares, and ewes supplied an ongoing food source, readily available without killing the creature that provided it. In time people also used large animals to pull plows and carts, imparting enormous advantages for farming, transport, and travel.

Agricultural Innovation and Expansion

Although West Asians were probably the first ones to develop agriculture, they were not the only ones. In places far from West Asia, adapting to their own environments, inhabitants developed different forms of farming and herding, using plants and animals native to their locales (Map 1.4). In the north-central African region called the Sudan, where grasslands then covered much of what is now the Sahara desert, people herded cattle and cultivated sorghum (a starchy grain), perhaps as early as 8000 B.C.E. In China's great river valleys, settlers grew millet and rice and raised pigs by about 7000 B.C.E. By this time, too, in New Guinea, people probably grew taro, a starchy root crop, on swamplands drained by digging ditches to channel away the water.

Farming and herding also spread through connections among cultures. By 7000 B.C.E., for example, agriculture had begun in ancient India's Indus Valley, and by 6000 B.C.E. it had started in Europe and Egypt's Nile Valley. The proximity of these areas to West Asia, and the fact that people there grew plants (such as wheat and barley) and animals (such as sheep and goats) domesticated in West Asia, suggests that agriculture probably spread there through intercultural connections. In exchanging goods and ideas, early societies also most likely exchanged knowledge about farming and herding.

But farmers and herders in these new areas were by no means mere borrowers. They cultivated native food crops (such as oats in Europe and figs in Egypt), domesticated local animals (such as different types of cattle in the Nile and Indus valleys), and eventually grew fibers (such as flax in Europe and cotton in Egypt and India) that could be woven into lightweight linens and clothes. But grains such as wheat and barley continued to predominate, especially as people learned to grind them into flour, bake the flour into bread, and brew the barley into a beverage like what we now call beer.

In the Western Hemisphere, where people had no connections with Africa or Eurasia, they developed different crops. In what is now southern Mexico,

How did agriculture expand and evolve through connections between cultures?

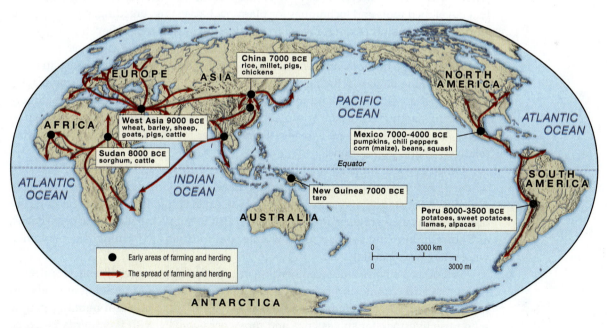

Map 1.4 AGRICULTURE DEVELOPS AND SPREADS, 9000 B.C.E.–1000 C.E. Over thousands of years, through human ingenuity and connections among cultures, agriculture developed and spread from its early areas of origin to other regions, as depicted by the arrows on this map. Note the large dots showing early areas of plant and animal domestication, with boxes indicating early food crops, domesticated animals, and estimated dates. What factors may have contributed to agriculture's development? Why did people raise different plants and animals in different parts of the world?

archeologists have found indications of farming as early as 7000 B.C.E., and evidence that, by 4000 B.C.E., farmers there grew corn, beans, and squash, cultivation of which later spread through much of North America. By 3500 B.C.E., and perhaps much earlier, people in what is now Peru grew potatoes and sweet potatoes (Map 1.4). In the Americas, however, since human hunters had earlier killed off most large domesticable animals, livestock herding was virtually unknown—except in Peru where people raised llamas and alpacas.

The spread of farming was also interwoven with population growth. As farmers and herders produced more food, the size of their societies grew, leading them to cultivate additional lands and clear away forests for farming. After all, only a small percentage of the plants in a forest were edible, while almost everything grown in a grain field could be used for human or animal consumption. An acre of crops fed far more people than an acre of woods.

Therefore, to increase the land available for farming, people cut and burned down forests. In the process they learned that burned-over forests were extremely fertile, as ashes from the burned vegetation served as superb fertilizer. After several years of nourishing crops, however, the soil was exhausted of nutrients and produced less food. So Neolithic farmers simply moved to other regions, cut and burned more forests, and repeated the process. This "slash-and-burn" practice, which ravaged the habitats of wild game and plants and thus undermined local foragers, enabled farmers to expand their food supplies and spread agriculture to additional places.

Foragers, Hunter-Farmers, and Pastoral Nomads

Which factors tended to promote settled agriculture, and which tended to lead to foraging and nomadic behavior?

Not all humans took up agriculture. Since raising crops and herds typically required more time and harder work than foraging, and often left people at the mercy of the weather and dependent on a few food sources, societies were unlikely to turn to farming unless compelled to do so by population growth and/or diminished food supply. Even then, they could do so only where climate and terrain made farming feasible, where local plants and animals were suitable for domestication, and where people had developed tools and techniques for planting, harvesting, breeding, pasturing, and storing. The transition from foraging to farming thus was a long, uneven process lasting thousands of years. Clearly farming and herding were not for everyone.

Some groups never farmed and continued to live as hunters and gatherers in small mobile foraging bands. In the far northern regions of Eurasia and North America, for example, where it was too cold to grow crops, people sustained themselves largely by hunting and fishing. In the arid plains and deserts of Australia, Africa, and central North America, where there was insufficient water for farming, foraging supported relatively sparse populations.

Other groups adopted farming but not herding, especially in the Americas, where there were few large domesticable animals. In eastern and southwestern North America, for instance, even after societies took up farming, hunting and fishing continued to play a key role, providing meat and fish to supplement crops of corn, beans, and squash. In many such societies women did most of the farming, since the men were often away hunting.

Still other societies embraced herding but not farming, especially in Central Asia, where the arid climate and sparse vegetation were suitable for grazing animals but not growing crops. Mobile herders such as these are called **pastoral nomads**: people who raise livestock for subsistence and move occasionally with their herds in search of fresh grazing grounds.

Always looking for new pasturelands, without which they could not endure, pastoral nomads occasionally came into contact with farming societies. Sometimes the two groups clashed, battling for use of lands both considered vital. But sometimes they traded, exchanging the herders' hides and fleeces for the farmers' grains and flour. Ranging across the open expanses between settled societies, the nomads created connections, conveying goods (such as carpets, cloth, and jewels) and techniques (such as horse breeding and metalworking) to distant and disparate cultures.

For many millennia, pastoral nomads coexisted uneasily with settled agricultural societies. Equipped by their harsh, itinerant existence with ruggedness and mobility, the nomads frequently prevailed in combat. In the long run, however, since agriculture could support far more people than nomadic herding or foraging, settled societies eventually gained huge advantages in population, weapons, possessions, and power—enabling them to defeat, attract, or displace almost all nomadic peoples. The future belonged mainly to societies based on farming.

Agricultural Society: Village, Family, and Land

What were the principal features of early agricultural societies?

Over time, the lives of farmers increasingly diverged from those of nomadic peoples. Although both farmers and pastoral nomads centered their societies on families and divided their duties by gender, many differences developed between them.

One key difference was permanence of place. Unlike nomads, who moved from place to place, farmers typically settled in one location. Almost everywhere they dwelt in **farming villages**, small settlements of homes in a compact cluster, surrounded by lands on which the villagers raised food. Village homes were mostly simple structures, fashioned from local materials such as earth, thatch, wood, or stone, and grouped together to facilitate socialization and defense. The lands around the village served as farm fields and sometimes also pasturelands for grazing livestock. A typical farming village was a permanent settlement, where people and their families often lived for generations.

Another key contrast was size. Agricultural communities frequently grew much larger than nomadic groups, whose numbers were limited by the need for mobility. A typical farming village, sustained by steady food supply and stabilized by permanence of place, might include a few hundred people, and sometimes substantially more. Furthermore, as neighboring villages formed connections with each other, creating networks based on mutual protection and support, agricultural societies grew even larger.

The growing size of these societies, and the need to parcel out farmlands among families, required a higher degree of structure than normal among nomads. Possession of land, scarcely a concern for nomads, became essential in many agricultural societies, where people's livelihood depended largely on the land. As families grew, they often sought to maintain and expand their access to lands and to pass them on to their offspring. Thus, as village families intermarried with each other and with families from other villages, it became increasingly important to keep track of who was descended from whom, in order to determine who would control which lands.

Family relationships in farming communities therefore were more structured than the informal kinship ties existing in nomadic societies. Marriages between farming families were typically arranged by the parents of the bride and groom, and often sealed by a transfer of assets, such as land or livestock, between the two families. Marriages between members of different agricultural societies, moreover, frequently were also alliances, designed to create closer connections and strengthen mutual support.

Farmers also diverged from nomads in terms of gender roles and status. In foraging bands, the role of women was crucial, since they supplied the plant food on which the group relied and often had to manage the group while the men were off hunting. Among pastoral nomads, where women were frequently responsible for tending, breeding, birthing, and milking the livestock, their role was also essential. In many farm communities, however, the men produced most of the food, laboring daily in the fields while women often stayed in the village. Their roles, which typically involved

Women and men doing farm work in the Americas.

raising children, maintaining the household, and helping in the fields when needed, came to be considered subordinate to those of men.

Family sizes further affected gender roles. In nomadic societies, where mobility was essential, large families could be a burden, so parents frequently kept families small, freeing women to assume many duties besides child-raising. In agricultural societies, however, where many hands were needed to help work the fields at sowing and harvest times, large families were considered desirable. Expected to bear, nurse, and raise many children, farming village women had limited ability to get involved in affairs outside the household.

Gender roles and status nonetheless varied among agricultural societies. In the Americas, for example, in farming villages where there was no livestock to provide meats and hides, the men often hunted while women did most of the farming. In such societies, since women were the primary food producers and men were often absent on the hunt, women sometimes played a key role in managing village affairs. And even in Eurasia and Africa, capable women with strong personalities often played a prominent role in running their families and villages. While many agricultural societies were **patriarchal** (*PĀ-trē-ARK-ul*), dominated by men as heads of households and community leaders, others were **matriarchal** (*MĀ-trē-ARK-ul*), run by women serving similar roles.

How did settled agriculture affect human societies?

The Impact of Agriculture

Initially, agriculture's impact was not always advantageous. Early farmers and herders typically had to work much harder than gatherers and hunters. Farmers had to clear land, till soil, sow seeds, tend fields, pull weeds, and shield crops from insects, animals, and birds. They also had to harvest, process, and preserve what they grew, while often also tending livestock and protecting it from predators. Furthermore, judging from excavations of early farming villages, Neolithic farmers appear to have been smaller, and probably less healthy, than nomadic foragers. From living in close contact with cattle and pigs, farmers acquired new illnesses, forerunners of deadly scourges such as smallpox and influenza. By settling continuously in one place, they accumulated garbage and waste, which fouled their water and attracted disease-bearing insects and rodents. And, unlike small nomadic groups whose mobility furnished access to varied plant and animal foods, settled farm societies typically relied on a few basic crops, leaving them vulnerable to disasters such as floods, droughts, crop failures, insect infestations, and famines.

But societies based on agriculture had a crucial advantage: they could produce surplus food. In good years the farmers could grow more than they consumed, and then store the surplus to meet future needs, initially in pits but later in bins and silos raised to protect against flooding.

Production of surplus food had immense implications. It provided agricultural societies with a backup food supply, helping to ensure their survival, even during deadly droughts and famines. It enabled farming families to support more children, allowing their communities to grow into settlements of hundreds or thousands of people, and contributing to an overall increase in human population. And it freed some people in settlements based on farming from the need to provide their own food, allowing them to specialize in other pursuits—including arts, crafts, commerce, religion, warfare, and governance. Agriculture thereby supported and sustained the development of large, complex, regional societies, which would increasingly dominate human history.

The Emergence of Complex Societies

1.3   **Account for and explain the emergence of complex societies.**

Toward the end of the Neolithic period, beginning in West Asia and North Africa, several factors combined to produce **complex societies**—large, organized, stable communities in which farm surpluses enabled many people to specialize in occupations other than farming. These societies included **towns and cities**, sizable permanent settlements supported by surplus food from surrounding farms. To manage their substantial populations, they typically formed governments, engaged in trade, organized religions, and extended control over surrounding lands, eventually creating very large and populous regional societies. The rest of this chapter discusses general features of these societies; the chapters that follow then examine their development as each was shaped by internal and external connections.

Towns, Cities, Occupations, and Religion

By 7000 B.C.E., as food supplies increased, some West Asian settlements were starting to grow quite large. Jericho (*JER-ih-kō*) in Palestine and Çatal Hüyük (*chah-TAHL hoo-YOOK*) in what is now Turkey, for example, developed into towns—large settlements, home to several thousand people, that served not only as residential centers but also as trading hubs. Jericho, an active trading center, had many huts made of mud-dried brick surrounded by a stone defensive wall. Çatal Hüyük, an even larger trading hub, had numerous mud-brick homes, shrines to various gods and goddesses, and marketplaces for exchanging foods and goods.

By the fourth millennium B.C.E., near the Tigris (*TĪ-gris*) and Euphrates (*yoo-FRĀ-tēz*) rivers in West Asia and the Nile in northeast Africa, some towns were growing into cities—very large, complex, densely populated settlements in which many people engaged in occupations other than farming. These early cities, housing upwards of 10,000 people and sometimes substantially more, also featured sizable buildings, bustling marketplaces, and extensive fortifications.

Although towns and cities depended on farming, their most influential inhabitants were those who did not farm. With their food supplied by farmers, these people could specialize in other occupations. Some, for example, were artisans who specialized in tool making, basket weaving, pottery, and carpentry, as shown by remnants of their handiwork at archeological sites such as Ur (*OOR*) and Uruk (*OO-rook*) in West Asia and Naqada (*nah-KAH-dah*) in Northeast Africa. Others apparently were merchants, who exchanged goods in the urban marketplaces unearthed at such sites. Still others may have been artists and sculptors, as suggested by excavations of shrines and temples embellished with wall paintings and statues of goddesses and gods.

These excavations also reflect the emergence of organized religion. Early peoples, as we have seen, probably engaged in rituals, summoning spirits to help secure food and ensure fertility. As societies grew more complex, the rituals grew more elaborate: people came to worship various gods and goddesses, divine beings believed to embody and control essential forces such as sun and rain, plants and animals, storms, rivers, forests, and fertility. Hoping to please or appease them, priests and priestesses—people specializing in religious rituals—conducted ceremonies and sacrifices in urban shrines and temples. These religious structures also may have reinforced the authority of rulers, depicting them as divinities or as agents of the gods.

Other excavations add to the impression that rulers exercised great power. Fortifications and weapons found at early cities suggest that they must have had numerous laborers to build the walls and watchtowers, soldiers to defend against outsiders, and governing officials with the authority to organize and supervise large groups of

How did specialized occupations emerge in early towns and cities?

workers and warriors. Also uncovered at such sites were remains of palaces, and royal tombs in which officials and servants were buried alongside the rulers, adding to the evidence that early cities were run by strong central governments.

States and Civilizations

How and why did large societies develop complex governance structures?

Before complex societies emerged, there was little need for strong central governments. Decisions could be made and conflicts resolved in foraging bands by the whole group, and in villages by family leaders. If one villager injured another, for example, the heads of households could meet to determine punishment and compensation, usually in accord with community customs. Since everyone was acquainted, and frequently related, such informal mechanisms normally sufficed.

As settlements grew so large that not everyone knew each other, however, residents could no longer rely on family and village leaders to settle disputes or decide issues for the whole community. Large societies hence developed governments, often starting with a single strong leader who, as the need arose, empowered others to assist him. Over time the result was an array of officials who carried out decisions, maintained order, organized food reserves, supervised construction projects, and resolved conflicts among strangers. If one city resident harmed another, the injured party could thus appeal, not to family and friends, but to a government official with the authority to impose punishment and compensation.

A government's main functions, however, were to secure the society's sustenance, ensure the survival of its ruling elite, and defend against outsiders. Some cities, therefore, secured their food supply by exerting dominion over neighboring villages, using armed warriors to force village farmers to part with a portion of their produce. Some of this food then fed the ruler and officials, as well as other urban residents, and some might be stored as a hedge against future shortages. The ruler and his warriors, in return, protected the villagers from conquest by rival outsiders.

Using this system, commonly called tribute, city rulers managed to maintain their food supplies and control the surrounding countryside. By thus establishing governance over a specific territory, they effectively formed **states**—territorial entities ruled by a central government. After 4000 B.C.E., for example, towns and villages along the Nile River began uniting into small kingdoms that may have formed the first states. By 3500 B.C.E. some West Asian cities, including Ur and Uruk, were extending their control over nearby farming villages, thus creating small states. Several centuries later in North Africa, a legendary ruler called Narmer or Menes (*MĀ-nāz*) extended his sway over numerous Nile Valley settlements, creating history's earliest large state, an Egyptian realm stretching hundreds of miles.

Historians have long noted that these early states, and others emerging a bit later in India and China (Map 1.5), all arose in river valleys in semiarid regions. Some scholars have held that such environments prompted the formation of states, claiming that they were probably created to organize vast numbers of people to build banks and dikes for flood control and irrigation systems to bring river water to farm fields. Others, however, citing evidence that irrigation ditches existed before states in West Asia and China, have suggested instead that societies formed states mainly to manage and control their growing populations. Whatever the case, it is clear that the rivers, by supplying plentiful water for people, crops, and livestock, and by enriching valley soils with periodic floods that left behind fertile silt, facilitated the formation of permanent settled societies.

It is also clear that, by providing ready transportation, the rivers helped connect societies up and down the river valleys. Thus, over many centuries, through trade, alliances, and conquests, cities and states along these waterways formed commercial, cultural, and political connections. The result was the emergence of large, complex, regional societies along rivers in West Asia, North Africa, India, and China.

These large, complex regional societies are customarily characterized as history's first **civilizations**—a term applied to very large, complex societies, or regional groups

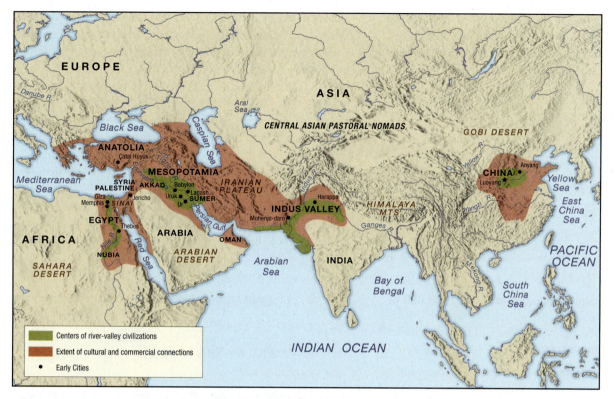

Map 1.5 **EARLY STATES AND CIVILIZATIONS EMERGE IN RIVER VALLEYS, 4000–2000 B.C.E.** In the fourth and third millennia B.C.E., early cities, states, and civilizations arose near rivers in Egypt, Mesopotamia, the Indus Valley, and China. Notice that these early complex societies also developed commercial and cultural connections with surrounding regions. What factors may have aided the emergence of early states and civilizations?

of complex societies, with widely shared or similar customs, institutions, and beliefs. At times, however, the word *civilization* has also been used to indicate an "advanced" level of social and cultural achievement, and hence by some peoples to claim they are superior to others. People in large, complex societies, for example, have frequently deemed themselves more "civilized" (that is, more culturally advanced) than outsiders, whom they have sometimes disparaged as savages and barbarians. To prevent ambiguity and elude this kind of cultural bias, we will avoid the latter usage of the word, while noting nonetheless that the emergence of the early civilizations, discussed in the next four chapters, traditionally marks the beginning of the historical era.

Chapter Review

Consequences and Connections

For tens of thousands of years, early humans lived in small, nomadic bands that were based on kinship and survived by hunting and gathering. Over time, as they adapted to a growing range of challenges and environments, our ancestors migrated to distant lands, eventually spreading throughout the entire world. They devised new tools and weapons, developed distinctive cultural expressions, divided their work along gender lines, formed marriage and family connections, exchanged information and goods, and occasionally engaged in conflicts with each other. Still, as long as they had to forage for food and move periodically from place to place, their societies remained simple and small.

Then came the advent of agriculture. People in some areas started to raise crops and animals and to form permanent settlements, some of which eventually grew into larger, more complex communities. In time some villages grew into towns, and some towns became cities, with large populations of people who specialized in nonfarming pursuits such as commerce, carpentry, tool making, warfare, religion, construction work, and governance. Some of these cities expanded their control over neighboring villages and towns, thereby creating states, which in turn formed the basis of large, complex, regional societies later called civilizations.

Henceforth, although nomadic cultures would long endure in areas unfit for farming, history would largely be dominated by complex, regional societies, and by the contacts and connections among them. The first such regional societies, discussed in the next chapter, emerged in the fourth millennium B.C.E. along rivers in West Asia and North Africa.

Reviewing Key Concepts

Paleolithic Period, p. 3
Cultural Adaptation, p. 3
Foraging Societies, p. 4
Gender Roles, p. 4
Great Ice Age, p. 5

Homo Sapiens, p. 6
Cultural Diversity, p. 7
Neolithic Agricultural Revolution, p. 9
Pastoral Nomads, p. 12

Farming Villages, p. 13
Complex Societies, p. 15
Towns and Cities, p. 15
States, p. 16
Civilizations, p. 16

Ask Yourself

1. How did hominid development differ from that of other animals? Why did hominids organize into nomadic kinship groups? Why did they divide their work along gender lines?

2. Why did some hominids, and later early humans, migrate to distant lands? Why did human societies develop diverse cultures?

3. Why did humans begin to grow their own food? What were the advantages and disadvantages of farming and herding? Why did some societies remain nomadic?

4. How did agricultural societies differ from nomadic ones? What were the major long-range impacts of agriculture?

5. Why did some people organize cities and states? What were the major features and advantages of these complex societies?

Key Dates and Developments

Paleolithic Period/Pleistocene Epoch 2,000,000–12,000 years ago

by 2,000,000 years ago	Early hominids use stone tools
by 1,800,000 years ago	Early hominids migrate from Africa to Asia
by 800,000 years ago	Early hominids migrate to Europe
by 200,000–150,000 years ago	Modern humans (*Homo sapiens*) emerge in Africa
by 100,000 years ago	Humans in Africa fish, mine, and carve symbols
by 100,000 years ago	Humans begin to inhabit Eurasia
by 50,000 years ago	Humans migrate to Australia
by 35,000–10,000 years ago	Humans produce cave art in Australia, Africa, Europe, South America
by 12,000 years ago (10,000 B.C.E.)	Humans migrate to the Americas

Neolithic Period 10,000–3000 B.C.E.

by 9000 B.C.E.	Farming begins in West Asia
by 8000 B.C.E.	Farming begins in the African Sudan
by 7000 B.C.E.	Farming begins in India, China, New Guinea, and Mexico
by 7000 B.C.E.	Towns emerge in West Asia
by 6000 B.C.E.	Farming begins in Egypt and Europe
by 3500 B.C.E.	Farming begins in Peru
by 3000 B.C.E.	Cities and states emerge in West Asia and Egypt

Chapter 2
Early Societies of West Asia and North Africa, to 500 B.C.E.

THE ZIGGURAT OF UR Early West Asian and North African societies produced impressive monuments, such as this massive "ziggurat" temple in the ancient Sumerian city of Ur, amply attesting to the power of their rulers and religions.

After reading this chapter, you should be able to:

2.1 Discuss the principal characteristics and contributions of early West Asian societies.

2.2 Analyze the ways in which early Northeast African societies adapted to their environment and developed complex civilizations.

2.3 Describe and explain the main Phoenician contributions and connections.

2.4 Discuss the evolution of the Jewish concept of monotheism.

Early West Asian and North
African Societies

According to legend, King Sargon of Akkad (*AH-kuhd*), regarded as history's first empire-builder, had very humble origins. Abandoned in infancy by his mother, who put him in a basket and set him adrift on a river, he was rescued and raised by a gardener. Thus favored by fertility goddess Ishtar, he became a local ruler's cupbearer and grew into a great warrior. Assembling an empire in West Asia in the twenty-fourth century B.C.E., he conquered Sumer (*SOO-mehr*), a prosperous region northwest of the Persian Gulf. But rather than destroy its great cities, he embraced their culture and later imposed it on other lands he conquered. He also expanded commerce, trading with lands as distant as India and Crete.

Sargon's story exemplifies the challenge of studying ancient times. Fragmentary records surviving from that era often were compiled much later, based on oral traditions and typically embellished by heroic legends and accounts of godly interventions. Historians thus find it hard to determine precisely what occurred. The actual events of Sargon's early life, for example, as well as the boundaries of his realm and the years of his reign, are open to question—as is the location of his capital city, which has yet to be found. Similar gaps exist in our knowledge of all ancient societies, which is based on fragmentary records and archeological evidence supplemented by scholarly speculation. The accounts that emerge are incomplete and often differ in details, but they are fascinating nonetheless.

Sargon's story also shows how connections were created among cultures. Sometimes warriors conquered cosmopolitan societies and then adopted their culture, as Sargon did when he annexed and emulated the cities of Sumer. Sometimes conquerors imposed their values on the people they vanquished, as Sargon did by spreading his adopted culture to other lands he ruled. And sometimes cultures influenced each other through commerce, exchanging both goods and ideas, a process Sargon encouraged by expanding trade.

Such connections were central to the growth of the complex societies that emerged in West Asia and Northeast Africa more than 5000 years ago. In each of these societies, people lived along rivers, whose waters sustained farming that produced sufficient food for large settlements. Each society formed cities and states, organizing and connecting people under powerful rulers. Each society worshipped many gods and goddesses, believing they could intervene in human lives. Each society was patriarchal, with governance, commerce, religion, and family dominated mainly by males. Through various connections, over several millennia, these societies interacted with each other and with peoples in other regions, leaving striking legacies that endure to this day.

Early West Asian Societies

2.1 Discuss the principal characteristics and contributions of early West Asian societies.

Agriculture, as we saw in Chapter 1, first arose in West Asia around 9000 B.C.E. In the following millennia, it was practiced extensively in the plains around the Tigris and Euphrates rivers (now part of modern Iraq), where periodic floods deposited silt that kept the soil fertile.

By the fourth millennium B.C.E., as farming flourished in this region, its population seems to have grown considerably. Shielded from outsiders by mountains and deserts and fed by ample food from fertile farmlands, people there formed increasingly complex societies. Farming villages merged into towns, and some towns grew into cities, with central governments, organized religions, and extensive commerce. Thus emerged one of the world's earliest civilizations, in a region later called Mesopotamia (*MESS-uh-puh-TĀ -mē-uh*), meaning "between the rivers." So impressive was it that later conquerors, including Sargon of Akkad, adopted and imposed its ways throughout West Asia and beyond.

Early Mesopotamia: The City-States of Sumer

By 3500 B.C.E. a number of cities, including Ur and Uruk, had emerged in a region called Sumer, near where the Tigris and Euphrates rivers connect (Map 2.1). By 3000 B.C.E. some of these cities, surrounded by protective walls, were more than a mile in diameter and home to more than 30,000 people. Most residents were farmers, living in huts made of sun-baked mud bricks, who tended their crops by day in nearby fields. But other city-dwellers, supported by the farmers' surplus food, specialized in other occupations. Their numbers included artisans, merchants, laborers, priests and priestesses, soldiers, and government officials.

Conflict was common among **Sumerian city-states**, independent urban political domains that controlled the surrounding countryside. Eager to enhance their power and wealth, larger city-states sometimes sought to swallow up others, provoking periodic wars. Leaders who emerged in combat often became kings and officials.

Over time the kings amassed power to command armies, levy tribute and taxes, dispense justice, and organize the building of roads, canals, and dikes. In many places kingship became hereditary, as rulers passed on power to their sons, reflecting the patriarchal structure of Sumerian society and families. Officials helped the kings

What were the principal cultural and technical contributions of the early Sumerians?

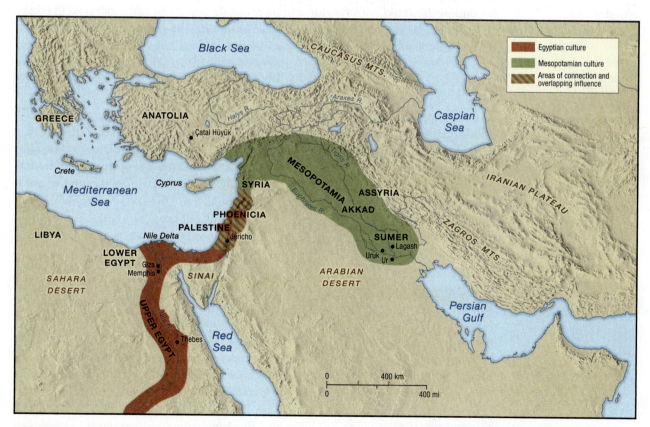

Map 2.1 COMPLEX SOCIETIES EMERGE IN WEST ASIA AND NORTHEAST AFRICA BY 3000 B.C.E. In the fourth millennium B.C.E., complex societies emerged in Mesopotamia and Egypt. Note that the lands along the eastern Mediterranean, later called Phoenicia and Palestine, connected them and were influenced by both. How did these connections develop, and how did each culture influence the other?

Gilgamesh and Enkidu defeating lions.

govern, while priests and priestesses exalted them as descendants of the gods. Royal authority was thus reinforced by religion.

SUMERIAN RELIGION AND WORLDVIEW   The most famous Sumerian ruler was King Gilgamesh (*GIL-guh-mesh*) of Uruk, hero of the ***Epic of Gilgamesh***, a magnificent narrative poem from the third millennium B.C.E. In this epic the handsome young king, described as part god and part man, is confronted by Enkidu (*EN-kih-doo*), a former wild man who was tamed by a prostitute. The two men battle ferociously but emerge as friends. Together they embark on many adventures. When fertility goddess Ishtar becomes infatuated with Gilgamesh, he brazenly spurns her advances, so in a rage she has her father the sky god send a wild bull to destroy him. Together, Gilgamesh and Enkidu slay the beast. But the gods respond by taking the life of Enkidu, who describes to Gilgamesh the dismal underworld awaiting people after death. Hoping to avoid this fate, Gilgamesh searches for immortality, only to learn that eternal life is beyond his grasp.

The epic exhibits fundamental features of Mesopotamian religion. Like many ancient belief systems, it was **polytheistic** (*PAH-lē-thē-ISS-tik*), meaning that people worshipped more than one god. Gods and goddesses personified forces central to agricultural society, such as earth, sun, water, sky, fertility, and storms. Deities such as Ishtar and her father were temperamental figures, portrayed in human form and believed to affect every aspect of life. People who pleased the gods by rituals and sacrifices could hope for assistance and good fortune, but those who (like Enkidu) displeased them could expect retribution. The overall outlook was gloomy: humans had to serve unpredictable and spiteful gods in this life, with little hope for better fate in the next life.

Religion nonetheless played a central role in early societies. It supplied an explanation for the forces of nature, and a way for people to try to influence those forces. It provided a focus for festivals, such as new year holidays in spring, celebrating life's natural cycles with rituals, dances, and songs. It exalted rulers as divine agents, enhancing their authority and helping them maintain order. Priests and priestesses, often family members or devoted followers of rulers, heralded the rulers as godlike beings descended from divinities and performed rituals intended to bring divine favor on the realm.

To further enhance their status and prestige, rulers built splendid temples to the gods and palaces for themselves. Some Sumerian cities constructed **ziggurats** (*ZIG-uh-rahtz*), massive brick towers ascending upward in tiers, typically topped by shrines for religious rituals. Dominating urban landscapes, ziggurats also served as symbols of power and as lookout towers for defense (see page 19). Governance and religion were thus intertwined, each supporting the other.

COMMERCE, INNOVATION, AND CUNEIFORM WRITING   Secured by this support and sustained by surplus food, Sumerians made great strides in other endeavors. They promoted regional commerce, pioneered the use of wheels, fashioned metals into tools and weapons, devised ways to keep track of time, performed architectural and engineering feats, and invented writing.

Although Sumer's farms produced abundant wheat and barley, and its sheep supplied ample wool, woods and metals there were scarce. So Sumerians traded with other lands, exchanging their textiles and grains for cedar wood and copper from the eastern Mediterranean, gold from Egypt, and gems from what is now Iran. To carry these goods, Sumerians fashioned wooden boats for rivers, cargo ships for seas, and wheeled carts to be pulled overland by animals.

Overland connections were vastly enhanced by the wheel, an innovation associated with Sumer but probably developed by nomads to its north. By 3000 B.C.E. Sumerians were transporting goods in carts with wooden wheels, and introducing wheels to other regions as they traveled. One of history's most useful inventions, wheels were later attached to chariots for war, thereby intensifying conflicts as well as connections among cultures.

Sumerians also made advances in metalwork. In the late Neolithic period, hoping to improve on their wood and stone implements, some West Asians started fashioning tools out of copper ore. At first they simply pounded copper into useful shapes; later they learned to heat it until it melted and pour it into clay molds to cool. However, although copper worked well for small tools and ornaments, it was too soft for larger tools and weapons. In the fourth millennium B.C.E., therefore, metalworkers began to mix molten copper with tin, thereby producing a sturdier metal called bronze, which was used to make swords and shields for soldiers and sometimes knives and axes for farmers.

Other innovations, too, are credited to Sumerians. They created a calendar based on cycles of the moon and a double-entry bookkeeping method. They devised a computation system based on segments of 12 and 60, still used now for dividing time into hours, minutes, and seconds. And they developed architectural and engineering skills to build palaces, temples, fortifications, and irrigation systems.

Furthermore, as trade and tribute expanded and society grew more complex, Sumerians devised symbols to record financial and administrative transactions. As this system improved, they also used it to record rituals, laws, and legendary exploits of rulers such as Gilgamesh. This momentous invention, which we call writing, facilitated governance, enhanced commercial connections, and vastly aided the preservation and transmission of knowledge.

Sumerians wrote by inscribing figures in wet clay, which hardened into tablets, some of which still exist today. They etched symbols from right to left, using wedgelike characters that scholars now call **cuneiform** (*KYOO-nē-ih-form*) **writing,** which means "wedge-shaped." At first these were merely stylized pictures (pictographs) of people, animals, and objects such as carts, houses, baskets, and bowls. Eventually, however, as characters were added to express ideas (ideographs) and sounds (phonetics), writing became very complex, so schools were set up in palaces and temples to train writing specialists, or scribes. To enter this prestigious profession, relied on by rulers to help manage their realms, students in these schools endured

Cuneiform writing.

memorization, recitation, copy work, harsh discipline by teachers, and harassment by older classmates.

Few Sumerians learned to write, but those who did played a key role in spreading and preserving their culture. So useful, indeed, was their writing system that it was adopted by outside conquerors seeking to unite and rule all Mesopotamia.

Akkadian Connections and the Spread of Sumerian Culture

What connections developed between and among Sumer, Akkad, and Babylon?

Conquest was crucial in spreading Sumerian culture. Beginning around 2350 B.C.E., Sumer's city-states were conquered by King Sargon of Akkad, the ambitious ruler depicted at the start of this chapter. Sargon went on to conquer most of Mesopotamia, connecting the region under his rule and creating one of history's first empires (Map 2.2).

Sargon also established a pattern repeated throughout history: conquerors learned from societies they conquered and helped spread their culture. The Akkadians (*ah-KĀ-dē-inz*), for example, adopted the Sumerian calendar, writing system, and computation methods, introducing them to other regions as the **Akkadian Empire** expanded. Akkadian conquests and connections thus spread Sumerian ideas across Mesopotamia and into lands along the eastern Mediterranean Sea.

The Akkadian Empire, which declined after Sargon's death, was overrun around 2230 B.C.E. by nomadic warriors from mountains to the northeast. The Sumerians later regained power, led by the city-state of Ur, which extended its rule over southern Mesopotamia until around 2000 B.C.E. The region then came under control of outsiders called the Amorites (*AM-uh-rītz*), who established their own empire.

Babylonian Society and Hammurabi's Code

How did Hammurabi's Code reflect the nature of Mesopotamian society?

The Amorites, warlike pastoral nomads from Arabia, came to Mesopotamia around 2000 B.C.E. possibly seeking grazing lands for their herds. Through a series of conquests, they extended control over most of Mesopotamia, which they

Map 2.2 AKKADIAN EMPIRE UNITES MESOPOTAMIA IN 24TH CENTURY B.C.E King Sargon of Akkad created the Akkadian Empire in the 24th century B.C.E. Note that it embraced all of Mesopotamia and some of the surrounding regions. What steps did Sargon take to connect and unify his realm?

ruled until about 1600 B.C.E. Like the Akkadians they embraced many aspects of Sumerian society, adapting the ruling and writing systems to their needs, and even settling in cities supported by farming. Since their capital city was Babylon (*BAB-ul-ahn*) on the Euphrates, their empire and culture are often called Babylonian (*bab-uh-LŌ-nē-in*).

Babylon's most notable ruler was Hammurabi (*hah-moo-RAH-bē*), who reigned from 1792 to 1750 B.C.E. and issued the famous law code bearing his name. **Hammurabi's Code,** a compilation of earlier Mesopotamian laws (such as the Code of Lipit-Ishtar), was carved on a black stone pillar and placed in a temple to promote public knowledge of the law. It sought to regulate matters such as trade and contracts, marriage and adultery, debts and estates, and relations among social classes. It assigned penalties based on retribution—the famous principle of "an eye for an eye"—attempting not only to deter crimes but also to limit retaliation by ensuring that punishments did not exceed the damage done.

The code provides many insights into Mesopotamian society. It reveals, for example, that society was hierarchical, divided into nobles, commoners, and slaves, with different penalties depending on social status. A noble who knocked out another noble's tooth, for example, would have his own tooth knocked out ("a tooth for a tooth"), but a noble who knocked out a commoner's tooth only had to pay a fine. A noble who hit a commoner likewise had to pay a fine, but a commoner who hit a noble would be whipped and a slave who hit a noble would lose an ear.

Property rights, as reflected in the code, were valued highly. Theft and robbery, for example, were punishable by death. Merchants and artisans were penalized for providing shoddy goods, but the principle in commercial transactions was "let the buyer beware." Tenant farmers were expected to give the landowner a portion of their crops. Slaves, who were most likely debtors, criminals, or prisoners of war, had limited rights but could own property, marry nonslaves, and even purchase their freedom (see "Excerpts from Hammurabi's Code").

The code also shows that society was patriarchal, with men having greater rights and status than women. Marriages were contractual, arranged by the parents of the bride and groom and sealed with a **dowry**—an endowment of money or property supplied by the bride's family (preserved today in a custom whereby the bride's family pays for her wedding). A husband could legally have a mistress, or even a second wife if his first one had no children. But a woman who cheated or ran off on her husband could be cast in the water to drown.

Women did have some rights: they could buy and sell goods and own property, which they were allowed to inherit and pass on to descendants. Records indicate that some women owned shops or taverns, worked as brewers or bakers, and even served as priestesses or scribes. But records also show that men sometimes sold their wives into slavery, and that women often died before age 40, victimized by infections from childbirth or worn out by ceaseless labor.

The code was not Hammurabi's only achievement. He built fortifications, temples, irrigation channels, and dams that could cut off water to potential enemies downstream—a potent military tool in a region that survived on river water. He also centralized state administration, appointing officials to control and collect regular taxes from the regions of his realm. This practice was more efficient and less disruptive than the old Sumerian tribute system, in which cities sent out armies to surrounding regions to collect tribute by force.

For all his accomplishments, Hammurabi failed to establish an enduring regime. Following his death in 1750 B.C.E., the Babylonian kingdom declined and was eventually overrun by warlike pastoral nomads using horse-drawn chariots.

Document 2.1 Excerpts from Hammurabi's Code

Hammurabi's Code had 282 articles, mostly assigning punishments for crimes or compensations for commercial and marital infractions. What insights do these articles provide about Mesopotamian culture, society, values, and gender roles?

6. If any one steal the property of a temple or of the court, he shall be put to death, and also the one who receives the stolen thing from him shall be put to death.

22. If any one is committing a robbery and is caught, then he shall be put to death.

104. If a merchant give an agent corn, wool, oil, or any other goods . . ., the agent shall give a receipt for the amount, and compensate the merchant . . . Then he shall obtain a receipt from the merchant for the money that he gives the merchant.

105. If the agent is careless, and does not take a receipt for the money . . ., he can not consider the . . . money as his own.

106. If the agent accept money from the merchant, but . . . quarrel with the merchant (denying the receipt), then shall the merchant swear before God and witnesses that he has given this money to the agent, and the agent shall pay him three times the sum.

108. If a tavern-keeper (feminine) does not accept corn . . . in payment of drink, but takes money, and the price of the drink is less than that of the corn, she shall be convicted and thrown into the water.

109. If conspirators meet in the house of a tavern-keeper, and these conspirators are not captured and delivered to the court, the tavern-keeper shall be put to death.

129. If a man's wife be [caught having intercourse] with another man, both shall be tied and thrown into the water, but the husband may pardon his wife and the king his slaves.

132. If the "finger is pointed" at a man's wife about another man, but she is not caught sleeping with the other man, she shall jump into the river for her husband.

142. If a woman quarrel with her husband, and say: "You are not congenial to me," the reasons for her prejudice must be presented. If she is guiltless . . ., but he leaves and neglects her, she shall take her dowry and go back to her father's house.

143. If she is not innocent, but leaves her husband, and ruins her house, neglecting her husband, this woman shall be cast into the water.

195. If a son strikes his father, his hand shall be hewn off.

196. If a man put out the eye of another man, his eye shall be put out.

199. If he put out the eye of a man's slave, or break the bone of a man's slave, he shall pay one-half of its value.

200. If a man knock out the teeth of his equal, his teeth shall be knocked out.

SOURCE: *Hammurabi's Code of Laws.* Translated by L. W. King. http://eawc.evansville.edu/anthology/hammurabi.htm

---

How did the Indo-European migrations create connections between and among European and Asian societies?

Indo-European Migrations

The warriors who challenged Babylon, beginning around 1600 B.C.E., spoke languages now classified as **Indo-European**. Since numerous languages in India, Iran, and Europe share many common features, modern linguists group them into a language family called Indo-European, divided into subfamilies such as Indo-Iranian, Balto-Slavic, Hellenic (Greek), Italic, Celtic, and Germanic (the branch to which English belongs). The ancient tongues from which they evolved differed greatly from Sumerian languages, which form their own language group, and from those spoken by Akkadians and Babylonians, which scholars place in the **Semitic** language family with Arabic and Hebrew.

The peoples who spoke ancient Indo-European tongues are also called Indo-Europeans. Although their origin is unclear, many scholars think they descended from pastoral nomads who had herded sheep, goats, and cattle since before 4000 B.C.E. on the grassy plains northeast of the Black Sea called steppes (*stepz*).

Early Indo-European achievements include domestication of horses, which were immensely useful for transport and warfare. When hitched to carts, horses hauled tents and supplies, helping people move more easily and travel longer distances. When attached to war chariots, developed in Central Asia by 2000 B.C.E., horses enabled warriors to maneuver with great speed, providing a huge advantage over foot soldiers. When harnessed to supply wagons, horses conveyed the provisions needed

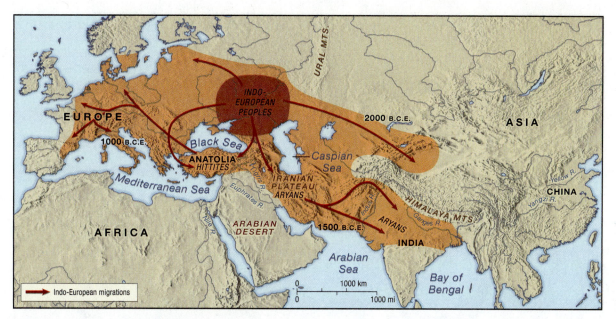

Map 2.3   **INDO-EUROPEAN MIGRATIONS CONNECT EURASIAN SOCIETIES, 3000–1000 B.C.E** In the third and second millennia B.C.E., according to scholars, peoples who spoke Indo-European languages migrated from their original homelands to distant regions. Notice that their migrations, as indicated by arrows, helped create connections across Eurasia. What factors facilitated these migrations, and what ideas and techniques did they spread?

to support an army on the move. Indeed, horses ultimately became the main form of military transport, remaining so until the Second World War in the twentieth century C.E. Long before that, however, horses aided some of history's greatest migrations.

In the third millennium B.C.E., perhaps as population growth outpaced the availability of good pastureland in the steppes, nomads apparently migrated great distances seeking fresh pastures for their herds. Aided by their horses, some went southwest to Anatolia (*an-uh-TŌ-lē-uh*), the site of modern Turkey, while others moved south to the Iranian plateau (Map 2.3). Later some went farther west, dispersing throughout Europe, while others migrated east toward northern India and western China. Both the widespread use of horses and the wide distribution of Indo-European languages can be attributed to these nomadic migrations.

The Hittite Connection

Among the Indo-European migrants were the Hittites (*HIT-tītz*), who settled in Anatolia around 2000 B.C.E. In the 1590s B.C.E., aided by horse-drawn chariots and attracted by Babylon's wealth, Hittite armies swept into Mesopotamia, conquering Babylon and ravaging the remnants of Hammurabi's realm. But unrest in Anatolia soon prompted Hittite armies to return. After 1400 B.C.E., however, the Hittites again expanded into Syria and northern Mesopotamia, clashing eventually with Egyptians expanding from Northeast Africa (Map 2.4). In these instances, as in many others, conflicts aided cultural connections, as Hittites adopted aspects of societies they encountered.

But the Hittites did not simply copy; instead, they took features of cultures they conquered and blended them into their own. They used cuneiform writing, for example, but modified it to fit their Indo-European language. They worshipped many Mesopotamian gods but absorbed them into their own polytheistic religion, in which the God of Storms was the main divinity. They established law codes like Hammurabi's but based them on their own pastoral customs, prescribing fines for the killing or theft of livestock—and death for men who had sex with cows or pigs. They adopted farming but adjusted it to their climate and soil, supplementing grain crops with grapes for making wines and olives for making oil.

What were the principal Hittite contributions and connections?

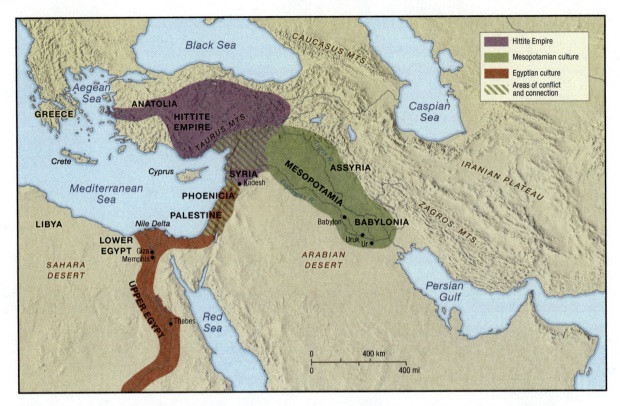

Map 2.4 **HITTITE CONNECTIONS AND CONFLICTS, 1600–1200 B.C.E.** Although the Hittite Empire centered in Anatolia, its expansion brought connections with Mesopotamian and Egyptian cultures. Note that Hittite influence extended into the region now called Syria, where Hittites fought Egyptians at Kadesh and then strengthened connections with them. What factors aided Hittite expansion, and what ideas and techniques did Hittites develop?

Hittites also developed **ironworking techniques** that proved historically momentous. At first they cast weapons and farm tools of bronze, as other West Asians had done. But copper and tin, the components of bronze, were relatively scarce in Hittite lands. Artisans long had tried making items of iron, a metal abundant in Anatolia and elsewhere, by melting and molding it as they did with bronze, but resulting cast iron goods proved brittle. By the thirteenth century B.C.E., however, Hittites learned to sear iron until red-hot, and then to shape it with hammer strokes before it cooled. Using this process, Hittites forged sturdy iron daggers, swords, spears, and shields, as well as hoes and other tools. Within several centuries, despite Hittite efforts to keep iron forging a military secret, it spread to other lands in Europe, West Asia, and North Africa and was developed independently in East Africa. By vastly increasing the availability of inexpensive tools and weapons, the use of iron greatly advanced both agriculture and warfare, enabling far more people to engage in such pursuits.

The Hittite kingdom, like most societies centered on agriculture and warfare, was hierarchical and patriarchal. Its farming villages were united under a warrior king, who was aided by an aristocracy in supervising soldiers, merchants, artisans, and slaves. Women were subordinate to men, but not entirely subservient: a man could have only one wife, a woman could sometimes reject the husband chosen by her parents, and queens could play key roles as diplomats and priestesses.

Although internal strife at times challenged its political unity, by 1300 B.C.E. the Hittite Empire stretched across Anatolia from the Aegean (*ih-JĒ-in*) Sea to upper Mesopotamia, and south along the Mediterranean coast toward Egypt. During the next century, the Hittites clashed and connected with the Egyptians (see below). But after 1200 B.C.E., the Hittites succumbed to new invaders, including the **Sea Peoples**, assorted marauders of uncertain origins who ravaged eastern Mediterranean lands, perhaps after being driven by famine from Aegean islands, western Anatolia, and the Black Sea region.

Later Mesopotamia: Assyrians and Chaldeans

Several centuries later, from the ninth through seventh centuries B.C.E., rugged warriors called Assyrians (*uh-SEER-ē-inz*) from the hill country near the northern Tigris amassed a new empire covering much of West Asia and Northeast Africa (Map 2.5). Noted for their brutality and well-organized chariot assaults, they used siege towers with battering rams and archers to breach enemy walls, then tortured, slaughtered, and exiled conquered peoples to prevent rebellions.

But Assyrians also made important cultural contributions. Their magnificent city of Nineveh (*NIN-uh-vuh*), built near the northern Tigris, boasted gardens and zoos, a system conducting fresh water from outlying mountains, and artworks displaying brutal realism. Nineveh's palace, for example, was adorned with sculptured reliefs depicting scenes from bloody battles and lion hunts, arranged so observers could follow the story of the conflict or hunt. And its library, unearthed in the nineteenth century C.E., housed more than 20,000 cuneiform tablets, brought from Babylon and elsewhere, preserving centuries of Mesopotamian writings, including the Gilgamesh epic.

But Assyria's cruelty provoked fierce hatred that finally proved its undoing. In 614 B.C.E. the Chaldeans (*kal-DĒ-inz*) from southern Mesopotamia, smarting from Assyrian brutality, allied with the Medes from east of Assyria to stage a massive assault. The empire that had tyrannized West Asia was shattered, and in 612 B.C.E. Nineveh was mostly destroyed.

What were the principal cultural contributions of the Assyrians and Chaldeans?

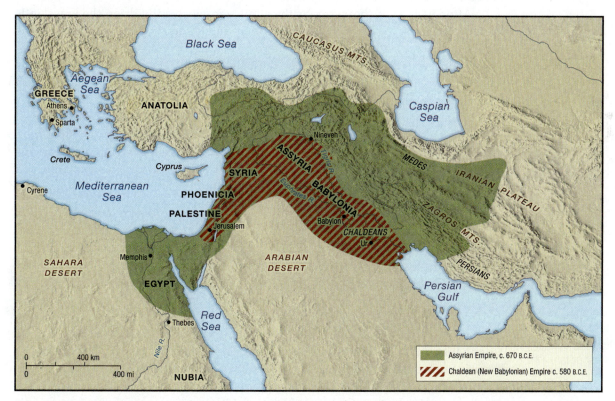

Map 2.5   THE ASSYRIAN AND CHALDEAN (NEW BABYLONIAN) EMPIRES, 9TH THROUGH 6TH CENTURIES B.C.E.
From the 9th through 7th centuries B.C.E., the Assyrians conquered a vast empire that connected Mesopotamia, Egypt, and surrounding regions. Notice that the Chaldeans, who helped destroy the Assyrian realm in 614–612 B.C.E., created a smaller "New Babylonian" empire. What were the key contributions of the Assyrians and Chaldeans?

The Chaldeans, also called New Babylonians, became Mesopotamia's new masters. Under King Nebuchadnezzar (*NEB-oo-kud-NEZ-ur*), who reigned from 604 to 562 B.C.E., Babylon again rose to greatness, surpassing even Nineveh's size and splendor. Its magnificent city wall, including the splendid Ishtar gate (named for the fertility goddess), was adorned with paintings of yellow and white animals against a bright blue background. And its remarkable Hanging Gardens, a set of stone terraces covered with plants and trees, were counted among the wonders of the ancient world.

But Babylon's new glory did not last. In 539 B.C.E. it was conquered by the Persians (discussed in Chapter 6), who eventually overran all West Asia and moved into Northeast Africa. There, along a river running through a desert, they encountered cultures as ancient and impressive as those of Mesopotamia.

Early Northeast African Societies

2.2 Analyze the ways in which early Northeast African societies adapted to their environment and developed complex civilizations.

North Africa is dominated by the Sahara Desert, a hot, dry wasteland as large as modern China. Only the Nile River, flowing north through the desert from sub-Saharan Africa (Africa south of the Sahara), interrupts the arid expanse. According to scientists, however, between 10,000 and 5000 B.C.E. much of this region was grassland, with enough water to support herding and farming. During this era, as seen in Chapter 1, people there herded cattle and grew sorghum, while Nile Valley residents learned to raise wheat, barley, sheep, and goats. By 5000 B.C.E., farming and herding were practiced across northern Africa (Map 2.6).

After 5000 B.C.E., however, as the climate grew steadily drier, the grasslands receded and desert expanded, forcing farmers and herders to settle where there was still water. Some settled near the Mediterranean coast, with its mild climate and seasonal rains, where they mainly herded cattle until after 1000 B.C.E., when coastal ports and colonies emerged with an expanding sea trade. Others settled in grasslands south of the Sahara, especially around Lake Chad and the Niger River, where they grouped into villages and clans, herded cattle, and raised sorghum and yams (a starchy root crop). Eventually, perhaps compelled by a shortage of farmland as the population grew, many of these people migrated south and southeast, bringing their agricultural ways to lands whose inhabitants had lived by foraging. Over several millennia the migrants, speaking languages now called Bantu (meaning "people"), may have helped to spread farming and herding across sub-Saharan Africa.

Most North Africans, however, settled near the Nile River, where they clustered in farming villages along its fertile floodplains. These villages eventually formed the foundations of large, complex, dynamic societies later called Egypt and Nubia.

Egyptian Culture and Society

What were the main features of Egyptian culture and society, and how did they differ from the cultures and societies of Mesopotamia?

In the fourth millennium B.C.E., as the Nile Valley population grew, towns and villages along the river united into small kingdoms. These early states organized irrigation works bringing river water to farm fields; they also traded and sometimes fought with one another. By 3100 B.C.E., through various conflicts and conquests, the northern realms combined into a Kingdom of Egypt, which became one of the ancient world's most powerful and prosperous realms.

In some ways, developments in Egypt paralleled those in Mesopotamia. As in Mesopotamia, smaller states combined by conquest into larger domains, with powerful rulers, polytheistic religions, writing systems, and extensive commerce. As in

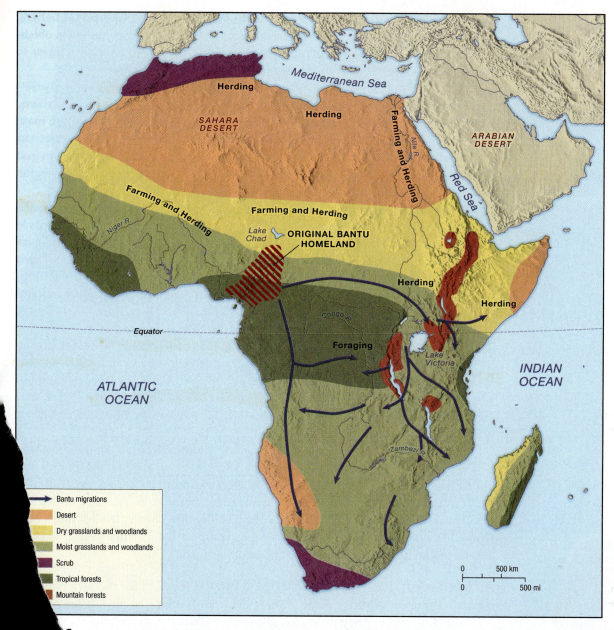

.6 AFRICAN ENVIRONMENT AND THE SPREAD OF FARMING AND HERDING, SECOND MILLENNIUM B.C.E.
UGH FIRST MILLENNIUM C.E. Africa's widely varied environment supported farming and herding in grasslands and
...ver valleys, as noted by labels on this map. Observe that people speaking Bantu languages, as indicated by arrows, migrated
throughout sub-Saharan Africa over several millennia. What factors facilitated these migrations, and what ideas and
techniques did they spread?

Mesopotamia, trade and conquest created connections, with Egyptians adapting ideas
from West Asians and from other Africans.

   In other ways, however, Egypt differed markedly from Mesopotamia. Separated
by seas and deserts from potential foes, and blessed by a river whose annual,
soil-enriching floods helped farmers produce ample crops year after year, ancient
Egypt was bountiful, powerful, extensive, and predictable, much like the wondrous
waterway that ran through it. Egyptian society seemed more stable, and its rhythms
of life more regular, than those in West Asia. Egypt's worldview was less gloomy, its
religion was more optimistic, and its women played more prominent roles than those
in Mesopotamia.

RELIGION AND WORLDVIEW   Religion was as integral to life in Egypt as it was
in Mesopotamia. Egyptians, too, worshipped many gods, including Egypt's rulers.

An elaborate system of priests and priestesses perpetuated traditional [
maintained numerous temples, performed sacred rituals, and sought to instil[
ence to the rulers. In time, belief in the prospect of life after death prompted ef[
preserve and house the remains of rulers and other prominent people.

Central to Egypt's worldview was the concept of *ma'at* (*mah-AHT*), the uni[
elemental order, which encompassed truth, justice, harmony, and balance. The [
eventually called pharaohs (*FARE-ōz*), were powerful, godlike figures whos[
duty was to maintain *ma'at*, without which there would be chaos. They were s[
descendants of Re (*RĀ*), also known as Amon (*AH-muhn*) or Amon-Re, the su[
and chief divinity, who ruled the heavens much as pharaohs ruled the earth. Re[
and governance in Egypt were one and the same.

Despite Amon-Re's preeminence, the two most popular deities came to be C[
(*ō-SĪ-ris*), god of vegetation and the Nile, and Isis (*Ī-sis*), goddess of the earth, who [
his sister and wife. According to legend, Osiris, a divine early ruler who taught Eg[
tians to farm, was slain and cut to pieces by his evil brother Seth, but Isis put Osi[
back together and restored him to life. Isis and Osiris thus became symbols of fertilit[
devotion, and the victory of life over death, inspiring an outlook far more hopefu[
than that of early Mesopotamian religion.

Sustained by such myths and the cycles of the Nile, whose annual soil-renewing [
floods were more regular and predictable than floods in Mesopotamia, Egyptians con[
cluded that life was renewable and cyclical. They came to believe that death was not [
the end of life, that Osiris judged the dead by weighing their hearts, and that those [
whose hearts were light from honorable living would merit eternal life. Religion thus [
reinforced morality, as the prospect of attaining life after death promoted honorable [
behavior.

The prospect of life after death also promoted **mummification**, an elaborate pro[
cess for preserving the bodies of prominent people after death. First the innards an[
brains were removed, and then the bodies were cleansed, packed in a special mi[
eral for months, tightly wrapped with linen strips, coated with gum, and sealed i[
wooden case. Anticipating immortality, the wealthy often had splendid tombs bu[
while they were alive, to house their remains and possessions after death. No ot[
culture has lavished such care on the bodies of the dead.

HIEROGLYPHIC WRITING AND OTHER INNOVATIONS Like the early Mes[
tamians, ancient Egyptians made momentous contributions to culture, know[
and communication. They produced impressive artworks, decorating temp[
tombs with splendid paintings and sculptures. They charted constellations, [
a calendar, and practiced medicine based on natural remedies. They even inve[
an accounting system and developed mathematics to advance their architectural an[
engineering skills.

Egyptians also devised a form of record keeping now called **hieroglyphic writing**
(*HĪ-ruh-GLIF-ik*). Like Sumerian cuneiform, it began in the fourth millennium B.C.E.
with pictographs, to which were added symbols for ideas and sounds. Like the
Sumerians, Egyptians trained scribes to master and use their writing system. Unlike
the Sumerians, however, Egyptian scribes wrote with ink-dipped reeds on papyrus
(*puh-PĪ-russ*), a paper-like material made from plants that grew along the Nile, and
rolled it into scrolls for easy storage or transport. Far less cumbersome than Sumerian
clay tablets, the scrolls helped Egyptians readily record their legends, laws, rituals,
and exploits.

Later, however, after Egypt abandoned early hieroglyphs for other writing systems, no one could read the early records. For many centuries, historians relied on
accounts of ancient Egypt written in Greek after 300 B.C.E. But in 1799 C.E., archeologists with French armies in Egypt discovered the Rosetta Stone, a large black slab on
which a ruler's deeds in the second century B.C.E. were inscribed in early hieroglyphs,

Decorated wooden "mummy" case
used for the remains of an ancient
Egyptian woman.

a later Egyptian writing system, and Greek. Working from the Greek, which they knew, linguists learned to read the others and decipher ancient Egypt's records.

SOCIETY, FAMILY, GENDER ROLES, AND WORK   The records thus deciphered, combined with archeological evidence, reveal that Egypt had a high degree of political and social stratification. They also show that life focused mainly on family, farming, and the Nile.

Egyptian society was structured by status and wealth. Upper classes of priests and state officials lived in luxury; middle classes of merchants, scribes, and artisans enjoyed some prosperity; and lower classes of peasants and laborers worked hard to barely survive. Most Egyptians were peasants: humble farmers and herders raising wheat, barley, cotton, sheep, and cattle.

Marriage and family were central to Egypt's society. Some men practiced polygyny, meaning they had more than one wife, but marriages were mostly monogamous. As in West Asia, husbands provided the homestead while wives brought a dowry and furnishings into the marriage.

Gender roles were well defined but not rigid. In lower-class households men mostly worked the fields, but they also might be hunters, miners, craftsmen, or construction workers. Women mainly did household tasks, such as cooking and making clothes. But women in Egypt seem to have had higher status than those in West Asia. Egyptian women could own and inherit property, seek and obtain a divorce, and pursue trades such as entertaining, nursing, and brewing beer. Furthermore, in contrast to West Asian households, Egyptian families often were **matrilineal,** with property descending through the female line, and wives in Egypt were recognized as dominant in the home. Egyptian priestesses played key roles in religion, and a few women even served as rulers. But governance and warfare were, as elsewhere, mainly the work of men.

The rhythm of work in Egypt followed the ebb and flow of the Nile, which typically flooded between July and September. In October, once the waters receded, the growing season began. Aided by oxen and other farm animals, peasants plowed fields and planted crops, then tended them, bringing buckets of water from irrigation canals. The harvest usually started in February, with women and children helping the men gather crops and thresh grain. The main crops were wheat and barley, but Egyptians also grew dates, grapes, and other fruits and vegetables. In years when food was abundant, the government stored some of the grain for use in times of scarcity. Large projects needing many workers, including construction and repair of palaces, temples, and irrigation systems, normally started once the harvest was over.

The Kingdoms of Egypt

For almost three millennia, with some interruptions, Egypt was ruled by kings, who came to be called pharaohs in the fifteenth century C.E. They governed through agents and officials who enforced royal edicts, collected taxes, dispensed justice, commanded soldiers, and supervised laborers in constructing buildings, monuments, and water control projects.

Although they disagree on precise dates, historians divide ancient Egypt into three great kingdoms and surrounding periods, whose approximate durations and main achievements are noted in the sections that follow. Scholars also have identified 31 dynasties throughout the whole era—each a succession of rulers from one royal family.

EARLY KINGDOMS AND HYKSOS RULE   The *Archaic Period* (roughly 3100–2700 B.C.E.) began when the legendary King Narmer, also known as Menes (*MĀ-nāz*), united Upper and Lower Egypt into a single state stretching hundreds of miles along the Nile (Map 2.7). Divine kingship and dynastic rule developed during this period.

What were the principal features and accomplishments of Egypt's kingdoms and empire?

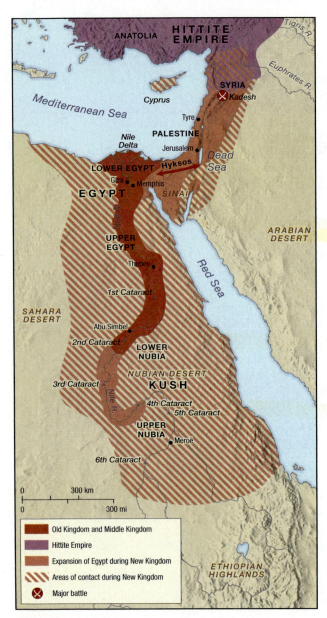

Map 2.7 EGYPTIAN KINGDOMS AND IMPERIAL EXPANSION, 2700–1075 B.C.E. Ancient Egypt was a long, narrow country stretching along the Nile. Notice, however, that during the New Kingdom (1570–1075 B.C.E.), Egyptians created an empire extending south into Nubia and northeast into Palestine and Syria, where they clashed and connected with the Hittites. How did connections with other cultures contribute to Egypt's wealth and power?

The Great Pyramid.

It was followed by the *Old Kingdom* (roughly 2700–2200 B.C.E.), during which Egypt's kings ruled a mostly peaceful and stable society. Internally they created a centralized state with an effective bureaucracy and tax collection system. Externally they established connections and traded with other societies, while largely avoiding warfare. Their most enduring achievements were the pyramids, monumental structures with triangular sides sloping upward toward a point. Used as burial chambers for departed rulers, the pyramids were built mostly between 2700 and 2500 B.C.E. The first one, erected as a tomb for King Zoser (*ZŌ-sur*), was composed of steps ascending toward a 200-foot peak. Not to be outdone, his successors commissioned ever more grandiose tombs, the largest of which was the Great Pyramid built for the monarch Khufu (*KOO-foo*). Standing almost 500 feet high, it was assembled by tens of thousands of workers using millions of tons of limestone blocks, carefully raised and fitted into place with a series of temporary ramps. It would later be acclaimed as the ancient world's foremost wonder.

The Old Kingdom ended with ruinous droughts, followed by an era of civil war and chaos known as the *First Intermediate Period* (roughly 2200–2050 B.C.E.). As central authority weakened, individual nobles carved out domains and battled among themselves, while bandits and marauders ravaged the land.

Unity was eventually restored by a ruler named Mentuhotep (*men-too-HŌ-tep*), from Thebes in southern Egypt, beginning the *Middle Kingdom* (2050–1700 B.C.E.). This era brought an increase in trade with other regions, including Mesopotamia, and a growing belief in life after death. Rather than build great pyramids, its kings undertook vast irrigation and land reclamation projects to expand farmland and enhance the realm's prosperity.

Around 1700 B.C.E. a warlike people called Hyksos (*HICK-sōs*), using horse-drawn chariots and bronze weapons that they brought from West Asia, conquered all of Egypt, beginning what is now called the *Second Intermediate Period* (roughly 1700–1570 B.C.E.). The conquest spawned cultural connections, as Egyptians learned to cast bronze tools and use chariots from the Hyksos, who in turn embraced Egypt's complex customs and religion. Egyptians nonetheless resented the Hyksos, deeming them culturally inferior, and ultimately united to expel them.

THE EGYPTIAN EMPIRE   The Hyksos were expelled by Ahmose (*AH-mōs*), another great Egyptian unifier from the south, initiating the *New Kingdom* (1570–1075 B.C.E.). Born of military insurrection, it was warlike and expansionist. Within a century, employing an army equipped with weapons and techniques derived from the Hyksos, its rulers established an **Egyptian Empire** stretching from Nubia in the south to Syria in the north. In the process emerged two new classes: one of professional soldiers who made up the standing army, and another of slaves who were captured as prisoners of war.

The New Kingdom had some remarkable rulers. One was Hatshepsut (*hat-SHEP-soot*), who became regent for her 6-year-old stepson around 1479 B.C.E. and later had the priests proclaim her king. Sidestepping Egypt's long tradition of male rule, she claimed that her father had made her his heir, dressed in men's clothing, was portrayed on monuments wearing a beard, and often wore one in public. But above all she ruled with vigor and determination, providing two decades of stability and commercial expansion.

After Hatshepsut died around 1458 B.C.E., her stepson Thutmosis (*thoot-MŌ-sis*) III, raised in the army during her rule, emerged as a great military leader. He extended his dominion north to the upper Euphrates, vanquishing various West Asian realms, and south up the Nile, conquering the people known as Nubians (Map 2.7). He was the first Egyptian monarch to use the title pharaoh ("great house"), which hitherto meant the king's palace, and the first known ruler to emphasize sea power, amassing a navy that made Egypt master of the eastern Mediterranean.

In the next century, however, Egyptian power waned when pharaoh Amenhotep (*ah-mun-HŌ-tep*) IV, along with his wife Nefertiti (*nef-ur-TĒ-tē*), attempted a religious revolution. Promoting the worship of a universal deity called Aton (*AH-tun*), the pharaoh changed his own name to Akhenaton (*AH-ken-AH-tun*), meaning "Aton is pleased." He also degraded traditional gods and expelled their temple priests, provoking vast resistance—especially among the priests, whose status was thus threatened, and the people accustomed to worshipping their favorite divinities. Obsessed with his religious reform, seen by some as an early attempt at **monotheism** (belief in a single god), Akhenaton failed to dispatch soldiers to protect Egypt's Syrian provinces from the Hittites, who were then expanding their West Asian empire. The results for Egypt were loss of territory, decline of tribute income, and revolts in the provinces against the pharaoh.

For most of his reign, Akhenaton seems to have ruled jointly with his wife Nefertiti, portrayed in the era's artwork as her husband's equal partner and a woman of great beauty. But late in his reign she disappeared from public life; perhaps she died or fell from favor. Then, when the pharaoh himself died a few years later, the religious revolution ended. The old religion and traditional gods were restored under Tutankhamon (*toot-ahn-KAH-mun*), Akhenaton's youthful successor, today best known as the famed "King Tut" whose fabulous tomb was discovered intact by British archeologist Howard Carter in 1922 C.E.

In the 1200s B.C.E., Egypt's foremost pharaoh was Ramses (*RAM-sēz*) II, the Great, who reigned more than 60 years. Early on, seeking to regain lands lost under Akhenaton, he fought the Hittites in an epic battle at Kadesh (*KĀ-desh*) in Syria. Although Ramses later claimed victory, his armies neither destroyed the Hittites' power nor drove them from Syria. So he turned to diplomacy, forming an alliance with his former foes and marrying a Hittite princess. To glorify his kingdom and himself, he ordered construction of colossal monuments and temples, using an abundance of slave labor.

Under Ramses' successors, however, Egypt was diminished by attacks from the Sea Peoples, the same raiders who ravaged the Hittites around 1200 B.C.E. A century later, the high priests of Amon-Re seized control of southern Egypt, dividing the realm and ushering in the *Post-Imperial Period* (1075–332 B.C.E.). Faced with new commercial and military challenges, Egypt's dominance waned, and power in northeastern Africa shifted to the south.

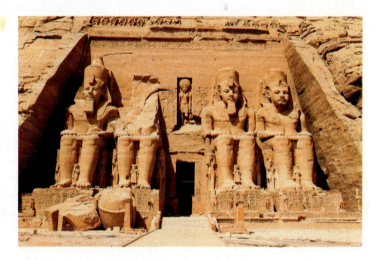

Statues of Ramses II at Abu Simbel.

Nubian Culture and the Kingdoms of Kush

Why was the Kingdom of Kush important in Egyptian history?

South of Egypt was the region known as Nubia, a name said to mean either "gold" (its most precious product) or "black" (the color of its people). Since before 7000 B.C.E, Nubians had raised cattle and grain along the upper Nile, forming a series of kingdoms in the fourth millennium B.C.E. Rich in gold and copper, Nubia also provided

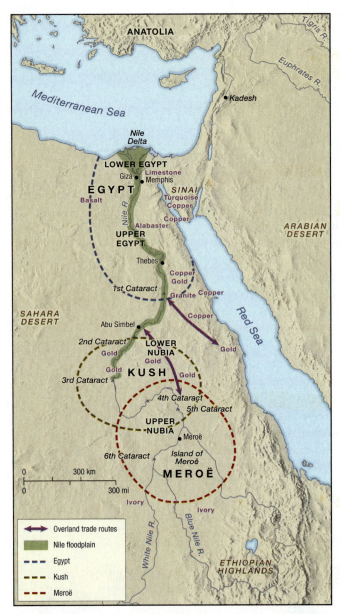

Map 2.8   EGYPT, KUSH, AND MEROË, SECOND AND FIRST MILLENNIA B.C.E. The Nubian Kingdom of Kush, which flourished up the Nile south of Egypt, had numerous connections with Egypt, which it conquered and ruled in the 8th and 7th centuries B.C.E. Note, however, that Meroë, which emerged somewhat later, was closer to sub-Saharan Africa, providing commercial and cultural connections between it and the Mediterranean world. How did these connections influence Meroë?

How did Meroë connect Sub-Saharan and Northeast African societies?

a link through the desert with lands to the south that produced precious ebony and ivory (Map 2.8). As Egypt grew wealthy and powerful, it sent caravans and armies to procure these valuable goods, trading and often clashing with the Nubians. During the Old and Middle Kingdoms, Egypt dominated northern Nubia; in southern Nubia a kingdom called Kush endured until the fifteenth century B.C.E., when it was conquered and then ruled by Egypt for the next four centuries.

Nubia and Egypt were thus closely connected for two millennia, during which Nubians combined various aspects of Egypt's culture with their own **Nubian cultures**. They adapted hieroglyphic writing to fit their various languages and blended Egyptian deities, such as Amon-Re and Isis, into the Nubian religion, which featured such divinities as Dedwen, the god of prosperity, and Apedemak (*ah-PEH-deh-mak*), the lion-headed god of war. In some crafts, such as ceramics and metalwork, Nubians were even more skilled than their northern neighbors.

With the demise of the Egyptian Empire in the eleventh century B.C.E., the Nubians regained their independence, eventually forming a new Kingdom of Kush. Effectively imitating the Egyptian pharaohs, the rulers of Kush expanded their dominion commercially and militarily, and in the eighth century B.C.E. they brought all of Egypt under their control. But they came less as conquerors than as restorers, reunifying the realm and assuming all the titles and traditions of Egyptian pharaohs. The Kushites returned the Nile Valley to peace and prosperity and helped revive art and architecture in Egypt. But in the seventh century B.C.E, they were driven back south by the expanding Assyrians, who briefly controlled the northern Nile. Egypt subsequently regained its independence, only to be swallowed up in the next century by the Persian Empire.

The Kingdom and Culture of Meroë

Up the Nile, as Egypt's influence waned, Nubia continued to flourish, but its cultural and commercial focus gradually shifted southward. In the sixth century B.C.E., its rulers moved south to Meroë (*MER-ō-ē*), a city with close connections to sub-Saharan Africa. Forsaking hieroglyphs, the Nubians devised their own writing system and emphasized new cultural and economic themes. These included increased worship of distinctive Nubian deities, an enhanced political role for women (as indicated by a growing number of female rulers), and increased reliance on camels for transport (rather than horses or donkeys). Iron smelting, developed independently in West Asia and East Africa, spread to Meroë and became a key feature of its economy.

Egyptian influence, although diminished, persisted in Meroë. Its people, for example, continued to entomb departed rulers beneath sandstone pyramids and to conduct regular commerce with Egypt. Lasting from the sixth century B.C.E. to the fourth century C.E., the Kingdom of Meroë provided the main link between sub-Saharan Africa and the Mediterranean world.

Nubians bringing gifts to Egypt.

West Asia and North Africa: The Phoenician Connection

2.3 Describe and explain the main Phoenician contributions and connections.

The Mediterranean world, meanwhile, was connected into a commercial network with the help of the Phoenicians (*fih-NĒ-shinz*), Semitic-speaking people who lived in what is now Lebanon on the eastern Mediterranean coast. Dwelling by the sea, without large armies or extensive farmlands, Phoenicians turned to sea trade and established commercial cities and seaports. By the twelfth century B.C.E., following the attacks on Egypt by the Sea Peoples, who may have been Phoenician allies, the Phoenicians gained sway over Mediterranean trade from the waning Egyptian Empire. Using hardy wood from the cedar trees of Lebanon, they built state-of-the-art ships with two decks of oarsmen to propel the vessel, a top deck of soldiers to protect cargo, and battering rams to smash enemy craft. Adept at both commerce and warfare, they formed a **Phoenician trading empire**, founding city-states and colonies in North Africa, Sicily, Sardinia, and what is now Spain. The Phoenicians thus connected West Asia with North Africa and the western Mediterranean (Map 2.9).

A simplified writing system, developed by Phoenicians, further enhanced connections by expediting communications. Employing only 22 symbols, or letters, each for a consonant sound, this system represented spoken words and phrases simply by combining these symbols. Far easier to learn and use than cuneiform or hieroglyphs, whose numerous symbols each represented a word, the **Phoenician alphabet** greatly aided the spread of writing and reading. As later modified by Greeks (who added vowels) and Romans, it provided a basis for phonetic alphabets eventually adopted throughout the Western world—including the one used in writing English today.

Of the colonies founded by Phoenicia, the greatest was Carthage on the North African coast, established around 800 B.C.E. In the following centuries, as Phoenician power waned, Carthage became independent. Building its own commercial empire in the western Mediterranean, Carthage grew into one of the world's largest cities, with a bustling harbor, a metropolitan population of perhaps 400,000, and a city wall more than 20 miles around. An urban republic ruled by its prominent merchants, Carthage dominated its region for centuries and even sent vessels into the Atlantic to explore the African and British coasts.

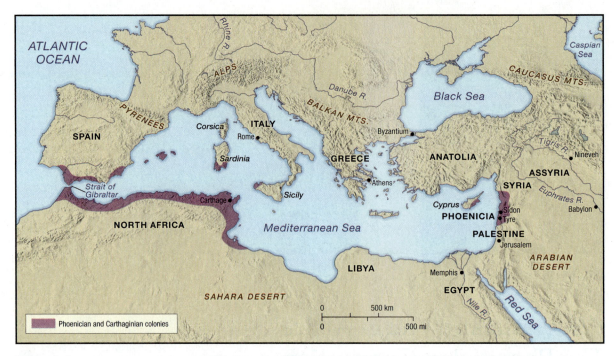

Map 2.9 **PHOENICIAN AND CARTHAGINIAN COLONIES, 12TH THROUGH 2ND CENTURIES B.C.E.** The Phoenicians conducted commerce and established colonies around the Mediterranean. Note their substantial connections in the western Mediterranean, where their colony, Carthage, grew into a great commercial and naval power. How and why did Phoenicians acquire such extensive influence?

The Israelites and Their God

2.4   **Discuss the evolution of the Jewish concept of monotheism.**

In terms of religious legacy, the most influential early West Asians were the Hebrews, a small group of tribes who spoke a Semitic tongue, herded sheep and goats, and were often conquered and controlled by others. In recording their exploits, first in oral and later in written form, some of them produced the **Hebrew Bible**, one of history's foremost religious and literary works. In the process, they developed a monotheistic faith that would serve as a basis for some of the world's most influential religions: Judaism, Christianity, and Islam.

The Children of Israel

What role did the Bible play in defining the identity of the Hebrews?

The Bible provides a striking story of the early Hebrews. According to its narrative, at the urging of his God, the patriarch Abraham left the realm of Ur in Mesopotamia to settle in the land of Canaan (*KĀ-nin*), later called Palestine. After several generations, the sons of his grandson Jacob, who was also called Israel, went to Egypt during a famine to find pastureland for their sheep. There these Hebrews, later called "Israelites" or "children of Israel," were eventually enslaved and spent years in bondage before being led by Moses, a prominent Egyptian born of Hebrew stock, in a flight to freedom called the Exodus (see "Excerpts from the Hebrew Bible"). On their way back to Canaan, the Bible asserts, the God of Israel embraced the children of Israel with his **covenant**, a binding agreement to protect them as his "Chosen People." He instructed them to worship him alone and keep the Ten Commandments, religious and moral laws he revealed to Moses. After wandering 40 years in the desert, the story goes on, the children of Israel finally returned to Canaan.

The Bible reflects Hebrew cultural connections with Mesopotamia and Egypt, based on oral traditions written down centuries after the events portrayed. It contains Hebrew versions of stories found in other narratives, telling for example of a great

Document 2.2   Excerpts from the Hebrew Bible

The Bible contains compelling stories of the Hebrews and their God. In what ways did their God differ from other ancient divinities? How did the Commandments compare with Hammurabi's Code?

CROSSING OF THE RED SEA. When the king of Egypt was told that the people had fled . . ., Pharaoh . . . made ready his chariot and took his army with him . . ., and he pursued the people of Israel . . . When Pharaoh drew near, the people of Israel lifted up their eyes, and behold, the Egyptians were marching after them; and they were in great fear . . . And Moses said to the people, "Fear not, stand firm, and see the salvation of the LORD . . ." The LORD said to Moses, ". . . Lift up your rod, and stretch out your hand over the sea and divide it, that the people of Israel may go on dry ground through the sea." . . . Then Moses stretched out his hand over the sea; and the LORD drove the sea back by a strong east wind all night, and made the sea dry land, and the waters were divided. And the people of Israel went into the midst of the sea on dry ground, the waters being a wall to them on their right hand and on their left. The Egyptians pursued, and went in after them into the midst of the sea . . . Then the LORD said to Moses, "Stretch out your hand over the sea, that the water may come back upon the Egyptians, upon their chariots, and upon their horsemen." So Moses stretched forth his hand over the sea . . . The waters returned and covered the chariots and the horsemen and all the host of Pharaoh that had followed them into the sea; not so much as one of them remained. But the people of Israel walked on dry ground through the sea . . .

THE TEN COMMANDMENTS. And the LORD came down upon Mount Sinai . . .; and the LORD called Moses to the top of the mountain, and Moses went up . . . And God spoke all these words, saying,

"I am the LORD your God, who brought you out of the land of Egypt . . . You shall have no other gods before me . . .

"You shall not make for yourself a graven image, or any likeness of anything that is in heaven above . . .

"You shall not take the name of the LORD your God in vain . . .

"Remember the sabbath day, to keep it holy. Six days you shall labor . . ., but the seventh day is a sabbath to the LORD your God; in it you shall not do any work . . .

"Honor your father and your mother . . .

"You shall not kill.

"You shall not commit adultery.

"You shall not steal.

"You shall not bear false witness against your neighbor.

"You shall not covet your neighbor's house; you shall not covet your neighbor's wife . . ., or anything that is your neighbor's."

flood like one described in the *Epic of Gilgamesh*. And its account of the infant Moses, placed by his mother in the river in a basket and later found by the pharaoh's daughter, is similar to the Sargon story at the start of this chapter. But the Bible's depiction of the Exodus, in which the pharaoh's army drowns in the Red Sea pursuing Israelites who had passed safely through it, is not found in existing Egyptian records. Scholars thus have difficulty determining exactly what took place, and there is much dispute about how much the Bible represents historical fact.

The first non-Biblical reports of the Israelites locate them around 1200 B.C.E. in Canaan, henceforth called Palestine, where they settled in tribes and fought sporadic wars against other local peoples. Among these foes were the Philistines (*FIL-ih-stēnz*), from whom the name Palestine derives, possibly one of the Sea Peoples that attacked the Hittites and the Egyptians. Within a few centuries, the military challenge posed by the Philistines compelled the tribes of Israel to combine forces under a warrior king.

The Kingdoms of Israel

How did the kingdoms of Israel evolve under David and Solomon?

The first such king, named Saul, united the Israelites under his rule but failed to defeat the Philistines decisively before his death around 1000 B.C.E. This task was thus left to his successor David, who won many battles, making his kingdom a prominent power in Palestine. King David also collected taxes, created a standing army, consolidated his realm, and established as its capital the city of Jerusalem. As a result, he is often revered as Israel's greatest ruler.

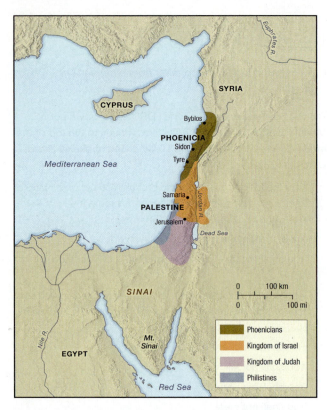

Map 2.10 ISRAELITES AND THEIR NEIGHBORS, 12TH THROUGH 8TH CENTURIES B.C.E. After fleeing Egypt across the Sinai, as related in their Bible, the Israelites settled in Palestine, emerging as a united kingdom by the 10th century B.C.E. Notice, however, that their realm later split into two kingdoms: Israel, whose people were later defeated and dispersed, and Judah, whose people, called Jews, survived later conquest and exile. How and why did they have such an enduring historical impact?

Israelite prominence reached its peak in the reign of David's son Solomon, lasting from about 960 to 920 B.C.E. Building on his father's foundations, Solomon transformed Jerusalem into a cosmopolitan city. His lavish construction projects included a city wall, a royal palace, and an elaborate temple to Israel's God. He also dispensed justice, gaining great renown for his wisdom and fairness. And he forged connections with other realms, often through marital alliances: according to the Bible his 700 wives included women from Arabia, Phoenicia, and Anatolia, as well as an Egyptian princess.

But Solomon's splendor caused problems. His massive projects, supported by harsh taxes and forced labor, offended the proud people whose ancestors reportedly fled such servitude in Egypt. The resulting dissent, after Solomon's death, helped split the realm into two kingdoms (Map 2.10). The northern one, called Israel, was later conquered by Assyrians who dispersed its people, hence called the "ten lost tribes." The southern one, called Judaea or Judah (after one of Jacob's sons), had a more lasting impact: its people, called Jews (a term derived from Judah), managed despite numerous hardships to preserve their unique religious heritage.

In the early sixth century B.C.E., Judah was conquered by Chaldeans (New Babylonians), who demolished the temple in Jerusalem and exiled the Jews to Babylonia. After Persia conquered Babylon in 539 B.C.E., the Jews were allowed to return to Jerusalem and rebuild the temple. But they remained part of the Persian Empire, free to practice their religion but lacking political autonomy. Later, as they were incorporated into other foreign empires, some Jews expected their God to send them a liberator or Messiah, who like Moses who would free them from oppression.

Why was Jewish monotheism so important in world history?

The God of Israel

Throughout their ordeals the Israelites developed their distinctive faith. Their deliverance from slavery and covenant with their God helped form their identity as a Chosen People. The unity imposed by their kings and reinforced by Jerusalem as their center of worship helped consolidate this identity. Through division, defeat, and Babylonian captivity, they struggled to maintain this identity. During times of trouble, prophets arose to speak for their God and remind them of the covenant and laws that bound them to him and each other, as passed on by word of mouth and later recorded in their Bible.

As a result, the Jews saw their God as unique. While other West Asian and Egyptian gods could be vengeful and fickle, theirs was forgiving and faithful, true to his covenant even when his Chosen People turned away. While other gods were portrayed in human forms or graven images, theirs was considered a spirit: immortal, invisible, all-powerful, and transcendent. While other gods could be unjust and unfair, theirs was perceived as just, proclaiming laws based on love of God and neighbor. Above all, Jews came to believe that their God stood alone: he was the one and only God, and all other gods were false.

This concept of a single divinity had vast potential significance, for it implied that the **God of Israel** was really the God of all. Centuries later, offshoot monotheistic religions such as Christianity and Islam extended this claim still further, proclaiming that the God of Israel was a universal God whose covenant and laws applied to all humanity. The Hebrew heritage has hence been central to many subsequent societies.

Chapter Review

Consequences and Connections

After their emergence in fertile river valleys in the fourth millennium B.C.E., the early societies of West Asia and North Africa developed their cultures and expanded their influence by forging connections. Sometimes they conquered their neighbors, as in the expansion of Egypt's New Kingdom, imposing on the vanquished the culture of the victors. Sometimes they were themselves overrun by warlike peoples, including the Akkadians, Amorites, Hyksos, and Assyrians, who then went on to adopt and spread the cultures of those they conquered. Sometimes other peoples, including Hittites, Nubians, Phoenicians, and Carthaginians, created connections through both conquest and commerce.

In the first millennium B.C.E., both Mesopotamia and Egypt came under foreign rule. But this circumstance also enhanced their influence, which was dispersed far and wide by their conquerors, including eventually the Persians, Greeks, and Romans (Chapters 6, 7 and 8).

Later cultures thereby learned much from ancient West Asia and North Africa. From Egyptians and Mesopotamians, they acquired extensive knowledge of astronomy, medicine, mathematics, art, sculpture, and architecture. From Hyksos and Hittites, they inherited the use of horses to pull carts and chariots, and metalworking to make tools and weapons. From Phoenicians, they adopted the use of ships to maintain distant colonies and commerce, and an alphabet to express sounds and ideas. From Jews they eventually inherited monotheism, in the forms of Christianity and Islam. Extensive indeed were the legacies of early West Asian and North African societies.

Reviewing Key Concepts

Sumerian City-States, p. 21
Epic of Gilgamesh, p. 22
Cuneiform Writing, p. 23
Akkadian Empire, p. 24
Hammurabi's Code, p. 25

Indo-European, p. 26
Ironworking Techniques, p. 28
Hieroglyphic Writing, p. 32
Egyptian Empire, p. 34
Nubian Cultures, p. 36

Phoenician Trading Empire, p. 37
Phoenician Alphabet, p. 37
Hebrew Bible, p. 38
God of Israel, p. 40

Ask Yourself

1. What were the similarities and differences between Mesopotamian and Egyptian civilizations? What circumstances account for the similarities and differences?

2. What roles did religion and patriarchy play in ancient societies? Why did rulers portray themselves as descendants and agents of the gods?

3. How did the invention of writing contribute to governance, commerce, religion, law, and the recording of history?

4. How did Hebrew religious beliefs compare with those of others? How did these beliefs help the Jews preserve their identity? What were the main implications of monotheism?

5. How did connections forged by conquest, culture, and commerce contribute to early civilizations?

Key Dates and Developments

	West Asia		North Africa
3500–2350 B.C.E.	Sumerian city-states in lower Mesopotamia	**4000–3100 B.C.E.**	Towns and villages along Nile unite to form small kingdoms
3000–1000 B.C.E.	Indo-European migrations	**3100–2700 B.C.E.**	Archaic Period (*Egypt unified*)
2350–2100 B.C.E.	Empire of Akkad in Mesopotamia	**2700–2200 B.C.E.**	Egypt's Old Kingdom (*pyramids built*)
2100–1900 B.C.E.	Sumerians again rule lower Mesopotamia	**2200–2050 B.C.E.**	Egypt's First Intermediate Period
1900–1600 B.C.E.	Babylonians (Amorites) rule in Mesopotamia (*Hammurabi's reign, 1792–1750: Law Code*)	**2050–1700 B.C.E.**	Egypt's Middle Kingdom
		1700–1570 B.C.E.	Egypt's Second Intermediate Period (*Hyksos rule*)
17th–13th centuries B.C.E.	Hittites dominate Anatolia	**1570–1075 B.C.E.**	Egypt's New Kingdom (*Egyptian Empire*)
11th–10th centuries B.C.E.	Kingdom of Israel flourishes in Palestine	**13th century B.C.E.**	Hebrews leave Egypt (*Moses*)
11th–9th centuries B.C.E.	Phoenicians flourish in Eastern Mediterranean	**10th–8th centuries B.C.E.**	Egypt under Libyan rule
10th–7th centuries B.C.E.	Assyrians dominate West Asia	**8th–7th centuries B.C.E.**	Egypt under Nubian rule (*Kingdom of Kush*)
		7th century B.C.E.	Assyrians invade Egypt
7th–6th centuries B.C.E.	Chaldeans (New Babylonians) dominate West Asia	**7th–3rd centuries B.C.E.**	Carthage flourishes in eastern Mediterranean
586–539 B.C.E.	Babylonian captivity of the Hebrews	**6th–4th centuries B.C.E.**	Persians dominate Egypt
6th–4th centuries B.C.E.	Persians dominate West Asia	**6th century B.C.E.– 4th century C.E.**	Kingdom of Meroë flourishes along Upper Nile

Chapter 3
Societies and Beliefs of Early India, to 550 C.E.

EARLY INDIAN SCULPTURE India's earliest complex societies, which flourished in the Indus Valley, left behind cultural artifacts, including this sculpture of a bearded man. Based on his stately attire and serene expression, he may have been a ruler or priest.

After reading this chapter, you should be able to:

3.1 Assess the effects of India's geographic diversity on its political development.

3.2 Describe how and why Early Indus Valley societies developed and then declined.

3.3 Analyze the significance of the Aryans as conquerors, creators, and connectors.

3.4 Describe the interaction of the concepts of samsara, dharma, and karma, and explain how that interaction affected India's social structure.

3.5 Compare and contrast the connections and divisions that arose in post-Vedic India.

3.6 Discuss how Indian culture and society provided stability and continuity within a divided, conflict-ridden subcontinent.

The **Mahabharata** (*muh-hah-BAH-ruh-tuh*), the world's longest epic poem, tells of a legendary war between related families in ancient India. The epic's most famous segment, the "Song of the Lord" or Bhagavad Gita (*BAH-guh-vahd GĒ-tah*), recounts the reluctance of the warrior Arjuna to fight and kill his own relatives. His chariot driver, a god in human form, explains to Arjuna that, as a member of the warrior caste, his sacred duty is to fight well in battle and *not* spare his kin, since even though the body is slain the soul will be reborn:

> For certain is the death of the born,
> And certain is the birth of the dead;
> Therefore that which is inevitable
> Thou shouldst not regret.

Emboldened by the god's wisdom, and reassured of the certainty of death and rebirth, Arjuna and his kin engage in deadly combat.

Early India

In many ways ancient India was like Mesopotamia and Egypt. In India, as in those regions, cities emerged near a river where farming had long flourished. Like Mesopotamia and Egypt, India had powerful rulers and priests serving numerous gods and goddesses believed to interact with humans. Like Mesopotamia and Egypt, India was overrun by outsiders who blended their culture with that of the conquered and spread the combined culture to surrounding regions. As in West Asia and North Africa, such connections produced diverse societies that engaged in commerce and conflicts and made major contributions to science, mathematics, literature, and art.

As reflected in Arjuna's story, however, India's society was unique in several ways. One was its belief that the spirits of the dead are reborn, or reincarnated, into new bodies. Other cultures believed in life after death, in another world or different form of existence, but people in India believed that the souls of the dead return to life in *this* world. Another distinction was India's segregation into hereditary occupational groups, such as Arjuna's warrior caste, which people had to stay in until they died and were reborn into another life. Other societies had social classes, but few were as rigid as India's. At the same time, despite the celebration of violence in the Mahabharata, India also produced belief systems embracing contemplation and nonviolence. In a region noted for political fragmentation and chronic conflict, the people of early India found hope in the prospect of a better incarnation, security in a rigid social structure, and peace through inner tranquility.

The Indian Subcontinent

3.1 **Assess the effects of India's geographic diversity on its political development.**

India is a subcontinent, a huge land mass separated from the rest of Asia by mountains and seas. To the north are the world's tallest mountains, the towering Himalaya (*HIM-uh-LĀ-uh*) and Hindu Kush (*HIN-doo KOOSH*) ranges. In the south, between the Bay of Bengal and Arabian Sea, is a vast subtropical peninsula centering on the Deccan, an extensive plateau surrounded by low mountain ranges. Between these regions, stretching across northern India, are broad plains drained by two great rivers: the Ganges (*GAN-jēz*) and the Indus (Map 3.1).

India's geographic diversity has often fostered political fragmentation. The challenges of conquering and ruling this vast, varied land have deterred or defeated all but a few empire-builders. Rare have been the rulers who united all of India for long.

The terrain and climate have also had other impacts. The northern mountains have been a buffer against both invasion and the icy winds of Central Asia, helping to make India, much of which is subtropical, almost relentlessly hot. Rainfall is seasonal and uneven, with annual monsoon winds bringing heavy rains from surrounding seas in summer and early fall, especially in coastal areas and the Ganges Valley. But other seasons and regions are very dry, and many areas experience recurrent drought.

In the north, the two great rivers provide abundant water for humans, animals, and irrigation of crops. The Ganges, rising in the Himalayas, flows south and east to the Bay of Bengal through fertile plains that favor human settlement. Although heavy rains in the Ganges Valley sometimes cause serious flooding, the Ganges is traditionally viewed as bounteous and benevolent. The Indus River, however, is less predictable, prone to significant changes in its depth and course. But it was the Indus, not the Ganges, that gave the subcontinent its name. For it was along the Indus that India's earliest complex societies emerged.

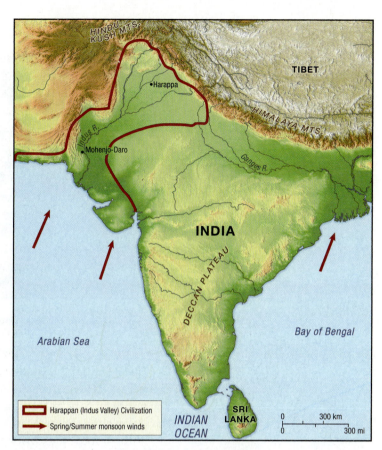

Map 3.1 INDIA'S GEOGRAPHY AND EARLY CITIES, THIRD MILLENNIUM B.C.E. India's geography includes northern mountains that separate it from the rest of Asia, the Indus and Ganges rivers that flow across northern India, and the vast southern peninsula embracing the Deccan Plateau. Note that India's earliest cities emerged in the Indus Valley. What factors account for their emergence in this region? Why did it have more contacts with other cultures than other parts of early India?

Harappan India: Early Indus Valley Societies

3.2   Describe how and why Early Indus Valley societies developed and then declined.

From the majestic Hindu Kush and Himalaya mountains, through the arid plains of what is now Pakistan, the Indus River flows southwest to the Arabian Sea. The river usually floods twice a year: in spring when it is swelled by melting mountain snow and in summer when monsoon winds bring heavy rains from the sea. As in Egypt, the receding floodwaters deposit rich silt, enabling farmers to plant and harvest two crops a year. Thanks partly to this fertility, and partly to farming's eastward spread from West Asia, agriculture came early to the Indus Valley. By 7000 B.C.E. it was home to many farming villages.

The Early Cities

As population increased, the villages grew larger, and by 3000 B.C.E. towns and cities emerged. As in Mesopotamia and Egypt, the growing population, combined perhaps with the need to control the river and irrigate the fields, led to the formation of larger, more complex, and better-organized communities, while farming advances supplied the food surplus to support them. Sustained by this surplus, from roughly 2800 to 1700 B.C.E. a cosmopolitan culture with large, thriving cities flourished in the Indus Valley.

How did towns and cities emerge in the Indus Valley?

Excavations at Mohenjo-Daro, with citadel in background.

The two main Indus cities unearthed by archeologists are called Mohenjo-Daro (*mō-HEN-jō-DAH-rō*), meaning "Mound of the Dead," and Harappa (*hah-RAP-puh*). The entire culture, including these cities and others, is called the **Indus Valley or Harappan civilization** (Map 3.1).

With 40-foot-thick brick walls, more than 3 miles around, and populations of 30,000 or more, Harappa and Mohenjo-Daro were similar to cities in ancient Egypt and Mesopotamia. But the early Indus cities were also like many modern ones, with dwellings aligned along straight streets arranged in gridlike patterns. Working-class districts, with rows of single-room barracks, bordered prosperous neighborhoods of multiroom brick houses with history's first indoor plumbing, served by an ingenious system of pipes that brought clean water from upriver and deposited waste downstream. Clearly there were disparities between the poor and the rich.

In each city there were temples, marketplaces, and a raised citadel with large buildings probably used by rulers and officials. Mohenjo-Daro had a beautiful public bath with a large brick-lined pool, while Harappa had a large grain storage facility with a raised floor to protect against floods. These features suggest that each city had a central authority with power to carry out urban planning and large public projects.

Farming, Culture, and Commerce

What were the principal features and connections developed by early Indus Valley civilization?

At its height, between 2500 and 2000 B.C.E., the Indus Valley civilization included hundreds of villages, towns, and cities and covered half a million square miles. Its people raised abundant food, produced high-quality goods, devised elaborate symbols, and traded with other societies.

Farming was the foundation of Harappan society. Although wheat was apparently the main food crop, residents also grew rice and barley and herded sheep, cattle, goats, and pigs. Key agricultural achievements included the domestication of chickens and cultivation of cotton, used to make lightweight clothing for the hot climate.

Central to Indus peoples' outlooks were family, nature, and fertility. Numerous carvings and figurines found in their cities, including children's toys and depictions of animals, indicate great respect for family and nature. Religious artifacts, such as phallic symbols and images of large-breasted women, suggest that their worship involved fertility rites. And the sculpture of a stately bearded man, shown on page 43, hints that they may have had a priestly ruling class.

Excavations have also uncovered numerous pottery vessels, farm tools, and utensils made of copper and bronze, displaying great metalworking skill. Yet few metal weapons have been found, suggesting perhaps that Harappan societies were less warlike than those of Mesopotamia.

Also uncovered have been numerous square seals, made of soapstone or baked clay, carved with symbols including depictions of humans, animals, and sacrificial rites. Some scholars see them as features of a writing system and speculate that Harappans spoke languages ancestral to those in the Dravidian (*druh-VID-ē-un*) language family now dominant in southern India. But other scholars think the symbols are religious and see no evidence of a Dravidian connection.

There is clear evidence, however, that Indus peoples had connections with distant cultures. Harappan clay seals and other Indus artifacts have been found in the Tigris and Euphrates valleys, while items made in Mesopotamia have been unearthed in India. Especially intriguing are sculptures, excavated at Harappa, that appear to depict Sumerian epic heroes such as Gilgamesh and Enkidu, about whom the Indians must have learned through contact with West Asia.

One of many inscribed square seals found in the Indus Valley cities.

Why did Harappan society decline?

The Decline of Harappan Society

In the centuries after 2000 B.C.E., the Indus Valley culture declined. Population seems to have fallen, perhaps on account of climate changes, diseases, or deforestation and soil exhaustion. There is evidence, too, that movements of the Earth's tectonic plates may have unleashed floods and earthquakes that changed the course of the Indus and dried up other rivers, fatally disrupting agricultural and urban patterns. Without surplus food to sustain them, large numbers of people—laborers, merchants, potters, metalworkers, and government officials—apparently left the cities, moving most likely to farming villages where they could raise food. By 1700 B.C.E., although farming and herding in the Indus Valley continued, the Harappan cities, with their commerce, governments, and specialized occupations, had been largely abandoned.

Vedic India: The Aryan Impact

3.3 **Analyze the significance of the Aryans as conquerors, creators, and connectors.**

As Harappan culture declined, according to many scholars, Indo-European pastoral nomads called Aryans (*AIR-ē-unz*) moved into the Indus Valley from the west and north (Map 3.2). Eventually they spread

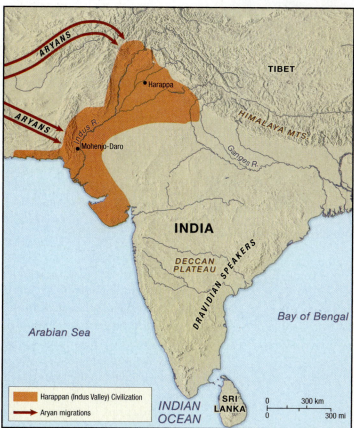

Map 3.2 ARYANS MIGRATE INTO INDIA, SECOND MILLENNIUM B.C.E. By 1500 B.C.E., Aryan-speaking peoples had moved into India from the northwest, creating historic connections with the people who already lived there. Notice that the Aryans came first to the Indus Valley, birthplace of Harappan civilization, and perhaps interacted with users of Dravidian languages, now spoken mainly in southern India. What were the major impacts on India of the Aryan migrations?

across northern India, interacting and clashing with the people who lived there. Over the next millennium, from before 1500 B.C.E. until about 500 B.C.E., these connections produced a blended culture, marked by political division and conflict but also by social stability and control.

Aryan Incursions and the Rise of Vedic Culture

How did the Aryans develop Vedic culture?

The **Aryan incursions** most likely were part of the Indo-European migrations described in Chapter 2. Like other early Indo-Europeans, the Aryans were pastoral nomads, herders of cattle and sheep, with metal-tipped weapons and horse-drawn chariots that made them formidable warriors. Reputedly light-skinned and ruthless, the ancient Aryans were much later hailed as racial forebears by Nazis and other white supremacists. Scholars, however, reject such racial claims, and instead use terms such as *Aryan* and *Dravidian* to designate language groups.

By 1500 B.C.E. many Aryans had moved into northern India, bringing their horses and imposing weapons. There they encountered farming peoples, including perhaps Dravidian speakers, with villages and fortified towns that may have slowed but did not stop the Aryan advance.

Over several centuries the Aryans prevailed, eventually forming many small contentious kingdoms ruled by warrior kings called rajahs (*RAH-jahz*). As these realms fought one another for regional dominion, attacking each other's domains and raiding their herds, conflict and political disunity emerged as hallmarks of Indian society. But conflict and disunity did not prevent the development of Indian culture.

The culture of Aryan India is often called **Vedic** (*VĀ-dik*) **culture**, as much of what we know about it comes from Vedas (*VĀ-dahz*), sacred hymns composed by Aryan priests for religious rituals. Since the Aryans initially had no writing, Vedas were composed in oral form, in meters and stanzas that made them easy to remember, and passed on by word of mouth for centuries. Only after 800 B.C.E., when a writing system emerged, were the Vedas written down.

Although religious in intent, the Vedas provide abundant information about Aryan culture. They depict Aryans as loving wine and music, living in patriarchal families, worshipping numerous deities, sacrificing animals to the gods, and believing in life after death. The Vedas further suggest that Aryans enjoyed competition and gambling, which may be why they are often credited with inventing both chess and dice.

Depiction of the war god Indra.

As portrayed in the Vedas, Aryans also glorified warfare, often fighting among themselves as well as against other peoples. The Rig Veda, oldest of the Vedas, exalts the war god Indra, wielder of thunderbolts and destroyer of towns, and asks him to help the nomadic Aryans destroy enemy settlements.

While thus acclaiming the Aryans, whose very name means "noble," the Vedas disparage the defeated peoples as Dasa (*DAH-suh*), a term meaning "subject" or "slave." This attitude reflects both the conquerors' contempt for the conquered and the nomads' disdain for settled farming peoples, whom they saw as shackled and enslaved to their lands, villages, and towns.

Eventually, however, as in West Asia and North Africa, the conquerors adapted ideas and ways from the conquered peoples. In time, for example, Aryans built towns, took up farming, and intermarried with Dravidian speakers and others. Aryan religion was infused with the spirituality of India's farmers, focusing on fertility, stressing nature's cycles of destruction and rebirth, and inferring from them that people's spirits are reborn in a new body after death. As a result of such blending, by 500 B.C.E., India was home to a diverse and multifaceted society.

The Emergence of Caste

Aryan society, as portrayed in the Vedas, was divided into classes called **varnas**, based on the functions fulfilled by their members. At the top were the priests, or Brahmins, who performed religious rituals and sustained sacred legends, and the warriors, or Kshatriya (*kuh-SHAH-trē-uh*), who protected society. At first the warriors apparently were preeminent, but over time the Brahmins, esteemed for gaining favor with the gods, acquired superior status. Below the priests and warriors were commoners, or Vaishya (*VĪSH-yuh*), who performed basic services such as farming, herding, and trading. Below them were servants, or Shudra (*SHOO-druh*), consisting initially of conquered peoples compelled to menial labor.

For centuries after the Aryan incursions, interclass mobility and marriage seem to have been fairly common, blurring class distinctions between Aryans and non-Aryans. Eventually, however, the system became more rigid. Upper-class families, anxious to protect their status, increasingly refused to socialize or arrange marriages with those of lower rank. The classes thus hardened into **castes**, exclusive and restrictive hereditary occupational groups, based on birth and ranked in hierarchical order. People were expected to fulfill their caste's occupational functions, to marry and share meals within their caste, and to observe its dress and behavioral codes.

Eventually numerous subcastes called **jatis** (*JAH-tēz*) developed, each typically identified with a certain trade, a specific region, and often a particular deity. Each jati, embracing hundreds of families, functioned as a community: its members ate, worked, socialized, and intermarried with each other, caring for one another during times of need. Jatis often vied with each other for higher ranking in the social structure.

The **caste system** also came to be connected with religious notions of purity and pollution. Brahmins were regarded as pure since they dealt with spiritual rather than bodily functions. But people whose work involved contact with dead bodies or human or animal waste were considered impure. Since touching such people could bring pollution, or spiritual contamination, they were widely shunned as "untouchables," ranking below the Shudra at the bottom of Indian society.

Family, Status, and Stability

Although Indian society limited freedom and mobility, it provided stability. Grouped by family, occupation, and heredity, people generally knew their place and what was expected of them. Within the family, for example, women were subordinate to men and children strictly subject to their parents. Within the larger society, occupations were determined by caste and duties were clearly prescribed. Each caste and subcaste supervised and protected its members, providing them security and employment. Deeply rooted in family and status, India's social structure was stratified, hierarchical, and stable.

Yet social interaction and mobility were not entirely impossible. Social interaction could occur when people of different castes worshiped together or participated jointly in village festivals and councils. Upward mobility could come in several ways. One was available to subcastes: an entire jati that excelled in its work could move up in the social hierarchy. Another was available to individuals: those who lived good lives and performed their duties well could hope for a higher standing in their next incarnation, according to India's distinctive religious beliefs.

How did the caste system evolve in Vedic India?

Why was the caste system so important for family life and social structure in India?

The Religions of India

3.4   Describe the interaction of the concepts of samsara, dharma, and karma, and explain how that interaction affected India's social structure.

The religious ideas that emerged in Vedic India, fostered largely by the Brahmin (priestly) caste, are often called the Vedic religion or Brahmanism. Centered on a universal spiritual source called Brahman, and including a wide array of divinities and rituals, this early faith set forth three basic concepts central to the Indian world-view: samsara (*sam-SAH-ruh*), dharma, and karma.

Samsara, sometimes called "reincarnation" or "transmigration of souls," was the basic belief that each being has a soul or eternal spiritual core called the Atman, identified with and encompassed in the Brahman, which is reborn into a new body when the old one dies. Each person thus has an ongoing series of lives. **Dharma** represented the faithful performance of duties pertaining to one's caste or station in life. **Karma** referred to one's fate or destiny in the next incarnation, based on performance of one's dharma in the current life. Those who dutifully carried out their dharma would have good karma and thus be reborn through samsara into a higher status. Those who did not fulfill their dharma would have bad karma and thus likely be reborn into a lower status. A servant who did her job well, for example, could improve her caste status in the next life, while a warrior who fought poorly could be reincarnated into a lower caste.

These three concepts reinforced the social structure. Fearful of acquiring bad karma, and thus undermining their chance for rebirth into a higher caste, lower caste members felt compelled to do their duties, accept their low status, and endure the dominance of priests and warriors. The privileged status of the upper castes was thus also preserved.

At the end of the Vedic era, however, around 500 B.C.E., some new religions challenged this social structure. Rejecting the concept of caste, Jainism (*JIN-iz-um*) and Buddhism saw karma and samsara not as means to a better life but as hardships trapping the soul in an endless cycle of lives. They thus sought to free the soul from this cycle and provide salvation from suffering.

Jainism: Reverence for All Living Things

What were the basic principles of Jainism, and why did relatively few people adhere to them?

Jainism was based on the teachings of a man called Mahavira (*mah-hah-VĒ-rah*), the "great hero," or Jina (*JĪ-nah*), the "conqueror," who lived from around 540 to 486 B.C.E. At age 30, according to tradition, he chose a life of **asceticism** (*uh-SET-ih-siz′m*), renouncing all possessions and practicing extreme self-denial, while also promoting pacifism and vegetarianism. His followers, called Jains, believed that all living things—including animals, insects, and plants—possess an eternal spirit and must be treated with reverence.

Jains therefore practiced **ahimsa (*ah-HIM-sah*):** nonviolence toward all living things. Some Jains even swept the ground ahead of them to avoid stepping on insects and wore face masks to avoid inhaling tiny flies. By showing profound reverence for life in all forms, Jains believed they could purify their spirits and eventually attain **moksha** (*MŌK-shah*) or liberation from the cycle of death and reincarnation.

Although Jains, who spurned the inequalities of caste, were widely admired among the lower castes, few people fully practiced Jainism. Most engaged in farming or herding, which sometimes involved killing insects or animals, contrary to Jainist teachings. Only people such as merchants and scholars, whose trades did not involve such killing, or monks and nuns, who renounced worldly pleasures, could hope to lead a fully Jainist life. Jainist ideals were influential, but few could fully follow them, so Jains remained throughout the centuries a small religious minority.

Buddhism: The Path to Inner Peace

What were the basic teachings of Buddhism, and why was it so attractive?

Buddhism, however, became one of history's most widely practiced religions. It grew out of the teachings of Siddhartha Gautama (*sih-DAHR-tah GOW-tah-mah*), whose influence compares to that of Moses, Confucius, Jesus, or Muhammad. Born into a princely family in the Himalayan foothills of what is now Nepal, Gautama reportedly lived from 563 to 483 B.C.E. According to Buddhist traditions, he enjoyed great comfort in his early life, protected by his parents from distress. But at age 29 he ventured outside his palace, eventually encountering an old man, a sick man, and a dead man. Determined to discover the meaning of aging, illness, and death, he left his wife and family to lead an ascetic life. For six years he practiced extreme self-denial, eating sparsely and avoiding other pleasures. But he found this life no more fulfilling than his earlier self-indulgence.

Finally, while meditating near the Ganges River underneath a tree, Gautama experienced enlightenment, a revelation enabling him to comprehend the secrets of salvation from human suffering. For the rest of his life, he traveled through northeastern India, gathering disciples and sharing the wisdom that had been imparted to him. He came to be called the Buddha ("enlightened one"), and his followers were later called Buddhists.

The Buddha's central teachings, known as the **Four Noble Truths**, can be summarized as follows: (1) Life consists of pain and suffering. (2) Pain and suffering are caused by desire. (3) To escape from suffering, one must curb desire. (4) Desire can be curbed by righteous living. To live righteously, one must follow the "Eightfold Path," which entails right thinking, right purpose, right conduct, right speech, right livelihood, right effort, right awareness, and right contemplation. Buddhists are expected to be kind, pure, truthful, and charitable, and to refrain from faultfinding, envy, hatred, and violence—although their adherence to ahimsa is typically less total than the Jains'. If the faithful absorb these truths and follow this path, they can eventually achieve enlightenment, like the Buddha himself, and escape the cycle of karma and samsara by attaining **nirvana** (*nir-VAH-nah*), a state of infinite tranquility.

These beliefs made Buddhism widely attractive. Like Jainism, Buddhism respected all beings and rejected caste inequalities, thus appealing to people of low caste, such as servants and farmers. But unlike Jainism, Buddhism counseled moderation, providing a simple and elegant formula for escape from suffering—not through extreme self-sacrifice or rigid ahimsa, but through self-awareness, meditation, curbing of desires, and pursuit of inner peace.

Hinduism: Unity amid Diversity

What were the principal beliefs of Hinduism?

Challenged by Jainism and Buddhism, which spread slowly throughout India in the centuries after 500 B.C.E., the Vedic religion adapted and endured as Hinduism, an assortment of beliefs and practices that eventually evolved into India's main faith. Unlike Jainism, Buddhism, and other major religions, Hinduism had no famous founder or teacher; instead it developed organically in concert with Indian society. Rather than becoming an organized church with fixed rituals and beliefs, Hinduism remained a flexible faith with a wide array of divinities, doctrines, and devotions. Supremely adaptable, it readily embraced new gods and beliefs, including concepts adapted from the Jains and Buddhists.

Hindu deities Vishnu and Lakshmi depicted in stone sculpture as sensuous lovers.

Like their Vedic ancestors, Hindus worshipped a multitude of divine beings. The god Brahma, typically portrayed with multiple heads, was considered the god of creation, but other gods and goddesses came to be more widely revered. Shiva (*SHĒ-vah*), the mighty "destroyer" and "lord of the dance," embodied the eternal cycle of destruction and renewal. Vishnu (*VISH-noo*), the valiant "preserver" and protector of the world against demonic powers, was said to take on different incarnations as needed—including Rama (*RAH-muh*), the ideal man and a model of virtue and reason, and Krishna (*KRĒSH-nuh*), a benevolent god involved in human affairs. Among the main goddesses were Lakshmi (*LUK-shmē*), identified with wealth and good fortune; Kali, linked with violence and death; and Durga, a multiarmed warrior often pictured riding a lion or tiger. All three were seen as manifestations of a supreme mother goddess, sometimes called Devi (*DĀ-vē*), a Hindu term for goddess.

Unlike Jains and Buddhists, Hindus accepted the caste system, believing that an honorable life meant fulfilling one's caste functions. Like Jains, however, Hindus came to believe that they could eventually achieve moksha—an eternal peace, somewhat like Buddhism's nirvana, that involved union of the personal soul or spiritual core (Atman) with the universal life force (Brahman). Hindus sought to secure this salvation by dedication to caste duties, devotion to the gods, meditation, and reverence for life.

Like Jains and Buddhists, Hindus revered all forms of life, but they developed a special veneration for certain places and beings. They regarded the Ganges, source of life-giving waters, as a sacred river, bathing in it for spiritual purification. They treated cows, source of nourishing milk, as sacred, letting them roam undisturbed through towns and villages as symbols of nature's benevolence. And they made pilgrimages to pray at numerous sacred sites and shrines. In a sense, Hindus were both *polytheistic*, with a rich array of divinities, and *monotheistic*, seeing them all as expressions of Brahman—the single, unifying, universal force.

Post-Vedic India: Connections and Divisions

3.5 **Compare and contrast the connections and divisions that arose in post-Vedic India.**

Two key developments marked India's transition from the Vedic era, traditionally seen as ending around 500 B.C.E., to the post-Vedic era. One was the rise of Buddhism, which eventually gained great influence throughout India and beyond. Another was the conquest of northwestern India, between 518 and 513 B.C.E., by Persians, whose rule of that region vastly increased India's connections with other cultures. In the centuries that followed, both would play important roles in shaping Indian society.

Conflicts and Contacts with Persians and Greeks

Why was the Persian conquest so important for India's connections with other cultures?

In the late Vedic era, northeast India's dominant kingdom was Magadha (*MAH-guh-duh*), around the lower Ganges in a hilly area laden with iron ore deposits. Although it prospered from its iron mines, agriculture, and control of the Ganges regional trade, its efforts to dominate its neighbors gained only limited success.

Meanwhile new intruders arrived in the northwest. Around 518 B.C.E. the Persians, whose realm had recently expanded across West Asia, entered the Indus Valley, eventually conquering and ruling it until 326 B.C.E. (Map 3.3). Although the Persians ruled only the northwest, their rule affected much of India, bringing commerce and

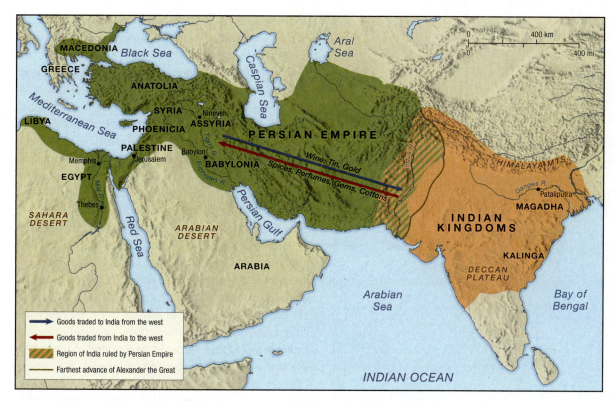

Map 3.3 **PERSIAN EMPIRE CONNECTS INDIA WITH WEST ASIA AND NORTH AFRICA AFTER 518 B.C.E.** From about 518 until 326 B.C.E., the Persians ruled northwestern India, enhancing its commercial and cultural connections with West Asia and North Africa. Note, however, that the rest of India was ruled by independent principalities and kingdoms, most notably the wealthy Magadha realm in the lower Ganges region. What were the main impacts on India of the Persian connection?

connections with Persian-ruled peoples throughout West Asia and North Africa. These contacts enabled Indians to export spices, perfumes, gems, and cotton textiles in return for wine, tin, and gold from the west.

By spreading awareness of India's vast resources and potential wealth, however, these connections eventually brought new conflicts. In 326 B.C.E. the famed Macedonian warrior Alexander the Great, having overrun Persia with his Greek and Macedonian armies (Chapter 7), invaded India in hopes of bringing its lands and wealth under his control. One Indian rajah tried to halt the intruders with a force of 200 war elephants. But Alexander's soldiers fired flaming arrows, frightening the elephants, who then stampeded and trampled the rajah's infantry.

Alexander, however, could not follow up on his victory. His men, far from home, refused to go farther, compelling him to turn back. He left behind officials and soldiers to run northwestern India, but they were unable to perpetuate his rule. His unexpected death in 323 B.C.E. created widespread confusion, clearing the way for the formation of India's first full-fledged empire.

The Rise of the Mauryan Empire

What were the Mauryan Empire's origins and main connections?

In the muddled situation surrounding Alexander's death, Chandragupta Maurya (*chahn-druh-GOOP-tah MOW-rē-ah*), ruler of a minor Ganges Valley principality, saw a chance to expand his power. Having fought Alexander's forces, he adopted some of their methods to defeat his Indian rivals. By 321 B.C.E. he ruled Magadha and much of the Ganges basin. He then moved northwest to the Indus Valley, vacated by Alexander's departure, and added it to his domains. In 305 B.C.E. he turned back an effort by Seleucus Nikator (*sih-LOO-kus nih-KAH-tor*), Alexander's former lieutenant and founder of the Seleucid (*sih-LOO-sid*) kingdom in Persia, to retake the Indus

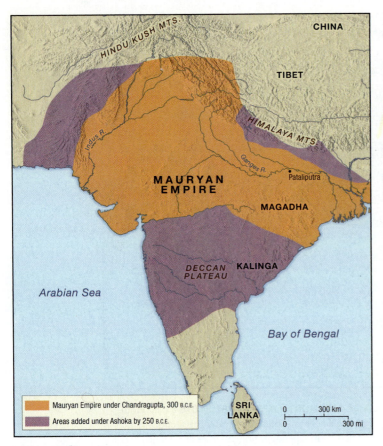

Map 3.4 MAURYAN EMPIRE UNITES MUCH OF INDIA,
321–184 B.C.E. The Mauryans united most of northern India by 300 B.C.E.
Notice that by 250 B.C.E., during the reign of Ashoka, their empire connected
much of the subcontinent. How did the Mauryans benefit from contacts
with other cultures? What were the main impacts on India of Mauryan rule?

region. In exchange for 500 war elephants, Seleucus
agreed to withdraw from northwestern India, leaving
it under Chandragupta's rule.

Chandragupta Maurya thus created the **Mauryan**
(*MOW-rē-un*) **Empire**, uniting much of India in a prosperous and populous domain that lasted from 321 to
184 B.C.E. (Map 3.4). The empire exemplified cultural
connections, combining Indian religion and social
structure with Persian administrative methods and
Macedonian military techniques, while expanding
India's commerce with the Mediterranean world.

The Mauryan Empire developed impressive roads
and public works, a magnificent capital at Pataliputra
(*PAH-tah-lih-POO-trah*)—now called Patna (*PUTT-
nah*)—on the Ganges, and a large bureaucracy to
administer the realm. It also had a huge standing
army, reportedly with half a million soldiers, and a
vast network of spies and agents to protect its ruler
against rebellion or assassination. Imperial laws and
decrees were rigidly enforced, and offenders were brutally punished. But according to legend, in his final
years Chandragupta embraced Jainism and practiced
ahimsa, giving up his throne to become a simple monk.

By then, around 300 B.C.E., Chandragupta's realm
included most of northern India. His policies were
continued by his son, who conquered and annexed
the vast central Indian plateau called the Deccan. But
it was Chandragupta's grandson Ashoka (*ah-SHō-kah*),
reigning from around 270 until 232 B.C.E., who proved
the most memorable of the Mauryan rulers.

Why was Ashoka so important to
India's development?

Ashoka's Reign: Buddhism and Paternalism

Ashoka's reign began in violence, when he defeated his older brothers in a bloody
civil war and then embarked on a course of military expansion. In conquering the east
coast region of Kalinga, his armies killed thousands of people. But the carnage is said
to have so sickened Ashoka that he had a change of heart, renouncing violence and
expressing remorse for the misery he caused. He became a Buddhist, gave up hunting
and eating meat, and embraced ahimsa.

Ashoka then used his imperial powers to propagate his new faith. He traveled about
preaching Buddhist values and had his officials do likewise. Calling himself "Beloved of
the Gods," he built many Buddhist temples and shrines, patronized Buddhist scholarship and art, and established Buddhist religious communities. He had huge stone pillars,
carved with his edicts and Buddhist teachings, erected throughout his realm. He hosted
Buddhism's Third Great Council, helping to standardize doctrines and resolve religious
disputes. According to tradition, he even sent his daughter and son as Buddhist missionaries to the island now called Sri Lanka off India's southern coast. Buddhism, formerly
practiced only in northern India, thus spread across the subcontinent and beyond.

Ashoka also practiced what he preached, creating a paternalistic government
devoted to his subjects' welfare. He dispatched agents throughout the realm to learn
people's needs and ensure that officials treated them with kindness and respect. To
encourage commerce and religious pilgrimages, he built numerous roads, with rest
houses, shade trees, and watering spots along the way. To improve people's lives, he
constructed hospitals, water wells, and irrigation systems. Despite his devotion to

Buddhism, he practiced religious toleration, respecting and supporting Hindus and Jains by helping to maintain their shrines and promote their worship. He personified the ideal Buddhist king, setting a humanitarian standard few other monarchs would match.

Ashoka's rule was nonetheless based on political control, sustained by his large bureaucracy and army. His officials and soldiers collected taxes, enforced laws, and supervised public works projects, effectively administering a huge kingdom with numerous people and languages. He used force sparingly, but the threat of it helped hold his vast realm together. And his promotion of Buddhist nonviolence, while no doubt sincere, also helped to discourage violent resistance.

India After Ashoka: New Connections and Contacts

Ashoka's successors were neither as humane nor as capable as he. The Mauryan Empire under their rule was weakened by corruption and revolts, and by financial problems worsened by the huge costs of the bureaucracy and army. As its power steadily declined, so did its territory. The empire finally ended in 184 B.C.E., when its last ruler was killed by one of his commanders.

The empire's collapse began five centuries of Indian political disunity. In both the north and south, a series of small kingdoms emerged. As in Vedic times, India's great size and diversity hindered centralization.

But disunity was no disaster. In this era, despite their divisions, Indians expanded connections with other cultures. Sea lanes linked India with Egypt and Arabia across the Arabian Sea, and with Southeast Asia across the Bay of Bengal, while land routes connected it through Persia with the West and through Central Asia with China (Map 3.5). Indian monks traveled to Southeast and Central Asia, and from there to

What factors contributed to Buddhism's spread and division, and to Hinduism's emergence as India's main religion?

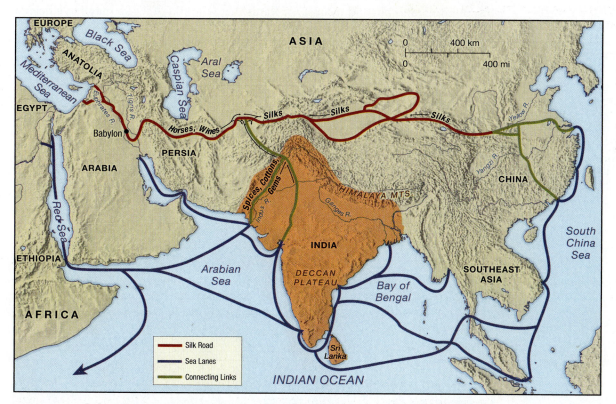

Map 3.5 **TRADE ROUTES LINK INDIA WITH OTHER LANDS BY LATE FIRST MILLENNIUM B.C.E.** In the centuries of disunity following the Mauryan Empire's collapse in 184 B.C.E., Indians expanded their commercial and cultural connections, using land and sea routes linking India with other parts of Asia. Notice that, to avoid the Himalaya Mountains, the land routes to China went north to Central Asia and then east along the Silk Road (Chapter 4). Note also that sea routes connected India with cultures to its east and west. What impacts did these connections have on Indian culture and commerce?

China, preaching the Buddha's message. Indian merchants traded extensively with other lands, exporting pepper and other spices, cottons, and precious gems, while importing horses, metalwares, silks, and wines.

Meanwhile southern India, separated from the rest by the Deccan Plateau and adjacent mountain ranges, remained largely indifferent toward the north. Buddhist missionaries traveled between north and south, and merchants conducted trade, but given the length and danger of the land routes, commerce was not extensive. The southern kingdoms preferred sea trade, first with West Asia and Africa and later with Southeast Asia. They also warred with one another and showed no interest in unity.

THE KUSHAN EMPIRE AND BUDDHISM'S SPREAD   In the north the Kushans (*koo-SHAHNZ*), who were part of a group of nomadic peoples that had earlier been driven out of northwestern China, eventually established an impressive empire centered in the upper Indus Valley. For about two centuries, from around 50 to 240 C.E., the Kushans dominated much of northern India and the lands to its northwest. Their realm sat astride the trade routes connecting India with China and West Asia, making it a crossroads of commerce and ideas. From the west came products such as wines, jewelry, and horses, as well as such ideas as the seven-day week, the 60-minute hour, and the solar calendar. From China came porcelain wares and especially silk, a cloth so prized that the main east–west trade route was called the Silk Road (Chapter 4). From India came spices and cotton cloth, scholars, artists, and poets, and above all, Buddhist ideals, which spread from India to Central and East Asia by way of the **Kushan Empire**.

The most influential Kushan king was Kanishka (*kah-NISH-kah*), whose reign of several decades began at some point between 78 and 144 C.E. A man of broad vision and ambition, he expanded south toward central India and north into Central Asia, creating a large, multicultural kingdom. But he is best known for spreading Buddhism throughout his kingdom and beyond (Map 3.6). Kanishka, who like Ashoka may have been a

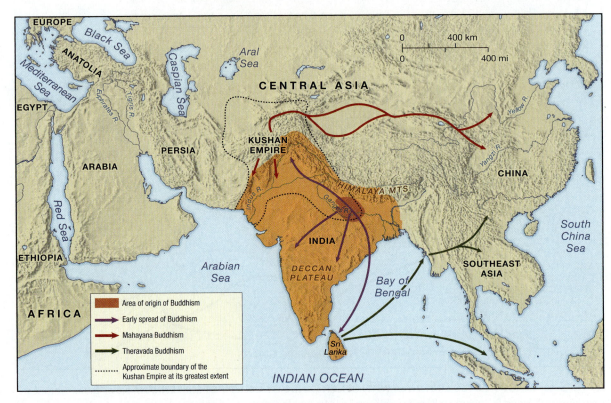

Map 3.6   THE KUSHAN EMPIRE (50–240 C.E.) AND BUDDHISM'S SPREAD Over many centuries, Buddhism spread from its birthplace in northern India throughout much of Asia. Notice that the Kushan Empire (50–240 C.E.), where Mahayana Buddhism flourished, sat along the trade routes (Map 3.5) connecting India with Central Asia and China. How did the Kushans contribute to the development and spread of Buddhism?

Buddhist convert, sent Buddhist missionaries into Central Asia where they preached to merchants and others in towns along the trade routes. From there Buddhism spread to East Asia, where it later flourished in China, Korea, and Japan. Like Ashoka, Kanishka promoted Buddhist architecture, sculpture, and art. The famous popular depictions of the Buddha, seated in meditation with his legs crossed, originated in the Kushan era.

Kanishka was aided by Ashvaghosha (*ahsh-VUH-gō-shuh*), a gifted Indian dramatist and poet who seems to have been the Kushan king's spiritual advisor. Raised as a devout Hindu of the Brahmin caste, Ashvaghosha reportedly opposed Buddhism until he was won over in a debate with a noted Buddhist teacher. Author of elegant essays, plays, and poems, including a *Life of the Buddha* in poetic verse, Ashvaghosha was influential at Buddhism's Fourth Great Council, hosted by Kanishka, which confirmed the division of Buddhism into two main branches.

In the centuries before the council, Buddhism in northwestern India had evolved into an elaborate religion, later called **Mahayana** (*mah-hah-YAH-nah*) **Buddhism**, marked by devotions to various divinities and holy persons. Its followers saw the Buddha not just as a man who gained enlightenment but also as a god who could help them gain salvation from suffering. They also venerated many other buddhas and bodhisattvas (*bō-di-SAHT-vuhz*), saintly figures who, having gained enlightenment, were moved by compassion to postpone their nirvana so they could help save others.

Devotees of this form of Buddhism called it Mahayana, the "greater vehicle," claiming it saved more people than traditional forms, which shunned such devotions and stressed withdrawal from worldly pursuits. Merchants, artisans, officials, and others unwilling or unable to avoid worldly pursuits thus tended to favor Mahayana, which enabled them to seek salvation through compassion to fellow humans and devotions to divinities. Mahayana supporters, including Ashvaghosha, dominated the Fourth Great Council, which affirmed their teachings. As the form of the faith embraced by the Kushans and spread by them to Central and East Asia, Mahayana became the larger branch of Buddhism and the one that later flourished in China, Korea, and Japan.

Scorned by Mahayana supporters as Hinayana (*HĒ-nah-YAH-nah*), the "lesser vehicle," traditional Buddhism nonetheless endured. Its main form, Theravada (*ter-ah-VAH-dah*), the "way of the elders," promoted strict adherence to the Buddha's original principles, focusing on righteous living and enlightenment rather than devotions to divinities. It flourished in Sri Lanka and spread to Southeast Asia, where it remains the main belief system today.

HINDUISM'S EVOLUTION AND ENDURANCE   Kanishka's reign marked a high point of Kushan power. His successors, less talented than he, failed to maintain their hold on the regions he had conquered. By 240 C.E. the kingdom had lost most of its lands and influence.

Kanishka's reign also marked a high point of Buddhist influence in India. Afterward, divided into factions and deprived of powerful patronage by the Kushan decline, Buddhism slowly waned in India even as it spread to other Asian cultures.

Buddhism's decline coincided with Hinduism's evolution into a popular religion. Hinduism competed successfully with Buddhism partly by co-opting the Buddha, making him an incarnation of the Hindu god Vishnu, but mainly by evolving in ways that widened its appeal, softened its asceticism and elitism, and better met the needs of the lower classes.

As practiced over time by the masses, popular Hinduism invited believers to fully enjoy life within the context of their caste. Although Hindus still had to fulfill their caste's occupational functions, within this framework they were encouraged to seek material success. Merchants or farmers, for example, could pursue prosperity by doing their caste duties honorably and well, thus improving both their comfort in this life and their status in their next incarnation. Likewise, although Hindus still had to socialize and marry within their caste, within this context they were encouraged to experience the pleasures of sexuality, so central to the family, and social engagement, so central to the community. Buddhism, even in its Mahayana form, urged people to curb worldly desires, but popular Hinduism urged them to enjoy life's pleasures.

Evolving over the centuries, popular Hinduism also let its followers tailor their devotions to their individual needs. Rather than relying on rituals performed by Brahmins, Hindus increasingly formed personal relations with a certain god or goddess, typically an incarnation of Vishnu, Shiva, or Devi. By invoking the name, singing the hymns, and visiting the shrines of their personal deity, Hindus could hope to create a bond that would help them gain moksha. Over time, Hinduism's ability to meet the daily needs of diverse peoples, combined with its multiple divinities and devotions, helped it to adapt better than Buddhism to the needs of Indian society.

How did the Mauryan and Gupta empires differ, and in what ways were they similar?

The Gupta Empire and Its Commercial Connections

Hinduism's rebound was reinforced by the rise of the **Gupta Empire** (320–550 C.E.), India's first centralized Hindu state. It was founded by the Guptas, a Hindu family whose control of the iron-rich central Ganges region provided it with abundant weapons and commercial wealth.

The dynasty's founder, Chandra Gupta I (320–335 C.E.)—no relation to the Mauryan Empire's Chandragupta Maurya—urged his son Samudra (*sah-MOO-drah*) to rule the entire known world. Falling short of that goal, Samudra Gupta (335–375 C.E.) nonetheless overthrew at least 20 northern Indian kings, gained control of both the Indus and Ganges valleys, and even conquered several states on the Deccan Plateau. His son Chandra Gupta II (375–415 C.E.) went on to expand Gupta influence over west-central India. Together they created an empire embracing all of northern India (Map 3.7), but they and their successors never managed to subdue the south.

They did, however, inaugurate an era of stability and prosperity in the north. As Hindus, the Guptas promoted their own faith, supporting the construction of numerous Hindu temples, but they also tolerated Buddhists and Jains and subsidized their shrines and monasteries.

Controlling major land routes and ports on the Bay of Bengal and Arabian Sea, the Guptas also fostered commercial connections. Under them trade continued to flourish with the West, where Indian perfumes, spices, ivory, and wood were highly prized. But commerce with the East became even more extensive, as Indian ivory, brass, and cotton cloth were sent to China in return for Chinese amber, silk, porcelains, and oils. Trade went by camel caravan through Central Asia, or increasingly by sea, as a growing commerce with resource-rich Southeast Asia made it worthwhile for merchant ships to risk the threat of ocean storms and pirates.

At home, where climate and soil supported good harvests of wheat, rice, fruits, and sugarcane, Gupta prosperity rested mainly on farming. Because of Hindu religious prohibitions, Indians rarely ate meat, but dairy products were widely available. The main obstacle to agriculture was weather, especially periodic regional floods and long periods of intense heat. But famine was rare in Gupta India, where peasants paid a portion of their harvest as a tax, and government ownership of metal and salt mines supplied the regime with substantial additional income.

Gupta prosperity eventually waned in the reign of Skanda Gupta (455–467 C.E.), when ruthless Central Asian nomadic warriors called Huns penetrated northern India. Other nomadic tribes followed,

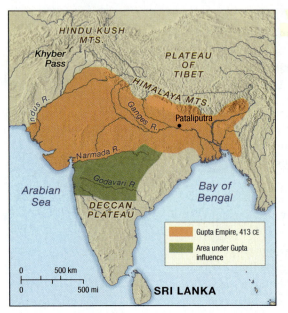

Map 3.7 THE GUPTA EMPIRE IN 413 C.E. India's size and geography (Map 3.1) deterred centralization, so unified governments were often confined to certain regions. Note that the Guptas, based along the Ganges, brought unity and stability in the north. What cultural and commercial connections did the Gupta Empire facilitate?

disrupting the empire's trade and severely reducing its income. Economic setbacks combined with Hun aggression caused northern India's political unity to crumble. The Gupta Empire collapsed by 550 C.E.

Indian Society and Culture

3.6 Discuss how Indian culture and society provided stability and continuity within a divided, conflict-ridden subcontinent.

Invasion and disunity, of course, were nothing new to India. Except for some periods of peace and unity under Mauryan and Gupta rule, most of India's early history was marked by conflict and political fragmentation. But these conditions did not prevent the emergence of a stable social structure and flourishing culture. Like ancient Mesopotamia, India showed that society and culture could thrive amid regional divisions, political disunity, and religious diversity.

Caste, Family, and Gender

How did family and gender roles evolve in Indian society?

Hindu society was dominated by the caste system, which influenced almost every aspect of life. Each caste had its own dharma, with specific rights, obligations, and restrictions. Beyond it was a general dharma applicable to all: deference to the Brahmins, devotion to the gods, and reverence for the Ganges and for sacred cattle. Procreation, too, was considered a sacred duty: large families were seen as blessings from the gods, and any attempt to limit family size was scorned. Since reproduction was essential to reincarnation, for most people marriage and parenthood were moral obligations. Some Jain and Buddhist monks and nuns might seek sanctity in the single life, but for Hindus prolonging virginity was considered perverse.

To fulfill their dharma, Hindus had to marry within their caste. Unwilling to leave such a crucial concern to romance or personal choice, parents arranged unions for their children, sometimes at ages as young as 8 or 9, before sexual attraction could complicate things. Marriages based on romantic love were possible but rare.

Indian society was patriarchal, centered on male-dominated villages and clans. The villages, where most people lived, were run by councils typically composed of male heads of households. Households were largely supported by the labor of the men, who performed the occupational duties of their caste, which for most meant farming and herding. Families were ruled by senior males, who exercised ownership of family possessions and authority over women and children.

In Vedic days women were not entirely subordinate: they could participate with men in religious rituals and, within the framework of marriages arranged by their parents, they could have some say in selecting their spouse. As a rule they could leave home on their own to shop, visit friends or family, and attend celebrations. If widowed, they were usually free to remarry, provided their new husband was from the same caste.

In post-Vedic times, however, women were increasingly barred from religious and social activities, forbidden to remarry after their husbands died, and confined to home and family. Girls were often engaged before age 10, and then wed at the onset of puberty to men in their twenties, a practice promoting both bridal virginity and male domination. Within the family framework, as in other societies, a woman might gain substantial influence. But her primary dharma was to serve her husband, and performing it with grace and devotion could presumably bring better status in her next incarnation.

Probably from the Persians, the Hindus adopted **purdah** (*PURR-dah*), the confinement of married women to certain rooms of the house. Under this custom a woman could show her face only within the family and had to wear a thick veil whenever out in public. But purdah was not imposed on Buddhists or Jains, and Hindus often adapted it to local custom.

How did India's religions and connections influence its visual arts?

Bronze statuette of a dancing girl, found at Mohenjo-Daro.

Statue of the Buddha from Central Asia, third century C.E.

What were India's main contributions to science and mathematics?

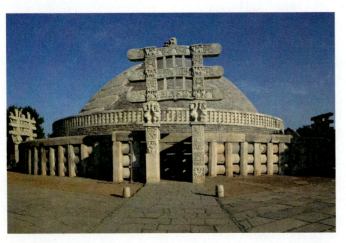

The Great Stupa at Sanchi in India, commissioned by Emperor Ashoka.

The most extreme example of female subordination was **sati** (*suh-TĒ*), a practice whereby widows were cremated alive on their dead husbands' funeral pyre (a wood-pile used to burn a dead body rather than burying it). Although sati, which means "loyal wife," may have predated Vedic India, in Vedic times the widow could lie briefly on the pyre and get off before it was lit. But in post-Vedic times, the practice resumed its lethal form. Brahmins at first condemned it but later accepted and even promoted it as a display of marital fidelity. Denounced by Buddhists and others, and not practiced extensively, sati survived in some segments of Indian society until the twentieth century C.E.

The Visual Arts

Early Indian society, while stressing stability and structure, produced a culture noted for delicacy, intricacy, and subtlety. In areas such as sculpture, art, and architecture, India ranked among the ancient world's most creative societies.

Early Indian sculptors produced superb statues and reliefs, portraying gods and goddesses, animals, and humans in exquisite detail. The sculptors often depicted women in alluring and sensuous poses, reflecting fascination with beauty, grace, pleasure, fertility, and sexuality.

Buddhism's spread later shifted the focus of Indian sculpture and art from sensual to spiritual. At first the Buddha's followers, anxious to avoid idolatry, refused to depict him in any lifelike way. In time, however, contacts with Greek culture and the rise of Mahayana Buddhism overcame their concerns. By the second century C.E., sculptors were producing scores of statues of buddhas and bodhisattvas, some of which still adorn the landscapes of southern and Central Asia.

More impressive still was India's architecture. Before the coming of the Persians and Greeks, buildings in India were made mainly of wood, but thereafter stone construction became more common. In Mauryan times, especially under Ashoka, artisans erected thousands of shrines, some carved into mountainsides and hewn out of solid rock. Even more spectacular were the many **stupas**, massive domed edifices constructed of stone, initially built to house relics of the Buddha and later used as temples for pilgrimage and worship. The faithful flocked to these stupas and typically prayed while walking around them on a circular path. Later, as Hinduism flourished in the Gupta era, many magnificent Hindu temples were constructed, setting the tone for Indian architecture in centuries to come.

Science and Mathematics

Early Indian thinkers, like those in West Asia and Egypt, made crucial contributions to science and mathematics. Indian astronomers, for example, accurately plotted the paths of the planets and stars—and even determined that the Earth is a sphere revolving on its axis. And ancient Indian mathematicians devised an early form of algebra.

India's most valuable mathematical innovation, however, was its method of expressing numbers. As early as 250 B.C.E., Indians used a place-value system of numeric notations based on the number ten. A thousand years later, Arab scholars adopted this system and spread it to the West, where the notations were called Arabic numerals. This system, far more functional than the cumbersome symbols (such as Roman numerals) used in other ancient cultures, so vastly facilitated numeric computation that it is used almost everywhere today.

Philosophy and Literature: Upanishads and Epics

How did literature and philosophy shape Indian cultural life?

Like the Gilgamesh epic, the Hebrew Bible, and other West Asian works, early Indian literature focused on connections between physical and spiritual forces. Its main works were the **Upanishads and epics**. The **Upanishads** (*oo-PAH-ni-shahdz*) were philosophical and religious texts composed by learned writers over many centuries, beginning in late Vedic times, but they also included precepts and epics recorded in post-Vedic India. Composed in Sanskrit, an Aryan language used for religious and literary purposes, these works served as the basic Hindu scriptures.

Unlike the works of ancient West Asia, the Upanishads look inward rather than outward for answers, valuing intuition and flashes of insight over intellectual speculation. They puzzle over such basic questions as where we came from, why we are here, how we should live, and where we are going. The answers, consistent with Hindu tradition, connect mortal beings with the immortal and divine. One's spiritual core is Atman, the soul and depth of one's being; the core of the world is Brahman, the life force of all existence. Properly understood, the Atman and Brahman are identical; thus, each person is one with the divine. The Upanishads provide guidance for attaining internal peace, rather than analysis of the external world. They thus reflect the intuitive introspection often said to distinguish Eastern thought from more worldly and analytic Western thought. Yet some forms of Indian philosophy, most notably **yoga**, a discipline stressing self-awareness and control of one's mind and body, eventually became widely known in the West.

More worldly was the **Code of Manu**, a series of instructions for virtuous conduct, probably written down between 200 B.C.E. and 200 C.E. Prescribing the dharma for each caste, among other things it directs Hindus to speak truth, do no harm to others, depend not on others, avoid eating flesh, and gain purity by tranquility. A wife must be faithful to her husband, even after he dies; but a man whose wife dies may remarry after her cremation.

Even more worldly were India's two great epic poems, the Mahabharata and the **Ramayana** (*RAH-mah-YAH-nah*), written in post-Vedic India based on Vedic oral traditions. The Mahabharata is a massive masterpiece that not only recounts an ancient war, full of legends and godly interventions, but also prescribes proper conduct and devotion to duty. As noted in this chapter's introduction, it includes the splendid Bhagavad Gita, regarded as one of India's central ethical and spiritual works. The Ramayana describes the adventures of Rama, heir to the throne of a northern Indian kingdom caught up in a great war. Later revered as a human manifestation of the god Vishnu, Rama was considered a model of courage, fidelity, and devotion. These virtues were displayed in the loving relationship between him and his wife Sita (*SĒ-tah*), whose hand he won by bending and breaking her father's great war bow, and who remained loyal to him through many ordeals (see "Ramayana Excerpts: Rama and Sita," page 62).

For centuries these epics were recited from memory at family meals and at roadside inns, delighting and entertaining listeners. Their elegance and directness are enchanting, even to many people today who do not share India's religious traditions.

To Indians for thousands of years, however, these works have been sources of inspiration, not just entertainment. Often incorporated into religious rituals, they have served as guides to proper conduct, illustrated by valiant role models who enact the search for answers to life's most basic questions. Over the ages, millions have followed the precepts of the Upanishads and epics, hoping thereby to be cleansed of imperfections and eventually to attain moksha.

Early India's culture, developed through connections among India's diverse peoples, was characterized by complexity and inner depth. It was also shaped by contacts with other cultures and profoundly influenced by the teachings of Hinduism, Jainism, and Buddhism. It reflected a society that sought unity amid diversity, order amid instability, tranquility amid turmoil, beauty amid bedlam, and virtue amid violence.

Document 3.1 Ramayana Excerpts: Rama and Sita

In these excerpts from the Ramayana, heroic Rama, son of King Dasa-ratha, wins the hand of the princess Sita by bending and breaking the great war bow of her father, King Janak of Videha. What virtues and values do Rama and Sita represent?

Rich in royal worth and valour, rich in holy Vedic lore,

Dasa-ratha ruled his empire in the happy days of yore . . .

Janak, monarch of Videha, spake his message near and far,

He shall win my peerless Sita who shall bend my bow of war,

Suitors came from farthest regions, warlike princes known to fame,

Vainly strove to wield the weapon, left Videha in their shame . . .

Stalwart men of ample stature pulled the mighty iron car

In which rested all-inviolate Janak's dreaded bow of war, . . .

"This the weapon of Videha," proudly thus the peers begun,

"Be it shown to royal Rama, Dasa-ratha's righteous son" . . .

Rama lifted high the cover of the pond'rous iron car,

Gazed with conscious pride and prowess on the mighty bow of war.

"Let me," humbly spake the hero, "on this bow my fingers place,

Let me lift and bend the weapon, help me with your loving grace."

"Be it so," the rishi answered, "be it so," the monarch said,

Rama lifted high the weapon on his stalwart arms displayed,

Wond'ring gazed the kings assembled as the son of Raghu's race

Proudly raised the bow of Rudra with a warrior's stately grace,

Proudly strung the bow of Rudra which the kings had tried in vain

Drew the cord with force resistless till the weapon snapped in twain! . . .

And the chiefs and gathered monarchs fell and fainted in their fear,

And the men of many nations shook the dreadful sound to hear!

Pale and white the startled monarchs slowly from their terror woke,

And with royal grace and greetings Janak to the *rishi* spoke:

Now my ancient eyes have witnessed wond'rous deed by Rama done,

Deed surpassing thought or fancy wrought by Dasa-ratha's son,

And the proud and peerless princess, Sita glory of my house,

Sheds on me an added lustre as she weds a godlike spouse,

True shall be my plighted promise, Sita dearer than my life,

Won by worth and wond'rous valour shall be Rama's faithful wife . . .

With a woman's whole affection fond and trusting Sita loved,

And within her faithful bosom loving Rama lived and moved,

And he loved her, for their parents chose her as his faithful wife,

Loved her for her peerless beauty, for her true and trustful life,

Loved and dwelt within her bosom though he wore a form apart,

Rama in a sweet communion lived in Sita's loving heart!

SOURCE: R.C. Dutt, translator, *The Ramayana: The Great Hindu Epic*, Book I: The Bridal of Sita. http://hinduism.about.com/library/weekly/extra/bl-ramayana1.htm

Chapter Review

Consequences and Connections

In many ways ancient India was a study in contrasts. Its Aryan-inspired literature glorified violence and war, but its Jain and Buddhist traditions exalted nonviolence and compassion. Its religious structure accommodated numerous gods, but also insisted that all beings are one with each other and with the divine in an infinite cycle of life. Its political climate was marked by disunity and conflict, but its social system emphasized stability and control.

These contrasts are hardly surprising, given India's vast size and great geographic and cultural diversity. Ancient India was no single society but a wide assortment of societies interacting through various connections. These connections were shaped not only by Harappan, Aryan, and Dravidian influences, but also by those who at times ruled parts of India, including especially the Persians, Greeks, Mauryans, Kushans, and Guptas.

Nor is it surprising that ancient India produced no long-enduring empire. In the ancient world, only a few great realms were able to rule vast, diverse, and populous regions for centuries. The most successful, discussed in upcoming chapters, were empires established by the Chinese, Persians, and Romans.

Reviewing Key Concepts

Indus Valley or Harappan
  Civilization, p. 46
Aryan Incursions, p. 48
Vedic Culture, p. 48

Caste System, p. 49
Samsara, Dharma, Karma, p. 50
Four Noble Truths, p. 51
Mauryan Empire, p. 54

Kushan Empire, p. 56
Mahayana Buddhism, p. 57
Gupta Empire, p. 58
Upanishads and Epics, p. 61

Ask Yourself

1. In what ways were India's societies and cultures like those of West Asia and North Africa? In what ways did they differ?

2. How did the caste system develop in ancient India? What were its advantages and disadvantages? How did dharma and samsara reinforce the system?

3. What were the basic beliefs of Hinduism, Jainism, and Buddhism? How did they support, and how did they challenge, the political and social structures?

4. How and why did Buddhism divide into separate branches? How and why did Hinduism endure as a popular religion?

5. What factors hindered political unity in India? What factors helped Indian societies flourish despite political disunity?

Key Dates and Developments

by 7000 B.C.E.	Farming in Indus Valley
2800–1700 B.C.E.	Harappan (Indus Valley) civilization
by 1500 B.C.E.	Indo-European Aryans arrive in India
1500–500 B.C.E.	Vedic Age: Vedas, caste system, early Upanishads
563–483 B.C.E.	Siddhartha Gautama (Buddha): founder of Buddhism
540–486 B.C.E.	Mahavira (Jina): founder of Jainism
518–513 B.C.E.	Persian conquest of northwestern India
500–300 B.C.E.	Initial compilation of Mahabharata and Ramayana
327–326 B.C.E.	Alexander the Great's invasion of northwestern India
321–184 B.C.E.	Mauryan Empire
321–297 B.C.E.	Reign of Chandragupta Maurya
270–232 B.C.E.	Reign of Ashoka
50–240 C.E.	Kushan Empire; spread and division of Buddhism
320–550 C.E.	Gupta Empire

Chapter 4
The Origins of the Chinese Empire, to 220 C.E.

THE FIRST EMPEROR'S UNDERGROUND ARMY The tomb of China's First Emperor, guarded by a huge underground clay army rediscovered in 1974, attests to ancient China's power and grandeur.

After reading this chapter, you should be able to:

4.1 Analyze the impact of China's geographic diversity on connections between various parts of China, and between China and other cultures.

4.2 Explain why and how early Chinese societies developed along the Yellow River.

4.3 Discuss the importance of the Zhou era in the early history of China.

4.4 Compare and contrast the Chinese systems of Confucianism, Daoism, and Legalism.

4.5 Assess the significance of the Qin dynasty in early Chinese history.

4.6 Evaluate the successes and failures of the Han dynasty and its influence on China's development.

4.7 Describe and discuss the social structures, innovations, and connections developed in China during the Han era.

In 1974, workers drilling a well near the Chinese city of Xi'an (*shē-AHN*) made a spectacular discovery. Much to their surprise, they unearthed a huge underground chamber filled with thousands of elaborate statues: an army of life-sized clay horses and soldiers, each one distinct from the others. Nearby chambers, seemingly guarded by this clay army, were later found to have hundreds of additional artifacts, scores of human remains, and a magnificent bronze mausoleum. Scholars soon determined that this subterranean sepulcher, dating from the third century B.C.E., was the tomb of an ancient Chinese ruler known as the First Emperor.

The realm of the First Emperor centered on a culture that arose in northern China long before his time. Here, as in Mesopotamia, Egypt, and India, early societies emerged along a waterway, in this case the Yellow River. Here, as elsewhere, farming villages grew into towns and city-states that expanded into larger domains. Here, as in West Asia and India, moral and religious concepts developed that over the ages influenced millions of people. Here, as in other ancient empires, the land was united by a mighty ruler, in this case the First Emperor.

Despite such similarities, however, ancient China was distinctive in many ways. The Chinese adopted an outlook on governance that justified revolts against rulers who failed to maintain public welfare—an outlook most uncommon in the ancient world. The Chinese developed a view of reality as balancing complementary forces, unlike other cultures that saw life as a struggle between good and evil. The Chinese produced goods, such as paper and silk, found in no other early cultures. And Chinese leaders, building upon the centralized state created by the First Emperor, assembled a professional civil service system to administer one of history's most extensive, populous, and enduring empires.

Early Chinese Empire

China's Geographic Diversity

4.1   Analyze the impact of China's geographic diversity on connections between various parts of China, and between China and other cultures.

China's geography provides a study in contrasts. The west and southwest are mountainous and bleak. The north is arid and barren, dominated by the Gobi (*GŌ-bē*) Desert and Mongolian Plateau (Map 4.1). Desolate and forbidding, these regions inhibited—but did not prevent—connections with other cultures.

Eastern China is defined by two great rivers. In the south is the Yangzi (*YAHNG-DZUH*) River, or Chang Jiang (*CHAHNG jē-AHNG*), sometimes called "China's blessing." A broad, deep waterway that seldom floods, it is excellent for transport and irrigation. The climate is warm, the growing season long, and rainfall abundant, as seasonal monsoon winds bring moisture from seas to the south. The terrain is lush, sustaining a variety of fruits, vegetables, and grains. In the north, by contrast, is the Yellow River, or Huanghe (*HWAHNG-HUH*), also known as "China's sorrow." It is shallow and flows through flat plains, with frequent floods and occasional course changes devastating those who live nearby. The climate is cold and dry, the growing season short, and nature harsh, with recurrent danger of drought, floods, and frost.

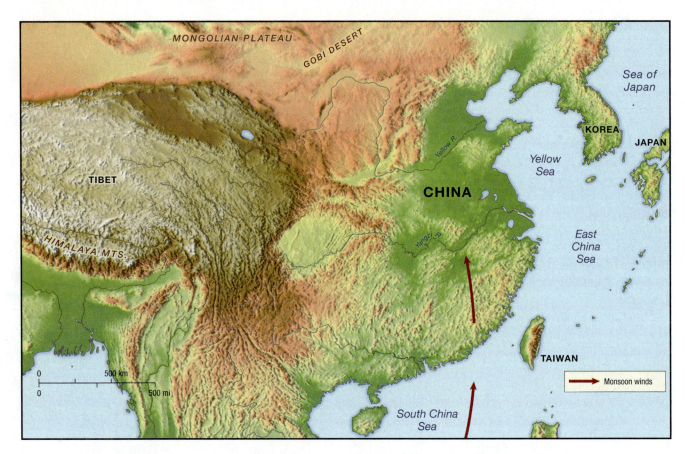

Map 4.1 CHINA'S GEOGRAPHY AND ENVIRONMENT, THIRD MILLENNIUM B.C.E. China's northern deserts and western mountains made connections with other cultures challenging. Note, however, that China's great rivers aided internal connections and facilitated farming, while monsoon winds from the south brought regular rainfall. How did good internal connections and productive farmlands help form the foundations for a strong Chinese state?

Early Chinese Societies

4.2 Explain why and how early Chinese societies developed along the Yellow River.

Despite its harsh environment, the north was home to China's first settled societies. Several factors help explain this development. One is the brownish-yellow silt carried by the Yellow River, giving it its appearance and its name. Deposited on surrounding lands by periodic floods, this rich silt regularly restored the soil's fertility. Farming thus came early to this area, helping to sustain the growing population needed to form cities and states. Another key factor may have been the Yellow River's unpredictability, compelling those who lived nearby to organize into communities large enough to build dikes and channels to control the current.

Responding to the benefits and challenges of their environment, from the seventh through second millennia B.C.E. the region's people developed a culture that served as the basis for later Chinese societies. They adopted farming and herding, settled with their families in villages, instituted religious rituals, and learned to produce silk. In time they built towns and cities, fashioned bronze tools and weapons, established a social class structure, created a centralized state, and devised a writing system. By the second millennium B.C.E., many basic features of Chinese civilization already existed in the Yellow River region.

Predynastic China

Aided by the silt-enriched soil, people started farming near the Yellow River as early as 7000 B.C.E. Farmers there, as elsewhere, resided in villages and raised food on surrounding lands. For protection from the wind and cold, they lived in pits dug in the ground and covered with thatch roofs. They grew millet, and eventually cabbage and wheat, produced fine pottery, and domesticated cattle, sheep, goats, and pigs. Later some also cultivated silkworms, little short-lived caterpillars that eat mulberry leaves and spin cocoons of fine soft thread. After painstakingly unraveling these cocoons, Chinese peasants wove the thread into silk, the world's finest cloth.

What were the focal points and key features of predynastic Chinese society?

The Yellow River.

According to legend, **Predynastic China**—the era before China was governed by a succession of ruling dynasties—was blessed with heroic benefactors. Fuxi (*FOO-SHĒ*) supposedly established the family and taught people how to raise animals. Shennong (*SHUN-NUNG*) allegedly developed farming and basic farming tools. Huangdi (*HWANG-DĒ*) is said to have invented silk, the bow and arrow, boats, and a writing system. He is also considered the first of China's predynastic rulers, fabled monarchs who reigned before the rise of ruling dynasties.

Legend also credits the last predynastic ruler, a former poor peasant named Shun, with selecting a man named Yu to harness the Yellow River's floods. The ingenious Yu purportedly dug channels to divert the floodwaters, creating northern China's other rivers. Shun was supposedly so impressed that he made Yu his successor. Then, when Yu died, the Chinese made his son their next ruler. Thus began the pattern of familial rule, initiating a series of dynasties that would dominate China from then until modern times.

Although they are legends, these accounts reveal ancient Chinese perceptions and priorities. They show that the Chinese saw family, farming, writing, river control, and dynastic rule as central to their culture. Furthermore, when augmented by archeological evidence, these stories help historians discern the general features of China's society under its first two dynasties.

Xia and Shang Societies

Yu and his son are traditionally regarded as the first two rulers of the **Xia** (shē-AH) **dynasty**, which governed the central Yellow River region from about 2200 to 1750 B.C.E. (Map 4.2). Once seen as a figment of folklore, the Xia is now considered China's first historical dynasty, as cities and towns unearthed in the area offer evidence of a real Xia realm. One large city called Erlitou (*ER-lē-TŌ*), possibly the capital, had paved roads, stately palaces and tombs, and a foundry for making bronze tools and weapons.

What were the key characteristics and connections of Chinese societies in the Xia and Shang eras?

Bronze metallurgy probably came to China via Indo-European migrations, discussed in Chapter 2, which provided early connections among Eurasian cultures. Much as Hittites moved to Anatolia and Aryans to India, other Indo-European

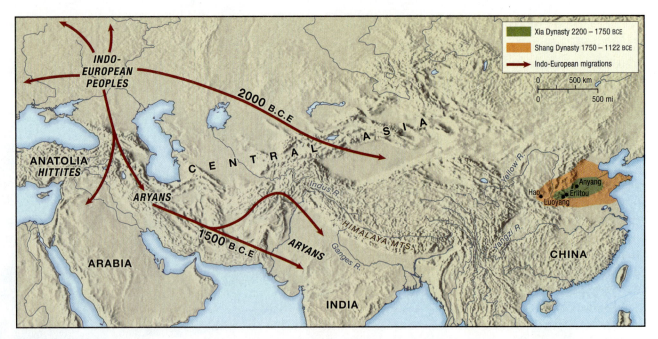

Map 4.2 **CHINA'S EARLY DYNASTIES AND CENTRAL ASIAN CONNECTIONS, SECOND MILLENNIUM B.C.E.** China's earliest cities and dynastic states were located in northern China around the Yellow River. Observe that Indo-European nomads apparently migrated to the region west of China by around 2000 B.C.E. What ideas and techniques might the Chinese have learned through connections with these nomads?

pastoral nomads moved toward northwest China during the Xia dynasty, bringing horse-drawn chariots and bronze weapons. The subsequent appearance of such devices in China, and similarities between old Chinese and Indo-European words for wheels and chariots, suggest that China learned of these devices through connections with the nomads.

Some Chinese warriors made good use of these vehicles and weapons. In the eighteenth century B.C.E., according to both legend and archeological evidence, the Xia regime was defeated and displaced by a new dynasty, the Shang (*SHAHNG*), whose warriors used bronze spears, bronze armor, and war chariots.

Since the **Shang dynasty** (roughly 1750 to 1122 B.C.E.) produced some written records, historians know much more about it than the Xia. These records, along with excavations of Shang settlements such as the capital, Anyang (*AHN-YAHNG*), portray a complex, warlike, stratified society.

By Shang times, a number of city-states had emerged in northern China. Although each had its own ruler, many of them were tied by allegiance and/or kinship to the Shang royal family. These connections created some political unity.

Shang society was stratified into several classes. At the top were the king and his warrior nobles, who lived in city centers in palatial homes, wore silk garments, and consumed food and beverages from bronze vessels. Below them were artisans, living elsewhere in the cities in homes of earth and wood, who produced bronze vessels and weapons, lacquered wood containers, and fine pottery for the upper classes. Less well off were the peasants, living in pit homes in rural villages and working the fields to supply the society's food. And at the bottom were slaves, often prisoners of war, who worked as servants in royal and noble households and as forced laborers in constructing walls, roads, palaces, and dikes.

Remains of early Chinese chariots.

Although Shang leaders worshipped a main deity and numerous lesser gods, the most common religion was probably **ancestor worship**, veneration of a family's departed relatives and forebears. Based on belief that spirits of the dead can aid their living relatives by influencing the gods, this worship involved rituals performed at graves and shrines set up to honor dead kinfolk.

The early Chinese apparently sacrificed animals, and sometimes even slaves, to win divine favor. They also studied the sun and stars, presuming this study would help discern the will of the gods. In the process they devised a calendar and a form of mathematics.

Chinese Writing and Regional Connections

Ancient **Chinese writing** likewise evolved from religious practices. For centuries Chinese oracles—spiritual leaders who sought communication with the gods—inscribed little pictures on a tortoise shell or cattle shoulder bone and then heated it until cracks appeared. The oracles then followed the cracks to connect the pictures, each representing a word, in a sequence believed to convey divine messages. By inscribing pictures denoting clouds, sun, rain, and upcoming days, for example, and then seeing how the heat cracks connected them, oracles could theoretically foretell the weather. By using other pictures and symbols, oracles could similarly predict the results of battles, hunts, and harvests.

Shang rulers, anxious to foresee the outcome of such endeavors, made extensive use of these "oracle bones," thousands of which have been found in modern China. Scholars have deciphered the oracle bone symbols and found them to be early versions of modern Chinese characters.

In Chinese writing, each character represents a word, not just a sound as in Western alphabets derived from the Phoenicians (Chapter 2). To read and write Chinese has hence meant mastering thousands of symbols. But since it was not closely tied to spoken sounds, the system proved useful in China, where people in one region often could not understand dialects spoken elsewhere. Since each written character conveyed the same concept no matter what the dialect, people could communicate in writing even if they could not understand each others' speech. The written character for horse, for example, conveyed the concept of horse to people who spoke different dialects, even if the spoken words for horse did not sound the same. Chinese writing thus helped create the connections needed to unite a vast and diverse land. And, as elsewhere, writing enabled people to record their history and ideas.

State and Society During the Zhou Dynasty

4.3   **Discuss the importance of the Zhou era in the early history of China.**

By the late twelfth century B.C.E., according to traditional accounts, Shang kings had become oppressive and corrupt, provoking rebellions against them. The victor was King Wu, ruler of Zhou (*JŌ*), a realm west of the Shang domain. In 1122 B.C.E. he defeated the Shang and started a new dynasty that lasted more than 800 years. The **Zhou dynasty** is traditionally divided into two periods: Western Zhou (1122–771 B.C.E.), when the kings resided at Hao (*HOW*) in the west (Map 4.3), and Eastern Zhou (770–256 B.C.E.), when they lived farther east at Luoyang (*LWŌ-YAHNG*).

The Mandate of Heaven and the Dynastic Cycle

Composed by Zhou era writers, traditional accounts of the Shang's overthrow denounce the old dynasty and exalt early Zhou leaders—especially King Wu's brother, the legendary Duke of Zhou. Based on these accounts, after King Wu died

How did Chinese writing develop, and how did it help to connect a vast, diverse realm?

Shang oracle bone.

What were the Mandate of Heaven and the dynastic cycle, and what were their implications for Chinese governance?

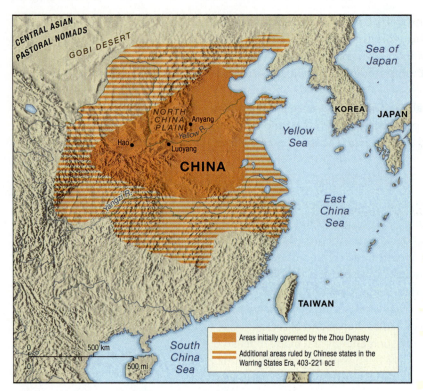

Map 4.3 **THE ZHOU DYNASTY, 1122–256 B.C.E.** The Zhou dynasty connected much of northern China, extending its rule through the Yellow River region and beyond. Note, however, that in the Warring States era (403–221 B.C.E.), various nobles with their own large armies came to control a vast area as independent warlords. What commercial and cultural developments continued to connect Chinese society?

in 1116 B.C.E., the duke served as regent for Wu's son, the new king, who was too young to rule on his own. The duke reportedly solidified Zhou rule, destroyed vestiges of the Shang, and capably ran the realm. When the new king came of age to rule, the duke then stepped aside, loyally affirming the father–son succession and setting a precedent for future public servants.

The Duke of Zhou's main contribution, however, may have been to lay the philosophical foundations for Chinese dynastic authority. To justify his family's ouster of one dynasty and creation of another, he allegedly developed the idea of the **Mandate of Heaven**. This concept asserts that, to rightfully rule China, a dynasty must have authorization from "Heaven," perceived not as a place but as the god of the skies and ancestor of Chinese rulers. This mandate empowered the ruler to reign as "Son of Heaven" but also required that he govern justly and humanely. If a ruler grew corrupt and oppressive and the people suffered, Heaven would withdraw the mandate and bestow it on someone else, who would take power and rule with virtue and benevolence. This principle thus legitimized the Zhou overthrow of the Shang.

In claiming this mandate, however, Zhou leaders unwittingly supplied both precedent and pretext for future rebels to challenge a reigning dynasty, establishing a pattern that recurred throughout Chinese history. Known as the **dynastic cycle**, it had four main phases. First, a strong leader conquered all of China, creating a powerful, effective regime. Then he passed on power to his heirs, continuing the dynasty and its era of stability and prosperity. But eventually the rulers grew corrupt, taxes increased, and prosperity declined, as natural and military disasters signaled the loss of Heaven's Mandate. In the cycle's final phase, a new hero arose to claim the mandate and challenge the old dynasty. If he failed to gain power, he was seen as lacking Heaven's favor; if he succeeded, he started a new dynasty, beginning the cycle anew.

The rise and fall of ruling families was not unique to China; Egypt, for example, also had a long chain of dynasties. But the Mandate of Heaven and the dynastic cycle set up expectations that were distinctively Chinese. In China, a dynasty was expected to provide stability and prosperity. If it failed, it forfeited its mandate, giving people a right to rebel.

Conflict, Chaos, and Commerce

What factors kept China connected during the Era of Warring States?

This implicit right of rebellion, combined with China's vast size and cultural complexity, made governance a formidable challenge. Rather than try to control their territories directly, early Zhou rulers developed a decentralized regime in which regions were governed by subordinates, who received landholdings for their service. These lands were handed down from father to son, producing a hereditary nobility based on service to the king. But for kings this system could be risky, as powerful nobles with their own lands and armies could potentially threaten the regime.

This threat almost ended the Zhou dynasty in 771 B.C.E., when rebellious nobles joined with nomadic invaders to overthrow a king named You. According to legend, King You sometimes amused a female consort by lighting beacon fires signaling his soldiers to prepare for enemy attack, then having her watch in delight as armies assembled to meet the nonexistent threat. But eventually the soldiers, tired of this game, did not respond to the beacon fires when real attackers appeared. They overran the capital, ransacked the palace, and killed King You.

Whatever the truth of this tale—patriarchal societies often have legends blaming women for men's misfortunes—it helped justify You's removal. But his heir fled east to the city of Luoyang, making it his capital and starting a new era now called the Eastern Zhou.

In the Eastern Zhou era (770–256 B.C.E.), many Chinese nobles surpassed the king in wealth and power, acting as independent warlords in their own domains. The result was an Era of Warring States (403–221 B.C.E.), during which all sense of unity and central authority ceased (see Map 4.3).

Yet as conflict divided China, commerce formed new connections. The Eastern Zhou era produced many new cities, which served as trading centers, with markets where farmers, artisans, and merchants exchanged goods. Roads and canals connecting these cities, built by rulers to move troops and supplies, were traveled by traders transporting such items as metal tools and utensils, lacquered wood plates and boxes, silk, pottery, gems, salt, and lumber. A money economy emerged, using copper coins called cash, with center holes for stringing them together for counting and carrying. China's towns and cities were likewise linked into a large economic system. Trade between China and distant lands was difficult and dangerous, but by the era's end commerce was conducted by sea with Southeast Asia and by land routes crossing Central Asia.

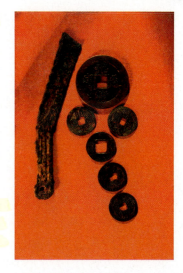

Copper coins called cash.

The Central Asian Connection

Central Asia, a vast expanse to China's north and west where the climate was too dry for farming (Map 4.2), was home mainly to pastoral nomads who grazed herds on its plateaus and plains. Skilled on horseback, the nomads occasionally attacked Chinese settlements to carry off goods and supplies, but they also spread commerce and useful knowledge. Some nomads, for example, exchanged their hides, wool, and horses for Chinese silk, pottery, metalware, and wood products and then traded these items with other societies across Central Asia. Over time, connections with the nomads, and through them with other Eurasian societies, had major impacts on China.

Nomadic connections, for example, transformed Chinese warfare in the Eastern Zhou era. From the nomads Chinese armies adopted horseback riding, replacing charioteers with mounted riders who moved and maneuvered more quickly. The nomads in turn began using the crossbow, a Chinese invention that could kill with precision from a distance.

Even more momentous was ironworking, a West Asian innovation that spread through Central Asia to China in this era. Since iron was far more abundant than copper and tin for making bronze, it produced far more shields and daggers, enabling rulers to field much larger forces. No longer limited to modest forces of bronze-armed noble warriors on horseback, Chinese armies now fielded tens of thousands of peasant foot soldiers armed with iron weapons.

Ironworking also brought China economic benefits. Crop cultivation was vastly enhanced by iron plows and seed drills, pulled by oxen hitched to a wooden harness, and by iron-bladed spades, used in tilling soil and digging irrigation ditches to expand arable farmland. Iron picks and shovels were used in building earthen dams and dikes to protect against floods, earthen walls to defend against nomad attacks, and roads and canals to aid movement of armies and goods. Central Asian connections thus helped to expand China's warfare, farming, and commerce.

How important were Central Asian connections in the development of China?

Chinese peasant using seed drill.

The Classical Age of Chinese Philosophy

4.4   Compare and contrast the Chinese systems of Confucianism, Daoism, and Legalism.

The Eastern Zhou era, with its ongoing warfare and economic growth, also furnished ideas intended to promote harmony and stability. These ideas laid the basis for China's main belief systems: Confucianism, Daoism, and Legalism.

Historians have noted that this era, from the eighth through third centuries B.C.E., also produced Buddhism, Jainism, and the Upanishads in India, the Avesta (sacred book) of Persia, the major Hebrew prophets, and the foremost Greek philosophers. Although China's great thinkers lacked direct contact with those in distant societies, increasing connections among these societies doubtless fed the intellectual ferment that inspired some of history's great belief systems.

Confucianism: Noble-Minded Conduct and Familial Respect

What were Confucianism's main ideals, virtues, and implications for human relations and governance?

The central Chinese philosopher was Kongfuzi (*KŌNG-FOO-DZUH*) or Master Kong the Sage (551–479 B.C.E.). Later known in the West as Confucius, he laid the foundations for China's foremost ethical system. Like other famous teachers, including the Buddha and Jesus, Confucius left no writings, making it hard to separate his views from those later added by his followers. His impact nonetheless has been immense.

Raised in a minor noble family, in humble conditions following his father's early death, Confucius aspired to a political career. He dreamed of becoming a wise official who, like the legendary Duke of Zhou, would help some ruler create a just society. For years he sought such a post but only held a few brief positions. Frustrated by this indifference to his ideas, he became a wandering teacher, earnestly preaching to a growing group of disciples.

After Confucius died his followers compiled his ideas in the *Analects*, a collection of sayings typically prefaced by "The Master said. . . ." They depict a man, deeply troubled by chaos and corruption, eager to bring social order and harmony to his violent era. The *Analects* envision a society regulated not by rigid laws but by virtuous behavior of leaders and citizens, idealizing "noble-minded" public servants who inspire by example and treat people with wisdom, compassion, and respect. Over the next few centuries, these ideas developed into **Confucianism**, a system of thought that dominated China for more than 2000 years.

Although Confucians recognized the deity called Heaven and later built many temples, Confucianism was less a religion than an ethical philosophy. Based on the *Analects* and Five Classics, a set of Chinese literary works compiled over many centuries, Confucian philosophy focused on human behavior rather than divine worship. Its main virtues included

Confucius and his disciples.

- *ren* (*RUN*), or "humanity," involving compassion, humane conduct, and benevolence;
- *li* (*LĒ*), or "ritual," the courtesy and etiquette by which people should treat one another; and
- *xiao* (*shē-OW*), or "filial piety," the devotion that a son owed his father (and, by extension, that all people owed their parents, ancestors, and leaders).

In promoting these virtues, Confucianism envisioned a hierarchical society in which all people knew their place, based on mutual respect between rulers and subjects, parents and children, spouses, siblings, and friends (the "five relationships"). Its main premise was that people would follow and imitate noble-minded leaders. Although elitist in upholding an all-male ruling class of scholars and gentlemen, Confucianism favored nobility of spirit rather than nobility of birth. Although conservative in championing the virtues and values of the past, it was progressive in stressing rulers' duties to provide good government (see "Excerpts from the *Analects*").

Document 4.1   Excerpts from the *Analects*

*In the **Analects**, followers of Confucius recorded his sayings and ideas about living a noble-minded, honorable life. How would these ideas contribute to stability in China?*

The Master said: "Worthy admonitions cannot fail to inspire us, but what matters is changing ourselves. Reverent advice cannot fail to encourage us, but what matters is acting on it . . ."

The Master said: "Above all, be loyal and stand by your words. Befriend only those who are kindred spirits. And when you're wrong, don't be afraid to change."

Adept Lu asked about governing, and the Master said: "Put the people first, and reward their efforts well . . ."

Adept Lu asked: "To be called a noble official, what must a person be like?" "Earnest and exacting, but also genial," replied the Master . . .

The Master said: "The people should be broadly educated by a wise teacher for seven years—then they can take up the weapons of war."

The Master said: "Sending the people to war without educating them first: that is called *throwing the people away*."

The Master said: "The noble-minded seek within themselves. Little people seek elsewhere."

The Master said: "The noble-minded stand above the fray with dignity. And when they band together with others, they never lose track of themselves."

The Master said: "The noble-minded don't honor a person because of something he said, nor do they dismiss something said because of the person who said it."

The Master said: "We're all the same by nature. It's living that makes us different."

Adept Chang asked Confucius: "What makes a person fit to govern?" "Honoring the five graces and despising the four deformities," replied the Master . . . "What are the five graces?" asked Adept Chang. "The noble-minded are generous without expense, hard working without resentment, wishful without greed, stately without arrogance, stern without cruelty . . ." "And what are the four deformities?" asked Chang. "Killing instead of teaching, which is called terror. Expecting results without telling people what you want, which is called tyranny. Issuing vague orders and expecting prompt action, which is called plunder. Grudging and miserly when giving people what they deserve, which is called officialdom."

SOURCE: English translation copyright © 1998 by David Hinton from *The Analects* by Confucius. Reprinted by permission of Counterpoint.

The Confucian ethic had vast implications for governance. The Master was not a revolutionary, but he detested political oppression, as recorded in this parable: One day the Master came upon a woman weeping by the mouth of a cave. When he asked her what was wrong, she replied, "First my father-in-law, then my husband, and now my son were all killed by a tiger at this place." When Confucius asked why she insisted on living in so dangerous an area, the woman replied, "There is no oppressive government here." Confucius then said to his students, "My children, remember this. It is better to live among tigers than to live under a bad government."[1]

The Master may not have meant his message as subversive, but many of his followers taught that unjust leaders should be held accountable. His foremost follower was Mengzi (*MUNG-DZUH*), or Mencius, an eminent sage who lived from roughly 370 to 290 B.C.E. He held that all humans are equal and good, and that a ruler must practice and promote the virtue of *ren*. A ruler who failed to do so forfeited Heaven's Mandate, and his subjects had the right to rebel.

By holding rulers and officials to high moral standards, Confucianism over the centuries promoted good governance and discouraged oppression. Several Chinese regimes sought to suppress Confucianism but had little lasting success.

Daoism: The Way That Cannot Be Spoken

What was the Daoist conception of living in harmony with nature?

Another prominent school of ideas was **Daoism** (*DOW-izm*), a naturalistic philosophy that, unlike Confucianism, had little use for organized institutions. It served as both an antidote and a complement to Confucianism.

The main text of Daoism was the *Daodejing* (*DOW-DUH-JING*), or "Classic of the Way and Its Power," supposedly written in the sixth century B.C.E. by a legendary figure called Laozi (*LAOW-DZUH*), the Old Sage, but probably compiled later from sayings ascribed to him. Centered on a mysterious, unchanging cosmic force called *Dao* ("The Way"), Daoism called for living in harmony with nature. It was passive, and even escapist, urging people to "be bland like melting ice," let go of control, avoid ambition, and accept whatever came their way. It delighted in noting that if there were no property there would be no theft, if there were no law there would be no crime, and if there were no fame there would be no disgrace. Beginning as a simple, romantic worldview, Daoism developed into a religion with numerous rituals and shrines (see "Excerpts from *Daodejing*").

Daoism in many ways contrasted with Confucianism. While Confucians relished intellectual and political discourse, Daoists tended to be anti-intellectual and anti-political, focusing instead on silence, contemplation, and passivity. These values were reflected in Daoist precepts, often expressed as paradoxical sayings, such as, "Those who talk do not understand; those who understand do not talk," and "The way that can be spoken of is not the true Way."

Although Confucianism and Daoism might seem contradictory, many Chinese people espoused both. They saw them not as opposites but mutual correctives, both necessary, each complementing the other. One could, for example, be Confucian in one's public life and Daoist in one's private life. Confucianism produced scholars and politicians, while Daoism inspired artists and poets, but each was essential to Chinese culture and character.

Yin and Yang: The Balance of Forces in Nature

How did the concepts of yin and yang complement each other and provide a framework for bringing balance into people's lives?

The balancing and blending of dissimilar concepts, such as those of Confucianism and Daoism, was reflected in another key concept that emerged in ancient China, the notion of **yin and yang**. Rather than see life as a conflict of opposing forces, such as

[1]James Legge, *The Life and Teachings of Confucius* (London, 1895), 67.

Document 4.2   Excerpts from *Daodejing*

As reflected in **Daodejing** *("Classic of the Way and Its Power"), Daoism urged simplicity, passivity, avoidance of ambition, and unity with a silent, shapeless cosmic force called* **Dao** *("The Way"). How did Daoism's basic ideals compare and contrast with Confucianism?*

When you never strive, you never go wrong . . .

Just do what you do and then leave: such is the Way of Heaven . . .

Way is perennially nameless, an uncarved simplicity. Though small, it's subject to nothing in all beneath heaven . . .

Heaven mingling with earth sends down sweet dew, and the people free of mandates share justice among themselves . . .

Way flowing through all beneath heaven: it's like valley streams flowing into rivers and seas . . .

Way is perennially doing nothing, so there's nothing it doesn't do . . .

Uncarved nameless simplicity is the perfect absence of desire, and the absence of desire means repose: all beneath heaven at rest of itself . . .

Bustling around may overcome cold, but tranquility overcomes heat. Master lucid tranquility, and you'll govern all beneath heaven.

What calamity is greater than no contentment, and what flaw greater than passion for gain? The contentment of fathoming contentment—there lies the contentment that endures.

You can know all beneath heaven though you never step out the door, and you can see the Way of heaven though you never look out the window.

The further you explore, the less you know. So it is that a sage knows by going nowhere, names by seeing nothing, perfects by doing nothing . . .

. . . To work at Way brings less each day, still less and less until you're doing nothing yourself. And when you're doing nothing yourself, there's nothing you don't do.

To grasp all beneath heaven, leave it alone. Leave it alone, that's all, and nothing in all beneath heaven will elude you . . .

. . . a tree you can barely reach around grows from the tiniest rootlet; a nine-tiered tower starts as a basket of dirt; a thousand-mile journey begins with a single step.

Work at things and you ruin them; cling to things and you lose them. That's why a sage does nothing, and so ruins nothing, clings to nothing, and so loses nothing.

SOURCE: English translation copyright © 2000 by David Hinton from *Tao Te Ching* by Lao Tzu. Reprinted by permission of Counterpoint.

good versus evil and hatred versus love, yin and yang expressed cosmic harmony and unity, with alternating forces supporting and completing each other. Yang represented light, heat, daytime, dryness, and masculinity, while yin signified darkness, coolness, nighttime, moistness, and femininity. Yang was active, aggressive, logical, and rational; yin was passive, nurturing, intuitive, and emotional. Yang was dominant in spring and summer; yin in fall and winter. Yang was rock and yin was water; yang had strength and yin had stamina; yang was sun and yin was moon.

As complementary forces, yin and yang blended with and yielded to each other, just as sun yielded to moon, day yielded to night, and summer yielded to fall. Nature needed both sun and rain, heat and coolness, and, of course, male and female. Society required both reason and emotion, strength and stamina, logic and intuition, action and passivity. Yin and yang depicted a natural order based not on conflict and competition but on harmony, symmetry, and balance.

Traditional yin-yang symbol, with light (yang) side blending into dark (yin) side to signify harmony and unity.

Yin and yang gave the Chinese a framework for understanding nature and bringing balance to their lives. Farmers, for example, needed both strength and stamina, parents had to be both assertive and nurturing, and the same person might be a Confucian scholar by day and a Daoist poet by night. Indeed, Confucianism was rooted in rationality and logic, coinciding with yang, while Daoism relied on intuition and inspiration, corresponding with yin.

Legalism: Regulation, Coercion, and Control

The late Zhou era produced another approach that, unlike Daoism, saw harmony and order not as natural but as needing to be imposed by force. It evolved from the insights of Xunzi (*SHOON-DZUH*), a Confucian scholar who lived from around 300 to 230 B.C.E. Living in the chaotic and violent Era of Warring States, Xunzi concluded

What was Legalism, and why did it develop during the Era of Warring States?

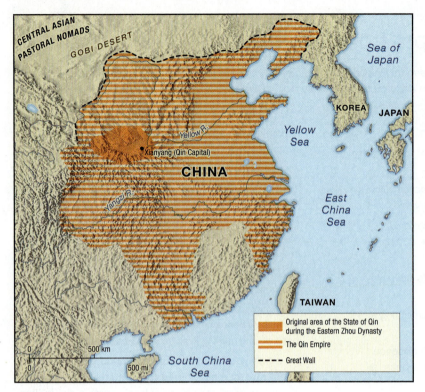

Map 4.4 THE QIN EMPIRE, 221–206 B.C.E. From 231 to 221 B.C.E., the state of Qin in west-central China conquered most of the country, creating China's first empire. Note that the First Emperor, who conquered and ruled this vast area, expanded China's northern fortifications to create the first "Great Wall." How did the Qin Empire help set the stage for larger and longer-lasting empires?

that humans are by nature brutal and selfish, and that their behavior must be controlled by strong laws and institutions. Although Xunzi was a Confucian, his disciples Hanfeizi (*HAHN-FĀ-DZUH*) and Li Si (*LĒ-SUH*) expanded his ideas into **Legalism**, a philosophy promoting strict enforcement of stringent laws by a powerful authoritarian state.

Legalists believed above all in law and order, maintaining that only an authoritarian regime could instill the fear and discipline needed to impose unity and control. For the state to be strong and prosperous, Legalists asserted, the ruler must have both the power and will to enforce strict laws and punishments and suppress all dissent and disunity.

The Birth of the Empire Under the Qin Dynasty

4.5   Assess the significance of the Qin dynasty in early Chinese history.

In 247 B.C.E., eager to enforce his ideas, the Legalist Li Si became a key official in Qin (*CHIN*), a state in northwest China that nine years earlier had overthrown the last Zhou king. Under Li Si's guidance, an ambitious new Qin ruler set out to create a mighty empire. In one eventful decade, from 231 to 221 B.C.E., he conquered all the other northern states and much of southern China as well (Map 4.4). For the first time ever, almost all of China was united under one ruler. He came to be called Shihuangdi (*SHUR-HWAHNG-DĒ*), that is, the First Emperor, the man whose spectacular tomb was described at the start of this chapter.

The First Emperor

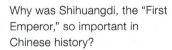

Why was Shihuangdi, the "First Emperor," so important in Chinese history?

Assisted by Li Si, the First Emperor ruled a regime remarkable for both its achievements and its brutality. He abolished the conquered states, disarming their forces and executing their rulers. He divided China into provinces and districts headed by officials selected for their talent and loyalty. Rather than appoint members of the old nobility, he chose capable civil servants wholly accountable to him and made the old nobles move to his capital so he could keep close watch on them. Inspired by Legalism and his own ambitions, he maintained a huge army, a pervasive surveillance system, and a brutal penal code—branding, burning, boiling, or burying alive those who defied his will.

Nothing, it seemed, could deter the First Emperor's drive for unity and control. To expedite connections and commerce, he standardized the written language and laws, coins and taxes, weights and measures, and even the width of roads and axle width of carts. To intimidate his subjects, he made periodic grand inspection tours of his realm. To suppress dissent he reportedly banned the study of philosophy and history, burned the books on them, and buried several hundred scholars alive (ensuring his later vilification by Chinese historians).

Using vast armies of forced laborers at a huge cost in lives, the First Emperor constructed massive projects that showcased his magnificence and megalomania. His extravagant palace, unearthed in 2012, measured over 170,000 square meters and could house up to 10,000 persons. Even more colossal was his tomb, guarded by its vast army of terracotta warriors. His more practical projects included a complex irrigation system, a network of canals connecting China's rivers, and more than 4000 miles of roads, 50 paces wide, which extended like spokes to connect his capital with the regions of his realm (Map 4.5). But his most renowned achievement was connecting all the northern fortifications built to protect against nomadic invasions. The resulting structure, 1400 miles long, later rebuilt and extended, came to be known as the Great Wall of China.

Over time, as his inhumane policies alienated his people, the First Emperor grew increasingly paranoid. After several assassination attempts by embittered subjects, he became obsessed with fear of death. He had oracles and magicians try to find a formula for everlasting life, and he even sent a sea expedition to search for "islands of immortality." These efforts apparently failed: in 210 B.C.E., on one of his inspection tours, the First Emperor fell ill and died.

China's Great Wall, now built of brick, began as an earthen barrier under the First Emperor.

The End of the Qin Dynasty

The First Emperor intended that his **Qin dynasty** would last 10,000 generations. Instead, it outlived him by four years. His death was followed by revolts plunging China into chaos, and by intrigues that killed both Li Si and the Second Emperor, leading in 206 B.C.E. to the Qin dynasty's fall. The rebels then battled among themselves until one, a former peasant named Liu Bang (*L'YOO BAHNG*), perceived as a man of the people, emerged victorious in 202 B.C.E. Building upon the centralized state created by the First Emperor, but ruling more humanely, Liu Bang assumed Heaven's Mandate, beginning a dynasty called the Han (*HAHN*) that lasted more than 400 years.

How and why was the Qin dynasty replaced by the Han?

The Growth of the Empire Under the Han Dynasty

4.6   **Evaluate the successes and failures of the Han dynasty and its influence on China's development.**

The **Han dynasty** (202 B.C.E.–220 C.E.), started by Liu Bang, ruled one of the world's largest and wealthiest domains. In size and population, it matched the vast Roman Empire, then flourishing in the West. The Han Empire also produced a large, effective imperial administration, a sophisticated urban culture and intellectual life, and major advances in technology and commerce. The dynasty's impact was so enduring that the Chinese have since called themselves the Han people.

How did early Han China strengthen its governance by synthesizing Confucianism and Legalism?

The Early Han: Confucian Bureaucracy and Military Expansion

Liu Bang, later known as Emperor Gaozu[2] (*GOW-DZUH*), achieved great success by extending the Qin state bureaucracy and reducing its severity. During his brief reign (202–195 B.C.E.), he lowered taxes, moderated punishments, and invited Confucian scholars, repressed by the Qin regime, to serve as state officials. Under his successors, these scholars came to run the bureaucracy, and Confucianism became the official ideology. The result was a ruling synthesis, combining Legalism's central authority with Confucianism's humane civility, that lasted two millennia—a shining example of China's ability to balance and blend dissimilar forces into a successful system.

Over time Han bureaucracy grew more formal. Initially, emperors simply asked local officials to recommend gifted young men for government posts. In 165 B.C.E., however, the emperor started examining these candidates to determine which were best qualified. Then, to improve preparation of candidates, in 124 B.C.E. the dynasty established an imperial university at Chang'an (*CHAHNG-AHN*), the capital, not far from modern Xi'an. Later the regime would use written exams, based on mastery of Confucian thought, to test potential appointees. These developments laid the groundwork for what would become a key feature of Chinese governance—a **Confucian civil service** made up of educated scholars. Elsewhere officials were often warriors trained in military combat; in China they were scholars educated in Confucian civility and ethics.

But China did not lack warriors. After early Han rulers consolidated their realm, Han Wudi (*WOO DĒ*), the Han Martial Emperor (141–87 B.C.E.), built China's army into an expansive force. Using it, he extended his empire south into northern Vietnam, north into southern Manchuria and northern Korea, and west into distant Central Asia (Map 4.5). He also attacked the Xiongnu (*shē-ŌNG-NOO*), warlike nomads who menaced northern China, beginning a struggle that continued under his successors. At its height the Han Empire extended more than 3000 miles east to west and 2000 miles north to south, embracing almost 60 million people.

How was the Han dynasty weakened after the reign of the Martial Emperor (141–87 B.C.E.)?

Rebellion, Reform, and Ruin

But Wudi's wars, with mass recruitments and high taxes imposed to support them, exhausted Chinese resources and patience. His successors were further weakened by repeated Xiongnu raids and internal revolts. The imperial court was racked by intrigues between the emperor's in-laws and his **eunuchs**, castrated males who ran his palace and guarded his many **concubines**, women who served him sexually to ensure him a male heir. As the only males besides the emperor permitted contact with his concubines, these men were rendered sexually impotent to ensure that any sons born to these women were really the ruler's. Nonetheless, as palace managers with regular access to the emperor, ambitious eunuchs often gained great influence and clashed with the royal in-laws, who likewise sought to use their status to gain power and wealth.

In 22 B.C.E., as intrigues between eunuchs and in-laws crippled the court, revolts erupted throughout the empire. The dynasty seemed to be losing Heaven's Mandate. Then, in 9 C.E., a palace coup deposed a child emperor and replaced him with Wang Mang (*WAHNG MAHNG*), a devoted Confucian from the young ruler's regency council.

---

[2]Chinese emperors often received a historical name that differed from their given name. *Gaozu*, for example, means *High Progenitor*. The historical name is sometimes preceded by the dynasty name, for example, *Qin Shihuangdi, Han Gaozu*. The *first* name is the *family* name in China.

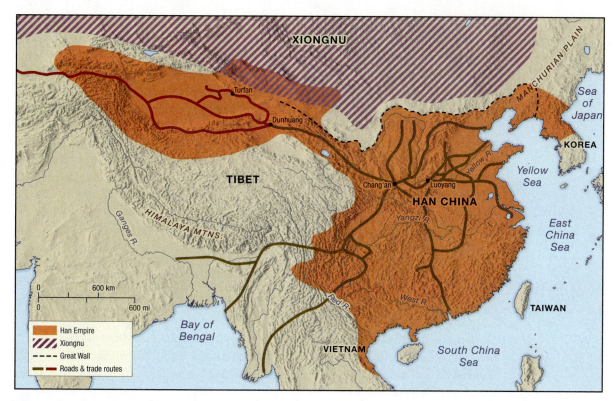

Map 4.5   THE HAN EMPIRE, 202 B.C.E.–220 C.E. China's Han dynasty extended its rule into Central Asia, Southeast Asia, Manchuria, and Korea, thereby connecting a vast area. Observe that a network of roads and trade routes, begun under the First Emperor, extended like spokes from the country's capitals to distant parts of the realm. How did these roads and routes help to expedite connections, unify China, and reinforce imperial rule?

Idealistic and egalitarian, Wang Mang launched reforms to improve the people's welfare. He abolished slavery, for example, and tried to take land from rich landlords for use by poor peasants. He also declared himself emperor, intending to start his own dynasty. But droughts and bad harvests interrupted his plans, and his attempted land transfers sparked fierce opposition from the landlords. In 11 C.E., a catastrophic Yellow River flood drowned hundreds of thousands and left millions homeless. As China descended into chaos, various groups rebelled, demanding the Han dynasty's return. In 23 C.E., when victorious rebels beheaded Wang Mang and ate the rest of his body, it was clear that they did not believe he possessed the Mandate of Heaven.

The Later Han: Revival and Decline

Han rule was restored under Guangwudi (*GWAHNG-WOO-DĒ*), the Shining Martial Emperor, who reigned from 25 to 57 C.E., initiating an era called the Later Han (25–220 C.E.). Signifying a fresh start, he moved the capital east to Luoyang, which was near his power base. For a few generations, he and his heirs maintained peace and prosperity, thanks to conscientious rule, disaster-free weather, and internal strife among the Xiongnu who threatened northern China. In 89 C.E., Chinese generals took advantage of this strife to overpower them, ending for a while the Xiongnu threat. In the next decade, the generals restored Chinese rule in Central Asia. By 100 C.E. the Han realm had recovered much of its former size and wealth.

During the next century, however, dynastic decline resumed. A succession of youthful and short-lived emperors set off new conflicts between their in-laws and eunuchs. In the 160s, dismayed by these developments, groups of Confucian civil servants and students rebelled, only to be butchered in a wholesale purge. Then came floods and droughts, locust infestations that destroyed crops, and a deadly epidemic

Why did the Han dynasty decline and eventually collapse?

(perhaps smallpox or plague), apparently brought by Central Asian nomads, that took millions of lives. The massive suffering and death seemed to show that the Han had lost Heaven's Mandate.

Exploiting the anarchy, many landlords subjected the peasants to serfdom, a slave-like status binding them to service on the land. These actions triggered peasant revolts led by the Yellow Turbans, a rebel group whose head cloths signified solidarity with the earth, associated in China with the color yellow. Han armies crushed these revolts, but generals then took the land for themselves and emerged as regional warlords. After 190 C.E., when a general seized Luoyang, deposed the reigning ruler, and slaughtered his relatives and eunuchs, all semblance of central authority ceased. In 220 C.E., after even more chaos and civil war, another general forced the last Han emperor to abdicate, ending one of China's greatest dynasties.

Society, Technology, and the Silk Road

4.7   Describe and discuss the social structures, innovations, and connections developed in China during the Han era.

Nonetheless, while the Han dynasty lasted, China had one of the world's most productive and innovative societies. As it expanded into Central Asia, China also increased its connections with other cultures along a network of trade routes later called the Silk Road.

Han Society

How did Chinese gender roles and social structures develop under the Han dynasty?

Han society, like that of other ancient civilizations, was based mainly on village farming and herding. In northern China, where it was cool and dry, farmers grew wheat and millet. In the south, where it was warmer and wetter, they mainly raised rice in fields that were flooded to provide continuous moisture. Many peasants also raised chickens and pigs, and some had oxen or water buffalo to help plow the fields. But most farm labor was accomplished by human effort.

Chinese peasants' lives were centered on their families, which included not just parents and children but all living relatives and even departed ancestors, widely believed to be actively concerned with the fortunes of their descendants. Families were ruled by their patriarchs, elder males who made the major decisions, and these men consulted with the spirits of family forebears and conducted ceremonies to venerate both their ancestors and the gods. All family members were expected to obey their elders and superiors.

Chinese women, as a rule, were considered subordinate to men. A bride's father arranged her marriage, typically providing a dowry, and she then became part of her new husband's family. Owing to such customs, daughters were often seen by their parents as a burden, to be raised and fed as children only to join and benefit another family as adults. Girls were thus treated as inferior to boys, and young women were trained chiefly to serve as wives and mothers. Wives were required to cook, make clothes, and clean—in Chinese script the character for wife was a woman using a broom. They were also expected to help in the fields when needed and, above all, to bear and raise sons to carry on the family. Women's lives were said to be governed by the "three submissions"—first to their fathers when they were young, second to their husbands when they were married, and third to their sons when they were ultimately widowed.

Despite their duties and submissions, Chinese women were to some extent protected by Confucian doctrine, which said that fathers, husbands, and sons should treat them with respect and dignity. In addition, Chinese custom made women the household managers, giving those with strong characters an opportunity to exercise substantial influence within the home and family.

The lives of most peasants were likewise confined. In theory, farmers were valued, since the food they grew was vital to survival. Indeed, the Confucian social order ranked farmers higher than merchants, since the former were producers while the latter were viewed as mere traffickers and traders. But in reality this ranking meant little. Most peasants lived in poverty, in villages of wood and bamboo huts, often toiling in service to a wealthy landlord. They worked the fields, tilling, hoeing, and harvesting, with little protection from the heat, wind, rain, or cold. Peasants also had to pay taxes, provide periodic labor for public works projects, and often serve in the army. Rural life was dreary, with few diversions to break the daily routine.

Urban life was far more diverse and sophisticated. Cities such as Chang'an and Luoyang, the two great Han capitals, had metropolitan populations approaching a quarter million people, with about 100,000 living within the city walls. Wealthy officials and merchants resided in two- or three-story homes made of stucco or wood, with gardens and terraces, plentiful food, and servants tending their needs. Poorer residents, mostly artisans and laborers, lived in much humbler conditions, but unlike peasants they had access to urban recreations and diversions. Major cities had palaces, parks, marketplaces, and temples; Chang'an even had a zoo. Entertainment ranged from music, art, and poetry to magic shows, juggling acts, and puppet performances.

Urban life in Han China also had a seamy side, with gambling houses, brothels, and gangs of youths roaming the streets. Public executions, designed to deter crime and disloyalty, typically attracted large crowds. Still, officials posted in small provincial towns, deploring their humdrum existence, often dreamed of reassignment to one of China's large, vibrant cities.

Model of a Han era house.

Technical and Commercial Creativity

Han cities were also centers of creativity, commerce, and craftsmanship. Here scholars, officials, doctors, inventors, and artisans, freed from the need to farm, developed ideas and techniques that would distinguish Chinese culture as enterprising and ingenious.

Scholars and bureaucrats, for example, exchanged ideas and kept records by writing with small brushes on paper—a product invented in Han China. Astronomers charted the paths of planets and recorded sunspots; other scientists studied acoustics and measured earthquakes. Doctors diagnosed diseases, prescribed herbal remedies and drugs, and discovered circulation of the blood. Physicians also used acupuncture, the insertion of thin needles at various points in the body, to relieve pain and cure ailments, theoretically by restoring the body's yin and yang balance. Farmers benefited from innovations such as wheelbarrows to help carry their loads, water mills to grind their grain, iron plows to turn their soil, and harnesses to better utilize the labor of their oxen and buffalo.

Commerce and craftsmanship also reflected Chinese ingenuity. Metropolitan markets had a wide array of shops and stalls run by manufacturers and merchants. Their wares were produced by skilled artisans, who worked with bronze, pottery, lacquer, jade, and silk to make tools, utensils, plates, vessels, jewelry, and clothing. These goods were sold either to consumers or to merchants who took the products elsewhere and resold them at a profit. Their travels were aided by a network of canals and roads, complete with suspension bridges. Carts and wagons traversed the roads, while boats plied the rivers and canals, carrying commodities all across China—and, increasingly, beyond (Map 4.5).

What were the principal technical and commercial innovations of Han China?

What were the origins, functions, and connective importance of the Silk Road and sea lanes?

The Silk Road and the Sea Trade

As conquest and commerce increased intercultural connections, Chinese products came to be highly prized in other lands. By the second century B.C.E., several land and sea routes linking Han China with Central and South Asia were in operation. But long-distance trade was risky, due to bandits, storms, and treacherous terrain.

Then, in 126 B.C.E., a Chinese general named Zhang Qian (*JAHNG chē-AN*), after spending many years in Central Asia, returned to China with reports of peoples, plants, and products hitherto unknown there. He told of lands far beyond the western wastelands, such as Bactria, Ferghana (*fur-GAH-nuh*), and Persia, with bountiful vineyards whose grapes produced fine wines, and splendid horses superior to any in China. He also said that in markets of these regions he had sometimes seen Chinese products, including bamboo canes and silk cloth, no doubt conveyed there along early trade routes.

Based on these reports, the Han Martial Emperor (Wudi) sent armies into Central Asia, adding cities and realms to his domains as tributaries of China. For many of them this arrangement was beneficial, as Chinese soldiers provided protection from bandits, while Han officials sent valuable silk to retain the tributaries' allegiance. The Chinese presence also helped to establish and sustain the long-distance trading network later called the Silk Road.

The **Silk Road**, named for the precious Chinese fabric often conveyed along its route, was actually a series of trails that connected trading towns across the heart of Asia. The route extended from China westward for thousands of miles across Central Asia, with links from there through Bactria into India and through Persia into Mesopotamia and the eastern Mediterranean (Map 4.6). The Silk Road thus provided a commercial connection, though rather tenuous and treacherous, among Eurasian societies.

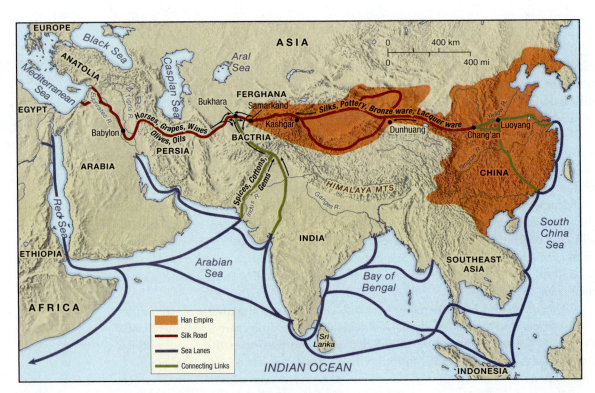

Map 4.6 THE SILK ROAD AND SEA TRADE, BY FIRST CENTURY B.C.E. The Silk Road, opened by about 100 B.C.E., was a complex series of trade routes linking towns across Asia, providing connections among many diverse regions. Note that land routes connected the Silk Road to several seaports, from which goods were shipped by sea lanes to many distant lands. What products were shipped along the Silk Road, and how were they transported? Along with goods, what else did the Silk Road and sea trade convey?

Merchants typically did not travel the whole length of the road; instead, they went back and forth between certain trading towns, where they exchanged the goods they brought for goods coming from the other direction. Merchandise was thus transported in a series of stages, passing through many hands along the way. Since all who handled it wished to make a profit, and since local princes often imposed tolls and fees, items typically cost many times more at their final destination than they did at their origin.

Nonetheless, the Silk Road flourished for more than a thousand years, as did the bustling cities and towns along its route. Located at key passes and junctures, cities such as Dunhuang (*DUN-WAHNG*), Kashgar (*KAHSH-gar*), Samarkand (*SAH-mur-KAHND*), and Bukhara (*boo-KAH-ruh*) teemed with traders, money changers, camel breeders, guides, and markets with exotic goods. Less celebrated, but no less important, were smaller towns along the way, where travelers found rest and recreation as well as food and water for their horses and camels. Some of the towns were independent, with their own ruling families, but many in time came under the protection of larger domains such as China.

Traffic on the trade routes typically consisted of items not produced in the destination country. From the west came fine horses, treasured in China, as well as grapes and wines, olives and oils, precious stones and metals, jewelry, arts, and crafts. From the south came Indian cottons, along with cinnamon, ginger, and other Asian spices highly valued for flavoring food and for making medicines, perfumes, and magic potions. From the east came Chinese pottery, bronze ware, and lacquerware, prized throughout Eurasia. But of all the choice items that made their way westward, perhaps the most treasured were the fine fabrics for which the Silk Road was named. By the first century B.C.E., Chinese silk clothing, with its brilliant colors and exquisite texture, was in fashion among the wealthy as far west as Rome.

Cargoes were conveyed along the Silk Road sometimes by horses and wagons, but often by caravans of camels, especially the dual-humped Bactrian variety, whose shaggy hair helped them endure the harsh, windy Central Asian winters. In time camel keepers crossbred these creatures with single-humped Arabian dromedaries, producing a larger and stronger camel that still had a warm shaggy coat. Saddled with bulging sacks, draped on both sides to equalize the weight, and led by skilled guides across mountains and deserts, these ill-tempered but invaluable animals carried loads weighing hundreds of pounds for dozens of miles a day.

Some Chinese merchants, especially those located near the seacoast and far from Central Asian land routes, conducted their trade by sea. But as with the land routes, so along the sea lanes (Map 4.6), merchants and vessels rarely made the entire trip from one end to the other. Instead, Chinese vessels typically traveled the South China Sea to trade with Southeast Asia and the islands of what is now Indonesia. From there some goods were transshipped, in Malayan or Indian vessels, to India and Sri Lanka, and thence in Persian or Arab crafts to Persia, Arabia, and Egypt. From Egypt some items were resold and shipped to East African or Mediterranean societies.

Along with goods, diseases and beliefs were sometimes conveyed on the Silk Road. Epidemics of smallpox and plague, including deadly outbreaks that ravaged both China and Rome in the second century C.E., spread through Central Asia along the trade routes. In that same century, as we saw in Chapter 3, Buddhist beliefs spread from India to Central Asia, and from there eventually to China along the Silk Road.

Despite the importance of the Silk Road and sea lanes, however, the connections they provided were tenuous and indirect. The Chinese got acquainted with the goods of other lands but learned little about their people. And the Western societies that valued Chinese goods had little real knowledge of the Eastern culture that produced such marvelous merchandise.

Bactrian camel.

Chapter Review

Consequences and Connections

In many ways, early China was like other ancient societies. Like the others, Chinese society began along a river, was based on agriculture, and developed extensive trade networks and large cities. Like the others, it was ruled by monarchs with semidivine status and governed with officials and armies. Like the others, its society was stratified, with a noble elite, urban classes of merchants and artisans, and a rural peasantry making up most of the population.

In other ways, however, China was distinctive. The Mandate of Heaven, for example, could justify rebellion against rulers who failed to furnish stability and security, a concept unknown in most other early cultures. The Confucian ethic, which held state officials accountable for public welfare, conveyed the relatively rare idea that government should serve society. The notion of yin and yang, focusing on balance and harmony, provided a perspective that differed from the view of reality as a struggle between good and evil. And China's civil service, with its stress on education and ethics, gave China a government run by scholars rather than military leaders.

As China's connections with other cultures grew, it was increasingly influenced by them. From Central Asian nomads, the Chinese learned to use chariots and cast bronze, and later to ride horses and forge iron. From the Silk Road and sea trade, China became acquainted with goods from India, Persia, and West Asia, while Chinese products became available there. China nonetheless remained distinctive, a land whose products were prized, but whose ways were largely unknown, in expansive societies far to China's west, such as Persia, Greece, and Rome.

Reviewing Key Concepts

Predynastic China, p. 67
Xia Dynasty, p. 67
Shang Dynasty, p. 68
Chinese Writing, p. 69
Zhou Dynasty, p. 69

Mandate of Heaven, p. 70
Dynastic Cycle, p. 70
Confucianism, p. 73
Daoism, p. 74
Legalism, p. 76

Qin Dynasty, p. 77
Han Dynasty, p. 77
Confucian Civil Service, p. 78
Silk Road, p. 82

Ask Yourself

1. In what ways was China like other ancient cultures and in what ways was it distinct? How do you account for these distinctions?

2. What were the advantages and disadvantages of China's writing system? How did it benefit an empire that was vast and linguistically diverse?

3. What were the advantages and disadvantages of the Mandate of Heaven and the dynastic cycle? How did these concepts affect China's development?

4. How did the concept of yin and yang differ from notions of good versus evil? How did the concept help the Chinese embrace disparate belief systems?

5. Why was Legalism effective in creating a vast empire but unable to maintain it for long? Why was the Han synthesis, combining Legalism and Confucianism, so successful and enduring?

Key Dates and Developments

by 7000 B.C.E.	Farming in Yellow River valley
2200–1750 B.C.E.	Xia dynasty
1750–1122 B.C.E.	Shang dynasty
1122–771 B.C.E.	Western Zhou dynasty
770–256 B.C.E.	Eastern Zhou dynasty
551–479 B.C.E.	Confucius
by 500 B.C.E.	Laozi and origins of Daoism
403–221 B.C.E.	Warring States era (Mencius, Xunzi)
231–221 B.C.E.	China united by Qin Shihuangdi
221–210 B.C.E.	Reign of Qin Shihuangdi (First Emperor)
202 B.C.E.**–6** C.E.	Early Han dynasty
202–195 B.C.E.	Reign of Han Gaozu (Liu Bang)
147–87 B.C.E.	Reign of Han Wudi (Martial Emperor)
by 100 B.C.E.	Origins of the Silk Road
9–23 C.E.	Reign of Wang Mang
25–220 C.E.	Later Han dynasty

Chapter 5
Early American Societies: Connection and Isolation, 20,000 B.C.E.–1500 C.E.

PUEBLO BONITO, CHACO CANYONE, NEW MEXICO Early Americans settled in many different parts of the Western Hemisphere. Their settlements conformed architecturally to their differing locations, as the ruins of this site in New Mexico are appropriate to a desert canyon setting.

After reading this chapter, you should be able to:

5.1 Evaluate the historical controversy over the timing of the arrival of Amerinds in the Western Hemisphere.

5.2 Analyze the differences between North American Amerind societies.

5.3 Trace the development of Amerind societies in Mesoamerica through the Preclassic, Classic, and Postclassic periods.

5.4 Explain how Amerind societies of the Andes coped with and compensated for geographic and topographic challenges.

Early in May 1945, as Soviet troops captured Berlin and ended World War II in Europe, a young Soviet soldier saw that the German National Library was on fire. He was able to save one book from the flames: an exceedingly rare collection of three manuscripts written by the Maya, an American Indian society that flourished in present-day Guatemala and Mexico before the tenth century C.E. Fascinated by the symbols in the manuscript, the soldier, Yuri Knosorov, returned to the Soviet Union, left the army, and earned a degree in linguistics at Moscow State University.

In 1952 Knosorov quietly published an article, titled "Ancient Writing of Central America." Scholars had been unable to decipher Mayan writing, but his study of it convinced him that the symbols, called glyphs, represented ideas rather than sounds, as experts had previously thought. If true, this would make Mayan writing similar to the hieroglyphic writing of ancient Egypt and would suggest ways to decipher it. In 1953 his article caught the attention of Tania Proskouriakoff, who had fled the Russian Revolution as an 8-year-old girl in 1917 and had earned a degree in architecture at Penn State. Proskouriakoff had studied Mayan architecture for two decades. She concluded that the figures depicted in Mayan pictorial writing were not gods but ordinary people. This insight, combined with that of Knosorov, led to one of the great intellectual breakthroughs of modern times: the decipherment of Mayan writing. Finally, three decades later, scholars were confidently translating Mayan glyphs and reaching deeper understandings of Mayan society, one of the most complex of those formed by the peoples known as American Indians. Without the work of Knosorov and Proskouriakoff, much of what this chapter will say about the Maya would have remained unknown.

Areas of Amerind Settlement

Origins and Arrival of the Amerinds

5.1 **Evaluate the historical controversy over the timing of the arrival of Amerinds in the Western Hemisphere.**

Human life originated in eastern Africa and spread outward to other continents through migration. North and South America, remote from eastern Africa, were the last continents to be populated by humans. When groups of hunting-gathering peoples entered North America through Alaska and pushed southward in search of food and a milder climate, they found abundant wildlife that had never been hunted by humans and did not fear them. Some of these people remained hunter-gatherers, pursuing many mammal species to extinction; others, thousands of years later, turned to agriculture in regions with fertile soils and abundant rainfall.

In most of the Western Hemisphere, human communities remained small and isolated from one another. Some developed towns and even long-range trade networks, and some attempted to combine their societies into larger confederations, but their small populations generally did not require complex political and social systems. In two regions, however, complex societies did develop: **Mesoamerica**, which comprises Mexico and northern Central America, and that portion of the Andean mountain range that stretches from Ecuador through Peru to Bolivia and northern Chile. Peoples in these regions were the only ones able to mount organized resistance to the Europeans who invaded in the sixteenth century C.E.

The Europeans mistakenly thought that the islands of the Caribbean where they first landed were part of the Spice Islands, or eastern "Indies," and so they called the people they encountered *Indians*. This term is still used. In recent years the term *Native Americans* gained popularity with some Indian and non-Indian groups, but it is technically inaccurate, since no human life was "native" to the Western Hemisphere. This book designates these people as **Amerinds** (*AM-uh-rinds*), or American Indians, to distinguish them from the Indians of Asia (Chapter 3).

The first humans to reach the Western Hemisphere either walked or traveled in boats from Asia. Anthropological evidence clearly points to their Asiatic heritage. Amerind languages are similar in syntax to those of northeastern Asia; Amerinds physically resemble the Mongolian peoples of Central Asia, an ethnic group that at one time populated most of northeastern Asia; and, in overwhelming numbers, Amerinds have Type O blood carrying a specific antigen found only in Mongolian peoples.

Clovis arrowheads found at sites in New Mexico, Arizona, and Colorado.

Most Amerinds, however, do not accept anthropological conclusions regarding their ancestry, preferring native religious accounts that tell of their origins in the Western Hemisphere. Navajo accounts of the Creation, for example, assert that the first American Indians ascended through three subterranean worlds before finally settling in this one, the fourth world. Snohomish lore states that the Creator and Changer began making the world and its peoples in the East, after which he slowly moved westward, creating as he came. The Amerinds, according to the Snohomish, were created in the West, in what came to be called the Americas.

Presuming that linguistic and biological evidence is correct raises another question: how did the Amerinds cross from Asia to America? At least twice during the Ice Ages of the Pleistocene period, first between 50,000 and 40,000 B.C.E. and again between 26,000 and 8000 B.C.E., tremendous quantities of water were trapped in immense ice caps and glaciers, lowering ocean levels by several hundred feet. The Bering Strait, separating Siberia from Alaska, is only 120 feet deep; during the Ice Ages it stood hundreds of feet above sea level, forming a land bridge between Siberia and Alaska. At one point around 18,000 B.C.E., the land bridge was approximately 1000 miles wide from north to south.

The Bering land bridge was used by caribou, reindeer, wooly mammoth, camels, and giant sloths. Some of these species survived in the Western Hemisphere, while others were hunted to extinction by Amerinds. Since there is archeological proof of human occupation of the Americas beginning between 12,000 and 10,000 B.C.E., most scholars assume that Amerinds crossed around that time, during the second period in which the land bridge was exposed. There are no cultural artifacts or human bones datable to the earlier era of the land bridge, more than 40,000 years ago. Moreover, the absence of evidence of fur clothing and subterranean (or pit) houses, either in America or in northeastern Asia earlier than 15,000 years ago, supports the more recent dating, as protective clothing and underground dwellings would have been essential to the survival of nomadic groups in the frigid Siberian-Alaskan climate.

Complicating this theory is evidence of an extensive, impassable barrier of ice separating the area now called Alaska from northwestern Canada between 21,000 and 11,000 B.C.E. Only after that time did the climate warm sufficiently to create ice-free corridors along the continental divide (Map 5.1). Humans could pass through these corridors southward to Mesoamerica and from there to South America. Simultaneously the land bridge flooded, and future human migration would have been possible only by boat. Many scholars therefore conclude that people crossed from Siberia to Alaska around 14,000 years ago, remained there for at least a millennium, and moved south sometime after 11,200 B.C.E.

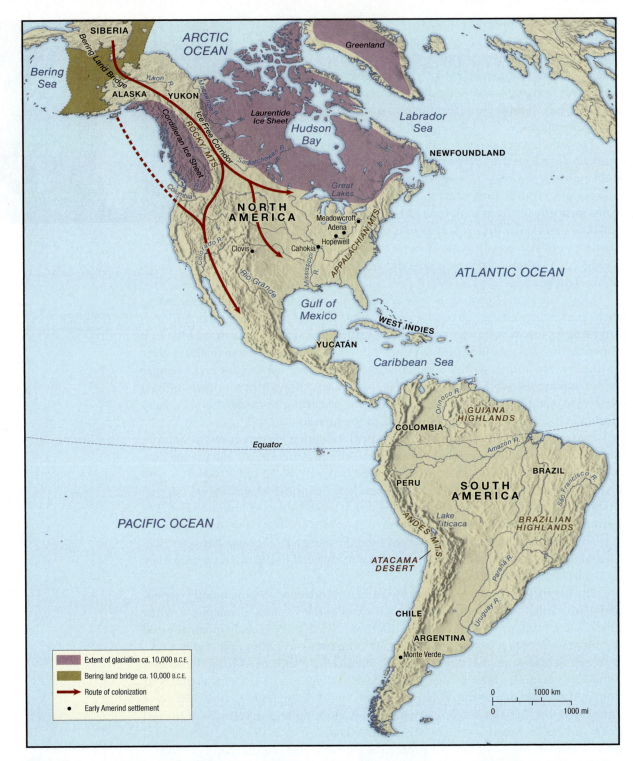

Map 5.1 **POPULATING THE WESTERN HEMISPHERE, CA. 20,000–6000 B.C.E.** Arrows indicate the probable arrival and dispersal routes of the Amerinds. Note the enormous ice sheets that covered much of present-day Canada, and the southward flow of peoples from present-day Alaska through an ice-free corridor. This arrival pattern is the most widely accepted hypothesis, but not the only one: some archeologists suggest that Amerinds may have arrived before the North American glacier began melting and then traveled down the coast in boats rather than moving overland. If the most widely accepted hypothesis is true, why would many Amerinds have continued moving southward, rather than stopping in the present-day United States?

Most artifacts and skeletal remains found in the Americas are consistent with this explanation. However, DNA evidence from living South American Indians analyzed in 1994 indicates a probable human arrival date between 27,000 and 20,000 B.C.E. Dramatic archeological findings at Monte Verde in southern Chile in the 1990s appeared to confirm the existence there of an Amerind village dating to between 14,000 and 10,500 B.C.E. That would place Amerinds at the southern tip of South America before the ice sheets had melted sufficiently to permit human passage. In 2011, archaeologists disclosed that projectile points found at the Buttermilk Creek site in Texas prove that human hunter-gatherers had reached there around 13,500 B.C.E. Two years later, paleontologists in Uruguay published their conclusion that humans had hunted giant sloths there as long ago as 28,000 B.C.E. And in 2014, researchers at the Serra da Capivara National Park in northeastern Brazil announced that, in addition to the park's long-famous cave paintings, stone tools found at the site demonstrated human arrival around 20,000 B.C.E.

But if the DNA evidence is true and the artifacts are authentic, why have no human remains from 40,000–13,000 B.C.E. been found in the Western Hemisphere? Is it because no such remains exist? Or have archeologists not been digging in the right places, or not yet dug deeply enough? Today we know that the Amerinds arrived in the Americas from somewhere in Asia, but that is all we know for certain…or do we?

The Amerinds of North America

5.2   **Analyze the differences between North American Amerind societies.**

The first people to set foot in North America were nomadic hunter-gatherers. Agriculture appeared about 4000 years later, apparently beginning before 3000 B.C.E. in southern Mexico. Maize (or corn) appeared in central Mexico around 5000 B.C.E. and in southern Mexico 2500 years after that. Between 2000 and 1000 B.C.E., farming villages emerged in central Mexico. Available evidence suggests that the idea of domesticating plants spread northward and southward from Mesoamerica. In North America, farming reached what is now the southwestern United States between 3500 and 2500 B.C.E., the "Eastern Woodlands" of the United States by 1000 B.C.E., and southern Canada sometime around 500 B.C.E. Agriculture therefore spread north from Mesoamerica thousands of years after its appearance in the river civilizations of Asia, delaying the development of North American settled societies for an equivalent period.

Since few North American Amerinds had written languages, what we know of their early societies is based largely on archeological evidence and oral tradition. Scholars have categorized their societies (before the European invasion) into four principal types: hunter-gatherer bands, limited-scale tribal societies, full-scale tribal societies, and complex mound-building and trading societies.

Two Hunter-Gatherer Bands

Two North American societal groups, the Arctic and the Great Basin, lacked any genuine political organization. The environments these groups lived in hindered organizational development. In the *Arctic*, where the Eskimo (or Inuit) people lived, frozen, snow-covered ground and brief or nonexistent growing seasons made organized agriculture impossible. Their icy shelters often melted during the summer, further discouraging permanent settlement. The preinvasion Eskimo lived in small nomadic bands under the informal leadership of whoever happened to be the most proficient hunter. The *Great Basin* societies of Utah and Nevada, such as the Paiute (*PĪ-oot*) and Shoshone (*shō-SHŌ-nē*) peoples, were similarly nomadic, moving about the desert in family units during the lengthy summers and coming together in villages during the winters. Each family had its own leader.

How did hunter-gatherer societies in North America adapt to environmental conditions?

What sort of societal organizations and functions were developed by limited-scale tribal societies in North America?

Totem poles from western Canada, carved from Western Red Cedar and depicting real or mythical events.

Five Limited-Scale Tribal Societies

More complex political organization emerged in five regions, where societies sometimes coalesced into **tribes**—large associations of villages, bands, or clans that share a common language and often a common leader. But tribes functioned only occasionally—during wartime, for example. Most of the time, these Amerinds associated in individual villages, bands, or clans. Authority was therefore mixed: family elders decided some issues, clan leaders others, and tribal leaders yet others.

In the eastern Canadian *Sub-Arctic* (Map 5.2), the Algonquian (*al-GON-kwē-un*) peoples banded together for the purpose of hunting caribou, a staple of their diet and an animal that, since it traveled in large herds, was best hunted by groups of at least a few dozen people. Hunting thus required that hunting bands combine into tribes, although the affiliation was loose and the tribes had little other impact on everyday life.

Along the *Northwest Coast*, from present-day Oregon north to Alaska, lived maritime peoples whose access to rich food sources encouraged the formation of densely populated fishing villages. These people lived largely by hunting and by fishing the rivers and coastal waters for salmon and seafood. From the region's great evergreen forests, they built splendid wooden homes and carved large dugout canoes and elaborate totem poles that traced their genealogies. Some of their villages combined to form tribes, while others remained fiercely independent. In the neighboring *Plateau* region, encompassing the inland areas of Washington, Oregon, and Idaho, people were originally grouped into individual villages but eventually learned tribal organization from others to their southeast.

In the *Southwest* there emerged a wide variety of societies, ranging from Navajo (*NAH-vuh-hō*) and Apache (*uh-PATCH-ē*) nomadic bands to the town-dwelling Pueblo (*PWĀ-blō*) Indians, who built walled settlements with central plazas and residences made of adobe (*ah-DŌ-bē*) brick or masonry. Flourishing from the second through fourteenth centuries C.E., the early Pueblo peoples, also called Anasazi (*ah-nuh-SAH-zē*), grew maize, squash, and beans using complex irrigation techniques and produced fine pottery, woven baskets, and cotton cloth. At one point, perhaps for protection, they built cliff dwellings and multistory terraced apartment houses guarded by watchtowers. After 1300, however, Anasazi society declined, probably as a result of drought and invasions by warlike outsiders. In *California*, the Amerinds lived in extended families organized as small tribes.

Four Full-Scale Tribal Societies

What sort of societal organizations and functions were developed by full-scale tribal societies in North America?

Four groups developed full-scale, continuously functioning tribal organizations. Each tribe was composed of thousands of people ruled by a variety of political chiefs, war chiefs, and religious leaders.

The *Plains* Indians included many seminomadic tribes that cultivated maize along the region's rivers and hunted great buffalo herds with bows and arrows. Perhaps the most highly organized among them were the Cheyenne, ruled by a council of 44 chiefs selected on merit. These chiefs oversaw the frequent moves from one camp to another and the tribal buffalo hunt, the success of which depended on teamwork and skill. Men hunted the animals while women repaired bows, made arrows, and sewed garments from the hides. The peoples of the *Prairies*, such as the Sioux, were predominantly agricultural until the availability of horses imported by Europeans revolutionized the art of hunting buffalo. Prairie Indian tribal organization remained centered on village life.

In the *Southeast*, Amerinds formed powerful tribes such as the Cherokee and the Natchez, in which chiefs exercised total authority over their subjects. Some, such as the Natchez, had rigid hereditary castes ranging from "Suns" down to "Stinkards."

Map 5.2 NORTH AMERICAN AMERIND CULTURE AREAS, CA. 1500 C.E. Many Amerind peoples moved through Canada and settled in what is now the United States. The more temperate climate there made agriculture possible, and the Great Plains were filled with buffalo and other large mammals that could be hunted for food and hides. Observe the distribution of peoples across this temperate climate zone: no region was free from settlement. What distinctions in lifestyle might be expected across such a wide area?

Others, such as the Choctaws and Creeks, constantly waged war against one another. Southeastern Amerinds blended agriculture with hunting and gathering.

Finally, in the *Eastern Woodlands*, a variety of farming peoples grew squash, beans, and maize, fished the rivers and streams, and hunted deer in the forests. They typically lived in villages surrounded by log walls for protection. The

Haudenosaunee (hō-d'nō-SAW-nē) of what is now New York State lived communally in wooden dwellings called longhouses. Their clans were led by clan mothers, who appointed tribal chiefs. Eventually the Haudenosaunee formed a five-nation alliance called the Great League of Peace and Power, which in turn created a political organization known as the Iroquois Confederacy. This organization fought neighboring Indians and allied with European settlers but never achieved complete political unity.

Three Complex Societies

What might explain the complexity of the Adena, Hopewell, and Mississippian societies?

Three North American Indian groups developed urban economies and complex governance structures similar in some respects to early river civilizations of Asia and Northeast Africa. These complex Amerind societies, emerging in the valleys of the Ohio and Mississippi rivers, were eventually centered in large cities with specialized occupations and extensive trading networks.

ADENA AND HOPEWELL   One of these societies was that of the Adena people of the Ohio River Valley, which flourished between 1000 and 300 B.C.E. The Adena constructed small villages near the Ohio River and enhanced them with immense earthworks and mounds. These impressive sites, the most famous of which is the 700-foot-long Great Serpent Mound in present-day Ohio, were apparently used for ceremonial purposes such as burials. Construction of these mounds would have been impossible without a large agricultural surplus to support the laborers who built them. It therefore seems likely that the Adena had specialized occupations, one of the key features of complex societies.

After 300 B.C.E., the Adena were absorbed into what archeologists call the Hopewell culture, centered in Ohio but managing a network of trade contacts with dependent tribes throughout a vast region bounded on the north by Ontario, on the east by New York, on the south by Florida, and on the west by Wisconsin. Hopewell consisted of a series of towns, ranging in size from a few hundred people to a few thousand, each ruled by a chief. Its commercial networks were extensive: graves at Hopewell sites in Ohio contain copper from Minnesota, shells and sharks' teeth from the Gulf of Mexico, obsidian (ob-SID-ē-un), a sharp, black stone made of volcanic glass, from Arizona, and grizzly bear teeth from west of the continental divide.

Although agriculture is typically the economic foundation of complex societies, Hopewell was an exception. The natural environment was so rich in fish, game, and plant life that even large towns could prosper through foraging for food. But this subsistence strategy meant that everyone did similar work, and occupational specialties never developed in the way that they did in the river civilizations in Mesopotamia, Egypt, India, and China. The reasons for Hopewell's disappearance around 400 C.E. remain unclear, but the culture's commercial networks survived.

MISSISSIPPIAN SOCIETY   Of all the North American Amerind societies, the one most comparable to Asian and North African river civilizations was that of the people now called Mississippians. Developing along and just east of the Mississippi River between 700 and 1500 C.E., their agriculturally based society benefited from the river's rich deposits of silt. Their trading networks connected settlements within and beyond their region. The most noteworthy Mississippian center was Cahokia (kah-HŌ-kē-ah), the ruins of which lie near the city of East Saint Louis in southwestern Illinois. With between 10,000 and 30,000 inhabitants, Cahokia had a population comparable in size to that of many Eurasian cities, and surpassing that of any other Amerind settlement north of Mexico. Indeed, more people may have lived in Cahokia than in the entire Iroquois Confederacy.

The Mississippian people, like the Adena and the Hopewell, were mound builders. One of Cahokia's many mounds was the largest such structure in all of North America, a colossal earthwork 100 feet high and 1037 by 790 feet at its base. Cahokia was a ceremonial and administrative center, surrounded by residential areas and shops and supported by the cultivation of adjacent fields. Mississippians, like the Haudenosaunee of the Eastern Woodlands, grew corn, beans, and squash—the "Three Sisters" whose cultivation originated in Mexico—suggesting some level of contact between these regional cultures.

Such a connection is also suggested by archeological evidence. In the only mound that has thus far been excavated at Cahokia, archeologists discovered the carefully positioned bodies of a nobleman and 260 other adults. The number 260 is also characteristic of sacrificial burials found in Mesoamerica, where a 260-day ritual calendar was widely used, dating from centuries before Cahokia. In addition, some of the skeletons found at Cahokia had their front teeth filed. Virtually unknown elsewhere in North America, this practice was widespread in Mesoamerica. The Cahokia skeletons may be remains of visitors or traders from Mesoamerica.

The possibility of contact between Cahokia and Mesoamerica cannot, however, be conclusively substantiated, since Cahokia left no written records. The city was devastated by an earthquake around 1250 C.E., and no subsequent Amerind culture built on its foundations. Some evidence suggests that by this time Cahokia was beginning to evolve into a complex society with a variety of occupational roles, including soldiers, officials, artisans, and priests. But its collapse leaves more questions than answers.

A modern photograph of Monk's Mound in Cahokia, where ancient Amerind temples once stood.

The Amerinds of Mesoamerica

5.3   **Trace the development of Amerind societies in Mesoamerica through the Preclassic, Classic, and Postclassic periods.**

Farther south, in what are now southern Mexico and northern Central America, civilizations developed to levels of social and political complexity unknown in North America. In this region, which scholars today call Mesoamerica, ample rainfall and rich soils supported a series of highly complex civilizations based on agriculture. Archeologists often divide the early history of this region into three periods: Preclassic (1800 B.C.E.–150 C.E.), comprising the Olmec and early Maya societies; Classic (150–900 C.E.), the era of the full-fledged Mayan society; and Postclassic (900–1500 C.E.), consisting first of the Toltec, and later the Aztec society.

The Olmec of the Preclassic Period (1800 B.C.E.–150 C.E.)

What were the achievements and contributions of Olmec civilization?

Mesoamerica's earliest complex society was discovered by accident. In the 1930s, archeologists were excavating ruins presumed to be from the Classic Mayan era (150–900 C.E.) when they realized that the huge carved stone heads they kept finding in swampy, tropical river plains along the Gulf Coast came from an earlier culture. The archeologists named the newly discovered culture **Olmec** and demonstrated that Mayan civilization was constructed on Olmec foundations. The center of Olmec culture lay south of the Gulf of Mexico and west of the Yucatán Peninsula. Rainfall there averages nearly 120 inches per year, causing the rivers to flood regularly, depositing rich silt in floodplains that extend for miles from the riverbanks. Well suited to tropical agriculture, the Olmec heartland resembled in many ways the areas where the river civilizations of Asia and Northeast Africa began.

OLMEC CITIES   Olmec society apparently emerged about 1800 B.C.E. and lasted until 150 C.E., encompassing the Preclassic period. The city now called San Lorenzo, founded around 1200 B.C.E., was the most important of a cluster of Olmec cities near the Coatzacoalcos (*kō-AHT-za-kō-AL-kōs*) River (Map 5.3). There the Olmec created immense stone heads and monuments out of basalt mined 50 miles away. The massive stones must have been dragged to the river, floated downstream on rafts, and dragged up from the riverbank to the plateau on which the city is located. In the absence of large domesticable mammals, carts with wheels were unknown.

The human labor involved in the transportation of these stones must have been enormous, since some of the heads of San Lorenzo are more than 9 feet high and weigh up to 25 tons. Equally impressive was the carving of the stones—done entirely with obsidian, not metal, tools. Obsidian implements were imported from other parts of Mexico and from Guatemala, indicating that the Olmec state's networks of commerce and trade covered large distances.

San Lorenzo was destroyed around 900 B.C.E. by some sort of revolution or invasion, but the Olmec culture survived, relocating its focus northeast to La Venta, 18 miles south of the Gulf of Mexico. There the Olmec built a mammoth clay ceremonial pyramid in the shape of a volcano. At the Olmec city of Tres Zapotes (*TRĀZ zah-PŌ-tāz*), about 100 miles northwest of La Venta, archeologists unearthed Stela C, one of the oldest dated monuments in the Western Hemisphere. This tall, stone column bears the date of September 3, 32 B.C.E., or (7).16.6.16.18 in the Long Count calendar used by the Mesoamericans.

THE LONG COUNT CALENDAR   Before the 1930s it was universally believed that the Maya had created the **Long Count calendar**, but Stela C suggests its Olmec origin. The Long Count enabled Mesoamericans to date events from a starting point that

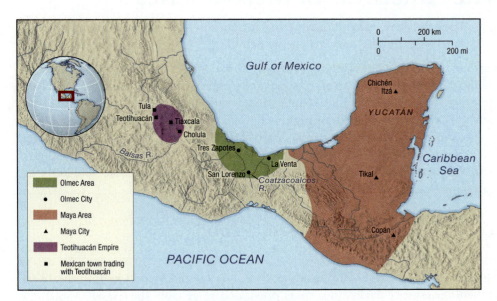

Map 5.3   MESOAMERICAN HOMELANDS AND CENTERS, CA. 2500 B.C.E.–700 C.E. Olmec settlement was localized, while Mayan city-states were concentrated in the Yucatán Peninsula of Mexico and modern-day Guatemala. A good comparison can be made between city-state development in the Yucatán, in Teotihuacán, and in ancient Greece: all three societies evolved in confined geographic areas, developed written languages, and formed intricate trade networks. What sort of connections would need to be forged with other peoples in order to permit complex societies to develop in such confined regions?

corresponds to August 13, 3114 B.C.E., in our modern (Gregorian) calendar. Used by both Olmec and Maya, the Long Count calendar served a number of purposes, including astronomy, astrology, agriculture, genealogy, and even prophecy, as Mesoamericans believed that the world is repetitively created, destroyed, and re-created at precisely measured intervals. The calendar employed two huge cogwheels, one with 365 notches for the days of the solar year, the other with 260 notches for the days of the "sacred almanac," which embodied the sequence of Olmec and Mayan ritual and ceremonial life. When the wheels were turned, each intersection of two dates would recur only once every 52 years. The world came to an end (and was re-created in fire) approximately every 5125 solar years. This was called the "great cycle," and since the current cycle began in 3114 B.C.E., the present world was scheduled to end on December 21, 2012, in the Gregorian calendar. The fact that this did not happen calls into question the predictive capability of the Long Count calendar, but not the chronological accuracy of the calendar itself.

Olmec head carved from basalt and found at La Venta.

The Long Count calendar testifies to Mesoamericans' convictions concerning the eternity of the world and the endless cycle of life. Inscriptions on several Olmec objects appear to be early versions of Maya glyphs, but no Olmec writing has been discovered.

THE SPREAD AND COLLAPSE OF OLMEC CIVILIZATION   Some scholars theorize that the Olmec spread their religion and way of life over a wide area of southern Mexico by force of arms. Others suggest they were a peacefully inclined theocracy with a wealthy merchant class. The Olmec depicted themselves in sculpture as ferocious warriors, clubbing their enemies to death and torturing their captives. Whichever theory is true, the Olmec clearly spread their commerce, art, and ideas through trade.

Eventually, however, Olmec civilization collapsed. By 300 B.C.E. La Venta had been abandoned, and the population of Tres Zapotes had declined steeply. Well before the Preclassic period ended around 150 C.E., Olmec culture had been absorbed by Amerinds who would evolve into one of Mesoamerica's most complex civilizations: the Maya.

The Maya of the Classic Period (150–900 C.E.)

Time and again in world history, civilizations developed and prospered, only to be conquered by peoples from less complex societies, who then adopted elements of the conquered civilization that they found useful or appealing. Examples include the Akkadian and Babylonian conquests of Sumer, the Hittite conquest of Babylon, the Hyksos conquest of Egypt, and the Aryan conquest of the Indus Valley. But this pattern did not occur in Mexico, as the Preclassic period gradually flowed into the Classic. The **Maya**, a Mesoamerican people of Guatemala and Mexico's Yucatán Peninsula, built on Olmec foundations and surpassed Olmec achievements.

What were the achievements and contributions of Mayan civilization, and how did it build upon Olmec culture?

AGRICULTURE, TRADE, AND CULTURAL CONTACTS   During the Preclassic period, the Maya developed village-based agriculture. Between 7000 and 1500 B.C.E., the world was considerably warmer than it is today, and in much of North America and Mesoamerica the hot, dry weather, combined with excessive hunting by Amerinds, wiped out the giant bison, camels, horses, and mammoths that had once been abundant. Hunting therefore gradually became less important than agriculture, which served as the foundation of Mayan civilization.

Mayan agriculture provided a nutritious diet of corn, beans, squash, chili peppers (rich in several vitamins), and tropical fruits. Protein came from wild birds, deer, peccaries, armadillo, and a breed of barkless dog. Sea salt preserved meat. The Maya, particularly the nobles, snacked on the cacao bean, the source of chocolate, and drank a chocolate beverage.

The cacao bean was traded, as were obsidian, jade, and colorful feathers from a large bird called the quetzal (*ket-ZAL*). Such products were exchanged not only among the Maya themselves, but also with other civilizations in Mexico and Central America. In the process, the Maya established commercial and cultural connections with cultures both more and less socially complex than their own.

Like most other civilizations, the Maya did not evolve in isolation. From the Olmec they learned astronomy and mathematics, developed social and political structures, and adapted a belief system that sought to explain the meaning of human life. And they also had contacts with smaller and weaker groups of people, many of whom they dominated or absorbed.

SOCIETY AND RELIGION Mayan society was hierarchical, with a privileged hereditary elite exercising political power. Priests, high-ranking warriors, and wealthy merchants were all nobles. Commoners were free peasants and soldiers, while the lands of the nobles were worked by a group resembling serfs. Below them were slaves, typically commoners captured in battle; although slavery was hereditary, freedom could be purchased by relatives. Politically, the Maya organized themselves as autonomous city-states rather than in a strong central government.

At the top of the hierarchy in each city-state was a sacred king who was both a political and spiritual leader. Kings were brave warriors and shrewd political negotiators who defended the interests of their people. But they also served those interests as spiritual intermediaries between this world and the next. In the Mayan world, political leadership, success in warfare, and religious power were closely linked.

The Maya pictured the earth as flat, with 13 layers of heaven above it and nine levels of underworld. An enormous number of gods populated the heavens, while the lower regions were the domain of the nine Lords of Death (see "Excerpt from the Council Book of the Quiché Maya, or *Popol Vuh*"). The Maya were terrified of death, believing that most ordinary people went to the underworld rather than to the heavens, where only kings and heroes could live. Special rituals to appease the gods were believed to be capable of holding death back, at least for a while, and also of ensuring the community's prosperity. Rulers and priests led these ceremonies, but ordinary people practiced them too, using their kings as role models.

These rituals involved **bloodletting**, a practice that connected the temporal and spiritual worlds and allowed departed spirits to materialize in the body of the bloodletter. That person, usually male, pierced some part of his body—often the ear lobe, lip, or penis—with a sharp thorn. Then he drew a knotted cord through the wound to force the blood to run. This type of sacrifice was believed to please the gods and bring good harvests, adequate rainfall, victory in warfare, personal happiness, cures for diseases, and many other benefits. Bridging the chasm between worlds brought creation into proper balance, harmonizing the relationship between spirits and mortals.

When the king himself was the bloodletter, he became the portal between the two worlds. The spirits would enter the realm of the living through the wounds he inflicted upon his body. Simultaneously, his own spirit would pass through the wounds into the domain of the dead, where it could influence the gods on behalf of the king's people. The sacrifice and pain involved in bloodletting would earn the king the respect of the gods and spirits; in return, they would grant favors to him and his subjects. In a few cases, women became kings, a status that also required them to serve as bloodletters, drawing the knotted cord through their ear lobes, lips, breasts, or genitals.

MAYA CULTURE The Maya developed a complex, intellectually sophisticated culture. Using an intricate pictographic system of writing, they carved inscriptions on stone pillars and compiled libraries of thousands of books written on long strips

Document 5.1   Excerpt from the Council Book of the Quiché Maya, or *Popol Vuh*

The Popol Vuh, *or "Council Book" of the Maya living in the city of Quiché in southwestern Guatemala, told of the origins and development of Maya civilization. Along with all but four of the thousands of books written by the Maya, it was burned by the Spaniards in the 1520s. Thirty years later, several members of the Quiché Maya nobility reconstructed the* Popol Vuh *using the Latin alphabet. Their manuscript was seen in Quiché between 1701 and 1703 by a Spanish friar, Francisco Ximénez, who copied it by hand and added his own Spanish translation. The original manuscript has been lost, and the reproduction and translation prepared by Fr. Ximénez has been in the Newberry Library in Chicago since 1911.*

Historians must use such a document with caution. Maya glyphs represented concepts rather than words and were intended to be used in combination with pictures. Both the glyphs and the pictures were burned in the 16th century. How well did the Maya authors remember the precise details of the Popol Vuh *30 years after they had last seen it? How accurate was their effort to change glyphs and pictures into words? When Fr. Ximénez copied their manuscript, did he change it in any way? These questions cannot be answered. Finally, what we have is not the* Popol Vuh *itself, but a document written in the 1550s, decades after the last events described in this chapter. Yet what we have suggests to us how the Maya saw their world, and this excerpt is presented for that purpose.*

The excerpt relates the conclusion of the story of the "hero twins," Hunahpú (hoo-nah-POO) and Xbalanqué (zhbahl-ahn-KĀ), who made too much noise while playing a Maya ritual ball game and were summoned to Xibalbá (zhih-bahl-BAH), the Underworld, by the Lords of Death. There they endured many torments and trials, all of which they overcame. But the twins knew that they could not defeat the Lords of Death by force but could only escape from Xibalbá by trickery. This is the story of their deception. What does this excerpt tell us about the personal qualities the Maya valued?

[The twins disguised themselves as poor orphans and performed amazing dances for the people of Xibalbá.] . . .

they worked many miracles. They burned houses as though they were really burning and instantly they were as they had been before . . . they cut themselves into bits; they killed each other; the first one killed stretched out as though he were dead, and instantly the other brought him back to life. Those of Xibalbá looked on in amazement at all they did . . .

Presently word of their dances came to the ears of the Lords of Death, Hun-Camé (*HUHN-kah-MĀ*), or One Death, and Vucub-Camé (*voo-COOB-kah-MĀ*), or Seven Death. Upon hearing it they exclaimed, "Who are these two orphans? . . . Tell them to come here, so that . . . we may admire them and regard them with wonder."

[So the boys appeared before the Lords of Death, who ordered them,] "Dance! And do the first part in which you kill yourselves; burn my house, do all that you know how to do. We shall give you pay . . ."

Instantly they put fire to the lord's house, and although the lords were within the house, they were not burned. Quickly it was whole again . . . the lords were astounded. "Sacrifice yourselves now, let us see it! We really like your dances!" said the lords . . . And [the twins] proceeded to sacrifice each other. Hunahpú was sacrificed by Xbalanqué, and instantly he returned to life . . .

Then One Death and Seven Death gave their commands. "Do the same with us! Sacrifice us!" they said. "Cut us into pieces, one by one!"

And so it happened that they first sacrificed the one, who was the chief lord of Xibalbá, the one called One Death, king of Xibalbá.

And when One Death was dead, they sacrificed Seven Death, and they did not bring either of them back to life.

The people of Xibalbá fled as soon as they saw that their lords were dead and sacrificed . . . In this way the Lords of Xibalbá were overcome. Only by a miracle and by their [own] transformation could [the boys] have done it.

SOURCE: Excerpts from *Popol Vuh: The Sacred Book of the Ancient Quiché Maya.* English version by Delia Goetz and Sylvanus G. Morley, from the Spanish translation by Adrián Recinos (Norman: University of Oklahoma Press, 1950), 156–160. Copyright © 1950 Reprinted with the permission of University of Oklahoma Press.

of tree bark paper. (The invading Spaniards burned all but four of these books in the sixteenth century.) The Maya also created a numerical system using zero as a number rather than a placeholder, an idea unknown to their contemporaries in the Roman Empire. Their adoption of the Long Count calendar from the Olmec testifies to their belief in recurrent historical cycles, a conviction similar to those held by people in ancient Egypt and China.

The Long Count calendar, the sophisticated numerical system, the intricate glyphic writing system, and the intense interest of the Maya in astronomy led most historians to conclude that they were a contemplative, scientific, and essentially peace-loving people. But that was before Mayan writing was fully deciphered. Following the work of Knosorov and Proskouriakoff described at the start of this chapter, scholars began to translate Mayan texts in 1988, and what they read overturned that

Venus table from the Mayan *Dresden Codex* showing the phases of the planet Venus.

How did the city-state of Teotihuacán serve as a connector?

assumption. Writings on bark paper and in stone indicate that the Maya were warlike and territorial, like many other cultures in America and elsewhere. Warfare was a full-fledged institution, with not only sacrifice and the taking of captives to serve as slaves, but also with complex rites of purification and fasting in preparation for battle. Perhaps this Mayan love of combat was ultimately responsible for bringing down one of the great civilizations of the ancient world in the mid–ninth century, at approximately the same time that another notable Mesoamerican culture was collapsing, that of the city of Teotihuacán.

Teotihuacán: Rise and Fall of a Great City-State

The Maya were not the only complex society in Mexico during the Classic period. By 500 C.E. the city-state of Teotihuacán (*tā-ō-tē-wah-KAHN*) in the Valley of Mexico, just north of modern-day Mexico City, held a population that may have reached 200,000 people, making it one of the largest cities of its time.

Located near a rich source of obsidian and trading actively with other cities of central Mexico, Teotihuacán grew into a politically and commercially significant city (Map 5.3). With 600 pyramids, it was central Mexico's preeminent religious and ceremonial center. Two thousand apartment complexes and an immense market compound made Teotihuacán the largest and most significant Mesoamerican city-state of the Classic period and one of the principal cities of the world. It was clearly the focal point of a powerful empire.

Teotihuacanos, unlike the Maya, did not seem to revere kings as supreme political authorities and intermediaries between two worlds. Indeed, since artistic depictions of the rulers are lacking and no written records have survived, it is impossible to determine precisely how Teotihuacán was governed. It did, however, maintain an army, probably to protect its commercial relationships with other Mesoamerican cultures, including the Maya. The army may also have forced peasants from the surrounding countryside to supply the city's political and religious elites with food.

Teotihuacán maintained commercial connections with Mayan, Zapotec (*za-PŌ-tek*), Mixtec (*MISH-tek*), and other Mexican civilizations. More than 400 workshops unearthed in its ruins indicate that its artisans fabricated exotic ornaments from seashells, onyx, and jade. In exchange, the Maya sent quetzal feathers, and the Zapotec sent fragrant incense made from copal gum.

In the late Classic period, however, all of these societies crumbled. Teotihuacán was deserted and burned, possibly as early as 650 C.E., certainly no later than 850 C.E. Several Zapotec cities and Mayan states were destroyed around the same time. Epidemic diseases, volcanic eruptions, earthquakes, and invasion by other Amerind tribes have all been proposed as causes. A major war lasting from 526 to 682 C.E. between two powerful Mayan city-states centered at Tikal and Calakmul certainly weakened the Maya heartland the way the Peloponnesian War between Athens and Sparta from 431 to 404 B.C.E. weakened Greece.

These highly urbanized societies may also have collapsed from internal stresses. An expanding population, coupled with increasing demands by the warrior and ceremonial elites for food and goods, may have overstrained the food supply and embittered the peasantry whose labor supported the entire structure. In this theory, a rebellion

The Pyramid of the Moon in the city of Teotihuacán.

of peasants against the urban center destroyed the great cities, whose inhabitants scattered into small village communities of the kind the Spaniards found in the sixteenth century. Today this theory seems to be the most plausible explanation for the catastrophic end of the great civilizations of Mexico.

The Toltec: Conflict Between Warriors and Priests

How was the Toltec state significant?

Warrior tribes quickly filled the power vacuum created by this collapse. The most successful of these was the **Toltec** (975–1200 C.E.) of northern Mexico. The Toltec established their capital at Tula, about 30 miles northwest of Teotihuacán, around 960–970 C.E. The Toltec ruling elite appears to have been divided between priests and warriors, with each faction struggling to dominate the other. According to legend, an early Toltec priest-king encouraged devotion to the god Quetzalcóatl (*kwet-zahl-KŌ-ah-tul*), or "Feathered Serpent," while the warriors opposed him in the name of a rival deity, Tezcatlipoca (*tetz-cat-lē-PŌ-kah*), or "Smoking Mirror." The two factions quarreled, and the worshippers of Quetzalcóatl were defeated and forced to leave Tula for the east, apparently in 987 C.E.

According to legend, Quetzalcóatl vowed revenge, claiming that he and his followers would return one day on boats across the Gulf of Mexico. Appearing as white-skinned men, oddities which no Mesoamerican had ever seen, they would reclaim their rightful heritage and redeem their people from bondage. Interestingly, Mayan sources describe the arrival in 987 on the Yucatán Peninsula of a man from the west named Kukulcán (*koo-kul-KHAN*), which means "Feathered Serpent" in Mayan; he apparently conquered the Yucatán Peninsula and built the city of Chichén Itzá (*chi-CHAIN ēt-ZAH*) for his capital. Was Kukulcán a Toltec worshipper of Quetzalcóatl forced to leave Tula? Murals at Chichén Itzá depict a Toltec army defeating Maya warriors around that time. And when Spanish invaders led by Hernán Cortés landed in ships and marched into central Mexico in 1519, those Maya who remembered the Toltec legend were convinced that the prophecy had been fulfilled and Quetzalcóatl had returned.

In the year 1000 C.E., the Toltec capital of Tula served as the hub of a militaristic empire stretching across Mexico from the Pacific to the Gulf. Its warriors dressed themselves as jaguars, coyotes, and eagles; they proudly carried Toltec rule to peoples who would soon learn to hate and fear them. Human sacrifice, an occasional practice in Mayan lands, became more frequent under the Toltec.

Although the brutality and efficiency of its warriors permeated all aspects of Toltec society, the Toltec did not lack appreciation for beauty and grace. In Chichén Itzá, Toltec and Mayan architectural forms merged to create magnificent stepped temples and light, airy hallways bordered by colonnades. The Mayan ritual pastime of the ball game, in which teams competed in an effort to propel a small rubber ball through a stone ring 25 feet above the ground using only elbows, hips, or knees, was adopted enthusiastically by the Toltec. Their ball court at Chichén Itzá was the largest in Mesoamerica, 490 feet long with walls 27 feet high. The game was played for very high stakes, since the captain of the losing team (and sometimes of the winning one as well) was often sacrificed.

The Toltec maintained the commercial connections forged by Teotihuacán and the Maya city-states, expanding them by exporting exquisite metal crafts, mosaics composed of quetzal feathers, and statuettes and jewelry made from precious gems. Toltec artisans skillfully blended their own methods with techniques learned from Mayan craftsmen. They used turquoise from modern-day New Mexico, gold from Central America, and obsidian and jade from their own realm to create stylized artifacts stunning in their simplicity. Their artistry was so breathtaking that, 500 years later, the artisans of the Aztec Empire were called *tolteca*.

Massive stone statues of Toltec warriors stand atop the pyramid at the ruins of Tula de Allende, Mexico.

No doubt the Toltec believed their militancy would ensure their dominance, but in the 1160s Tula was torn apart and sacked. Its destruction may have been the result of irreconcilable animosity between warriors and priests or of some sort of internal uprising. In the Yucatán, Chichén Itzá gradually decayed, and in 1224 it was abandoned. No one knows why the Toltec empire collapsed, and no empire replaced it until the coming of the Aztecs in 1325.

South America: Societies of the Andes

5.4 **Explain how Amerind societies of the Andes coped with and compensated for geographic and topographic challenges.**

The civilizations of Mesoamerica were built by only a small fraction of the Amerinds. Many never penetrated that far south, remaining in North America, north of the Rio Grande. Many others passed through the region and continued into South America. Forbidding in terms of topography and climate, South America remains the least explored of the earth's inhabited continents. The migrating peoples who first entered it confronted sweltering rain forests, snow-capped mountain ranges, and waterless deserts. There they created civilizations carefully adapted to such challenging environments.

Chavín, Nazca, and Moche Societies

How did early South American Amerind societies cope with topographic obstacles and isolation?

On the Pacific side of South America, the environment is shaped by the **Andes Mountains**, part of a geologic formation running from Cape Horn north through Peru 11,000 miles to the north slope of Alaska. With peaks more than 14,000 feet high, the Andes stand as a barrier to cultural connections across the South American continent. Chile and Argentina would probably have evolved as a single cultural region had not the Andes stood between them. Part of the "Ring of Fire" surrounding the Pacific Ocean, these mountains include many active volcanoes. Earthquakes and mudslides, some of them extremely damaging, are common.

Unlike the rest of the continent, however, the Andean highlands are home to three large mammals, the llama, alpaca, and vicuña. Useful for carrying burdens and as a food source, these animals never spread beyond the Andes because they could not thrive in the heat of lower-lying regions. Hunter-gatherers arrived in the Andean region at some time around 10,000 B.C.E. Four thousand years later, a significant population increase along the seacoast suggests the evolving importance of fishing. Lima beans were domesticated around this time, although the rockiness and aridity of Andean soils delayed the full development of agriculture until irrigation was employed. Sometime after 4000 B.C.E., irrigated fields stimulated the growth of the first Andean society in northern Peru.

This early society vanished, and an Andean successor state, the Chavín, emerged during what archeologists call the Early Horizon period (1200–200 B.C.E.). Centered on the ceremonial site of Chavín de Huantar (*cha-VĒN dā WAHN-tar*) in central Peru, it was organized around a polytheistic belief system whose gods were worshipped throughout the central Andes for centuries after Chavín's collapse. Almost nothing is known of Chavín political structures, but this civilization produced durable textiles, pottery, and metalwork, whose uses reflected Chavín religious convictions.

Isolation was the most significant handicap facing the Chavín state. Cut off from contact with other South American Indian societies by the Andes and separated from the Olmec civilization of Mexico by 1600 miles of ocean and 2000 miles of rugged terrain (Map 5.4), the Chavín people did not have the opportunity to adopt new technologies and ideas. All the Andean societies succeeding the Chavín were similarly isolated. Even today, there is no road connecting Mesoamerica to the Andes because the border between Panama and Colombia remains impassable.

During the Early Intermediate period (200 B.C.E.–500 C.E.), two post-Chavín societies developed, the Nazca and the Moche. Archeological evidence indicates that they fought each other, but not that they developed commercial or other peaceful connections.

Little is known of Nazca political organization, but its artistic accomplishments continue to impress modern-day observers. Based in southern Peru, the Nazca traced immense patterns on the desert by removing surface debris to expose the underlying strata of rock. These designs, visible only from the air, depict birds, spiders, monkeys, fish, and cats. Some scholars believe that the designs were offerings or signals to the gods; others contend that they were ritualized pathways connecting local shrines. Delicately painted polychrome ceramics and elaborate mummification of the dead also characterized Nazca civilization (as they did the Chavín).

Map 5.4 PRE-INCAN ANDEAN EMPIRES AND CULTURE AREAS, CA. 800 B.C.E.–1400 C.E. Several complex early cultures emerged in what is now Peru. Middle and South America's challenging topography isolated peoples from one another; the Tupí of the Amazon, for example, never learned of the existence of Andean societies, while the distance between the Chavín Empire and the Olmec society of Mexico was too great to be traversed with available means of transportation. Even in the 21st century C.E., no roads connect southeastern Panama with northwestern Colombia. How might such isolation have disadvantaged Amerind societies once they were confronted by peoples from less isolated regions?

The Moche (*MŌ-chā*) society of northern Peru dominated that region without creating a formal imperial structure. Complex irrigation channels transported water from up to 75 miles away, allowing the Moche to develop a diversified agricultural base that they supplemented with meat from their herds of alpacas and llamas. An elaborate religious hierarchy presided over worship services performed in structures like the Pyramid of the Sun, an adobe building 1140 feet long and 130 feet high. The first Andean culture to develop accurately representational art, the Moche created ceramic portrait vases and objects of silver and gold. They also took a dim view of medical malpractice: physicians who killed their patients through incompetence were staked out to be eaten alive by birds of prey.

Moche women, like women in other early American Indian societies, centered their lives in the home. There they raised fruits and vegetables, tended animals, cooked meals, nurtured children, made clothing, and appeased the gods through rituals. Political life, military service, hunting, and labor on roads and buildings were tasks reserved for men. This gender-based division of labor was so consistent throughout the Americas that scholars have been tempted to speculate, in the absence of concrete evidence, that the Amerinds brought it with them from Central Asia.

The Moche thrived in northern Peru for the first six centuries of the Common Era, finally collapsing under the pressure of a series of earthquakes, floods, and droughts that deprived the ruling elite of its political legitimacy. Apparently the Chinese were not the only people to monitor the environment for signs of Heaven's Mandate.

Tiahuanaco, Huari, and Chimor

How did the successor states of Tiahuanaco, Huari, and Chimor build on and exceed the accomplishments of their predecessors?

The Moche were succeeded by three societies during the Middle Horizon period (500–1000 C.E.). Two developed in the Andean highlands and one on the Pacific coast.

First of the mountain societies was the Tiahuanaco (*tē-wah-NAH-koo*), named for its impressive capital at 13,000 feet above sea level near Bolivia's Lake Titicaca. The city's population ranged between 30,000 and 40,000, making it the highest large city of the Andes but small in comparison to Teotihuacán. Tiahuanaco's agriculture centered on fields reclaimed from lakeside swamps by means of an intricate drainage system. Commercial relationships over long distances were maintained by caravans of sure-footed llamas. Ceremonial buildings were constructed of stones joined together with such artistry and precision that no mortar was necessary; even the blade of a knife could not pass between them. The city of Tiahuanaco featured running water and a closed sewer system.

The second highland civilization of this period was the Huari (*WAH-rē*), located in the mountains of southeastern Peru. This culture developed later than Tiahuanaco and was similar to it technologically and tied to it commercially. In building their commercial enterprises, the two civilizations competed for the copper, obsidian, and turquoise deposits of local valleys. But the Huari culture differed in some ways from that of Tiahuanaco. Huari public buildings were much smaller than those of Tiahuanaco and were built from adobe rather than cut stone. Its capital was larger in area than Tiahuanaco but much less densely populated.

Neither of these highland cultures developed elaborate administrative structures, and like all early Andean civilizations, their lack of a system of writing makes it difficult to learn much about them. Huari collapsed around the year 800 C.E., bringing to an end 2000 years of urban settlements in southern Peru. Tiahuanaco lingered for several centuries, declining slowly well before the arrival of the Europeans. No reasons for the weakening of either culture can be stated with certainty.

On the Pacific coast, the Moche were succeeded by Chimor (*chē-MOR*), a major imperial power that dominated coastal Peru until the emergence of the Inca in the fifteenth century C.E. Chan Chan, constructed in the heart of Moche territory on a huge site directly on the coast, became Chimor's capital and cultural center. The city was notable for its massive ceremonial structures, large warehouses, and extensive one-story living compounds, built without roofs, since rain occurred infrequently along the Peruvian coast. Chimor arose as a successor state to the Moche around 700 C.E. but does not appear to have developed into an expansionistic state before 1300. Once it did, it created the first Andean empire.

Chimor's social structure was hierarchical, topped by a warrior aristocracy supported by priests. Beneath these classes, artisans developed distinctive techniques of pottery making, textile manufacture, and metal craft. Close in status to the artisans, merchants organized and carried on commerce with the remotest regions of the empire and with other Andean cultures. Peasants, at the bottom of the social hierarchy, supported Chimor's social and economic structure with agriculture, fishing, and livestock raising. This social structure, especially the warrior class and the widespread commercial contacts, indicates that Chimor was intent on spreading its culture and control as far as the imposing mountainous topography of the region would allow.

Indeed, the people of Chimor, known as Chimú, conquered a number of less formidable neighbors, but they do not seem to have oppressed them or treated them as captives. Instead, unlike the Moche and Huari, they deliberately incorporated them into their empire, giving them a stake in the power and prosperity of Chimor. Imperial administration was aided by a far-flung system of roads and bridges that encouraged communication, commerce, and coercion. Given their cultural achievements, the Chimú might have been far better known today had they not been conquered between 1462 and 1470 by the Inca, who adopted many Chimú practices and policies on their way to becoming South America's most powerful civilization.

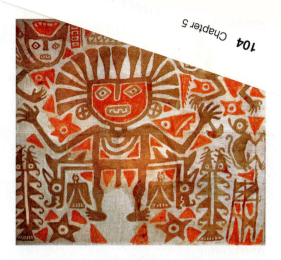

A painted textile panel from Chimor depicting a central figure wearing an elaborate headdress. The two felines on either side of him may signify that he is a shaman or a chieftain.

Chapter Review

Consequences and Connections

The first groups of Central Asian nomads who crossed the Bering land bridge and entered the Western Hemisphere were probably very similar to one another in genetic composition, hunting techniques, weaponry, customs, and social life. Their descendants, however, who spread through North and South America through countless generations, diverged from one another in many ways as they adapted to widely varying environments.

In the Arctic and Sub-Arctic regions of North America, brief growing seasons and frozen, snow-covered ground made organized agriculture impossible. The peoples who remained in these regions maintained their hunter-gatherer lifestyles. In the southwestern corner of the present-day United States, arid soils and the absence of huge rivers for irrigation projects similarly limited agriculture. At the same time, agriculture seemed unnecessary in the Pacific Northwest, the Prairies, and the Great Plains, which teemed with abundant fish and game. In the Eastern Woodlands, the Iroquois founded an innovative confederacy based on agriculture, but its small population base prevented the sort of large-scale, complex development found in Mesoamerica.

The Mississippi people seemed to be modeling their society on Mesoamerica when they built Cahokia, but its unexplained abandonment ended this experiment.

In Mesoamerica, organizationally complex societies arose, including the Olmec, the Maya, the Teotihuacanos, and the Toltec. In lands with plentiful rainfall, rich soils, a lengthy growing season, and a wide variety of possible crops, these peoples turned from hunting and gathering to agriculture, and agricultural surpluses made possible the development of complex political and social organizations. Mesoamerican civilizations developed elaborate belief systems, advanced mathematical and astronomical knowledge, considerable architectural and engineering skills, and impressive military establishments.

Farther south, the civilizations of the Andes met the challenges of their natural environment. Irrigating the dry soils and carefully shepherding livestock, they constructed a firm agricultural base in an arid environment. With each successive civilization building on the achievements of its predecessors, the Chavín, Nazca, Moche, Tiahuanaco, Huari, and Chimú societies built temples and public halls, created goods of fabric and metal, threw bridges across raging rivers at dizzying heights, and gradually evolved toward imperial conquest. The later Inca civilization appreciated the accomplishments of the Chimú and adopted many of their practices.

Beginning their development much later than the civilizations that originated in Asia, Africa, and Europe, some Amerind societies had evolved to complex levels

of social organization by 1500 C.E. Others, restricted by their environments, continued the ways of their ancestors. Some evolved in isolation from one another, but most had connections and conflicts. Over many centuries, they fought each other, traded with each other, and learned from each other. All did, however, develop in isolation from the cultures and civilizations of the Eastern Hemisphere until 1500 C.E.

Reviewing Key Concepts

Mesoamerica, p. 86
Amerinds, p. 87
Tribes, p. 90

Olmec, p. 93
Long Count Calendar, p. 94
Maya, p. 95

Bloodletting, p. 96
Toltec, p. 99
Andes Mountains, p. 100

Ask Yourself

1. How did North American Amerinds react to their differing environments?

2. How did Olmec society influence the subsequent development of Maya civilization?

3. How did leadership in Maya civilization reflect the political, spiritual, and military aspects of society?

4. How did the Toltec build on the accomplishments of previous civilizations?

5. How did early South American societies influence one another?

Key Dates and Developments

North American Chronology:

ca. 1000 B.C.E.	Adena society emerges in Ohio River Valley
ca. 100 C.E.	Adena merges with Hopewell society
400	Adena-Hopewell society disappears
700–1200	Anasazi society in southwestern United States
700–1500	Mississippian society along and east of the Mississippi River
1050–1250	Zenith of Cahokian society

Mesoamerican Chronology:

1800 B.C.E.– 150 C.E.	Olmec society: The Preclassic period
1700 B.C.E.	Foundation of San Lorenzo
1200 B.C.E.	Foundation of Tres Zapotes
100 C.E.	Foundation of Teotihuacán
150–900 C.E.	Maya society: The Classic period

ca. 750	Destruction of Teotihuacán
800–900	Abandonment of Mayan urban centers
ca. 970	Foundation of Tula by the Toltec
ca. 990	Foundation of Chichén Itzá
1156	Destruction of Tula
1224	Abandonment of Chichén Itzá

South American Chronology:

1200–200 B.C.E.	Early Horizon period: Chavín society in Peru
200 B.C.E.– 500 C.E.	Early Intermediate period: Nazca and Moche societies in Peru
500–1000	Middle Horizon period: Tiahuanaco, Huari, and Chimú societies in Bolivia and Peru
1300–1465	Chimú military expansion culminating in rivalry with Inca Empire

Chapter 6

The Persian Connection: Its Impact and Influences, 2000 B.C.E.–637 C.E.

A PERSIAN SOLDIER The sculpted figure of a Persian policeman guards the entrance to one of Persia's royal palaces. This stylized image shows the braided hair and beard worn by Persian men, the long pike considerably taller than a man, and the attitude of vigilance and resolution that Persian emperors expected from their soldiers (page 113).

After reading this chapter, you should be able to:

6.1 Discuss the advantages and disadvantages involved in creating a state on the Iranian Plateau.

6.2 Identify the administrative, legal, and commercial developments in Persia under Darius the Great, and note Mesopotamian influences on those developments.

6.3 Explain the appeal of Zoroastrianism to Persians and account for its usefulness to the emperors.

6.4 Analyze the consequences of the Ionian Revolt and explain Persia's repeated failures to defeat the Greeks.

6.5 Discuss the successor states to the Persian Empire (Macedonians, Seleucids, Parthians, and Sasanians), demonstrating their continuing ability to connect various cultures.

In 529 B.C.E., a solemn procession filed from northwest India across Afghanistan and onto the plateau of Iran. Its members were carrying the mutilated remains of one of the most powerful rulers of the ancient world. As his body was placed in the sturdy tomb that had been built for him years earlier, priests chanted hymns and recited prayers. Sacrifices were made on his behalf to the fundamental forces of fire and water. Then the tomb was sealed and guards were placed around it to safeguard his royal dignity even in death. Cyrus the Great of Persia had come home.

The Persian Empire

Cyrus, like other kings of his day, was a fearsome warrior. But a list of his military conquests would tell only part of his story. The Persian Empire he founded left a legacy that included an efficient system of government, a tolerant society, a model for fostering commerce and cooperation among many cultures, and a conception of a universal god who rewards those who lead good lives and work for justice. Though often portrayed as foreign and therefore barbaric by the Greeks, Persian civilization was rich in its own right. The empire might well have dominated southwest Asia for centuries had Alexander the Great not arisen in Macedonia and decided to destroy it. Even after its fall, the Persian Empire's legacy profoundly influenced Islamic culture and present-day Iran. The king whom the Persians buried in 529 B.C.E. was an extraordinary ruler who set in motion a series of events and influences that long outlived him.

The Persian Empire

6.1   **Discuss the advantages and disadvantages involved in creating a state on the Iranian Plateau.**

Mesopotamia, Egypt, India, and China all originated in fertile river valleys. Persian society, in contrast, developed on the arid **Iranian Plateau**. In that challenging environment, the Persians constructed an empire that at its height would encompass most of southwestern Asia.

Geographic Challenges Confront the First Persians

What geographic and topographic challenges confronted the first Persians?

The Iranian Plateau, comprising nearly one million square miles, is relatively inhospitable. It contains two immense salt deserts, and the small rivers that cross it are difficult to navigate and offer little water for agriculture. Even entering the plateau can be difficult. It is guarded on the west by the Zagros (*ZAH-grus*) Mountains; on the northwest by the Caspian Sea, Caucasus (*KAW-cuh-suhs*) Mountains, and Elburz (*el-BURZ*) Mountains; on the east by the mountain ranges and arid depressions of Afghanistan; on the southeast by the Baluchi (*buh-LOO-key*) Desert; and on the south by the Persian Gulf (Map 6.1). The easiest way to ascend the plateau is from the northeast, where broad corridors through the mountains link Iran to Central Asia.

Archeological evidence suggests that people domesticated sheep and goats and cultivated wheat and barley in the Zagros foothills at least 10,000 years ago. Little is known of these early Iranians, but artifacts made of obsidian, a mineral not native to the region, indicate the existence of early trading networks. Pastoral nomadism dominated the Iranian Plateau, where wide variations in water supply made regular farming impossible. Central Asian nomads arrived on the plateau through the northwest corridors about 5000 years ago.

The Central Asian steppes were no more inviting than Iran, but they were much more difficult to defend against invaders. For thousands of years, hostile tribes had

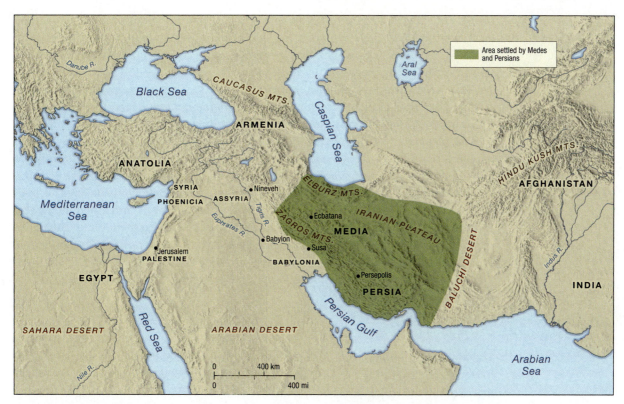

Map 6.1 THE PHYSICAL GEOGRAPHY OF THE IRANIAN PLATEAU The geography of the region provided natural defenses for Indo-European peoples settling on the Iranian Plateau. Notice that the Zagros and Elburz mountain ranges, the Persian Gulf, the Caspian Sea, and the Baluchi Desert made access to the region difficult for invaders. Sparse rainfall made the population dependent on irrigation systems that channeled runoff from mountain snows that melt in spring. Why might such an easily defensible region have appeared undesirable to earlier settlers?

fought each other for control of the region, often contending at the same time with formidable empires such as China. Winners expelled losers and were driven out in turn. Some of these tribes went to Iran, undismayed by its uncertain water supply, and grazed their herds on the plateau.

The first migrants were influenced by the Sumerian culture they found among peoples living on the plateau, but they blended it with their own customs and preferences. Archeological remains indicate that these early immigrants were skilled artists, particularly in ceramics. Then around 1000 B.C.E., an Indo-European tribe from Central Asia migrated down the eastern shore of the Caspian Sea into western Iran. This group was a branch of the Aryans who had earlier moved into India, and they gave their own name to the plateau they occupied: Iran means "land of the Aryans" (Map 2.3).

The two principal subgroups of Aryan migrants were the Medes (*MĒDZ*), who took up residence in the Zagros Mountains, and the Persians, taking their name from Farsia, the central region of the Iranian Plateau. Both spoke the same language, which today is known as Farsi (*FAHR-sē*). They had different accents, but the Greeks, who encountered them during the Greco-Persian Wars, were unable to distinguish between the two and called all of them Persians.

Although they periodically fought against invaders from the Assyrian Empire, the Medes were relatively well protected by the Zagros and established a thriving economy and culture. They mined minerals such as gold, silver, precious gems, marble, iron, copper, and lead, which they used in artistry and traded with neighboring cultures.

The mountain snows provided the only reliable source of water for agriculture in a land that averages fewer than 12 inches of precipitation per year, so the Medes developed a sophisticated irrigation system. They trapped the waters of the melting snows and diverted them to fields. In one of the many valleys of the Zagros, they built Ecbatana (*eck-BAH-tuh-nuh*), the seat of their government and center of their economy. Eventually, however, the Assyrian Empire conquered both the Medes and the Persians, forcing them to pay tribute although never completely subjugating them.

When Babylonia and Assyria erupted into civil war, the Medes and Persians took advantage of the conflict to free themselves from the invaders. First the Median king Cyaxares (*sī-AX-ar-ēs*) strengthened his army, reducing the Persians to the status of vassals. Cyaxares (640–584 B.C.E.) then allied with the Chaldeans against Assyria. But his plans were delayed by the arrival of Scythians (*SIH-thē-ahns*), nomadic warriors from Central Asia, who invaded Iran through the passage between the Caspian Sea and the Caucasus Mountains. Forced to pay tribute to the Scythians, Cyaxares decided to give a banquet for their leaders—at which he got them drunk and killed them. This enabled him to return to his original plan, and by 612 B.C.E. the Medes and Chaldeans had destroyed the Assyrian capital of Nineveh. Cyaxares ruled northern Mesopotamia until his death in 584, while the Chaldeans (or "New Babylonians") ruled in southern Mesopotamia (or "Babylonia"). The Assyrian Empire was shattered, making way for the creation of the Persian Empire.

Cyrus the Great

What principles of governance were developed by Cyrus the Great?

The Median kingdom lasted for only a few decades before its Persian vassals started intriguing against it. The Persian ruling family, called the Achaemenids (*ah-KĒ-muh-nids*), married into the ruling house of Media. Cyrus, a child of this union, managed to unify the Persian tribes and wage war against the Median king, his grandfather. In 550 B.C.E. he united Medes and Persians under the Achaemenid house. Three years later he defeated the king of Lydia and expanded the Persian Empire to the Aegean (*ih-JĒ-uhn*) Sea, gaining control of several Greek city-states on the shores of Anatolia. Although Cyrus made no move against the Greek mainland, the Greeks were unnerved by the proximity of an empire with a large, well-equipped army that enjoyed a reputation for winning. During the following decades, they watched the Persians carefully.

Cyrus next moved east, conquering the lands of Parthia and Bactria (modern-day Afghanistan) and extending his dominion from the Aegean in the west to the Hindu Kush Mountains in the east. In 539 B.C.E., he invaded southern Mesopotamia, then controlled by New Babylonia. By allying himself with various tribes struggling against New Babylonia and portraying himself as their liberator, Cyrus was able to enter the city of Babylon without a fight. By the time of his death in 530 B.C.E., he had clearly earned the title of Cyrus the Great, one of history's most successful empire-builders.

ASSIMILATION AFTER CONQUEST   The importance of Cyrus extended beyond his conquests. For its time, his rule was remarkably sophisticated in its approach to subjugated peoples. Conquerors of that era normally pillaged defeated cities and enslaved their populations. Cyrus, by contrast, had a shrewd instinct for governing that allowed him to win the trust of those he defeated. An examination of some of the **principles of government of Cyrus the Great** illustrates this instinct.

First, Cyrus demonstrated early in his reign that he would rule through persuasion and compromise rather than force and humiliation. When he conquered the Medes, he granted their leader honors and respect, and he united the Medes with his own people rather than subjugating them. He retained not only Median administrative and military structures but also the Medes who directed them. In this way he won the trust of the Medes and reduced the possibility of rebellion against his rule.

Second, Cyrus treated conquered peoples benevolently, allowing deported peoples to return to their homelands rather than enslaving them. He won the gratitude of the Jews when he freed them from captivity in Babylonia and allowed them to return to Jerusalem. He even encouraged them to rebuild their temple, which the Babylonians had destroyed.

Finally, Cyrus permitted the peoples he defeated to retain their own religions and cultures while simultaneously offering them partnership in the Persian Empire. This two-pronged approach persuaded various ethnic groups to accept his rule; in doing so, they understood that they would not be humiliated and would retain their self-respect. Cyrus also realized that his own people could learn from many of the societies he conquered. His officials sought out and copied the most useful practices of their new subjects. He also standardized taxes and measurements, codified laws, and fostered commercial and cultural connections within his vast domains.

Cyrus's policies of tolerance were based not so much on benevolence as on pragmatism. He acted in ways he knew would work. He understood that people treated humanely were not likely to rebel, and he also understood the nature of nomadic societies that occupied the Iranian Plateau. These groups, often called tribes, usually resisted joining settled societies. They tended to pursue their own interests, migrating at will to various parts of the plateau and following their own traditions and governing methods. Tribal fighters were bound to their chiefs by ties of loyalty cemented by blood relationships and patronage, the voluntary submission of a family or clan to a powerful leader (or patron). Thus, chiefs commanded considerable leverage that could be used to support a central leadership, as long as that leadership did not monopolize power or impose its culture on others. In such circumstances, Cyrus acted prudently, accepting conditions he could not change and turning necessity to his advantage by granting autonomy generously.

That generosity was not, however, unlimited. Tribal leaders were expected to place their own interests within the context of the empire's broader goals, recognizing that cooperation would benefit everyone. Defense and trade were empire-wide priorities. Permitting the Jews to return to Palestine helped Cyrus assimilate the Phoenician and Palestinian remnants of the Babylonian Empire, and the rebuilding of the temple at Jerusalem was followed by the construction of fortifications designed to protect the western regions of the empire against invasion from Egypt. The Jews were expected to cooperate in this task, and evidence suggests that they did. So did the Babylonians, whose merchants welcomed membership in an empire that offered them secure trade routes to markets in Egypt and Syria. Cyrus's ability to transform conflict into connection created an extensive commercial network in Southwest Asia.

Persian Governance and Society: Links with Mesopotamia

6.2 Identify the administrative, legal, and commercial developments in Persia under Darius the Great, and note Mesopotamian influences on those developments.

The Persian Empire dominated both Iran and Mesopotamia by the middle of the sixth century B.C.E. Then its rulers consolidated their hold over their subjects and projected Persian influence westward toward an eventual confrontation with Greece.

From Cyrus to Darius

After the conquest of Babylon, Cyrus presided over the largest empire on earth. He had won the loyalty of most of his subject peoples by treating them humanely. Only one corner of his realm resisted his rule, and the King of Kings finally overreached himself. The Massagetae (*mahs-ah-JET-ē*), a nomadic people of Scythian origin in northwestern India, were contemptuous of Persian ideals and indifferent to Persian control. In 530 B.C.E., Cyrus, now in his sixties, led his army into the region to subdue the nomads. The battle went badly for the Persians, and Cyrus himself was knocked

How did Darius's principles of political leadership differ from those of Cyrus?

from his horse by Tomyris (*tum-Ē-riss*), queen of the Massagetae. She severed his head with a single blow of her sword and returned his mutilated corpse to the Persians, who retreated westward and buried him in the tomb described at the beginning of this chapter.

Cambyses (*kam-BĒ-sēz*), Cyrus's son, succeeded him and wisely decided to leave the Massagetae alone. Instead, he invaded Egypt, bringing the Nile Valley under Persian control. But the campaign there took three years and Persians at home, unnerved by Cyrus's defeat and tired of war, revolted in 522 B.C.E. Cambyses (r. 530–521 B.C.E.) rushed back from Egypt to suppress the uprising, but he died along the way. The Persian Empire had never established a routine order of succession, and with three different heirs of the Achaemenid dynasty contending for power, the empire fell into disarray.

The eventual winner was Darius (*duh-RĪ-us*), a 28-year-old soldier who married both Cambyses's grieving widow and a daughter of Cyrus the Great (Persian rulers sometimes married more than one woman for political gain). But he was widely viewed as a usurper, and rebellions broke out throughout the empire. Claiming divine support, Darius (r. 521–486 B.C.E.) put down the uprisings by force. Prudently, he waited a few years before resuming Persia's imperial expansion, using the time to reorganize his army. But he did not wait too long, for he understood that the arrogance he had shown in claiming the throne would have to be justified by victories. In 517 B.C.E. he struck eastward, driving into southwestern India and putting its gold mines to the service of the empire. His victories in the Indus Valley (Map 6.2) completed Persia's conquest of three of the four great river civilizations. Only China remained outside his grasp, and it is unlikely that he ever thought of going there. Instead, he moved

Map 6.2 THE PERSIAN EMPIRE EXPANDS, 549–490 B.C.E. The Persian Empire stretched across portions of three continents on a broad east–west axis. Note that Persia recentered power in Southwest Asia eastward away from Mesopotamia, controlling territory from Libya and Macedonia in the west to the Indus Valley in the east. The Royal Road facilitated communication and connections across this geographically challenging region, while local governors known as satraps enforced the Persian king's will in areas the monarch himself never visited. What effects would Cyrus the Great's policies of assimilation have had on the peoples of such a vast and diverse region?

westward, securing Egypt and Libya, and then struck north into southeastern Europe, pressing as far as the Danube River by 512 B.C.E. With future conquests in mind, he settled down for the time being to solidify his rule.

Administration of the Empire

What were Darius's principal administrative innovations?

Cyrus, Cambyses, and Darius had built an enormous empire, many times larger than the Assyrian Empire that Cyrus had overthrown (Map 6.3). Ruling that realm—a vast expanse of many different peoples and cultures—would require a carefully structured bureaucracy. Central control had to be ensured, even as local autonomy was preserved, in order to avoid inefficiency, rebellion, or both.

Darius chose strong central rule. Whereas Cyrus had governed through cooperation backed by the ever-present threat of force, Darius emphasized authority. Cyrus called himself "King of Kings," emphasizing that he was first among equals; Darius called himself "the Great King," emphasizing the opposite. More distant from his people than Cyrus and less willing to permit autonomy, Darius grounded his government on the unswerving loyalty of political appointees.

This objective led Darius to divide the Persian Empire into 20 provinces, each known in Farsi as a **satrapy** (*SĀ-trap-ē*) and ruled by a governor called a satrap. Most satraps were not Persians but members of the ethnic group they were expected to rule. In this way, Darius strengthened central control while perpetuating the local autonomy characteristic of nomadic society. Linked to the Achaemenids through marriage or birth, satraps were referred to as "the eyes and ears of the Great King."

Selected for their loyalty and familiarity with local conditions, satraps exercised considerable authority, reinforced by rapid communication. A carefully maintained

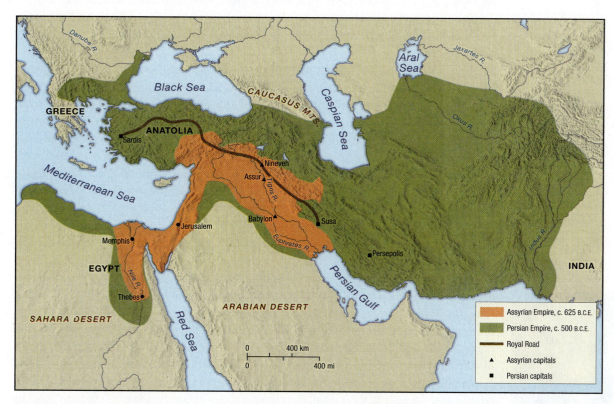

Map 6.3 THE ASSYRIAN AND PERSIAN EMPIRES COMPARED, 625–500 B.C.E. The sprawling Assyrian Empire had dominated Southwest Asia, but observe how the conquests of Cyrus, Cambyses, and Darius I dwarfed it. Ruling an empire as enormous as Persia was an unprecedented task, requiring administrative innovations such as satrapies. It also required a willingness to grant substantial autonomy to local rulers and leaders, a feature that had characterized Persian governance even before Cyrus. What other policies or institutions might have been devised to permit efficient rule of such an enormous realm?

highway system, dominated by the **Royal Road** running from Sardis, near the Aegean Sea, to Susa (*SOO-suh*), near the Persian Gulf, guaranteed that information would travel quickly. Persia's superb mounted postal service could, under the best conditions, carry a message more than a thousand miles in the course of a week. Foot soldiers, however, even if marching at the breakneck pace of 19 miles a day, would take three months to travel the Royal Road. Beyond Susa, the roads eastward to India were less satisfactory, and the terrain rougher.

Darius knew, of course, that the swift delivery of a royal message did not necessarily guarantee compliance. The emperor might be master of all he surveyed from his capital, but beyond that horizon he depended on the willing cooperation of subordinates. He needed men, particularly in remote areas, who would carry out his commands without question and who would act in his own best interests. Satraps were the men he chose.

The satraps were crucial to the prosperity and peace of the empire they served. They conducted diplomacy with border states and warrior peoples. Both inside and outside the empire, they followed their rulers in blending persuasion and force. The stability they ensured allowed trade and commerce to thrive. In addition, they collected royal taxes; if they failed at this task, the empire would collapse. That its fall came with defeat by a military genius, rather than as a consequence of poor administration, is a tribute to the diligence and skill of the satraps as well as the administrative system designed by Darius the Great.

Mesopotamian Influences: Law, Administration, and Commerce

How were Darius's policies in the areas of law, administration, and commerce influenced by Mesopotamia?

As Persia expanded and as its bureaucracy grew, its connections with other cultures multiplied. The emperors were particularly attracted by Mesopotamia, birthplace of the Sumerian, Babylonian, and Assyrian cultures and worthy of imitation in several respects.

Law was one area in which Persians learned from Mesopotamia. Darius needed a legal system applicable throughout the empire to support his administration. Adhering to Cyrus's principle of tolerance for subject peoples, Darius permitted local customs and regulations to remain in place. But he established a system of royal judges to ensure that local laws would be enforced in a manner consistent with the interests of the empire. Hoping to be known as a lawgiver like the Babylonian king Hammurabi, Darius authorized the codification of Persian laws. But while Hammurabi's Code survived on a black stone column in Susa, Darius's *Ordinance of Good Regulations*, written on parchment (treated sheepskins or goatskins), completely disappeared. The few indirect references to it found in contemporary Babylonian commercial documents suggest that it was modeled on Hammurabi's Code but altered to apply Persian ethics to civil and criminal matters.

Mesopotamia also influenced Persian governance. The Aryans who entered Iran brought with them a simple social structure adapted to life on the steppes of Central Asia. But Cyrus's invasion of Mesopotamia brought Persia into contact with a complex civilization. Ruling it required levels of organization beyond those present in a nomadic society. The Babylonian Empire used a system of provincial governors, many of whose duties were now taken over by Persian satraps and their subordinates, such as tax collectors, police officials, and record keepers. These officials constituted an administrative class of their own, developing codes of conduct specific to their roles in Persian life. In addition, the military occupation of Mesopotamia and its assimilation into the Persian Empire forced the satraps to share power with local warriors, who resented the Persians for their literacy and their knowledge of diplomacy. Soldiers did not generally have these skills, and Persian administrators, responding to their antagonism, gradually became more militaristic.

Persepolis: the east stairway to the great audience hall of Darius I, showing visiting dignitaries bringing tribute.

The conquest of Mesopotamia also brought Persia into contact with western Asia and northwestern Africa. International trade expanded, fostered by the empire's political stability, control of sea routes, and well-maintained roads. Persia traded extensively with Syria, Egypt, Greece, and Ethiopia, connecting those regions with Central Asia through Afghanistan. Far more cosmopolitan than its Mesopotamian, Egyptian, and Indian predecessors, the Persian Empire forged connections between cultures separated by thousands of miles.

Persian Society and Culture

How did society, culture, and family life develop under the Persian Empire?

Contact with Mesopotamia also affected Persian society. To meet the needs of an expanding empire, social classes began to develop in Persian cities. Artisans now needed to fabricate more than saddles and weapons: they created items of metal, fiber, and leather required by an urbanizing society forsaking its nomadic past. Merchants carried on local and long-distance trade via the Royal Road and Silk Road. Nomads had no need for elaborate systems of irrigation, but settled societies based on arid plateaus did, and the skilled and unskilled workers who built and maintained them were highly valued.

In addition, Persian society included a slave class. Persia had a history of slave owning—in Central Asia the Aryans had owned slaves—and when invading Persians occupied Mesopotamia, they saw Babylonians using slaves on construction projects. Most Persian slaves were prisoners taken in battle, but others were debtors forced to sell themselves or even their families into slavery to repay their creditors. Slaves were the property of their owners and could make no decisions (including marriage) without permission. Although some slaves became highly skilled at their tasks and were rewarded with increasing levels of responsibility and respect, most led short lives of hard labor and deprivation.

What little we know of Persian family structure suggests a self-reliant society. A Persian man could have more than one wife, provided that he could afford to maintain each one above the poverty level, a restriction that limited polygamy to the upper classes. The fact that men were frequently away from home on business or at war meant that elite Persian women enjoyed substantial independence. They administered family estates, organized celebrations, and traveled freely throughout the empire with or without their husbands. Most men and women, of course, lived from one meal to the next and never acquired wealth. These families, on whose labor the empire depended, had little time to contemplate anything other than survival.

Everyone, however—elites, ordinary people, and slaves—benefited from the Persian love of celebration. Festivals were common throughout the empire, particularly once Zoroastrianism took root. That religion, described below, obligates people to seek happiness and considers fasting and penance to belong to the realm of demons. Accordingly, Persians enjoyed feasts filled with music, dancing, and fun. The staple food was barley bread, supplemented by fruits, vegetables, and date or grape wine. Merrymakers were required to give to the poor and invite even the most destitute to join the revelry. The spring festival of Nō Rōz (*NO ROSE*), commemorating the creation of fire, was celebrated with special foods, the exchange of gifts, and the wearing of new clothes and ornaments. In addition to seven "high feasts," there were many local fairs and frolics. The love of celebrations gave the Persians a spirit of joy that counterbalanced the empire's military might and administrative control.

Persians also enjoyed fine jewelry and clothing. Like their Median and Scythian ancestors, they wore a wide variety of bracelets, necklaces, chains, and earrings, often made of gold or silver. Contemporary non-Persian accounts often refer to Iranians as taking great pride in their appearance and their homes. Bowls, goblets, and ceremonial

Persians loved objects made of gold or silver, like this silver figurine of an antelope.

A photograph of the ruins of the entrance to the Palace of Darius in Persepolis.

vessels were made of brass, gold, and silver, and appear to have been widely used not only by the elite but by many ordinary households.

Much of the empire's cultural inheritance came from the Medes and Persians. The Persians spoke Farsi, which featured a 36-character alphabet, an intricate grammatical structure, and a rich, expressive vocabulary. This language was written not on clay in the Sumerian style, but with pen and ink on parchment.

Another original aspect of Persian culture was architecture. Once the formerly nomadic Persians became sedentary, they constructed huge monuments depicting bulls and lions with wings. Surviving Persian art generally consists of sculpture and reliefs carved into the walls of buildings. These monuments reveal a culture sensitive to beauty and aware of its political uses. For example, the emperor, his generals, and courtiers were portrayed as regal, powerful persons of great dignity. Often they were depicted as stylized, mythical heroes, adorned with wings or engaged in single-handed combat with lions or bulls. Delegations from subject kingdoms like Babylonia and Lydia were shown bearing tribute and paying homage to Cyrus or Darius, particularly on the walls of the city of Persepolis (*per-SEH-puh-lis*), the most visually striking of Persia's cities.

The emperor maintained official residences in three cities, enabling him to rule the empire from whichever one he happened to be visiting. During the winter this was usually Susa, centrally located in Mesopotamia; Ecbatana or Babylon served as the capital in the summer. Shortly after seizing the throne, Darius began building a ceremonial capital at Persepolis, intending to demonstrate his greatness through building and sculptures. He died before the work was completed, and his son Xerxes (*ZURK-z_ez*) finished the task. Festivals, celebrations, and major imperial functions were held there in an atmosphere suggesting that the largest empire of its day would last for thousands of years.

Persepolis survives today only as ruins, but even those fragments are impressive. It contained a series of massive public buildings, including the royal treasury and several superbly designed reception halls. Colossal monuments portrayed the power and ferocity of the Persian emperor. Anyone witnessing such grandeur would conclude that Persia in 500 B.C.E. was truly the center of the world. But just as Cyrus the Great had been unexpectedly brought down in battle by a small tribe of nomads far to the east, his successors would inadvertently lead the empire to destruction in wars with seemingly unimportant people on its western frontier.

Zoroastrianism

6.3 Explain the appeal of Zoroastrianism to Persians and account for its usefulness to the emperors.

Those assimilated into the Persian Empire participated in a dynamic, expanding state with a flourishing economy. Many also practiced a religion that gave divine sanction to the ambitions of Persian emperors: **Zoroastrianism** (*zohr-ō-ASS-trē-ahn-iz′m*).

At first Medes and Persians were polytheistic, worshipping a variety of deities including two powerful gods, Ahura and Mazda (*uh-HOOR-uh* and *MAHZ-duh*). Like other polytheistic peoples, they incorporated religion into their daily lives, believing that various gods represented natural forces such as wind, rain, and sunlight and praying to the one whose benefits they sought. This belief system changed significantly in the sixth century B.C.E. with the empire's adoption of the ideas of a holy man who had lived centuries earlier on the Iranian Plateau.

A Religion of Good and Evil

What were the principal beliefs of Zoroastrianism?

Zoroastrianism was based on the ideas of the prophet Zoroaster—or Zarathustra (*zah-rah-THOO-strah*), as he is more commonly known today—who apparently lived in Persia sometime between 1300 and 1000 B.C.E. Zoroaster sensed that two powerful Persian gods, Ahura and Mazda, were in fact a single god, whom he called **Ahura Mazda**. He perceived Ahura Mazda as the universal god of light who had created human beings and given them free will to choose between right and wrong. To explain the existence of evil, Zoroaster maintained that Ahura Mazda had a malignant twin, **Ahriman** (*AHR-ē-mun*), whom Ahura Mazda had defeated and banished from paradise but who still sought to influence human behavior as lord of the forces of darkness.

Zoroaster's promotion of monotheism (belief in one god) won few converts until he blended it with an ancient cult emphasizing fire worship. Zoroastrians built fire temples to enshrine the light of Ahura Mazda. They conceded that lesser gods existed but characterized some as attributes of Ahura Mazda, while others were manifestations of **The Lie**, a set of false doctrines propagated by Ahriman to lead people astray.

Once the Persian emperors adopted Zoroastrianism, they gave control of it to the **Magi** (*MĀ-ji*), scholar-priests who guarded the temples and compiled Zoroaster's ideas in the **Avesta**, a sacred text (see "Excerpt from the *Avesta*"). The Magi, who later played a role in the Christian story of the birth of Jesus of Nazareth, came to see all creation as a cosmic struggle between good and evil. At the end of life, each individual would be judged by Ahura Mazda: those who had led lives of goodness and truth would be rewarded with eternal bliss; those who had practiced wickedness and deceit would be doomed to everlasting pain. At the Last Judgment, righteousness would overcome The Lie.

Many beliefs later important to Judaism, Christianity, and Islam first appeared in Zoroastrianism: the existence of one God of justice and benevolence, the conflict between God and the Devil, the divine judgment of individuals based on moral behavior, and the notions of heaven and hell. Zoroastrianism was the first religion whose fundamental beliefs are itemized in a categorical declaration of faith. It was also the source of the cult of Mithras (*MITH-rahs*), a divine-human "god of day" revered as Ahura Mazda's main deputy, which spread widely in the Greek and Roman worlds. Zoroastrianism survived for more than a thousand years, until, in the seventh and eighth centuries C.E., it was displaced by Islam. Refugees fled to the area surrounding Bombay in India, where Zoroastrianism survives today, practiced by Parsees, the descendants of these refugees.

Document 6.1   Excerpt from the *Avesta*

The Avesta, *the Holy Scripture of Zoroastrianism, is a collection of prayers to Ahura Mazda and to lesser spirits and beings. What similarities and differences can you detect between documents 2.2, 6.1, and 8.2?*

Purity is the best good. Happiness, happiness is to him: Namely, to the best pure in purity. Broken, broken be Satan Ahriman, whose deeds and works are accursed. May his works and deeds not attain to us. May Ahura Mazda be victorious and pure.

Let Ahura Mazda be king, and let Ahriman, the wicked holder-aloof, be smitten and broken.

All the evil thoughts, evil words, evil deeds, which I have thought, spoken, done, committed in the world, which are become my nature—all these sins, thoughts, words, and deeds, bodily, spiritual, earthly, heavenly, O Lord, pardon; I repent of them.

In the name of God, the Lord, the Increaser. May he increase in great majesty. I praise and exalt Ahura Mazda, the Brilliant, Majestic, Omniscient, the Perfecter of deeds, the Lord of Lords, the Prince over all princes, the Protector, the Creator of the created, the Giver of daily food, the Powerful, Good, Strong, Old, Forgiving, Granter of forgiveness, Rich in Love, Mighty and Wise, the pure Supporter. May thy right rule be without ceasing.

SOURCE: *The Avesta*, translated by Arthur Henry Bleeck (New York: Gordon Press, 1974), 3–6.

What was Zoroastrianism's social message, and how did Darius make use of it?

Social and Political Content

Zoroastrianism was more than theology: it carried a strong social and political message about how people should conduct themselves. Zoroastrians believe that the purpose of the struggle between good and evil is the improvement of life on earth before the Last Judgment, and that individuals will be judged not only by what they have believed but by what they have done. Zoroastrians thus feel compelled to engage in government, political affairs, and social justice struggles.

After 521 B.C.E., the Zoroastrian faith was strongly supported by Persian emperors, who portrayed themselves as Ahura Mazda's earthly agents. Darius the Great had the magnificent Behistun relief carved to depict his triumphs over his enemies through the divine assistance of Ahura Mazda, who appears in the relief as a winged god blessing the proceedings. Zoroastrianism's sociopolitical ethic proved very useful to Persian emperors: it established a moral order in Persia and designated the Great King as God's vice-regent on earth. To disobey his commands was equivalent to sinning against God and humanity.

Neither Darius nor his successors imposed Zoroastrianism on Persia's subject peoples; to do so would have violated the cultural autonomy that formed the basis of Persian rule. But Darius seems to have believed that Ahura Mazda had bestowed upon him the awesome yet appropriate duty of unifying the known world into a single empire based on justice and peace. In pursuit of that sacred goal, the emperor believed he had to respect the various cultures of the peoples entrusted to his care. He also had to give them positions of responsibility (such as satrap) and demonstrate that obedience to the empire carried with it not slavery but opportunity. In this way Zoroastrianism reinforced attitudes that Darius had already learned to value. Or perhaps, given his enormous influence, it was the other way round.

Confrontation with Greece

6.4 **Analyze the consequences of the Ionian Revolt and explain Persia's repeated failures to defeat the Greeks.**

The Persian Empire first came into contact with Greece when Cyrus conquered Lydia. Several Greek city-states in Ionia along the western coast of Anatolia fell under Persian domination, since Lydia had previously protected them. The Greeks knew little about Persian culture prior to Lydia's defeat and liked little of what they learned thereafter. Zoroastrian monotheism and musings about social justice baffled polytheistic people who believed that justice for humans was not a high priority for the gods. To the fiercely independent Greeks, Persia's tolerance for its subject peoples seemed only a strategy for making bondage less offensive. For their part, Persians regarded Greeks as no more sophisticated or dangerous than other peoples the empire had subdued. The conquerors of Assyria and Babylon were not intimidated by a land divided into competing city-states that seemed to lack military potential. For several decades after the defeat of Lydia, these city-states reluctantly accommodated themselves to Persian rule. Then in 499 B.C.E. the **Ionian Revolt** began.

The Ionian Revolt and the Persian Response

Why did Persia feel it necessary to invade Greece after putting down the Ionian Revolt?

The uprising in Ionia took Persia by surprise. The Persians had followed their standard policy of working with local leaders, but in Ionia those leaders discredited themselves with their own people by collaborating with Persia. The rebellious cities were far from Susa, and the Greeks, who never understood Persians, apparently thought that this distance would discourage retaliation. Almost as an afterthought, the rebels appealed for aid to the Greek city-states across the Aegean Sea. Athens, a leading city-state, responded by sending a fleet, which Persia defeated in 494 B.C.E. The revolt

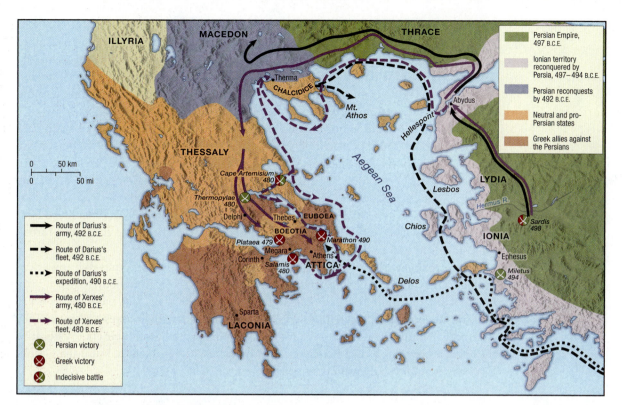

Map 6.4 CONFLICT BETWEEN PERSIA AND GREECE, 492–479 B.C.E. Persia's suppression of the revolts of the Ionian city-states in western Anatolia provoked Greek intervention. Persia responded with two separate invasions of the Greek peninsula. Note that Persia, a land-based empire, was forced by geography to construct a powerful navy in order to fight the Greeks. Persia's inability to conquer Greece meant that Greek civilization would continue to evolve apart from Eastern influences and would eventually form part of the foundation of what came to be known as Western civilization. Had Persia been victorious, what might have happened to Greek society and culture?

disintegrated, and Darius sought to consolidate his victory by directing the city-states of the Greek mainland to submit to Persian domination of Aegean commerce. He was astounded when Athens and Sparta, another important city-state, killed his messengers, an act of sacrilege from the Persian perspective and an insult to the emperor. Deeply offended, Darius prepared for war.

In 492 B.C.E., a powerful Persian fleet heading for Greece was wrecked near Mount Athos. A second force was dispatched two years later and landed in the Bay of Marathon (Map 6.4). The Persians expected to defeat their enemy easily—an expectation the Athenians in fact shared. Persia's army of 20,000 soldiers outnumbered the Greeks two to one, but in the Battle of Marathon more than 6000 Persians perished, while the Greeks lost only 192 men.

The Greeks believed that their victory at Marathon had frustrated Persia's intention to conquer the entire Greek mainland. But to the Persians, Marathon was only a small setback that did nothing to change Darius's strategy of ensuring Persian domination of the Aegean Sea. He had intended to punish the Greeks for their revolt, not conquer them, but the debacle at Marathon convinced him that conquest was necessary. Darius intended to return with a much larger army but died before his forces were ready. It was a foregone conclusion, however, that his son and successor, Xerxes (r. 486–465 B.C.E.), would renew the struggle.

Xerxes and the Invasion of Greece

Xerxes had learned from Marathon not to underestimate his opponents, so in 481 B.C.E. he left Susa at the head of a massive army. The Greek historian Herodotus (*hair-AH-duh-tuss*), who chronicled the **Persian Wars**, reported that an invading

Why was Persia unable to defeat the Greeks in 481–480 B.C.E.?

host of 2,641,000 men drank entire rivers dry when camping for the night. This was a wild exaggeration—there probably weren't 2 million men of military age in all of Persia—but Xerxes could have brought about 250,000 soldiers, enough to frighten the usually quarrelsome Greeks into an anti-Persian alliance. Sparta provided leadership on land, while Athens mobilized a formidable navy. At stake in the struggle was the future leadership of Greece, western Anatolia, and the entire Aegean basin.

The Persians struck simultaneously by land and sea. At a narrow mountain pass near the town of Thermopylae (*thur-MAH-puh-lē*), 360 Spartans held out against more than 10,000 Persians. The Spartans died to the last man, delaying the Persian advance long enough to permit their comrades to mount a successful defense on the plains beyond. Today a plaque at the entry to the pass commemorates the Spartan ideal that inspired such sacrifice: "Go tell the Spartans, stranger passing by / That here, obedient to their laws, we lie." Shortly thereafter, the dramatic Greek victory at Salamis forced the Persians to withdraw.

In retrospect it is clear why the Persians lost. They faced massive logistical problems in trying to sustain such huge military forces so far from home. Their lightly armed soldiers, equipped for mobile fighting on the plains of Asia, were surprised to find the Greek infantry better equipped to fight in the narrow passes and rocky hills of Greece. Finally, the Greeks were more highly motivated than their enemy because they had more to lose. The Persians could withdraw to fight again, but if the Greeks lost, they would lose their independence.

Stalemate

What explains the stalemate between Persia and the Greeks between 480 and 431 B.C.E.?

Their defeat in Greece astounded the Persians and convinced Xerxes to return home. He had been absent too long and he faced a rebellion in Babylonia, probably provoked by news of his difficulties in Greece. If he failed to put it down, his throne stood in jeopardy.

But the Greco-Persian conflict was far from over. Misinterpreting Xerxes' withdrawal as evidence that the Persians had given up, Athens and its allies landed troops in western Anatolia to pursue the Persians and secure Ionian independence. After nearly three more decades of intermittent warfare, the two sides signed the Peace of Callias (*KAHL-ē-us*) in 448 B.C.E.: Athens agreed to leave Anatolia to the Persians, who in turn promised to stay out of Ionia and the Aegean Sea.

What had begun as the small-scale Ionian Revolt had turned into an unanticipated stalemate, and Persian ambitions were frustrated. Persia's reach exceeded its grasp: it could land forces on the Greek mainland and devastate the countryside, but it could neither conquer Greece nor hold Ionia. The Greeks had seen the benefits of cooperation in the face of a powerful enemy, but they learned little from the experience. Athens and several of its allies, after driving Persia from Ionia, soon took up arms against Sparta.

Xerxes returned home in 479 B.C.E., and though he had intended to return to Greece, he had made no preparations to do so by the time he was assassinated in 465 B.C.E. Thereafter, Persia endured a succession of weak rulers who were unable to deal effectively with rebellion in Egypt and rising discontent at home. But in 431 B.C.E., when the Greek city-states went to war with one another, the Persians found themselves with a new opportunity for conquest.

Persian Resurgence

What events allowed Persia to become "the real winner of the Peloponnesian War"?

From 431 to 404 B.C.E., Greece was racked by the **Peloponnesian** (*pell-luh-puhn-Ē-zhē-un*) **War**. Rival alliances led by Athens and Sparta clawed at one another and left the Greek mainland open to intervention or invasion. At first Persia alternated between supporting one alliance or the other, but eventually it funded the expansion of the Spartan fleet. That fleet enabled Sparta to challenge Athens's longstanding control of the sea and eventually defeat the Athenian alliance, Persia's most persistent antagonist. Artaxerxes (*AR-tuh-zurk-zēz*) II, Persian emperor from 404 to 358 B.C.E., then took advantage of Greek exhaustion and moved to reclaim the Ionian city-states.

Had the Greeks united, it is likely that they could have defeated the Persians, whose army, consisting largely of draftees, suffered from low morale. But Persian diplomacy and bribery combined with centuries of Greek rivalry to keep the Greeks divided. Finally, in 387 B.C.E., Artaxerxes gained enough leverage to impose a treaty called the King's Peace (or the Treaty of Antalcides), withdrawing his forces from Greece in exchange for recognition of his control of Ionia. After 16 years of struggle, Persia emerged as the real winner of the Peloponnesian War. The Persian city of Susa was now the capital of the Aegean world.

The Macedonian Conquest and Its Successor States

6.5   **Discuss the successor states to the Persian Empire (Macedonians, Seleucids, Parthians, and Sasanians), demonstrating their continuing ability to connect various cultures.**

The days of the Achaemenids, however, were numbered. The satraps, sensing the weakening of royal authority, enriched themselves in the provinces at the emperor's expense. Artaxerxes III (358–338 B.C.E.) proved too distracted by these troubles to pay attention to Macedonia, a new threat to Persian power arising north of Greece (Map 6.4).

The End of the Persian Empire

In 341 B.C.E., Persia refused to assist Athens in its war against Philip II of Macedon (*MASS-uh-dun*), preferring to negotiate with the Macedonian leader. It was a shortsighted policy. By 339 B.C.E., Persian troops had been drawn into the war, and in the following year Philip (r. 359–336 B.C.E.) united all Greece under his leadership. Artaxerxes was poisoned by satraps, and his eventual successor, Darius III (336–330 B.C.E.), was not an effective leader. Suddenly vulnerable, Persia stood alone against the new Macedonian power in the West.

Philip would have been a formidable enough adversary even for Cyrus the Great, but his murder at his daughter's wedding in 336 B.C.E. brought to the Macedonian throne his son Alexander III, later known as Alexander the Great, a military genius whose talents have never been surpassed. Alexander, whose story is told in Chapter 7, defeated the Persian army in a series of battles in 334–333 B.C.E. Darius III and his counselors underestimated the abilities of this 22-year-old novice. The Persian Empire had lost many battles but had always won the wars, provided that its leadership had the sense to play for time.

The problem was that the impetuous Alexander had no intention of letting the Achaemenids stall. He sacked Persepolis in 330 and stood over the corpse of Darius III, murdered that summer by his own troops while fleeing from Alexander's advance. The Achaemenid dynasty died with Darius III, and by officiating at his funeral ceremony, Alexander designated himself as that dynasty's rightful heir. The former Persian Empire, which had conquered so many peoples itself, was subjugated to the Macedonian empire of Alexander the Great (Map 7.4).

How was Alexander the Great able to defeat Persia?

Part of a mosaic illustrating the Battle of Issus, in which Darius III (in chariot) led the Persians to defeat against Alexander the Great.

How were the successor states to Alexander's empire created?

Persia Under Macedonian Rule

Persian government, always tolerant of subject peoples, was now forced to accept Greek political institutions and culture. Alexander wisely retained most of the local Achaemenid administrative structure, but he encouraged the mixing of Greeks and Persians, taking several Persian wives himself, and significant numbers of Macedonian and Greek soldiers settled permanently in Persia. Alexander's policies appear to have worked well, since no noticeable unrest marred his rule and no rebellions followed his unexpected death in 323 B.C.E. at the age of 33.

Soon after, one of Alexander's generals, Seleucus Nikator (*sell-LOO-kus ni-KĀ-tur*), assumed control over most of the former Persian Empire; the new state was called the Seleucid (*sell-LOO-sid*) kingdom (Map 7.5). But in an effort to secure his position with the Macedonian leadership, Seleucus (r. 305–280 B.C.E.) promoted Macedonian officials over Persians and displayed no sympathy for or connection to the Persian culture or language. Soon he lost the support of the Persian nobility on the old empire's eastern fringes. Rebellions broke out there, and by 304 B.C.E. Seleucus was forced to turn control of western India over to Chandragupta Maurya, founder of the Mauryan Empire. Thus the disintegration of the Persian Empire helped create a new empire in India. By 129 B.C.E., the Seleucid kingdom had fallen apart, with two principal successor states emerging: the Greco-Bactrian kingdom, comprising northern Afghanistan and part of northwestern India, and the Parthian Empire, extending from Armenia southeastward to the Arabian Sea.

Why was the Parthian Empire commercially important?

The Parthian Empire

The collapse of the Seleucid kingdom opened the way for the Parthians, a Central Asian tribe that had moved onto the Iranian Plateau during the Achaemenid dynasty. The Parthians ruled formerly Seleucid lands through kings who were vassals of the Parthian emperor. After Roman armies were routed by the Parthians in 53 B.C.E., the Parthian and Roman empires fought many times along their common border, but neither gained a lasting advantage over the other.

Parthian Persia was a critical crossroad of Asian trade because of its strategic location along the Silk Road (Map 6.5). The Parthians eagerly participated in trans-Asiatic commerce, serving as middlemen between China and Southwest Asia while maintaining safe roads and centers of hospitality for passing merchant caravans from many different cultures. Parthian merchants filled Chinese orders for alfalfa plants, grape vines, and Persia's magnificent Ferghana horses. Their contact with China also promoted the transmission of Indian goods and Buddhist doctrines eastward during the third century C.E. Like the Persians, the Parthians connected East and West. But the Parthians lacked the forceful leadership necessary to win back the westernmost provinces of the former Persian Empire. Following their collapse as a result of internal intrigue in 224 C.E., the imperial throne passed to a people known as the Sasanians (*suh-SAY-nee-uns*).

What was the Sasanian concept of the circle of equity, and how was it connected to Zoroastrianism?

The Sasanian Empire

The Sasanians had arrived in Fars, just north of the Persian Gulf, even before the Medes and Persians. Now they seized an opportune moment, first to help the Parthians fight the Romans, and then to replace the Parthians and construct their own empire. They fought the Roman Empire for several decades, taking Mesopotamia in 256 under the leadership of King Shapur (*shah-POOR*) I (r. 240–271 C.E.). Four years later, the Roman emperor Valerian (r. 253–259) personally commanded the Roman legions in a campaign to expel the Sasanians from the Roman province of Syria. Shapur's forces defeated the Romans, captured Valerian, and kept him prisoner in Persia for the rest of his life. The Sasanians then drove through Syria into central Anatolia.

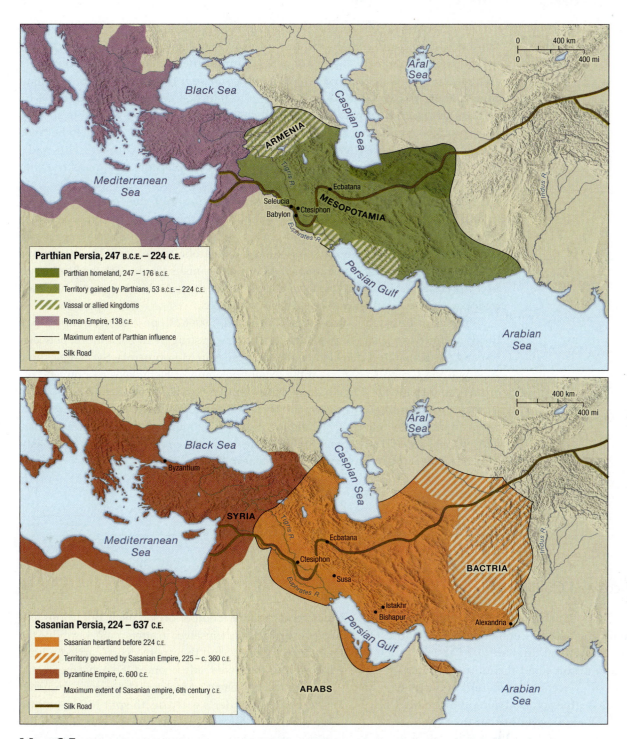

Map 6.5 THE PARTHIAN AND SASANIAN EMPIRES, 247 B.C.E.–637 C.E. The Parthians and Sasanians occupied pivotal positions in turn. Notice that Persia's location on the Silk Road made it important in trans-Asiatic commerce, while its location at the eastern edge of first the Roman and then the Byzantine Empire connected it to those regimes, making it sometimes a natural partner and sometimes an antagonist. Neither Parthians nor Sasanians, who owned not a single inch of Mediterranean coastline, were as economically powerful as Rome or Byzantium, but they were nevertheless significant forces in Southwest Asia. Why might Rome and Byzantium have chosen to coexist with these empires rather than try to conquer them?

Shapur stood firmly in the tradition of the Achaemenians, ruling diverse ethnic groups simultaneously through satrapies and administrative flexibility. He tolerated the practice of Judaism, Christianity, and Buddhism, but he institutionalized Zoroastrianism as Persia's state religion and made it a powerful ally of the Sasanian monarchy. Shapur's successors were strict Zoroastrians who ended toleration and persecuted those who followed other faiths.

Zoroastrianism reinforced the Sasanian ruling concept of the **circle of equity**: there could be no monarch without an army, no army without prosperity, no prosperity without justice, and no justice without the monarch. Zoroastrianism's emphasis on social justice and ethical conduct made it the ideal faith for Sasanian rulers. They insisted that the emperor, who had been chosen by God, must be obeyed, but he in turn had to ensure prosperity and a just and equitable society. They proclaimed that the circle of equity limited the emperor's authority because that authority depended on his own righteous conduct. But, coupled with traditional Persian respect for local autonomy, it also enabled the Sasanians to claim divine sanction and compel popular support.

Persia's struggle with Rome continued throughout the Sasanian period, intensifying after Emperor Diocletian's division of the Roman Empire in 284 C.E. (Chapter 9). The eastern portion of the Roman Empire, later called the Byzantine Empire (Chapter 10), fought the Persians for control of Anatolia and eastern Mediterranean trade routes. Under King Khusrau I (531–579), the Sasanians fought with the Byzantines over Arabia. Both sides cultivated client tribes in southern Arabia, hoping to dominate trade routes between the Red Sea and the Arabian Sea.

But one of Khusrau's successors, Khusrau II (590–628), pushed the quarrel with the Byzantines too far. Taking advantage of a power struggle in Byzantium, between 604 and 619 Khusrau II defeated Byzantine armies in Mesopotamia, Syria, Palestine, Anatolia, and Egypt. At that point the Byzantine emperor Herakleios reorganized his armies, counterattacked against the overextended Sasanian forces, and by 628 had pushed them out of all the territories they had conquered. This disaster threw the Sasanian monarchy into disarray and left it open for conquest by Islamic Arab armies between 637 and 651 (Chapter 11). In 651 the last great pre-Islamic Persian dynasty ceased to exist, and Persia became part of a new Arab empire.

Chapter Review

Consequences and Connections

Starting from an inhospitable plateau in Southwest Asia, the Achaemenid dynasty of Persia created the largest empire the world had yet known. The Persians ruled by a combination of force and flexibility. Though they could be brutal, they were also tolerant and practical, allowing various degrees of local autonomy among the many cultures and ethnic groups that they conquered. By permitting those they subdued to retain their cultural identities while enjoying the benefits of Persian order and prosperity, the Persians won their loyalty. Persia's excellent road system and centralized governmental organization enabled its emperors to govern this huge region effectively. In Zoroastrianism, those emperors had a belief system whose clearly developed social ethic enabled them to cast themselves and their officials as warriors for truth and light against evil and The Lie.

In its efforts to centralize its control and its methods of governing, Persia stood in the company of the great river civilizations. In its attempts to expand rapidly over vast expanses of territory, it outperformed them. But Darius and Xerxes overreached themselves in attempting to subdue the mainland of Greece, and their persistence carried with it repercussions that eventually doomed the Achaemenians.

Alexander the Great's Macedonian Empire conquered Persia, but its founder's early death split his realm into three parts. The former Persian Empire was then ruled by three successor states: the Seleucids, Parthians, and Sasanians. Persia's strategic location across Asian trade routes such as the Silk Road assured its continued economic viability, and Khusrau II's dramatic victories over the Byzantine Empire seemed to signal the reestablishment of the western boundaries of the Achaemenian Empire. But the Byzantines struck back, leaving the Sasanians open to the unanticipated invasion of Arab armies that ended the Persian Empire. Persia's administrative efficiency and social tolerance, both well in advance of similar developments elsewhere in the world, continue to mark its place in world history.

Reviewing Key Concepts

Ask Yourself

1. Do Cyrus and Darius merit the title "Great"? In what ways were they different from rulers who preceded and followed them?

2. What was distinctive about Zoroastrianism? In what ways did it differ from Hinduism and Buddhism?

3. Why were Persia and Greece frequently at war? Why did the Persians eventually fail to defeat the Greeks?

4. In what ways did the Persian Empire create connections with other peoples and cultures?

Key Dates and Developments

ca. 1300–1000 B.C.E	The Prophet Zoroaster preaches that there is one god, Ahura Mazda
ca. 1000 B.C.E	Medes and Persians settle on Iranian Plateau
612 B.C.E.	Destruction of Nineveh by Median king Cyaxares
550 B.C.E	Persian king Cyrus unites Medes and Persians under the Achaemenid dynasty
550–530 B.C.E.	Reign of Cyrus the Great
546 B.C.E	Persia conquers Lydia
539 B.C.E	Persia conquers Babylonia
530–522 B.C.E	Reign of Cambyses
525 B.C.E	Persia conquers Egypt
521–486 B.C.E	Reign of Darius the Great
	Construction of Persepolis and the Royal Road
	The *Ordinance of Good Regulations*
517 B.C.E	Persia conquers the Indus Valley
512 B.C.E	Persian forces reach the Danube River (Europe)
499 B.C.E	Ionia revolts against Persian rule
490 B.C.E	Athens defeats Persia at Marathon
486–465 B.C.E	Reign of Xerxes
480–479 B.C.E	Xerxes invades Greece and is defeated
448 B.C.E	Peace of Callias: Stalemate with Greece
334–330 B.C.E	Alexander the Great defeats Persia
323 B.C.E	Death of Alexander; creation of the Seleucid kingdom
240 B.C.E– 224 C.E.	The Parthian Empire
227–642 C.E.	The Sasanian Empire

Chapter 7
Greek Civilization and Its Expansion into Asia, 2000–30 B.C.E.

GREEK ATHLETES Runners in ancient Greece sprint in a race depicted on a glazed Athenian vase. Athletic events, such as the Olympic Games, were extremely important in Greek culture and were often portrayed on ceramic pieces.

After reading this chapter, you should be able to:

7.1 Explain why ancient Greece found it difficult to unify politically.

7.2 Discuss the expansion of Greek culture throughout the Mediterranean world.

7.3 Evaluate the Greek response to the Persian challenge and show how the Peloponnesian War negated earlier Greek accomplishments.

7.4 Describe the most influential contributions of ancient Greece in the fields of architecture, art, drama, and philosophy.

7.5 Discuss the characteristics of society and religion in Classical Greece.

7.6 Explain the importance of Alexander's empire and evaluate his legacy.

7.7 Describe the impact of Hellenization in culture, commerce, and politics.

In 334 B.C.E. an army of Greeks and Macedonians entered Gordium in Anatolia (modern Turkey), capital city of the fabled King Midas whose touch turned all things to gold. Led by an energetic young Macedonian who sought to become a legend in his own right, the army paused before the Temple of Jupiter, inside which was a large wagon designed to be pulled by yoked oxen. An immense knot—three feet in diameter—was tied around both the yoke and the wagon pole. Popular belief held that the man who could untie this Gordian Knot would conquer Asia.

The young commander, who indeed sought to conquer Asia, tried for nearly two hours to untie the knot. Eyewitness accounts disagree over what happened next. Some say that in a rage, he severed the knot with a single stroke of his sword. Others claim that after staring silently at the knot for several minutes, he simply removed the pin connecting the yoke to the pole and slipped the knot off. The first version calls attention to the commander's strength and ruthlessness, the second to his practicality. In either case, the commander—known to history as Alexander the Great—possessed all these traits in abundance. He went on to conquer much of southern Asia.

The Greco-Macedonian World

Centuries before Alexander, numerous small city-states had emerged in the mountains and islands of Greece. Fiercely independent, these city-states had often clashed and occasionally cooperated. In the fifth century B.C.E., many banded together to fight off Persian invaders, but later they returned to warring among themselves. In the fourth century B.C.E., weakened by wars, they were conquered by the northern armies of Macedonia. United under the leadership of Alexander, the Greeks built a vast empire that included Egypt, Palestine, Mesopotamia, Persia, and northwestern India. Although Alexander's empire proved short lived, it spread Greek culture to all these regions, connecting far-flung realms to what would evolve into Western civilization.

Early Greece

7.1   **Explain why ancient Greece found it difficult to unify politically.**

Mesopotamia, Egypt, India, and China emerged in the valleys of great rivers, while Persia developed on the Iranian plateau. In the final millennium before the Common Era, a new society took shape on the Greek mainland in southeastern Europe and on nearby islands in the Aegean Sea.

Greek civilization developed on a rocky land. An extension of the Balkan Peninsula, Greece has neither fertile plains nor irrigating rivers, and its mountains cut the peninsula into isolated areas. River travel allowed rapid communication in Mesopotamia, Egypt, India, and China; in Persia, the relative flatness of the Iranian plateau made land travel easier than in Greece. These drawbacks meant that early Indo-European inhabitants of Greece needed to be hardy and resilient, able to survive on the sides of rugged mountain ranges (Map 7.1). From their hardships, they created a rich body of heroic legends and epics that would serve as a basis for Greek religion and culture. As the mountainous terrain proved a barrier to political unification, they organized into independent city-states with distinctive forms of governance.

Because it lacked a single centralized kingdom, Greek civilization appeared less complex than the other early societies. Eventually, however, it spread through much of the ancient world. During its expansion it changed significantly, as it absorbed elements from the cultures it encountered.

Map 7.1 GREECE AND WESTERN ANATOLIA The Greek peninsula has a rugged topography. Greece's mountains impeded communication between settlements only a few miles apart, while its numerous islands and peninsulas further made travel difficult. Note that Greek city-states are separated from each other not only by mountains, but also by the Aegean Sea. What impact did this isolation have upon Greek economic and political development?

Mycenae and Crete

How did Mycenae and Crete help lay the foundations for Greek civilization?

The early centuries of Greek history are enveloped in myth, but historians and archeologists have gradually uncovered the reality behind the fables. Indo-European migrants, speaking a language that evolved into ancient Greek, settled on the Greek peninsula before 1650 B.C.E. and called it Hellas. No records of a previous population exist. The first well-organized Greek civilization on the peninsula is called Mycenaean (mī-SĒ-nē-an), after a site named Mycenae, mentioned in ancient Greek legend and excavated in the late nineteenth century C.E. by a German amateur archeologist, Heinrich Schliemann (SHLĒ-mahn).

Mycenaean culture seems to have been influenced by a civilization that flourished on the island of Crete, about 60 miles southeast of the Greek peninsula. This culture, called *Minoan* after a mythical Cretan ruler named Minos (MĪ-nus), built impressive monuments and government complexes. Minoans possessed a system of writing that scholars have never deciphered. Mycenaeans appear to have borrowed from the Minoans a variety of artistic and architectural techniques, the principles of centralized bureaucracy, and the idea of using a palace as the seat of government. They also appear to have conquered Crete around 1450 B.C.E.

Mycenae developed a diversified civilization. By 1450 B.C.E. it was a thriving center of trade, with satellite cities at Athens and Thebes. Mycenaean metalwork was traded as far west as Sardinia and as far south as the Upper Nile. Mycenaeans used a system of writing similar to the Minoan script, which has been translated successfully. Mycenaeans used writing not to describe heroic feats or to create poetry or drama, as the Greeks later did, but to compile inventories of nearly everything made in the kingdom. From these massive lists emerges a picture of a highly centralized government intensely interested in every aspect of the economic life of its people. Its rulers, however, like those of Crete, remain unknown: no representations of them have been uncovered. Only through the *Iliad* do we know the name of the most famous Mycenaean, Agamemnon.

The *Iliad* and the *Odyssey*, two epic poems allegedly written in the eighth century B.C.E. by a Greek poet named Homer, may actually have been composed by several writers using earlier traditions. The *Iliad* tells the dramatic stories of the Mycenaean siege of Troy (a city in what is today western Turkey), the quarrel between Mycenae's King Agamemnon and the warrior hero Achilles (*ah-KILL-ēz*), and the interaction between gods and men during the battle. The *Odyssey* depicts the adventurous journey home of Odysseus (*ō-DISS-ē-us*), one of the Greek heroes of the Trojan War.

The people depicted in **Homeric poetry** were long believed to be entirely mythical. Then in 1876 C.E., Schliemann, who believed the poems had a historical basis, discovered evidence of a complex culture at Mycenae. Six years later Schliemann unearthed the ruins of Troy, which indicated that the story told in the *Iliad* might be based in fact. Archeological evidence suggests that Troy was destroyed around 1200 B.C.E., perhaps following the siege described in the Homeric poems. Whatever the proportion of myth and reality in these epics, they encouraged the Greeks to perceive themselves as a warlike, heroic, and resourceful people.

The Polis

Homer's writings were composed during the so-called Dark Age of Greece (1200–750 B.C.E.), a chaotic era during which the Greeks evolved from Mycenaean monarchy to a political form more suited to the regional isolation imposed by terrain. The English word *political* is derived from the Greek word **polis** (*PŌ-liss*), meaning "city-state," referring to a city, its people, and the surrounding countryside that they controlled.

Early Greek city-states were small. The largest, Thebes, contained about 40,000 adult males, who alone were citizens exercising full civil rights. Women, children, slaves, and resident aliens had no such rights. Over the centuries, some city-states extended their domination over large rural areas, which provided them with the population required for economic expansion and military power.

The Greeks developed several methods for governing a polis, all of which entered the political vocabulary of the Western world. One-man rule was known by Greeks as **monarchy**; rule by a select few, as **oligarchy**; rule by a class of well-born families, as **aristocracy**; and rule by the entire body of citizens, as **democracy**. These four methods were all considered legitimate, differing from **tyranny**, the illegal seizure of power (usually in a time of emergency) by someone who had no right to it and who thereby became a "tyrant" for the duration of the crisis.

Of all these systems, many Greeks thought democracy the least efficient. Since *all* citizens had the right to participate in *every* decision, democracy was cumbersome. It was also impractical: in Athens, for example, votes were cast and counted at a meeting place in the center of the city, so some citizens who lived at a distance were unable to participate. Both then and in subsequent centuries, democracy was considered inappropriate for city-states or countries with large, dispersed populations. These almost always chose one of the other methods of rule.

How did the various methods of governing the polis differ from one another?

Gold mask of Agamemnon.

In the Greek city-states, individualism flourished, voters knew the leaders they elected, and large bureaucracies were unknown. This political arrangement was very different from centralized empires such as Egypt and China, where governments were remote from their subjects. The polis became both a significant force in Greek history and culture and a model for future civilizations to adapt or imitate.

Archaic Greece, 750–500 B.C.E.

7.2   **Discuss the expansion of Greek culture throughout the Mediterranean world.**

Greek techniques of government matured during the era later called the **Archaic Period**. During this time, overpopulation and a shortage of land suitable for farming prompted many Greeks to colonize Sicily, Italy, France, Spain, and North Africa. In this way, Greek culture came to dominate and define the Mediterranean world. At the same time, those remaining in Greece responded to overpopulation through other changes in society and government.

Greek Colonization and the Spread of Greek Culture

Why did the Greeks find it necessary to colonize non-Greek areas?

Rocky terrain limited the size of Greek farms, and although some crops, such as olives, could be grown on hillsides, the available soil could not support significant population expansion. Midway through the eighth century B.C.E., many city-states began to look to overseas colonization as a safety valve by which to reduce population pressures. In the course of a few decades of **Greek colonization**, Greek settlements were established on the shores of the Black Sea (Map 7.2), on the coast of North Africa in present-day Libya, in southern Italy and Sicily, and in southern Gaul (today France).

These new holdings expanded significantly the total amount of land available for cultivation. Since the climate and topography of much of the Mediterranean and

Map 7.2 THE GREEK COLONIES, 750–550 B.C.E. Faced with an expanding population and limited arable land, Greek city-states exported their surplus people to colonies throughout the Mediterranean basin. Notice that these colonies, which cover a distance of 2300 miles from east to west, are all located on the shores of the Mediterranean, Aegean, and Black seas. Colonial expansion by water came naturally to the Greeks, a maritime people who looked at the sea as a highway rather than an obstacle. How might this extensive colonization forge connections between Greeks and other peoples?

Black sea basins were essentially similar to that of Greece itself, the transfer of Greek agricultural techniques was relatively simple. As in any migration of populations, some settlers went willingly, even eagerly, while others would rather have remained at home. The city-states gave every willing person the opportunity to go and forced others to leave.

As Greeks spread throughout the region, they carried their culture with them. Greek words, coins, and religious practices were transmitted to areas hundreds of miles away. As the colonists encountered other peoples, they built trading networks with merchants in cities on the Greek peninsula, linking Greece not only to its new colonies but also to previously unfamiliar cultures. From these peoples, such as the Phoenicians in North Africa, the Greeks learned new methods of plowing fields, new ways to lay out cities, and new ideas about the nature of existence. Colonization proved to be a two-way street, connecting Greece to parts of Europe, Africa, and Asia in ways that enriched all these peoples and cultures. The Mediterranean basin became active and vibrant with the exchange of commerce and culture.

Rivalry Between Sparta and Athens

How did the Spartan and Athenian societies differ from one another?

Most Greeks, of course, remained on their peninsula, dealing with overpopulation and land scarcity in ways other than colonization. Two of these ways are illustrated by two city-states that developed on the peninsula, becoming bitter rivals for influence and power. The first of these, Sparta, created a society organized along militaristic lines and entrusted power to an oligarchy. The second, Athens, chose a limited democracy in which all adult male citizens enjoyed the right to cast votes that counted equally. Later, cooperation between these two states would enable Greece to beat back a dangerous invasion from Persia, although their competition resumed once the Persian threat disappeared. Eventually divided into two antagonistic armed camps, the peninsula became vulnerable to an equally dangerous invasion from Macedonia, in the north.

SPARTAN MILITARY OLIGARCHY   Sparta expanded its economic base by conquering nearby regions, creating a highly militarized society in the process. Territorial expansion increased the available farmland and food supply, which in turn kept Spartans satisfied. Sparta's very name, meaning "The Scattered," suggests its origin as five small villages on the plain of Lacedaemon (*lah-sih-DĀ-mun*), a location so well protected by mountain ranges that Sparta found it unnecessary to build city walls for defense.

Spartans believed that under Lycurgus (*lī-SUR-juss*), a legendary lawgiver who may have lived in the seventh century B.C.E., they had rejected their individuality in favor of the collective mentality of a garrison state. Every aspect of society was directed toward military strength. Boys left home at age 7 to live in barracks, where they spent 12 years in rigorous physical and military training before becoming soldiers. Even after marriage, they took all meals with their regiments. The basic food served was black broth, consisting of pork simmered in blood and seasoned with vinegar and salt; most non-Spartans found it disgusting. Spartan girls were also raised under strict discipline, in the belief that regular physical exercise would help them produce strong children.

Sparta was not, however, a military dictatorship. All adult male citizens were eligible to attend the public assembly, at which laws were passed and policies made. Execution of the laws was entrusted to Sparta's two hereditary kings, acting with a council of 28 members. The councilors were chosen for life terms by the public assembly. Spartan government was an oligarchy, responsive to the wishes of this assembly.

The regimented organization of Spartan society was not imposed on a reluctant people but sprang from the needs of daily Spartan life. Spartans had to coax a

Spartan warrior.

living from rocky soil and suppress local peoples resentful of Spartan domination. The oligarchs perceived these needs, but the citizens recognized them, too. Indeed, the basis of Sparta's rivalry with Athens was neither economic nor militaristic, but political. The Spartans were convinced that regimentation and oligarchy offered the best guarantee of social peace, while Athenians found them offensive.

During this period Greek city-states frequently fought among themselves. After 550 B.C.E., however, Sparta attempted to minimize conflict by persuading neighboring states to join the **Peloponnesian** (*pel-uh-puh-NĒ-zhun*) **League**, so called since most of its members lived on the large peninsula known as the Peloponnesus (*pel-uh-puh-NĒ-suss*). By 510 B.C.E. that alliance had enough power outside the Peloponnesus to force Athens into a form of dependency, thus ensuring its cooperation against possible external enemies, particularly Persia.

ATHENIAN DEMOCRACY   Although Spartan military oligarchy offended Athens, the involvement of all adult male citizens in the responsibilities of government did not. During the Archaic Period, the Athenian aristocrat Draco (*DRĀ-kō*) developed a legal code, the first of its kind in Greece, to regulate a similar political participation among Athenians. Published in 621 B.C.E., this code was harsh and in parts brutal (hence our adjective *draconian*, meaning "severe"), but it held that the law belonged to all citizens and must exist in written form so that all might consult and understand it. Citizenship, however, was limited to adult males who owned property, so most residents of Athens were not citizens. At this time Athens was an aristocracy, although its evolution in the direction of democratic forms had already begun.

Building on this foundation, the chief magistrate Solon (*SŌ-lun*) reformed the Athenian state in the 590s B.C.E., banning enslavement for debt and guaranteeing basic rights to everyone. Solon was a skilled political operator, undermining aristocratic privileges and allowing all citizens to participate in government, while positioning himself as mediator between aristocrats and commoners. Finally, beginning in 508 B.C.E., the Athenian aristocracy transformed itself into a democracy. An assembly of adult male citizens accepted or rejected proposed laws; a council of 500 proposed those laws and supervised major governmental committees; and a board of ten officials called *archons* administered the polis, handling all military and legal issues. This type of participatory governance was not radically different from Spartan practice, except for the absence in Athens of hereditary kings.

Excluded from voting, and all other political rights, were women, slaves, males under the age of 18, and those who owned no property. Athenian democracy therefore differed significantly from present-day conceptions of democracy, which are based on political equality and on the participation of every citizen above a certain age, regardless of gender or social class. Most important positions in Athens were still held by aristocrats, since ordinary men had neither the leisure nor the money to undertake full-time state service. Yet, however exclusive Athenian democracy was, it offered a clear alternative to the Spartan model. In Athenian democracy, the state existed for the citizen rather than the citizen for the state. The citizen therefore served the state as a matter of self-interest, a principle that has inspired and challenged democracies from Athenian times to the present.

Classical Greece, 500–338 B.C.E.

7.3   Evaluate the Greek response to the Persian challenge and show how the Peloponnesian War negated earlier Greek accomplishments.

The Peloponnesian League provided an initial framework for defending Greece against outside invasion. That defense, however, was sorely tested during the

Classical Period (500–338 B.C.E.), an era in which classical Greek philosophy, art, and drama were flourishing. Early in that period, the Greeks combined to repel the attacks of the powerful Persian Empire. Later, however, the city-states resumed fighting among themselves, weakening each other and opening the way for the conquest of Greece by Macedon.

The Persian Wars

As we saw in Chapter 6, the revolt of the Ionian city-states in western Anatolia provoked war between Persia and Greece. Darius I and Xerxes invaded Greece between 492 and 479 B.C.E., but Persian forces were unable to overcome a Greek alliance that included Athens, Sparta, and their respective allies. By 479 B.C.E. Persia had abandoned the struggle and retreated to Anatolia.

The Persian Wars influenced Greece significantly. Victory boosted its self-confidence and strengthened its identification with accountable government rather than what Greeks saw as arbitrary Persian rule. Yet the image of heroic Greeks resisting Persian invaders ignores the fact that most Greeks failed to fight at all: hundreds of city-states collaborated with the Persians, remained neutral, or tried to ignore the threat. Not all Greeks were convinced of the value of cooperation.

How did the Persian Wars affect Greece?

Athenian Dominance and the Spartan Response

The dramatic demonstration during the Persian Wars of the strength to be found in cooperation might have impelled the Greeks toward unity. Instead, however, it promoted division and eventual disaster. With hindsight, the Greeks probably should have left the Persians alone. But in 477 B.C.E., Athens formed the **Delian** (*DĒ-lē-un*) **League,** an alliance that embarked upon a 30-year naval campaign aiming to drive Persia out of the Aegean, secure the independence of the Ionian city-states, and ensure Athenian domination of the region. Indeed, Athens soon dominated the League, forcing its allies to pay tribute and threatening Spartan influence. Spartan skepticism at the prospect of chasing the Persians into Asia, coupled with its fear of Athenian power, ended the fragile collaboration between the two dominant Greek states. The Spartans used their own Peloponnesian League to counter the Delian League. Now Athens and Sparta, without the common danger of Persia to unify them, faced off against each other as heads of rival alliance systems (Map 7.3).

It was not the Spartan militaristic oligarchy but the proud Athenian democracy that created this predicament. The confrontation began during a period considered the pinnacle of Athenian greatness, often termed the **Age of Pericles**(*PAIR-ih-clēz*). It was named for an Athenian aristocrat who was repeatedly elected to the highest positions in government between 467 and 429 B.C.E. Under his leadership the Acropolis, a hilltop citadel in the midst of the city, was transformed into a magnificent architectural display of Athenian power. Building on its extensive agricultural base, its population of over 300,000, and its large merchant fleet, Athens under Pericles' leadership became an economic and commercial power unlike anything previously imagined in Greece.

That sort of domination generated envy and fear in Sparta. Athenians defended their political and economic dominance on the ground that their city needed to protect its commerce. But Pericles exerted Athenian power throughout the region, putting down uprisings in several smaller cities that resented paying tribute. The city-state that revered liberty and democracy at home became an agent of expansion abroad. Sparta regarded the Athenian policy of establishing democracies in its satellites as a threat to the continued existence of oligarchic and aristocratic governments and called on its Peloponnesian League.

Why did Athens and Sparta develop a bitter rivalry after the Persian Wars?

Pericles.

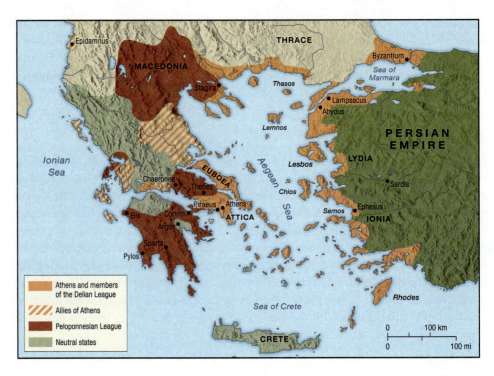

Map 7.3 **THE DELIAN AND PELOPONNESIAN LEAGUES, 431 B.C.E.** Cooperation between the most powerful Greek city-states prevented the Persian Empire from conquering Greece, but that cooperation did not survive the withdrawal of the Persian threat. Observe that Athens and its allies in the Delian League controlled the area surrounding the Aegean Sea, while Sparta and its Peloponnesian League partners, like Thebes and Corinth, tended to be land-based. Eventually these two alliance systems fought the Peloponnesian War against each other between 431 and 404 B.C.E. How did this conflict make the eventual conquest of Greece by Philip of Macedon possible?

What was the impact of the Peloponnesian War upon Greece?

The Peloponnesian War

In confronting the Peloponnesians, Pericles had to choose between Athenian expansion and retreat. He preferred war, and he was not alone. As Thucydides (*thoo-SID-uh-dēz*), the first major historian to report events accurately and analytically, wrote in his *History of the Peloponnesian War*, "The Peloponnesus and Athens were both full of young men whose inexperience made them eager to take up arms." In 431 B.C.E. a commercial dispute led Sparta to demand that Athens grant all Greek cities independence. In essence, such a policy would have dismantled the Athenian empire. Athens refused, and the competing alliances went to war. Thucydides concluded, "The thing that made war inevitable was the growth of Athenian power and the fear this caused in Sparta." It was the first thesis statement written by a genuine historian, and the conflict it spoke of is often called "the suicide of Greece."

The Peloponnesian War (431–404 B.C.E.) devastated Greece, bringing destruction of property, famine, disease, and death. It lasted more than two decades due to a central paradox: because Sparta had a powerful army but no navy, while Athens had a superb navy but a small army, neither found it easy to engage the other. Although Sparta eventually defeated Athens, the duration and severity of the conflict ensured that there would be no real winner—at least not in Greece itself.

Exhausted, the warring city-states fell to an outsider: Philip II of Macedon, who between 359 and 336 B.C.E. turned his primitive realm on Greece's northern frontier into a formidable political and military power. Modifying the phalanx (a closely arrayed formation of troops difficult for infantry to penetrate) by lining it with men wielding pikes 18 feet long, Philip swept down from the north in 338 B.C.E. to defeat the Athenians and Thebans. Greek independence was thus extinguished by foreigners, who took command of the temples and palaces of Athens. These catastrophes might have been avoided had Sparta and Athens not weakened each other in the Peloponnesian War.

The Arts and Philosophy in Classical Greece

7.4 Describe the most influential contributions of ancient Greece in the fields of architecture, art, drama, and philosophy.

Greece in the Age of Pericles was not focused exclusively on politics and war. This was also a golden age of Greek culture. In Greece, the division of the peninsula into separate city-states seems to have fostered an appreciation of the virtues, capabilities, and rights of individual people. Although often inspired by belief in the gods, Greek artistic forms also demonstrate a profound fascination with the human person.

The Parthenon.

Architecture, Sculpture, and Pottery

Ancient Greek gods and goddesses inspired the magnificent temples of the Acropolis, a hilltop complex of public buildings in Athens. The Acropolis was dominated by the Parthenon, a temple of Athena, goddess of wisdom, for whom the city was named. Avoiding thick walls, Greek architects used a variety of handsome columns, on the Acropolis and elsewhere, to support the roofs of public buildings in a graceful yet functional style.

> What were the characteristics of Greek architecture, sculpture, and pottery?

Inside the Parthenon, a variety of lifelike sculptures paid tribute to Athena. Since Greeks believed their gods and goddesses looked and acted like humans, Greek sculpture portrayed them in human form. They were shown in action rather than in frozen, artificial poses. Greek sculpture was therefore qualitatively different from the comparatively static, stylized depictions of humans in the art of Egypt, Persia, and China. The Greeks also portrayed the human form on their pottery, which combined artistic beauty with utilitarian value. Potters created an extensive array of jars, bowls, urns, vases, cups, and other vessels, glazed in vivid colors and fired in kilns. Decorating these pieces were depictions of men and women in realistic, active poses, some of them heroic (such as in combat against soldiers or wild beasts), some of them ordinary (for example, weaving, cooking, or farming). Greek art and architecture mark the beginning of a lengthy transition to styles today's observers would recognize as modern.

Galloping horses pull a chariot across the face of a ceramic Greek vase.

Greek Drama

In Greek literary life, the Classical Period produced four Athenian dramatists whose works remain influential in the present. The earliest of these was Aeschylus (*ES-kuh-luhs*), who lived 525–456 B.C.E. He wrote complex plays dealing with people trapped in

> Why has Greek drama remained interesting long after the end of Classical Greek civilization?

Document 7.1   Excerpt from Sophocles' *Oedipus the King*

Oedipus, King of Thebes, attempts to find his father's murderer by consulting the blind prophet Teiresias. The tragedy of the play is that Oedipus, who never knew his father, is himself the murderer. Teiresias tries to show him the truth, but Oedipus is proud and contemptuous of those beneath him and will not listen.

TEIRESIAS

Alas, how terrible is wisdom when
it brings no profit to the man that's wise!
This I knew well, but had forgotten it,
else I would not have come here . . .
I say you are the murderer of the king
whose murderer you seek . . .

OEDIPUS

Do you imagine you can always talk
like this, and live to talk of it hereafter?

TEIRESIAS

Yes, if the truth has anything of strength.

OEDIPUS

It has, but not for you; it has no strength
for you because you are blind in mind and ears
as well as in your eyes.

TEIRESIAS

You are a poor wretch
to taunt me with the very insults which
everyone soon will heap upon yourself . . .

Eventually Oedipus learns the truth, and, in despair over having inadvertently killed his father and then married his own mother, blinds himself. The Chorus of the play deplores the pride which led him to his fate:

CHORUS

If a man walks with haughtiness
of hand or word and gives no heed
to Justice and the shrines of Gods
despises—may an evil doom
smite him for his ill-starred pride of heart!—
When such things are done, what man shall contrive
to shield his soul from the shafts of the God?

conflict between their personal wishes and the claims of justice and reason. A generation later, Sophocles (*SAH-fuh-klēz*) wrote carefully crafted dramas such as *Antigone* (*an-TIH-guh-nē*) and the *Oedipus* (*ED-ih-pus*) cycle. The works of Sophocles (496–406 B.C.E.) draw a precise line between the divine and the human; when pride causes men and women to think that they can cross that line, the consequences for themselves and their families are tragic.

Oedipus, whose career is described in Sophocles' trilogy of plays, was a fictional ruler fated by the gods to inadvertently kill his father and unknowingly marry his mother. Terrible results flowed from these actions, and Oedipus stood as a warning to those who would doubt the awesome power of destiny (see "Excerpt from Sophocles' *Oedipus the King*"). People may not understand divine law, but they must obey it for the sake of order and rationality in the world.

The third dramatist was Sophocles' contemporary Euripedes (*yoo-RIP-ih-dēz*). Euripedes (ca. 480–406 B.C.E.) focused on the tragic flaw of human beings: the tendency to subordinate reason to emotion. These three eminent tragedians were complemented by Aristophanes (*air-ih-STAH-fuh-nēz*, ca. 445–386 B.C.E.), a comic writer who poked fun at the famous and powerful. In their examination of human personality as well as divine law, of the demands of reason and justice as well as the necessity of action and heroism, these dramatists served as a bridge between the more limited horizons of ancient literature and the psychologically complex plays of later Western culture.

Philosophy

How were Socrates, Plato, and Aristotle significant in the development of Western culture?

Greek philosophy was even more foundational than drama to Western culture and thought. Following the "pre-Socratic" thinkers, who inquired into the nature of the universe, philosophers in the early Classical Period, called Sophists, taught rhetoric, mathematics, science, and philosophy to young men throughout Greece.

The Sophists' most influential critic was the Athenian philosopher Socrates (*SOCK-rah-tēz*, ca. 470–399 B.C.E.), who taught that fulfillment meant attaining the good, the beautiful, and the true through the pursuit of excellence in learning. "The unexamined life is not worth living," Socrates asserted, and he taught his pupils by means of **Socratic dialogue**—rigorous questioning and analysis of ethical issues. The Socratic dialogue was meant to draw students out by pressing them to answer a series of leading questions, such as "Is democracy the most reasonable form of government?"

Eventually Socrates ran into difficulties with Athenian authorities, who convicted him on charges of undermining the gods and teaching young people to question their elders. At his trial, Socrates refused to apologize for his conduct, claiming that his actions were proper behavior for an educated, inquisitive person. Sentenced to death, he met his fate with dignity and grace, drinking a cup of hemlock (a potent poison) and continuing to converse with his followers until he died. But Socrates' teachings guaranteed him immortality. Although he wrote nothing himself, his student Plato (427–346 B.C.E.) recorded the master's reasoning and founded his own school of thought.

Born during the Peloponnesian War and shaped by its turbulence, Plato saw civil society as deeply flawed. Many of his dialogues, including *The Republic*, aimed to nudge the Athenian elite toward a more effective form of government. He contended that the state exists to serve its people, and that only a philosopher-king, a statesman whose education equips him to know the truth, is genuinely qualified to lead. For Plato, democracy was absurd: it gave power not to the most knowledgeable individual but to the most popular. Government should be led by the most competent, he argued, and only an aristocracy that honors learning and the quest for truth can produce competent leaders.

Plato's most brilliant student, Aristotle (*AIR-ih-STAH-tul*), became one of the most influential thinkers of all time. Philosopher, scientist, poet, and student of politics, Aristotle (384–322 B.C.E.) took the entire universe as his field of study. He wrote on physics, chemistry, biology, geography, and cosmology. The classification of political systems discussed earlier in this chapter is Aristotelian, based on his rigorous analysis of 158 Greek city-states. Aristotle proposed that the universe is composed of five elements: earth, air, fire, water, and ether, this last being an invisible medium through which stars and planets supposedly move around the earth. Those celestial bodies, he argued, were impelled by a "prime mover," a force that initiates all motion but that cannot itself be moved.

In his later years, Aristotle became tutor to Alexander the Great, molding that Macedonian conqueror into an enthusiast for, and transmitter of, Greek culture. Aristotelian ideas and principles, preserved and transmitted by Muslims and Byzantine Christians, shaped the thought of the medieval Islamic and Christian European worlds.

Classical Greek Society and Religion

7.5   **Discuss the characteristics of society and religion in Classical Greece.**

Most Greeks, of course, never had the opportunity to learn from Socrates, Plato, or Aristotle. They were artisans, farmers, slaves, and women whose labors allowed little time for philosophy, and who believed that their destinies were not in their own hands, but were controlled by an assortment of unpredictable gods.

What was the nature of slavery in Classical Greece?

Free Labor and Slavery

As with societies in other ancient civilizations, labor in the Greek economy was organized around both rural and urban activities. Daily life in the countryside was simple and primarily agricultural. Greeks ate grains and fruits, enjoying vegetables and fish on occasion. The goats and sheep they raised provided milk and cheese, while pigs provided the modest amount of meat that Spartans ate every day. In the cities, men earned their living as artisans or skilled laborers. The unskilled worked alongside slaves in manual jobs such as garbage removal and street-sweeping, with the same daily wage going to both the enslaved and the free.

Slavery was common in Greece, as in most of the ancient world. Greek slaves generally shared the material standard of living of their owners, who were not necessarily wealthy. They were paid modest wages for their work and might eventually save enough to purchase their freedom. Most slaves were foreigners captured in warfare or in slave raids. Well-born prisoners of war were usually ransomed by their families, so slaves tended to come from the ranks of the poor. Criminals, debtors, and orphans were also sometimes forced into slavery, but because most Greeks considered all non-Greeks to be inferior, foreigners were more likely to be enslaved than native Greeks.

Slavery differed in various parts of Greece. In Athens, slaves constituted nearly one third of the total population. Since male prisoners of war were routinely imprisoned or killed, nearly all Athenian slaves were women. They helped the master with his farm or business, or the mistress of the house with her domestic chores. Legally they were human property. They could be beaten, usually for disobedience or laziness, but not killed. They were clearly inferior to citizens in civil rights and considered inferior also in natural abilities.

In Sparta, slaves were bound to the land that they worked on their masters' behalf but otherwise enjoyed considerable freedom of action. Although many Spartan slaves were foreigners, others were *helots* (HĒ-lots or HELL-uts), named after the nearby town of Helus, which Sparta had conquered. Most Spartan slaves were male, in contrast to the situation in Athens, and the Spartan oligarchy lived in permanent fear of helot revolts. This fear helps explain the intense militarization of Spartan society.

The Status of Women

What was the status of women in Classical Greece, and how did the roles of women in Sparta and Athens differ from one another?

Greek women enjoyed a status above that of slaves but below that of free men. In Sparta, women were highly valued for their ability to bear and rear healthy young warriors who would defend the city-state and make possible its expansion. Girls were therefore raised in much the same way as boys, with an emphasis on physical training and horsemanship. Spartan girls as well as boys competed naked in athletic events, and unmarried teenage girls were required to audition for marriage and motherhood by dancing naked before audiences of young men.

Spartan women usually married at 18, later than women in other Greek city-states, while men married in their mid-20s. Since men remained in the barracks until age 30, young husbands visited their wives secretly at night, and they might father children before ever seeing their wives by daylight. As a consequence, the mother was the dominant figure in Spartan family life. Women could own property and transact business without the consent of their husbands, who spent most of their time in the barracks or away on military campaigns. Women were also guaranteed full civil rights except for voting, a right no Greek polis ever granted them.

Greek women.

Athenian women, in contrast, were confined to the home, except for infrequent occasions such as celebrations or funerals. As full citizens of a state that relied on substantial male political participation, Athenian husbands possessed nearly total authority over their households and everyone living in them. A woman was protected by her father or male guardian until she married; if divorced or widowed, she returned to him. Virginity before marriage was highly prized for both men and women. After marriage, wives were expected to remain faithful, but a husband's casual adultery, particularly when away from home, was not considered immoral. Wives ran their households, supervised slaves, and wove clothing for family members. Once menopause occurred, Athenian women enjoyed greater freedom, working as midwives, nurses, and seamstresses.

The subordination of women to men was written into Greek law. Protections for women also protected the rights and interests of their husbands. In Sparta, women were honored as mothers of the next generation of warriors; in Athens, women were prized for conveying economic and political rights to their male children. Authority in Greece was a male monopoly.

Homosexuality

How did Greek culture view homosexuality?

Male authority was also a contributing factor to the prevalence of homosexuality in upper-class Greek society. A homosexual relationship between a young man and his older patron or mentor was often taken for granted as part of the younger person's apprenticeship. Such relationships in adolescence were usually considered preludes to heterosexual relationships beginning in a young man's 20s and did not preclude marriage and fathering a family. Nor did homosexuality constitute an impediment to military service, as male couples were permitted to serve together in the armies of Thebes, Corinth, and Sparta, among other city-states.

Greek culture celebrated the human body in art and athletic competition, and Greek society's commitment to raising and educating boys and girls separately did nothing to discourage same-sex relationships. But acceptance of unconcealed homosexuality was limited to the elite. Commoners either avoided such relationships or hid them, and laws against homosexual conduct existed in most city-states.

Greek Religion

How were Greek gods and goddesses similar to and different from human beings?

What is now called Greek mythology was originally a belief system reflecting ancient Greek culture. The twelve major Greek gods were said to live on **Mount Olympus**, the highest mountain in northwest Peloponnesus. Unlike divinities in other early civilizations, the Greek gods were not believed to have created the universe or the earth; both were assumed to be eternal. The major Greek gods were believed to have created men and women, but not out of dust and a rib (as in Jewish and Christian tradition), nor out of a clot of blood (as in Islamic belief). Instead they engaged in sexual intercourse with mortals to produce heroic humans whose own offspring then became the human race.

Among themselves, the gods had love affairs that produced additional gods. Zeus, figuratively and literally the "Father of the Gods," sired Ares (*AIR-ēz*), the god of war, by his wife Hera, and six other gods by a variety of women. The children of Zeus also included Apollo, Athena, and Aphrodite (*aff-rō-DĪ-tē*), gods and goddesses of exceptional beauty and varying sexual appetites. Poseidon (*puh-SĪ-dun*), god of the sea, was Zeus's brother, and Demeter (*dih-MĒ-ter*), goddess of grain, their sister. All played significant roles in Homer's *Iliad*, as they intervened on one side or the other during the Trojan War.

Greek deities were clearly more powerful than humans, but they had human traits. They could be greedy, generous, lusty, chaste, envious, kind, angry, and affectionate.

Asklepios, the Greek god of medicine.

Generally the gods on Mount Olympus took little direct interest in humans, but from time to time, out of boredom, they sought pleasure in manipulating human affairs, playing with people on earth as children play with dolls and toys. Other deities, who did not reside on Olympus, lived closer to mortals, affecting their lives each day by rewarding or punishing them. All gods and goddesses were believed to crave worship, adoration, and sacrifices of food and drink, which fearful humans provided to win divine favor.

For example, every fourth year men and women competed in a great festival of athletic events in honor of the deities they worshipped. These Olympic Games, named for the mountain on which the main gods lived, consisted of nine events, including a chariot race. The Olympic Games attracted participants and spectators from throughout Greece, and warfare between city-states stopped whenever the games were held. Presumably the gods' enjoyment of these sports disposed them more kindly toward humans. The ancient games were last held in 395 c.e. but were revived by Europeans in 1896.

The Greek gods live today in Western literature and drama, but in ancient times they were believed to be never far away from their people. That humans served as their puppets did nothing to diminish this closeness. The gods could feel pain (when a god was wounded in battle, his blood ran black), and what kept them immortal was their diet of ambrosia and nectar. They quarreled with each other and took delight in frustrating each other's plans. For Greeks, the gods were not remote beings but a part of everyday life.

The Empire of Alexander the Great

7.6   **Explain the importance of Alexander's empire and evaluate his legacy.**

When Philip of Macedon conquered Greece in 338 B.C.E., Greeks did not feel the gods had deserted them. They simply believed that Philip, for all his power and glory, was just one more tool in the hands of the Olympians. When he was assassinated in 336, only two years after his dramatic triumph, his new subjects nodded knowingly to one another: the gods had grown tired of him. The chief murder suspect was his first wife, Olympias, who had been cast aside by Philip in favor of a younger woman, also killed, along with her young daughter, soon after the king's murder. Since these events left Olympias and her 20-year-old son Alexander in control of the kingdom, many Macedonians suspected that Alexander had been part of the plot, though there is no evidence of his involvement. These sorts of intrigues, of course, would have been typical among the gods, and therefore familiar to both Greeks and Macedonians.

Why was Alexander the Great such a successful military commander?

Alexander the Great.

Alexander's Conquests

Alexander III of Macedon (336–323 B.C.E.), who quickly succeeded Philip, was a young man of unusual political and military talents. Tutored in his youth by Aristotle, he had developed a profound admiration for Greek culture, especially as his native Macedonia was looked upon by Greeks as a backward frontier area. Alexander, whose mother claimed descent from Achilles, immersed himself in Homeric poetry and by his late teens had become, in the words of one scholar, "self-confident, endlessly curious, and reckless," much like Achilles himself. After his father's murder, Alexander moved swiftly to ensure the loyalty of the army and to kill anyone questioning his claim to rule. Then he descended upon Greece, destroying the powerful city of Thebes and forcing the Greeks to recognize him as Philip's legitimate successor.

After subduing Greece, Alexander resumed the invasion of Persia that Philip had planned. That invasion appeared wildly risky. Persia was not the power it had been under Darius I and Xerxes, but it had a strong army, and its immense size placed invaders at a disadvantage. In addition, Alexander's position at home, resting (unlike his father's) on no domestic achievements whatsoever, was not yet secure. But he was eager for conquest and moved quickly against Persia with a mixed army of Macedonians and Greeks. In 334 B.C.E., at the Granicus (*grun-Ī-kus*) River in northwestern Anatolia, he won his first major victory. After that, as he entered Asia by way of the bridge at Gordium, he cut the Gordian Knot.

Alexander justified his attack on Persia by claiming to be the champion of Greek culture against barbarian values and the instrument of Greek revenge for Xerxes' invasion in 480. Despite these justifications, Alexander's principal objective was heroic conquest, and he was talented enough to achieve it. In battle, Alexander was able not only to plan a sequence of moves but also to anticipate his enemy's likely responses and to be ready with countermeasures. He was also able to change his course of action in the midst of the confusion of battle. Complementing these impressive abilities was Alexander's religious faith. The incident of the Gordian Knot convinced him that the gods had willed that he rule Asia. Seeing himself as a second Achilles, he had no doubt he would succeed.

Alexander met the Persians in battle at Issus, in southwestern Anatolia, in 333 B.C.E. The Persian Emperor Darius III was an experienced military leader, and his army was more than twice as large as Alexander's. The outcome was in doubt at first, but Alexander personally led a headlong cavalry charge that broke through Darius's bodyguard and forced the Persian emperor to flee. Next Alexander moved south through Syria and Palestine into Egypt, adding to his dominions the rich former realm of the pharaohs and founding there the city of Alexandria, destined to become one of the world's great cultural centers. This conquest of Egypt secured the Mediterranean coastline so that Persia could not use it as a springboard for invading Greece.

No longer underestimating Alexander, Darius offered to surrender to him all of the Persian Empire west of the Euphrates. To the dismay of his commanders, Alexander rejected the offer. He marched northeast to Mesopotamia, where he again vanquished the Persians, paving the way for his conquest of their entire empire. Storming across Persia, he crossed into Afghanistan and through the Khyber Pass (Map 7.4) into India. By 326 B.C.E. he was east of the Indus River and dreamed of pressing on to the "eastern sea" (which may have been either the Ganges River or the Bay of Bengal), but his men, having been away from home for eight years, refused to continue. Compelled to turn back, Alexander returned to Persia but never saw Greece again.

The Fate and Impact of Alexander's Empire

What was the significance of Alexander's empire for Asia?

Ruling the former Persian Empire turned out to be more difficult than defeating it. But Alexander was insightful about how an empire should be run and wise in his decision to retain satrapies and other features of Persian government. Like previous outsiders who had overrun complex civilizations, the Macedonian leadership quickly adopted useful techniques from its new subjects.

Alexander tried to fuse Persian and Greek cultures, taking several Persian wives, encouraging his commanders and officials to do the same, and placing both Greeks and Persians in important political and administrative positions. These moves won him more praise in Persia than in Greece. In Persia, Alexander sought to have his rule recognized as a continuation of the imperial tradition by retaining the satrapies and by officiating at the burial services of Emperor Darius III. In Greece, however, he was still resented as an outsider. Most Greek cities feared Macedon more than Persia, and during Alexander's long absence they frequently rebelled. Accustomed to independence, they resented centralized rule under Macedonian governors and charged (without evidence) that Greeks were being denied privileges that Alexander was granting to Persians.

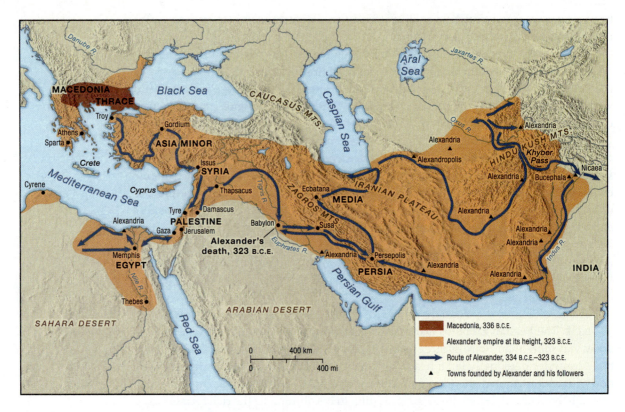

Map 7.4 THE EMPIRE OF ALEXANDER THE GREAT, 336–323 B.C.E. The armies of Alexander the Great created Greek-based connections across Southwest Asia. Note that his enormous empire, constructed in only 13 years, duplicates almost exactly the Persian Empire of Cyrus, Cambyses, and Darius I (Map 6.3). Alexander's conquests placed a permanent Greek imprint on millions of people, while Eastern concepts like despotism flowed westward into Greece. What kinds of changes would have occurred during this blending of such varied cultures?

Alexander adopted Persian governing practices, but he had little use for Persian culture. According to his Greek biographer Plutarch, he considered himself "a governor from God and a reconciler of the world." He hoped that Greek culture would, through his actions, permeate all of Asia, inspiring its peoples to pursue virtue, excellence, wisdom, and truth. This heroic idealism blended with practicality in his plan to develop the Tigris, Euphrates, and Indus rivers as commercial waterways linking all of Asia.

These undertakings promised to be long and difficult, however, and Alexander was an impatient man. His soldiers' unwillingness to proceed past the Indus was a great disappointment to him, for which he compensated by exalting his own greatness and indulging in festivals and celebrations. At one in 323 B.C.E., he reportedly consumed more than a gallon of wine in half an hour. He quickly developed a fever, grew weaker, and died several days later from symptoms consistent with tropical malaria. He was only 33 years old.

Alexander's sudden death threw his empire into confusion. Each of his most important generals seized a portion for himself: Ptolemy (*TAHL-em-ē*) took Egypt, Antigonus (*an-TIH-guh-nuss*) held Greece and Macedonia, and Seleucus Nikator controlled all the rest, from western Anatolia to the border of India. The Seleucid Empire, as we saw in Chapter 6, was the first of a series of successor states to the Asian portions of Alexander's empire. It was followed by the Greco-Bactrians, Parthians, and Sasanians, none of whom were able to reconstitute the Persian Empire that Alexander had conquered.

Although Alexander's empire was no longer unified, the importance of his accomplishments remained. He had defeated the immense Persian Empire, spread Greek culture throughout Southwest Asia, and connected Europe, Asia, and Africa in ways that would later benefit the Roman Empire. These connections are delineated later in this chapter.

At the same time, Alexander's legacy should not be romanticized. Although he championed Greek civilization, he developed no appreciation for the achievements of the Persian Empire he opposed. He demolished one of the great powers of the ancient world without replacing it with a culture that demonstrably improved the lives of its people. In addition, his model of kingship, which exalted an aloof, militaristic, divinely inspired monarch, blended West with East but benefited neither. Finally, Alexander's conquests, for all their brilliance, were personally motivated. Despite his love for Greek culture and his desire to fuse the Greek and Persian worlds, he never thought seriously about establishing political and economic institutions that could have helped unify a realm stretching from Macedonia to Egypt and from Greece to India.

Connections and Conflicts in the Hellenistic World

7.7 Describe the impact of Hellenization in culture, commerce, and politics.

Alexander's diffusion of Greek values and practices eastward was accompanied by the westward spread of values and practices from the civilizations of the East. His penetration of Southwest Asia and Egypt created a set of new societies and political entities that were not simply Greek, Persian, Egyptian, or Indian but a blend of them in varying combinations. To distinguish it from the earlier **Hellenic culture** developed by the Greeks, this new culture is traditionally called **Hellenistic culture**.

Commercial and Cultural Connections

Nowhere was this convergence of cultures more obvious than in economics. The post-Alexander monarchies of Southwest Asia (Map 7.5) used confiscated Persian wealth to construct roads and harbors for the promotion of trade. These improvements kept Mediterranean goods flowing eastward and Asian luxuries moving westward. Foodstuffs were shipped by sea, while luxury goods traveled overland by camel caravans, protected by the Seleucid and Ptolemaic states. Spices from India and silks from China became widely prized in Greece, while exquisite examples of Greek sculpture and pottery were popular in India and China. Greek law and custom became the foundation on which business was transacted. Greece benefited immensely from this commerce, particularly in agricultural commodities: the grain produced in surplus in the eastern Hellenistic monarchies improved the nutrition of people throughout the rocky peninsula who had always lived on the edge of malnutrition. Greek fish, wine, and olive oil were exported to the East in return.

Cultural contact in the Hellenistic world extended beyond trade and commerce. In astronomy, physics, mathematics, and medicine, Greek thinkers profited from the knowledge and techniques of the East. In Egypt, Alexandria grew into a renowned center of learning and inquiry. Most of its population spoke Greek, which rapidly became the tongue of educated people throughout the Hellenistic world. Alexandria's library was justly famous, and in 245 B.C.E. its chief librarian, Eratosthenes (*air-uh-TAHS-thuh-nēz*), calculated the circumference of the earth at 24,675 miles—an error of only seven-tenths of one percent. More than 17 centuries before Columbus, he also predicted that a ship leaving Spain could reach India either by sailing around the southern tip of Africa or by sailing west. Educated people throughout the ancient world knew that the earth is round and had a good sense of its size.

Another Hellenistic astronomer, Aristarchus of Samos (*air-ih-STAR-kuss, SĀ-mus*), constructed his ideas on Babylonian foundations. More advanced in his thinking than

What were the principal commercial and cultural connections created by the Hellenistic kingdoms?

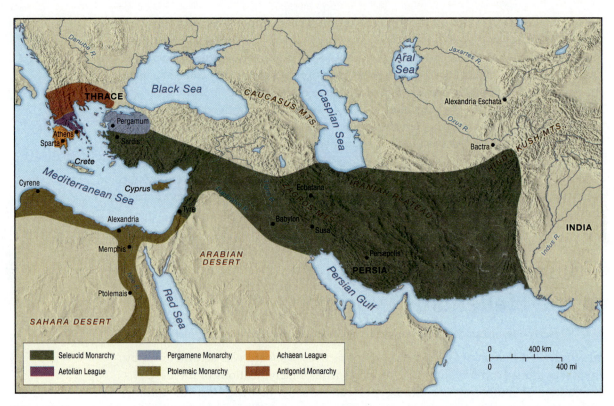

Map 7.5 **THE HELLENISTIC KINGDOMS, 323–146 B.C.E.** No one knows whether Alexander the Great could have held together the enormous territories he conquered. We do know that after his death at age 33, none of his successors could do so. The division of Alexander's empire into a variety of kingdoms ended the temporary political unity of Southwest Asia and created a region in which the only unifying factor was Hellenistic culture. Notice the unequal distribution of lands between Alexander's three successors and their dynasties. Which do you think would prove the most powerful and influential? Why?

Aristotle, Aristarchus (310–230 B.C.E.) proposed that the earth revolves around the sun and that the stars orbit neither the earth nor the sun. But Aristarchus's view, though correct, did not prevail. The astronomer Claudius Ptolemy (85–165 C.E.), working in Egypt, endorsed Aristotle's concept of heavenly bodies moving around the earth, and Ptolemy's writings proved so influential that the idea of a heliocentric (sun-centered) system was not taken seriously until the publication of the work of Copernicus nearly 14 centuries later.

More influential than Aristarchus was Archimedes (*ark-ih-MĒ-dēz*) of Syracuse (285–204 B.C.E.), a master of mathematics, physics, and mechanical engineering. The creator of the science of hydrostatics (fluid pressure), Archimedes determined that an object immersed in a container of liquid displaces from the container the precise equivalent of its own volume in liquid. According to legend, he solved this problem while stepping into his bathtub and became so excited that he ran through the streets naked, shouting, "Eureka!" (Greek for "I have found it!"). Less dramatic but equally significant were his discoveries of a compound pulley to raise heavy weights and a screw system to lift water to higher levels.

Alexander the Great's dynamic conquests also affected the pursuit of philosophy in Greece. In response to changes wrought by Alexander, Hellenistic thinkers sought permanence and stability. Epicurus (*EP-ih-KYOOR-us*) (341–270 B.C.E.), for example, advised that nothing is to be gained by trying to appease the gods, who are indifferent to human problems. As all matter, including the gods, is composed of atoms, he argued, the soul dies with the body. Pleasure is simply the absence of pain. Epicureans therefore held that one should not be troubled by change, resent fate, or try to alter destiny. Zeno (*ZĒ-nō*) refuted this position with a complex philosophy called Stoicism. Release from pain is not an end in itself, he charged, and Epicurean withdrawal into private life is wrong. Stoics must show courage, cultivate wisdom, and do their duty, remaining steadfast in time of crisis even in the face of overwhelming odds. It is not success that matters, but the virtuous pursuit of duty. Neither Epicureanism nor Stoicism became the dominant philosophy of the day. Most people were attracted by one and then by the other, depending on the circumstances.

In religion, the two-way flow of ideas benefited West more than East. The cults of Greek deities like Apollo and Athena moved eastward with the spread of Greek culture, but they had little theological content and enjoyed limited appeal among Eastern peoples interested in problems involving sin and salvation. Even Greeks who emigrated eastward eventually found Greek religious views sterile. The westward flow, on the other hand, brought Eastern mystery religions (also called "salvation religions") to the Greek world, with profound historical consequences.

Mystery religions addressed directly the problems of human weakness, divine redemption, and eternal life. In each of them, a god or goddess either became human or became deeply involved with human beings, teaching his or her followers certain divine secrets or mysteries. Through initiation into these mysteries, new converts were believed to become one with the deity, whose sacrifices redeemed the sins of the newcomers and promised them immortality. Once the initiation was complete, the convert felt "born again" into a new life.

Mithras slaying the sacred bull.

Two of the most important Hellenistic mystery cults centered on the god Dionysus (*dī-uh-NĪ-suss*) and the goddess Demeter. Dionysus was the god of fruitfulness and wine. His festivals, preceded by solemn performance of the mystery rituals he allegedly taught his followers, included choral singing, pantomime, free-spirited sexual activity, and great quantities of wine. Worshippers believed they were linked with deceased ancestors, fellow revelers, and generations of believers yet to be born.

Rituals devoted to Demeter, the goddess of grain, were called the Eleusinian (*el-yoo-SIN-ē-un*) Mysteries because they were celebrated only at Eleusis, a city-state near Athens. Demeter's followers memorialized the cycle of life as represented in the sowing, sprouting, and harvesting of grain. The grain that is scattered on fertile soil germinates, sprouts, and is reaped for bread and future seeding. Similarly, a girl is taken from her parents, is "seeded" through sexual intercourse, and produces offspring. When men and women die, they are buried in the earth and remain part of the cycle of life. New life springs forth from every grave, and those devoted to Demeter look forward to eternal life.

Mystery religions became extremely popular in the Hellenistic world. The cult of Mithras, a Persian god who created the universe by catching and sacrificing a sacred bull, eventually reappeared in Western culture. Devotions to the Egyptian deities Isis and Osiris, involving a god who is slain but then restored to become the judge of humankind (Chapter 2), also became highly influential in Greco-Roman civilization. But in the long run, the main beneficiary of Eastern religious influences was Christianity. In the first century C.E., the Apostle Paul preached the message of this Eastern-inspired religion to a Greek population already familiar with many of its basic conceptions.

Politics and Governance

Politically, too, the impact of Hellenization was two-sided. Alexander's conquests removed the Persian Empire from world history and spread the Greek language and Greco-Macedonian military techniques into southern Asia. But distinctively Greek forms of government were not transmitted in the same way. Athenian democracy and Spartan oligarchy may have been suitable forms of governance for small, internally cohesive city-states, but they were not suited to sprawling, multiethnic empires. For leaders wishing to rule such diverse states, monarchy seemed to work best, as

What was the Hellenistic attitude toward monarchy and democracy?

it permitted the creation of royal dynasties in which the authority of the king was believed to come from the gods. The royal family thus became the symbol of political unity within the empire, transcending tribal loyalties and language differences.

Although monarchy was nothing new to the Greeks—the word itself is Greek—it belonged to the legendary past. Homer's *Iliad* sang of kings like Agamemnon and Priam, but the Greeks of the fourth century B.C.E. thought that monarchy had been replaced by better forms. Then the Eastern empires that Alexander conquered made them appreciate the power of a central authority. Emperors disposed of their subjects like Athenians disposed of used clothing, and they cared little for the opinions of the people. To an ordinary Greek, this was tyranny, not monarchy, but to Ptolemy, Seleucus, and their successors it was convenient.

Yet the post-Alexandrian empires were ruled entirely by Greeks, even if the form of government they adopted was Eastern. Greeks held every influential political, diplomatic, military, and administrative post. Hellenistic rulers were anxious to recruit Greeks and Macedonians for their armies and navies, as they believed that relying on local warriors would be politically dangerous. Cities laid out in the Greek style, designed and constructed by Greek architects and engineers, were built throughout the new empires, and Greek immigration into these empires was encouraged.

The political structures of Hellenistic expansion proved strikingly fragile. Although there were too many Greeks for their rocky homeland, there were not nearly enough to staff every important position in southwestern Asia. The Hellenistic kingdoms could not sustain the vigor, curiosity, and enthusiasm of Alexander the Great. They declined slowly for a hundred years and eventually collapsed when challenged by a dynamic new dominion arising in the west, centered on the city of Rome.

Chapter Review

Consequences and Connections

The Greeks developed sophisticated forms of government, created magnificent works of poetry and drama, formulated enduring answers to fundamental questions about the nature of reality, and made striking advances in scientific inquiry. But their refusal to cooperate with one another ultimately delivered them into the hands of conquerors. Their short-lived alliance against the Persians ran aground on the rocks of Athenian ambitions, and the ensuing Peloponnesian War so weakened them that they fell to Macedonia.

Nevertheless, the accomplishments of Greek culture spread throughout the Mediterranean basin with Greek colonies, and Alexander's soldiers carried them into Egypt and across southern Asia to the Indus Valley. Greek learning enriched the lives of hundreds of millions and altered the course of history. Europeans were particularly fascinated by Greek culture. They adapted its methods for governing the polis to their own states. Words such as *tyranny*, *aristocracy*, *oligarchy*, and *democracy* continue to be used to describe governmental systems throughout the world. Europeans produced their own philosophies, dramas, and architectural forms on foundations laid by Greece. Alexander spread Greek culture eastward, but its long-range influence lay to the northwest, in its appeal to a Europe that did not yet exist in the era of great confrontations and connections between Greece and Persia.

Reviewing Key Concepts

Homeric Poetry, p. 127
Polis, p. 127
Monarchy, p. 127
Oligarchy, p. 127
Aristocracy, p. 127
Democracy, p. 127

Tyranny, p. 127
Archaic Period, p. 128
Greek Colonization, p. 128
Peloponnesian League, p. 130
Classical Period, p. 131
Delian League, p. 131

Age of Pericles, p. 131
Socratic Dialogue, p. 135
Mount Olympus, p. 137
Hellenic Culture, p. 141
Hellenistic Culture, p. 141
Mystery Religions, p. 143

Ask Yourself

1. Why were the Greek city-states unable to create a permanently unified state?

2. How did the Persian Wars affect the Greeks, both for good and for ill?

3. How did Greek religion differ from Eastern "mystery religions"? What does Greek religion tell us about the Greeks themselves?

4. Describe the connections forged between ancient Greece and other civilizations.

Key Dates and Developments

1200–750 B.C.E.	The "Dark Age"; Homer's writings are composed
750–550 B.C.E.	Greece colonizes the Mediterranean basin; The Archaic Period
621 B.C.E.	Draco's legal code in Athens
594 B.C.E.	Solon's reforms in Athens
ca. 560 B.C.E.	Formation of the Peloponnesian League
500–338 B.C.E.	The Classical Period
499 B.C.E.	Beginning of the Ionian revolt against Persia
490 B.C.E.	Athenians defeat Persians at Marathon
480 B.C.E.	Sparta's sacrifice at Thermopylae
480 B.C.E.	Athenian victory over Persians at Salamis
478 B.C.E.	Formation of the Delian League
461–429 B.C.E.	Age of Pericles at Athens
431–404 B.C.E.	The Peloponnesian War
399 B.C.E.	Trial and execution of Socrates
338 B.C.E.	Philip of Macedon conquers Greece
336–323 B.C.E.	Conquests of Alexander the Great
323–30 B.C.E.	Era of the Hellenistic kingdoms

Chapter 8
The Romans Connect the Mediterranean World, 753 B.C.E.–284 C.E.

ROMULUS AND REMUS A statue of Romulus and Remus being suckled by a she-wolf. This legend encouraged Romans to consider themselves tough, resilient people accustomed to overcoming hardships.

After reading this chapter, you should be able to:

8.1 Describe the structure of the Roman Republic and explain its attitudes toward law and citizenship.

8.2 Discuss the erosion of support for the Roman Republic, and evaluate Julius Caesar's solution to its problems.

8.3 Explain how Caesar Augustus created the Roman Empire while protesting that he was doing no such thing.

8.4 Explain how and why Christianity posed a lethal threat to the Roman Emperor.

8.5 Discuss the transition of Rome from its golden age to its decline.

According to Roman legend, in the early eighth century B.C.E., the daughter of a local king in central Italy was impregnated by Mars, the god of war. She gave birth to twin sons, and her uncle, who wanted the throne for himself, feared the boys as future rivals and left them on a roadside to die. But a she-wolf discovered them, and rather than devouring the helpless infants, she nursed them. Eventually the twins were discovered by passing shepherds, who adopted them and raised them as their own.

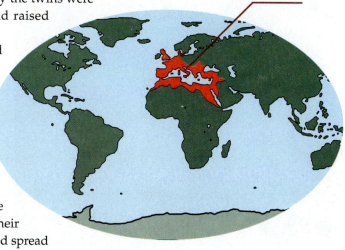

The Roman Empire

The twins of this legend were named Romulus and Remus. Their upbringing was unconventional, and their adolescence was tempestuous: Romulus killed his brother and fled from the shepherd family that had raised him. Then in 753 B.C.E., on the banks of the River Tiber in the fertile plain of Latium (*LĀ-shē-um*) in west-central Italy, he founded a village that, according to the story, became the city of Rome.

Although legendary, this account of Rome's origin reflects the Romans' image of themselves as offspring of the god of war, toughened by the milk of a she-wolf. Proud of their origins, the Romans created influential institutions and helped spread the cultural contributions of ancient Greece and Christianity as they conquered and then managed one of history's most adaptable, effective, and enduring empires.

The Roman Republic to 133 B.C.E.

8.1 **Describe the structure of the Roman Republic and explain its attitudes toward law and citizenship.**

The true story of Rome's founding is less dramatic than its legendary one. Around 1000 B.C.E. three tribes built a village in Latium, in west-central Italy, on seven hills surrounding a place on the Tiber River that could be bridged. The hills gave it natural defenses against land-based attacks, while the 14 miles that separated it from the Mediterranean Sea provided defense against both pirates and naval landings. As the city's later inhabitants also learned, their central location in the Mediterranean basin was close to major trade routes and a good place from which to rule the entire region. Potential competitors, such as Sicily's Syracuse and North Africa's Carthage, were also well located, but, being seaport cities, they were more vulnerable to naval assaults.

The Roman Republic and Its Foundation in Law

At first the Romans were ruled by the kings of Etruria (*ih-TRUR-ē-uh*), a plain northwest of Latium (see Map 8.1). The people of Etruria, known as Etruscans, had adapted the Greek writing system to fit their local language, thereby creating what came to be known as the Latin alphabet. They also brought Rome into a Mediterranean commercial network. But an Etruscan tyrant provoked the ambitious Romans to revolt in 509 B.C.E. Rome's expulsion of the Etruscans was commemorated by Romans for centuries as the end of tyranny and the beginning of rule by a *res publica* (*RĀZ POOB-lick-ah*, or "public possession"). Thus began the Roman Republic, a flexible form of government by elected representatives that proved capable of military conquest and administrative efficiency.

The government of the **Roman Republic** was grounded in principles and practices unlike those developed earlier in Greece. Athenian democracy was based on the right of all adult male citizens to debate, deliberate, and vote. This type of government—a direct democracy—was possible in a city-state with a limited population, but Rome was larger than Athens, and it kept growing. The Romans therefore governed

How important was the rule of law for the development of the Roman Republic?

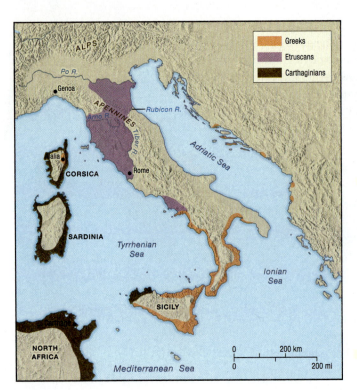

Map 8.1 ITALY IN 600 B.C.E. Italy in 600 B.C.E. was heavily influenced by non-Italian peoples. Observe that Carthaginians controlled Corsica, Sardinia, and western Sicily, while Greeks dominated the remainder of Sicily and the southwestern tip of the Italian peninsula. Etruscans controlled most of Italy north of Rome. Rome's victory over Etruria guaranteed the Romans domination over Italy and laid the foundation for their rivalry with Carthage for control of the Mediterranean. Why would the Greek colonies, as outposts not of a centralized Greek state but of individual city-states, be unable to intervene decisively in the Roman-Carthaginian rivalry?

themselves through a **republic**—a system in which all adult male citizens voted not on the issues of the day but for representatives elected to a variety of assemblies that drafted, debated, and passed laws. If the citizens did not approve of the laws, they could vote the representatives out of office in the next election.

The Roman representative assemblies, however, did not have full authority over public affairs. The Republic's principal political institution was the **senate**, an advisory body composed of the most prestigious statesmen of Rome. The senate was dominated by patricians, wealthy landowners who led Rome's military units and who constituted the majority of the educated class. Senators selected new members of the senate, often nominating their own sons or relatives. The senate elected Rome's two consuls, officials who administered the state for one-year terms.

The governments of Mesopotamia, Egypt, China, and Persia were based largely on the power and personalities of individual rulers, but Rome's government was based on laws. In those other civilizations, rulers made the laws; in Rome, rulers were subject to the laws. Roman law distinguished between civil and criminal procedures. It aimed at developing solutions that would be fair to all parties in a dispute. In this pursuit it proved remarkably flexible, sometimes relying on precedent, sometimes on concepts of both common and individual good, and sometimes on common sense. As Rome expanded beyond its traditional boundaries, it amplified its civil law into "**law of peoples**," which applied to Romans and foreigners alike. The "law of peoples," in turn, evolved into **natural law**, a Roman vision of legal principles applicable to all societies regardless of time or circumstance. The necessity of ruling non-Roman peoples encouraged Roman jurists to develop universally valid legal standards, and these influenced subsequent legal systems and laid the foundations of international law.

This legal system helped regulate a bitterly divisive social contest between patricians and plebeians known as the **Struggle of the Orders**. Common people, or plebeians (*plih-BĒ-uns*), frustrated in their attempts to attain a meaningful voice in state affairs, went on strike in 494 B.C.E. and withdrew from the city, creating their own assembly apart from the senate. This new assembly elected tribunes, or spokesmen who were charged with protecting the plebeians' rights and presenting their concerns to the senate. Even more alarming to the patricians, however, was the plebeians' refusal to serve in the army. Since commoners were the foot soldiers, without whom there would be no army, the patricians were forced to give in. Over the next two centuries they yielded their privileged legal and political positions bit by bit.

By 471 B.C.E. the patricians accepted the assembly, although its decisions did not enjoy the status of law until 287 B.C.E. In 450 B.C.E., plebeian agitation forced patricians to publish the famous Law of the Twelve Tables (see "Excerpt from the Twelve Tables"), a series of laws displayed on 12 tablets along with regulations governing legal procedure. Published and public laws thus opened the legal system to full use by all free men, breaking the patricians' monopoly. By 342 B.C.E. the patricians yielded further, agreeing to the plebeian demand that one of the two consuls be a plebeian. Gradually, wealthier plebeians moved into the patrician class, which grudgingly allowed them a role in governing the Republic. But when the Struggle of the Orders ended in 287 B.C.E., all Roman citizens were equal before the law. Roman practicality

Document 8.1   Excerpt from the Twelve Tables

The Roman Republic encapsulated its most important laws in the book of Twelve Tables, which the great orator Cicero praised as follows: "Though all the world exclaim against me, I will say what I think: that single little book of the Twelve Tables, if anyone look to the fountains and sources of laws, seems to me, assuredly, to surpass the libraries of all the philosophers, both in weight of authority, and in plenitude of utility." (Cicero,De Oratore, I, 44.)

TABLE I

1. If anyone summons a man before the magistrate, he must go. If the man summoned does not go, let the one summoning him call the bystanders to witness and then take him by force.
3. If illness or old age is the hindrance, let the summoner provide a team. He need not provide a covered carriage with a pallet unless he chooses.

TABLE II

2. He whose witness has failed to appear may summon him by loud calls before his house every third day.

TABLE IV

1. A dreadfully deformed child shall be quickly killed.
2. If a father sell his son three times, the son shall be free from his father.
5. A child born after ten months since the father's death will not be admitted into a legal inheritance.

TABLE V

1. Females should remain in guardianship even when they have attained their majority.

TABLE VIII

3. If one is slain while committing theft by night, he is rightly slain.
4. If a patron shall have devised any deceit against his client, let him be accursed.
13. It is unlawful for a thief to be killed by day . . . unless he defends himself with a weapon; even though he has come with a weapon, unless he shall use the weapon and fight back, you shall not kill him. And even if he resists, first call out so that someone may hear and come up.

TABLE IX

4. The penalty shall be capital for a judge or arbiter legally appointed who has been found guilty of receiving a bribe for giving a decision.

SOURCE: Oliver J. Thatcher, ed. *The Library of Original Sources*, Volume III: *The Roman World* (Milwaukee: University Extension Co., 1901) 9–11.

---

and flexibility prevailed, and rather than being plunged into civil war, the Republic evolved into a healthier, stronger system of government.

The equality of all citizens before the law naturally exalted **Roman citizenship**, a privilege conferred upon all adult males who, by birth or adoption, belonged to one of the tribes that had founded the city. Roman citizenship entitled the holder to a number of rights, including the right to appeal any official decision to the highest authorities. Citizens of Rome were safe from unjust imprisonment, and the authorities were required to treat them with respect. The highest positions in the Republic were open to any citizen, regardless of ancestry or wealth.

Like Persia, Rome tried to assimilate the peoples it conquered, and eventually the benefits of citizenship were employed in this process. The most talented and useful males in tribes or ethnic groups subdued by Rome were offered full citizenship and the opportunity to advance their careers in the service of a great and powerful state. This practice made Roman citizenship one of the most highly prized distinctions of its day. The proud boast, *"Civis Romanus sum"* (CHIH-vis ro-MAHN-us SOOM, "I am a Roman citizen"), commanded immediate respect throughout the Roman Empire. Some foreigners even sold themselves into slavery to Rome, hoping someday to be freed and become citizens. But Rome's decision to grant citizenship to some foreigners while withholding it from others transformed citizenship from a right into a privilege. The legacy for some modern European nations has been to use citizenship as a reward that can be revoked if a citizen's conduct proves offensive to the state.

Romans were proud of their government and laws. Representative government, the Twelve Tables, equality before the law, and citizenship as privilege combined to make it possible for Rome to rule the Mediterranean basin.

Why was Rome's victory over Carthage so significant?

The Punic Wars and Rome's Mediterranean Domination

Rome's domination of the Mediterranean basin was first achieved, however, by its powerful army. The Roman army was divided into legions of approximately 5000 men each, subdivided into centuries of 100 men, each of which was commanded by a centurion. Every adult male was required to serve in the army for as long as he was needed, and no man was permitted to run for public office unless he had served at least 10 years. In ordinary times, between 10 and 15 percent of men served in the legions; in emergencies, this figure rose to 25 percent. No society matched this degree of militarization before World War I, and Rome managed it for centuries.

Rome's army was superbly trained and equipped. Infantry legions were accustomed to 20-mile forced marches, the distance being measured by counting the soldiers' steps: each double (left-right) step was about 5 feet, and 1000 such steps took them a "mile" (derived from *mille*, the Latin word for "thousand"). Food consisted of bread and vegetables, a diet so ingrained that on one occasion soldiers objected when they had to eat meat instead. Courage was richly rewarded through promotions and honors, while cowards were stoned or flogged to death. If a century broke and ran in the face of the enemy, the penalty was *decimation*: every tenth soldier in the entire legion would be executed.

This combination of harsh discipline and constant training, together with skilled, experienced commanders, gave the legions a degree of self-assurance bordering on arrogance. Like tightrope walkers who remain unafraid because they *know* they will not fall, the armies of the Roman Republic moved steadily from conquest to conquest, losing an occasional battle but never a war. They reacted to defeat with bemusement and returned until they finally won. Magnanimous in victory, they aimed not merely to conquer but also to rule diverse peoples and integrate them into the Roman state.

Rome's principal rival for control of the Mediterranean was the city of Carthage, the former Phoenician colony (see Chapter 2) that had become a great naval power on the central North African coast (Map 8.2). Carthage tried for decades to conquer the large island of Sicily, off the tip of southern Italy, which it intended to use as a staging area from which to expand into continental Europe. From Rome's perspective, however, Carthaginian control of Sicily would threaten its control of Italy. From 264 to 146 B.C.E., the two cities fought what would later be called the three Punic (*PYOO-nik*) Wars. In the first of the **Punic Wars** (264–241 B.C.E.), Romans gained control of Sicily by applying land-based military techniques to war at sea. They developed powerful ships with iron-tipped bows designed to ram opposing vessels. In the tumult following a ramming, a gangplank would slide from the bow of the Roman ship onto the deck of its enemy. Foot soldiers would run down the gangplank, board the crippled vessel, and fight what amounted to a land battle on a ship. Given the power of its infantry, Rome usually won such engagements.

Now Rome owned territory outside Italy and would have to defend, tax, and govern it. Within three years, Rome also took control of the Mediterranean islands of Sardinia and Corsica. Sicily, Sardinia, and Corsica were designated as provinces, subordinate regional units, each of which had its own governor and local administration and was not directly subject to the authority of the senate, an arrangement that later contributed to the fragmentation of the Republic.

Carthage fought back, led by Hannibal, a brilliant military tactician outraged by Rome's seizure of Sardinia and Corsica. Hannibal began the Second Punic War (218–201 B.C.E.) by crossing the Mediterranean to southern France, then invading Italy from the north, crossing the Alps with troops and war elephants. Hannibal's innovative tactics enabled him to surround and crush the **Roman legions**, but he never marched on Rome itself, probably realizing that subjugating and occupying the city would be beyond the strength of Carthage. From his viewpoint, the most desirable

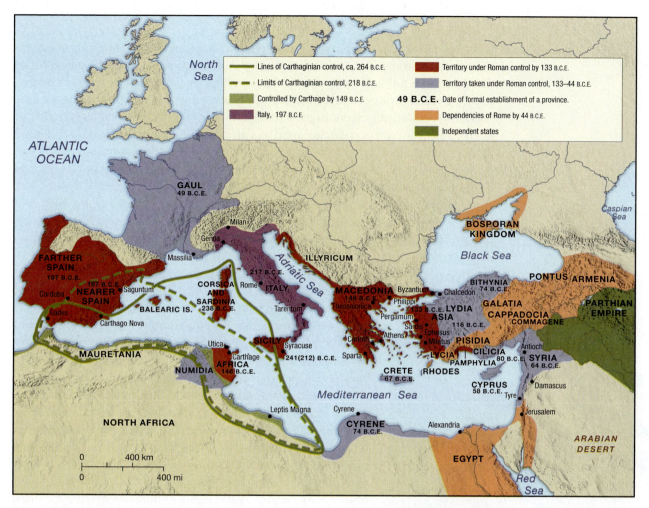

Map 8.2   THE MEDITERRANEAN WORLD AT THE TIME OF THE ROMAN REPUBLIC, 264–44 B.C.E. Rome grew from a centrally located city on the Italian peninsula (Map 8.1) to the dominant power in the Mediterranean basin. Success in the Punic Wars against Carthage removed Rome's military and commercial rival in North Africa and facilitated its conquest of Gaul, Anatolia, and Syria, thereby connecting the entire Mediterranean world. Notice that Rome's conquests and dependencies spanned a distance of nearly 3000 miles. What impact did the vastness of Rome's holdings by 133 B.C.E. have on its republican institutions?

outcome would be Rome's surrender of its overseas provinces. But Hannibal was eventually forced to return to Carthage when Roman forces conquered coastal Spain, and there he lost the Second Punic War.

Over the next 53 years, the Mediterranean balance of power was firmly reoriented in favor of Rome. During this period, the Republic acquired an extensive empire. The senate authorized the pacification of Spain and the subjugation of Macedon and Greece, placing each of these areas under a Roman governor and designating them as provinces. In the Third and final Punic War (149–146 B.C.E.), Rome completely destroyed the city of Carthage, sold the survivors into slavery, and claimed Carthage's empire. The new Roman province of Africa's grain surpluses henceforth fed Romans.

The Punic Wars constituted a major turning point in the history of the Mediterranean basin. Carthage neither shared nor appreciated Rome's devotion to the rule of law, representative government, and equality of all citizens. A Carthaginian victory would have relegated Rome to the status of a historical oddity, a high-minded political experiment that was unable to compete effectively with less sophisticated states. Rome's triumph, on the other hand, helped to preserve these political values while ensuring Rome's domination of the Mediterranean. By 133 B.C.E., the Roman Republic had established nine non-Italian provinces, making it an empire in all but name and changing it considerably.

How did Rome's victory over Carthage alter Rome's structure, its gender relations, and the institution of slavery?

Changes in Society and Culture

Rome's domination of the Mediterranean led to changes in social stratification, gender relations, and the institution of slavery. The first change altered Rome's social divisions from political to economic. The wealth that came with conquest obscured the old patrician–plebeian distinction and replaced it with a gap between those who profited economically from expansion and those who did not. The newly rich as likely came from plebeian background as patrician. Now talent, ambition, and good fortune, rather than birth alone, were the means to success. The new gap that developed between rich and poor proved more difficult to bridge than the old distinction between patrician and plebeian.

Changes in Roman society also gave women a more elevated status than that found in other societies of the time. Persia and Greece had relegated women to the private life of the family, but in Rome, women routinely appeared in public and presided at meals where both sexes were present. Within the family the patriarch ruled, but clearly women were active participants in decision making, consulted by their husbands in all matters pertaining to the family's welfare. They enjoyed their own religious rituals, cults, and festivals from which men were excluded.

A contemporary mosaic shows female Roman students wearing togas.

Outside the home, Roman women enjoyed a significant measure of independence—able to own property, conduct monetary transactions, and even manage businesses. A few women became physicians, practicing gynecology, and many plebeian women became midwives. Even at the highest levels of male-dominated society, women's influence was felt: Roman senators spoke freely of being lobbied by their wives, and under the empire, women such as the Empress Livia, second wife of Caesar Augustus, exercised considerable indirect power over political affairs. From time to time the Roman assemblies passed laws restricting the rights or mobility of women. These laws sparked formal protests, most notably in 195 B.C.E., when numerous women picketed the senate and forced the repeal of a law forbidding women to ride alone in carriages. Men retained ultimate authority in private and public life, but few of them underestimated or ignored female influence.

A third change altered the Roman institution of slavery. Like many other ancient civilizations, Rome enslaved people to labor on behalf of others. In Rome's early days, many citizens owned a few slaves, who worked as domestic servants or agricultural laborers. These slaves were almost always from the Italian peninsula, usually captured through warfare with non-Roman tribes. Chronic debt, alcoholism, or mental incompetence could cause even native Romans to become slaves, and in some cases, parents who could not afford to raise their own children sold them into slavery. This situation changed after the Third Punic War. Rome's succession of military conquests brought tens of thousands of captive foreigners to Italy as slaves. It then became a mark of status for a Roman to own many slaves and to employ them not only for manual labor but also as skilled workers, musicians, and tutors.

Slaves, of course, resented their condition. They lacked freedom and were forced to labor for someone else's prosperity or pleasure. Although some worked for owners who were decent and compassionate, many others endured brutal punishments. Those who worked in mines or as part of agricultural work gangs experienced particularly harsh forms of servitude. At times slaves rebelled. While slave revolts were not frequent, they terrified the Romans and were suppressed with deadly force, much as the Spartans suppressed the helots. The most famous such revolt, led by a gladiator named Spartacus in 73 B.C.E., involved more than 70,000 slaves and lasted two years.

Rome sent a succession of legions to crush the uprising, but Spartacus and his forces defeated all of them but the last. In 71 B.C.E. Spartacus was killed, and thousands of his followers were crucified.

Slavery in Rome declined after the string of Roman conquests ended, but it never disappeared as long as Rome lasted. The use of forced labor and the fear of slave revolts remained ingrained in Roman life until the empire collapsed.

Dissatisfaction with the Republic

8.2   **Discuss the erosion of support for the Roman Republic, and evaluate Julius Caesar's solution to its problems.**

The Roman ability to adapt and synthesize was put to the test once the Punic Wars ended. The governing system of multiple assemblies advised by a senate had to be restructured to serve the needs of an increasingly complex and extensive empire. A tax system was required to fund a permanent standing army and to pay administrators to govern distant provinces. Otherwise, the senate feared, military leaders might rule those lands and use them as a base for challenging senatorial authority. The senate also hoped to organize the entire Mediterranean basin into a vital center of commerce and manufacturing. Yet this wealth encouraged an opulent lifestyle among the Roman elite and growing resentment among Rome's lower classes.

Social Discontent and Decline in Popular Rule

The expanding Roman state faced serious social problems. The Punic Wars laid waste to much of the Italian countryside, and since most of Rome's citizen-soldiers were farmers in civilian life, their frequent absences on military campaigns left their families unable to sow and harvest crops. Upon returning home, many veterans sold their devastated or run-down farms to wealthy buyers, who pieced the lands together to form immense private estates. The veterans then worked for inadequate wages in cities, where they competed with slave labor. Their discontent threatened Rome's stability as their plight threatened its defense: only landowners could serve in the army, and given the harm done to the land and the declining number of landowners, Rome's ability to field its famous armies was threatened.

The senate tried to address the problem by dividing some public lands among the poor, but this practice affected only a small number of families. Ominously, generals began accepting propertyless men into the legions, promising them farms upon their retirement. These men were, quite naturally, more loyal to their commanders than to the senate, and many Romans began to think that the senate had lost touch with the needs of the people.

As Rome's domain expanded, the Republic lost control of events. The more territory it occupied, the more borders it had to defend. The greater the burdens of defense became, the more power was delegated to military commanders. The more powerful military commanders became, the less willing they were to take orders from the senate. As this sequence spiraled out of control, the advocates of republican rule found themselves isolated.

In 91 B.C.E. the senate defeated a bill to extend citizenship to all Rome's allies in the Italian peninsula. Many of the disappointed allies revolted, and civil war was waged sporadically until 79 B.C.E., when the Roman general Sulla (*SOO-la*) put down the strife and emerged as **dictator**—a tyrant ruling for the duration of the crisis. His seizure of power effectively ended the Roman Republic, although he tried unsuccessfully to restore it and many of his successors claimed to be loyal to it. But the Republic's usefulness was over: it could no longer control its own generals and it had failed to evolve to meet the changing needs of an expanding state. Generals such as Sulla and

Why did the Roman Republic weaken gradually?

Pompey, who served in Spain, pretended to bow to the senate's will while effectively ignoring it. They made their own policy at the far-flung extremities of empire.

Why was Julius Caesar important in Roman history?

Julius Caesar

With the Republic approaching its end, ambitious generals followed Sulla's lead. After Pompey colonized Spain, he used that province as a base for advancing his power. Elected consul in 59 B.C.E., he formed a political alliance, the First Triumvirate, with two other prominent generals, Caius Crassus and Julius Caesar. Caesar enjoyed military success in Spain and also in Gaul (today France), which he used as a power base for splitting the Triumvirate. In 48 B.C.E. he defeated Pompey at the battle of Pharsalus. Pompey fled to Egypt and was murdered there. Three years later, Julius Caesar proclaimed himself dictator of Rome.

Julius Caesar ruled Rome for only one year, but he left an enduring mark on world history. Descended from Rome's original aristocracy, he was educated by tutors and studied oratory and rhetoric in Greece. He blended political ambition with military genius in pursuit of his overriding goal: to restore order to the Greco-Roman world. Caesar accomplished a great deal in his one year as dictator: he revised the Roman calendar, made the senate more representative of the citizenry, and gave discharged soldiers and even the urban poor the opportunity to own a bit of land. A masterful literary stylist whose works are still enjoyed two millennia after his death, Caesar spread Roman culture into the lands he helped conquer. Popular in many quarters for his willingness to implement reforms, he was resented in others for his ambitions and his betrayal of Pompey. He rewarded his non-Italian supporters with Roman citizenship, ensuring their loyalty but angering many citizens of Rome.

As dictator, Caesar was remarkably magnanimous, granting pardons to many of his enemies. Within a short time this generosity destroyed him. On March 15, 44 B.C.E. (the famous "Ides of March"), he was stabbed to death in the Roman Forum by several conspirators, two of whom (Gaius Cassius and Marcus Brutus) were among the opponents he had pardoned. Caesar's assassination terminated the brief stability he had created, plunging Rome into renewed civil strife.

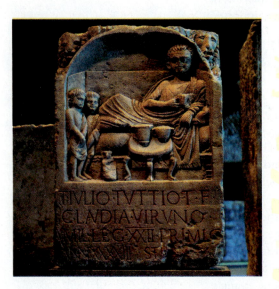

Tombstone of a Roman soldier.

The Birth of the Roman Empire

8.3 Explain how Caesar Augustus created the Roman Empire while protesting that he was doing no such thing.

Caesar's assassination was followed by a struggle for power in which his grand-nephew and adopted son Octavian (ock-TĀ-vē-un) emerged triumphant. Octavian then reshaped the governing institutions of Rome, molding them into a structure that would support his military dictatorship while seeming to remain republican in nature. As Caesar Augustus, Octavian served as a towering transitional figure between the Roman Republic and the Roman Empire.

What strategies did Octavian use in outmaneuvering his rivals to become sole ruler of Rome?

The Rise of Octavian

Caesar's killers were swiftly defeated by his followers, led by the Second Triumvirate: Caesar's eloquent defender Marcus Antonius, immortalized as Marc Antony in Shakespeare's *Julius Caesar*; the skillful and subtle politician M. Aemilius Lepidus; and Octavian, then only 18 years of age. Rome, however, was not large enough for two dynamic leaders such as Octavian and Antony. Lepidus was shunted off to Africa, and Octavian took Rome's western possessions while Antony took Greece, Egypt, and the East. Caesar had dreamed of uniting Rome and Egypt, hoping to transfer his capital eastward. He had courted the Queen of Egypt, the clever Cleopatra VII, last of the Ptolemaic dynasty that had ruled that land since the death of Alexander the Great. Caesar had acknowledged to friends his paternity of her son Caesarion (*seh-ZAIR-ē-un*), born in 47 B.C.E. Now Antony seemed to take Caesar's place, spending the winter of 41–40 B.C.E. with Cleopatra in Alexandria and, in 32 B.C.E., marrying her.

Octavian resolved to destroy Antony, fearing that if Antony became sole leader of Rome, he and Cleopatra would probably subordinate Italy to Egypt. Cleverly Octavian declared war against Cleopatra rather than Antony, mobilizing Rome's forces in a patriotic struggle to preserve Italian supremacy. Antony and Cleopatra responded by urging eastern princes to fight for their liberation from the tyranny of Rome.

In September 31 B.C.E., Octavian's forces defeated Antony and Cleopatra at the battle of Actium (*ACK-tē-um*). The following year Octavian's armies attacked Egypt itself. Antony, hearing a rumor that Cleopatra had been killed, took his own life by falling on his sword; the Queen of Egypt, after her lover's suicide and her empire's defeat, put an asp to her breast and died from its venom. Returning to Rome in triumph, Octavian was hailed as the man who ended decades of civil war. In 27 B.C.E. the senate voted him the title **Augustus**, meaning "one who rules with majesty and grandeur." Octavian now called himself Caesar Augustus.

Octavian's victory shifted Rome's focus toward the east. As Caesar Augustus, Octavian claimed the Egyptian throne and began Egypt's gradual absorption into Roman civilization. Alexandria, which for nearly three centuries had been the world's center of Hellenistic learning and culture, now became subject to Rome. The cultures of the eastern provinces, including Egypt and Syria, were attractive to the Romans. And now with northern Africa and Palestine, Rome's Mediterranean empire was a "Greco-Roman world" and the Mediterranean Sea Rome's *Mare Nostrum* (*MAH-rā NAHS-trum*), "our sea."

From Republic to Empire

At the time, however, Rome seemed the center of the world, and its governance, following 15 years of turmoil, was a matter of some concern. Ironically Caesar Augustus, the first Roman Emperor (27 B.C.E.–14 C.E.), hated dictatorial rule and wanted to restore the Republic. Although he tried to reinvigorate republican institutions, especially the senate, most of his political innovations enhanced his own authority.

Technically Augustus ruled not as king or emperor, but as one man holding a broad variety of republican offices. He served a succession of one-year terms as consul, giving him influence over those who served one year only. The senate appointed him to several magistracies and conferred on him powers normally reserved to tribunes. Thus, as consul, he spoke to the people on behalf of the government, while as tribune he spoke to the government on behalf of the people. All these positions were republican, but they were not designed to be held by one man. Augustus made himself emperor in everything but name, and in so doing he transformed Rome into an empire while claiming loyalty to the Republic.

The Roman Empire evolved gradually. Spain, Germany, the Balkan Peninsula, and much of southeastern Europe fell to Augustus's legions. Virtually the entire coastline of the Mediterranean was Rome's, giving substance to the claim of *Mare Nostrum*. Rome's control of the waves eased communication between the empire's remotest regions, overcoming the administrative problems that distance might have created. Augustus also constructed fortified camps and connected them to one another with well-built Roman roads. These camps extended Roman rule and brought Rome's culture to many parts of continental Europe.

How did the Roman Republic gradually become the Roman Empire?

Caesar Augustus, Emperor of Rome.

The distant regions were inhabited mainly by tribal peoples who spoke Germanic languages and whom the Romans labeled "barbarians." As Rome defeated one tribe after another, Augustus and his successors consolidated their control by offering command positions in Roman armies to the highest-ranking Germanic chieftains and Roman citizenship to some of their most important followers. This clever use of privilege and citizenship to win over the most powerful Germans helped Rome lay the foundations of a truly multiethnic empire while reducing foreign pressure on its extended borders. The result was the *Pax Romana* (*POCKS rō-MAHN-ah*), or "Roman peace." Until his death in 14 C.E., Augustus presided over a stable and prosperous society.

Greco-Roman Culture

What were the principal achievements of Greco-Roman culture?

The *Pax Romana* was founded on a number of interlocking factors: military superiority, Augustus's political skills, integration of foreigners into the empire, and material prosperity. In addition, **Greco-Roman culture**, rich and attractive, helped keep Roman society stable. Rome's familiarity with Greek culture began through contacts with Greek colonies on the Italian peninsula and Sicily, continuing when Rome conquered Greece. For centuries Rome had envied and attempted to imitate Greek arts and letters, in the process preserving Greek literary and philosophical masterpieces and making them known throughout the immense, multiethnic Roman Empire. This cultural transmission was enhanced by the incorporation of Egypt into the empire, especially Alexandria, where a fabulous library contained many Greek manuscripts. Some Greek philosophical schools, such as the Stoics, appealed to the Romans, who appreciated the Stoic insistence on living in harmony with natural forces. Now the "**Augustan Age**," or age of Augustus, brought forth a dazzling display of poetry that rivaled anything produced by the Greeks. Much of it sang the praises of the *Pax Romana* and of the ruler who created it.

Virgil, one of Rome's most noteworthy poets, lived from 70 to 19 B.C.E., long enough to enjoy the early years of the age of Augustus. Using a Greek literary form, the epic poem, Virgil in the *Aeneid* (*ih-NĒ-id*) narrates the legend of Aeneas (*ih-NĒ-us*), a Trojan warrior who fled from Troy as the Greeks sacked it. In the legend, Aeneas makes his way to Italy, where he acquaints early Romans with the ancient splendor of Greece. The *Aeneid* provides an alternative creation story for the origins of Rome, shifting the Roman self-image away from the tough and ruthless descendants of Mars who were nursed by a she-wolf and toward the refined and enlightened bearers of Greco-Roman culture. Virgil portrayed Rome as the benefactor of the known world, enlightening barbarian peoples and staunchly upholding Greek ideals of the good, the beautiful, and the true. The *Aeneid* remains, with the *Iliad* and the *Odyssey*, one of the world's great epics.

Ovid (*AH-vid*) (43 B.C.E.–ca. 17 C.E.), a generation younger than Virgil, wrote for a less learned audience. He immortalized Rome's religious and seasonal festivals in verses that nearly everyone who could read could enjoy. But Ovid was surpassed in popular appeal by Virgil's contemporary Horace (65–8 B.C.E.), whose eloquent, soaring odes praised the accomplishments of Caesar Augustus. All educated Romans, and many learned people since that time, memorized Horace's stirring lines celebrating Greco-Roman virtues and exalting the heroic victories of the noble Romans over the so-called barbarians. In Virgil, Ovid, and Horace, Rome had a trio of poets whose work, by incorporating Greek themes and styles, immortalized Roman civilization.

The language of the Roman Empire was Latin, the language of Latium. Rome's newly acquired subject peoples continued to speak their own languages, but any who wished to take advantage of Roman contacts had to learn Latin. Gradually, Latin became the empire's common language, first of the educated classes and then of ordinary people. Over centuries, many of Europe's languages evolved from it, including French, Italian, Portuguese, Romanian, and Spanish; these are called "romance languages" because of their Roman origins. Latin's dominance demonstrated that Rome's conquests were linguistic and cultural as well as military and economic.

The Romans also made permanent contributions to architecture, and Roman building can still be seen not only in Italy, but also in southern France, Spain, and North Africa. Rome went beyond the graceful pillars of Greek architecture to create enormous domed interior spaces, vaulted ceilings, and arches. Central to these innovations was Rome's invention of concrete, a combination of water, sand, and powdered limestone that provides impressive strength and durability when set. Concrete enabled Romans to create not only buildings of great beauty, but also large sports arenas and utilitarian projects such as aqueducts, long conduits supported by arches that brought fresh water from mountain lakes to lower-lying urban centers, using nothing more than gravity. Many Roman aqueducts still exist 2000 years after their construction, and a few remain in service, a convincing testament to both the durability and the usefulness of Roman architecture.

Roman aqueduct, Segovia, Spain.

Challenges to Augustus's Work

When Augustus died in 14 C.E., Rome was undisputed master of Europe, the Mediterranean, and much of Southwest Asia (Map 8.3). No other state of the day could challenge Rome's control of its empire. There were, however, three factors threatening the stability of Augustus's imperial domain.

Why was Augustus's work challenged soon after his death?

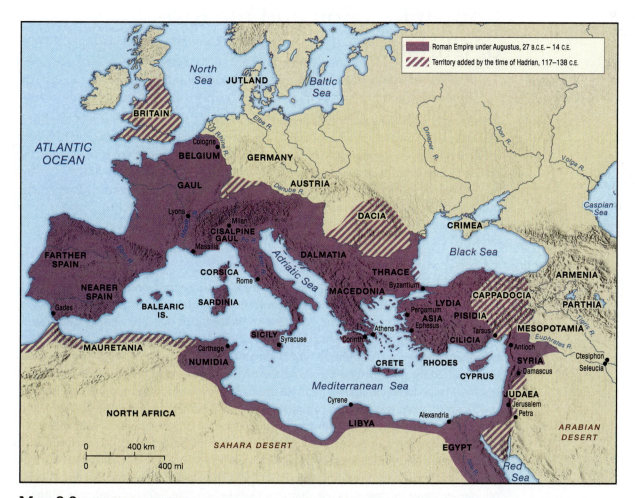

Map 8.3 THE ROMAN EMPIRE, 138 C.E. The Roman Empire, using the conquests of the Republic as a foundation (Map 8.2), expanded into Britain, Dacia, Cappadocia, Thrace, Judaea, and Mauretania. Note that the extent of the empire from northwest to southeast was greater than its extent from east to west. Why would this impressive expansion actually weaken Rome's security and place the continued existence of the Roman Empire in jeopardy?

First, Augustus himself never formalized his position within the empire. Insisting that the Republic would one day be restored, he called himself *princeps civitatis* (PRIN-cheps chi-vē-TAH-tis), "first citizen of the state," a modest title that died with him. His other title, *Imperator*, was purely military in nature, but his control over the army was personal rather than institutional. His generals were loyal to him because of his personal attributes. If future emperors lacked such qualities, the army would destroy them and replace them with more suitable candidates—possibly one of the generals themselves. Augustan rule was personal rather than institutional.

Second, the empire itself was too large. Sea travel on the Mediterranean made possible rapid communication between distant points, and Rome's willingness to purchase loyalty with citizenship and privilege helped it hold the borders for many years, even expanding them northward into Britain. But although the Roman legions constituted an unparalleled fighting force, those borders were too extensive to be held forever by armies of the ancient world. Sooner or later, invaders would probe enough points simultaneously to uncover a weak spot and break through. Skilled leadership could delay but not prevent eventual collapse.

Finally, Rome's expansion and multiethnic diversity brought it into contact with monotheism, which differed substantively from the traditional Roman polytheistic religion. As monotheistic religious beliefs spread throughout the empire, they presented significant challenges to the core values of the Roman world.

Roman Religion and the Rise of Christianity

8.4   **Explain how and why Christianity posed a lethal threat to the Roman Emperor.**

Rome's original belief system reflected what it regarded as the civic virtues of tolerance and cultural pluralism, in which various conquered societies were permitted to retain their own cultures. Roman polytheism also permitted the gods of the conquered to be incorporated into the larger pantheon of Roman deities. Monotheism, however, is by its very nature intolerant of what it considers "false gods." The monotheistic religions of Judaism and Christianity, at first merely irritating to the cosmopolitan Romans, represented serious challenges to a belief system that had served the Romans well.

Rome's Polytheistic Religion

Rome's principal gods, such as Jupiter, Juno, Mars, Neptune, and Bacchus, presided over a great many lesser deities, each identified with some natural or human-made force: Mars was the god of war, Neptune of the sea, and Bacchus of wine. Each god had his or her personal cult of devotions and rituals. If appropriate ceremonies and sacrifices were offered, the god was appeased and would protect the worshipper. Those who ignored the gods earned their wrath, expressed in the form of natural disasters and personal tragedies. Roman religion was another manifestation of fundamental Roman practicality, based not so much on morality as on a contractual relationship with the gods. Those who fulfilled the contract would be rewarded with good fortune on earth.

Polytheism served Rome's complex, sophisticated society well, constituting yet another example of the adaptability of Roman culture. In particular, polytheism's tolerance for previously unfamiliar gods enabled the empire to assimilate conquered peoples without forcing them to abandon their beliefs. Foreign gods, such as Mithras of Persia and Osiris of Egypt, were simply added to the Roman array of deities after their native lands were conquered. All that was expected was that conquered peoples would be courteous enough to respect the festivals of the principal Roman gods,

How did polytheism prove useful to the Roman Empire as it attempted to assimilate conquered peoples?

such as Jupiter, thereby appeasing those gods and deflecting their wrath.

Jewish Resistance and Eastern Cults

When Rome overran Judaea in the eastern Mediterranean region, however, it discovered that Jews, who believed in a single, all-powerful God, were intolerant of all other belief systems and unwilling to participate in Rome's rituals. Perplexed by this conduct, the Romans isolated the Jews, a policy that worked fairly well, since the Jews considered themselves the **Chosen People** and prized their separateness. They had no interest in converting Romans to their own faith and simply wanted to be left alone; the more militant among them hoped that Rome would someday be overthrown or simply go away.

Excavations at Qumran, northwest of the Dead Sea, reveal how the Essenes lived around 150 B.C.E.

The intolerance of the Jews irritated the Romans, and Roman rule embittered the Jews, who revolted on the death in 4 B.C.E. of Herod, a puppet king whom Rome had elevated from among the Jewish people. Augustus sent his legions to put down the insurrection and 10 years later assigned to Judaea an official called a procurator who reported directly to the *Imperator*. Rome attempted to make peace with the Jews by assigning responsibility for Jewish religious matters and local affairs to the Sanhedrin (*san-HED-rin*), the highest Jewish judicial body.

How did Jesus of Nazareth fit into the relationship between Romans and Jews?

Nevertheless, Jews continued to resist Roman domination, especially the taxes that Augustus imposed in order to pay for legions permanently stationed in Judaea. Some Jewish sects, advocating direct action, not only refused to pay taxes but also engaged in serious though futile efforts to dislodge the Romans. Best known among these groups were the Zealots (*ZELL-uts*), who practiced terrorism and assassination not only against Romans but also against Jews who collaborated with the occupying legions. Other sects revived traditional Jewish prophecies of the coming of a Messiah who would liberate God's Chosen People from earthly oppression—in this case, from the Roman Empire. John the Baptist, a desert preacher, prophesied that the Messiah would soon arrive. In contrast to these groups, Jewish apocalyptic sects such as the Essenes (*ESS-ēnz*) concluded that the world would end soon and that pious people should withdraw from public life and prepare for the end.

Simultaneously, interest in Eastern mystery religions was spreading across the Roman Empire, affecting not only Jews but polytheists as well. Alexander's conquests had acquainted Greeks with Eastern cults that promised personal immortality through the sacrifice of a god who had died and risen from the dead. Mystery cults became widely popular in Greece and the eastern Mediterranean region. Rome's absorption of Hellenism spread familiarity with those cults to all parts of the empire, including Judaea. It was in Judaea that Jesus of Nazareth preached.

JESUS OF NAZARETH Born around 4 B.C.E. in Bethlehem, Jesus was raised in the town of Nazareth in the Zealot stronghold of Galilee and was thoroughly familiar with the apocalyptic predictions of the Essenes. But as a man of peace, he disagreed with the Zealots, and his teachings regarding how to live in this world, rather than only preparing for the next, also distinguished him from the Essenes. Jesus, who declared that he did not intend to change Jewish law, was permitted to preach in the synagogue. Like the great Jewish rabbi Hillel (30 B.C.E.–9 C.E.), with whose teachings he was undoubtedly familiar, Jesus taught in texts such as the Sermon on the Mount (see "Excerpt from the Sermon on the Mount") that Jews must love one another as they loved God and treat others as they themselves wished to be treated. A small group of his followers thought he was the Messiah, and Jesus reportedly revealed himself to them as exactly that. But he did not intend to destroy the Roman Empire; he sought to establish a spiritual kingdom, not a political one.

Document 8.2   Excerpt from the Sermon on the Mount

Soon after the beginning of his public ministry in 26 C.E., Jesus of Nazareth spoke from a mountain to a large crowd. His address, as recounted in the Gospel of St. Matthew, has become known as the Sermon on the Mount. It contains many of his most fundamental teachings.

And seeing the multitudes, He went up on a mountain, and when He was seated His disciples came to Him.

Then He opened His mouth and taught them, saying,

"Blessed are the poor in spirit, for theirs is the kingdom of heaven.

"Blessed are they who mourn, for they shall be comforted.

"Blessed are the meek, for they shall inherit the earth.

"Blessed are those who hunger and thirst for righteousness, for they shall be filled.

"Blessed are the merciful, for they shall obtain mercy.

"Blessed are the pure in heart, for they shall see God.

"Blessed are the peacemakers, for they shall be called sons of God.

"Blessed are those who are persecuted for righteousness' sake, for theirs is the kingdom of heaven.

"Blessed are you when they revile and persecute you, and say all kinds of evil against you falsely for My sake.

"Rejoice and be exceedingly glad, for great is your reward in heaven, for so they persecuted the prophets who were before you . . .

"You have heard that it was said, 'An eye for an eye and a tooth for a tooth.'

"But I tell you not to resist an evil person. But whoever slaps you on your right cheek, turn the other to him also.

"If anyone wants to sue you and take away your tunic, let him have your cloak also.

"And whoever compels you to go one mile, go with him two.

"Give to him who asks you, and from him who wants to borrow from you do not turn away.

"You have heard that it was said, 'You shall love your neighbor and hate your enemy.'

"But I say to you, love your enemies, bless those who curse you, do good to those who hate you, and pray for those who spitefully use you and persecute you, that you may be sons of your Father in heaven; for He makes His sun rise on the evil and on the good, and sends rain on the just and on the unjust . . ."

And so it was, when Jesus had ended these sayings, that the people were astonished at His teaching . . .

SOURCE: *The Holy Bible*, The New King James Version (1983), Matthew 5:1–12 and 38–45, 7:28.

Jesus' emphasis on the spirituality of his rule disappointed Jews who hoped that the Messiah would deliver them by force from Roman bondage. Other aspects of Jesus' teachings alarmed more traditional Jews, particularly those connected with the Sanhedrin. To them, Jesus appeared as a radical reformer threatening their established place within the Jewish hierarchy, or as a troublemaker who might provoke their Roman rulers.

There was nothing politically revolutionary in Jesus' thought, but he was clearly an unsettling figure within Judaism. Pontius Pilate (*PUNCH-us PĪ-lut*), Roman procurator of Judea from 26 to 36 C.E., a tough former legionary turned political official, was indifferent to Jewish religious quarrels and concerned solely with the maintenance of peace and order. The crowds acclaiming Jesus in Jerusalem during the Jewish Passover festival in 29 C.E. alarmed him. To avert civil unrest and possible riot and bloodshed, Pilate condemned Jesus to death by crucifixion.

How did Paul of Tarsus develop and spread Christianity?

Paul of Tarsus and the Spread of Christianity

After Jesus' death, unrest subsided in Jerusalem, where his disciples continued to live. Pilate did not attempt to suppress them, assuming they were just one among many different Jewish cults. As rumors began to circulate that Jesus had risen from the dead, however, his followers grew increasingly outspoken. They came to be known as Christians, or those who believe that Jesus was the Christ (a Greek word meaning Messiah).

The head of the Christian sect was Peter, a Galilean follower of Jesus and a man of traditional Jewish beliefs who felt that Jesus' teachings were meant exclusively for Jews. The new sect continued to observe Jewish laws and customs, accepting only circumcised males and people who obeyed Jewish dietary regulations. To these it added new practices such as baptism (in which new members were sprinkled with or immersed in water as a symbol of new spiritual birth) and communion (at which believers consumed bread and wine in commemoration of Jesus' Last Supper with his disciples). Without Paul of Tarsus, Peter's sect might have remained a purely Jewish offshoot, ignored by mainstream Jews.

Paul of Tarsus (a town in today's Turkey) was a Jewish Roman citizen fluent in Hebrew, Latin, and Greek. He helped persecute Christians until, while traveling from Tarsus to Damascus in Syria around 31 or 32 C.E., he experienced a vision that convinced him of the truth of Christian belief. Paul promptly converted to Christianity and, noting that the sect was largely ignored by ordinary Jews, decided to proclaim it to non-Jews, whom the Jews called Gentiles. He taught that Judaism was essentially preparation for the arrival of the Messiah, who by his coming had fulfilled the ancient prophecies and inaugurated a new age. Paul proclaimed that Jesus was not only the Messiah but also the Son of God, and that his teachings were meant for all people on earth.

Traveling and preaching throughout Greece, Turkey, Syria, and Palestine, Paul spread Christianity among the Gentiles. Many, familiar with Eastern mystery religions, embraced the new faith. They were drawn to its forgiveness of sinners who repented, its promise of personal immortality, its emphasis on community, its inclusiveness (e.g., treating women and slaves as the spiritual equivalents of free men), and its message that each individual had a part to play in the completion of God's work on earth. A small, physically unimpressive man, Paul was a compelling preacher whose devotion and intensity inspired many conversions.

Paul's decision to preach to the Gentiles transformed Christianity from a minor Jewish sect into a distinct, dynamic new religion. Insisting that male converts should not have to endure the Jewish rite of circumcision (the Greeks considered circumcision a form of mutilation), he made it possible for people to become Christians without first becoming Jews. Soon Gentile communities of Christians were larger than the original community of Christians in Jerusalem, which persisted in vainly attempting to convince other Jews that the Messiah had come. When Judaea revolted against Rome in 66 C.E., Christianized Jews were accused of collaborating with the Romans, and by the close of the first century it was apparent that Christianity's future lay solely with the Gentiles.

Paul's vision of Christianity as a religion speaking to all humanity distinguished the new faith not only from Judaism but also from other mystery religions. It gave Jesus' message a universal character rather than limiting it to one ethnic group selected by God. The only initiation required was baptism. Within the Roman Empire, Christianity began to challenge polytheism, offering converts a sense of mission and a place in God's plan for the redemption of the world. It also, of course, offered a powerful reward that polytheists considered absurd: eternal life. In time, Christianity's strong appeal and consequent spread transformed the Roman Empire, and the teachings of a Galilean preacher became the foundation of one of the principal religions of the world.

ROME'S VIEW OF CHRISTIANITY   Traditional Roman religion, with its intricate rituals and great range of deities, continued to serve most of the empire's citizens. But Rome's integration of the eastern Mediterranean made it relatively easy for Christianity to spread throughout the region. Paul traveled along well-established trading routes to Greece and Anatolia, while other missionaries carried the new faith to Syria and Egypt. In the northern and western reaches of the empire, however, Christianity encountered indifference bordering on hostility. By 250 C.E. fewer than 10 percent of Romans were Christian.

Nevertheless, imperial authorities distrusted Christianity. Its practitioners owed their allegiance to a king who, although his kingdom was spiritual, seemed to rival the emperor. In addition, unlike public Roman rituals, Christian ceremonies were conducted privately, appearing to be secret and thus potentially subversive. Finally, Christians' intolerance of all other gods and refusal to offer sacrifices to the

St. Mamai of Georgia, a Christian martyred by the Romans, is shown with a cross in one hand while riding a lion, symbolizing his triumph over death and ignorance.

official Roman pantheon—including deceased emperors, whom Romans openly worshipped—threatened the stability of the state.

By the reign of Emperor Nero (54–68 C.E.), Christianity had become enough of an annoyance within Rome itself to provoke this unstable and incompetent ruler to atrocities and persecutions. Between 64 and 312 C.E., several imperial persecutions consigned Christians to martyrdom by fire, beheading, crucifixion, or mauling by wild beasts. Sometimes Christians were slaughtered in front of tens of thousands of spectators in the Colosseum, a large stadium in Rome. Those who died during persecutions were considered by Christians to be holy martyrs. Their memories were honored and their heroism used to spread the new religion even further. But as long as the force and power of the state remained arrayed against it, Christianity could never attract more than a small minority of Romans.

From Golden Age to Disarray

8.5 **Discuss the transition of Rome from its golden age to its decline.**

Nero's relentless pursuit of Christians did not obscure his inadequacies as a ruler. He was so ineffectual that the army ousted him in 68, and two years of political turmoil finally ended with the triumph of Vespasian (*vess-PĀ-zē-un*), a general who abandoned all pretense of ruling a republic and openly established his own imperial dynasty, the Flavians (*FLĀ-vē-uns*).

The next century was the golden age of Rome. By 180 the emperor was recognized as a guarantor of peace, stability, and prosperity. An enormous commercial network integrated the entire Mediterranean basin and attracted trading partners from Asia and Africa. After 180, however, a combination of epidemic disease, political incapacity, and external pressures weakened the empire and left its continued existence in doubt.

Why did Rome become commercially dominant in the Mediterranean basin, and what sort of connections did that dominance create?

The Roman Coliseum.

Commercial Connections and Imperial Expansion

Economic prosperity made it grand to be a Roman citizen during the golden age. The city of Rome itself was exciting. Noisy and cosmopolitan, with a multiethnic population exceeding 600,000, it was the most impressive European city of its time. All citizens received free grain, wine, and oil; those who were not citizens were fed at low, government-subsidized prices. Chariot races, gladiatorial combats, and other athletic contests provided entertainment.

Roman economic productivity increased, and Roman commerce dominated the Mediterranean world (Map 8.4). The Roman Empire after Augustus developed a productive agricultural system. The number of small farms increased, many of them worked by retired military veterans who settled in the regions where they had been stationed. The result was the cultivation of large expanses of rich farmland in Gaul, Britain, and central and eastern Europe, ensuring Romans an abundant supply of food.

The Romans also built an enormous interconnected area of free trade and transport. They developed a system of paved, well-maintained roads connecting Rome to all parts of its vast empire. These roads ensured the regular flow of goods into and out of the city, and of soldiers to frontiers and trouble spots.

Rome's provinces were encouraged to trade not only with the capital but also among themselves. Wine from Gaul and Italy, wool from Britain, olive oil from Syria, and grain from Egypt traveled in Roman ships across the Mediterranean, transshipped at ports connected by land routes to the far-flung reaches of the empire. Prosperity and security stimulated the growth of manufacturing, particularly in northern Europe, which grew to rival Italy itself in the production of glass, pottery, brass, and bronze.

Rome's commercial expansion affected the eastern Mediterranean profoundly. Roman ships cleared the sea of pirates and incorporated it into the empire's

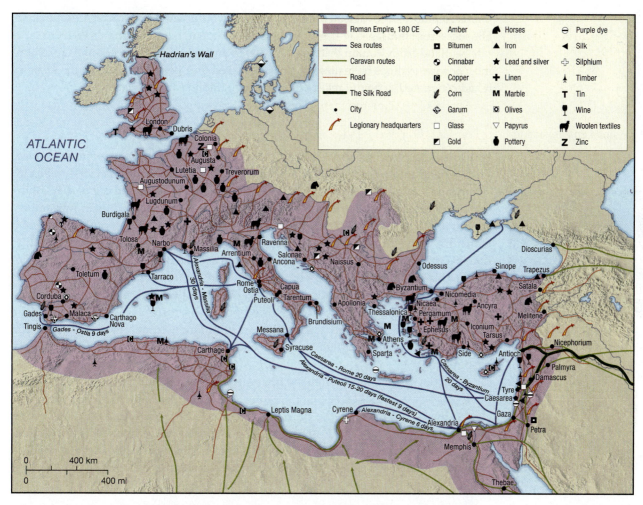

Map 8.4 ROME'S ECONOMIC ORGANIZATION OF THE MEDITERRANEAN WORLD, 180 C.E. The economic linkages forged by Rome united the Mediterranean world into an enormously powerful economic engine. Roman roads, most of them paved with stone, linked cities throughout the empire and connected Rome to caravan routes serving Asia and Africa. Notice that the shipping times indicate how rapidly Roman galleys could cross the Mediterranean. Observe also the large number of products listed in the legend, which demonstrates the complexity of trade within the Roman world. But what does the clustering of legionary headquarters in northern Europe and the eastern Mediterranean suggest about the negative aspects of the extent of the Roman Empire?

commercial network. In addition, Rome used its eastern lands to connect with the Parthian and Sasanian empires, which had consolidated the remnants of the Persian and Alexandrian empires. This easterly orientation that began after Actium brought Rome into contact not only with Persian and Macedonian successor states but also with India and China.

In the second century C.E., Roman mariners sailed regularly from ports in Egypt through the Indian Ocean to the Indus River, trading goods of Roman manufacture for the varied wares of the Indian subcontinent, especially fragrant and flavorful spices. Earlier, in the first century B.C.E., Han Wudi, China's Martial Emperor, had opened the Silk Road between China and the Parthian Empire; in the course of this commerce, Chinese merchants often met their Roman counterparts. Chinese silk and porcelain sold well in Roman markets, and in 96 C.E. China dispatched an ambassador to Roman Syria, where he observed the Greeks and Romans and filed a report of his impressions. But neither Chinese nor Roman rulers concluded that the other civilization had much of interest to offer, and this intriguing set of contacts resulted in nothing that would alter either's view of the world or of itself.

Rome's commercial dominance was complemented by the expansion of the empire to its greatest extent. The Flavian emperor Trajan (98–117), a capable administrator noted for his common sense, defeated the Parthians and occupied Babylon and Mesopotamia. His successor Hadrian (117–138), cautious and prudent, built "Hadrian's Wall" to separate Scotland from Roman Britain (Map 8.4) in an effort to seal the empire's northernmost border; perhaps he realized that Rome lacked the power to defend all the territory it had conquered. If he did realize this, that recognition came too late.

Why did the Roman Empire start to decline?

A modern photo of the Appian Way, part of the network of Roman roads that facilitated travel and commerce throughout the empire.

The Empire in Disarray

Near the close of the second century C.E., the golden age of the Roman Empire ended. The Flavians and their successors, known as the "**five good emperors**," had ruled efficiently and effectively. They kept the army under control, defended the borders of the empire, reformed and revitalized the bureaucracy, and consolidated their own authority. But during the reign of Marcus Aurelius (165–180 C.E.), the last of the "five good emperors," a deadly epidemic of smallpox drastically reduced the empire's population, eventually even killing the ruler himself. To make matters worse, the incompetence of his son Commodus soon plunged the empire into civil war.

In 235 the empire fell under the rule of the so-called barracks emperors, a succession of generals who typically gained power by force and quickly lost it the same way. Between 235 and 284, more than 20 different emperors tried to rule. The administrative structure that Augustus had established degenerated into military despotism.

Such developments would have been dreaded even under normal circumstances, but it was Rome's misfortune that they coincided with intense pressure on its frontiers caused by the migration of the Germanic peoples, whom the Romans called barbarians. In the second and third centuries C.E., some of these Germanic tribes, originating in northern and eastern Europe, began to force their way across the borders of the Roman Empire, attracted by Rome's prosperity and the fertility of the lands it controlled.

Chapter Review

Consequences and Connections

Rome, which began in the eighth century B.C.E. as a tiny city in the midst of the Italian peninsula, eventually assembled an empire that surpassed the Persian Empire in size and wealth. Victory over Carthage gave the Romans dominance over the Mediterranean basin, enabling them to build an extensive trading network that would spread their goods and influence. However, Rome's republican form of government, admirably suited to a small city-state, could not satisfy the demands of a far-flung seaborne empire. Roman generals contended for the right to exercise political power, and in 27 B.C.E. Octavian eliminated his opponents and became "the first citizen of the state."

As Caesar Augustus, Octavian managed the transition from republic to empire by perpetuating the institutions of the former while employing the broad powers of the latter. But Octavian's successors never created a coherent philosophy of government with which to supplant the Republic, and Rome's golden age eventually degenerated into misrule as military dictators sought unsuccessfully to defend lengthy frontiers.

Rome's genius lay in winning conflicts and forging the cooperative connections that often grew out of them. Its legions stormed across the Mediterranean world, conquering all rivals and dominating the region for centuries. Its rulers brought the lands and peoples they defeated into a multiethnic realm that rewarded ability with citizenship. Romans rarely rejected a good idea, taking the achievements and even the gods of their subject peoples and making them their own. The very extent of the empire ultimately doomed it, but it lasted for centuries.

Benefiting from Roman cultural connections, Christianity spread across the Roman world and eventually grew into one of the most influential of the world's religions. Paul of Tarsus transformed the message of Jesus of Nazareth from the belief system of a small Jewish sect into a compelling faith that promised salvation and resurrection to all people. Paul's travels and preaching probably would not have been possible had not Rome united the eastern Mediterranean region and had not Paul himself possessed Roman citizenship.

Eventually, however, the Roman Empire's control of the Mediterranean world weakened. The leadership of the "five good emperors" gave way after 180 C.E. to the military rule of the barracks emperors, marked by power struggles and assassinations. The Chinese principle of the dynastic cycle explained the inevitability of good rulers being succeeded by bad ones and prescribed a change of dynasties as the proper cure for such troubles. But China was not pressed on all sides by the ambitious invaders who sensed Rome's weakness and sought to exploit it.

Reviewing Key Concepts

Roman Republic, p. 147
Senate, p. 148
Law of Peoples, p. 148
Natural Law, p. 148
Struggle of The Orders, p. 148
Roman Citizenship, p. 149

Punic Wars, p. 150
Roman Legions, p. 150
Dictator, p. 153
Augustus, p. 155
Mare Nostrum, p. 155
Pax Romana, p. 156

Greco-Roman Culture, p. 156
Augustan Age, p. 156
Princeps Civitatis, p. 158
Chosen People, p. 159
Five Good Emperors, p. 164

Ask Yourself

1. How did the Roman Republic differ from Athenian democracy? In what ways did the Roman Republic's governing framework respond to the political needs of Romans?

2. How did Rome use citizenship as a tool of governance?

3. How was the Roman Republic transformed into the Roman Empire?

4. How did the Roman Empire's organizational structure facilitate the spread of Christianity? What challenges did this new religion present to Rome?

Key Dates and Developments

The Roman Republic

753 B.C.E.	Traditional date for the founding of Rome
509 B.C.E.	Establishment of the Roman Republic
494–287 B.C.E.	Struggle of the Orders
450 B.C.E.	Law of the Twelve Tables
264–241 B.C.E.	First Punic War
218–201 B.C.E.	Second Punic War; Hannibal crosses the Alps
149–146 B.C.E.	Third Punic War; destruction of Carthage
200–133 B.C.E.	Rome's conquest of the eastern Mediterranean
91–88 B.C.E.	Conflict between Rome and its allies
45–44 B.C.E.	Julius Caesar's dictatorship

March 15, 44 B.C.E.	Assassination of Caesar
44–42 B.C.E.	The Second Triumvirate defeats Caesar's murderers
41–30 B.C.E.	Antony and Cleopatra

The Roman Empire to 284 C.E.

27 B.C.E.–14 C.E.	Caesar Augustus's rule as *Imperator*; conquest of Spain, Germany, southeastern Europe
ca. 4 B.C.E.	Birth of Jesus of Nazareth
29 C.E.	Crucifixion of Jesus in Jerusalem
45–58 C.E.	Paul of Tarsus: preaching Christianity in the eastern Mediterranean
54–68 C.E.	Misrule of Emperor Nero
69–180 C.E.	Rome's golden age
235–284 C.E.	Rule of the barracks emperors; onset of the Germanic migrations

Chapter 9
Germanic Societies and the Emergence of the Christian West, 100–1100 C.E.

EMPEROR CONSTANTINE I Roman Emperor Constantine I, whose vision on the eve of battle is depicted in this painting, legalized Christianity and moved the empire's capital east from Rome to Constantinople. The western part of the empire, including Rome, was then overrun by Germanic peoples who in time developed a new culture, blending Roman, Christian, and Germanic ways to create the Christian West.

After reading this chapter, you should be able to:

9.1 Discuss the nature of Germanic society.

9.2 Analyze how and why the Western Roman Empire declined and collapsed.

9.3 Assess the impact of Germanic peoples and the Christian Church on Early Medieval Europe.

9.4 Discuss the reasons for the decline of the Western Christian Church and show how it recovered.

In 312 C.E., Constantine (*KON-stun-tēn*), son of a Roman emperor who had died in 306, advanced on Rome with an army to secure his own claim to the throne. His main rival, with a much larger army, was blocking access to Rome at the Milvian Bridge. According to legend, as Constantine prepared for battle, he saw in the sky a symbol of Christ and the phrase "In this sign you will conquer." Adopting the symbol as his battle standard, the next day he won a great victory.

The Christian West

Constantine became one of Rome's most pivotal emperors. Interpreting his vision and victory as signs from the Christian God, he legalized Christianity, which had been banned and periodically persecuted since 64 C.E. He moved the empire's capital east from Rome to Byzantium, a city he rebuilt as a grandiose New Rome, soon called Constantinople. And he defended the empire against Germanic peoples who threatened it from the north.

Constantine thus set the stage for Europe's transformation in the centuries that followed. His legalization of Christianity, and its designation by his successors as the Roman state religion, helped make it Europe's main faith, embodied in a wealthy and powerful institution called the Church. And his new capital, Constantinople, reinforced the empire's eastward orientation at the West's expense. The prosperous eastern half of the Roman realm, later called the Byzantine Empire, was ruled from Constantinople for another millennium (Chapter 10). But the western half was conquered in the fifth century by Germanic peoples, whose connections with the Romans and their heritage eventually produced a new civilization, often called the Christian West, combining Germanic and Roman elements with Christian religious beliefs.

The Germanic Peoples

9.1   **Discuss the nature of Germanic society.**

North and northeast of the Roman world were assorted tribal societies, now collectively called Germanic peoples, since most spoke languages in the Germanic branch of the Indo-European language family. These peoples included, among others, Franks, Angles, Saxons, Lombards, Alemanni (*AH-luh-MAH-nē*), Vandals, and Goths (Map 9.1). Their tribal warrior societies, disparaged by Romans as "barbarian," eventually would overrun Rome, Germanicize the Christian West, and help to shape Western civilization.

Germanic Society: Kinship and Combat

Initially the Germans were pastoral nomads who lived in northern Europe by herding, hunting, and fighting. They herded cattle to get meat, milk, and cheese for food and hides for making clothes. They hunted deer and other wild game for additional meat and hides. They made swords and spears from iron, an ore abundant in northern and central Europe, and used these weapons to stage raids and attacks on neighboring peoples. The Germans were not much for commerce, preferring instead to get their goods from raids and warfare.

Germanic societies were based on kinship and patriarchy rather than on territory or formal institutions. Members of each tribe, linked by family connections, saw themselves as an extended clan with common ancestry and heritage. These kinship loyalties frequently led to blood feuds: if an outsider killed a tribe member, the victim's kinsfolk felt bound to get vengeance by killing the murderer or someone from

How were kinship, combat, and patriarchy important in Germanic society?

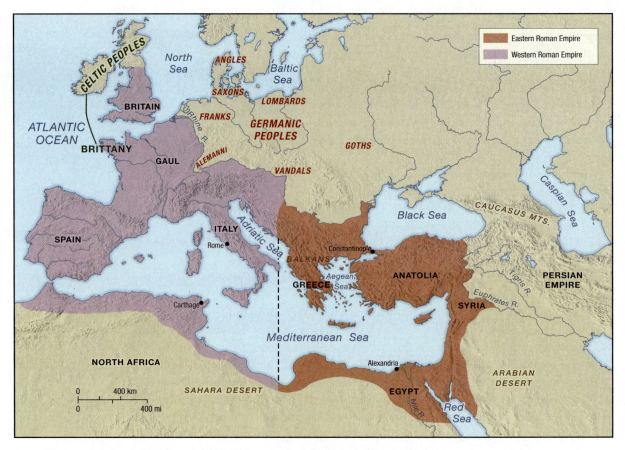

Map 9.1 **GERMANS, CELTS, AND ROMANS, 1ST THROUGH 4TH CENTURIES** c.e. In the early centuries c.e., Germanic peoples connected and conflicted with Celts and Romans. Note that under Germanic pressures, the Celts from Central and Western Europe resettled in what are now Scotland, Wales, Ireland, and Brittany. What advantages did Germanic peoples have in their clashes and contacts with the Romans? Why were the Germanic invasions and infiltrations such a threat to the Roman Empire?

the murderer's clan, often triggering battles between tribes. These tribal connections foreshadowed the notion of **nation**, a political community united by its people's sense of common heritage and culture, which later played a key role in European history.

The tribes were often organized as chiefdoms, ruled by a chief elected by a warrior assembly. Attached to the chief by bonds of mutual loyalty, the warriors were expected to protect him with their lives or die with him in battle. Eventually some chiefdoms matured into monarchies, with the chief becoming king and his warriors the nobles who served on his royal council. Germanic tribal structure thus helped to shape later Europe's stratified societies, dominated by warrior-kings and nobles.

Much as male warriors ran Germanic societies, senior males dominated Germanic families. In these patriarchal households, women were valued mainly for their reproductive roles and service to male warriors. Men of status could have more than one wife, and fathers could sell their daughters in marriage to whoever made the best offer. The women's main role was to support the men, who fought the wars that protected the society and secured the food that sustained it—a function and relationship that prevailed throughout much of European history.

Like most other early societies, Germans were polytheistic, worshipping numerous gods and goddesses who personified aspects of the world around them. The main deities included Woden (*WŌ-dun*), creator of the earth and sky; Tiu (*TĒ -oo*), the god of war; Thor, the god of thunder; and Friia (*FRĒ-uh*), the goddess of fertility and love. Although Germans later became Christians and abandoned these deities, their names would survive in Anglo-Saxon weekdays such as Tuesday (Tiu's day), Wednesday (Woden's day), Thursday (Thor's day), and Friday (Friia's day).

Sometimes the Germans called on divinities to decide legal issues brought before the chief and his assembly. Believing that the gods would protect a guiltless person from harm, the chief might order a trial by ordeal, putting the defendant to a test to determine innocence or guilt. An accused woman, for example, might undergo ordeal by fire: if she walked through flames without being burned, she would be considered innocent. Or, when faced with conflicting testimony, the chief might have an accused man face his accuser in combat, typically with swords. This practice endured into the Christian era, when it took the form of a duel, in which combatants appealed to "God's judgment" to bring victory for the side embodying justice and truth.

Judicial duel.

Germanic Migrations and Their Threat to Rome

In the last few centuries B.C.E., while Rome built its Mediterranean empire, many Germans began moving south into central and western Europe, driven perhaps by food scarcity resulting from population growth. By the first century C.E., attacks by Germans and Romans had displaced from these regions the peoples who spoke Celtic (*KELL-tik*) languages (another branch of the Indo-European family), lived in farming villages and fortified towns, and worshipped numerous gods served by priests called Druids (*DROO-ids*). As Celtic tribes resettled in what are now Scotland, Wales, Ireland, and Brittany (in western France), Germans moved toward the Roman frontiers, where they increasingly took up farming and interacted with the Romans (Map 9.1).

The Germans thus became more settled but no less warlike. They came to reside in villages, where they lived in wooden huts and grew wheat, oats, and barley on the surrounding lands. Women did much of the fieldwork and most household chores, boiling grains to make thick gruel, grinding them into flour for flat, baked bread, and fermenting them into lush, hearty beer that has long been beloved by Germans. The men helped with planting and harvesting but still hunted and herded, made war on other tribes, raided Roman towns and farmlands, and even fought the famed Roman legions.

The Romans countered these **Germanic migrations** partly by fighting the German "barbarians" and partly by seeking to assimilate them. Roman leaders recruited many Germans as soldiers, awarded German leaders with command positions, and sometimes even made them Roman citizens. In so doing, the empire secured the services of its foes but also brought growing numbers of Germans into the Roman armies. As Germans thus increasingly bore much of the empire's defensive burden, they began to believe they should enjoy some of its riches. The pressure on the empire from Germans in its armies was further compounded by war among German tribes. The losers, forced off their lands, typically moved toward the fertile soils and wealth of the Roman world.

Beset by internal power struggles during the third century, the Romans proved unable to pacify the Germans, who invaded and raided at will. Hence, by the late third century, the Roman Empire was in serious danger.

What were the Germanic migrations, and how did they affect the Celtic Peoples, Germanic peoples, and the Roman Empire?

The Decline of the Western Roman Empire

9.2   Analyze how and why the Western Roman Empire declined and collapsed.

In the late third century, to deal with the crisis, Roman rulers divided the empire into eastern and western sectors, hoping to make it easier to defend. This division, however, combined with the capital's eastward relocation from Rome to Constantinople in the early fourth century, strengthened the eastern sector at the West's expense. In the fourth and fifth centuries, while Christianity replaced polytheism as the empire's main religion, the West was wracked by continued Germanic invasions, culminating in the fall of Rome and the end of the **Western Roman Empire**.

The Divided Empire and Its Eastern Orientation

Why and how did Diocletian divide the Roman Empire, and what were the impacts of this division and Constantine's construction of a new capital?

In the third century c.e., as noted in Chapter 8, a prolonged crisis shook the Roman Empire. Increasing Germanic attacks coincided with internal revolts that proclaimed as emperor more than 20 different generals within 50 years (235–284), bringing to power "barracks emperors" more focused on fighting for power than defending the frontiers. In the West, repeated German raids and infiltrations disrupted commerce and caused social chaos. In the East, the Sasanian Persians drove the Romans out of Mesopotamia. The Roman world seemed in disarray.

But desperate times produced an exceptional leader in 284, when Diocletian (*dī-uh-KLĒ-shun*), a soldier who had risen through the ranks, seized power as Roman emperor. Faced with continual revolts and invasions, he concluded that the empire was too vast for one man to rule alone. So he divided it along a line running north and south between Italy and Greece (Map 9.1), keeping himself in charge of the East and naming a co-emperor to administer the West. Later he added a junior ruler to assist each emperor, creating a four-ruler system called a tetrarchy (*TET-rar-kē*). For a while this reform seemed to work, enabling the leaders to restore order and fight invasions more effectively.

Diocletian's retirement in 305, however, led to a new power struggle, eventually won by Emperor Constantine I (312–337), whose 312 victory at Milvian Bridge is noted at the start of this chapter. He restored the empire's unity, defeating all rivals and emerging as sole ruler by 324. He also shored up its defenses, enlarging the army and stationing more forces along the frontiers. And he moved the capital east from Rome to Byzantium, where he built a splendid New Rome that came to be called Constantinople.

In many ways the new capital's site was superb. Surrounded by water on three sides, the New Rome was much easier to defend than the old Rome in the West. Situated astride the trade routes connecting Europe with Asia, Constantinople flourished for centuries, both as the seat of imperial power and as a great commercial and cultural center. The new capital's location strengthened the realm's wealthy eastern sector politically and militarily. But the change of capitals also relegated the less prosperous West to secondary status, portending its continuing decline under ongoing Germanic onslaughts.

The Triumph and Transformation of Christianity

How did Christianity triumph within the Roman Empire, and what accounts for its transformation?

Constantine's reign also heralded the triumph of Christianity, which by then had gained a large following despite Roman persecutions (Chapter 8). After his vision and victory in 312 at Milvian Bridge, Constantine strongly supported the Christian faith. He was not at once baptized a Christian, in part because as emperor he was high priest of Rome's polytheistic state religion. But he legalized Christianity in 313, played an active role in its affairs, and was baptized into it before he died in 337, preparing the way for its later adoption as the empire's official religion.

Constantine's delay in accepting baptism reflected Rome's ambivalence toward the Christian faith. Like its parent Judaism, Christianity was monotheistic and intolerant of all other gods and religions. Roman officials did not demand that Christians adopt polytheism, only that they pay homage to the Roman gods and then worship in their own way as other cults and creeds did. But Christians refused to participate in the Roman state religion, thereby defying imperial authority. To many Romans they thus seemed narrow minded, intolerant, and disloyal.

By Constantine's time, however, many Romans were losing faith in the traditional gods, who were supposed to protect the empire in return for Roman performance of proper rituals. As German invasions continued, it was obvious these rituals were not working, and devotion to the old gods steadily declined.

Meanwhile Christianity gained influence. Its promise of potential salvation for all, whatever their social status, attracted many converts among women and the urban poor. Constantine's military success, achieved in the name of Christianity, showed Romans that it could perhaps protect imperial interests better than the old gods did. His legalization of Christianity hence met little opposition, even among prominent polytheists, whom Christians called pagans ("country-dwellers"), since many lived on rural estates.

It also helped advance the Christian faith, so much so that in 380 a later emperor, Theodosius (*thē-uh-DŌ-shus*) the Great, issued a decree that made it the official state religion, and pledged to punish those who failed to follow its teachings. Christianity was thus trans-

Statue of Constantine I

formed, within a few generations, from a persecuted movement with little power and wealth into a powerful and wealthy institution called the Church. Theodosius and his successors supported this Church by banning pagan worship, closing temples to Roman and Greek gods, and even ending the Olympic Games, which had been held to honor Greek gods for more than a thousand years. In return, the Church became a pillar of the Roman state, calling on Christians to support imperial leaders (see "Decree Making Christianity the Official Roman Religion").

Document 9.1   Decree Making Christianity the Official Roman Religion

In 380 C.E., Emperor Theodosius the Great issued the following decree, making Christianity the Roman state religion and promising to punish those who disagreed with Christian teachings. How was Christianity transformed from a persecuted sect into a state church that persecuted other beliefs?

It is our desire that all the various nations which are subject to our Clemency and Moderation, should continue in the profession of that religion which was delivered to the Romans by the divine Apostle Peter, as it hath been preserved by faithful tradition; and which is now professed by Pontiff Damasus and by Peter, Bishop of Alexandria, a man of apostolic holiness. According to the apostolic teaching and the doctrine of the Gospel, let us believe in the one deity of the Father, the Son and the Holy Spirit, in equal majesty and in a holy Trinity. We authorize the followers of this law to assume the title of Catholic Christians; but as for the others, since, in our judgment, they are foolish madmen, we decree that they shall be branded with the ignominious name of heretics, and shall not presume to give to their conventicles the name of churches. They will suffer in the first place the chastisement of the divine condemnation, and in the second the punishment which our authority, in accordance with the will of Heaven, shall decide to inflict.

SOURCE: Henry Bettenson, ed. *Documents of the Christian Church*, 2/e. Copyright © 1962 Oxford University Press, UK. Reprinted with permission.

The Church also organized itself along Roman imperial lines, with numerous priests as its local agents and above them **bishops**—Church officials who presided over districts called dioceses (*DĪ-uh-sis-iz*). Atop this hierarchy was the bishop of Rome, also known as **pope** (from the Latin for "father"), who headed the Church much as Roman rulers headed the empire, and who acted as the vicar (or agent) of Christ on earth. The popes saw themselves as successors to Peter, leader of Christ's disciples, whom Christians considered the first head of the Church. Pope Celestine (*suh-LES-tēn*) I (422–432) even asserted that the pope held the "keys of the kingdom of heaven," which Christ had entrusted to Peter (see "Bible Passage on 'The Keys of the Kingdom'").

Document 9.2   Bible Passage on "The Keys of the Kingdom"

In this passage from the Christian scriptures, Jesus promises to build his Church upon his disciple Peter (whose name means "rock") and to give Peter "the keys of the kingdom of heaven." How could the popes later use this passage to claim that, as Peter's successors, they held the keys to eternal salvation?

Now when Jesus came into the district of Caesarea Philippi, he asked his disciples, "Who do men say that the Son of Man is?"

And they said, "Some say John the Baptist, others say Elijah, and others Jeremiah or one of the prophets."

He said to them, "But who do you say that I am?"

Simon Peter replied, "You are the Christ, the Son of the living God."

And Jesus answered him, "Blessed are you, Simon Bar-Jona! For flesh and blood has not revealed this to you, but my Father who is in heaven.

And I tell you, you are Peter, and on this rock I will build my church, and the powers of death shall not prevail against it.

I will give you the keys of the kingdom of heaven, and whatever you bind on earth shall be bound in heaven, and whatever you loose on earth shall be loosed in heaven."

SOURCE: *The Bible*, Revised Standard Version, Matthew 16:13–19 (New Revised Standard Version Bible), copyright 1989, Division of Christian Education of the National Council of the Churches of Christ in the United States of America. Used by permission. All rights reserved.

Thus developed the concept of **papal primacy** (supremacy of the pope), later to become Church doctrine, which held that the pope had authority over the whole Christian Church. Claiming to be vicars of Christ, a poor preacher who said his kingdom was "not of this world," the popes paradoxically headed a Church with great wealth and power in this world. Their claims of papal primacy also fueled discord with eastern Church leaders—a discord deepened by the empire's east–west division and by growing German domination in the West.

Crisis and Chaos in the West

What were the main aspects and effects of the confrontation between the Western Roman Empire and its Germanic opponents?

Christianity's triumph coincided with the empire's disintegration, as Constantine's successors proved unable to preserve its unity or protect it from Germanic invasions. After Constantine's death in 337, his sons divided the empire anew and fought among themselves, initiating decades of sporadic civil wars and succession struggles. On several occasions the realm was reunified, but not for long. By the century's end, it effectively had become two separate states: an Eastern and a **Western Roman Empire**, each with its own ruler.

The empire's vast size continued to compromise efforts to defend it. The Romans could defeat either the Germans in the West or the Persians in the East, but not both. Since a normal day's march was 20 miles, and since 2000 miles separated the western and eastern frontiers, Roman armies could not move quickly back and forth. Sooner or later, the empire's enemies were bound to wear it down on one frontier or the other.

Persia in the East, though a formidable foe, was a single state with specific lands and borders to defend; Romans there could thus focus their forces against a well-defined adversary. But in the West were many German tribes with ill-defined homelands who often struck in several places at once. And the Germans, with their nomadic roots, were flexible and mobile: when defeated in battle, they simply moved elsewhere to attack.

Facing this danger, Constantine's successors sought valiantly to stabilize the West. Some took a forceful approach: Emperor Valentinian I, who ruled in the West from 364 to 375, imposed heavy taxes for imperial defense and led large armies north into France (then called Gaul) and Germany to crush Germanic forces. Other emperors pursued assimilation, trying to pacify warlike tribes by giving them farmlands on Roman frontiers while employing their best warriors and generals in the Roman legions.

Such efforts might have worked had not a new threat emerged in the fourth century. Around 370, the Huns, aggressive nomads probably related to the Xiongnu who tormented China, swept in from Central Asia and attacked the Goths, Germanic peoples living north of the Black Sea (Map 9.2). The eastern Goths, or Ostrogoths (*OST-ruh-goths*), fell to the Huns and were ruled by them for eight decades. The western Goths, or Visigoths, were driven south into the Balkan Peninsula, where they defeated Roman armies in 378. Theodosius the Great (379–395), the Roman ruler who made Christianity the official religion, bought them off by giving them lands in the eastern Balkans, where they settled and converted to the Christian faith.

After Theodosius died, however, his sons split the empire (which their father had reunified) between them and angered the Visigoths by not giving a Roman command post to Alaric (*AL-uh-rik*), their gifted young leader. The Visigoths rebelled, moved south into Greece, and later invaded Italy. The Western Roman Empire fought them

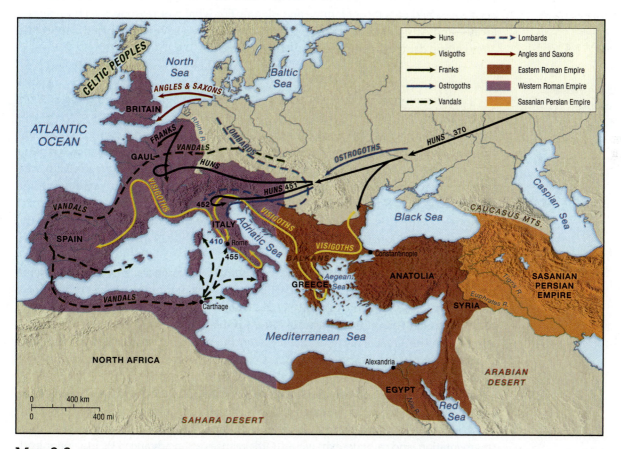

Map 9.2 HUNNIC AND GERMANIC INVASIONS, 370–500 C.E. Beginning around 370 C.E., invading Huns from Central Asia drove Germanic peoples to the west and south, leading to further invasions of Roman lands. Note that Visigoths invaded Italy and sacked Rome in 410, that Huns invaded Central Europe in the 450s, and that Vandals attacked Rome by sea in 455, setting the stage for its fall in 476. Why was the Western Roman Empire unable to withstand these onslaughts?

off for a time in northern Italy with forces led by Stilicho (*STILL-ih-kō*) the Vandal, a Germanic general who emerged as Rome's most effective commander. But then the Roman leaders, distrusting Stilicho because of his ambitions and his Germanic heritage, accused him of treason and beheaded him in 408, depriving the realm of its finest commander at an hour of maximum danger.

Angered by news of Stilicho's alleged treason, Romans massacred hundreds of Germans living in the Western Empire, including Germans who were Roman soldiers and their families. Many German soldiers who escaped swore vengeance and joined Alaric, whose army grew to exceed 30,000 men, while the Western Empire lacked an effective commander. Alaric asked for a Visigothic homeland in return for his army's commitment to defend the empire. Distrusting the Germans, the Romans refused, so in August 410 the Visigoths attacked Rome itself—and for the first time in eight centuries the city fell to foreigners. After sacking the city, Alaric's forces moved south in search of further plunder, but their leader died of an illness later that year.

The pope saw Alaric's death as God's punishment for the sack of Rome; the Goths attributed it to his having eaten some spoiled meat. Either way, the resulting respite for the Romans proved brief. In 434 a warrior named Attila (*uh-TILL-uh*) became leader of the Huns, and in 441 he began threatening the Eastern Roman Empire. Constantinople bought him off with tribute, so in 451 he turned west.

Attila the Hun, called the "scourge of God," was brutal—but so were most warriors of his day. As the Huns devastated northern Italy, fear spread that they would move south and lay waste to Rome itself. This fate was avoided in 452 when Pope Leo the Great, venturing north from Rome to the Huns' encampment, met Attila and apparently persuaded him to withdraw. Possibly Attila learned from his scouts that Constantinople had sent an army to attack the Huns; probably Attila's forces had been weakened by a recent famine and plague. For whatever reasons, the Huns turned away—and Attila died in his sleep the next year from a severe nosebleed, reportedly after getting drunk to celebrate his own wedding.

The Fall of Rome and End of the Western Roman Empire

How and why did the Western Roman Empire collapse?

Rome had been saved from the Huns, but the Western Roman Empire's crisis continued. Germans continued to invade, often meeting little resistance, driving into Britain, Gaul (France), Spain, northwestern Africa, and Italy itself (Map 9.2). Interregional commerce, hampered by constant warfare, virtually vanished in the West, as did collection of imperial revenues. People subsisted in self-contained local economies, with little access to goods or information from other parts of the empire. Commerce still flourished in the East, but in the West connections increasingly unraveled.

The Western emperors could no longer control the provinces or even defend Rome itself. The Vandals sacked the city in 455, marking the beginning of the end. Twenty-one years later, a Germanic general called Odoacer (*Ō-dō-Ā-sur*) forced the abdication of a boy named Romulus Augustulus (*ROM-yoo-lus ah-GUS-tyoo-lus*), the last Roman emperor in the West. This action completed the process, begun by Diocletian and Constantine, of reorienting the Roman Empire to the east. In the West, with Rome itself in German hands, the empire ceased to exist in 476 C.E.

Historians have long debated the reasons for the **fall of Rome**. Chief among them clearly were the empire's overextension, which made it hard to defend both East and West, and the Germanic incursions, which disrupted commerce and brought chaos, fragmentation, and military exhaustion. Other causes often advanced include poor leadership and lack of clear succession systems for selecting emperors, deadly epidemics in the second and third centuries, social tensions caused by economic and agricultural decline, a growing gap between rich and poor, and even the rise of Christianity, which some say weakened the Romans by making them more humane.

Technically, of course, the Roman Empire did not end in 476. Having lost its former capital and western provinces, it nonetheless endured in the East for almost another millennium. Emperors reigned in Constantinople until 1453, claiming all the while to rule the Roman Empire.

Yet the end of the empire in the West did bring momentous changes. Ravaged and then ruled by the Germanic "barbarians," Rome ceased to be a center of imperial authority. In succeeding centuries the popes, who as bishops of Rome held the most prestigious post remaining in the West, would assert secular as well as spiritual authority, placing the Christian Church at the center of European culture, politics, and society. And with Germans controlling Rome, the rulers in Constantinople, later called Byzantine emperors, could no longer exercise authority in the West. Although it would take centuries for Europeans to recognize this reality, the Western Roman Empire was gone, and the future of the West would hence be shaped by its Germanic conquerors.

Early Medieval Europe: Germanic and Christian Connections

9.3   **Assess the impact of the Germanic peoples and the Christian Church on Early Medieval Europe.**

In Europe the period from the fall of Rome through the fourteenth century, since it came between ancient and modern times, is called the Middle Ages, or **medieval** (*mē-dē-Ē-vul*) era. In the **Early Middle Ages** (fifth through eleventh centuries) European societies, dominated by Germanic tribes that had overrun the Western Roman Empire, were characterized by tribalism and localism. In central and western Europe, Roman cities, roads, trade, and money fell into disuse. Learning and literacy declined, interregional commerce dwindled, and central administration virtually disappeared.

Eventually, however, conflict and fragmentation in the West helped foster creative new connections. Europeans gradually developed a new culture, blending Germanic and Celtic customs with Christian beliefs and remnants of the Roman heritage. In the early 800s, a Germanic empire reunited much of the West, but it soon disintegrated and Europe was beset by new nomadic invasions and raids from the north, east, and south. Nonetheless, by the eleventh century, led by a landed warrior nobility and an energized Christian Church, Europe experienced a political and cultural revival.

The Emergence of Germanic Kingdoms

How did dynastic monarchies emerge in Germanic Europe?

At the start of the Middle Ages, the Germans were still grouped in tribes, united by kinship and ruled by chieftains typically elected from among the strongest warriors. Although hunting and fighting remained central, most tribes by this time practiced farming, dwelling in villages and tending crops and herds. Families remained patriarchal, dominated by male heads of household, with women in supportive roles. Men tended cattle and raised grains such as wheat and barley, while women ground the grain, baked bread, and helped work the land. Wealth was measured in cattle and land, often acquired by the warriors, who thus formed an early kind of rural nobility.

As farming increased food supplies, supporting population growth, some Germanic groups—including Ostrogoths and Lombards in Italy, Visigoths in Spain, Angles and Saxons in England, and Franks in what is now France—set up **Germanic kingdoms** (Map 9.3). Unlike tribes, which were groups of people, kingdoms were

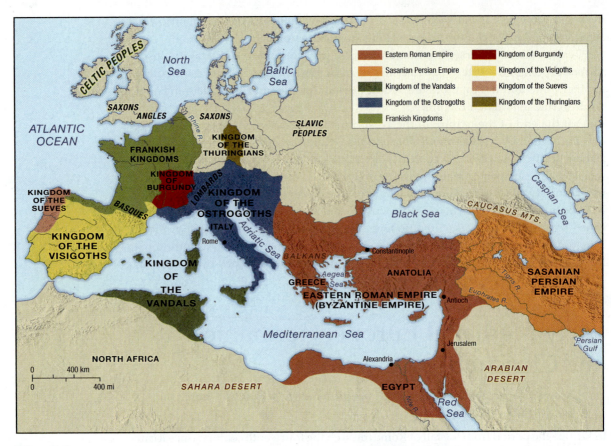

Map 9.3 GERMANS DIVIDE THE WEST INTO KINGDOMS, 5TH AND 6TH CENTURIES C.E. In the 5th and 6th centuries, as they overran the Western Roman Empire, Germanic peoples divided its lands into separate kingdoms. Notice, however, that the East remained united under the Eastern Roman (or Byzantine) Empire. How did Germanic rule affect the culture and religion of the former Roman West?

large units of territory, ruled by monarchs often chosen from the same royal family, or dynasty. The national monarchies that later grew out of these kingdoms eventually became Europe's main form of governance.

The Early Medieval Church: Expansion and Adaptation

What roles did monasticism play in the development of Western Christian society?

The central institution of the **Early Middle Ages**, however, was not Germanic kingship but the Christian Church. Led by the popes in Rome, the Church won the allegiance of the Germans and Celts, preserved elements of learning from the Roman era, cared for the poor and the sick, and provided religious unity in the midst of political fragmentation. By maintaining its Roman heritage, while adapting the Christian faith to Germanic and Celtic cultures, the Church also helped to shape a new European society.

The Church strove to Christianize the Germans and Celts, usually by working through tribal chiefs or kings and by blending Christian beliefs with local customs. In the mid-fifth century, a bishop from Britain named Patrick, who as a youth had been a slave in Ireland, used this approach to convert that island's Celtic tribes. Around 496 King Clovis of the Franks adopted Christianity, reportedly after prayers to his Christian wife Clotilda's God helped him win a great battle. In 597 a Roman monk named Augustine (*AW-gus-tēn* or *ah-GUS-tin*), heading a mission sent by the pope to convert the Anglo-Saxons in England, began by baptizing one of their kings and several thousand of his people. Later, after Ireland and England became Christian strongholds, Irish and English missionaries promoted Christianity elsewhere in Europe.

In adopting Christianity, however, Celts and Germans did not abandon their traditional ways. Instead, with Church approval, they converted their old shrines into Christian churches and modified their festivals into Christian holy days. Rather than praying for good fortune to their traditional gods, the people now asked Christian saints to help them gain God's blessings. Rather than conducting trials and ordeals based on tribal ritual, priests and bishops now presided at them in the name of Christ. The Christian faith was thus adapted to fit Celtic and Germanic cultures.

In adjusting to these rural tribal cultures, Western Christianity increasingly diverged from the urbane cosmopolitan Christianity of the Byzantine East. Aware of the growing gap, the Church in the West sought to preserve some semblance of Christian learning and Roman culture, especially in Christian monasteries.

Medieval Europe thus was shaped by **monasticism** (*muh-NASS-tih-siz-um*), a movement in which devout men (called monks) and women (called nuns) withdrew from secular society to live in religious communities (monasteries for monks and convents for nuns), where life was characterized by prayer and self-denial. During the Middle Ages, Christian monasteries played a prominent role in Western scholarship, education, agriculture, hospitality, charity, and health care. They worked effectively to spread the Christian faith, and later to reform the Christian Church.

Although Christian monasticism had emerged earlier in Egypt, its most influential Western expression was developed by Saint Benedict (480–543). An earnest and devout young man from a wealthy family, Benedict withdrew from urban Rome's affluence to live in poverty and prayer in the wilderness, in time attracting other men to join him as monks. He eventually founded a monastery on a hill called Monte Cassino and wrote for the monks a *Rule*, or set of regulations for monastic life, which his sister Scholastica (*skuh-LASS-tih-kuh*) later adapted for women. Throughout the Middle Ages, the *Rule* of Saint Benedict would set the standards not only for his followers, known as Benedictines, but also for most other Western monastic communities (see "Excerpts from the *Rule* of Saint Benedict").

In keeping with Benedict's *Rule*, monks and nuns took vows of poverty, chastity, and obedience, pledging thereby to forsake personal possessions, abstain from sex, and fully submit to their monastic superior. They lived in communities based on equality and hard work: whether sons of nobles or slaves, monks were expected to labor in the fields and live lives of self-denial. They promoted learning by setting up local schools, maintaining libraries, writing books, and copying religious manuscripts. They advanced agriculture by clearing swamps and woods and by implementing new farming methods. They provided charity for people in need, hospitality for travelers, and sometimes even health care for the sick. In a fragmented and dangerous world, monasteries provided a safe haven for prayer, learning, farming, and charity. They also promoted Christian beliefs throughout Europe, with significant assistance from the rulers of the Franks.

Abbey of Monte Cassino, on the site of Saint Benedict's first monastery.

Document 9.3   Excerpts from the Rule of Saint Benedict

In founding his monastic movement, Saint Benedict (480–543) wrote a Rule, a set of regulations for monks, which his sister Scholastica adapted for nuns. As reflected in the following excerpts, how does this Rule prescribe a life of poverty (rejecting personal possessions), chastity (repressing "desires of the flesh"), and obedience (submitting to one's superior)?

Holy Scripture, brethren, cries out to us, saying, "Everyone who exalts himself shall be humbled, and he who humbles himself shall be exalted" (Luke 14:11) . . .

The first degree of humility, then, is that a person keep the fear of God before his eyes and beware of ever forgetting it. Let him be ever mindful of all that God has commanded; let his thoughts constantly recur to the hell-fire which will burn for their sins those who despise God, and to the life everlasting which is prepared for those who fear Him. Let him keep himself at every moment from sins and vices, whether of the mind, the tongue, the hands, the feet, or the self-will, and check also the desires of the flesh . . .

As for self-will, we are forbidden to do our own will by the Scripture, which says to us, "Turn away from your own will" (Eccles. 18:30), and likewise by the prayer in which we ask God that His will be done in us . . .

And as for the desires of the flesh, let us believe with the Prophet that God is ever present to us, when he says to the Lord, "Every desire of mine is before You" (Ps. 37:10). We must be on our guard, therefore, against evil desires, for death lies close by the gate of pleasure . . .

The second degree of humility is that a person love not his own will nor take pleasure in satisfying his desires, but model his actions on the saying of the Lord, "I have come not to do My own will, but the will of Him who sent Me" (John 6:38) . . .

The third degree of humility is that a person for love of God submit himself to his Superior in all obedience, imitating the Lord, [who] ". . . became obedient even unto death."

. . . Let no one presume to . . . have anything as his own—anything whatever, whether book or tablets or pen or whatever it may be—since they are not permitted to have even their bodies or wills at their own disposal . . . Let all things be common to all, as it is written (Acts 4:32), and let no one say or assume that anything is his own.

SOURCE: *The Rule of Saint Benedict.* Copyright © 1948 by The Order of Saint Benedict, Inc. Published by Liturgical Press, Collegeville, Minnesota. Reprinted with permission.

The Franks and Their Effort to Reunite the West

How were Charlemagne and the Franks able to reconnect much of Europe?

The Franks had the most expansive Germanic kingdom. King Clovis (481–511) not only accepted Christianity but also expanded his domain to include most of what is now France and western Germany (Map 9.3). His heirs, less capable than he, eventually let an official called the mayor of the palace run their affairs. One such mayor was Charles Martel, who in 732 or 733 defeated Muslim forces near Tours (*TOOR*) in central France (Chapter 11), thereby gaining fame as Europe's savior from Islamic conquest. He also supported Benedictine monks from England, led by Saint Boniface (*BAH-nih-fiss*), in their efforts to Christianize Central Europe. In return, Boniface anointed Martel's son Pepin (*PEP-in*) as King of the Franks in 751, helping him take the throne from an ineffective ruler. Charles Martel's descendants, later called the Carolingian (*kar-uh-LIN-jun*) dynasty (from *Carolus*, Latin for Charles), thus came to rule the Frankish realm.

These events set the stage for the remarkable reign of Pepin's son Charles (768–814), known as "Charles the Great," or Charlemagne (*SHAR-luh-MĀN*). Standing well over 6 feet tall in an age when most men were much shorter, Charlemagne was the most commanding and successful of the early medieval warrior-kings. In a pivotal series of conflicts, he conquered the Saxons in northern Germany, the Lombards in northern Italy, and various other Germanic peoples; he also took land from the Muslims in northeastern Spain and the

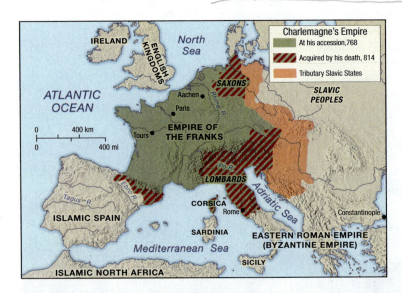

Map 9.4 CHARLEMAGNE'S EMPIRE REUNITES THE WEST, 768–814 C.E. Charlemagne, as ruler of the Franks, created an empire that reunited much of western and central Europe. Note, however, that his empire was Germanic, not Roman, with its capital in the north at Aachen [Aix-la-Chapelle] rather than in Rome. How did Charlemagne differ from the former Roman rulers, and how did his empire differ from the former Roman realm?

Byzantines in eastern Europe (Map 9.4). He thereby reunited most of western and central Europe for the first time since the fall of Rome.

The symbolic climax of Charlemagne's career was provided by the pope. In 799, attacked by his enemies in Rome, Pope Leo III (795–816) escaped and found refuge in northwestern Germany with Charlemagne, who then restored the fugitive pope to the papacy (office of the pope) in Rome. Leo soon found a dramatic way to express appreciation and to assert the Church's political authority. On Christmas Day 800, as Charlemagne knelt in worship during a visit to Rome, the pope suddenly crowned him "Charles Augustus, . . . Emperor of the Romans." It looked as if the Roman Empire had been revived in the West.

But the **Empire of the Franks** was not the Roman Empire. Charlemagne's realm, vast as it was, was still a Germanic kingdom. Its capital was not in Rome but at Aachen (*AH-ken*)—also known as Aix-la-Chapelle (*EX-lah-shuh-PELL*)—in northwestern Germany. Its center was not the Mediterranean Sea but the Rhine River; its rulers were not Romans but Franks; and its emperor, for all his talent, was a semiliterate warrior-king. Indeed, Charlemagne's coronation horrified the Byzantine rulers at Constantinople, who regarded their realm as the real Roman Empire and resented the new Germanic imitation of it in the West.

Undeterred, Charlemagne strove to consolidate and educate his empire. He compelled the Saxons and other polytheists in his realm to adopt Christianity. Aided by Alcuin (*AL-koo-in*), a learned English Benedictine monk, he assembled scholars who copied manuscripts, founded libraries, and set up schools at monasteries and cathedrals throughout Europe. Alcuin's curriculum, divided into a *trivium* (*TRIV-ē-um*) of grammar, rhetoric, and logic, and a *quadrivium* (*kwah-DRIV-ē-um*) of arithmetic, astronomy, geometry, and music, became the standard for medieval European education.

Charlemagne's efforts, however, had limited long-term impact, as very few people received an education. By this time most people in the West spoke Germanic dialects, which later evolved into languages such as German and English, or regional offshoots of Latin, which developed into languages such as French, Italian, and Spanish. Only the literate elite, mostly monks and Church officials, could read and write formal Latin, which remained the language of learning throughout the Middle Ages.

Furthermore, after Charlemagne died in 814, his empire did not long endure. In 843 his three grandsons, after fighting among themselves, divided the realm into three kingdoms (Map 9.5). The middle kingdom soon fragmented further, while the western one went on to form the basis for medieval France, and the eastern one the basis for medieval Germany.

Charlemagne's chapel at Aachen (Aix-la-Chapelle).

What new connections were created in the West by the Vikings, Muslims, and Magyars?

Vikings, Muslims, and Magyars: Invasions and Connections

Christian Europe after Charlemagne also experienced new invasions. In the ninth and tenth centuries, it was assaulted by outsiders, coming first by sea from the north and the south and later by land from the east. Although these invaders pillaged towns and ravaged the countryside, they also helped create new connections between Europe and other cultures.

By sea from the north came Norsemen, or Vikings, seafaring warriors who exploded out of Scandinavia in the ninth and tenth centuries, propelled perhaps by growing population and scarcity of food. With superior seamanship and shallow-draft ships, using both sails and oars, they ravaged

Map 9.5   CHARLEMAGNE'S GRANDSONS DIVIDE HIS EMPIRE, 843 C.E.
After Charlemagne died in 814, his empire remained intact for only a generation. Observe that his grandsons divided up the realm in 843, with Charles the Bald taking the west, Lothair the center, and Louis the German the east. How did this division affect the future development of western and central Europe?

Viking ship.

Europe's coasts and rivers, plundering towns for booty and slaves and pillaging churches and monasteries for precious vessels and vestments.

But the **Viking invasions** were not always destructive. Many Norsemen settled along European coasts, trading with Muslims and Byzantines and eventually adopting Christianity. Some Norsemen, known as Normans, took control of the region now called Normandy in northwestern France, from which their successors in 1066 conquered England and became its kings and nobles. Other Norsemen, called Varangians (*vuh-RAN-junz*), reportedly served as early rulers of Kievan Rus (*KĒ-ev-un ROOS*), the first Russian state, which forged commercial and religious connections with the Byzantine Empire (Chapter 10). Still other Norsemen explored the North Atlantic, founding settlements in Ireland, Iceland, Greenland, and even for a time on the coast of North America (Map 9.6). Like so many great conquerors and invaders, the Norsemen produced extensive devastation and consequential connections.

By sea from the south came Muslims, also known in Europe as Saracens (*SAIR-uh-senz*). In the mid-ninth century, seaborne marauders from Islamic North Africa staged

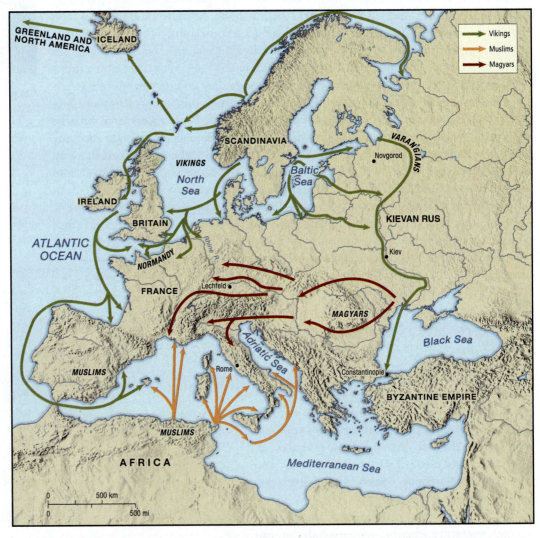

Map 9.6 VIKING, MUSLIM, AND MAGYAR INVASIONS, 9TH AND 10TH CENTURIES C.E. In the 9th and 10th centuries, Europe was hit by attacks from all directions. Note that Vikings came by sea from the north, ravaging coastal and river settlements from western Europe to Russia, while Muslims came by sea from the south and Magyars by land from the east. How did these invasions, which brought widespread destruction, also help to expand commercial and cultural connections?

periodic raids along Europe's Mediterranean coast. Unlike the earlier Muslim warriors defeated by Charles Martel, who came to conquer lands and spread Islam, the skillful Saracen sailors came to plunder, even pillaging the city of Rome in 846. Still, these Muslim raiders, by plying sea routes between Europe and North Africa, helped create a basis for commercial connections between the Islamic and Western Christian worlds.

By land from the east came Magyars (*MAH-jarz*), warlike tribes that moved into eastern Europe in the late ninth century and raided central Europe in the tenth, pillaging towns and plundering the land. In 955 they were defeated in a decisive battle at Lechfeld (*LEK-feld*) by King Otto I (936–973), ruler of the Frankish domains in Germany. Settling in what is now Hungary, the Magyars, later called Hungarians, adopted Christianity and combined their Eastern culture with Western Christian ideals. Their conqueror, known as Otto the Great, was crowned by the pope as emperor in 962. Claiming connections with the Christian Church of Rome and the imperial Roman heritage, Otto and his successors were called Holy Roman Emperors—although they were really Germanic warriors whose realm was mostly German, not Roman.

Germanic warriors in fact proved vital to Europe's eventual recovery, but this recovery relied on regional warlords rather than on monarchs ruling large domains. Their security shattered by outside raiders and invaders, and their hopes for unity dashed by the dissolution of Charlemagne's empire, Europeans increasingly looked to warrior nobles to protect their society.

Europe's Warrior Nobility: Protection, Land, and Power

How and why did central power in Europe decline, and how did regional warlords fill the void?

Responding to the invasions and political fragmentation of the ninth and tenth centuries, Europeans developed a new set of arrangements to restore the security and stability needed for a farming economy. Rather than submit to a strong central state, like the Roman or Frankish Empire, they depended for defense on autonomous regional warlords. Connected by complex allegiances and sustained by landed estates, these warlords developed into a hereditary landed nobility.

Although rooted in the warrior assemblies that long had served Germanic chieftains, the landed nobility arose directly from the ruins of the Frankish realm. To administer their vast domain, the Franks had divided it into counties, each managed by a count, and later also created large duchies, regions directed by dukes. As central authority waned in the decades after Charlemagne's death, these counts and dukes eventually became autonomous warlords. Treating their positions as hereditary, they amassed landed wealth and assembled powerful armies.

With the onslaught of outside invaders in the 800s and 900s, lesser lords and landowners accepted the protection of these great warlords and became their **vassals**, subordinate warlords who swore allegiance and pledged military service to a higher lord, their overlord. In return for such service, the overlords often gave their vassals grants of land called fiefs (*FĒFZ*). In the absence of strong central government, these warlords exercised political and military power on the local and regional level. Strengthened by their warrior status and sustained by their possession of land, they evolved into hereditary nobles. Typically comprising less than 5 percent of the population, they exercised enormous influence based on their family's rank and status, the extent of their landholdings, the size of their armies, and the number of their vassals.

Warfare was central to the status and family life of the medieval nobility. The lords (noblemen) fought wars, training for combat and hunting between conflicts to sustain their military skills, while the ladies (noblewomen) managed the households, caring for children and supervising servants so the lords could hunt, train, and fight. Noblemen served on horseback as **knights**, armed mounted warriors whose code of conduct entailed strict devotion to their overlords and to the Christian Church. As early as age 7, looking forward to future knighthood, boys in noble families were taught by their fathers to ride horses, to hunt, and to use bows and arrows, swords, shields, lances, and armor. Girls in noble families often also learned to ride and hunt, but they were trained mainly for marriage, motherhood, and household management, duties that typically precluded most women from engaging in combat.

Although later observers characterized the arrangements between lords and vassals as a comprehensive system called **feudalism**, there was really no set system or consistent feudal order. Instead there were numerous individual agreements, often quite different from each other, creating an extremely complex web of relationships. Many vassals, for example, served several lords, based on separate agreements with oaths of service to each. Most lords in turn served as vassals to higher lords. A count, for example, might be a powerful lord with vast landholdings and numerous vassals of his own, but he might also be the vassal of a duke, who might in turn be the vassal of a king. Thus, during wartime, a count and his vassals could be called into service of a duke who had been called into service of a king. Yet medieval kings, despite their lofty status, were not absolute rulers: they depended on the support of their vassals, the noble warlords, some of whom might have stronger armies than the king.

Economy and Society: Manors, Lords, and Serfs

What was peasant life like under medieval European manorialism?

The nobles, occupied with military duties, did not raise their own food. Instead, their **manors**, or landed estates, were worked by peasant farmers. Under this arrangement, later called **manorialism**, each noble typically owned at least one manor. Some were huge, with a massive castle and vast stretches of forest and field; others were much smaller. But even the lowest noble was the lord of his manor and master of all who dwelt there. The peasants, who lived on the manor in a village and farmed the surrounding fields (Figure 9. 1), were typically required to give the lord a portion of their crop, and perhaps labor several days a week on land set aside to feed the lord and his family. The peasants thus supported the lord so he could fight, providing some protection and security in a dangerous world.

The peasants, who made up 80 to 90 percent of the population, varied widely in status. Some remained free, and a few even prospered. Most, however, became **serfs**, bound to the manor and under the control of its lord. Without the lord's permission, serfs as a rule could not own or inherit property, leave the manor, or even get married. Unlike slaves, serfs supposedly had rights—they did not have to serve in the army, they were not supposed to be bought and sold apart from the land, and the lord was expected to provide them with plots of land to farm. In practice, however, **serfdom** differed little from slavery: there were few restraints on the lord, who could punish his serfs for perceived transgressions by flogging and beating them, sometimes even to death.

Peasant life centered on fields, family, and church. Men mainly worked the land and tended the herds, the mainstays of economic life. But women played numerous crucial roles, grinding grain, baking bread, brewing beer and ale, curing cheese, cooking meals, making clothes, raising children, and often also helping to care

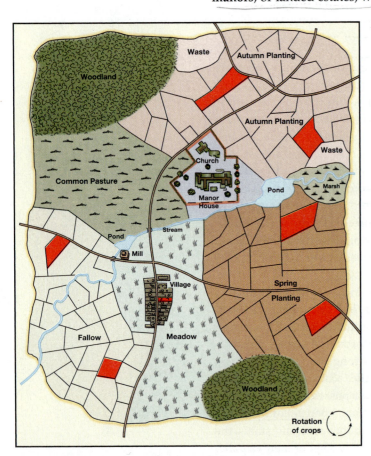

Figure 9.1 DIAGRAM OF A MEDIEVAL MANOR. On a typical manor, the lord and his family lived in a large manor house, while peasants lived in a separate village. Each peasant family had a hut in the village and strips of land in each surrounding field to farm, as shown by the hut and strips of one family shaded here in red. Each year crops were rotated according to a three-field system, with one field planted for spring-summer crops, another for autumn-winter crops, and a third left fallow (uncultivated) to regenerate its soil.

for animals, cultivate fields, and harvest crops. Peasants ate mostly dark bread, supplemented by cabbage and carrots, peas and beans, and perhaps eggs and cheese, washed down with wine, beer, or ale. Some peasant families had wood or brick homes with two or more rooms; others lived in one-room windowless huts with dirt floors, thatch roofs, and walls of mud or clay. Peasants got no formal education, rarely traveled beyond the manor, and had few diversions aside from celebrating baptisms, weddings, and holy days at the village church—their main link to the larger Church and hence to the outside world.

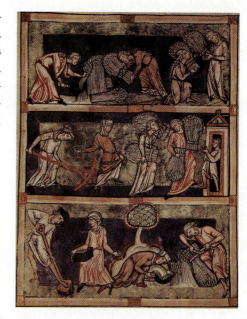

Medieval peasant women helping with the harvest and grinding grain into flour.

The Decline and Revival of The Western Church

9.4   **Discuss the reasons for the decline of the Western Christian Church and show how it recovered.**

Despite its exalted status, by the tenth century the Church in the West was in trouble. In some ways its problems were symptoms of success, since its great wealth and power attracted unscrupulous men to its service, fostering corruption and intrigue. In other respects the decline of the Church was connected with the rise of the regional warlords, who often managed to gain control over local Church offices. The lords used their power to fill Church positions with relatives and supporters, at times even selling these positions to the highest bidder. Chosen thus for loyalty and not ability, and provided with little education, local priests were often illiterate and incompetent, while bishops were frequently dishonest and corrupt. In Rome the papacy itself was controlled by powerful local clans, who secured the selection of their family members and agents. A series of scandalous popes led lives of open debauchery, commanding neither influence nor respect.

From Scandal to Reform

In 963 Pope John XII (955–964), a dissolute man who had become pope through his powerful father's influence, was deposed by a council of bishops for adultery, incest, and murder. Declaring the council illegal, he violently reclaimed his throne, only to die soon thereafter—reportedly from a stroke suffered during an adulterous affair, or from a beating by his lover's angry husband.

What reforms helped the Western Christian Church revive in the eleventh century?

Eighty years later, Pope Benedict IX, another immoral man who became pope through his father's influence, was ousted by the people of Rome, who replaced him with their own choice as pope. The next five years (1044–1049) saw a rapid succession of popes, as Benedict regained the papacy, sold it to another man, and then later claimed it back. In the meantime, Holy Roman Emperor Henry III placed several of his handpicked German bishops on the papal throne.

This sorry spectacle actually marked the onset of the Church's revival. The Germans installed by Henry III were the first of a number of reforming popes, many of whom had close connections to Cluny, Europe's most influential monastery. Founded in the tenth century, this French Benedictine monastic institution had been made subject directly to the pope to free it from the control of local rulers and nobles. Known for their piety and rigor, its monks by 1050 had founded more than 60 daughter houses, all ruled by the mother house at Cluny. Its leaders pushed openly for Church reform, calling for strict priestly **celibacy** (*SELL-ih-buh-sē*), or abstinence from marriage and sex, and an end to **simony** (*SIM-uh-nē*), the sale of Church offices. The popes who were connected with Cluny resolutely attacked Church abuses, restoring the papacy as Europe's preeminent institution. Their efforts had far-reaching consequences.

What caused the Great East–West Schism of 1054?

The Great East–West Schism of 1054

One crucial consequence of this papal revival was to reinforce the growing rift between Eastern and Western Church leaders. Ever since Rome had fallen to Germanic tribes, the cosmopolitan Christians of the Eastern Roman Empire had found it hard to accept the supremacy of the Church in the West, increasingly run by Germanic leaders the Easterners saw as "barbarians." The four main centers of the Eastern Church—Constantinople, Antioch, Jerusalem, and Alexandria—were each led by a patriarch who saw himself as equal to the pope, who was bishop of Rome. In the interest of Church unity, the Eastern patriarchs had often been willing to accept the pope as "first among equals," but they resented papal claims to overall supremacy.

By the eleventh century, moreover, these long-standing frictions had worn away their willingness to compromise, and recent papal scandals had intensified their disdain for the papacy and the Western Church. Now the new reforming popes, in an effort to attack abuses, were asserting even greater powers and claiming unlimited primacy over the whole Church. The Eastern patriarchs found these papal assertions offensive and threatening.

A climax came in 1054, when the patriarch of Constantinople issued an insulting letter to a Western bishop that found its way to the dying Pope Leo IX (1049–1054), who then sent envoys to Constantinople to press the patriarch for an apology. Although Leo died several weeks after they arrived, the envoys had several tense meetings with the patriarch and then issued an edict of "excommunication," formally banning him from Christian worship and from the Christian community. The patriarch responded with a similar edict against the papal envoys.

This episode produced an enduring split between Eastern and Western Christendom, often called the Great East–West Schism or **Great Schism of 1054**. Although deepened by long-standing disputes about the wording of the official creed (profession of beliefs) approved during Constantine's reign, the rift was actually rooted in the conflict concerning whether the pope should have total supremacy over the entire Church. The division was not really caused by a single event, but rather by a series of political, cultural, and theological developments occurring over many centuries. The result was the emergence of two separate branches of Christianity: an Eastern Orthodox religion over which the patriarchs and Byzantine emperor presided, and a Western, or Roman Catholic, Church, ruled by the pope in Rome.

How did the increasing power of the popes help revitalize the Western Christian Church?

The Power of the Popes

As divisive as it was, the schism freed the papacy from its involvement in affairs of the Eastern Church, thereby allowing subsequent popes to focus on reform in the West—and to assert their authority over all other Western religious and political leaders. The stage was thus set for conflict between the Roman popes and Europe's secular rulers.

In 1059, to ensure that future popes would not be chosen by powerful families or rulers, Pope Nicholas II decreed that new popes must henceforth be elected by a group of specially designated bishops called cardinals. In 1073, the cardinals elected a radical reformer named Hildebrand who had spent time at Cluny. As Pope Gregory VII (1073–1085), he extended the concept of papal primacy into secular affairs, holding that all lords and princes were his subjects and that he could depose or punish them if he judged their conduct immoral. To free the clerics who served the Church from family attachments and distractions, he made celibacy the rule for all priests and bishops in the Western Church. And he insisted that only the pope could appoint Church officials.

This attack on corruption and insistence on papal appointment directly threatened Europe's kings and lords, who were used to selecting loyal supporters as bishops in their realms. When Gregory banned **lay investiture**, a practice in which secular ("lay") rulers conferred on new bishops the symbols of spiritual authority, the German emperor Henry IV openly defied him, refusing to forsake this practice. The pope responded in 1076 by excommunicating and deposing Henry, giving German nobles a convenient pretext to rebel against him. Alarmed but inventive, in January 1077 the deposed emperor went to Canossa in Italy and reportedly stood barefoot in the snow to beg forgiveness of Gregory, who was compelled as a priest to pardon the penitent prince. Henry thus regained his title and later even drove Gregory into exile. But the specter of an emperor humbling himself before the pope nonetheless reinforced the notion of papal authority over secular rulers, paving the way for an even more sensational exercise of papal power.

In 1095 Pope Urban II, a former Cluniac monk and disciple of Gregory VII, dramatically proclaimed a great crusade, or holy war, calling on Europe's lords and princes to restore Christian control over "holy lands" in Palestine where Christ had lived and died. Urban's call touched off a series of crusades that created further connections and conflicts between the Germanic West and the Byzantine and Muslim worlds (Chapter 16).

Chapter Review

Consequences and Connections

The Germanic migrations and division of the Roman Empire transformed the West. The German tribes attacked, infiltrated, and eventually ended the Western Roman Empire, replacing it with their own tribal institutions, developing over time into territorial kingdoms. Despite sporadic efforts to restore the empire in the West, central authority waned and Roman institutions fell into disuse. Political, social, and economic life became largely regional and rural, dominated by warlords who also controlled the land. The peasant farmers who tilled the soil eventually sank into serfdom, effectively forsaking freedom in return for security and protection.

The main exception to this decentralization was the Christian Church, which remained based in Rome despite the end of the Western Roman Empire. The Church's administration, modeled on the old empire's, helped preserve some central authority in the West, while the Church's monasteries helped sustain a semblance of Latin learning. In the absence of other strong central institutions, the Church became Europe's dominant religious and cultural organization, with the popes who led it wielding vast religious and political power. In converting and incorporating the Germans, however, the Church in the West was altered by their culture and customs. Eastern Christians hence found it hard to accept the leadership of the Germanicized West, which they considered culturally inferior. Eventually Christianity split into Western and Eastern Churches.

In the West, as the warrior nobles and manorial economy helped restore stability following the Viking, Muslim, and Magyar invasions, a reformed and reenergized papacy asserted its authority over secular rulers. In the East, although the Eastern Roman Empire survived, it too developed new institutions and ideals, forming the basis of what would later be called the Byzantine world.

Reviewing Key Concepts

Ask Yourself

1. What were the main characteristics of Germanic societies? How and why did they connect and conflict with the Roman Empire?

2. Why were the Romans unable to protect the western part of their empire from the Germanic invaders? How did the empire's division contribute to the fall of the West?

3. How did Christianity become the Roman Empire's main religion? How did this change in status transform the Christian Church?

4. Why did the Western Church become medieval Europe's central institution? How did it adapt to Germanic cultures? How and why did the Western and Eastern Churches diverge?

5. Why did Europe's warrior nobility become so powerful in the ninth and tenth centuries? What were the main roles of lords, vassals, manors, and serfs?

Key Dates and Developments

100s–200s	Early Germanic attacks on Roman territory
284–305	Reign of Diocletian (division of the Roman Empire)
312–337	Reign of Constantine (building of Constantinople)
380	Proclamation of Christianity as the Roman state religion
410	Sack of Rome by Alaric and the Visigoths
432	Beginning of Patrick's efforts to Christianize Ireland
451–453	Invasion of Italy by Attila and the Huns
476	Abdication of the last Western Roman emperor
496	Adoption of Christianity by Clovis and the Franks
529	The *Rule* of Saint Benedict
597–605	Augustine's efforts to Christianize England
732 or 733	Defeat of Muslim forces by Charles Martel at Tours
768–814	Reign of Charlemagne, formation of Frankish Empire
843	Division of Frankish Empire by Charlemagne's grandsons
800s–900s	Viking, Magyar, and Saracen invasions
1054	Schism of 1054 (Eastern Orthodox vs. Roman Catholic)
1073–1085	Reign of reforming Pope Gregory VII (Hildebrand)
1095	First Crusade proclaimed by Pope Urban II

Chapter 10
The Byzantine World, 284–1240

THE BASILICA OF SAINT SOPHIA, CONSTANTINOPLE Interior of the former Basilica of Saint Sophia in Constantinople, a Byzantine church converted to a mosque in 1453. Notice the domed Romanesque architecture and imagine the impression such a magnificent building would have made on citizens of Constantinople during the Byzantine Empire.

After reading this chapter, you should be able to:

10.1 Show how the Byzantine Empire continued the governing traditions of Greece and Rome.

10.2 Examine the ways in which the East Roman Empire completed its transition to become the Byzantine Empire.

10.3 Explain how the Byzantine Empire coped with medical, military, and cultural challenges.

10.4 Describe the Byzantine Empire's quick revival and account for its even swifter decline.

10.5 Analyze the significance of Kievan Rus's conversion to Eastern Christianity.

Justinian, the ailing Roman emperor's nephew and recently appointed co-ruler, prepared to enter a magnificent church on April 4, 527. It was the day of his formal coronation. At his side was his wife, Theodora, who would be crowned as empress. The imperial couple were greeted by black-robed priests who covered them in clouds of fragrant incense. Once inside the church, Justinian and Theodora proceeded slowly through a throng of guests down a long aisle leading to the main altar. Waiting there was another group of priests, robed in cloth-of-gold and wearing jeweled crosses and rings. These priests stood in front of a glittering screen made of gold and silver; on it paintings of holy men and women of early Christianity were displayed. Choirs chanted hymns and prayers as Justinian and Theodora knelt, beginning the six-hour ceremony.

Byzantine Claims in Europe

Kievan Rus

The Byzantine Empire

Justinian was crowned Roman emperor, but his coronation took place hundreds of miles east of the city of Rome. The ceremony took place in Constantinople, the "New Rome" founded in the fourth century by Emperor Constantine I. Rome itself was conquered by Germanic invaders in 476, and only the eastern portion of the empire survived. There a new society evolved, preserving Rome's heritage but grounded in its own variant of Christianity and its own conception of the relationship between political and spiritual authority. The realm would be known as the Eastern Roman Empire and later as the Byzantine Empire, after the old city of Byzantium on which Constantinople had been built. Situated where Europe and Asia meet, the Byzantine world, often called simply Byzantium, blended elements of East and West but was truly part of neither.

Still, the empire's eastern rulers, however distinct their civilization was becoming, had no intention of writing off the western half. For centuries they would claim it and occasionally succeed in temporarily retaking portions of it. The Byzantine Empire endured without the West for a thousand years. And even after it declined, its legacy lived on in Russia, which in the tenth century adopted Eastern Christianity and joined the Byzantine world.

The Foundations of Byzantine Governance

10.1 Show how the Byzantine Empire continued the governing traditions of Greece and Rome.

When Constantine legalized Christianity (Chapter 9) he did not know that he would soon be compelled to resolve its internal disputes and thereby assume leadership in the Christian Church. And when moving his capital to Constantinople, he scarcely envisioned that the empire's western section would eventually fragment into separate Germanic kingdoms, leaving only the eastern portion intact. But these events set in motion trends that allowed the Eastern Roman Empire to develop separately, with governing structures substantively different from those in the West.

How and why did the Emperor Constantine intervene in the affairs of the Christian Church?

Constantine and the Christian Church

No sooner had Constantine become sole emperor in 324 than he became involved in a serious dispute among Christians. For a decade or so, an Egyptian Christian priest named Arius (AIR-ē-us) had been preaching that since God had created Christ,

God the Father was older than and superior to God the Son. This perspective differed from the prevailing Christian belief that the Father, Son, and Holy Spirit were coequal persons of the Blessed Trinity. Arius's teaching, which his opponents branded a **heresy**—a religious opinion contrary to accepted Church doctrine—left the Christian Church sharply divided. In fact, the Arian Heresy, as it was called, threatened to produce a **schism**, or division of the Church into separate, competing churches.

Constantine was perplexed: why should anyone want to quarrel about something that was irrelevant to everyday life and could never be proven or disproven? He instructed the opposing parties to settle the issue amicably. But this advice enraged both sides, provoking Constantine into calling an ecumenical (*eck-ū-MEN-ih-kull*), or worldwide, council of Christian bishops and theologians. It convened in 325 in the Byzantine town of Nicaea (*nī-søĒ-uh*), near Constantinople (Map 10.1), with the emperor himself presiding.

Assuming the role of practical counselor in matters of religion, Constantine intended to enforce uniformity within the Church to which he did not formally belong but with which he sympathized. His presence at Nicaea demonstrated that he was in charge, and he shaped the council's findings in a manner that satisfied the great majority of bishops. The Nicene Creed, a statement of belief drafted by the council that is still recited today in many Christian churches, declared that Christ was "of the

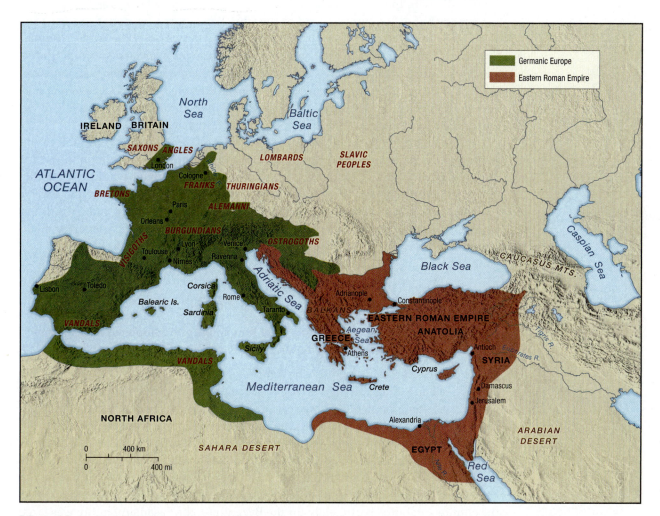

Germanic Europe	
Eastern Roman Empire	

Map 10.1   THE EARLY BYZANTINE EMPIRE, 481 C.E. After Constantine reoriented the Roman Empire eastward, Germanic tribes gradually overran the western portion of the realm. Following the abdication of the last Western Roman emperor in 476, only the Eastern Roman Empire, known as the Byzantine Empire, remained. Notice that the Byzantine Empire controlled the prosperous commercial region of the eastern Mediterranean. How might this location have assisted the Byzantines in defending the legacy of Rome?

same being" as God the Father. A few delegates, including Arius, refused to sign this creed; they were expelled from the council and exiled by the emperor.

The Union of Church and State

What is caesaropapism, and how did it develop?

Constantine's forceful intervention in the Council of Nicaea illuminates how governance would develop in the East Roman Empire. While Western institutions were influenced by Germanic concepts of kingship, the Byzantines amplified the authoritarian legacy of the caesars. Their political institutions were also derived in large measure from the monarchist principles of Alexander the Great and his successors, in which the ruler was exalted above all. For example, the East Roman emperor was referred to as "lord of the world." After Emperor Theodosius the Great proclaimed Christianity the official religion of the empire in 380, he and future rulers were called "equal of the Apostles." The interchangeable use of these two titles reflected the combination of secular and spiritual authority in one man.

In Constantinople, the rulers embraced Christianity fervently. The emperor was considered God's vice-regent on earth, a sacred person who headed Church as well as state and who acted with both divine and human authority. This was the Byzantine concept of **caesaropapism** (*sē-zar-ō-PĀ-pizm*), the vesting of all spiritual and political authority in a single person—a man who served as both caesar and pope. It contrasted profoundly with the position taken by the bishop of Rome, who claimed no political supremacy but called himself head of the Christian Church (or pope) and used his spiritual authority to curb the ambitions of kings and princes after the Western Roman Empire collapsed in 476. In the East, however, patriarchs exercised spiritual leadership over Christian communities equivalent to that exercised by bishops in the West. Each of the four Eastern patriarchs—of Constantinople, Antioch, Jerusalem, and Alexandria—considered himself equal to the bishop of Rome and subject solely to the emperor in Constantinople, the true leader of the Christian Church.

In the emerging Byzantine world, then, Church and state were united in the person of the ruler. In relocating the capital of the empire, Constantine infused it with the spirit of a new, dynamic faith that half a century later would become the empire's official religion. These actions revolutionized both government and society in the Eastern Roman Empire, accelerating the decline of paganism and embedding Christianity in the popular culture. This all-embracing, vigorous Christianity made caesaropapism work and laid the foundations of Byzantine governance.

From East Rome to Byzantium

10.2 Examine the ways in which the East Roman Empire completed its transition to become the Byzantine Empire.

In the two centuries following Constantine's death in 337, the Roman Empire's western section gradually gave way to Germanic pressure and its own internal weaknesses—and the stability of the eastern part was by no means ensured. First, religious problems continued to distract the empire. In 361 Emperor Julian (361–363) tried to revive paganism and reverse the trend toward Christianization. For his actions he was called "the Apostate"—a person who abandons a religion and returns to a previous belief system. Julian's return to paganism might have led to civil war had he not been killed fighting the Persians in 363. Sasanian Persia constituted a second threat to the empire's stability. Fortunately for the Byzantines, the Sasanian Empire was large and cumbersome, and if it sent too many soldiers against Constantinople, it risked uprisings among non-Persian peoples along its own eastern frontiers.

As Germans overran the West Roman Empire in the next century, Constantinople survived, too strategically situated and too well defended to be attacked directly.

When the West Roman Empire collapsed in 476, the East Roman Empire was holding off the Ostrogoths in southeastern Europe. Constantinople could not have dispatched a powerful army to save Rome without endangering itself. Now only the Eastern portion of the empire remained. Although future emperors would long refuse to acknowledge the loss of the West, their efforts to regain it proved futile.

Justinian and Theodora

Gradually the Eastern character of the empire intensified. The Emperor Justinian, who ruled from 527 to 565, exercised power even more forcefully than Constantine had. He was determined to make the most of the awesome powers of caesaropapism.

Born in Macedonia in 482, Justinian became in his mid-thirties the power behind the throne of his uncle, Emperor Justin. Through Justin he negotiated a reunification of the Christian Church, which had been divided since the Roman pope and patriarch of Constantinople had excommunicated one another in 484. Justinian stood firm in his belief in unity, both religious and imperial: just as there was one God, so must there be one Church and one Roman Empire. When he came to the throne in 527, he was determined to restore and maintain those unities under God, of whose will he considered himself the chief executive on earth.

Justinian was a disciplined autocrat—a ruler whose authority was unlimited. He was also a shrewd judge of men and a gifted administrator. In addition, he married a woman whose skills complemented and enhanced his own. Theodora, a comic actress and strip-tease dancer whose parents were circus people, had enthralled Justinian when she performed at his court. He promptly overcame the horrified protests of his counselors and made her his wife. When he was crowned emperor in 527, he insisted that she be crowned empress— a formal designation as co-ruler. With an iron will and outstanding political judgment, Theodora worked tirelessly in the service of her husband and the empire.

In 532, when a violent uprising against his rule threatened his life, Justinian consulted his advisors and decided to flee Constantinople. But Theodora disagreed, arguing that in an hour of peril a ruler must not abandon his responsibilities. Neither emperor nor advisors would ordinarily have taken that sort of rebuke from a woman, but Theodora was empress, a regular participant in imperial deliberations and a superb politician. Shamed by her courage and logic, Justinian and his advisors remained in Constantinople and put down the rebellion.

CODIFICATION OF ROMAN LAW   Justinian and Theodora were autocrats, but they ruled by Roman law and not by whim. Germans might be in control of the West, but law remained the foundation of East Roman society, and Justinian decided to codify and streamline it. He appointed prominent jurists to compile all the laws of Rome that were still in force; they were published in 529 as the **Code of Justinian**. This path-breaking collection of statutes made Roman law the most influential legal system in history. The Byzantine Empire preserved it for centuries, eventually returning it to Western Europe.

The Code not only preserved Roman law, however, but also inadvertently froze it. Exalted by the Byzantines as a perfect system, Roman law was closed to the possibility of further change. It remains the foundation of the modern legal systems of many Western nations but never displayed the flexibility that would later characterize Anglo-American law (see "Excerpt from the Code of Justinian").

ATTEMPTS TO REUNITE THE EMPIRE   Justinian's Code was the foundation of his efficient administration. But his government was in constant financial distress, largely because of its extensive and expensive military commitments. Throughout his reign, Justinian waged war to reunify the Roman Empire.

What was Justinian's impact on Byzantine law and imperial reunification?

Given the circumstances of the day, reunification was unlikely. By the time of Justinian, two distinct cultures had evolved, the one Byzantine, the other a blend of Roman and Germanic. Their political and religious institutions were so different that permanent reunification could have been achieved only by occupation, and an army large enough to secure Italy was too large for the Byzantines to afford. The Germanic tribes were powerful forces in their own right, and in any case Byzantine troops were needed to defend the empire against Sasanians on its eastern border.

Nevertheless, Justinian's political and economic realism was overridden by his religious faith. Not only did a Roman Empire without Rome seem absurd, but the emperor was spiritually troubled by the heretical Germanic kingdom that ruled Rome. Those Germans were Arian Christians, believing that Christ was a divine creature made by God. The Arian Heresy had been condemned at the Council of Nicaea in 325, and Justinian would not tolerate its presence in Rome.

So for the next three decades, the undermanned Byzantine Empire waged war. Whenever Byzantium advanced in Italy and reoccupied Rome, the Persians attacked in the east. When Byzantine troops shifted to the east, the Germans took back Italy. The arrival of **bubonic plague** in 541—its first recorded appearance in the eastern Mediterranean region—further weakened Byzantine forces.

As the Byzantine Empire became less Roman, it became increasingly Greek. Constantine's creation of a new capital had at first expanded knowledge of Latin in

Empress Theodora and attendants.

Document 10.1 Excerpt from the Code of Justinian

"The compilation of Roman law which was enacted under the Byzantine emperor, Justinian I . . . has been without doubt the most important and influential collection of secular legal materials that the world has ever known. The compilation preserved Roman law for succeeding generations and nations. All later Western systems borrowed extensively from it." (Allen Watson, page xxiii)

BOOK ONE, PART I

10. Justice is a steady and enduring will to render unto everyone his right. The basic principles of right are: to live honorably, not to harm any other person, to render to each his own. Practical wisdom in matters of right is an awareness of God's and men's affairs, knowledge of justice and injustice.

11. The term "law" is used in several senses: in one sense, when law is used as meaning what is always fair and good, it is natural law; in the other, as meaning what is in the interest of everyone . . . it is civil law.

BOOK ONE, PART III

31. The emperor is not bound by statutes.

BOOK ONE, PART IV

1. A decision given by the emperor has the force of a statute. This is because the populace commits to him and into him its own entire authority and power . . .

BOOK ONE, PART V

1. All our law concerns [either] persons or things or actions.

3. Certainly, the great divide in the law of persons is this: all men are either free men or slaves.

4. Freedom is one's natural power of doing what one pleases, save insofar as it is ruled out either by coercion or by law. Slavery is an institution . . . whereby someone is against nature made subject to the ownership of another. Slaves are so-called, because generals have a custom of selling their prisoners and thereby preserving rather than killing them.

9. There are many points in our law in which the condition of females is inferior to that of males.

BOOK TWENTY-FOUR, PART II

3. A true divorce does not take place unless an intention to remain apart permanently is present. So things said or done in anger are not effective unless the parties show by their persistence that they are an indication of their considered opinion. So where repudiation takes place in anger and the wife returns shortly afterward, she is not held to have divorced her husband.

BOOK TWENTY-FOUR, PART III

1. An action for the dowry takes precedence at all times and in all circumstances; for it is in the public interest for women to keep their dowries, since it is absolutely essential for women to have dowries so that they can produce offspring and replenish the state with their children.

SOURCE: Allen Watson (ed.), Excerpt from *The Digest of Justinian*, Vol 1. Copyright ©1985. Reprinted with permission of The University of Pennsylvania Press.

the East, since much of the empire's administration was transferred to Constantinople. But Greek remained the spoken language of the Eastern Roman Empire, and gradually it replaced Latin in official transactions. Greek was also more prestigious than Latin: public speeches in Constantinople were normally given in Greek, and it was the language of instruction in most Byzantine schools. Justinian was the last native Latin-speaking Byzantine emperor.

Justinian's death in 565 was a significant event in turning the empire away from Rome. His successors, lacking his commitment to reunification, did little to realize it. As Rome receded in significance, Byzantium concentrated on Persia (Map 10.2). Then, from the seventh century onward, the Arabs in the southeast proved even more dangerous foes. Eventually, Constantinople had little choice but to let go of the West.

Byzantine Society

What were the principal characteristics of Byzantine economy and society?

During the two centuries from Constantine to Justinian, Byzantine society prospered. The Roman emperors brought from the West a privileged imperial court; a large, generally efficient, and well-compensated bureaucracy; legions of ambitious entrepreneurs; and clever con men on the lookout for every angle.

This transplanted society's showplace was Constantinople, whose population approached 400,000 in the early sixth century C.E. Ships docked in the **Golden Horn**, the city's inner harbor, bringing treasured goods from Asia and Africa. The city's artisans created splendid wares and textiles. The imperial court glistened with jewels, while visitors admitted to the emperor's presence passed by artificial trees filled with mechanical songbirds crafted in gold.

Constantinople's superb location gave it control of the trade routes of the eastern Mediterranean, and its vibrant economy justified Constantine's decision to build his

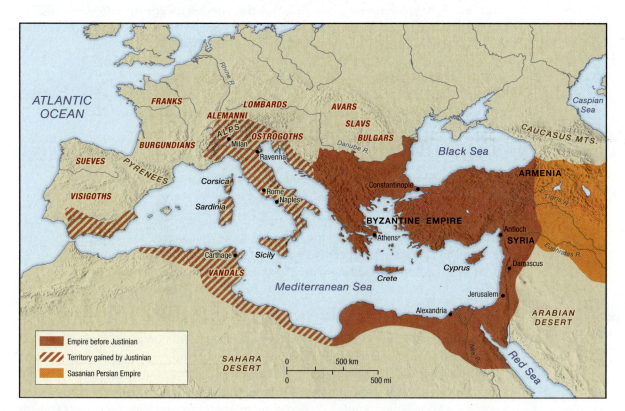

Map 10.2 **THE BYZANTINE EMPIRE DURING JUSTINIAN'S REIGN, 527–565** Justinian, last of the Latin-speaking emperors, never accepted the loss of the Western Roman Empire. In comparing this map with Map 10.1, note that Justinian's armies reconquered sizable segments of the West. Pressure from other areas, however, made it impossible for Justinian to hold his gains and prevented his successors from undertaking further westward initiatives. Where might this pressure have come from?

Constantinople.

capital there. Grain and cotton from Egypt, spices from India, and silks from China were traded on the docks not only of Constantinople but also of other cities throughout the realm. Transporting goods by sea instead of land made trade in bulk profitable and lowered prices on imported goods enough so that they could be purchased not only by aristocrats but also by a developing middle class.

As the Byzantine Empire's urban economy expanded, it was run by an increasingly wealthy and confident commercial class. City women enjoyed substantial mobility and freedom of action. Many owned shops, kept the books for merchant houses, and bartered with traders from three continents. But this prosperity rested not only on trade but also on the labors of peasants who worked the land and supplied food and soldiers for the empire. Rural people remained largely impoverished, tied to farming and the reproduction of enough children to keep the ranks of farmers and soldiers filled. Social mobility between farm and city was virtually unknown, and rural and urban people seemed to inhabit two different worlds.

Social life for peasants centered on weekly religious services, religious holidays, and celebrations of family events such as baptisms and weddings. Activities in cities were more varied; many involved the Church, but secular attractions were also available. Crowds gathered in large outdoor arenas, known as hippodromes, to watch chariot races, combats between men and wild animals, and athletic competitions. Young male spectators cheered for their favorite teams—the "Blues" or the "Greens"—wearing the team colors, cutting their hair in outlandish styles, and often fighting in the stands against supporters of the opposing side.

By the seventh century c.e., it no longer made sense to define Byzantium as the East Roman Empire. A distinctively Byzantine society and culture had developed, celebrated by splendid religious rituals and grounded in a prosperity supported by intercontinental commerce. These foundations enabled the empire to survive the conflicts and challenges that lay ahead.

Connection and Conflict in the Byzantine World

10.3 Explain how the Byzantine Empire coped with medical, military, and cultural challenges.

The Byzantine Empire was never free from threats, some originating outside its borders and others within. Given the nature of these challenges, it is surprising that the empire survived and prospered as long as it did. Its splendid geographic advantages were partly responsible, along with the strength and resilience of its spirit.

Disease and Warfare

What were the biological and military impacts of plague on the Byzantine Empire?

A seismic disturbance thousands of miles away set in motion a series of events that ravaged the empire. Around 535 the Indonesian volcano of Krakatoa erupted in an enormous explosion, spewing millions of tons of ash into the atmosphere. The ash produced cool, wet, dark summers throughout the world for the next several years. As Susan Wise Bauer points out, declining temperatures provided a perfect growth environment for bacteria; Byzantines were hungry and weak from poor harvests, and their immune systems were depressed; and efforts to import grain from warmer regions brought more and more ships to Constantinople. Some of those ships carried not only grain but also the plague.

Plague germs are ingested by fleas that suck the blood of infected black rats. The fleas then move from rats to humans and pass on microbes by biting their new hosts. Before the development of broad-spectrum antibiotics in the twentieth century, mortality rates from the three varieties of plague were very high. Pneumonic plague, spread by a victim coughing directly into the face of an uninfected person, killed 50 percent of its victims; septicemic plague, occurring when a flea transmits the germs directly into a blood vessel, killed 100 percent. But the most common form of the disease was bubonic plague, occurring when a flea bites soft tissue anywhere on the human body. Mortality was about 35 percent 15 centuries ago and is approximately 20 percent today.

Bubonic plague, which Europeans later called "the Black Death," appeared in the Byzantine Empire in 541 when ships from North Africa carrying infected rats docked in Byzantine ports. Victims died horribly, their bodies covered with "buboes," or large nodules filled with blood that turned black. The high fevers, delirium, and intense pain that accompanied the plague terrified the uninfected population; frightened citizens left the sick untended and bodies unburied in the streets. Epidemics hit the urban centers particularly hard, disrupting commerce and culture and causing millions to perish. To make matters worse, the 541 pandemic was caused by an unusually deadly variety of the plague, a new strain to which Byzantines had no acquired immunity. The Byzantine population declined drastically, producing death rates in the first wave of nearly 50 percent, making it impossible for Justinian to consolidate his conquests in the West and weakening the empire for the next two centuries.

In this fragile state, Byzantium was forced to confront serious external threats. Between 613 and 628, the Sasanian emperor Khusrau II advanced to the gates of Constantinople in an ambitious effort to conquer the Byzantine Empire. In response, Byzantine emperor Herakleios (610–641), with weaker forces and far less money, outmaneuvered Khusrau, advanced deep into the heart of Persia, and decisively defeated the Sasanians. But the devastation of two decades of war left both Persia and Byzantium vulnerable to an unanticipated threat from the Arabian Peninsula.

Out of Arabia in the 630s swept formidable desert warriors who spread the world's third major monotheistic religion—Islam—by conquest. The military forces of this vigorous new faith, whose rise is described in Chapter 11, quickly overran Syria, Mesopotamia, Palestine, Egypt, and much of North Africa, depriving the Byzantine Empire of many of its richest lands, and also subjugating Persia by 642. In 655 the Muslims, as practitioners of Islam are known, destroyed the Byzantine navy, enabling them to besiege Constantinople from 673 to 678. But the Byzantines were able to break the siege with the help of a secret weapon called **Greek fire**, a flaming liquid sprayed on the hulls and sails of enemy ships. Since it was oil based, any of the substance that missed its target floated on the water and continued to burn, spreading to other ships and incinerating anyone who fell or jumped overboard. In 678 the frustrated Muslims turned their energies to the conquest of North Africa. Then, moving across the Straits of Gibraltar and through Spain into Europe, they were finally blocked in 732 near Tours, by Franks led by Charles Martel (see Chapter 9).

Although the Byzantine Empire survived the initial Arab onslaught, its territorial holdings were greatly diminished. Commerce declined as Byzantine trade routes with Mesopotamia and Syria passed into Islamic hands. This trade reduction weakened the self-confident Byzantine commercial class and coincided with an alteration in the status of women. Theodora had been the first in a series of important Byzantine empresses: seven governed as regents for their young sons, two ruled the empire themselves, and others were quietly yet effectively influential. But in spite of the prominence of such powerful women, the situation for women in general deteriorated after the onset of the plague. As in Persia and Arabia, women were now required to veil themselves in public and to remain at home for most of their lives, their social contacts with men restricted to members of their own families. As Byzantine society became more agrarian and less commercial, women's lives became increasingly confined and their roles increasingly subordinate to those of men.

Disease and warfare did not destroy the Byzantine Empire in the seventh century, but they gravely weakened it. They also amplified the divisions and weaknesses within the Christian Church, threatening the empire's continued stability.

Eastern Christianity's Culture and Conflicts

What doctrinal and political struggles occurred within Eastern Christianity?

The Christian Church dominated the empire's spiritual and cultural life in penetrating, vibrant ways. As one historian observed, for the Byzantines, "Christ, his Mother, and the Saints were as real as members of their own families." To be Byzantine was to be deeply Christian and to express that faith in elaborate rituals. Byzantine church services were usually between four and six hours long. The emperor took part in all major worship services held in Constantinople, often marching to church at the end of a procession that could include as many as 50,000 gloriously robed officials. During services, the churches resounded with chants and hymns; clouds of incense perfumed the air. Christianity was the connective tissue of Byzantine life and the worldview that gave life meaning.

Culturally, Christianity inspired architectural works of exquisite beauty. Beginning around 450, the Church built basilicas, shrines, and monasteries from one end of the empire to the other. Byzantine architecture was noted for its massive, elegant domes. For example, the Basilica of Saint Sophia in Constantinople commissioned by Justinian featured an immense dome held up by several smaller ones. The ceilings were adorned with elaborate ornamental mosaics depicting scenes from the life of Christ, the lives of the saints, and the principal events of the Jewish and Christian Scriptures. Angels and holy people were portrayed in colorful, stylized paintings called **icons** that hung on the walls. As the exteriors of these structures were frequently rather plain, those entering them were often awed by the grandeur inside.

Yet despite the devotion of its faithful and the grandeur of its culture, Eastern Christendom involved itself in destructive internal and external disputes. First, the Church engaged in recurring doctrinal quarrels over the precise nature of Jesus Christ. The **Monophysites** (*mah-NAH-fizz-ītz*) contended that Christ was purely divine, while the Nestorians asserted that he was actually two persons, one human and the other divine. In 681, an ecumenical council in Constantinople agreed on an official definition: Jesus was one person with two distinct natures, one divine and one human, each the equal of the other. This statement should have settled the issue, and over time it did. But in the short term, Monophysitism (*mah-NAH-fizz-ih-tizm*) remained strong in the empire's eastern provinces, such as Armenia and Anatolia, which were the crucial source of much of its food and most of its soldiers. The loyalty of these vital regions was questionable. Not until the eleventh century did the issue of Monophysitism vanish, and then not by agreement among Christians, but rather because these provinces were conquered by Muslims.

While struggling with the insoluble issue of Jesus' true nature, the empire was also divided by a controversy over icons—religious paintings of Jesus, Mary, and the saints that were distinctive to Byzantine art. Popular belief held that divine graces flowed through these images to anyone who looked at them with reverence. One consequence of this belief was icon worship, a form of idolatry and arguably a violation of the Second Commandment, which decreed that "Thou shalt not make any graven images." Under different circumstances this might have been considered a spiritual matter for each person to work out individually, but as stated earlier, Byzantine Christianity was more than a set of rituals: it was a worldview that gave life meaning.

Byzantines believed that although the world was infested by demons that pestered and annoyed people, the only real power in the universe was God. Since the emperor was the only legitimate ruler of the inhabited world, his failures and defeats were always punishment for his sins and the sins of his people. Byzantines believed in a logical, orderly, purposeful universe in which disasters do not happen by chance. They did not believe in coincidence.

What, then, could explain the devastation caused by the sudden onslaught of the Muslims? Punishment for sin. Muslims considered all pictorial representations of holy people idolatrous and banned them. In 726, Byzantine Emperor Leo III, fearing that God was punishing Byzantium for the idolatrous sin of icon worship, banned all icons and ordered them destroyed, hoping thereby to atone for this sin and regain God's favor. Presumably, God would then allow the Byzantines to defeat the Muslims.

Leo's prohibition provoked a wave of **iconoclasm** (*ī-KAHN-ah-klah-zum*), or image breaking, throughout Byzantium, resulting in the destruction of priceless works of art and triggering a bitter dispute that tore the empire apart.

The former Basilica of Saint Sophia in Constantinople, with its massive dome surrounded by four graceful Islamic minarets following its conversion into a mosque.

A revolt against iconoclasm then broke out in Greece, and in Rome the pope, supporting the use of icons, denounced Leo. The destruction of icons was prohibited at a Church council in 787, restored by another in 815, and banned again in 843. For two more centuries iconoclasm remained a divisive force in Byzantine life, although it was gradually overshadowed by the growing division between the Eastern and Western Churches.

The Christian Church's most threatening problem was the prospect of a rupture between Eastern and Western Christendom. Ever since the founding of Constantinople, the two branches of the Church had developed radically different organizational structures. At various times between 476 and 1054, the bishop of Rome attempted to assert his authority over Constantinople; at other times, Byzantine patriarchs and sometimes emperors adopted initiatives designed to enhance their privileges.

From a Byzantine perspective, the struggle was doctrinal as well as political. The Byzantines, designating the emperor as an equal of the apostles, could not subordinate him to the pope in theological matters. Church tradition held that questions of doctrine could only be solved by an ecumenical council, at which the Holy Spirit would make its wishes known. Although the pope asserted authority over both the emperor and an ecumenical council, Byzantines could not accept what to them would have amounted to a redefinition of Christianity and of the emperor's role within it. At the same time, from a Western perspective, the Eastern Church's tendency to debate obscure theological issues was dangerous to Christian unity.

So many issues separated the two branches of Christianity that when the formal schism finally came in 1054 (Chapter 9), it merely ratified a reality that had existed for centuries. Henceforth, despite occasional short-lived efforts at reconciliation, the **Eastern Orthodox Churches**, functioning under their own patriarchs and caesaropapist rulers, remained independent of the pope in Rome and the Roman Catholic West.

Icon of St. Michael the Archangel.

Byzantium's Ascendancy and Decline

10.4 Describe the Byzantine Empire's quick revival and account for its even swifter decline.

Beginning in the mid-800s, Byzantine power rapidly revived. The Arab threat waned, and in the tenth century rejuvenated Byzantine armies destroyed Arab bases in Syria. Later the Byzantines conquered much of Bulgaria and established a strong imperial position in the Balkans. From 867 until 1025, the Byzantine Empire prospered under a series of forceful, farsighted leaders. Its position was stronger than at any time since the age of Justinian. Then it declined even more swiftly, and this time it never fully recovered.

The Macedonian Era, 867–1025

Why was the Macedonian dynasty so important in Byzantine history?

Under the **Macedonian dynasty**, founded by Basil I in 867, Byzantium's struggle for survival turned into an offensive against the Arabs that peaked in the tenth century. The ground lost to Islam in the seventh century was largely regained, including almost all of Syria and Palestine and a large section of Mesopotamia by 975. Then Basil II took over in 976 and concentrated most of his resources against the Bulgars, ruling for 49 years and earning the title "Basil the Bulgar-Slayer."

Bulgaria, south of the Danube River and northwest of Constantinople, was a much more serious threat to Byzantium than the Arabs. If Bulgaria was weak, it was useless as an ally against other powers, and its weakness would invite those powers to occupy it and menace the Byzantine Empire. If Bulgaria was strong, it threatened the empire's very existence. Basil II realized this and, after 42 years of effort, finally defeated the Bulgars in 1018.

By 1018 eleventh-century Byzantium resembled the third-century Roman Empire. After a lengthy period of prosperity and security, pressures from beyond the frontiers prodded the military into constant intervention in politics. In the 56 years between 1025 and 1081, there were 13 Byzantine emperors, many of them generals. They fought off repeated Pecheneg invasions from the north, definitively defeating them in 1091, but the most serious threat to the empire came from the east.

Byzantines fighting the Bulgars.

The Turkish Conquests

What were the impacts of the Turkish conquests upon Byzantium?

During the eleventh century, central Asian nomads called the Seljuk (*SELL-yook*) Turks gradually conquered Persia and Mesopotamia. In the process they became Muslims, and as part of an overall plan to unify Islamic lands, they intended to strike next at Egypt. To do so they would have to move from Mesopotamia to the east and south of the Byzantine Empire, whose eastern Anatolian provinces they plundered but whose existence as the region's major power they had no intention of challenging.

Adjacent to the Turks' new Mesopotamian territories was Armenia, populated by Monophysite Christians who had been antagonized by Byzantine policies of religious discrimination and crushing taxation. The Turks decided to take advantage of Armenia's dissatisfaction with Byzantine rule, hoping to secure their borders before attacking Egypt. In 1064, led by Sultan Alp Arslan, Turkish forces destroyed the capital of Armenia and penetrated Byzantine Anatolia, where they met only sporadic resistance. Six years later, hoping to prevent further Turkish advances, the Byzantine emperor Romanus IV Diogenes (*rō-MAH-nus dī-AH-juh-nēz*) concluded a truce with the sultan.

The truce was almost immediately broken by raiding parties composed of Southwest Asians who spoke a language related to Turkish but who refused to accept Seljuk control. Romanus, erroneously concluding that Alp Arslan was behind these raids, moved eastward to punish him in 1071. At the same time, the sultan, considering the truce still in force, moved southward against Egypt. When he learned that the Byzantines had broken the truce, however, he turned north to intercept Romanus.

The two armies met on August 26, 1071, at Manzikert in Armenia, where the Byzantines were soundly defeated. The battle proved disastrous for the Byzantine Empire. Romanus was captured, and the new Byzantine emperor soon broke the generous treaty

Map A

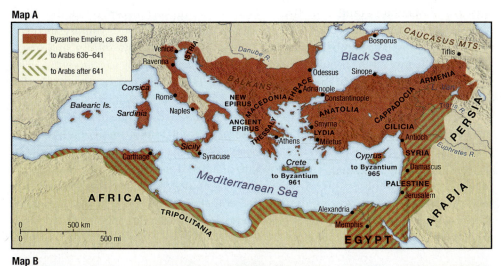

Map B

Map C

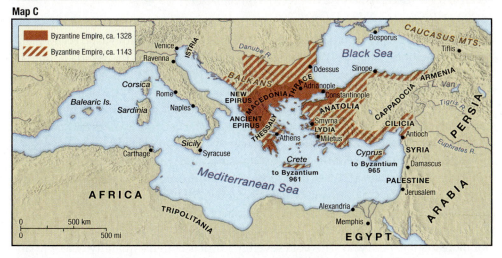

Map 10.3   THE GRADUAL RETRACTION OF THE BYZANTINE EMPIRE, 628–1328   By 1200, the

Byzantine Empire was considerably smaller than in 481 (Map 10.1). Arabian invasions from the south in the 7th century surprised the empire's leaders, forcing them to divide their forces between Persian and Arab threats. Observe that the empire was gradually pushed westward, losing all its North African territories to the Arabs. At the start of the 13th century, Byzantium's long-term survival was clearly questionable. How might the loss of these regions have handicapped the Byzantine emperors?

that Alp Arslan had granted the Byzantines after Manzikert. Exasperated, the sultan gave up his Egyptian plans and moved forcefully against the empire. Military and civilian factions fought each other over succession to the throne of Byzantium, and one of them actually invited the Seljuks to help them. The sultan was only too happy to oblige, receiving in return access to the city of Nicaea, only 60 miles from Constantinople. The contours of the Islamic and Byzantine worlds had been changed forever.

The Byzantine Empire still held the coasts of the Mediterranean and Black Seas and western Anatolia (Map 10.3). But eastern Anatolia and Armenia had been the empire's source of food and soldiers, and, once lost, these valuable territories could be neither retaken nor replaced. The Turks, who had had designs on eastern Anatolia but had never thought of conquering Byzantium itself, now held the strategic initiative and possessed the resources necessary for eventual victory. It came in 1453, when the Ottoman Turks, successors to the Seljuks, completed the Islamic conquest of West Asia and defeated the Byzantine Empire.

Kievan Rus Connects to the Byzantine World

10.5 Analyze the significance of Kievan Rus's conversion to Eastern Christianity.

The Byzantine Empire was largely shattered after Manzikert, but Byzantine influence lived on in the north. There, in 988, the grand prince of an area called Kiev had converted to Eastern Christianity. His decision meant that even after Byzantium's collapse, its culture and religion would continue in his realm. This area of Byzantine influence eventually grew into an enormous country known as Russia.

Russia's Difficult Climate and Terrain

How did geography affect Russian development?

Russian territory stretches from Eastern Europe across northern Asia. Endless forests blanket its northern expanses, while its south is covered with vast treeless plains known as steppes (Map 10.4). Although Russia today possesses thousands of miles of seacoast, throughout most of history it was essentially landlocked. Its long northern coastline borders the Arctic Ocean, ice-bound for much of the year, while access to its Baltic and Black Sea ports, acquired in recent centuries, is controlled by countries that have often been hostile. This landlocked condition blocked trade routes and frustrated Russia's development for centuries.

Not only is Russia landlocked, but it also is cold, the most heavily populated frigid land in the world. Even its southernmost portions lie no farther south than North Dakota. The Gulf Stream, which moderates the climate of continental Europe, touches only a tiny portion of Russia. Siberia, in Asian Russia, is known for its brutally cold conditions, and in the northern part of European Russia the soil remains frozen for more than half the year. This cold severely restricts both the quantity of arable land and the length of the growing season. Central Asian Russia suffers from both severe cold and inadequate moisture, making agriculture impossible there without irrigation. Finally, as nearly all the region's principal rivers flow north or south, rather than east or west, travel across Russia has always been difficult, hindering commerce and exploitation of its natural resources.

The First Period: Early Rulers and Campaigns

What was the significance of Olga's creation of a connection between Kiev and Constantinople?

The origin of the people who called themselves "Rus" (ROOS) is disputed. Some scholars argue that they were Norsemen from Scandinavia, also known as "Varangians," who allegedly arrived in northwestern Russia around 862 and imposed order on the

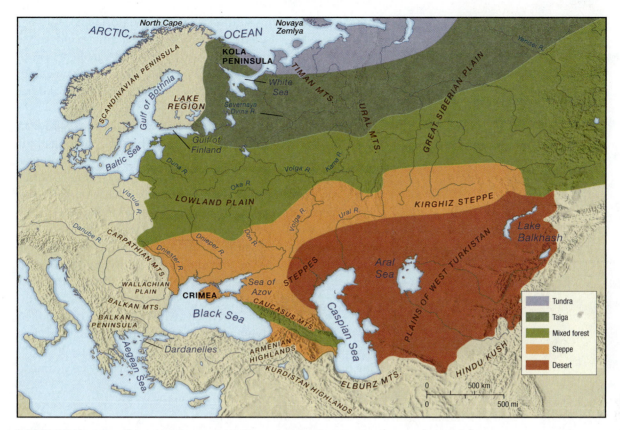

Map 10.4 **THE TOPOGRAPHY OF RUSSIA** Russia's formidable topography impeded its settlement and development for centuries. Its great rivers flow north–south rather than east–west, dead-ending travelers from its southern regions in the frigid Arctic rather than linking its Baltic and Pacific coasts. Notice that between taiga and desert lie vast expanses of forest and grassy steppes, areas in which large-scale farming has always been difficult. Battling these geographic challenges, the grand princes of Kiev laid the foundations of the Russian Empire. How might Russia's location across extreme northern latitudes restrict its development?

Slavs who lived there. Other historians contend that the Rus lived in the south and were known to both Arab and Byzantine observers before 862. Late in the ninth or early in the tenth century, the Rus, wherever they originated from, founded the state known as Kievan Rus. By 988 this state had become part of the Byzantine world.

Kievan Rus's history is customarily divided into three periods. During the first, from approximately 882 until 972, the state was established and consolidated. Its first ruler was Oleg, a prince who gradually extended control over neighboring East Slavic tribes. They were forced to pay tribute to him in Kiev, his capital, a town on the lower Dnieper (*ně-YEH-pur*) River in southern Russia (Map 10.5). In 907 Oleg fought an inconclusive series of skirmishes against the Byzantine Empire. Constantinople bought off the Rus with a generous commercial treaty.

Oleg's successor, Prince Igor (913–945), conducted a series of campaigns designed to maintain Kiev's domination over its tributary peoples. He also fought a large-scale war against the Byzantines from 941 to 943, plundering the suburbs of Constantinople. But Greek fire kept him from conquering the city, and in 945 he was killed while collecting tribute (always a dangerous undertaking) from one of the East Slavic tribes. His widow Olga assumed his powers, ruling Kiev as regent for their young son Sviatoslav (*svě-AH-tuh-slav*) from 945 to 962.

Olga became the first prominent female leader in Kievan Rus, in part by relentlessly enforcing her control over tributary groups, and in part by coming to terms with the Byzantine Empire. She converted to Eastern Christianity and traveled to Constantinople, where she met the emperor himself. The two appear to have

Map 10.5   KIEVAN RUS, CA. 900 While the Orthodox Christian Byzantine Empire contended for supremacy in Southwest Asia with the Muslims (Chapter 11), a new Orthodox Christian monarchy was emerging farther north. Grand Prince Vladimir's conversion to Orthodoxy in 988 oriented Kievan Rus to the south and west, turning it away from Asia and toward Europe. Note that Kievan Rus's location, on the western edge of Asia and the eastern fringe of Europe, would have supported a turn in either direction. This made Vladimir's adoption of Orthodox Christianity decisive for future Russian development. Could Kievan Rus have offered any support to the Byzantine Empire in its ongoing struggle with the Muslims?

Why was Vladimir of Kiev's conversion to Christianity so important?

concluded a cautious alliance, giving Sviatoslav a degree of security on his southern frontier when he became grand prince (or ruler) of Kiev in 962. Although her son did not convert to Christianity, ultimately Olga's efforts on behalf of her new faith were recognized by the Orthodox Church, which canonized her as a saint.

Sviatoslav's ten-year rule was a pivotal decade for Kievan Rus. In 965 he boldly attacked the Khazars, sacking their capital and fatally weakening their state. But this action was shortsighted, since the Khazars had been useful as a buffer against nomadic Central Asian tribes, particularly the ferocious Pechenegs (*PEH-chen-egs*). Three years later Sviatoslav, as the ally of Byzantium, conquered Bulgaria. The Pechenegs seized upon his absence to besiege Kiev, and in 969 Constantinople suddenly awoke to the dangers of instability on its northern border. The Byzantine emperor broke his alliance with Kiev, and in 971, after two years of bitter warfare, Sviatoslav withdrew from the Balkans. On his way home in 972, he was killed by the Pechenegs, who boiled the flesh off his skull, and then made it into a cup from which they drank in the hope of imbibing his courage. The first period of Kievan Rus's history came to a discouraging end.

The Second Period: Connections to Christendom

Eight years later, following civil war among Sviatoslav's three sons, Vladimir (*VLAD-i-mēr* or *vlad-Ē-mēr*), the youngest, emerged victorious. His accession as grand prince in 980 ushered in Kiev's second and most glorious era, which lasted until 1054. Vladimir did much to unite and consolidate his realm, secure its borders, and enhance both its culture and its commerce. But his most momentous step was conversion to the Christian faith and his insistence that it be adopted throughout his realm. Vladimir's historic conversion took place in 988–989, when Christianity was spreading swiftly into Scandinavia, Poland, and Hungary. As part of a complex set of arrangements with Constantinople, he not only was baptized a Christian but also married the Byzantine emperor's sister.

Russian legend offers an explanation for the conversion. According to popular accounts, Vladimir summoned to Kiev representatives of the three great monotheistic religions, requiring each delegation to argue in support of its beliefs. After the presentations, he and his advisors decided against Judaism because its principles had not prevented the conquest of Judea by the Romans or the more recent defeat of the Jewish Khazars by Kiev itself. Islam was attractive as a dynamic, expanding movement, but its expansion slowed considerably after 732. A more practical problem was that the Islamic faith forbade the use of alcohol, and Russians could not imagine getting through the harsh winter months without it. Impressed with the majesty and beauty of Byzantine ritual, Vladimir chose Christianity and connected his realm with the Christian world.

It is significant that Russia adopted Eastern rather than Western Christianity. By 988 those two branches had diverged dramatically from one another, and the Great Schism of 1054 formally divided them into two distinctly regional religions.

Vladimir's preference for the Byzantine branch, known after 1054 as the Orthodox Church, carried with it three monumental consequences for Russia.

First, Russia attached itself to a Christian church that remained firmly anchored in the rituals, practices, and doctrines of early Christianity. Western Christendom, by contrast, had gradually revised many of these traditions, exalting one bishop (the pope) above all others, altering the liturgy of divine worship, forbidding the marriage of priests, and later fragmenting with the rise of Protestantism in the sixteenth century. The rigorous internal questioning and self-criticism characteristic of Western Christendom remained alien to Russia, as did the notion of a spiritual authority that was separate from the secular state. The Russians instead inherited the Eastern caesaropapist tradition, which closely connected the Church and state and placed both under the authority of the ruler of the realm.

Second, the slow weakening and eventual collapse of the Byzantine Empire eventually made Russia, by default, the leader of the Orthodox world. Outside of Russia, the Orthodox Church was increasingly marginalized and reduced to the status of a weak minority faith. Russia thus became the flagship of Eastern Christianity.

Finally, Vladimir's choice made his country the beneficiary of the Byzantine cultural heritage. Orthodox Christianity linked Kiev to a rich, dynamic collection of traditions that enriched its austere Slavic culture. Byzantine art, with its extensive use of gold and vivid depictions of Christian saints and events, left an indelible stamp on Russian symbolism. Orthodox worship services, chanted and sung in a liturgical language developed for Slavic peoples (rather than in Hebrew, Arabic, or Latin, as would have been required had Russia converted to Judaism, Islam, or Western Christianity), played a key role in the development of the Russian language. So did the Cyrillic alphabet, adapted from the Greek with extra letters added to represent Slavic sounds. Over the centuries, these and other influences, flowing from the Byzantine connection, contributed to the formation of an energetic and inspirational Russian culture.

Vladimir was later canonized a saint in the Orthodox Church. His actions provided a platform for the accomplishments of his successor, Iaroslav (*YAHR-ah-slahv*) the Wise (1019–1054), who governed at the height of Kievan power. Iaroslav's military campaigns against Pechenegs and Poles consolidated a state ranging from the Black Sea to the Baltic. He authorized the preparation of Russia's first legal code, built churches and monasteries throughout the land, and transformed Kiev into a vibrant center of commerce and culture. He also appointed a Russian as Metropolitan of Kiev, Russia's leading Church official, giving Russia its first native-born Church leader. But his decision to divide his lands among his five sons upon his death in 1054 condemned Kievan Rus to political turmoil and civil war. Taking advantage of this instability, a new wave of Turkic-speaking invaders from the steppes, the Polovtsy (*pah-LAHV-tsē* or *pah-lahv-TSĒ*), appeared in the southeast and harassed the Kievan state for decades.

The Third Period: Chaos and Conflict

With this civil war and the subsequent Polovtsy invasion, the third era of Kievan Rus began, a lengthy period of chaos and conflict (1054–1240) during which its survival was often in doubt. Iaroslav's grandson Vladimir Monomakh (*MAH-nō-MAHK*), who served as grand prince from 1113 to 1125, fought constantly to defend the state, primarily against the Polovtsy but also against other invaders from the west and south. Monomakh managed to preserve his realm but was unable to guarantee its long-term survival. His successors quarreled among themselves, sacked Kiev, and eventually transferred the capital northeast to the city of Vladimir. Repeatedly raided by the persistent Polovtsy and increasingly detached culturally and commercially from the declining Byzantine Empire, Kievan Rus fragmented into feuding principalities. By the time Kiev fell to the Mongols in 1240, the center of Russia had shifted to the

What difficulties were experienced by Kievan Rus after 1054?

northern forests, affording its people a more defensible position against the seemingly unending stream of invaders moving across the southern steppes.

Economy and Society

What were the principal characteristics of the economy and society of Kievan Rus?

Agriculture was the source of Kievan prosperity. Because of Russian geography, the growing season was brief, but Kiev's black soil was rich and plentiful. Northern areas produced barley, oats, and rye, while wheat was the principal crop farther south. Farmers divided their lands into two parts, leaving each one fallow, or uncultivated, in alternate years. Eventually this alternation evolved into a three-field system, in which a parcel of land would be sown in one year with a spring crop, in the second year with a winter crop, and in the third with no crop at all. This system enhanced the fertility of the soil and increased food production.

Grain cultivation was supplemented by cattle raising and beekeeping, which supplied candle wax to light homes and honey to sweeten food and drink. Fishing and hunting were also important. Russia was a snowy land, but its vast forests and numerous lakes and rivers contained enough game and fish to feed a population much larger than the one that lived there. The majority of that population, of course, was rural; most townspeople, including artisans who practiced skills in tanning, metalworking, and woodworking, also worked on the land.

Townspeople were also merchants. Kiev's location on the Dnieper River north of the Black Sea gave it easy access to the principal trade routes of southwestern Russia. The grand prince was the chief merchant as well as the chief executive. Collecting tribute in the form of honey, beeswax, furs, hides, and slaves, he presided over a complex trade with Byzantium, Bulgaria, and Baghdad. Relations with Constantinople were commercial as well as cultural and religious.

In addition to directing trade, waging war, and regulating affairs of state, the grand prince presided over a social and governing elite centered on his siblings and cousins. His courtiers intermarried with local Kievan nobles to form the **boyar class**, an aristocracy that played a significant role throughout much of Russian history. Most Kievan peasants were free, although some fell into debt so burdensome that they were scarcely better off than the slaves who formed the base of the social structure.

From bottom to top, Kievan society blended with Byzantine Christianity. The Orthodox Church offered much more than divine services. It provided a colorful, enriching series of rituals designed to guide the believer from birth through life to death. It owned and administered early forms of charitable institutions, hospitals, and schools. It dominated Russian art, architecture, and literature, giving each a distinctively Byzantine flavor. In addition, its married clergy sent their children not only back into the Church but also into all other walks of life, spiritualizing Kievan society to a degree unmatched in Western Christendom.

The End of Early Russian Civilization

Why did Kievan Rus collapse?

The spiritual richness of Kiev, impressive though it was, could not prevent the state's collapse. Economically, in the eleventh century, Kiev began to lose its privileged commercial position, as Polovtsy occupation of the south disrupted its connections with both Byzantium and Islamic southern Asia. Socially, a gradual reduction in peasant status led to serious unrest in the twelfth century. Politically, Kievan Rus never became a fully centralized state, remaining a loose federation of principalities that only unusually talented rulers such as Vladimir and Iaroslav could hold together.

Recurrent civil strife left Kiev vulnerable to repeated attacks by Turkic-speaking nomads such as the Khazars, Pechenegs, and Polovtsy. Although Russia defeated them time and again, they continued to undermine its vitality. In 1240 the Mongols sacked Kiev, ending the third period of early Russian civilization.

Chapter Review

Consequences and Connections

When Emperor Constantine legalized Christianity, took a leading role in Church affairs, and moved the Roman Empire's capital to Constantinople, he laid the foundations of the Byzantine realm. After 476, when Germanic forces conquered Rome, the Eastern Roman Empire continued to develop a distinctive society, blending Roman traditions with Greek culture and a vibrant version of the Christian faith that united Church and state authority in the person of the emperor.

Byzantine emperors continued to claim all the western territory they had lost, but their efforts to retake it achieved no lasting success. Far more significant were the achievements of Byzantium itself. Among these was Justinian's Code, which systematized Roman law and guaranteed its survival into modern times. In the area of religion, Byzantine Christianity developed a rich set of rituals that preserved early Christian practices to the present day. And, beginning in the tenth century, Byzantine religion and culture took root in Russia, where they were destined to outlast the Byzantine Empire itself.

Byzantium's culture was splendid, its commercial connections extensive, and many of its emperors effective, capable leaders. Some, however, proved inept or corrupt. A political system that restrained executive power could have survived the mistakes of these incompetents, but the Byzantine Empire's caesaropapist heritage exalted the ruler's authority, even if he or she was disastrously ineffective. Although the emperors worked to unify their people religiously, Byzantium's chronic quarrels over insoluble doctrinal differences frustrated their efforts and weakened the empire in the face of its enemies.

In the end the empire's enemies proved its undoing. Drastically diminished by Arab conquests during the seventh century, the realm regrouped and regained a measure of power and prosperity, only to be battered by the Turks beginning in the eleventh century. Both Arabs and Turks were driven by a compelling, militant new faith that arose in Arabia in the early 600s. That dynamic force, to which we now turn, was known as Islam.

Reviewing Key Concepts

Heresy, p. 189
Schism, p. 189
Caesaropapism, p. 190
Code of Justinian, p. 191
Bubonic Plague, p. 192

Golden Horn, p. 193
Greek Fire, p. 195
Icons, p. 196
Monophysites, p. 196
Iconoclasm, p. 197

Eastern Orthodox Churches, p. 197
Macedonian Dynasty, p. 198
Boyar Class, p. 204

Ask Yourself

1. Why was caesaropapism important in the administration of the Byzantine Empire? How did Justinian and Theodora utilize it?

2. Why was Byzantium unable to reconquer and hold Rome?

3. Could the Great Schism of 1054 have been avoided? Why or why not?

4. How and why did Kievan Rus emerge as a powerful state in Russia? How was Kievan Rus affected by Byzantium?

5. Which features were distinctive about Byzantine civilization? Which of these features were passed on to later cultures?

Key Dates and Developments

	The Byzantine Empire		Kievan Rus
284 C.E.	Diocletian's division of the Roman Empire	700–200 B.C.E.	Scythians controlled southern Russia
325	Constantine's intervention at the Council of Nicaea	200 B.C.E.–200 C.E.	Sarmatians controlled southern Russia
527–565	Rule of Justinian and (until 548) Theodora	200–650 C.E.	Germanic invasions
		7th century C.E.	Arrival of the Khazars
529	Code of Justinian	ca. 862	Varangians arrived in northwestern Russia
541	Bubonic plague appeared in Constantinople	882–972	Foundation and First Period of Kievan Rus
681	Council of Constantinople defined the nature of Jesus	945–962	Regency and conversion of Olga
		962–972	Rule of Sviatoslav
726	Leo III's ban on icons and images; iconoclasm	980–1054	Second Period of Kievan Rus; Vladimir as grand prince (980–1019)
1054	The Great Schism	988	Conversion of Russia to Byzantine Christianity
1071	Battle of Manzikert Kievan Rus	1054–1240	Third Period of Kievan Rus
		1240	Mongol conquest of Kiev

Chapter 11
The Origins and Expansion of Islam, 100–750

THE GREAT MOSQUE AT MECCA The Great Mosque at Mecca during pilgrimage season. The large black structure at the center is the Ka'ba.

After reading this chapter, you should be able to:

11.1 Discuss the role of pre-Islamic Southern Arabia as a commercial connector.

11.2 Describe the early development of Islam.

11.3 Trace the creation and expansion of the Islamic Empire from 632 to 661.

11.4 Trace the expansion and eventual overthrow of the Umayyad Caliphate between 661 and 750.

11.5 Show how Islam connected diverse peoples by creating a blended society and culture.

The Expansion of
Islam, 632–732 C.E.

Night was approaching in the Arabian Desert. Moving eastward from the Red Sea, a caravan of camels laden with goods hastened to reach the gate of the city before darkness fell. Safely inside, the handlers fed and watered the camels while the merchants shook the dust from their clothing and bought food at a bazaar. Before retiring for the night, they visited the center of the city, an open square filled with shrines and statues. There they performed a series of rituals, thanking their gods for protecting them in the desert and leading them to safety.

This was the city of Mecca, a haven for travelers in an unforgiving wasteland. For centuries Mecca had provided food, water, rest, and sanctuary for anyone passing through its gate. Its food sellers, craftsmen, and peddlers prided themselves on making everyone welcome, regardless of the traveler's station in life or religious beliefs. The city's shrines offered every passerby a chance to worship his or her favorite god. But in the early seventh century, Mecca was changing. In 630, a man who had been born there six decades earlier returned to his home. He brought with him a new, monotheistic faith, preaching belief in one god, Allah, and rededicating Mecca to the worship of that god. In the following centuries, that new faith, known as Islam, spread throughout the world. Neither Mecca nor the Arabian Peninsula would ever be the same.

Pre-Islamic Arabia

11.1 Discuss the role of pre-Islamic Southern Arabia as a commercial connector.

By the sixth century of the Common Era, the world of the eastern Mediterranean had long been a commercial crossroad attracting all sorts of believers, including those who believed in no gods at all. It was a place where not only goods but also cultures, languages, values, and customs intermingled. On the fringe of this world lay the Arabian Peninsula, a land of searing heat at the southwestern tip of Asia. Arabia was not a centralized state but home to a collection of tribes and clans. The region was noted for fragmentation and rivalry rather than unity. Yet out of Arabia came **Islam**, a vigorous form of monotheism that aspired to unify not only its home peninsula, but also the entire world, under a banner of allegiance to one God. Islam excited the entire region, spreading its beliefs, its values, and its Arabic language over much of southern Asia and northern Africa within the next century. Lands once devoted to Greek, Roman, or Persian gods, to Judaism and Christianity, became part of a new Islamic world.

Camels and Commerce

Why was the camel so important to Arabian commerce?

Arabia in the centuries before Islam was an isolated area, even though it lay just south of the eastern Mediterranean basin, one of the busiest places in the world. An immense peninsula bordered by five seas should constitute an ideal location for oceangoing commerce, but Arabia had just two decent harbors. It has no rivers at all, so internal transportation was difficult and fresh water almost completely unavailable. Only the southwest receives ample rainfall. The rest of the peninsula consists of imposing mountains and arid, scorching deserts, culminating in the Empty Quarter of the southeast, the largest expanse of uninterrupted sand anywhere on the planet. Much of Arabia was unsettled, traversed only by Bedouin (*BED-oo-win*) peoples, nomads who moved from one oasis to another on camels.

Aptly nicknamed "ships of the desert," camels were indispensable to Arabian commerce. Able to carry 500-pound loads for distances up to 25 miles per day, camels can work for as much as three weeks without drinking, taking advantage of their huge stomachs and their ability to retain water until needed. Defiant and ill-tempered, camels were nevertheless crucial to travel, even though a sizable portion of each beast's load had to be reserved for food and no less than a gallon of water per day for the man who guided it. Despite this limitation, camels made trade possible across the forbidding interior of Arabia, and caravans of camels traveled up and down the Red Sea coast.

Camel transport sustained the economic life of both the nomads of the north and the more settled peoples of the fertile, rain-fed southwest. But given the importance of water in a desert land, it is not surprising that southern Arabia dominated the peninsula. City-states developed in that area after 1000 B.C.E., led by kings and fed by slaves. Compensating for lack of harbors, southern Arabians built ships that traveled the waters of the Arabian Sea and Indian Ocean in search of products and profits. By 400 B.C.E. the southerners had created a commercial network that operated in two directions, trading raisins, hides, leather goods, and perfumes for spices, textiles, olive oil, and weapons. Southward, their ships of the sea carried cargoes to and from eastern Africa, Persia, and India. Northward, their "ships of the desert" carried goods across oceans of sand, linking southern Arabia to Mesopotamia and the eastern Mediterranean. These trade routes connected with one created by the Phoenicians in the Mediterranean to form the longest commercial highway in history. Southern Arabians were primarily responsible for introducing Indian spices to the Mediterranean world, initiating a trade whose importance lasted more than a thousand years. In this commercial network, northern Arabia was subordinate to the southern city-states, which, protected by the same deserts and mountains that made their existence so precarious, did not fear their northern neighbors.

A camel caravan.

The Collapse of Southern Arabia and the Rise of Mecca

How and why did Mecca become a major Arabian sanctuary?

Eventually, however, southern Arabia's prosperity collapsed. The Ptolemaic (*tahl-ih-MĀ-ick*) Empire of Egypt, one of the successor states of the vast empire of Alexander the Great, had by 100 B.C.E. established its own commercial route linking Egypt to India by way of the Red Sea. Simultaneously, the Ethiopian kingdom of Axum on the western bank of the Red Sea, which actually owned territory on the Arabian Peninsula, threatened the commerce of the declining Arabian city-states. Finally, northern Arabians took this opportunity to interfere with overland trade routes, eroding southern control over the peninsula's interior (Map 11.1). By 300 C.E. the southern city-states had lost much of their power and wealth (Map 11.2).

As the city-states weakened, regional powers engaged in a military, commercial, and religious contest for Arabia. The capital of the Roman Empire was transferred from Rome to Constantinople, while the Sasanians, energized by Zoroastrianism, were revitalizing Persia six centuries after the Greco-Macedonian conquest. Byzantium, inspired by Christianity, also considered the Arabian Peninsula open for commercial exploitation and religious conversion.

Monotheistic beliefs had entered Arabia as early as 70 C.E., when the Roman destruction of the Second Temple in Jerusalem initiated a dispersal of Jews throughout Southwest Asia. Southern Arabian kings, observing that two of their most dangerous enemies, Byzantium and Ethiopia, were Christian, adopted Judaism in the early

Map 11.1 **PHYSICAL GEOGRAPHY OF THE ARABIAN PENINSULA** Mesopotamians, Assyrians, Babylonians, Egyptians, Persians, Greeks, and Romans all knew of the existence of Arabia, but none of them considered it important. Its forbidding geography explains this lack of interest. Observe the lack of rivers to channel the small amount of moisture that falls as rain. An enormous limestone plateau jutting into the Arabian Sea, the Arabian Peninsula bakes under intense heat and lacks subsurface supplies of fresh water. How might Arabia have forged connections with other societies if its topography had been less discouraging?

400s. But in 520 an Ethiopian invasion destroyed the southern city-states and established a Christian protectorate. Judaism was weakened through forcible conversion to Christianity, but Ethiopian military domination was never secure, and in the 570s Ethiopians were replaced by Persians. Under Persian rule, Judaism, Christianity, and Zoroastrianism were all tolerated in southern Arabia.

The destruction of the southern Arabian states ended the southern domination of the peninsula and created a politico-economic vacuum that neither Ethiopia nor

Sasanian Persia could fill. Bedouin nomads of the interior now gravitated toward the less highly developed towns of the north, linking them with the city of Mecca on the western edge of the Arabian Desert.

For several centuries Mecca had been a place of sanctuary where both travelers and the bandits pursuing them could refresh themselves undisturbed. It was also a religious center, housing tribal idols from throughout the peninsula and offering pilgrims an opportunity to view the **Ka'ba** (*KAH-bah*), a shrine containing large stone idols. As southern Arabia's commercial power vanished following the Ethiopian and Persian invasions, Mecca took on added importance as a resting place for camel caravans traveling up and down the Red Sea coast and across the desert. Making the most of this opportunity, the Quraysh (*kurr-ISH*) tribe, which rose to dominate the city around 500 C.E., became custodians of the Ka'ba, protectors of pilgrims, and traders determined to establish an international commercial dynasty.

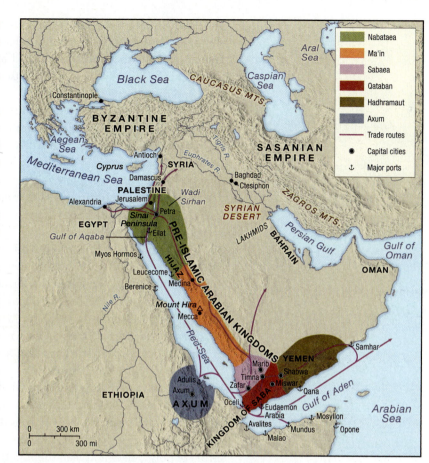

Map 11.2 ARABIA AND ADJACENT REGIONS, 500 C.E. Isolated and arid, the Arabian Peninsula in 500 C.E. was divided into states and subdivided into feuding clans. Nearby states like Axum traded with Arabian states but otherwise left them alone. Note that the eastern shore of the Red Sea could serve as a highway for camel caravans linking the kingdom of Saba to the ports of the eastern Mediterranean. What role could cities like Medina and Mecca play in the development of such commerce?

The Rise of Islam

11.2 Describe the early development of Islam.

As the sixth century closed, the Arabian Peninsula was changing rapidly. The powerful southern city-states were gone and no central authority took their place. Traditional trade routes had been disrupted and new ones were forming. Monotheistic religions had been introduced but none had succeeded in converting very many. Mecca, now flourishing as a religious and commercial center, seemed to offer a promising new focus for regional control.

Then a boy, born into a minor clan of the Quraysh tribe in Mecca, transformed the changing Arabian Peninsula. He was Muhammad ibn Abd'Allah (*muh-HAHM-ahd ibn abd-AHL-lah*), and he would become one of the most influential figures in history.

The Prophet Muhammad

Muhammad was born in 570, shortly after his father's death. The boy was raised by a grandfather and later by an uncle. He worked on caravans up and down the Red Sea coastline, first as a camel tender and then as a merchant, and at age 25 he married his employer, a wealthy widow named Khadija (*kah-DE-jah*). In Mecca he earned a reputation as a responsible businessman and camel merchant, and as a spiritual person committed to living an ethical life. Often he went to the mountains near the city to pray and meditate. While doing so, in 610 he experienced the first of a series of revelations. He described these revelations as transmitted to his unconscious mind by the Archangel Gabriel, a figure in both Jewish and Christian scriptures. But Muhammad claimed to have felt the words rather than having heard them and said that they came directly from Allah, the one and only God.

What role did Muhammad play in the emergence of Islam?

Allah's name was known to Arabians. He was one of a number of gods they worshipped, but no cult was devoted solely to him and his nature was not well defined. He was not the one God worshipped by the few Arabs who had come to believe in monotheism. But Muhammad said that his revelations identified Allah as the only God, and they clarified his nature.

At first the disclosures Muhammad reported concerned God's nature and his relations with humanity. Allah is omnipotent and merciful, Muhammad claimed; he created everything, and it is the duty of everyone to acknowledge his greatness and worship him. He expects the rich to assist the poor and requires that all people live honest, faithful, and upright lives in compliance with specific rituals and regulations. On the Last Day, according to Muhammad, Allah will bring all souls before him and will judge them according to their actions on earth, consigning some to heaven and others to hell.

Muhammad's definition of God and of people's relations with him paralleled those of other religions with which Meccans were familiar. Jews were uncompromising monotheists who accepted the Mosaic code of ethical conduct and followed well-defined religious practices. Christians believed in the Day of Judgment and described it in words and images similar to those transmitted to Muhammad. Zoroastrians believed in the eternal struggle between good and evil and in the eventual triumph of Ahura Mazda over Ahriman. But Judaism, Christianity, and Zoroastrianism had failed to win significant numbers of followers in Arabia, possibly because in a land fragmented into tribes and clans, polytheism seemed more reflective of the realities of daily life. Now Muhammad believed that Gabriel had instructed him to do much more than simply believe in a single god. He was to prophesy in the tradition of Moses and Jesus, to speak to men and women on behalf of Allah, to turn them away from the errors of polytheism and lead them to the worship of the one true God.

Muhammad's revelations provided a religious explanation for why other monotheistic religions had failed to convert Arabs. According to Muhammad's account, Gabriel had said that Jews and Christians possessed their own scriptural texts and were recognized by Allah as **People of the Book**. Their books—the Jewish and Christian scriptures—were valid but incomplete and only partially accurate. They had been copied, translated, and revised over the centuries until they no longer contained the fullness and purity of divine revelation. Muhammad's mission was to communicate the totality of God's teaching in its pure and final form. He was to be the last and greatest of the prophets, the Messenger of God.

This charge was a daunting prospect for an uneducated merchant, but Muhammad proceeded with his mission. He recited his revelations over and over to secretaries who recorded his words carefully in Arabic, and many of his followers memorized them. These recitations became the **Qur'an** (*kuh-RAN*), the sacred scripture of the religion that would soon become known as Islam (*IZ-lahm* or *is-LAHM*), Arabic for "submission" to the will of God. Organized neither topically nor chronologically but roughly by length of recitation (from the longest to the shortest), the Qur'an is a difficult text. But individual believers felt compelled to read it, and it became a powerful force in their lives (see "Excerpts from the Qur'an"). It was also a force in Arab history, as its compilation and eventual publication standardized classical Arabic, and the Qur'an and the Arabic language became principal unifying forces within the Arab world.

In 613 Muhammad began to preach publicly outside the circle of his own family and friends. He quickly encountered opposition from the merchant elite of the Quraysh, who realized that these new teachings would disrupt the polytheistic traditions and genial tolerance of the sanctuary at Mecca, which would rapidly lose its attractiveness as a haven for commercial travelers. They were clearly disturbed by Muhammad's claim that on the Day of Judgment, their fate would be decided by their conduct in life and not by their membership in a powerful tribe. Muhammad's

A hand-copied page from a 19th-century edition of the Qur'an.

Document 11.1   Excerpts from the Qur'an, 7th Century C.E.

The most holy book of Islam, the Koran (or Qur'an) means "the recital," and it contains, according to Islamic theology, the direct words of God (al-Ilah, or Allah), as told to his prophet Muhammad through the angel Gabriel. Muslims believe that the angel directed Muhammad to "recite" 114 suras, or books, beginning around 610 C.E. About twenty years after Muhammad's death in 632, an authorized text of these suras was compiled and publicized. The general arrangement of the Qur'an is according to the size of each document. It is important to note, therefore, that the Qur'an does not purport to be a continuous narrative, telling a series of stories, as is typical in other religious texts. This means that individual pronouncements can be taken out of context, and that various portions of the document can be quoted to different effects. The document here is assembled from excerpts, taken from one of the longest suras, entitled "The Cow."

PREAMBLE

In the Name of God, The Compassionate, the Merciful Praise be to God, Lord of the worlds! The compassionate, the merciful! King on the day of reckoning! Thee only do we worship, and to Thee do we cry for help. Guide Thou us on the straight path, The path of those to whom Thou hast been gracious; with whom thou are not angry, and who go not astray.

ESCHATOLOGY

Verily, they who have charged our signs with falsehood and have turned away from them in their pride, heaven's gates shall not be opened to them, nor shall they enter Paradise, until the camel passeth through the eye of the needle. After this manner will we recompense the transgressors. They shall make their bed in hell, and above them shall be coverings of fire! And this way will we recompense the evil doers.

But as to those who have believed and done the things which are right (we will lay on no one a burden beyond his power)-these shall be inmates of Paradise, for ever shall they abide therein.

And we will remove whatever rancor was in their bosoms; rivers shall roll at their feet, and they shall say, "Praise be to God who hath guided us hither! We had not been guided had not God guided us! Of a surety the apostles of our Lord came to us with truth." And a voice shall cry to them, "This is Paradise, of which, as the meed of your works, ye are made heirs."

And the inmates of Paradise shall cry to the inmates of the fire, "Now have we found what our Lord promised us to be true. Have ye too found what your Lord promised you to be true?" And they shall answer, "Yes." And a herald shall proclaim between them, The curse of God be upon the evil doers.

"Who turn men aside from the way of God, and seek to make it crooked, and who believe not in the life to come!"

And between them shall be a partition, and on the wall Al Araf [between heaven and hell] shall be men who will know all, by their tokens, and they shall cry to the inmates of Paradise, "Peace be on you!" but they shall not yet enter it, although they long to do so.

And when their eyes are turned towards the inmates of the fire they shall say, "O our Lord! place us not with the offending people."

And they who upon Al Araf shall cry to those whom they shall know by their tokens, Your amassings and your pride have availed you nothing.

"Are these they on whom ye swore God would not bestow mercy? Enter ye into Paradise! where no fear shall be upon you, neither shall ye be put to grief."

And the inmates of the fire shall cry to the inmates of Paradise, "Pour upon us some water, or of the refreshments God hath given you." They shall say, "Truly God hath forbidden both to unbelievers, who made their religion a sport and pastime, and whom the life of the world hath deceived." This day therefore will we forget them.

WARFARE

Fight for the cause of God against those who fight against you; but commit not the injustice of attacking them first. God loveth not such injustice.

And kill them wherever ye shall find them, and eject them from whatever place they have ejected you; for civil discord is worse than carnage. Yet attack them not at the sacred Mosque, unless they attack you therein; but if they attack you, slay them. Such is the reward of the infidels.

But if they desist, then verily God is Gracious, Merciful.

Fight therefore against them until there be no more civil discord, and the only worship be that of God. But if they desist, then let there be no hostility, save against the wicked.

CHRISTIANS AND JEWS

We believe in God, and in what hath been sent down to us, and what hath been sent down to Abraham, and Ismael, and Isaac, and Jacob, and the tribes, and in what was given to Moses, and Jesus, and the Prophets, from their Lord. We make no difference between them. And to Him are we resigned (Muslims).

Whoso desireth any other religion than Islam, that religion shall never be accepted from him, and in the next world he shall be among the lost.

Verily, they who believe (Muslims), and they who follow the Jewish religion, and the Christians, and the Sabeites - whoever of these believeth in God and the last day, and doeth that which is right, shall have their reward with their Lord. Fear shall not come upon them, neither shall they be grieved.

Make war upon such of those to whom the Scriptures have been given as believe not in God, or in the last day, and who forbid not that which God and His Apostle have forbidden, and who profess not the profession of the truth, until they pay tribute out of hand, and they be humbled.

SOURCE: J.M. Rodwell, trans., *the Quran.*

claim to be God's messenger also challenged their political authority. The elite tried to bribe Muhammad with an offer of membership in their inner circle. When he refused, they tried intimidation and then a boycott of his family and associates that prevented them from buying food in local markets. But nothing deterred Muhammad.

What roles did the *umma* and "five pillars" play in connecting Arabia and spreading early Islam?

From Mecca to Medina

By 619 Muhammad had some one hundred followers in Mecca, a small return on his investment of six years of preaching and teaching. At the same time, the oasis town of Yathrib, later renamed Medina (*meh-DĪ-nuh* or *meh-DĒ-nuh*), two hundred miles north, took an interest in his message. Medina was jealous of Mecca's economic domination, and the town was friendly to monotheism, since many of its residents were monotheistic Jews. In 622, after sporadic negotiations, 75 men from Medina invited Muhammad to move there: two tribes were fighting continually, and the delegation hoped Muhammad could stabilize the situation. Late that summer he, his closest relatives, and their families undertook a nine-day journey known as the **Hijra** (*HĒJ-rah*, sometimes rendered as "flight" or "severing of relationships"). They reached Medina on September 24, 622, making that year the beginning of the Islamic lunar calendar. It was the pivotal event of Islamic history, symbolizing a flight from polytheism to monotheism.

Medina had been divided by religious quarrels among various tribes, some polytheistic and some Jewish. Muhammad offered a monotheistic creed with scriptures in Arabic and a rigorous moral code that he himself would apply as a neutral judge. The polytheistic tribes accepted his arrival and soon converted to Islam, but the Jewish clans resisted despite Muhammad's willingness to incorporate some obviously Jewish practices into his evolving faith. The Jews rejected his claim to stand in the tradition of their great prophets Moses, Elijah (*ē-LĪ-jah*), and Isaiah (*ī-ZĀ-uh*).

Faced with Jewish resistance, Muhammad reported receiving a new series of revelations that became part of the Qur'an. These recitations disclosed that the Hebrew patriarch Abraham was a greater prophet even than Moses and that God had commanded him to build the Ka'ba in Mecca. Muhammad now claimed that Abraham was the father of the Arab people, a pure monotheist whose beliefs had been corrupted by subsequent generations of Jews, just as subsequent generations of polytheists had placed idols in the Ka'ba. Now, Muhammad asserted, Allah had directed him to make Islam a completely independent religion, replacing both Judaism and Christianity because it represented the ultimate revelation of God.

Over the next several years, Muhammad carried out this charge, building an **umma** (*OOM-mah*), a purely Islamic community under his leadership. Believers called themselves Muslims, or "those who submit" to the will of God. The foundation of the *umma* was five basic religious tenets; a Muslim is anyone who follows them, and following them, Muslims believe, will guarantee life in paradise with Allah after death.

The **five pillars**, as these tenets are called, were adapted from existing Christian, Jewish, and Arabian practices (see "The Five Pillars of Islam"). Together they constituted a foundation for the *umma*, giving it a religious charter and shared identity. In turn, the *umma* provided a means for social unity in fragmented Arabia, demonstrating that the belief in a single god carried with it serious political implications. If polytheism had proven attractive to Arabians because its fundamental disunity reflected their daily realities, then monotheism's insistence on obedience to one god had the potential to end social and political disunity, subjecting all believers to God's law in both temporal and spiritual matters.

Document 11.2   The Five Pillars of Islam

1. **Shahadah**, or *the bearing of witness*. The prayer reads: "There is no God but Allah, and Muhammad is His Messenger."
2. **Salat**, or *the practice of praying* at five specific times during the day while facing in the direction of the Ka'ba at Mecca.
3. **Zakat**, or *the practice of caring for the poor* of the *umma* through almsgiving or charity.

4. **Sawm**, or *the Ramadan Fast*. During the holy month of Ramadan, Muslims must abstain from food, drink, and sexual intercourse during daylight hours.
5. **Hajj**, or *performing the seven-day ritual of the pilgrimage* to Mecca at least once during one's lifetime.

SOURCE: John W. Langdon.

Muhammad instituted laws that bound all members of the *umma*, regardless of tribe, a concept that probably grew out of his experience as a merchant and his acquaintance with Byzantine and Sasanian legal forms. His construction of an *umma* at Medina gave him a base from which to convert Mecca. His followers plagued Meccan trading caravans, provoking the Meccan commercial establishment into open hostility. In three battles between 624 and 627, Meccans failed to destroy Islam, and Muhammad's survival was widely interpreted as evidence of divine approval of his mission. Then in 628 Muhammad led a large band of Muslims from Medina on a pilgrimage to the Ka'ba. This gesture of reconciliation, designed to show that Islam was an intrinsically Arabian belief system rooted in tradition, persuaded many Arabian tribes to support Muhammad. In 630 he returned to Mecca, bearing gifts and pardons for his former enemies.

With Mecca now supporting him, Muhammad was able to extend his influence over even the most polytheistic Arab tribes. The simplicity of Islam's five pillars made it highly attractive. Compared with Judaism and Christianity, with their complex doctrines, regulations, and rituals, Islam was easy to understand. By the time of his death in 632, Muhammad, now known as the Prophet, had unified most of the peninsula around his inspired leadership and religious vision. He had provided a spiritual and legal framework within which to resolve the blood feuds that had long devastated the region, based on his status as the final messenger of God.

The Shahadah: "There is no God but Allah, and Muhammad is His messenger."

Islam Expands, 632–661

11.3 **Trace the creation and expansion of the Islamic empire from 632 to 661.**

Islam's second generation demonstrated that this new religion would not remain confined to the Arabian Peninsula. Once certain internal leadership questions were settled, Arab warriors burst forth into Southwest Asia and the eastern Mediterranean basin. Their advance startled the rulers of the long-established empires of Persia and Byzantium, who had not anticipated either a military or a political challenge from desolate Arabia. Barely three decades after the death of the Prophet, Islamic forces were masters of an extensive empire of their own, held together by contacts and connections that were forged in conflict.

An Agreement Between Leader and Followers

Muhammad's death provoked a crisis in Mecca, but not a crisis of spiritual leadership. Obviously no one could succeed him as Prophet, since the Qur'an indicated that Allah would send no more such messengers. Besides, Islam was individualistic, based on a personal relationship between Allah and each believer. There was no self-evident need for continuing spiritual directorship such as that provided in Christianity by popes and patriarchs.

Political leadership was a different issue entirely. To leave the *umma* leaderless would be to undermine Muhammad's work in unifying the peninsula. Muslims from

How did the caliphate develop, and how did it employ jihad?

Medina, still suspicious of Meccans, decided to select their own head, a move that if implemented would splinter Islam. This threat was averted in a contentious all-night meeting that selected the Prophet's father-in-law, the Meccan Abu Bakr, as **caliph** (*KĀ-liff*), meaning "successor of the Messenger of God." The new caliph would lead the *umma*.

Abu Bakr, like his son-in-law, was a member of the Quraysh clan. His selection established the principle that future leaders must belong to the Prophet's tribe. Abu Bakr lived only two more years, but that was long enough to convince nearly everyone that the position of caliph should continue. The **caliphate**, or the territory governed by a caliph, developed into an institution that existed only in the Islamic world. Grounded in the idea that Islam must become more than an individualized, person-to-God relationship, it evolved into a contract binding all Muslims to one another within the *umma*. The caliph's appointment constituted an agreement between leader and followers, imposing a set of obligations on both. Any violation of these obligations was both a political breach of contract and a sin against God.

This combination of political and spiritual authority carried with it awesome responsibility. Abu Bakr did not hesitate to exercise the former and live up to the latter. Muhammad's death led to rebellions in several Islamic areas, and to prevent the *umma* from coming apart, the new caliph raised a large army and defeated the rebels. This left him with a substantial armed force that he decided to deploy against outside enemies in the service of the faith. Abu Bakr and his successors believed that, since Muhammad's revelations were true, Islam, as the only true faith, must be spread by the faithful throughout the entire world. The contractual understanding implicit in Abu Bakr's concept of the caliphate helped transform Islam from an Arabian version of monotheism into a dynamic faith committed to spiritual and political expansion. That expansion, taking place between 632 and 732 mostly through armed conquest, was justified by Islam's claim to be a superior religion and achieved by the superiority of Arabian military tactics. It transformed the futures of Asia, Africa, and Europe.

JIHAD AND THE TWO HOUSES   Islam's expansion conformed to the Qur'an's commandment to pursue **jihad** (*JĒ-hahd*). Often expressed in English as "holy war," jihad is literally translated as "striving" or "struggle." In the Qur'an and the sayings of the Prophet, it is used in the military context of waging war against unbelievers. Some theologians in Islam's early centuries, and some Muslim reformers in the nineteenth and twentieth centuries, suggested that jihad also should be interpreted as an injunction to wage an inner, spiritual struggle against sin and weak faith rather than solely military conquest for the purpose of spreading the faith. But most Islamic jurists and theologians interpret its original intent as military, as did the Muslim soldiers who conquered lands for Islam under the leadership of the caliphs.

The obligation to wage jihad, whether militarily or peacefully, is grounded in Islam's claim to be a universal religion. For Muslims, Allah's revelations apply not simply to Muhammad and his fellow Arabs but to all humanity. Those who have accepted these revelations are required to work diligently to convert those who remain in error. This obligation remains in force until all peoples have either embraced Islam or come under the rule of Islamic governments. While this struggle lasts, the world is divided into **two houses**, the House of Faith and the House of Disbelief. Conflict exists between these two houses and will continue until the final triumph of Islam throughout the world. A military interpretation of the commandment of jihad draws a clear, uncrossable line between Muslims and unbelievers and is consistent with the military expansion of Islam's first century. Interpretations that emphasize self-defense, or the individual's spiritual struggle to become holy, have become more prevalent in recent times.

THE CALIPHATE AS EMPIRE   For both political and spiritual reasons, Abu Bakr began to build an Islamic empire, sending forces in 632 against the Byzantine Empire's frontier posts in Syria and Sasanian Persia's installations in southwestern

Mesopotamia. Commanded by Khalid ibn al-Walid (*KAHL-ēd ibn ahl-wah-LĒD*), whom the Prophet himself had dubbed "The Sword of Allah," these remarkable fighters, emerging by surprise from the desert wastes on horses and camels, quickly established Islamic rule on non-Arabian soil for the first time. This force, though only a few thousand strong, used the desert to its advantage, withdrawing into it when danger threatened and returning only when it chose. The Arab invasions could not have come at a worse time for the Byzantines and Sasanians: exhausted from decades of fighting each other, they had ignored their frontiers with Arabia and now paid a heavy price.

In the midst of these military expeditions, Abu Bakr died and was succeeded by his kinsman Umar (634–644), who continued Islam's expansion (Map 11.3). Two years later, when Khalid's army took the Syrian city of Damascus, the Byzantines realized that this was no typical Arabian raiding party but a serious invasion. Jerusalem fell in 637, and only an outbreak of plague and the formidable mountains of northern Lebanon prevented the Muslims from expanding farther. In the same year, another Muslim force attacked Sasanian Persia, conquering it completely by 642 in exploits unmatched since the days of Alexander the Great.

Umar turned next against the Byzantine province of Egypt. Byzantine forces there were defeated in a series of engagements, and the patriarch of Alexandria surrendered the entire province in 642. But then geographic challenges—the mountains of northern Lebanon, the unfamiliar deserts of northern Africa (where native Berber warriors held the advantage), and the Iranian plateau—slowed them down. Meanwhile, the Byzantine Empire reconquered Alexandria with a naval expedition in 645. Arabs, accustomed to fighting on ships of the desert, now had to learn to fight on ships of the waves. They made the transition, but future conquests took longer than their first ones.

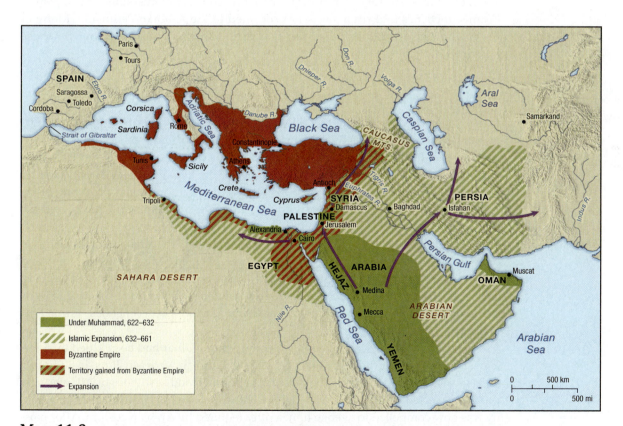

Map 11.3 ISLAMIC EXPANSION IN SOUTHWEST ASIA, 632–661 In the century following the death of the Prophet Muhammad, Islamic soldiers poured out of the Arabian Peninsula to conquer lands spanning three continents. Notice that they started with Southwest Asia before being blocked in their northwestward expansion by the Byzantine Empire. Spreading the Islamic faith and the Arabic language into the eastern Mediterranean, Mesopotamia, Persia, and the Indus Valley, they forged commercial and cultural connections that endure today. What similarities and differences can you see between the Persian Empire and this new Islamic empire, which Muslims called a caliphate?

Under Umar the caliphate became an empire composed of many different ethnic groups. In Syria, Persia, and Egypt, he ruled through local officials wherever possible and left farms in the hands of their owners. Unoccupied lands were awarded to his soldiers, who cultivated them with slaves taken from the conquered peoples. Arabs thus became an elite warrior caste rather than immigrants who assimilated into the peoples and cultures they conquered. But they never hesitated to learn from those peoples, borrowing Sasanian innovations in military organization, tactics, court procedure, and law enforcement, as well as Byzantine concepts of the rule of law and the connection between spiritual and temporal leadership.

This Islamic empire differed in several ways from the great empires of China, Persia, and Rome. It was significantly larger than any of those realms and too extensive to be governed by one man ruling from one capital. Unable to centralize authority in the caliph, Muslims delegated considerable power to his representatives, or *emirs*, who did not always follow his wishes. The Islamic empire was held together by religious faith, not by centralized authority, as in Persia, or military superiority, as in Rome.

The Arabs were set apart not only by their status as conquerors but also by their practice of Islam. Their aim was to take the pure truth of Islam to the world, but in the seventh century they did not force conversion on those they conquered. In fact, Christians and Jews in Arabia were permitted freedom of worship, as long as they submitted to Islamic rule. In Persia, Zoroastrians were initially extended these same rights. Umar considered Islam an Arab religion to be practiced by an ethnic elite, the people to whom Muhammad revealed the Qur'an. Those conversions that did occur were immediately suspect, since Muslims were exempt from tribute. There were, of course, entirely legitimate spiritual reasons for conversion. The appeal of Islam's doctrines and rituals was not confined to the Arabian Peninsula. Many of those who converted considered this new faith a distinct improvement over those it displaced.

The Challenge to a Unified Islam

How did the split between Sunnis and Shi'ites originate?

In 644 Umar was assassinated by a Persian slave. The new caliph, Uthman (*UHTH-mahn*), was chosen over his rival Ali by a committee of six Quraysh electors. Both men were sons-in-law of the Prophet. This election was closely contested, and Uthman's victory left a legacy of difficulties. A member of the Umayyad (*oo-MĪ-yahd*) family of Mecca, Uthman openly appointed his relatives to high positions, alienating many high-ranking Muslims. Ali's defeat drove his followers underground and placed the unity of Islam in doubt.

For the time being, warfare held the empire together. The Arab governor of Egypt built an Islamic fleet that captured Cyprus in 649, pillaged Sicily three years later, and in 655 moved against Constantinople. But these successes could not save Uthman from the consequences of his favoritism. Exasperated by his relatives, Arab garrisons in Mesopotamia and Egypt intrigued against him, and in 656 his enemies stormed his house and killed him.

Uthman's murder scandalized the Islamic world. Umar had been killed by a foreign slave bearing a grudge, but the assassins of Uthman were Muslims, including in their ranks a son of Abu Bakr. They were also kinsmen and associates of Ali, who was promptly elected caliph in his own right. Civil war broke out because Uthman's family was now compelled to avenge him, a duty required by Arabian custom. After massacres perpetrated by both sides, Ali was stabbed to death in 661 by one of his former followers. Muawiya (*moo-AH-wē-ah*), a kinsman of Uthman, was elected caliph after persuading Ali's eldest son to renounce his own claim.

Two major consequences flowed from this. First, Muawiya's selection created the **Umayyad Caliphate**, a succession of caliphs from the same family that presided over nine decades of Islamic expansion. Second, and in the long term more significant, the *umma* split permanently into two antagonistic groups. The Umayyads and their followers constituted the majority, calling themselves **Sunni** (SOO-nē, from the *Sunna* [SOO-nah], or traditional practices of the Prophet) and claiming to be the true heirs of Muhammad and the doctrinally pure practitioners of Islam. The followers of Ali and his line made up the minority, or *Shi'at Ali* (SHĒ-at ah-LĒ, "Party of Ali"), calling themselves **Shi'ites** (SHĒ-īts).

Doctrinal differences between the two groups were inconsequential in the beginning, but significant differences in practice emerged. For example, Shi'ite Muslims developed a religious hierarchy, while Sunnis did not. In addition, after Hussein (hoo-SĀN), second son of Ali and a grandson of Muhammad, led an uprising against the Umayyads in 680 in Iraq and was slain with nearly all his family, Shi'ites developed a sense of persecution and martyrdom that divided them emotionally from the majority.

The Umayyad Caliphate, 661–750

11.4 Trace the expansion and eventual overthrow of the Umayyad Caliphate between 661 and 750.

The split between Sunnis and Shi'ites changed the political nature of the Islamic empire. The Party of Ali never gave up asserting that they were the true heirs of the Prophet and that the Sunnis were usurpers. They constituted a minority within the caliphate, but they spread throughout it, preaching opposition to Sunni Islam in North Africa, Egypt, Syria, Mesopotamia, and Iran.

Muawiya was forced to deal with Shi'ite factionalism in his efforts to rebuild the moral authority of the caliphate. To limit fragmentation, he transformed the caliphate into a centralized authority, convincing its leaders to recognize his son Yazid as his successor before his own death. The elective system died out and was replaced by the dynastic principle. Muawiya hoped that this transformation would settle the issue of succession and block the Shi'ites from power. In practice, claimants to the title continued to emerge, particularly when the new caliph was very young, and the Islamic empire simply proved too large and unwieldy to centralize.

Umayyad Expansion

Factionalism within Islam slowed but did not stop the empire's dynamic expansionism. Muawiya had been proclaimed caliph in Jerusalem, but he promptly moved his government to Damascus, from which he could more readily threaten Byzantine power. His forces attacked Constantinople again in 669, blockading it between 673 and 678 but eventually failing, primarily because of the Byzantines' lethal incendiary weapon, Greek fire. Events farther east were more encouraging: Muslim armies overran eastern Afghanistan in 664 and penetrated western India as far as the lower Indus Valley. In North Africa, they reached the eastern border of Algeria by 670. However, in 680, Muawiya's passing led to a Shi'ite rebellion. When the Shi'ite leader Hussein was defeated and killed, Shi'ite hatred for Umayyad rule intensified.

For a time internal difficulties slowed the Islamic advance. In 682 rebellious Muslim forces besieged Mecca and burned the structure housing the Ka'ba. Meanwhile, centralization continued, with Arabic becoming the administrative language of the empire. Local officials were replaced by Arabians loyal to the caliphate, and a professional administrative elite replaced tribal chiefs. By 705, the caliphate rested on firmer foundations and was ready to return to conquest.

The wars that began in 705 differed substantively from earlier Islamic campaigns. With the nearby lands of Syria, Mesopotamia, Iran, and Egypt already in the caliphate, campaigns were undertaken in distant places that involved the cooperation of

In what ways did the Umayyad expansion differ from the earlier expansion of Islam?

non-Arabian armies. Islamic forces penetrated deep into western India and stormed across northern Africa while preparing for a mammoth, although ultimately unsuccessful, siege of Constantinople. This new expansionist wave spread the faith farther from Mecca and laid the foundation for Islamic commercial dominance throughout the region, linking the trade routes of the Mediterranean Sea, the Red Sea, the Arabian Sea, and the Indian Ocean.

In 711 a mixed expedition of Arabs and Berbers crossed the Strait of Gibraltar and invaded Spain. Within four years this army had pushed organized Christian resistance to the northern mountains of Iberia. For the first time, Islam was entrenched on the continent of Europe, and the Muslim advance appeared unstoppable. It appeared to be only a matter of time before all of the European kingdoms would fall, after which the Byzantine Empire could be assaulted from Europe as well as Asia.

Collapse of the Umayyad Caliphate

Why was the Umayyad dynasty overthrown?

The Islamic impulse had, however, reached its westward limits. After initial conquests in regions that were already Arab or that resented their governments, expansion became less easy. The Iranian highlands were subdued only after grinding, bloody warfare. Anatolia's Byzantines were Greek and tended to be loyal to Constantinople. North Africa stretched for 2000 miles from east to west, but only a few miles of its coastline were inhabitable. A joint Arab–Berber invasion of France was defeated in 732—or, as Roger Collins persuasively argues, 733—at the battle of Tours (Map 11.4) by a Frankish army commanded by Charles Martel. Unable to sustain a prolonged campaign so far north of their base in Spain, the invaders retreated south of the Pyrenees, ending a tumultuous century of Muslim expansion.

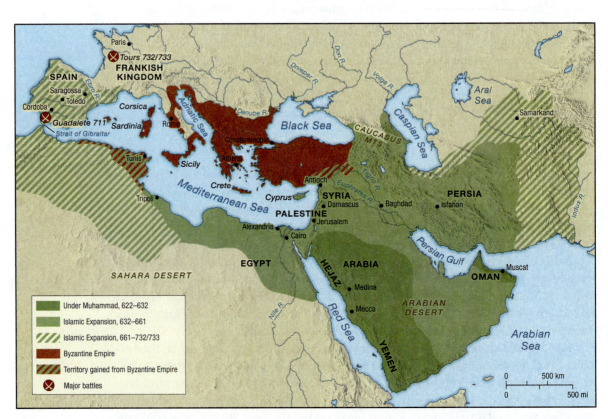

Map 11.4 ISLAMIC EXPANSION, 661–732/733 After expanding throughout Southwest Asia (Map 11.3), Islamic forces were blocked from entering southeastern Europe by the Byzantine Empire. They thereupon swept across North Africa, crossed the Strait of Gibraltar, and landed on the Iberian Peninsula in 711. Note that in present-day France, they were defeated at the battle of Tours by a Frankish army headed by Charles Martel. What sort of problems might such a far-flung empire pose for those trying to administer it?

During that century the Umayyad Caliphate had conquered immense stretches of territory from the Strait of Gibraltar to the Indus River Valley. This political empire had been unified economically into a Muslim zone of trade and commerce. Culturally, the spiritual principles of Islam and the widespread adoption of the Arabic language glued the far-flung realm together and gave it a sense of religious purpose. Ultimately, the economic and cultural connections forged by a century of Islamic conquest endured long after political unity had crumbled.

The crumbling of that unity was not far off. Shi'ites found support from another branch of the Sunni Quraysh, the Abbasids (*ah-BAH-sids*), descended from Abbas, one of the Prophet's uncles. The Abbasid clan advocated the overthrow of the Umayyads and reconciliation between Sunni and Shi'ite. Umayyad rule, based on exploitation of non-Arabs and lacking any mechanism to address their concerns, was increasingly viewed as illegitimate. In 747 revolts broke out in Afghanistan, Iran, and Mesopotamia, culminating in the seizure of the caliphate by Abbasid forces in 750. Umayyad rule was over, as was the heroic period of Islamic expansion. The Abbasids would emphasize consolidation over conquest.

Society and Culture in Early Islam

11.5 Show how Islam connected diverse peoples by creating a blended society and culture.

By 750 the Islamic empire stretched from Spain in the west, through North Africa, to Egypt, including Lebanon, Syria, and the Arabian Peninsula, and east through Mesopotamia, Iran, and Afghanistan into India. Unlike the other two major monotheistic religions, Islam combined a personal relationship with God, a dynamic military impulse, and a political succession based on blood relationship to a divinely inspired prophet. Preaching total submission to the will of God, Islam changed every society and culture it conquered, blending with them to produce a new Islamic society and culture.

Religious Observance: The Mosque

Among the distinctive creations of Islamic culture was the **mosque**, or Islamic house of worship, which architecturally blended the influences of many different societies. Immediately after conquering an area, Muslims marked it as their own by building mosques. Muhammad apparently did not intend to build any sort of temples, emphasizing personal prayer five times a day rather than prayer in communities. But his own home in Medina quickly became sacred space, and the Prophet himself decided that each such space should orient prayer in the direction of the Ka'ba in Mecca.

Mosques include no statues, portraits, or any other depictions of God, angels, or any person living or dead. The interior spaces are simply furnished. There are no chairs or benches for worshippers, and although some mosques contain a pulpit, this feature is not mandated. Walls are covered with artistic geometric designs and with verses from the Qur'an inscribed in Arabic; the rugs that cover the floors are similarly patterned. Minarets, or ornamental towers, are often attached to the sides of mosques so that an Islamic cleric can ascend to call the faithful to prayer at the appointed times of day.

In some cases, Muslims took existing churches in Christian lands they conquered and converted them to mosques. Usually, however, they built new structures, using them to demonstrate the supremacy of Islam over the "old" monotheistic faiths of Judaism and Christianity. The magnificent Dome of the Rock in Jerusalem, built by an early caliph, served that purpose by establishing an Islamic house of prayer on a site sacred to all three faiths. That place is the traditional site of King David's altar and

What were the purposes and characteristics of the mosque?

King Solomon's temple, making it significant to both Jews and Christians. In Islamic tradition, it is the spot on which Abraham was told by God to sacrifice his son Ishmael and from which Muhammad rode his horse into heaven during one holy night. Construction of a mosque on such a site carried the obvious implication that Islam had replaced what it considered ancient, inadequate forms of worship.

Byzantine and Persian motifs were often incorporated into Islamic architecture, not only in mosques but also in other public buildings and private residences. Arabian culture, primarily desert based, had few architectural styles of its own and readily adopted those from other lands that it found beautiful. Frescoes and mosaics decorated many such buildings. The overall impression of grace, beauty, and harmony is intended to replicate the ideal qualities of the universe as Muslims believe God designed it, and to reflect the God-centered nature of Muslim society.

The Dome of the Rock.

In what sense was the Shari'ah unlike other legal codes?

Legal Uniformity: The Shari'ah

The God-centric nature of Muslim society was probably most completely expressed in Islamic law, considered more important than theology to a practicing Muslim. Although pre-Islamic Arabia had no formal legal structure, the roots of the **Shari'ah** (*SHAH-rē-ah*), the Islamic legal code, are to be found there, and Muhammad himself was more an arbitrator, lawgiver, and judge than a theologian or politician. He endorsed many customs common to the pre-Islamic social order and enshrined them in the Shari'ah, a compilation of religiously sanctioned obligations and duties intended to regulate daily life so that men and women might more easily carry out the will of God in the *umma*. Consequently, the Shari'ah differs from secular legal systems, which use punishment to achieve social control. The Shari'ah, in contrast, prescribes the pathway to paradise.

Islamic law, in other words, is essentially moral and spiritual, the product of a new religion's concerted effort to turn a nomadic, tribal society away from the things of this world and toward the wishes of God. The Shari'ah accordingly prohibits gambling, intoxication, and the lending of money at interest. It restricts personal revenge and outlaws the blood feud that turned so much of Arabian tribal life into never-ending cycles of murder between rival families. It attempts to strengthen sexual morality and affirm the sanctity of marriage. It provides legal recourse for women, orphans, the disabled, the mentally infirm, the poor, and anyone else who might be termed defenseless within the social structure. In a culture that valued strength, the Shari'ah protected the weak.

Large sections of the Shari'ah are concerned with family life and gender relations. The wife is integrated into her husband's family and guaranteed a portion of his inheritance. Men are required to treat women with honor and respect. The insistence that women be veiled in public and spend much of their lives sequestered in their homes comes not from the Shari'ah but from Byzantine and Persian customs, which are designed in part to promote honor and respect for women. A man may marry as many as four wives, but if he does so, he must treat them equally in terms of financial support, sexual intercourse, household duties, and respect. Women are permitted to practice contraception, initiate divorce proceedings, remarry after divorce, and own property in their own names. Harsh penalties are provided for physical abuse of wives, adultery, and other such crimes.

Salat, or ritual worship, mandates a sequence of prayers to be performed five times each day.

The Shari'ah was compiled in the eighth, ninth, and tenth centuries C.E. and still forms the basis of civil and criminal law in some Islamic states. It provided legal uniformity throughout the early Islamic world and survived the subsequent deterioration of Islamic caliphates. But altering the Shari'ah in any meaningful way is considered impossible in Islamic society, as Muslims believe it represents the will of God as transmitted by the last and greatest of the prophets.

Thus, the same rigidity that helped perpetuate Islamic law's influence also made it increasingly obsolete as Islamic societies modernized and certain traditional practices and beliefs came into question. The status of women under the Shari'ah provides a valid example. Although it offered protections for women not available in eighth-century Arabia, it now places women in a position unequal to men. Women may sue for divorce only if they can show cause; a man needs no cause. Women can testify in court, but a man's testimony is weighted more heavily. Women are to be honored and respected but may have only one husband, while a man may have four wives. Penalties for adultery are much more severe for women than for men.

Tolerance of Other Faiths

In what ways and to what degree did early Islam tolerate other faiths?

Islamic law applied, of course, to all Muslims, and it formed the basis of civil law in all early Islamic states. But not all citizens of such states were Muslims. The dramatic expansion of Islam aimed to convert those unbelievers who were willing to accept Allah's message as delivered by Muhammad, and to subjugate those who would not convert. While conquered peoples were invited and encouraged to embrace Islam, forced conversions were rare and are in fact prohibited by the Qur'an. Non-Muslims were free to practice their religions under conditions imposed by Islamic law and were required to pay a heavy tax each year. This tax, which was not paid by Muslims, helped underwrite the expenses of the state. Obviously, if everyone converted to Islam, the financial impact on the government would have been negative. That fact made forced conversions both religiously forbidden and fiscally unwise. Tolerance for other creeds was characteristic of most Islamic societies, and Jews in particular often found it more congenial to live under Islamic rule than under Christian governments.

This level of tolerance, though impressive by the standards of the day, did not mean that people of other faiths accepted Islamic conquest. Christians in particular were horrified at the prospect of domination by rulers practicing a faith they considered heretical. The Byzantine Empire fought desperately to prevent the triumph of Islam, and Charles Martel's victory over the Muslims at Tours caused rejoicing throughout Europe. Although Muslims were required to tolerate other monotheists and treat them decently, they often treated those they conquered with thinly concealed contempt and sometimes with overt hostility. Polytheists and atheists, on the other hand, were barely tolerated, and many converted to Islam in order to improve their condition.

Chapter Review

Consequences and Connections

As the Umayyad Caliphate passed into history, Islam was only 140 years old. From a set of revelations claimed by an obscure merchant living on a desert peninsula, Islam evolved into a powerfully attractive monotheistic belief system with many more followers than Judaism or Zoroastrianism and only slightly fewer than Christianity.

The Prophet Muhammad provided a series of ideas that unified the previously fragmented Arabian Peninsula, setting aside tribal rivalries in the name of faith in Allah.

In addition to establishing Arab unity, Islam inspired warriors to spread their faith across thousands of miles

of Europe, Africa, and Asia. The new religion offered Spaniards, Berbers, Egyptians, Syrians, Mesopotamians, Persians, Afghans, and many others a set of easily comprehensible beliefs as well as a centralized governing structure that gave Muslims throughout the world a sense of community. The Shari'ah, a complex yet readily accessible religious law, helped ensure legal uniformity throughout the Islamic empire.

In the Golden Age of Islam, just ahead, this dynamic new culture would attain unprecedented heights as a dominant force in much of Africa and most of South Asia.

Reviewing Key Concepts

Ask Yourself

1. How did Islam transcend Arabian tribalism?

2. To what extent were Muhammad's beliefs original? In what ways were they derived from other belief systems familiar to Arabia?

3. Explain Islam's appeal to Arabs and to those they conquered.

4. What was the significance of the office of caliph in Islam's expansion between 632 and 732?

5. How and why do Sunni and Shi'ite Muslims differ?

Key Dates and Developments

520 C.E.	Ethiopian incursion into southern Arabia
570	Persian occupation of southern Arabia begins; Birth of Muhammad ibn Abd'Allah
610	Muhammad's revelations and the beginning of his preaching
622	The *Hijra,* or emigration from Mecca to Medina of Muhammad and his followers
630	Return of Muhammad to Mecca
632	Death of Muhammad; Caliphate of Abu Bakr (632–634)
634–644	Caliphate of Umar; Muslims take Damascus, Jerusalem, Persia, and Egypt
644–656	Caliphate of Uthman; Muslim naval victories
651	First compilation of the Qur'an

656–661	Caliphate of Ali, marked by blood feuds following Uthman's assassination
661–750	The Umayyad Caliphate, initiated by the murder of Ali; division between Sunni and Shi'ite Muslims
664	Muslim seizure of eastern Afghanistan
670	Muslims' arrival in eastern Algeria
673–678	Blockade of Constantinople
705–715	Islamic conquest of Algeria, Morocco, and Spain
713	Islam in India
732/733	Umayyad expansion halted by Charles Martel's victory at Battle of Tours
750–1258	The Abbasid Caliphate

Chapter 12
Religion and Diversity in the Transformation of Southern Asia, 711–1400

ANGKOR WAT The temples of Angkor Wat are reflected in the moat surrounding the temple complex in Siem Reap, Cambodia. Angkor Wat testifies to the influence of Hinduism in portions of Southeast Asia.

After reading this chapter, you should be able to:

12.1 Discuss Islam's eastward expansion, explaining why the Abbasids were unable to achieve political unification.

12.2 Show how Islam and Persia influenced each other.

12.3 Account for Islam's evolution from an Arabian to a cosmopolitan faith.

12.4 Explain the decline of the Abbasid Caliphate.

12.5 Describe the results and implications of the Islamic invasion of India.

12.6 Show how Hinduism and Buddhism transformed southern Asia.

Buddhism, Hinduism, and Islam Affect South Asia

In 711 an Arab ship passed the mouth of India's Indus River, sailing northwest from the island of Ceylon. Laden with spices, silks, and exquisite objects made from metal and jewels, it was bound for a Persian Gulf port at the mouth of the Tigris and Euphrates rivers. But the ship never arrived at its destination. From an inlet near the Indus, a pirate ship moved swiftly to intercept the Arab craft. The pirates captured the ship, killed the crew, and sailed off to tally the value of their plunder.

Hearing the news, the Umayyad governor awaiting the cargo was furious. How dare these pirates steal from Muslims? The governor probably realized that he could not locate the pirates or recover the cargo, but he could punish the entire region, as a warning that Arab ships were not to be disturbed. He promptly sent 12,000 mounted warriors against the rajahs (kings) of the western Indian region of Sind. Conquest proved easy, and suddenly the Muslims stood on the banks of the Indus, considering how attractive it might be to seize all of India for Islam.

This sequence of events, initiating direct contact between Muslims and Hindus, launched 13 centuries of conflict and connection between practitioners of the two religions.

Islam Expands Eastward

12.1 **Discuss Islam's eastward expansion, explaining why the Abbasids were unable to achieve political unification.**

Islam's defeats north of the Pyrenees deflected its further expansion into Persia, Afghanistan, and India, where its impact was dramatic. The **Abbasid Caliphate**, which assumed leadership of Islam by overthrowing the Umayyad dynasty in 750, relocated its capital eastward to Baghdad. It then extended its domination over the Iranian plateau and the remains of the Persian Empire. The Abbasids presided over Islam's Golden Age, a flourishing of learning and culture across the Muslim world from West and South Asia across North Africa to Spain. But this vast region was unified only by religion. In the long run, the Abbasids proved no more capable than the Umayyads of imposing centralized governance on such a diverse set of realms and peoples. They themselves fell victim to a series of revolts in outlying provinces, and in 945 a group of Iranian warlords reduced them to the status of a puppet government.

Islam was also beginning to penetrate the vast expanses of the Indian subcontinent, which since the collapse of Mauryan rule in 184 B.C.E. had been unified just once, under two centuries of Gupta rule (320–550). The arrival of Islam did not cause disunity but perpetuated it, as Hindus and Muslims persistently opposed one another, creating hostility that endures today.

Neither religion was able to prevail over the other, and as India divided between Hindus and Muslims, Hindu priests, Buddhist monks, and energetic merchants carried Indian culture into the mainland societies and islands of Southeast Asia. There a fascinating set of hybrid cultures emerged, influenced by India yet clearly distinct from its customs and traditions.

Islamic Persia and the Abbasid Caliphate

12.2 **Show how Islam and Persia influenced each other.**

The Islamic conquest of Iran was made possible by the decline of Sasanian Persia, weakened by its numerous inconclusive campaigns against the Byzantine Empire. Early in the seventh century, the Sasanian king Chosroes (*KAHS-ress*) II attacked the empire, taking Antioch, Damascus, Jerusalem, and Egypt (Map 12.1). But the Byzantines reconstructed their armies and in 622 launched a devastating drive into Sasanian lands. By 633 both Sasanians and Byzantines were exhausted, and at this precise moment Muslim warriors burst forth from Arabia. The Muslims' timing could not have been less convenient for the Sasanians, who were unable to mount an effective defense. Their armies were defeated by Islamic forces in 636, and their empire collapsed in 642.

Persia's conquest by the Muslims marked a dramatic break with its Zoroastrian religious heritage. Although the new rulers tolerated Zoroastrianism, its followers were subject to discrimination and taxation. Many converted to Islam, while others moved to western India near Bombay. A few persevered in remote corners of the Iranian plateau. Politically, the once-glorious Persian Empire was now absorbed into the Islamic empire. Muslim conquest marked the end of historic Persia as a powerful, independent political force.

Map 12.1 THE ABBASID CALIPHATE IN 800 C.E. Islam spread so rapidly that its practitioners were unable to develop political institutions that could govern its extensive acquisitions adequately. The Abbasid Caliphate sprawled from Syria to the Indus Valley, but the caliphs never exerted central control over their realm. Notice that their decision to relocate their capital from Damascus eastward to Baghdad testifies both to the importance of the eastern portion of the caliphate and to the difficulty of controlling the western portion. In the absence of political centralization, what techniques could the caliphs use to control their empire?

How did Persian influences modify Islam?

Persian Influences on Islamic Governance and Culture

Although the Persian Empire had ended, its culture survived in altered form under the Islamic regime. Persian culture blended with Islamic ideas of government to form a distinctive new culture exhibiting both Iranian and Arabian elements.

Muslims proved just as susceptible as Greeks to the attractions of Eastern forms of governance. Persian kings had exercised centralized powers far beyond those held by local Arabian tribal leaders, and the caliphs adopted as much of that authority as they dared. In particular, they admired the Persian policy of subordinating the religious authority of Zoroastrian priests to the political will of the emperor. Soon interpreters of Islamic law found themselves overruled by political officials who had deferred to religious authority during the Prophet's lifetime but intended to do so no longer. The power of the caliphate grew dramatically following the conquest of Persia. This enhancement of the caliph's authority, coupled with the growing importance of Arabic as a common language, provided a degree of unity in this region of the developing Islamic empire.

Arabic, of course, had always been the language of Islam. The Qur'an required that Arabic be used for all prayers. Thus, all converts had to learn Arabic, and many who did not convert realized that knowledge of that language was essential for dealing with their new masters. But the Persian language did not disappear, as Arabs were enchanted by its richness and beauty. Poets and scholars who wrote in Arabic began to adopt Persian expressions, imagery, and syntax; Persian plot lines found their way into Arabic folktales; Persian vocabulary supplemented and enriched spoken Arabic. The result was an Arabic language that grew beyond its roots to become a cosmopolitan tongue that Islamic conquerors could use to enhance their influence in Southwest Asia.

How important was Shi'ite support for the Abbasids?

The Impact of Shi'ite Opposition

The conquest of Persia took place within the context of the great Sunni-Shi'ite split, which divided the Islamic world after 661. Refusing to accept the Sunni leadership of the Umayyad caliphs, Persian Shi'ites made great progress preaching their beliefs on the Iranian plateau. That made it impossible for the Umayyads to impose a *Pax Islamica* (Islamic Peace) on their vast holdings. This failure annoyed merchants, who depended on political stability for their commerce to prosper.

Persians suffered from additional grievances. Non-Muslims in Iran were required to pay a special tax as the price of religious toleration. Upon conversion, this tax was supposed to disappear, but by 720 the Umayyad government, no longer able to enrich itself through easy conquests, was unable to balance its accounts and was therefore reluctant to lift this burden from converts. Moreover, the caliphate inexplicably refused to reinvest any of the income it derived from taxes in Persia itself, where arid conditions required constant, expensive irrigation. These grievances fueled a revolution in 747, led by a man who called himself Abu Muslim. His real name and ancestry are unknown, but his rhetorical and political skills energized Persian malcontents and attracted Shi'ite Arab dissenters.

The resulting turmoil squeezed the Umayyads between two angry groups, a situation that worked to the Abbasids' advantage when they overthrew the Umayyads in 750. The Abbasid revolt, which began in a northeastern Persian province in 747, was led by Muslims loyal to the family of a man named Abbas, an uncle of the Prophet Muhammad. Its success aided by uprisings in Persia, the Abbasid Caliphate took care to look after the needs of this province. Persia suddenly benefited from tax revenues, and Persian influence rose at the Abbasid court. Although Sunni Muslims themselves, the Abbasids strove to placate Persian Shi'ites, hoping perhaps to heal the century-old schism within the Islamic world or at least to ensure their continued domination of that world.

The Rise of Baghdad

The Abbasids also shifted the focus of the Islamic world eastward. The gateways to Europe through Constantinople and southern Africa through Ethiopia were barred by Christian states hostile to Islam. Northern Asia was mountainous and cold, filled with wolves and unfriendly Turkic tribes. Opportunity for Islamic expansion clearly lay in the east. In 763 the caliphate moved its capital east to a new city, which it built on the site of a tiny village known as Baghdad. Located in eastern Mesopotamia near the site of ancient Babylon, Baghdad's founding embodied the Abbasid transfer of emphasis from western to eastern Islam.

The caliphate's decision to relocate was considered carefully. In addition to being close to the eastern Islamic lands, Baghdad was strategically located at the juncture of the trade routes connecting Syria, Mesopotamia, and Persia. It had easy access to the Tigris and Euphrates rivers in one of the most fertile areas of Mesopotamia. Favored by its location, Baghdad quickly became the largest urban area in the history of western Asia, populated in the early 800s by somewhere between 300,000 and 500,000 people. By comparison, Constantinople at that point contained about 200,000 people. Baghdad proved to be central to the development not only of the Abbasid Caliphate but also of Islamic civilization.

What was the significance of the relocation of the caliphate's capital to Baghdad?

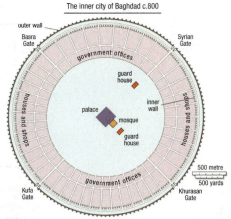

A sketch of the inner city of Baghdad around the year 800 C.E.

Cosmopolitan Islam

12.3 **Account for Islam's evolution from an Arabian to a cosmopolitan faith.**

Islam now developed a prosperous, cosmopolitan civilization. The Islamic faith had originated in the Arabian Peninsula, grounded in local Arab customs and culture. Its explosive century of expansion, however, had exposed it to a broad variety of ethnic and linguistic groups across southern Asia. For the leadership of Islam, a religion that claimed universality, the next step was both obvious and challenging: it must grow beyond its Arabian origins. To do so, it would have to reach out to people of diverse ancestries, offering them a path to salvation and combining their backgrounds and cultures into a new civilization that would be greater than the sum of its parts. To do otherwise would limit Islam's appeal, reserving its practice for an Arabian elite, denying its claim to worship the one true God, and perpetuating it as a conquering rather than constructing faith.

Baghdad enabled the Abbasids to take that next step. They made Islam a universal religion and inspired a golden age of Islamic civilization. Cosmopolitan and diverse, Baghdad welcomed Arabians, Mesopotamians, Syrians, Persians, Indians, Egyptians, Central Asians, Christians, Zoroastrians, Jews, and many others. In this new, vibrant city, these people were assimilated into a new, vibrant civilization built on a self-confident, dynamic faith that offered spiritual equality to all who embraced it. Growing into a major industrial and commercial center, Baghdad provided jobs for all who sought them and ample revenues to sustain Abbasid ambitions.

Abbasid Governance

Chief among Abbasid ambitions was correcting the errors of the Umayyads. While the Umayyads had reserved influential positions for Arabs, the Abbasids sought to advance talented people, regardless of ethnicity, to positions of responsibility. The government at Baghdad recruited personnel from throughout the empire with the promise of equality of opportunity in a large empire serving a universal faith. The privileged, elite status enjoyed by Arabs was abolished. Jews served the caliphate as bankers and financial advisors, Persians as bureaucrats and scribes, Mesopotamian Christians as engineers and diplomats.

How did the Abbasids revise the governance structures of the Umayyads?

Although Arabs supervised all these groups, they were Arabs completely devoted to the Abbasid regime. Exclusively Arab armies were replaced by a skilled force of paid professional soldiers of mixed ethnic background. No longer needed for conquest, they were assigned to maintain internal order and patrol the Byzantine frontier. Their leadership was Arabian, but their most important characteristic was loyalty rather than ethnic ancestry.

The Abbasids built on Umayyad governmental centralization and amplified it by adapting Sasanian Persian and Byzantine judicial and bureaucratic institutions. Control was maintained by the caliph and his advisors. Government bureaus collected taxes, kept records, handled correspondence, and disbursed tax revenues. Judges were charged with applying the Shari`ah to everyday life in every corner of the realm. A *wazir* (*WAH-zēr*) supervised and coordinated the entire politico-legal system in Baghdad. Governors closely tied to the caliph's family ruled outlying provinces with degrees of loyalty proportionate to their distance from the capital. As messages had to be transmitted slowly across the caliphate by either camel or ship, the caliph's operational authority dwindled significantly on the remote fringes of the empire. Conscious of the importance of centralization, the Abbasids strove to achieve it, but success eluded them.

Commerce and Culture in the Abbasid Caliphate

How did Abbasid intellectual achievements create connections across three continents?

The administrative stability of the Abbasid era promoted significant commercial and cultural achievements. Abbasid caliphs nurtured trade routes that crossed Asia, Africa, and Russia, while in the caliphate itself they fostered literature and the arts.

Perhaps because Muhammad himself had been a merchant, commercial activity was generally held in higher esteem in Islamic lands than in either Christian Europe or Confucian China. Abbasid caliphs, eager to increase their own immense wealth and the prosperity of the lands they ruled, lowered trade barriers, promoted the work of artisans and merchants, and encouraged long-distance commerce. A vast network of trade routes stretched by land across Central Asia and the Sahara Desert, and by water across the Mediterranean and the Red and Arabian Seas. Products widely traded included Chinese silks and Indian spices; gold, salt, slaves, and ivory from Africa; steel and leather from Spain; and magnificent handwoven carpets and textiles from southern and western Asia. Banking and credit helped finance expensive commercial enterprises. Widespread use of the Arabic language eased business transactions, and Arabic numerals simplified and standardized bookkeeping. The caliph Harun al-Rashid (*hah-ROON al-rah-SHĒD*), who ruled from 786 to 809, negotiated peace with the Khazars so that Arab merchants could pass west of the Caspian Sea and reach the Volga River. From there they could trade with Scandinavia, exchanging their gold and silver for luxurious furs (which quickly became status symbols in the caliphate's deserts).

Eager to imitate the Indo-Persian civilizations, the Abbasids led their empire into a spectacular cultural renaissance. Harun al-Rashid brought to Baghdad authors, artists, architects, and entertainers from as far

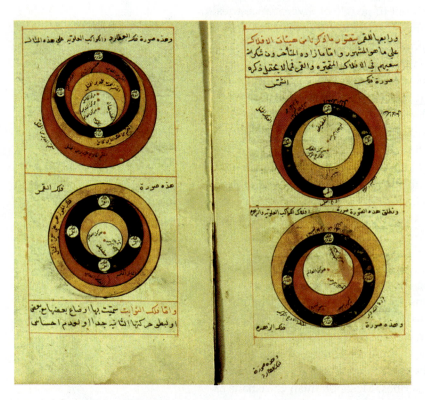

A page from a 12th-century Islamic manuscript dealing with alchemy.

away as Morocco in North Africa and Delhi in India, and they made the city a radiant cultural center. Harun's son established in Baghdad an academy called the House of Wisdom. There some scholars translated ancient Greek, Latin, and Sanskrit writings into Arabic, while others laid the foundation for the devotion to keen observation and objective thinking that became characteristic of Arab scientific and intellectual life.

From the eighth through the twelfth centuries, Islamic learning blossomed. The philosopher Ibn Sina (*ib-un SĒ-nah*), later known in Europe as Avicenna, translated and wrote commentaries on the works of Aristotle, which at this time were unknown in the West. Ibn Sina was also inspired by the discovery of Indian and Greek writings on medicine, which he and other Muslims translated, compiled, explained, and amplified. The Persian scholar al-Khwarizmi (*al-kwa-RIZ-mē*) analyzed the findings of various classical thinkers, including Claudius Ptolemy, whose detailed conception of an earth-centered universe was later revised by other Muslims and prevailed until the seventeenth century both in the Islamic world and the West.

A Muslim astronomer's depiction of the constellation Sagittarius, copied from the original manuscript in 1730.

Inspired by their contacts with India and China, Muslims under the caliphate proved to be talented innovators. For example, they developed the quadrant, the astrolabe, the celestial globe, and other instruments of navigation. Most of these had been invented by other peoples, but Muslims refined and used them to great advantage. Muslims also excelled at physics and optics, and they developed windmills, watermills, water clocks, new methods of irrigation, and instruments used in meteorology. Applying Persian and Indian mathematics, al-Khwarizmi devised both algebra and the Arabic numerals that are universally used today.

The production of paper provides an excellent example of Islamic development of an earlier invention. Paper had been invented in China sometime between 200 and 50 B.C.E. When Muslims encountered this product, they found that it was made of wood-based fibers derived from tropical plants like bamboo, hemp, and jute. Papers made from these fibers were not particularly durable, and since these plants did not grow in Islamic lands, Muslims looked for new sources of fiber. They began to use rags made from linen or from cotton cloth, which produce paper that is extremely durable. In 794, the first Islamic paper mill was built in Baghdad. Soon the availability of this paper throughout Muslim lands encouraged scholarly writing in every area of knowledge. Paper made it possible for Muslims to preserve, and eventually transmit, Greek and Byzantine knowledge and culture. When Europe first came into contact with this Islamic knowledge base in the twelfth century, its scholars were both impressed and intimidated.

Muslims considered education an act of worship, a quest for God that was required of all believers. Islamic schools, called **madrasas** (*mah-DRAH-saz*), educated males, while females were educated at home. Coeducation was just as unthinkable in the eighth-century caliphate as it would later be in nineteenth-century Europe, but that does not mean that women remained ignorant. Some males opposed the education of women, but theirs was a minority opinion.

Works of fiction and folklore also flourished in this era. The most famous of these was *The 1001 Nights*, also known in the West as *The Arabian Nights*. Embellished over the centuries, this assortment of fanciful and fantastic fables eventually came to include such well-known adventure stories as "Sinbad the Sailor" and "Aladdin and His Magic Lamp." Of the many marvelous works of poetry produced in this period, among the best known is *The Rubaiyat*, a collection of verses originally composed around 1100 by a famous scientist and mathematician named Omar Khayyam (see "Quatrains from *The Rubaiyat*").

Sufis and Fundamentalists

Not everyone in the caliphate participated in the economic and cultural achievements of Islam's Golden Age. Many devout Muslims worried that the age's emphasis on material prosperity, its encouragement of artistic expression, and its wide-ranging

In what ways did Sufism and religious conservatism attempt to revitalize Islam?

Document 12.1   Quatrains from *The Rubaiyat*

Omar Khayyam's collection of quatrains, or four-line poetic stanzas, was translated from Omar's elegant Persian into English by Edward FitzGerald in 1859. This translation made the work accessible to Western readers, and it has since been translated into more than one hundred languages. Omar was a master of astronomy, history, jurisprudence, mathematics, medicine, and philosophy as well as poetry. The Rubaiyat *reveals his fatalistic fascination with questions of eternal interest: Who are we? Why are we here? Where are we going? What is the nature of our relationship to God?*

The moving finger writes; and, having writ,
Moves on; nor all your piety nor wit
Shall lure it back to cancel half a line,
Nor all your tears wash out a word of it.

Oh, threats of hell and hopes of paradise!
One thing at least is certain: **this** life flies.
One thing is certain and the rest is lies:
The flower that once has blown forever dies.

SOURCE: From *The Rubaiyat*, translated by Edward FitzGerald.

intellectual efforts undermined the simplicity and spirituality of their faith. As various groups sought different ways to revitalize Islam and return it to its roots, several distinct responses emerged.

One was **Sufism** (*SOO-fizm*). Originating in eighth-century Iraq and Persia, Sufism was a mystic strain of Islam that advocated direct union with God through prayer, contemplation, and religious ecstasy. It complemented the public rituals of prayer and observance of the Shari`ah with private devotions leading to an inner emotional relationship with God. Sufism developed gradually during the first three centuries of Islamic history. In its early stages, it was characterized by rejection of the luxury and wealth that Islam had come to emphasize under the influences of Persia and Byzantium. Sufism favored a simple lifestyle, recalling the devout Muslim to the origins of the faith on the austere deserts of the Arabian Peninsula. In Arabic, *suf* (*SOOF*) means "wool," and Sufis (*SOO-fēz*) wore rough woolen clothing, obviously uncomfortable in the Middle Eastern heat, to symbolize their renunciation of worldly pleasures, a renunciation also practiced by Buddhist and Christian mystics and monks. Later Sufism also came to involve the pursuit of a mystical union with God through elaborate dances and ceremonies. Sufi doctrines varied widely as different brotherhoods of Sufis developed. One principal tradition was centered in Mecca and another in northeastern Persia, although Sufi brotherhoods also became common across the Islamic world.

Another response to the materialism of the Abbasid Caliphate was the growth of religious conservatism. Unlike Sufis, who strove mainly to withdraw from the secular world, conservatives sought to combat and repress it. In general, Islamic conservatives believed that Islam itself had become corrupted by secular influences, and that purification of the *umma* was necessary to restore fidelity to the original revelations of Allah transmitted through Muhammad. Like Sufism, Islamic religious conservatism took a wide variety of forms, including Wahhabism, which eventually became the dominant form of Islam on the Arabian Peninsula.

Inspired by a deep suspicion of intellectual pursuits, the conservatives who dominated eleventh-century Spain exiled both the great Muslim scholar-physician Ibn Rushd (*ib-un ROOSHD*), known in the West as Averroës, and the Jewish philosopher Moses Maimonides (*mī-MAH-nih-dēz*), charging them with polluting the Qur'an by trying to reconcile it with modern philosophy. Later Islamic governments in Spain appointed religious courts, instructing them to enforce the Shari`ah against any attempts at secularization.

Conservative resistance to secularization fostered a climate of intellectual repression. As Islamic scientific and technological curiosity was submerged in religious fervor, Islam found itself poorly prepared to face the cultural and military challenges posed by the West.

The Decline of the Abbasid Caliphate

12.4 **Explain the decline of the Abbasid Caliphate.**

Like all large empires before them, the Abbasids found their vast territory difficult to rule. Communication over thousands of miles separating Spain from Baghdad was challenging enough under the best of circumstances. Quarrels between rival leaders, disputes between Sunni and Shi'ite Muslims, and tensions between various ethnic groups also interfered with the ability of the Abbasids to govern effectively and frustrated their dream of conquering the world for Islam.

Forces of Disintegration

The glory of Islamic learning could not obscure the disintegration of the caliphate, which set in even before its consolidation was complete. First, Harun al-Rashid's two sons fought for the right to succeed him as caliph, causing four years of civil strife. Second, the succession conflict helped create a warlord nobility that undermined the Abbasid drive for centralization and provided a focus for Persian Shi'ite opposition to the Abbasid Sunni regime. These warlords rivaled and eventually replaced the caliph. Third, to increase their power the Abbasids established armies of Turkish slaves from Central Asia called mamluks (*MAM-lukes*).

These male slaves, purchased before they turned 13, were converted to Islam and segregated in military barracks. There they studied military tactics, developed loyalty and comradeship, and after several years, became soldiers in the caliph's armies. In theory, every mamluk was a disciplined servant of the state, without ties to family or region; his loyalty was to the caliph and the army. In practice, mamluks fought for the caliph only so long as he paid them well and proved a competent leader. They antagonized the people of Baghdad, most of whom considered them uncivilized foreigners, so Caliph al-Mu'tasim built a new capital at Samarra (*sah-MAR-rah*) in Mesopotamia in 836 and took the mamluks with him. The move solved one problem but created another by eroding the caliphate's authority.

Finally, growing disloyalty in the Abbasid bureaucracy accelerated the caliphate's decline. Dominated by factions based on family ties and cronyism, the bureaucrats began to peddle their services and influence to the highest bidders. As caliphs became less able to maintain control of the central government, discontented factions in outlying areas took advantage of the situation and revolted. Occasionally the caliphs were able to restore order, but only by using the unpopular mamluks. As the authority of the central administration disintegrated, the empire itself collapsed.

Although the last caliph did not leave the throne until his murder by the Mongols in 1258, the tenth century marked the end of effective Abbasid rule. One by one, provinces of the empire had broken away. Egypt was taken over by a mamluk family in 868 and then by the Shi'ite Fatimid dynasty in 969. The governor of Islamic Spain created his own independent caliphate in 929, confirming a separation that had actually begun much earlier. A mass revolt of frontier troops that could not be repressed resulted in the loss of Persia in the ninth century. By 935 the Abbasid caliph had lost control of every province outside the immediate vicinity of Baghdad. After a power struggle lasting nearly a decade, the Buyid

> What forces of disintegration affected the Abbasid Caliphate?

The Mosque of Ibn Tulun, Cairo.

(*BOO-yid*) dynasty of Shi'ite Persian warlords seized control of Baghdad in 945. The caliphs were allowed to remain as puppet rulers but exercised no authority; after 945 their rule was entirely symbolic.

Continuity of Islamic Unity and Expansion

How did the Muslims try to preserve unity as the caliphate's political centralization weakened?

Political fragmentation did not, however, destroy the unity of Islam. Despite its multitude of rulers and cultures, the Muslim community was still held together by Shari'ah and the Qur'an. Islamic law provided a code of conduct that differentiated Muslims from all other peoples. Stipulations that the Qur'an must be read only in Arabic helped make that language a unifying force across different Muslim cultures. Finally, the pilgrimage to Mecca, a common practice in pre-Islamic Arabia that Muhammad eventually required of all believers, helped create cohesion.

The pilgrimage symbolized the equality of all Muslims in the context of their complete submission to Allah. Pilgrims were greeted at the outskirts of Mecca, where they exchanged their clothing for simple white robes in which they entered the holy city. During the entire seven days of the pilgrimage, no distinctions of birth, race, wealth, or position separated one Muslim from another. All wore the same white robes, performed the same rituals, and professed the same unworthiness in the sight of Allah. The pilgrimage also promoted contacts and common values among pilgrims from diverse cultures, inspiring them to foster these values in their native lands.

Nor did political division put an end to Islamic expansion. Indeed, even as the caliphate declined and the various Muslim factions fought against each other, Islamic faith and Islamic armies were penetrating into India, clashing with the ancient cultures of that immense subcontinent.

The Islamic Impact on India

12.5 **Describe the results and implications of the Islamic invasion of India.**

The Arab invasion of the Sind in western India had begun in 643, but when the Caliph Umar realized how much wasteland lay between his forces and the rest of India, he called off the campaign. Then the piracy of an Umayyad ship in 711, described at the beginning of this chapter, provoked the Umayyad governor to conquer a 100-mile-wide stretch of land east of the Indus River. Those actions established contact between Muslims and Hindus that altered the economic and cultural frameworks of the Indian subcontinent. Eventually India became part of a sprawling Indian Ocean Islamic trading network, while tensions between Hindu polytheists and Muslim monotheists divided the region for centuries.

Islamic Invasions from Persia

In what ways was Mahmud of Ghazni a connective influence?

After the initial Umayyad incursion, northern India successfully resisted further Islamic advances until 998 when a new threat emerged, this time from Persia, which was now divided among three groups of Muslim warlords. The Buyids, who had conquered Baghdad and subordinated the Abbasid caliphs in 945, ruled Mesopotamia and western Persia from then until 1055; the Samanids (*sah-MAH-nids*) controlled eastern Persia from 819 to 999; and the Ghaznavids (*gaz-NAH-vids*) dominated northeastern Persia and Afghanistan from 962 until 1040 (Map 12.2). Baghdad's fall in 945 opened the frontiers between the Middle East and Central Asia to nomadic Turkish tribes that crossed between these regions at will. In the eleventh century, one of these

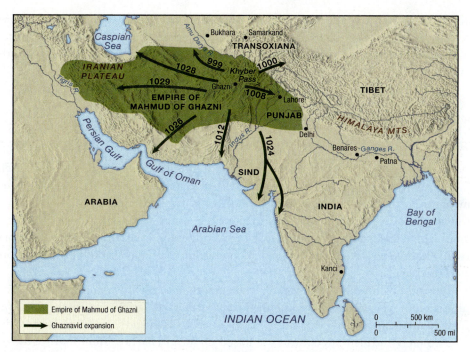

Map 12.2 **THE GHAZNAVID ISLAMIC EMPIRE, 1030** Early in the 11th century, Mahmud of Ghazni created an Islamic empire in northeastern Persia, Afghanistan, the Punjab, and western India. Observe that the Ghaznavid Empire, in creating political linkage across these regions, laid the foundation for economic, religious, and cultural connections between societies. How might such connections have affected Indian society and culture?

tribes, the Seljuk (*SELL-jook*) Turks, took both Persia and Anatolia from the weakened Abbasids, adding Turkish customs and genes to an already simmering stew of ethnicities.

The Buyids of western Persia legitimized themselves by propping up the caliphs and then governing like the warlords they were. In eastern Persia, the Samanids tried to replicate the early Abbasid bureaucracy. They presided over a cultural renaissance centered on the city of Bukhara (*boo-KAH-rah*), in which Arabic literary and legal forms blended with Persian, and Farsi joined Arabic as a language of transmission for Islamic culture. Finally, in northeastern Persia and Afghanistan, the Ghaznavid government of mamluks took control of both state and bureaucracy, creating a hybrid Persian-Islamic culture while attacking every non-Islamic area within reach. The most attractive area was India.

The Ghaznavids took their name from the Afghan city of Ghazni, just west of the Khyber Pass. From that stronghold they could plunder the trade routes between India and southwestern Asia. Between 998 and 1030, Mahmud of Ghazni (*MAH-mood of GAZ-ně*), known as the "Sword of Islam," led 17 raids on the northwestern Indian region of Punjab. He pillaged its cities remorselessly, destroying magnificent Hindu temples (whose idols, from his Islamic viewpoint, were abominations) and confiscating every jewel, coin, and woman he could find. This plunder enriched Ghazni, which quickly became a major cultural center of the Islamic world. Its glittering mosques and palaces were heavily influenced by Persian architectural concepts. But the empire was founded on bloodshed, rape, and destruction, all carried out in the name of God and in the interest of profit.

Shortly before his death in 1030, Mahmud annexed the Punjab. The Ghaznavid dynasty now controlled all of northwestern India, including the Indus Valley. But in Ghazni the political situation was deteriorating. Ignoring the advice of his Persian counselors, Mahmud had permitted the Seljuk Turks to use grazing pastures in Ghaznavid territory. The Seljuks responded by making war on the Ghaznavids and by 1040 had expelled them from northeastern Persia. Leaving that region to their enemies, the Ghaznavids relocated to northwestern India, which they plundered relentlessly while generating hatred and bitterness within the Hindu population.

What were the principal connections and conflicts between Muslims and Hindus in India?

Conflict and Connection: Muslims and Hindus

Hostility between Muslims and Hindus, which continues to plague the Indian subcontinent today, is rooted both in the behavior of the Ghaznavids and in religion itself. There was little compatibility between these two belief systems. Islam's rigorous, uncompromising monotheism holds that there is only one God and that all human beings must subordinate themselves to his will in every act of daily life. To Muslims, Hinduism, with its vast number of gods and goddesses, is simply polytheistic idolatry. To Hindus, however, the Muslims' monotheistic conviction is both presumptuous and preposterous.

Beyond this fundamental fissure, Islam asserts the essential equality and unworthiness of all people who stand before Allah. This view, grounded in ancient Arab tribal customs, gives any Muslim the right to address even the most exalted leader as an equal. Hinduism, in contrast, is based on a rigid caste system that reinforces inequality between different levels of society. To Muslims, a system that assigns a majority of the population to lifelong discrimination is offensive. Since a caste is a social class into which you are born and from which you cannot move, this system has always discouraged conversion to Hinduism: if caste is determined by birth and you are not born Hindu, how can you fit into Indian society? Many other differences between Hinduism and Islam exist, but these two distinctions—the number of gods worshipped and the value of equality—have proved sufficient to ensure more than a millennium of mutual suspicion.

Coupled with religious incompatibility was the behavior of the invading Ghaznavids. Their regime was created by slave soldiers who had been brutalized by decades of warfare with Central Asians and who were interested only in conquering and converting foreign peoples, not in assimilating them. Considering Hindus' polytheism, they placed little value on Indian culture, customs, art, or architecture, much of which they destroyed. The Hindus fought back, often, for example, setting fire to Ghaznavid mosques and burning the worshippers alive.

Consequently, the basic incompatibility between Islam and Hinduism was intensified by atrocities and persecutions on both sides. Yet despite this hostility, from the tenth century onward, Hindus and Muslims shared the subcontinent and eventually learned to live together. Lower-class people began to enjoy each other's religious festivals and often lived in mixed neighborhoods. Brahmins socialized easily with Islamic elites despite Hindu prohibitions against such contact. Even the Ghaznavid atrocities were mitigated by ethnic prejudice: many Indians held the invaders responsible not because they were Muslims, but because they were Afghans or Turks (and therefore barbarians). Indian Muslims, on the other hand, were not barbarians and were assumed to be friendly.

The Ghaznavids retained the advantage until 1186, when they were ejected by another Islamic Turkish tribe, the Ghurids (*GUR-ids*). Hindus put up fierce resistance against the Ghurids, having learned in the eleventh century exactly what Turkish occupation meant for their families and their culture. Buddhists suffered even more than Hindus, in part because their faith's rejection of violence made them reluctant to resist aggression, and in part because, like Islam, their faith sought converts and Muslims viewed it as competitive. The Ghurids destroyed Buddhist monasteries throughout India, driving the faith from its native soil. While flourishing in exile in Tibet, Japan, China, and Southeast Asia, Buddhism did not return to India with any significant presence until the 1950s, when India was unified under a secular democracy that granted toleration to all faiths (Chapter 35).

Despite Hindu resistance, the Ghurids eventually triumphed, establishing what came to be known as the Delhi Sultanate. From 1206 to 1526, a succession of sultans tackled the challenge of consolidating an Islamic regime in a region dominated by Hindu culture and beliefs. The result was a society combining both Hindu and Islamic characteristics. Although at first the Delhi Sultanate leveled Hindu temples and sought conversions, it soon changed course, staking its stability on values that Hindus and Muslims could share, including loyalty to kings, strong relationships between patrons and clients, and virtues such as service and honor. Delhi's ruling elite was primarily Islamic, but meritorious or wealthy Hindus were permitted to enter it while retaining their faith and customs. No more than a quarter of the northern Indian population converted to Islam, and for three centuries the Delhi Sultanate ruled a predominantly Hindu population through collaboration rather than confrontation.

Delhi brought stability to northern India and at one point was able to expand its holdings into the southern part of the subcontinent. But it could not hold all of India together: the subcontinent was simply too large and too diverse, linguistically and culturally. India continued to be buffeted and battered by internal conflicts and external attacks, and eventually it was conquered by invaders from the north.

The Quwwat-ul-Islam mosque in Delhi, featuring Hindu motifs such as tasselled ropes and bells.

India's Influence on Southeast Asia

12.6 Show how Hinduism and Buddhism transformed southern Asia.

Islam was not the only religion to transform southern Asia. As Muslim rule migrated across Southwest Asia and India, Hinduism and Buddhism spread into Southeast Asia, bringing India's influence to a vast region already affected by China.

Funan: The First Southeast Asian State

Geographically, Southeast Asia is divided into three subregions: the Southeast Asian mainland (sometimes called Indochina), the Malay (*MĀ-lā*) peninsula, and the Indonesian archipelago (*ahr-kih-PEL-ah-gō*), or group of islands. Southeast Asia is a seismically active area, part of the "Ring of Fire" surrounding the Pacific Ocean, and most of the islands are volcanic in origin (Map 12.3). Its tropical climate, abundant rainfall, and highly fertile soils give it great agricultural potential. But this promise has been difficult to realize. As much of the area is covered by teeming rain forests, farmland must be cleared again and again but without removing so much cover that the soil washes away. As a result, the large populations of Southeast Asia walk a fine line between survival and catastrophe.

Little is known of the origins of the first inhabitants of Southeast Asia. They had lived there for many centuries before the sustained immigrations from southern China that began around 3000 B.C.E. Many original inhabitants remained in the region, becoming the peoples now referred to as Malays. Others moved eastward across the Pacific Ocean or westward across the Indian Ocean, sailing in sturdy double-outrigger canoes built to compensate for strong oceanic swells. They populated many of the islands that dot those seas.

Southeast Asia lay across a trade route widely used in the first centuries of the Common Era to transport goods from China to India and from there to the

How did Indian and Chinese cultures influence the Funan Empire?

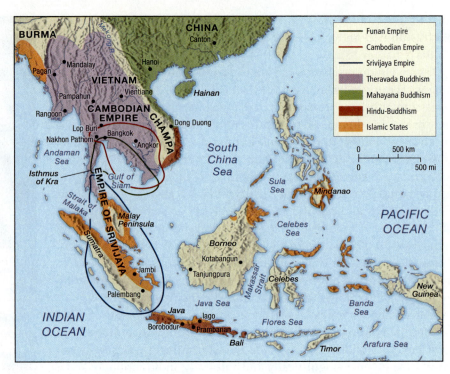

Map 12.3 SOUTHEAST ASIA, 800–1400 In Southeast Asia, Islam, Buddhism, and Hinduism coexisted at the crossroads of the Indian and Pacific Oceans. All three religions entered the region on ships carrying goods between India and China. Notice the strategic location of the Indonesian islands, perfectly placed as connectors between these two great oceans. In what ways did the convergence of these three religions, combined with the intense commercial activity typical of Southeast Asia, create unique societies?

Mediterranean basin. Eventually Malay merchants, who controlled oceangoing traffic, added spices from Southeast Asia to their shipments of Chinese silk. As a connection point for traders from both India and China, Southeast Asia eventually absorbed cultural elements from both of its wealthy and powerful neighbors.

In what is today southern Vietnam, the first Southeast Asian state emerged in the first century C.E. Chinese traders referred to it as Funan (*foo-NAHN*). Its point of origin was the Mekong (*MĒ-kong*) River delta, but quickly it expanded southward into the Malay Peninsula, enabling it to control trade across the strategically located Isthmus of Kra (*KRAH*), a narrow neck of land between the South China Sea and the Bay of Bengal. Merchants preferred to carry their cargoes across it rather than risk the lengthy ocean voyage around the Malay Peninsula. Funan's control of this transfer point increased its prosperity as well as its exposure to foreign peoples and cultures.

With the traders came their ways of life. Most of the actual transporting, buying, and selling was done by Indians. Accordingly, Buddhist monks and Hindu priests from India arrived in Funan shortly after the merchants. The learning of these religious men, as well as their familiarity with events outside the region, quickly made them sought-after counselors to local princes, and their religious beliefs and artistic tastes spread readily through the population. As intermarriage increased, a cultural synthesis occurred, featuring the adoption of Sanskrit as a written language and considerable mixing of cuisine and customs. Literary works native to India were also sometimes adopted by Southeast Asians, who added their own villains and heroes to the ancient Vedic sagas. For many years Indian influence was so pervasive that all of Southeast Asia was known as "farther India." The Chinese remained aloof from most of Southeast Asia, but they took a close commercial interest in Vietnam, and Chinese expansionism affected both Vietnam and Thailand.

Following Funan's lead, other Southeast Asian states began to consolidate after 600 C.E. In what today is Thailand, for example, the local tribes, fearful of Chinese territorial expansion, unified into a loose confederacy heavily influenced by Buddhism. They maintained a tense, uneasy relationship with the Chinese until both were overrun by the Mongols in 1253. Farther east, another state developed in Vietnam, partly in response to periodic Chinese invasions, some of which were followed by occupation but usually by reduction to tributary status. The country finally expelled the Chinese in the tenth century, but memories of its long, bitter subjugation linger to this day, as does a powerful Chinese influence upon Vietnamese culture. In particular, Confucian social doctrine and the prevalence of a highly educated bureaucracy recruited through merit endured in Vietnam until the middle of the twentieth century, as have many elements of Chinese cuisine.

The Cambodian Empire

Dominating the southern portion of the Southeast Asian mainland was the Cambodian Empire. Funan enjoyed well-developed links to the Khmer (*k'MARE*) people, the main ethnic group of modern Cambodia, who originated north of that state along the Mekong River valley in what is today Laos. Around 600 C.E. the developing Khmer state of Chenla absorbed Funan, and over the next two centuries the framework for a Cambodian empire emerged, locating its capital near the inland town of Angkor (*ANG-kor*).

Cambodia was heavily influenced by Hinduism, although Buddhism was welcomed and amiably tolerated. Strong Hindu influence was seen particularly in the construction of religious buildings. Over two centuries an extensive Hindu temple complex was constructed near the Khmer capital at Angkor Wat. Dedicated to the Hindu god Vishnu, its elaborate buildings and ceremonial rooms entranced visitors long after the collapse of the state that had built it. Following that collapse, the complex at Angkor Wat was abandoned and forgotten. Only in the nineteenth century was it rediscovered by French explorers.

Hindu influence was also apparent in Cambodian government. The king was assisted, and to some extent restricted, by an intricate Hindu bureaucracy dominated by military leaders and Hindu priests. But the Hindu caste system was never replicated in Cambodia, which retained an unusually egalitarian social structure.

The Cambodian Empire slowly expanded south to the Gulf of Siam. It endured until the early 1200s, when it was overthrown and replaced by a Thai tribal regime.

What was the impact of Hinduism on the Cambodian Empire?

Srivijaya: Coalition and Cultural Blend

The most complex of the early Southeast Asian states was centered not on the mainland, where Funan and the Khmer state were located, but on the Indonesian island of Sumatra (*soo-MAH-trah*). This was the Malay kingdom of Srivijaya (*srē-vē-JĪ-yah*), first described to the outside world by a Chinese Buddhist pilgrim in 671.

Srivijaya is a Sanskrit word meaning "great conquest." It appears to have been created as a maritime trading empire, catering to oceangoing traffic between China and India that was bypassing the overland portage across the Isthmus of Kra. As sailors became more familiar with the dangerous passage through the straits between Sumatra and the Malay Peninsula, the time saved outweighed the risks incurred, and the new kingdom prospered while Funan's power declined.

The capital of Srivijaya was the Malay port city of Palembang (*pah-lum-BANG*) on the coast of Sumatra. Its rulers were accomplished diplomats, stitching together a coalition of Malay maritime principalities through a careful balance of Buddhist spiritual leadership, bribery, and intimidation. Although known to history as an empire, Srivijaya was politically decentralized. It never expanded its territorial control even to the neighboring island of Java, preferring to influence principalities there through the same combination of tactics that worked so well on Sumatra.

What was the impact of Buddhism on the Malay kingdom of Srivijaya?

Relief sculpture at the temple complex of Borobodur in central Java, depicting scenes from the life of the Buddha.

While the Cambodian Empire was grounded in Hinduism, Srivijaya was overwhelmingly Buddhist. The spectacular Buddhist temple complex called Borobodur (*bō-rō-bō-DUHR*), built in central Java between 770 and 825, was constructed with more than 2 million cubic feet of stone. At the time it was the largest integrated network of buildings south of the equator. A ten-tiered megaplex, it represents the ten levels of increasing enlightenment passed through by the pilgrim on his or her spiritual journey to nirvana. Borobodur testifies to the pervasiveness of Buddhist cultural influence in Southeast Asia, as Cambodia's Angkor Wat testifies to Hindu influence.

But whether they adopted Hindu or Buddhist architecture, whether they adopted Sanskrit as a written language or translated Vedic epics into their own tongues, the Southeast Asian states did much more than *adopt* Indian culture. They *adapted* it to their own tastes and purposes, integrating it, for example, with their own customs of spirit worship and tribal rule. Ancient Indonesian deities were transformed into Hindu gods and goddesses, while traditional Indonesian dances and songs were blended with Indian rhythms and played on Indian instruments. These processes created a series of hybrid, blended cultures unlike any others.

Srivijaya flourished for several centuries, until it was weakened in 1025 by a devastating raid launched by one of its commercial competitors, the southeastern Indian state of Chola (*CHŌ-lah*). After that Srivijaya's fortunes declined sharply, and by the thirteenth century it had disintegrated into smaller maritime principalities. The Javanese king Kertanagara (*kur-tan-ah-GAH-rah*) constructed a short-lived successor state in the late 1200s, but after that no comparable system arose in the Indonesian archipelago until the Dutch East India Company arrived at the beginning of the seventeenth century.

Chapter Review

Consequences and Connections

Islam's Abbasid Caliphate looked eastward rather than westward, and its willingness to accept a synthesis of Arabic and Persian cultures on the Iranian plateau added greatly to the richness of Islamic civilization. The Abbasids presided over an Islamic golden age in commerce, culture, poetry, and power. But they were unable to unify the Islamic world, owing to the immensity and ethnic diversity of their conquests.

In the eleventh century, the caliphate was superseded by the rule of Central Asian warlords who carried Islam into India. They were no better at unification than the Abbasids. The Indian subcontinent's vastness, diversity of geographic features and cultures, and attachment to Hinduism consistently frustrated both external and internal efforts to impose unification. Between 1206 and 1526, the Delhi Sultanate attempted to create a hybrid Indian-Islamic system, with more success culturally than politically.

The peoples of Southeast Asia were influenced by commercial contacts with China and by the Indian religions of Hinduism and Buddhism. Funan, Cambodia, and Srivijaya developed states that tried to manage the trade flowing between China and India. They succeeded for a time but eventually dissolved in the face of external invasion or internal ethnic rivalry. Hinduism and Buddhism offered many insights into the nature of human life and the destiny of human souls but few into administrative organization and political power. Eventually, Islam and European imperialism would contend for dominance in Southeast Asia.

Reviewing Key Concepts

Abbasid Caliphate, p. 226

Madrasas, p. 231

Sufism, p. 232

Ask Yourself

1. How did Persia and Arabia influence one another in the seventh century C.E.? What were the consequences of this mutual influence?

2. Why was the Abbasid Caliphate at first so successful in ruling its vast territories? What accounts for its eventual failure and collapse?

3. How did Islam affect India?

4. How did Hindus and Muslims view one another? What impact did their rivalry have on India?

Key Dates and Developments

ca. 100	Funan, the first Southeast Asian state
ca. 600s	Establishment of the kingdom of Srivijaya
636	Muslim defeat of the Sasanian Empire
711	Arab rule in the Sind in western India
750	Establishment of the Abbasid Caliphate
770–825	Construction of Borobodur
786–809	Rule of Harun al-Rashid as caliph in Baghdad
ca. 800	Establishment of the Cambodian Empire
800–1000	Construction of Angkor Wat
945	Buyid warlords' seizure of Baghdad
962–1040	Ghaznavid rule in Khurasan and Afghanistan
969	Establishment of the Fatimid Caliphate in Egypt
998–1030	Mahmud of Ghazni's invasion of India
1040	Seljuk Turks' seizure of northeastern Iran
ca. 1100	*The Rubaiyat* of Omar Khayyam
1206	Establishment of the Delhi Sultanate by the Ghurids

Chapter 13
Early African Societies, 1500 B.C.E.–1500 C.E.

FIGURE OF A SACRED KING
This bronze sculpture of a sacred king was created in the Ife region of southwestern Nigeria between the 12th and 15th centuries C.E. Many African kings were sacred personages who served as intermediaries between the tangible world of human beings and the unseen world of the gods.

After reading this chapter, you should be able to:

13.1 Discuss early African political, social, and cultural characteristics.

13.2 Explain how Islam connected North Africa and Spain to Southwest Asia.

13.3 Describe the nature and importance of the trans-Saharan trade.

13.4 Explain how Ghana and Mali provided centralized government and economic organization to West Africa.

13.5 Account for Ethiopia's ability to resist Islam's expansion.

13.6 Discuss the development of the city-states of East Africa.

13.7 Explain how the Bantu provided connections between and within central and southern Africa.

It was just past midday on a humid summer's day in West Africa in 685 C.E. In a small village on the border between grassy plains and the desert, in what would later be the kingdom of Ghana, the men rested in whatever shade was available. They had spent the morning weeding their root crops of sorghum and yams. The women were preparing the midday meal. Children were tending a flock of goats and a few scrawny cattle. Then, from the north, they sighted an animal unlike anything they had ever seen before.

The children spotted it first and ran whooping to fetch their parents. Everyone rushed out to catch a glimpse of this amazing beast, awkward and ungainly, as it slouched across the sands toward the grassland. By the time the village assembled, there was not just one camel in view, but several dozen. They were loaded with cargo and led by men wearing loose-fitting white robes and turbans on their heads. The leader approached one of the men of the village and asked for water. But he spoke a strange tongue, and no one could understand his words.

Muslims had come to West Africa, bringing goods from the eastern Mediterranean, a written language, a monotheistic religion, and many other things. The region was about to change dramatically.

Africa Before Islam

13.1 Discuss early African political, social, and cultural characteristics.

Human life first evolved in Africa, but not written history. Although Egypt, Nubia, and the northern coast have recorded histories that date back thousands of years, most of Africa had no form of writing, and thus no written records, before the arrival of Islam. Consequently, most of what we know about early African history is known through legend and folklore, transmitted from one generation to the next by word of mouth, and through the work of modern archeologists and anthropologists.

Compounding the difficulty of knowing early African history is the means by which writing came to most of the continent. As it was introduced primarily by Islamic and Christian traders, invaders, and missionaries, Africa was often seen and interpreted by outsiders, and early African voices were ignored. Foreigners usually judged Africa by the standards and institutions of their own worlds, rather than evaluating the continent within its own frame of reference. These facts make the study of early African history particularly challenging.

Yet that study is also rewarding. African societies were as varied as the continent's geography and climate (Map 13.1). They ranged from the Mediterranean and desert societies of the north to the forest and grassland societies of central and southern Africa and from the wealthy farming and trading empires of West Africa to the commercial city-states of Africa's east coast. In some regions, especially those that came under Islamic influence, sophisticated systems of governance and commerce emerged. Elsewhere people lived largely in stateless societies, based mainly on clans and villages, without strong regional governments or rulers.

The Bantu Migrations: Cohesion in Diversity

Despite the geographic breadth and social diversity of African societies, there were connections among them. Between 500 B.C.E. and 1000 C.E., tribes of Africans known

How did the Bantu migrations connect various regions of Africa?

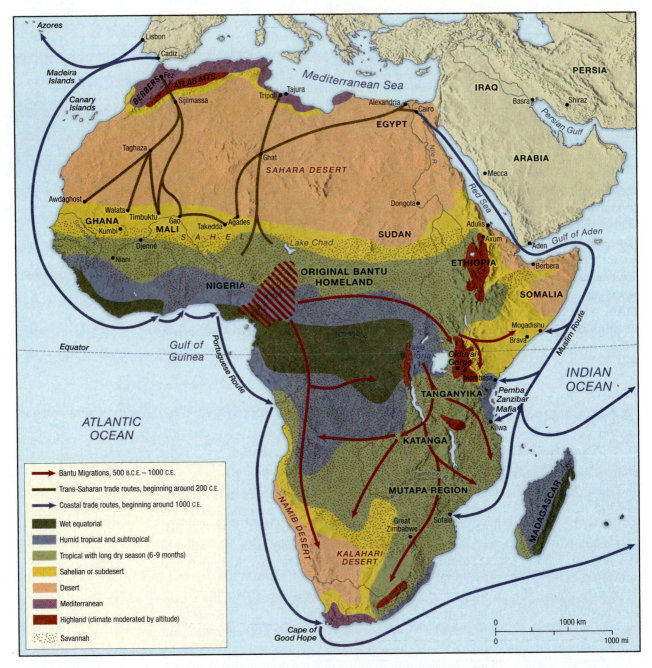

Map 13.1 **EARLY AFRICA, INCLUDING BANTU MIGRATIONS AND TRADE ROUTES, 1500 B.C.E.–1500 C.E.** The African continent, bisected by the equator, runs north–south through 70 degrees of latitude. This provides it with widely differing climates to accompany its diverse topography. Notice that Africa hosts a lengthy and varied coastline, tropical grasslands, equatorial rain forests, and enormous deserts. How did the Bantu migrations help Africans overcome the isolation this topography would encourage?

as **Bantu** (from their word for "people"), who spoke closely related languages also known by that name, migrated gradually from their homeland in West Africa, near the boundary between what are now Nigeria and Cameroon. Many historians believe that over the centuries Bantu peoples moved into eastern, central, and southern Africa, spreading their knowledge of farming and ironworking and a common set of Bantu languages and customs.

Although no written accounts of this migration exist, many scholars presume that it resulted from pressures on available land and food resources exerted by an expanding population. Bantu peoples had mastered agriculture before the migrations began, and by 500 B.C.E. they had acquired technology sufficient to smelt iron for tools, equipment, and weapons. Thus, they were able to clear forests rapidly and cultivate crops efficiently. They dominated and in some cases displaced the foraging societies they encountered as they spread across Africa.

Bantu peoples organized themselves into families and clans. Bantu villages, towns, and cities were governed by ruling councils composed of male heads of families. One of these men, elected chief, spoke for the community in dealings with other Bantu and non-Bantu societies. This decentralized method of rule served the Bantu well until population growth put pressure on resources of land and food. By the fourteenth century C.E., a centralized Bantu kingdom known as Kongo had emerged in Central Africa. The king of Kongo ruled through a multilevel administration to manage resources, dispense justice, and defend the kingdom against external threats.

As the Bantu migrations were ending, Islamic connections were beginning. Muslim merchants from Arabia and North Africa crossed the Sahara with caravans of camels, establishing commercial and cultural contacts with West African empires such as Ghana and Mali. At the same time, Muslim mariners sailed down the eastern coast of Africa, bringing their religion and the Arabic language to local city-states. These Islamic travelers forged links between West and East Africa, connecting both regions to the growing Islamic empire stretching from Spain to South Asia. The connections created by Muslims and Bantu continue to affect Africa today.

Regional Cultural Adaptations

The development of trade, travel, and cultural connections across Africa testifies to the creativity and adaptability of Africans, not to the hospitality of the African environment. This immense continent, home to the first human beings, presented significant challenges to the growth and prosperity of their societies.

Covering 20 percent of the land surface of the globe, Africa is the second largest continent (after Asia), a landmass of remarkable diversity in climate and topography. But in all its diversity, Africa, located almost entirely in the tropics and subject to extremes of heat, rainfall, and dryness, has never been an easy place in which to live. Most of its precipitation is seasonal rather than consistent, and in its vast desert regions—the Sahara (the world's largest desert), the Kalahari (*kah-lah-HARR-ē*), and the Namib (*NAH-mib*)—there is virtually no rain at all. Here agriculture is impossible and pasturage for livestock scarce. On both sides of the equator, however, lie dense rain forests with far too much moisture for raising grain crops and herds. Only the valleys of the Nile and Niger rivers, and the grassy regions that stretch across the continent both north and south of the tropical rain forests, offer opportunity for settled societies. Fortunately these grassy areas, known as savanna, constitute more than half of Africa's land surface; without them the continent would be largely empty of people and domesticable animals.

Africans adapted their cultures and societies to these topographical and climatic variations in several ways. In the relatively mild north, the Berbers, Caucasian peoples who had earlier adopted Phoenician culture and language, lived along the Mediterranean coast. They fished, farmed, and engaged in maritime commerce with the Egyptians and Phoenicians and later with the Greeks and Romans. Eventually they developed a series of trade routes by camel caravan across the scorching Sahara to the south. Even after being conquered by the Arabs, they maintained their way of life and distinct ethnic heritage.

South of the Sahara, but still north of the rain forest, across the region known as the Sudan, stretch endless expanses of savanna. Since the fifth millennium B.C.E., people in this area have herded cattle and raised crops such as sorghum, millet, and yams. As in most agricultural societies, these people lived in villages, grouping themselves into families and clans and organizing their lives around the care of their crops and herds.

How did African peoples adapt to climatic variations throughout the continent?

The San people of the Kalahari.

An Akuba wooden doll from Ghana, a classic African fertility symbol.

In what ways were clans and kingdoms important in early African political and social life?

Why might polytheism have seemed logical and appropriate to early African societies?

Cattle, prized as symbols of status and wealth, were often offered as part of the bargain in commercial and political agreements. A man's family offered them to the family of his bride as part of their marital agreement, though upon divorce the bride's family would be obligated to return the cattle. Cow's blood was considered a highly desirable beverage. The central position of these animals in the lives of their owners, even in modern times, is attested to by the decision of a small village in Kenya to send 14 cattle to the United States in 2002 as a gesture of condolence for the September 11, 2001, terrorist attacks on the World Trade Center and the Pentagon.

The most influential early residents of the Sudan were Bantu speakers. Beginning around 500 B.C.E., perhaps in search of more ample food and water to support their growing population, Bantu peoples gradually moved out of the Sudan into Africa's equatorial savannas and forests, where they raised livestock and cleared land so they could practice agriculture. Their knowledge of ironworking enabled them to fashion weapons and farming tools that gave them an advantage over the foraging societies they encountered, and they incorporated many of these foragers into Bantu culture. By the time they finally reached southeastern Africa, around 1000 C.E., the Bantu had created a large set of societies, related by language and culture, throughout the continent.

Clans and Kingdoms

Despite cultural and linguistic similarities, the Bantu developed differing social organizations. In the sub-Saharan savanna, kingdoms often emerged as large groups of villages combined under a regional ruler who exercised both spiritual and temporal authority. Farther south, although small groups of villages sometimes formed coalitions, societies tended to remain stateless, ruled autonomously by local chiefs and councils. Along the eastern coast, a series of city-states emerged, each with an independent ruler. Finally, in the central rain forests and eastern plains, some foraging societies managed to survive as small, nomadic clans.

Africans relied primarily for their protection and survival on their families and clans, which formed the foundation of their social, cultural, and religious life. Although some African societies were matrilineal (in which children trace their ancestry through their mother's lineage), the dominant figure in most families was the male head of household. This patriarchal figure was typically responsible for performing religious rituals, maintaining contact with the spirits of departed ancestors, and serving on the council of the village chief.

Men who had sufficient means often practiced polygamy, thereby establishing links with a number of families and creating an intricate network of kinship ties and loyalties that bound the community together. For example, a man marrying women from two different families could expect support—such as food in time of drought or assistance during illness or injury—from both. Moreover, the marriages also bound these families in relations of mutual support and hospitality.

African Traditional Religion

Local rituals that have survived into modern times suggest that most African societies were polytheistic, like their contemporaries in Mesopotamia, India, Southeast Asia, Greece, early America, and elsewhere. Each god represented a different natural force and was believed to perform a different function, bringing, for example, rain, wind, or sun to local people. Many such societies practiced **animism**, the belief that spirits existed that could either help or harm human beings. Africans believed it wise to worship all gods and spirits through carefully prescribed rituals.

In some African societies, a caste of priests or prophets performed the rituals. These people were believed to be able to communicate with the gods if the community desired rain, good harvests, or good health. In other African societies, the privilege of conducting these rituals was reserved for the king alone. This was a principal element of royal power as well as a foundation for the eventual development of large empires. Indeed, many African peoples believed that after death the king was rewarded by becoming a lesser god.

As in China, **ancestor worship** was widely practiced in early Africa. The spirits of deceased clan or family members were thought to exercise considerable influence over the day-to-day lives of their descendants. Bad luck or accidents were assumed to be reminders that living people must continue to perform ceremonies in honor of the dead. To stop such devotions would be to condemn ancestral spirits to extinction; they survived as spirits only as long as the living remembered them.

When Muslims arrived in Africa, they found a variety of creeds practiced by the peoples they encountered. Some elements of those beliefs, such as faith in a supreme creator, were similar to Islam and might ease conversion to the creed of the Prophet. Others, such as the king's ritualistic role, would discourage rulers from embracing the new Islamic faith, in which all people were equal before Allah. Still others, such as the Christianity practiced in Ethiopia, held that Jesus of Nazareth was the Son of God, a belief clearly incompatible with Islam.

Grass-skirted masks represent the spirits of ancestors among the Kuba people of the Congo.

What was the nature of the link between African religion and royal authority?

Early African Culture

In early Africa, religious beliefs and practices often affected artistic expression, which played many roles in daily life. Literature and poetry, set to music in the form of chants or songs, often performed a religious function. Music and chanting not only accompanied but also formed a crucial component of every stage in the lives of Africans: birth, coming-of-age rituals, weddings, political ceremonies, and funerals. Dancing served not only as a pastime but also as a method of communicating with ancestral spirits. Religious incantations and folk legends were transmitted from one generation to the next through music and song.

Architecture, too, fulfilled religious requirements. In most of Africa, ordinary people lived in huts constructed of readily available mud or thatch, but religious buildings were constructed of more durable stone. In northeastern Africa, Egyptians, Nubians, and Ethiopians built pyramids and religious monuments out of stone. In southern Africa stone structures seem to have served practical as well as ceremonial purposes. When Muslims arrived in West Africa, they introduced techniques of brick-making that Africans then used to build palaces and mosques.

Finally, woodcarving served explicitly ceremonial needs throughout Africa. Elaborate wooden headpieces and masks were carved to depict spirits and gods, and to communicate with them. Often these masks were used in rituals featuring dancing and chanting. The masks helped the clan elders teach lessons to the young and transmit the collective folk wisdom of the people from one generation to the next. With their great beauty and vivid expression, African masks testify to the artistic talents and deeply held beliefs of those who created them.

Islamic Africa and Spain: Commercial and Cultural Networks

13.2 **Explain how Islam connected North Africa and Spain to Southwest Asia.**

Even before Islam created strong commercial and cultural links that tied Africa to the larger world, North Africa was in touch with that world. Influenced by the Egyptian and Phoenician civilizations, with their links to the Persians and Macedonians, it was eventually absorbed into the Roman and Byzantine empires. Diocletian's division of the empire in 284 C.E. partitioned North Africa as well: modern-day Morocco, Algeria, and Tunisia remained with the western empire until its collapse in 476 while Libya and Egypt passed under Byzantine rule.

During all this time, North Africa remained on the margins of Mediterranean commerce, and its political connections with Rome and Constantinople were fragile. But when North Africa became part of Islamic civilization early in the eighth century, its entire orientation changed.

Islamic North Africa

How did Islamic conquest change North Africa?

Between 476 and 639, North Africa was isolated, not greatly influenced by either Germanic Europe or the Byzantine Empire. It was populated largely by Berbers who pursued their own heritage and scorned outsiders. In the northeast the Egyptians boasted a long, rich cultural heritage, but their civilization had been in eclipse for more than a thousand years. Although an outside influence, Christianity flourished in North Africa as a distinctively Egyptian faith—Coptic Christianity—whose Monophysite view of Jesus as a purely divine being was viewed as heresy by both Rome and Constantinople. Byzantine efforts to replace Monophysitism created hostility that Arab armies, bringing Islam, used to their advantage.

When it came, the Arab onslaught took North Africans by surprise. Between 639 and 642, the Arabs used a combination of force and generosity to conquer Egypt, whose fertile Nile Valley attracted and enriched the Islamic caliphate. More than one million Arabs moved to Egypt by 750. Most Egyptians converted to Islam, not only for spiritual but also for economic and practical reasons, as Muslims were exempt from taxation and free from intimidation or coercion. Within a century less than a third of Egyptians remained Christian.

Initial Arab plans to move south into Nubia were frustrated by the skills of Nubian archers and a Christian government that had substantial experience fighting Egyptian attacks. But prosperity and population growth made Egypt an ideal base for expansion to the west. In the next few decades, the Arabs moved across North Africa, taking advantage of the fact that the region's various inhabitants feared one another as much as they despised the Muslims. Refusing to cooperate, North African groups fell one by one. By 711, little more than 70 years after the Muslim invasion of North Africa began, the Islamic empire stretched across that entire region, and its soldiers were crossing the Strait of Gibraltar into Spain.

Cosmopolitan Umayyad Spain

What was the impact of Islam on Spain?

Muslims arrived in Spain as invited guests. The Germanic king of Spain died in 709, and in the contest over his succession one contender for the throne appealed to the Islamic *amir* (AH-mēr, or governor) of North Africa for help. The *amir* responded by sending an Arab-Berber expeditionary force under General Tariq ibn Ziyad (*tah-RĒK ibn zē-YAHD*), which landed in 711, defeated the other contender, and prepared to go home. But Tariq heard rumors that the legendary treasure of the ancient Jewish king Solomon was hidden in a cellar in Toledo (Map 13.2). He took the city and found nothing but rats in its cellars but saw to his astonishment that many of the residents welcomed his forces and converted to Islam. The next year the *amir* himself conquered Spain with an army of 20,000 men. About four fifths of the Iberian Peninsula (modern Spain and Portugal) came under Muslim control, while Christians were pushed into a few surviving kingdoms in the Spanish north. The Muslims called their newly acquired territory *al-Andalus* (*al-AHN-dah-loose*); Spaniards called it Andalusia. For the next five centuries, Spain was linked with North Africa as the westernmost part of Islam's growing commercial and cultural network.

From 711 to 756, Islamic Spain was ruled by the *amir*, who for most of that time reported to the Umayyad Caliphate in Damascus. From Spain the Muslims tried to advance into France but were defeated by the Franks at Tours in 732/733. When the Umayyads were overthrown by the Abbasids in 750, one of the Umayyad family's princes escaped from Damascus and governed Spain from Córdoba (*CŌR-duh-buh*). Al-Andalus thereupon became the last bastion of Umayyad rule during the Abbasid Caliphate. This unusual situation lasted for nearly two centuries: Iberia was a long way from Baghdad, the new capital of the Abbasids, and as long as Spain remained loyal to the Sunni brand of Islam, the Abbasids, Sunnis themselves, were willing to leave the Spanish Umayyads in peace.

Umayyad Spain fused Arabic culture and language onto a Spanish and Berber population base. The result was a civilization of distinctive cultural achievements. The Arab occupiers created exquisite irrigated gardens, splendid mosques and palaces like the Alhambra in Granada (*gra-NAH-dah*), elegant fountains and courtyards, and important works of science, poetry, and philosophy. They also married into Spanish families and assimilated into the local population to a degree unheard of in other Islamic lands. In so doing, they joined with the Spaniards to create a uniquely Hispano-Arab culture, vestiges of which endured for centuries after the collapse of Spanish Islam in 1492.

This cosmopolitan culture emerged gradually from Islamic Spain's flourishing urban centers of Seville (*suh-VIL*), Córdoba, and Granada. Poetry praising warrior virtues and romantic conquests was written either in Arabic or in a Spanish language thick with Arabic words and expressions; the rhyme schemes and meters were Roman. Scholars from throughout the Islamic empire came to Spain, building libraries, studying medicine and mathematics, and translating Aristotle's philosophy and the medical works of the Greek physician Galen from Arabic into Latin, all under the patronage of the state.

Economic prosperity and cultural connections made such achievements possible. Accustomed to sunny, dry climates, Arabs brought to arid Spain methods of irrigation perfected in Yemen and Syria, some based on timed water flow. Soon the Iberian Peninsula was abundant with figs, dates, tangerines, pears, oranges, apricots, and dozens of other crops whose cultivation was imported from the southern and eastern Mediterranean. As Byzantine naval power declined in the western Mediterranean, Islamic Spain established seaborne trading routes with Africa, non-Spanish Europe, and western Asia. Al-Andalus exported Toledo steel, timber, and West African gold, while crossbreeding of local mares with North African stallions produced the Andalusian breed of horses. This flourishing commerce made the Spanish Umayyads financially independent of Damascus, free to promote not only cultural magnificence but also political autonomy.

In 909, a political development in North Africa accelerated Spain's distinctive cultural development. The Shi'ite **Fatimid** (*FA-ti-mid*) family, descended from the Prophet's daughter Fatima, began a six-decade struggle to break away from Abbasid rule and establish a caliphate of its own centered in Egypt, which it conquered in 969. The *amir* of al-Andalus seized the opportunity provided by this distraction to claim the

Map 13.2 ISLAMIC NORTH AFRICA AND IBERIA, 910
The Sahara Desert cuts North Africa off from the rest of the continent and orients it toward the Mediterranean. When Muslims moved from east to west across the top of Africa, they eventually turned north toward Iberia rather than south toward the desert. Note that by 910, the Iberian Peninsula was divided into an Islamic caliphate, independent Christian kingdoms, and independent Muslim states. What do these subdivisions suggest about Muslim prospects for conquering Europe from a base in Iberia?

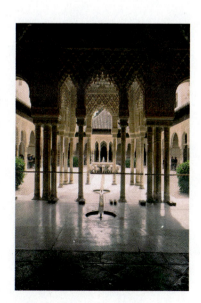

The Court of the Lions at the Alhambra in Granada, Spain.

Al-Azhar Mosque, Cairo.

How did the Fatimid Caliphate emerge in Egypt?

title of caliph for himself in 929. The unity of the *umma* was now shattered, with three different men claiming to be its true leader. The Islamic state of Spain, now known as the Caliphate of Córdoba, was a separate Sunni Muslim government presiding over a luxuriant hybrid culture unlike any other in the Islamic world.

Although the Caliphate of Córdoba lasted little more than a century, Hispano-Arab culture continued to prosper there. Córdoba's population grew to 500,000, and by the twelfth century the caliphate was noted for its immense paper mills. Its intellectual life blossomed with scholars such as Ibn Rushd, a philosopher and physician who argued that the Qur'an was an allegory requiring rational interpretation and who reintroduced the work of Aristotle and Plato to European readers. Jews and Christians were not only tolerated in Córdoba but also encouraged to contribute their talents to Islamic civilization.

Nevertheless, internal dissent undermined the caliphate: Arabs fought with Berbers, Arab clans intrigued against each other, and by the late tenth century Umayyad control was crumbling. In northern Spain, the surviving Christian kingdoms sensed weakness and began to pressure the Muslims.

Fatimid Egypt

As the Umayyads had managed to survive for centuries in Spain, remote from the Abbasid world, so in Egypt the Shi'ite Fatimids found refuge. Abbasid rule was always stronger in Asia and Arabia than in North Africa, particularly after the capital of their caliphate moved eastward from Damascus to Baghdad in 763. The Abbasids appointed mamluks, Turkish slaves from Central Asia, to rule Egypt on their behalf, but the resulting mamluk dynasties proved short-lived. Then, between 909 and 969, the Fatimids set forth their claim, not only to the province of Egypt but also to spiritual and political authority throughout the Islamic world.

The Fatimids were **Isma'ilis** (*iss-mah-ILL-ēs*), a branch of Shi'ite Islam. Isma'ilis claimed to be the true imams (or direct descendants of Muhammad's son-in-law Ali), and they denied the legitimacy of both mainstream Shi'ites and the Sunnis. Most Shi'ites believed that the last imam had hidden himself in a cave after 874 and would return one day as the Messiah. Isma'ilis disputed this belief and claimed direct descent from Isma'il, the last publicly seen imam, who died in 760. These doctrinal disputes, like those in Christian Byzantium, plagued the Islamic empire. In Baghdad, the Abbasid Caliphate was in decline, its power eroded by the size and complexity of its empire. Ultimately, it could not hold Egypt.

Having established their own caliphate, the Fatimids moved their capital from Alexandria to Cairo, a new city they founded in 969. They built magnificent mosques rivaling those at Mecca and Medina, such as the exquisite Al-Azhar Mosque in Cairo. But they left the Egyptian population undisturbed in its Sunni Muslim faith, a political necessity but a spiritual contradiction: if they were indeed the true imams, how could they fail to oppose Sunni Islam? This tolerance undermined their claim to universal legitimacy and eventually destroyed their caliphate. Lacking adequate support, the Fatimids were defeated first by European crusaders who took Jerusalem in 1099 and ultimately by the Muslim general Salah al-Din (*sah-LAH al-DĒN*), also called Saladin (*SAH-lah-dēn*), who brought together several Muslim states to fight the crusaders. Fatimid rule in Egypt ended in 1173.

Far from the seats of Islamic power in Damascus, Baghdad, and Mecca, North Africa developed as a series of distant states out of touch with mainstream Muslim spiritual and political evolution. Islam's impact on the continent of Africa was, however, profound. Through commerce as well as conquest, Islam spread from North Africa to the west and south, with consequences that shaped the course of African history for centuries to come.

Trade Across the Sahara

13.3 Describe the nature and importance of the trans-Saharan trade.

The Sahara resembled an ocean of sand that the Arabs navigated on camels, their ships of the desert. Muslim caravan trade brought Islam and other changes to West Africa, and Africans, in turn, reached out to the Islamic world.

Early Saharan Trade

In the first millennium B.C.E., long before the arrival of caravans from North Africa, kingdoms had been established in the western part of Africa's vast savanna region known as the Sudan. These early kingdoms were based on villages, each containing families and clans linked by kinship ties. Councils of elders advised the chief in governing each village; the chief represented the village in dealings with regional and provincial leaders, who in turn answered to a king.

West African kingdoms seem to have protected their peoples effectively and saw no compelling reason to expand until the development of north–south trade across the Sahara. The trade was made possible by the arrival of camels from Central Asia some time before 200 C.E. Without them the Sahara would have remained unexplored and uncharted; with them merchant caravans crossed the desert in search of profit.

Once the camel came, Berber tribes such as the Tuareg (*TWAH-reg*), accustomed to an arid environment, set out to cross the Sahara, exploring its vastness and mapping safe, direct trade routes. Financed by Jewish merchants operating out of oases in North Africa, Berber caravans carried salt, dates, and manufactured goods to the Sudan, exchanging these commodities for slaves, gold, ivory, and gum. By the seventh century, commerce by camel across the Sahara was regular and profitable.

How and why was the camel crucial to early Saharan trade?

Islam's Interaction with West Africa

Following Islam's conquest of North Africa, the trans-Saharan trade became part of a sprawling commercial and cultural network extending from Persia to Spain. Eager to expand both their faith and their fortune, Muslim merchants replaced Jewish

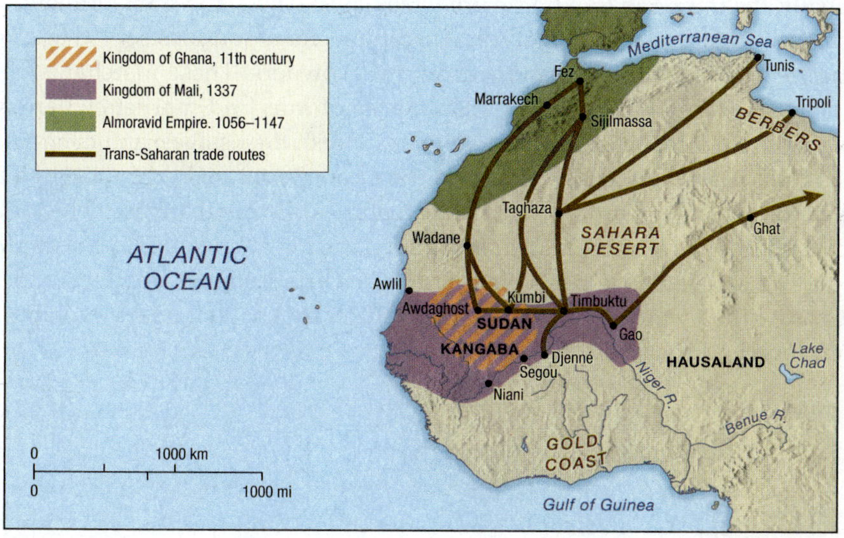

How did the Islamic world interact with West Africa?

Map 13.3 WEST AFRICA, 800–1400 The trans-Saharan trade connected West Africa to the Islamic world. Observe, both here and on Map 13.1, that trans-Saharan trade routes connected West Africa to the commercial highways of the Mediterranean Sea. Kingdoms such as Ghana and Mali emerged to organize traffic in salt, gold, and slaves. In addition to money and goods, what did Islamic traders supply in return?

financiers, and many traders and camel drivers converted to Islam. By the eighth century, trade across the Sahara was generating great wealth, and some caravans included thousands of camels, braving sandstorms, bandits, and withering heat on difficult journeys lasting for months.

The effects of trans-Saharan trade on West Africa were significant. First and foremost, it introduced Islam into the region. Berber and Arabian Muslims brought with them not only their faith but also their complex cultures. West African rulers and councils became literate in Arabic and began to keep written records. Islamic laws, institutions, and administrative forms also took shape. Muslims brought new goods to trade and taught Africans how to make bricks, enhancing the durability of buildings in societies that had previously used dried mud for walls. Beyond these advantages, West Africa became part of an extensive community of Islamic peoples.

Second, the trade created a tremendous potential market for African gold. West African mines provided work that raised standards of living across the area. The ready availability of African gold stimulated the economy of the entire Mediterranean basin, and gold became the medium of exchange for the silks and spices of India. Legends depicted Africa as an exotic realm of cities overflowing with gold, ruled by fabulously wealthy kings. The lure of gold linked Africa, Asia, and Europe.

Third, the camel caravans carried cargoes of slaves, and in this trade Islamic influence was decisive. Upper-class Muslims wanted African slaves for their households; Muslim military commanders purchased them for their armies; local operators of salt and gold mines in West Africa used them for labor. Muslims purchased, transported, and sold the slaves at huge profits. This trade involved moving the captives across the desert to the Middle East, a crossing that was stressful even for well-fed camel merchants but agonizing, and sometimes fatal, for slaves.

African slavery was not exclusively racial, since whites captured in war were also sold. But since there were no whites native to West Africa, the overwhelming majority of slaves were black. Some slaves were sold to owners in Islamic cities in Spain and Portugal during the medieval period, but slaveholding never spread to the rest of Europe. In contrast, it was widely practiced in Islamic lands. Only with Europe's discovery of the Americas in the late fifteenth century did slavery become a race-based global phenomenon.

Finally, the trans-Saharan traffic urbanized West Africa and transformed clusters of villages into centralized kingdoms. African merchant families served as middlemen between Muslim traders and African mine owners. These merchants opened caravanserais (*care-ah-VAN-sair-ās*), complexes of inns and markets where camel merchants could sleep, care for their animals, refresh themselves, and conduct their business. Shops and services expanded in these complexes, and urbanization quickly followed. Between the ninth and thirteenth centuries, the populations of cities such as Kumbi (*KOOM-bē*), Djenné (*jen-NĀ*), and Timbuktu, in what would later be known as Mali, grew to exceed 10,000 inhabitants each. What had been tiny kingdoms expanded as well, as Africans learned more about the sophisticated political systems of the larger Islamic world and adapted some of its features.

West African Kingdoms: Ghana and Mali

13.4 **Explain how Ghana and Mali provided centralized government and economic organization to West Africa.**

The expansion of trade stimulated by the camel caravans enhanced the wealth of West Africa, enabling its rulers to construct extensive empires on the foundations of what had been small kingdoms. Two of those empires, Ghana and Mali, provided centralized government and economic organization to a region previously divided along clan and tribal lines.

The Conversion of Ghana

The kingdom of Ghana (not to be confused with the modern republic of the same name) was located in the area north of the Niger and Senegal rivers (Map 13.3). It was founded by the Sondinke (*sahn-DIN-kā*) people between the second and fourth centuries of the Common Era. By 800, Muslim traders were calling it "the land of gold," and it began appearing on their maps in 833. Ghana was a prosperous kingdom, located between major sources of gold and salt. Its rulers did not control the gold mines, which were located in a southern forest belt that they could neither penetrate nor influence for long. But they did control the transport of gold from south to north, an extraordinarily profitable trade that made them rich.

At the same time, Berber tribesmen known as Sanhaja (*san-HAH-yah*) conducted a valuable salt trade from north to south. Salt was essential to life in a prerefrigeration age, as it offered an effective method of preserving meat. The continual exchange of salt for gold was carried out in Ghana's capital city of Kumbi, where a swarm of royal officials collected tribute, customs duties, taxes, and revenues.

The Sanhaja brought Ghana not only salt and manufactured goods but also Islam. The ruling elite learned Arabic and accepted Muslim aid in organizing an efficient bureaucracy. Few Ghanaians (*GAHN-ē-ans*) converted at first, however. Because the king's authority was religious as well as political, he was reluctant either to convert from animism personally or to urge spiritual changes on his people.

By the tenth century, however, Ghana's kings had become wealthy enough to expand their domain northward until the kingdom dominated an area nearly as large as Texas. In the process they took control of the salt trade routes from the Sanhaja, who simultaneously were being squeezed out of their trans-Saharan trade routes by competition from Berbers to the north. Irritated by these events, the Sanhaja found inspiration in a militantly puritanical sect of Islam called *al-Mirabitun* (*al mē-RAH-bih-TOON*), whose followers were known as **Almoravids**.

The Almoravids believed that to be successful in a war against unbelievers, the faithful Muslim must first conduct an inner struggle to purify his soul against the remnants of unbelief. This Berber movement inspired the religious fervor the Sanhaja needed to fight back. In 1076, after more than a decade of fighting, they conquered Ghana and converted its people to Islam. Historians debate whether conversion came primarily by force or persuasion. Available evidence indicates that the Almoravids blended trade, preaching, and military intimidation in a successful effort to Islamicize the most important kingdom in West Africa.

Ghana's conversion altered its society and politics. Prior to widespread acceptance of Islam, the capital city of Kumbi was actually two distinct towns. In one, the king and his people lived and held court in buildings constructed largely from mud; in the other, Sanhaja traders lived and conducted their business in stone dwellings. With the coming of Islam, mosques were built all over Kumbi as the two cities merged into one. Stone houses replaced those built of mud, and literacy in Arabic grew dramatically. The sacred role of the king gradually vanished before the worship of Allah, while Islamic prayer and ritual replaced Ghanaian magic.

This fractured the bases of Ghana's power. Kings, no longer seen as holy men, could not lead their people on the basis of their sacred powers. Ghana's agriculture never recovered from the Almoravid

What were the economic bases of Ghana's power and prosperity?

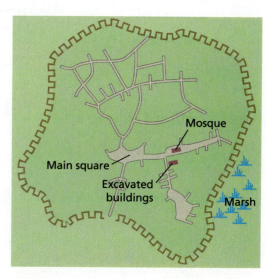

Kumbi.

occupation, and its trade routes had been severely disrupted. Political uncertainty prompted trans-Saharan caravans to bypass Ghana. Such routes were less convenient but also less troubled, and this shift in commerce proved fatal to Ghana's prosperity and power.

How did Mali connect to trade routes and the Islamic world?

Islamic Mali, 1200–1450

The alteration of trade routes worked to the advantage of the Islamic Mandinke (*man-DIN-kā*) people. Living close to the Niger in a region more suitable for agriculture than Ghana's northern areas, they controlled the lengthy central trade routes and seized the opportunity to break free of Ghanaian control. In 1235, following a lengthy struggle among Mandinke tribes, King Sundiata (*soon-JAH-tah*) emerged victorious and constructed Mali, a successor state to the ruined kingdom of Ghana.

The Mandinke, who were linguistically tied to the Sondinke and who had been part of the kingdom of Ghana, built their successor state on the upper Niger River. Constructed on lines similar to those of Ghana, this new kingdom of Mali enjoyed a rich agricultural base. Rainfall in this sector of West Africa was more abundant in the twelfth century than it is today, and temperature ranges appear to have been less severe. A secure food supply combined with Ghana's traditional position astride the gold–salt trading route ensured population growth and employment opportunities necessary for success.

All that was needed was capable leadership, and the Mandinke were fortunate to have the dynamic Sundiata, who ruled Mali from about 1235 until 1255. Sundiata was one of 12 royal brothers who together were heirs to the throne of the tiny West African kingdom of Kangaba. A neighboring king, Sumanguru, overran Kangaba early in the thirteenth century and murdered 11 of the brothers, sparing only Sundiata, a sickly child who was not expected to live to adulthood.

But Sundiata survived, grew into a strong warrior, and in 1235 defeated Sumanguru in battle. Within a few years, Sundiata's forces made Mali the clear winner of the struggle among the Ghanaian successor states. Sundiata's capital in the Niger River town of Niani (*nī-AH-nē*) became both a base for military conquest and a vibrant commercial center. His fame spread across Africa, and his immediate successors continued his expansionistic policies and consolidated Mali's wealth. Sundiata's son, Mansa (or "Emperor") Uli (1255–1270), was secure enough to leave his kingdom and become the first of his line to make the pilgrimage to Mecca.

Uli achieved that level of security through his consolidation of Mandinke control of the Songhai (*sahn-GĪ*) people and the central Saharan trade routes. Building on Mali's power and prosperity, Kankan Musa (*MOO-sah*), monarch from 1312 to 1337, eventually ruled almost twice the amount of territory once controlled by Ghana. Like rulers in France and China, he enhanced centralized control by selecting provincial administrators from within the ranks of his own family. Those men governed an empire that now commanded the only approaches to the salt deposits in the north, the gold mining district in the south, and the copper mines to the east. Mansa Musa, at the height of his powers, was the most formidable and wealthy ruler in the recorded history of West Africa, before or since.

Mansa Musa put Mali on the map, both literally and figuratively, during his pilgrimage to Mecca in 1324. Passing through Cairo on his way to Arabia, the emperor visited the sultan of Egypt. His caravan of thousands of camels, 100 elephants, a vast number of servants and courtiers, and an incredible quantity of gold (which he lavished on innkeepers, camel tenders, and princes alike) made a powerful impression on the Arab world. Muslims in Southwest Asia marveled at a visit from a monarch whose holdings were equivalent in size to all of Arabia. For his part,

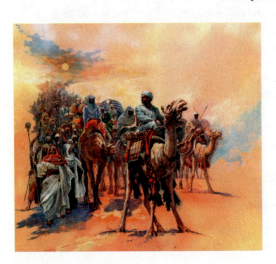

Mansa Musa on pilgrimage.

Musa learned about the Mediterranean world and Islam's role in it. His pilgrimage was glorified in song and story for centuries.

Mansa Musa's caravan aimed to do more than enable a West African emperor to make the pilgrimage to Mecca and fulfill one of the five pillars of Islam. The spectacle must have been intended to strengthen Mali's connections to the principal cities of the Middle East. Indirect evidence indicates that Mansa Musa succeeded. A dormitory was established in Cairo for students from West Africa, and on his return to Mali, the emperor set about making Timbuktu into a center of learning and culture. Poets, mathematicians, astronomers, and theologians came to Mali from across the Arab world, drawn by the prospect of riches and the excitement of building a new empire of knowledge in yet another desert. Aided by a Spanish Muslim architect, Musa built new mosques in Timbuktu and Gao (*GAOW*), along with flat-roofed houses in the Mediterranean style. Having become a renowned center of Islamic scholarship, Timbuktu attracted not only permanent residents but also North African visitors such as Ibn Battuta (*ibn bah-TOO-tuh*), who traveled through Mali in 1352–1353 (Map 15.7).

Ibn Battuta left a written record of an impressively sophisticated civilization (see "Ibn Battuta's Travels in West Africa"). He found the roads and cities clean and safe. The emperor, he wrote, was a just judge, quick to punish wrongdoers in accordance with Islamic law; and scholars, poets, and scientists made Mali an intellectual oasis. But other accounts suggest that Ibn Battuta, who spoke no African languages and could communicate only with the Arabic-speaking elites, overestimated both the sophistication of Mali and the extent of its practice of Islam. Mansa Musa apparently told visitors in the 1330s that he was reluctant to force the Mandinke to surrender their animist beliefs in spirits and magic. His own authority was derived in large measure from his status as a sacred person, and disturbing animist beliefs might jeopardize the mining of gold. A modern view of fourteenth-century Mali might characterize it as a pyramid, Islamic at the apex and animist at the base.

Mali was ruled by a Muslim emperor who claimed to be partly divine and whose immense wealth permitted him to employ a standing army of nearly 100,000 men.

Document 13.1   Ibn Battuta's Travels in West Africa, 1352

Ibn Battuta spent three decades during the fourteenth century traveling across the Islamic world. This excerpt from his account of his journeys illustrates the challenges of mining salt in West Africa.

From Marrákesh [in Morocco] I traveled with the suite of our master [the Sultan] to Fez, where I took leave of our master and set out for the Negrolands. I reached the town of Sijilmása, a very fine town, with quantities of excellent dates . . . At Sijilmása I bought camels and a four months' supply of forage for them. Thereupon I set out [in 1352] with a caravan including, amongst others, a number of the merchants of Sijilmása. After twenty-five days we reached Tagházá, an unattractive village, with the curious feature that its houses and mosques are built of blocks of salt, roofed with camel skins. There are no trees there, nothing but sand. In the sand is a salt mine; they dig for the salt, and find it in thick slabs, lying one on top of the other, as though they had been tool-squared and laid under the surface of the earth. A camel will carry two of these slabs. No one lives at Tagházá except slaves, who dig for the salt; they subsist on dates, camels' flesh, and millet imported from the Negrolands. The negroes come up from their country and take away the salt from

there . . . The negroes use salt as a medium of exchange, just as gold and silver is used [elsewhere]; they cut it up into pieces and buy and sell with it. The business done at Tagházá, for all its meanness, amounts to an enormous figure in terms of hundredweights of gold-dust.

We passed ten days of discomfort there, because the water is brackish and the place is plagued with flies. Water supplies are laid in at Tagházá for the crossing of the desert which lies beyond it, which is a ten-nights' journey with no water on the way except on rare occasions . . . We passed a caravan on the way and they told us that some of their party had become separated from them. We found one of them dead under a shrub, of the sort that grows in the sand, with his clothes on and a whip in his hand. The water was only about a mile away from him.

SOURCE: Ibn Battúta, *Travels in Asia and Africa 1325–1354* (London: George Routledge & Sons, Ltd., 1929), 317–318.

That sort of force bought a great deal of social control in West Africa. It did not, however, ensure a long life for Mali. By 1400 the Songhai tribe, which had been subdued by Mansa Uli, was reasserting itself, reviving its long-lost monarchy and pressing for independence. Between 1464 and 1492, the Songhai king, appealing to animism against Islam despite his own status as a Muslim, carried on a relentless military campaign that eventually destroyed Mali. In its place the Songhai king Ali erected a new realm that dominated the region for most of the next century.

Ethiopia's Christian Kingdom

13.5 **Account for Ethiopia's ability to resist Islam's expansion.**

Islam's expansion in Africa was neither steady nor consistent. Unqualified success in converting the north guaranteed nothing more than partial victory in the west. In the northeast, Muslim intentions to expand southward from Egypt and southwestward from Arabia were blocked not only by traditional animists but also by Christians in Ethiopia.

Human remains at least 1.5 million years old have been found in Ethiopia, and Egyptian writings speak of a civilization there nearly 2000 years before the Common Era. The Jewish Scriptures record the visit of the Ethiopian Queen of Sheba to King Solomon of Judaea in the tenth century B.C.E. Apparently, she came bearing great riches and irresistible charms, for legend says that after she returned home she bore a son, through whom all future kings of Ethiopia claimed descent from Solomon. Direct evidence of Ethiopian culture dates from the sixth century B.C.E., recorded in inscriptions and monuments unearthed by archeologists. These indicate settlement by southern Arabians who blended with the African population to create a hybrid Arab-African culture centered on the city of Axum (*ahk-SOOM*) (Map 13.4).

Like other African societies at this time, this civilization practiced a religion based on polytheism and animism. But its religious practice changed between 320 and 340 C.E., when the Ethiopian king Ezana (*eh-ZAH-nuh*) made Christianity the state religion. Converted by Byzantine Monophysite priests from Egypt, Ezana consecrated polytheist temples to the worship of Christ and created a Christian commonwealth in sub-Saharan Africa.

Ethiopia enjoyed abundant rainfall and rich soil, and Axum became a major participant in Red Sea trade. A favorable combination of commerce, agriculture, and cattle raising enabled this Christian land to prosper despite its isolation from surrounding polytheist communities. Ethiopia's resources encouraged its Christian rulers to project Axum's power across the Red Sea into southern Arabia, thus involving Ethiopia in Arabian tribal conflicts. In the early seventh century, Arabians periodically and unsuccessfully crossed the Red Sea to invade Ethiopia.

In 615, several of Muhammad's followers who had fled Mecca arrived in Axum, where they were treated with great courtesy. Their presence in Ethiopia improved Axum's relations with Arabia, and they informed Muhammad of Ethiopia's friendship. The Muslims observed that the early forms of Christian ritual still practiced in Ethiopia were in some ways compatible with rules in the Qur'an, and the Prophet instructed Muslims not to attempt conversions. To this good will was added Ethiopia's military and naval strength, making it a discouraging target for invasion.

But eventually Islamic expansion cut Christian Ethiopia off from the Red Sea trade and, after Muslims conquered Egypt in 642, from any consistent contact with the Byzantine Empire. Still, surrounded by Islam, Ethiopia for centuries maintained both its political independence and its Christian faith. Rumors of its continued existence fascinated twelfth-century European crusaders. They spread stories of a legendary ruler named Prester John, whose Christian kingdom in East Africa might assist

Europeans in seizing the Holy Land from Islamic control. Though the crusaders made no connections with Ethiopia, the land retained its Christian heritage and its strong monarchical rule into the twentieth century.

The City-States of East Africa

13.6 Discuss the development of the city-states of East Africa.

Organized settlement along the East African coast is less than two thousand years old. A few small tools dating to 500 B.C.E. have been discovered, but these seem to have been used by small nomadic bands of foragers. These hunters traded with

Map 13.4 CITY-STATES OF EAST AFRICA, 1500 East Africa's city-states used the Indian Ocean as a highway across which to market products from the interior of Africa. This connected them to the Muslim-dominated Indian Ocean commercial network and turned their political and mercantile elites Islamic. In southern Africa, Great Zimbabwe developed as the center of an empire built on agriculture, animal husbandry, metalworking, and trade in gold, using Sofala as a port. Note that the trade routes hug the African and Asian coastlines. Why would mariners be reluctant to sail directly across the Indian Ocean, for example, from Goa to Kilwa?

Greeks and Romans, furnishing them with African products such as ivory, rhinoceros horns, fragrant spices, and black slaves, but they built no permanent ports. Persians and Chinese certainly knew of East Africa, but they showed no more interest than Greeks or Romans in colonizing it. No organized coastal settlements traceable to pre-Islamic times have been found. The history of East Africa changed, however, as first the Bantus and then the Muslims arrived and blended their cultures with those of the local foragers, as well as with each other.

Development of a Bantu-Arab Culture

How did a blended Bantu-Arab culture emerge in East Africa?

When people arrived in East Africa to settle rather than forage, they appear to have come from two different directions: overland as part of the Bantu migrations from the west and across the Indian Ocean from Muslim lands. The Bantu came first, arriving from central Africa with cattle, kings, and castes of both warriors and priests. They also brought their Bantu language, which eventually combined with Arabic elements to develop into modern-day **Swahili**, a term designating not only the language but also all of Bantu-Islamic East African culture. The first recognizable ruins in East Africa date from the ninth century C.E. and are clearly Bantu, consisting of small agricultural communities of huts and mud houses, with an occasional stone structure that was probably a religious shrine.

An Arab dhow.

The Muslims came next, down the coast ("Swahili" means "coasters" in Arabic) from Egypt and Arabia in small, swift boats called dhows (*DOWS*), settling along the Somali shoreline and on the Indian Ocean island of Zanzibar. Islamic settlements, usually beginning as Muslim quarters in existing Bantu towns, began in earnest after 1100. The Arabs turned Bantu towns such as Kilwa, Mombasa, and Malindi into ports attracting oceangoing commerce. This trade in turn encouraged the creation of a series of East African city-states (Map 13.4).

Muslim expansion into India, the extension of Egyptian influence southward from the Red Sea, and the conversion of Indonesians to Islam all encouraged the development of an Indian Ocean community of states and peoples. African traders sailed across the Indian Ocean not only to India but also to Indonesia, and the traffic flowed in both directions: Indians settled all along the East African coast, while Indonesians, accustomed to living on islands, preferred the huge offshore island of Madagascar, which they named Malagasy.

As Islam spread throughout East Africa, city-states built an Islamic culture upon Bantu agricultural foundations. In the thirteenth and fourteenth centuries, great mosques were built at Kilwa, Mombasa, and Mogadishu (*mō-gah-DĒ-shoo*). Ibn Battuta, visiting the coast in 1331, described Mogadishu as a bustling port filled with wealthy Muslim merchants and a highly ritualized court life. Recent excavations at Kilwa have uncovered the foundations of an imposing royal palace, probably built in the Abbasid Islamic style in the early fourteenth century.

This Swahili East African culture suggests the power exerted by connections among differing civilizations. East Africa's strength and prosperity emerged not from the Bantu or Islamic traditions alone but from their blending, a synthesis that existed nowhere else on earth.

East and West Africa Compared

What similarities and differences can you detect between East Africa and West Africa?

The societies of West and East Africa were both influenced by the Bantu, but they evolved in very different ways. In economic structure, commercial relations, political organization, and contact with non-African cultures, their differences were more pronounced than their similarities.

East African city-states, located on the coast, were oriented toward oceangoing trade. They depended on inland regions for food, which, given the ample rainfall and fertile soil of the East African savanna, was abundant. West African cities were located inland, in the midst of agricultural regions, rather than on the coast. The Atlantic was uncharted and unusable for trade. West African trade was land based, traversing the Sahara, while East Africa used the Indian Ocean—charted and easily navigable—as a commercial highway.

In West Africa, this inward-looking organizational structure led eventually to the creation of extensive empires like Ghana, Mali, and Songhai. Each East African city-state, in contrast, had its own council, headed by a king or sheikh, and was jealously protective of its own rights and distinctive trading networks. While West African empires produced gold, salt, and copper, each East African city-state developed a specialty. One produced tools, another cotton goods, and a third perfumes. Some produced gold, but others did not.

In East Africa, the slave trade was not as profitable as in the west. But in both east and west, Muslims expanded that trade, shipping black captives to Arabia, Iraq, Persia, India, and China. In India and China, however, the demand for African slaves was limited by the large size and pervasive poverty of native populations, while in Southwest Asia Muslims found it easier to get slaves from West Africa by means of the trans-Saharan trade routes. Slavery nonetheless persisted in East Africa, where slaves were used to provide heavy labor and to transport goods.

The Bantu Connection: Central and Southern Africa

13.7 **Explain how the Bantu provided connections between and within central and southern Africa.**

Of all the regions of Africa, the central and southern zones were least affected by the outside world before the fifteenth century C.E. The spread of Islam, which had such an important impact on other parts of the continent, had minimal influence in the center and south. Instead, it was the long-enduring Bantu migrations that provided these regions with some degree of ethnic and linguistic cohesion.

The Bantu Influence

Central Africa consists primarily of tropical woodlands and grassy plains, ideal environments for bands of hunter-gatherers, including the diminutive peoples once referred to as Pygmies but known among themselves by such names as Mbuti. Many Central Africans lived in rain forests in informal groups, moving from camp to camp to secure food. Farming and herding apparently came to this region with the Bantu. Linguistic evidence indicates that people speaking Bantu languages migrated out of West African savannas and into Central Africa. Archeological evidence suggests that this migration took place over many centuries, primarily between 700 B.C.E. and 800 C.E.

The Bantu brought herds of livestock, iron-making skills, and experience in raising crops such as millet and yams, which unfortunately did not grow as well in the tropical forests as they did in the savanna. Eventually the Bantu began to depend on bananas, the cultivation of which spread, in the fourth and fifth centuries C.E., from Indonesia through Madagascar to Central Africa. Many Bantu remained in the region, interacting and intermarrying with its native peoples, while others moved on to the east and south.

Settlements in Central Africa, as elsewhere on the continent, were organized along village lines, with several villages sometimes combining to form a chiefdom and several chiefdoms occasionally constituting a kingdom. Several Bantu states had

How did the Bantu influence Central Africa?

developed by the thirteenth century, including the kingdom of Kongo, which covered a large area around the Congo River. Within these realms, each village or group of villages was led by a hereditary chief, and the king was typically selected from among the chiefs by a group of electors. Elsewhere in the region, however, the people continued to live in stateless societies.

For the most part, Central Africa remained agricultural and maintained only limited contact with peoples and civilizations from other parts of the continent. The dense rain forests and woodlands, the intense equatorial heat, and the presence of dozens of tropical diseases, such as encephalitis and yaws, ensured the region's isolation.

Farther south, however, the climate is variable and temperate, free from the parasites and insect-borne diseases that plague much of the continent south of the Sahara. The Bantu arrived there in the eighth century C.E., bringing with them their knowledge of ironworking and their agricultural skills. They developed a society in relative isolation. Southern Africa's remoteness from Arabia and Europe protected it from invasion until the sixteenth century.

Beginning in the twelfth century, governmental systems in southern Africa appear to have become more sophisticated than those of their predecessors, characterized by more elaborate social stratification and mining of gold and copper. Numerous prehistoric mines have been located in present-day Zimbabwe (*zim-BAHB-wā*) and in the Transvaal (*TRANZ-vahl*) region of South Africa. Some of this gold reached the Indian Ocean trade through the East African city-state of Kilwa. The towns and trading centers of southern Africa never attained any degree of political unity, although they were influenced to some extent by Swahili culture. They also maintained commercial connections with an Islamic world that seems to have had little interest in venturing inland.

Great Zimbabwe

What explains the prosperity of Great Zimbabwe?

The most fascinating of the southern African kingdoms is the unnamed one that built the imposing stone building complex known as Great Zimbabwe. Although more than 150 stone ruins have been discovered in an area extending from southwestern Zimbabwe into Mozambique, most are fragmentary. But the ruins of Great Zimbabwe, an impressive set of buildings northeast of Johannesburg, South Africa, are comparable to no other ancient sites in Africa. Their rounded stone towers, walls, and battlements suggest raw power similar to that conveyed by medieval European fortifications.

Great Zimbabwe was constructed over several centuries. Its earlier, less complex structures date from the eighth century, while the most recent buildings were erected between 1700 and 1750. This complex served as the political and ceremonial hub of a far-flung southern African empire, possibly as large as Mali. Like Ethiopia, this empire's prosperity rested upon a combination of agriculture, cattle raising, and commerce; unlike Ethiopia, its trade was based on gold. Abandoned gold mining sites abound throughout the region. Regrettably, we know almost nothing of this state's culture, religion, or political organization, since neither the people who built it nor the local Arab and African traders left any written records. In the nineteenth century, Great Zimbabwe's ruins were explored and mapped by a German geologist, who promptly but mistakenly declared that one of its buildings was a copy of King Solomon's temple. Today we know that Great Zimbabwe was built by Africans from local granite without reference to Solomon's temple or any other non-African architectural achievements. But we know nothing beyond what archeological analysis can suggest.

Great Zimbabwe.

Chapter Review

Consequences and Connections

Throughout most of their early history, African societies developed largely in isolation from each other, separated by distance, desert, forest, and heat. Two major developments, however, helped foster connections among the continent's cultures.

One was the great Bantu migration, a process lasting many centuries, which spread herding, farming, and iron-working across Africa's sub-Saharan lands and created ethnic and linguistic links among their assorted peoples. Another development that built connections was the spread of Islam, which came about much more quickly and brought to Africa's northern, western, and eastern regions a militant new religion and a common written language. Through Islam, these regions were connected to a vast commercial and cultural network that ranged from Spain to South Asia.

Neither of these developments, however, did much to intrude on the dramatic diversity that has continuously characterized the African continent. In many ways, they added new elements to its rich and diverse history. Early Africa was influenced by many different peoples: Arab, Bantu, Berber, Mandinke, Mbuti, Sondinke, Tuareg, and numerous others. Today we enjoy only limited knowledge of the accomplishments of these peoples, and Africa's past is still inadequately understood. Archeology, anthropology, and oral tradition can only supplement the scant written record.

Reviewing Key Concepts

Bantu, p. 244
Animism, p. 246
Ancestor Worship, p. 247

Fatimid, p. 249
Isma'ilis, p. 250

Almoravids, p. 253
Swahili, p. 258

Ask Yourself

1. Why were the Bantu migrations so important to the cultural development and cohesion of early African civilizations?

2. How did the arrival of the Muslims change North Africa?

3. How did the trans-Saharan trade change both West Africa and the Islamic world?

4. How did the Indian Ocean community affect the economic and political development of East Africa?

Key Dates and Developments

3000 B.C.E.–700 C.E.	The Bantu migrations
320–340	Establishment of Christianity in Ethiopia
639–642	Islamic conquest of Egypt
700–1750	Construction of Great Zimbabwe
702	Islamic conquest of the Berbers
711	Islamic conquest of Spain
800–1100	Zenith of the kingdom of Ghana
929	Establishment of the Caliphate of Córdoba in Spain
969	Establishment of the Fatimid Caliphate in Egypt
1050–1100	Rise of the Almoravids in Morocco and Spain
1085–1492	The Reconquest in Spain
1100–1800	City-states in East Africa
1235	Sundiata founds the kingdom of Mali
1324	Pilgrimage to Mecca of Mansa Musa
1352–1353	Ibn Battuta visits Mali
1433	Sack of Timbuktu by the Tuaregs

Chapter 14

The Evolution and Expansion of East Asian Societies, 220–1240 C.E.

PRINCE SHOTOKU AND SONS Prince Shotoku, Japan's regent from 593 to 622, adopted Buddhism and many other ideas and practices from China, while adapting them to fit Japanese culture. In adapting Chinese ways while asserting Japan's autonomy, his rule reflected the complex connections in East Asian societies from the 3rd through 13th centuries.

After reading this chapter, you should be able to:

14.1 Describe and explain China's internal decline and Buddhism's ascendance during China's Age of Disunity.

14.2 Discuss the main characteristics and accomplishments of the Sui, Tang, and Song dynasties.

14.3 Analyze the key innovations and attributes of Chinese society during the Tang and Song dynasties.

14.4 Explain how Vietnam was able to become and remain autonomous despite the power of China.

14.5 Compare and contrast the experiences of Korea and Vietnam in gaining and maintaining autonomy from China.

14.6 Explain how Japan developed a society and culture both similar to and different from China's.

Although revered as the father of Japanese culture, Prince Shotoku (*shō-TŌ-koo*), regent of Japan from 593 to 622, borrowed many ideas from neighboring China. He actively promoted Buddhism, which had spread from China to Japan. He sent Japanese missions to China, brought Chinese artisans and artists to Japan, adopted China's calendar, and instituted a government bureaucracy based on the Chinese model. He even asserted equality with the Chinese emperor, sending him a letter addressed "from the ruler of the land of the sunrise to the ruler of the land of the sunset." According to Chinese sources, the emperor was not impressed—his reply was haughtily addressed "the emperor speaks to the prince."

East Asian Societies

Shotoku's story illustrates several aspects of East Asian history in the centuries following the collapse of China's Han dynasty in 220 C.E. (Chapter 4). One was the expansion of Buddhism. In the third through sixth centuries, as China endured a long era of disunity, Buddhism spread from India to China and became China's main faith. From China it spread to Korea and Japan, where it was integrated into the cultures and used by leaders such as Shotoku to enhance their authority.

Another key aspect of East Asia in this era was Chinese preeminence, reflected in Shotoku's borrowing from China and in the Chinese emperor's refusal to address Japan's prince regent as an equal. In the late sixth century, reunited after centuries of chaos, China reemerged as a powerful and prosperous empire with unsurpassed cohesion, commerce, technology, and influence. So successful was China that neighboring countries, including Prince Shotoku's Japan, often imitated Chinese ways—as did the nomadic warriors who conquered northern China in the twelfth and thirteenth centuries.

A third aspect, embodied in Shotoku's assertion of equality with China's emperor, was the ability of smaller East Asian countries to preserve their cultural autonomy. Vietnam, Korea, and Japan adopted Chinese concepts but altered them to fit their own cultures, thus creating their own unique variants of East Asian civilization. And the northern nomadic invaders, after conquering parts of China, used Chinese methods to organize and exploit the lands they had conquered. Connections with China helped neighboring peoples adopt and adapt Chinese ways, which in turn helped them to hold their own against China.

China's Age of Disunity, 220–589

14.1 Describe and explain China's internal decline and Buddhism's ascendance during China's Age of Disunity.

China's preeminence had been established during the Han Empire (206 B.C.E.–220 C.E.), which rivaled the concurrent Roman Empire in size, population, and influence. After the fall of the Han, however, China endured an **Age of Disunity** (220–589 C.E.) in some ways similar to Europe's Early Middle Ages. Like the Western Roman Empire, China was beset by internal divisions and nomadic invaders. As in the West, imperial decay brought decline in learning and commerce. And as in the West, where people in troubled times sought comfort in Christianity, East Asians likewise found a new faith, turning to Buddhism for consolation amid chaos.

The Three Kingdoms Era

The fall of China's Han dynasty in 220 C.E. resulted in the emergence of three separate kingdoms in the north, south, and west, none able to defeat the others (Map 14.1).

Why was the Three Kingdoms Era so disastrous for China?

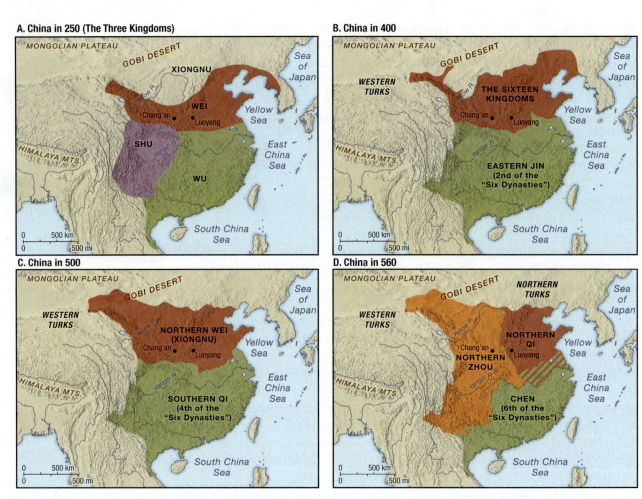

Map 14.1 **CHINA'S AGE OF DISUNITY, 220–589** China's Age of Disunity began with the Three Kingdoms era (220–280), depicted in Map A. Notice that, after splintering into small states in the Sixteen Kingdoms era (304–439), shown in Map B, northern China was reunified under Toba (Northern Wei) rule from 439 to 534 (Map C) but again divided by the mid-500s (Map D), while southern China endured a succession of Six Dynasties. How did this age of disunity affect China's culture and religion?

Led by powerful families and warlords, they engaged in endless brutal battles, while China was ravaged by diseases and natural disasters. By the year 280, China's population, nearly 60 million at the height of the Han, had declined to 16 million by official counts. It was a terrifying time.

Despite the devastation, however, the Chinese later came to see the era as a time of heroic exploits and adventures. The *Romance of the Three Kingdoms*, China's most beloved epic tale, was told, retold, and embellished over the ages until finally published in its modern form in the sixteenth century. Countless generations of Chinese people have thrilled to its stories of three heroic blood brothers who, in the Han's declining years, joined in the famous "Oath of the Peach Garden" to fight together for their country. At times they outwitted their mortal enemy Cao Cao (*TSOW-TSOW*), a character based on a real Chinese general who seized power in northern China at the end of the Han era. In the long run, however, the three heroes failed to reunite China or preserve the Han dynasty (see "Excerpts from *Romance of the Three Kingdoms*").

The actual **Three Kingdoms era** (220–280) was disastrous for China. For decades descendants of the real Cao Cao fought against descendants of his foes, wreaking widespread havoc. By 280 a general from the north had conquered the south and west, briefly reuniting the realm under the short-lived Jin (*JĒN*) dynasty. But after he died, his 25 sons vied for power, dividing the domain into numerous warring states. Then one of them unwisely asked for assistance from

Document 14.1   Excerpts from *Romance of the Three Kingdoms*

Told and retold over the centuries until published in its modern form, **Romance of the Three Kingdoms** *is China's most beloved epic tale. What aspects of Chinese culture does it highlight? How well does it reflect the real Three Kingdoms era?*

Empires wax and wane; states cleave asunder and coalesce . . . The rise of the fortunes of Han began with the slaughter of the White Serpent. In a short time the whole Empire was theirs and their . . . heritage was handed down until the days of Kuang-Wu . . . A century later came to the throne the Emperor Hsien, doomed to see the beginning of the division . . . known to history as the Three Kingdoms . . .

The Government went quickly from bad to worse, till the country was ripe for rebellion . . .

Yüan-tê was twenty-eight when the outbreak of the rebellion called for soldiers. The sight of the notice saddened him and he sighed . . . Suddenly a rasping voice behind him cried, "Noble Sir, why sigh if you do nothing to help your country?" Turning quickly he saw standing there a man . . . with a bullet head like a leopard's, large eyes, a pointed chin, and a bristling moustache. He spoke in a loud bass voice . . . "Chang Fei is my name . . . I live near here where I have a farm; and I am a wine-seller and a butcher as well. And I like to become acquainted with worthy men . . ."

Yüan-tê replied, "I am of the Imperial Family, Liu by name, and my distinguishing name is Pei. . . . I would destroy these rebels and restore peace to the land, but alas! I am helpless."

"I am not without means," said Fei. "Suppose you and I raised some men and tried what we could do."

. . . The two betook themselves to the village inn to talk over the project. As they were drinking, a huge, tall fellow appeared pushing a hand cart . . . He had eyes like a phoenix and fine bushy eyebrows like silkworms. His whole appearance was dignified and awe-inspiring. "I am Kuan Yü" said he; ". . . I have been a fugitive . . . for five years because I slew a ruffian who . . . was a bully. I have come to join the army here."

Then Yüan-tê told him his own intentions and all three went away to Chang Fei's farm . . . Said Fei, "The peach trees in the orchard behind the house are just in full flower. Tomorrow we will institute a sacrifice there and solemnly declare our intention before Heaven and Earth . . ."

All three being of one mind, the next day they prepared the sacrifices, a black ox, a white horse, and wine for libation. Beneath the smoke of the incense burning on the altar they bowed their heads and recited this oath: "We three, Liu Pei, Kuan Yü and Chang Fei, though of different families, swear brotherhood, and promise mutual help to one end. We will rescue each other in difficulty, we will aid each other in danger. We swear to serve the state and save the people. We ask not the same day of birth but we seek to die together. May Heaven, the all-ruling, and Earth, the all-producing, read our hearts, and if we turn aside from righteousness or forget kindliness may Heaven and man smite us!"

SOURCE: Lo Kuan–Chung, *Romance of the Three Kingdoms* (Tokyo: Charles E. Tuttle Company, 1959) I: 2, 4–6.

---

the **Xiongnu** (*shē-ŌNG-NOO*), warlike Turkic nomads from Central Asia who had long threatened northern China. This request gave the Xiongnu, many of whom had entered the empire during its years of division, a new opportunity to overrun northern China. And they did so with a vengeance. By 317 they had laid waste to northern China's great cities and driven out the Jin dynasty. The Xiongnu rulers also claimed the Mandate of Heaven, thereby asserting that they had divine approval to rule over China (Chapter 4).

Division, Invasion, Adaptation, and Migration

For the next century, the Yellow River region, birthplace of Chinese culture, endured further ruin as Xiongnu and others ravaged the land and warred among themselves. This painful period was known in the north as the Sixteen Kingdoms era (304–439) for its rapid succession of short-lived regimes. It finally ended in 439 when the Toba (*TŌ-BAH*), a Mongolian nomadic tribe, gained control over the entire northern region (Map 14.1).

Then, as so often happened after conquests, the victors adopted features of the conquered society, thus connecting and combining the cultures. To reinforce their rule, the Toba established a Chinese-style administrative system, staffed it with Chinese officials, and created a new dynasty called the Northern Wei (*WAY*) that restored some

How did invasions and internal conflicts affect China between 220 and 589?

stability to northern China for about a century. In the 490s they even moved their capital to Luoyang, which had been the Later Han capital, and made Chinese their realm's official language.

In time these adaptations produced new conflicts. The adoption of Chinese language created discord among Toba warriors, who resented the submersion of their own Mongolian tongue. Their resentment fueled internal strife, and by the 530s northern China was again divided into different domains.

Meanwhile, China's ongoing turmoil prompted mass migrations. As chaos enveloped the north in the third through sixth centuries, thousands of wealthy and educated Chinese families fled to the south, which gradually emerged as China's cultural center as well as its most populous and prosperous zone. Largely spared the ravages that befell the north, southern China nonetheless experienced recurrent power struggles throughout the Age of Disunity as six successive short-lived regimes, later called the "Six Dynasties," sought but failed to achieve a long-lasting reign.

Central Asian Connections and the Arrival of Buddhism

How did Buddhism come to China and blend with Chinese traditions?

During these tumultuous times, a new religion flourished in China. Founded by the Buddha many centuries earlier in northern India, Buddhism embraced his Four Noble Truths that called for avoiding life's pain by curbing desire and living righteously. After spreading throughout India, it had been adopted by the Kushans (*koo-SHAHNZ*) to India's northwest, and fostered by them in Central Asian towns and cities (Chapter 3). From there it had been carried by merchants and others along the Silk Road, the great trading route whose commercial connections conveyed not just goods but ideas, and it had arrived in China during the Later Han dynasty (Map 14.2).

Buddhism, meanwhile, had split into two branches. Theravada (*ter-ah-VAH-dah*) Buddhism, prevailing in Sri Lanka and Southeast Asia, largely remained true to the Buddha's simple teachings. But Mahayana (*mah-hah-YAH-nah*) Buddhism, the branch that came to China through Central Asia, had all the trappings of an organized religion, with priests, sects, monasteries, convents, and bodhisattvas (*bō-dih-SAHT-vuhz*). Said to be former mortals who had earned the endless peace called nirvana but postponed it to help others get there, bodhisattvas were revered as saviors by Mahayana Buddhists, who sought to follow their examples of mercy, hope, and love.

Mahayana Buddhism had features that coincided with certain aspects of the Confucian and Daoist traditions, long prevalent in China. Its stress on charity, compassion, and good works, for example, paralleled the Confucian ethic of benevolence, civility, and public service. At the same time, its basic Buddhist emphasis on meditation and curbing desire concurred with Daoism's focus on silence and passivity. Furthermore, like Mahayana Buddhism, Daoism had evolved over time into a complex religion with numerous devotions and divinities, priests and officials, monasteries and convents. In fact, although Daoism and Buddhism retained their separate identities, to China's common people they were often indistinguishable from each other. Chinese people could thus adopt Buddhism without forsaking their traditional beliefs.

The Spread of Buddhism in China

Why and how did Buddhism spread throughout China?

Initially Buddhism had little impact in China. As long as the Han dynasty flourished, Confucianism reigned as the official philosophy, and Confucian bureaucrats who ran the country enjoyed great prestige as preservers of stability and order. Foreign religions such as Buddhism, dismissed by Confucians as alien cults, attracted little following.

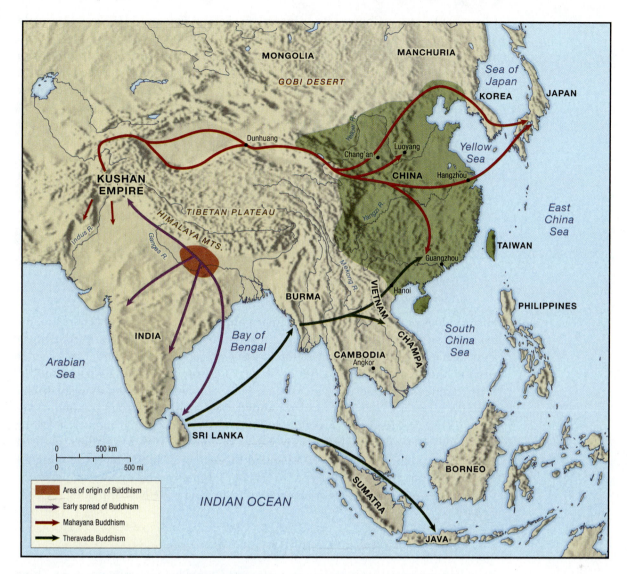

Map 14.2 **BUDDHISM SPREADS TO EAST ASIA, 2ND THROUGH 6TH CENTURIES** C.E. In the early centuries C.E., Buddhism expanded from its origins in India throughout eastern Asia. Notice that, while Theravada Buddhism spread to Southeast Asia, Mahayana expanded through Central Asia to China, and eventually from there to Korea and Japan. What factors and conditions facilitated Buddhism's spread?

In the Age of Disunity, however, the cultural climate changed. As nomadic invasions and civil wars shattered China's stability, the prestige of the Confucians declined, and Chinese cultural confidence gave way to confusion and anxiety. People began to look for relief in creeds such as Buddhism and Daoism, which promised inner peace and relief from life's burdens.

In the fourth century, then, in chaotic northern China, Buddhism began to thrive. With its emphasis on avoiding desire and ambition, it was fostered by Xiongnu warlords hoping to keep power by promoting people's passivity. Buddhism's premise that life was painful reflected people's perceptions, while its promise of escape from pain consoled them. It offered hope of salvation from suffering and of attaining nirvana, perpetual peace. Its numerous shrines and temples gave Chinese artists and sculptors opportunities to express creativity, while its monasteries and convents, like the ones in Christian Europe, provided refuge for those who felt called to lives of contemplation and devotion. By 400 C.E. much of northern China had accepted the new faith.

By this time Buddhism had also penetrated the south. Partly it came from northern China, and partly it arrived over land and sea routes from India and Southeast Asia.

Buddhist temple in northwestern China.

From 399 to 414, a Chinese Buddhist monk named Faxian (*FAH-shē-YAN*) made a pilgrimage from China to India, crossing treacherous mountain passes on foot. After spending a decade in India, visiting Buddhist shrines and talking with Indian Buddhists, he returned by sea to southern China with hundreds of Indian Buddhist texts, which he painstakingly translated into Chinese. His efforts and those of other monks and missionaries helped make Buddhism popular in southern China.

In 517, Buddhism was proclaimed the official religion in the south by Liang Wudi (*lē-AHNG WOO-DĒ*), the so-called Bodhisattva Emperor, a ruler so devout that, much to his advisors' dismay, he twice gave up his throne to become a Buddhist monk. By 589, when China reemerged as a unified empire, it had become a bastion of Buddhist beliefs, which also spread from China to neighboring Korea and Japan.

China's Age of Preeminence, 589–1279

14.2 Discuss the main characteristics and accomplishments of the Sui, Tang, and Song dynasties.

History does not repeat itself, but similar patterns do at times recur. There are, for example, striking parallels between China's initial unification in the third century B.C.E. (Chapter 4) and its reunification in the sixth century C.E. In both cases a ruler from the north united China after centuries of chaos, establishing a powerful but brief regime that paved the way for a far more eminent, enduring dynasty. In the third century B.C.E., the First Emperor ended the Warring States Era by conquering all of China, founded the short-lived Qin dynasty, and opened the way for four centuries of Han dynastic rule. In the sixth century C.E., a northern general named Yang Jian (*YAHNG jē-AHN*) ended the Age of Disunity by conquering all of China, founded the short-lived **Sui** (*SWAY*) **dynasty**, and opened the way for six centuries of Chinese preeminence under the Tang (*TAHNG*) and Song (*SŌNG*) dynasties.

China Reunited: The Sui Dynasty, 589–618

How did the Sui dynasty restore strong central rule to China?

Yang Jian, a general for a regime in northwest China, helped unite northern China under its rule, and then became regent when a young boy inherited its throne. Seizing the opportunity, in 581 Yang deposed the boy monarch and claimed Heaven's Mandate for himself, starting a new dynasty called the Sui. Using skillful propaganda, carefully cultivated Buddhist support, and a well-planned river and land campaign, he went on to conquer the south. So by 589, for the first time in centuries, one man ruled all of China.

Yang Jian, who reigned from 581 to 604 as Emperor Wendi (*WUN-DĒ*), focused on forging and restoring connections. He devised a nationwide law code and restored the civil service system begun by Han rulers. He centered his regime at Chang'an, earlier the Han capital, and built it into one of the world's great cities. He also began construction of the Grand Canal, a momentous waterway connecting the north with the south. By easing transport of troops and grain, the canal combined the north's military might with the south's agricultural prosperity, serving for centuries as a key conduit of Chinese power and wealth.

Yang Jian's son and heir, however, was a disastrous ruler. Yangdi (604–618) is described in Chinese annals as a despot who reportedly poisoned his father to hasten his own rule, then alienated his people by imposing harsh taxes and sacrificing millions of laborers' lives to erect an extravagant palace, complete the

The Grand Canal.

Grand Canal, and rebuild the Great Wall. He also launched catastrophic wars that ruined the economy and prompted widespread rebellions. Then he fled to the rural south where he lived in luxuriant debauchery until murdered in 618. That same year the Duke of Tang, one of Yangdi's most effective governors and generals, declared himself emperor and assumed Heaven's Mandate, ending the Sui dynasty.

China Triumphant: The Tang Dynasty, 618–907

The Duke of Tang's seizure of power ushered in a new regime called the **Tang dynasty**. Under its long reign (618–907), China attained new heights in political stability, economic prosperity, military expansion, cultural sophistication, and technological innovation.

The Tang's most capable leader was the duke's son Li Shimin (*LĒ SHUR-MIN*). After persuading his father to claim the throne, the 18-year-old Li led skillful campaigns against numerous rebels and northern nomadic invaders. He then ambushed and killed his two older brothers, forced his father to abdicate, and assumed the throne himself at age 26. Bold and energetic, Li then reigned from 626 to 649 as the Emperor Taizong (*TI-ZŌNG*).

Nothing seemed impossible to Taizong. He forced the northern nomads to become his vassals and allies, then with their help invaded Central Asia and conquered Turkestan (Map 14.3). He even sent an army to India to arrest a local ruler who had

What were the Tang dynasty's main achievements and how were they advanced by Emperor Taizong and Empress Wu?

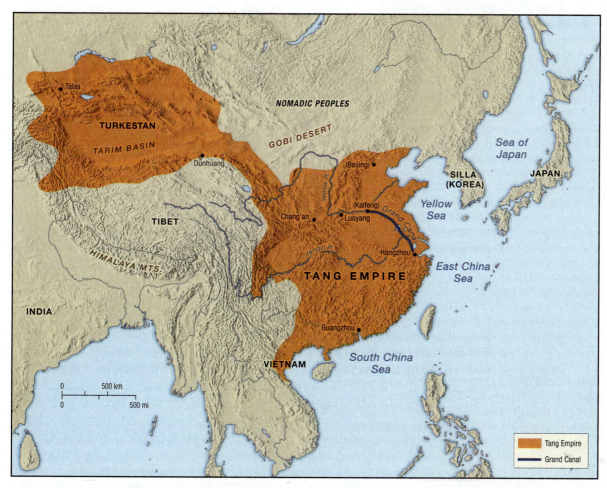

Map 14.3 CHINA UNDER THE TANG DYNASTY, 618–907 Under the Tang dynasty, China expanded into Central Asia, reopening trade routes and cultural connections. Observe that the Grand Canal, built under the Sui dynasty (589–618) and expanded under the Tang, enhanced commerce and connections between China's north and south. How did good internal connections contribute to the China's wealth and power?

insulted his ambassador. In China he promoted education, patronized the arts, and revitalized the civil service. Although a Confucian, he promoted religious toleration and devotion among the Buddhist and Daoist masses. Revered as a hero, he attained a legendary status among the Chinese people.

Another notable Tang leader was Wu Zhao (*WOO JOW*), later known as Wu Zetian (*WOO dzuh-t'YEN*) and as Empress Wu. According to traditional accounts, as one of Taizong's many concubines she was obliged to enter a Buddhist convent after he died. But she was only 24 and reportedly a reluctant nun. When the next emperor visited her convent, the accounts assert, she seduced him and won his heart, becoming his full-time consort and later his empress. In 660, when his eyesight failed, she acted as informal regent and skillfully ruled the realm, staffing the government with her supporters and killing those who got in her way. In 683, when the emperor died, she had their sons locked in the palace and ruled as regent till 690, when she claimed the throne for herself. Finally, in 705, a palace coup ousted the aged Empress Wu, forcing her to resume her long-lost calling as a nun.

Although disgruntled male Confucian historians later denounced her as a brutal opportunist, Wu Zhao actually accomplished a great deal. During her long period of power, she granted tax relief, improved the civil service, decreased the power of the old nobility, fostered military expansion, and promoted economic prosperity.

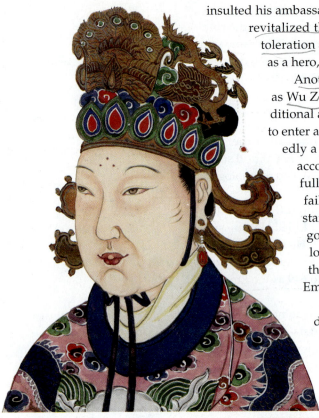

Empress Wu.

Not long after her removal, one of her grandsons took the throne as Emperor Xuanzong (*shu-WAHN-ZONG*), reigning from 713 to 756. His early reign was peaceful and prosperous, full of impressive achievements. He patronized the arts, lengthened the Grand Canal, reformed the bureaucracy and coinage, and maintained a magnificent court. But later he fell madly in love with a princess called Yang Guifei (*YAHNG GWĒ-FĀ*), neglected his duties, and let her relatives run things. In 751, as the empire drifted without strong direction, Islamic forces drove its armies from Central Asia. In 755 a massive revolt led by An Lushan (*AHN LOO-SHAHN*), a Chinese general of Turkish descent, forced the emperor and Yang Guifei to flee. Thus began a civil war that resulted in Yang Guifei's strangulation, Xuanzong's abdication, and China's devastation.

The Tang dynasty survived the An Lushan revolt but never regained its earlier domination. Local warlords took advantage of the turmoil to assert their power, while palace eunuchs guarding the emperor's concubines increasingly ran the court. Religious strife arose in the mid-800s, as Confucian civil servants, resenting the untaxed wealth of Buddhist monasteries, worked to suppress Buddhism as a foreign cult. A Daoist emperor, hating all things foreign, had thousands of Buddhist shrines and monasteries destroyed. Later a famine in eastern China sparked a mass rebellion and convinced many that the Tang had lost Heaven's Mandate. In 907, as local warlords carved up the country, one of them overthrew the dynasty, leading to a new age of disunity.

What factors account for the decline of central rule in China between 907 and 960?

China in Turmoil: Ten Kingdoms and Five Dynasties, 907–960

Fifty-three years of dynastic disruption followed the Tang demise. The south was split into warring states, later called the Ten Kingdoms. The north retained some unity under a string of brief regimes (the "Five Dynasties") but lost a number of provinces to the Khitans (*KĒ-TAHNZ*), a people from Manchuria who posed a new nomadic threat. Establishing a capital at what is now Beijing (*BĀ-JĒNG*), the Khitans formed a realm called the Liao (*lē-OW*) Empire, which for the next few centuries ruled Manchuria, Mongolia, and parts of northern China (Map 14.4).

Meanwhile, in 960, a Chinese general named Zhao Kuangyin (*JOW KWAHNG-YIN*) began to reunify the rest of China. He overthrew the last of the north's Five Dynasties at the urging of his troops, who proclaimed him emperor and pledged him absolute allegiance. Once they had done so, he compelled his key commanders to retire, thus preventing their emergence as warlords and ensuring that none of them could threaten his rule. He then annexed most of the south's Ten Kingdoms, exploiting their peoples' hunger for unity and peace.

China Resurgent: The Song Dynasty, 960–1127

In reuniting China, Zhao Kuangyin founded the **Song dynasty**, which lasted from 960 to 1279. It never matched the size or military success of the Han and Tang dynasties, and in its later years it ruled only the south. But its political and economic vitality was second to none.

Zhao Kuangyin, who reigned from 960 to 976 as Emperor Taizu (*TĪ-DZUH*), took many decisive steps. He restored and strengthened the Confucian civil service, promoting professional governance. He banned court eunuchs from high state office, preventing conflicts between them and the civil servants. He centralized control over the army, reducing the influence of local nobles and warlords. And he decreed that he would be succeeded, not by his young son, but by his talented brother, who then completed the conquest of the south to consolidate dynastic control.

Unlike their predecessors, however, Song rulers made little attempt to conquer foreign lands, judging that such ventures mainly drained China's resources. In 1004, after failing to subdue the Khitans and win back the northern border provinces, the Song made peace and agreed to pay them a large annual tribute. Similar settlements, far less costly than conquest and control, were also arranged with others on China's borders. This policy, reversing China's age-old practice of making weaker neighbors pay tribute, enabled China to buy peace with tribute in silver and silks.

Instead of expanding outward, the dynasty focused its energies on China itself. To stop the rise of local warlords and armed revolts, it tightly managed the army, frequently rotating commands among generals to keep them from turning forces they led into their personal armies. To limit the power of nobles who had dominated regional affairs, it enticed them to move to the new capital, Kaifeng (*KĪ-FUNG*), where they lived in splendor but had little local power.

To administer the realm, the Song consolidated the **Confucian civil service**. **Civil service exams**, established initially in the Han era and revived by the Sui and Tang, were now standardized and strengthened,

In what ways did the Song dynasty restore connections, stability, and order to China?

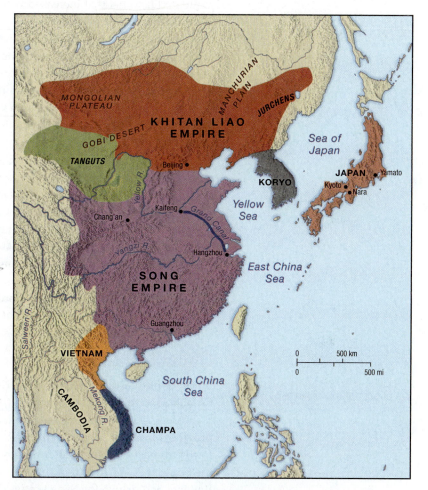

Map 14.4　SONG CHINA AND THE KHITAN LIAO EMPIRE, 960–1125 Under the Song dynasty (960–1279), China enjoyed renewed stability and prosperity. Notice, however, that northernmost China was controlled by the Khitans and their Liao Empire (907–1125). How did the Song approach to nomadic peoples differ from that of the Tang?

requiring of applicants comprehensive knowledge of Confucian classics. Potential state bureaucrats had to pass a series of extremely rigorous exams, first on the regional and then on the national level. So competitive were the tests that less than 1 percent of the candidates became state officials. Those who did, once in office, had to earn promotions through performance. As a result, their loyalty was largely to those who could promote them—the emperor and central government, which hence became more autocratic than ever.

Chinese civil servants typically were quite conservative. Trained in the ancient classics, which many learned by heart, Confucian bureaucrats were steeped in tradition and devoted to the system that reinforced stability, fostered civility, and brought them power and prestige. Most came from wealthy families, since they could afford to send their sons to schools or hire tutors to prepare them for exams. To ensure they had the means to do so, families of state officials often intermarried with those of wealthy landowners. This practice over time helped create a Confucian **scholar gentry**—an educated elite supported by both official state posts and large rural estates—that was self-perpetuating and resistant to change.

As the Song searched for ways to finance its vast army and bureaucracy, however, one civil servant tried to enforce change. From 1069 to 1085, Wang Anshi (*WAHNG AHN-SHUR*), the emperor's main advisor, sought to boost revenues by increasing the wealth of the farmers and merchants who paid the state taxes and duties. He intervened in the economy, establishing price controls and government monopolies, introducing a graduated land tax that increased with the soil's productivity, and providing peasants with low-interest loans to buy seeds and tools to increase their harvests. He engaged the government in commerce, acquiring products in one area and selling them elsewhere at a profit. He even tried to open civil service exams to more talented young men. But his actions horrified other members of the Confucian elite, who disdained merchants and commerce and feared that his reforms would dilute their power. When floods, droughts, and famine, sparking widespread unrest, seemed to show that Heaven did not favor Wang Anshi, his enemies managed to get him dismissed and undo most of his reforms.

Wang's enemies, however, could not undo the commercial class's growing influence. Although ranked by Confucians as nonproducers at the bottom of the social scale, merchants generated huge advances in money and banking, trade and transport, manufacturing and technology, fostering a Chinese commercial revolution. Combined with vast increases in agricultural output, these advances promoted urbanization: by the twelfth century China had at least 50 cities with more than a 100,000 people. With abundant capital and resources, expanding foreign and domestic markets, many miles of roads and canals, merchant ships, textile mills, printed books, flourishing farmlands, and advanced military technology, Song China seemed to have all it needed for sustained economic and industrial growth—and perhaps even global domination.

China Divided: Jurchens and Southern Song, 1127–1279

Why did China ally with the Jurchens and what were the effects of this alliance?

In the twelfth and thirteenth centuries, however, warlike nomads again disrupted China's growth. In 1114 the Jurchen (*JUR-chen*) nomads in Manchuria rebelled against the Khitans' Liao Empire. Seeing this revolt as a chance to regain some northern border provinces from the Khitans, the Song allied with the Jurchens. The result was disaster for the dynasty. In the 1120s, after crushing the Khitans, the Jurchens turned against the Song. By 1127 they had overrun all of northern China, plundered the capital at Kaifeng, and driven the Song armies deep into the south (Map 14.5).

The Song regime eventually rallied but never regained the north, where the Jurchens ruled for the rest of the century. Song rulers could only secure and stabilize the south. Establishing a new capital in 1138 at the bustling eastern port of Hangzhou (*HAHNG-JŌ*), they maintained their regime in southern China until 1279.

In this era, called the Southern Song, the regime ruled only half the country. But the half it ruled was probably the most prosperous place on earth. Agriculture, technology, cities, and commerce continued to advance and thrive. Although reduced in size and power, the realm was as rich as ever. Nonetheless, despite its great wealth and technical sophistication, it would not survive the great challenge of the thirteenth century, when first the Jurchens and later the Song would fall to the Mongol conquests (Chapter 15).

Highlights and Hallmarks of Chinese Society

14.3 **Analyze the key innovations and attributes of Chinese society during the Tang and Song dynasties.**

From the sixth through twelfth centuries, during the Tang and Song dynasties, China may have been the world's most prosperous and cosmopolitan culture. It had extensive trade, innovative technology, inspiring poetry and art, robust religious institutions, large vibrant cities, and intense intellectual creativity. But many Chinese people, including most peasants and women, gained little from this commercial and cultural preeminence.

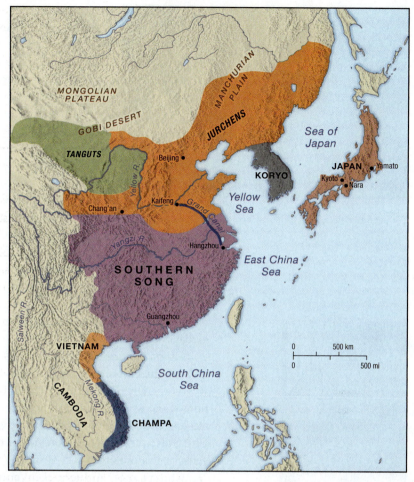

Map 14.5 **THE JURCHENS AND THE SOUTHERN SONG, 1127–1279** After conquering the Khitans in the 1120s, the Jurchens, nomadic warriors from the Manchurian Plain, attacked the Song dynasty and overran all of northern China. Note, however, that Song rule continued in the south, which flourished until the Mongol conquests of the 13th century. How did southern China continue to prosper despite the loss of the north?

Commercial and Technological Innovations

China's commercial preeminence was based on internal stability and interregional connections. The Tang and Song regimes, with their capable civil servants and soldiers, typically provided the effective law enforcement and security from foreign threats needed for commerce to thrive. They also constructed and maintained thousands of miles of waterways and highways, including the bustling Grand Canal and the tree-lined roads alongside it, connecting China's productive farmlands with its urban commercial economy.

Government-forged connections also promoted China's agricultural abundance. Tang and Song domination of northern Vietnam introduced Chinese farmers to new fast-growing rice developed in Champa (now central Vietnam). Since Champa rice matured in three months, rather than in five like other strains, farmers could double their output by growing two crops in succession, rather than one, each year. Other agricultural innovations, including use of animal-powered pumps and waterwheels to bring new lands under irrigation, also increased China's food supply.

Agricultural advances in turn sustained population growth, from less than 50 million in the eighth century to more than 100 million in the twelfth, and facilitated commercial farming. As cultivating rice took up less of their time, Chinese farmers additionally produced and sold marketable goods such as silk, cotton, and tea, a distinctive Chinese drink that eventually gained global popularity. And the growing food supply supported

What were the origins and impacts of Tang and Song China's main commercial and technological innovations?

Terraced rice fields in southern China.

large numbers of merchants, manufacturers, artisans, and inventors, some of whom developed innovations that transformed the world.

Some innovations improved domestic commerce. As copper and silver grew scarce, and as coins made from them proved cumbersome for interregional trade, enterprising Tang-era merchants introduced "flying cash" (mobile money)—paper notes that could be bought in one region and redeemed in another. These notes prepared the way for checks, credit certificates, and government-issued paper money during the Song era. The invention of the abacus, a computing device with sliding counters grouped in multiples of ten, also aided commercial calculations.

Other innovations enhanced international trade. As bandits and brigands endangered land trade along the Silk Road (Chapter 4), especially after Tang armies lost control of Central Asia in 751, Chinese merchants increasingly traded silks, ceramics, tea, and other goods by sea. Giant ships, sailing from Chinese ports, were equipped by Song times with multiple masts, watertight compartments, and magnetic compasses. By helping ships stay on course for great distances with no land in sight, the compass, adopted from the Chinese by Arab sailors and later used by European explorers, eventually helped open an era of global trade and travel.

Other Chinese innovations also had global impact. Gunpowder, which later revolutionized warfare around the world, was originally used in Tang China for fireworks, then by Song armies in rockets, grenades, flame-throwers, and crude early cannons. Coal was first used in northern China as fuel and later to smelt iron and make steel, eventually providing sturdier weapons and farm tools the world over. Song-era China also developed, among other things, mechanical clocks and cotton textile mills centuries before other societies.

China's most influential invention, however, may have been the printing process. The printing of books, using blocks of wood that were carved for each page and brushed with ink to make impressions on paper, began in Tang China and improved in Song times. Song-era printers also experimented with moveable type, using small blocks of print for each character, but since Chinese writing uses thousands of characters, most Chinese printers found it simpler to make a block for each page. Printing later spread westward from China to the Muslim and Christian worlds, revolutionizing learning, communications, and interregional connections.

Early carved woodblock used for printing.

How did Buddhism and Confucianism influence Chinese culture during the Tang and Song eras?

Spiritual, Intellectual, and Cultural Creativity

In China, printing was used first to publish Buddhist scriptures and later to record the works of religious thinkers, scholars, philosophers, and poets. By providing writers, artists, and artisans with security and food so they could specialize in diverse pursuits, stable governance and agricultural abundance also aided China's flourishing intellectual and cultural life.

In the early Tang era, while Buddhism had broad support, several innovative Buddhist sects became very influential. One was **Pure Land Buddhism**, which claimed that humans could not achieve enlightenment by their own works and instead preached salvation by faith in the Buddha of Infinite Light who ruled the Western Paradise, or "Pure Land." Another was **Chan** (*CHAHN*) **Buddhism**, known in Japan as **Zen**, which taught that meditation was the only path to enlightenment and which stressed love of nature, simplicity of life, and individual self-discipline.

In the late Tang era, as noted earlier, Confucian officials began suppressing Buddhism as a "foreign cult," initiating a Buddhist decline and Confucian revival. But the "neo-Confucianism" that emerged in the Song era was far more complex and theoretical than the simple, pragmatic system devised by Confucius more than a millennium earlier. Responding to Buddhism and Daoism, neo-Confucian thinkers grappled with such concepts as the nature of reality and meaning of life. Unlike Buddhists and Daoists, however, neo-Confucians concluded that reality is understood through education and reason rather than meditation, and that life derives meaning from action and involvement rather than withdrawal. By the twelfth century, when the great philosopher Zhu Xi (*JOO-SHĒ*) created a neo-Confucian synthesis stressing tradition, education, and personal morality, neo-Confucianism reigned supreme among the educated elite. Buddhism retained a following but ceased to be China's main faith, while Daoism continued to thrive among peasants, poets, artists, and others who had close connections with nature.

China's most beloved poets, Li Bai (*LĒ-BĪ*) and Du Fu (*DOO-FOO*), flourished in the early Tang era. Li Bai (701–763) was a homeless wanderer and Daoist free spirit, undisciplined and romantic, a lover of nature and wine. He wrote more than 20,000 poems, including the haunting "Drinking Alone by the Moonlight," which contains these lovely but lonely lines:

> A cup of wine, under the flowering trees;
>
> I drink alone, for no friend is near.
>
> Raising my cup, I beckon the moon to join me;
>
> For he, with my shadow, will make three men . . .
>
> SOURCE: "Drinking Alone by the Moonlight" from *Drinking Alone by the Moonlight: Three Poems,* by Arthur Waley (New York: Alfred A. Knopf, 1919).

According to legend, Li Bai's career ended during a drunken nighttime boat ride, when the sentimental poet drowned while trying to embrace the moon's reflection on the water.

Although a friend and admirer of Li Bai, Du Fu (712–770) was a more refined and sober poet who wrote in structured verse and was known for his Confucian compassion and strong social conscience. Having failed the civil service exams as a young man, he lived for years in poverty and endured many hardships. Some of his poems contrast the wasteful indulgence of the rich (who often lived and dined lavishly in estates behind red gates) with the sufferings of the common people, as reflected in these famous phrases:

Fan Kuan, *Travelers amid Mountains and Streams.*

> Inside the red gates the wine and meat go bad;
>
> On the roadside lie the bones of men who died from cold . . .
>
> SOURCE: A. R. Davis, *Tu Fu* (New York: Twayne Publishing, 1971).

Turning from Confucianism, a system that stamped him a failure, Du Fu became a Buddhist and spent his last years as an impoverished pilgrim. On one of his journeys he met an official who had read and cherished his poetry. The delighted official took the poet home, wined and dined him, and gave him his own bed to sleep in. Du Fu died the next morning.

Chinese arts likewise flourished in Tang and Song times. Tang sculptors produced splendid statues for Buddhist temples, and lifelike figures of horses and soldiers to guard emperors' tombs. Skilled artisans fashioned fine porcelain vessels prized throughout East Asia and beyond. Song-era painters, working with flexible brushes on silk, created brilliant portraits, striking scenes from Chinese life, and exquisite studies of birds, bamboo sprigs, and flowers. But they are best known for developing the art of magnificent landscape painting. Among its foremost practitioners were Fan Kuan (*FAHN KOO-AHN*) and Guo Xi (*GWŌ-SHĒ*), whose naturalistic masterpieces capture the majestic serenity and grandeur of northern China's mountains, woods, and streams.

Guo Xi, *Old Trees, Level Distance.*

In what ways were women subordinate to men in the cities and in the villages of Tang and Song China?

Urban and Rural Society

China's commercial and cultural life was centered in urban areas, especially the imperial capitals, which ranked among the world's biggest and busiest cities. While urban dwellers enjoyed abundant goods and cultural activities, however, village farmers, who made up most of the population, lived in stark simplicity. Women of all classes were typically subordinate to men.

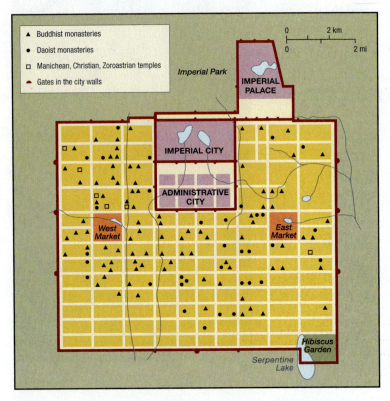

Map 14.6 CHANG'AN: CHINA'S IMPERIAL CAPITAL, 589–907
Chang'an, China's capital in the Sui and Tang eras, featured rows of blocks and boulevards in a rectangular layout. Observe that it also included markets, temples, monasteries, gardens, lakes, and government facilities. What other features and diversions did this great city provide?

Chang'an, the Tang capital, was the era's grandest city, with an overall population of almost 2 million, half of whom lived within its walls. It was laid out as a rectangle, roughly 5 by 6 miles, with wide north–south and east–west boulevards connecting its main gates and dividing it into a huge grid (Map 14.6). The city was dotted with Buddhist and Daoist temples and monasteries. Its two large markets boasted goods and visitors from all over Asia, as well as performers, musicians, artists, craftsmen, and fashionably dressed shoppers. The emperor's palace sat in the north, behind the Imperial City, a section of Chang'an that served as government headquarters.

Kaifeng and Hangzhou, the Song capitals, strove to imitate Chang'an's size and splendor. Kaifeng, located near where the Grand Canal connected with the Yellow River, was a commercial hub that had shops, warehouses, shipyards, restaurants, and hotels but lacked Chang'an's elegant symmetry. Hangzhou, south of the Yangzi River at the canal's other end, was a striking seaport brimming with bridges and waterways, merchants and shops, cabarets and teahouses, entertainers, artisans, public baths, and brothels. In the thirteenth century, long after Hangzhou's prime, European observer Marco Polo described it as the world's "finest and noblest city."

The peasants, who made up most of China's population, knew little of this urban elegance. Dwelling in rustic rural villages, they rarely traveled farther than the nearest market town. The young men worked the fields around the village, and the elder males reigned as family patriarchs. But women typically ran the household, preparing meals, raising children, tending chickens and silkworms, and helping in the fields when needed.

Women of all classes were subject to men: first to their fathers, then to their husbands, and finally (if widowed) to their sons. Parents arranged marriages as contracts between families, often engaging in complex negotiations to decide such matters as the size of the dowry supplied by the bride. Society demanded virginal brides and faithful wives but placed no such requirements on men, who might have mistresses or concubines if they could support them. Property and inheritance laws favored men, as did education and civil service systems. A few Tang-era women, such as Empress Wu and Yang Guifei, exercised great influence, but they did so mainly by working through men.

By Song times, economic advances and the development of printing enabled some women to get an education and even to own property and pursue careers. Women served as innkeepers, entertainers, midwives, mediums, and poets. But changing social standards in well-off families also brought increased seclusion of women in the home and subjection of girls to **foot binding**, a process in which their feet were tightly wrapped with strips of cloth for years, beginning in early childhood. Foot binding was designed to restrict the foot's growth and achieve a "lily-foot" effect, with toes and heels pointed down to resemble a bell-shaped lily flower. Since many Chinese men considered women with tiny feet sexually attractive, and men of means saw it as a sign of status to have wives with feet so dainty that they could not work, mothers often bound their daughters' feet to help attract wealthy husbands. But the process was extremely painful, and the resulting deformation frequently made it hard to walk without a cane. Foot binding thus became a social status symbol, distinguishing idle upper-class ladies from hardworking peasant women.

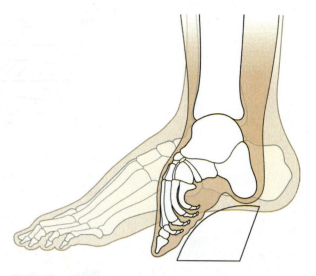

Foot reshaped by foot binding compared with normal foot.

Vietnam and the Chinese Impact

14.4 **Explain how Vietnam was able to become and remain autonomous despite the power of China.**

Overshadowed by China's size and wealth, the lands on its borders often served as its colonies or tribute-paying vassals, while their societies imitated Chinese ideas and ways. China's neighbors nonetheless managed to preserve key elements of their traditional cultures and even, over time, to secure and sustain their political autonomy. Especially successful in these endeavors were the Vietnamese.

Vietnam Under Chinese Dominion

Vietnam occupies the easternmost part of the Southeast Asian peninsula, which extends out from southwestern China, west of the South China Sea (Map 14.7). A lush subtropical region with abundant sunshine, rainfall, mountains, forests, rivers, and plains, it was one of Asia's first agricultural areas, with early farmers raising yams, rice, chickens, and pigs. In what is now northern Vietnam, a thousand miles from China's early societies, people produced fine works of bronze, traded throughout Southeast Asia, and developed a distinctive culture centered on village societies in which women played a leading role.

The region was invaded by Chinese forces during the Qin dynasty (221–206 B.C.E.), but China's influence there waned after that dynasty's demise. In 111 B.C.E., however, the Han Martial Emperor (Wudi) conquered the northern part and brought it under Chinese dominion. For much of the next millennium, China ruled the region, imposing on it Chinese language and writing, Confucian ideals, and bureaucratic structures. Vietnam briefly regained independence under the legendary Trung Sisters, who reportedly rebelled and reigned as independent queens from 39 to 41 C.E., and later during China's Age of Disunity (220–589), when the region was divided, like China itself, among local warlords. It again came under Chinese rule during the Sui dynasty (589–618) and throughout the Tang era (618–907).

Thus, unlike the rest of Southeast Asia, which was heavily influenced by India's culture, northern Vietnam was overlaid with Chinese ideals and institutions. While Theravada Buddhism spread through the rest of Southeast Asia, for example, the Vietnamese adopted from China the Mahayana branch of that faith, combining it with Confucianism and Daoism to form a blended belief system called the **Three Religions**. Vietnam also adapted

How was Vietnamese culture influenced by the Chinese and how did it remain distinct?

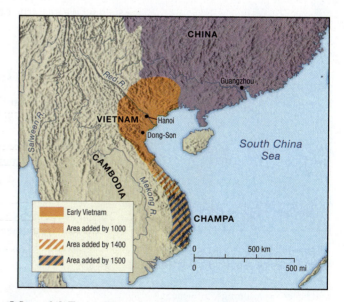

Map 14.7 EARLY VIETNAM AND ITS EXPANSION IN THE TENTH THROUGH FIFTEENTH CENTURIES For most of its history, Vietnam was linked with China by political and cultural connections. Notice, however, that after gaining its autonomy from China in the mid-900s, Vietnam expanded southward over the Champa region in ensuing centuries. What social and cultural patterns distinguished Vietnam from China?

various aspects of Chinese education, urban life, architecture, and administration to fit traditional Vietnamese culture.

Vietnam thereby retained its distinctive social and family patterns, which gave women a relatively prominent role. Among both rural villagers and urban dwellers, Vietnamese women enjoyed higher status than women in China. A Vietnamese woman, for example, could take an active part in selecting her spouse, receive from his family a wedding endowment rather than giving him a dowry, and have him come to join her family's household rather than going to join his. Thus, supported by ongoing connections with their families of origin, Vietnamese women apparently could also seek and obtain divorces, inherit and bequeath family wealth, and even keep their own family names after marriage. These practices, which predated the imposition of Chinese culture, were never completely eradicated by it.

Vietnamese Autonomy

How did Vietnam manage to gain and maintain autonomy while continuing connections with China?

With its distinctive society and distance from China's power centers, Vietnam maintained its cultural identity through centuries of Chinese rule. Finally, in 939, during the chaotic decades following the fall of the Tang, the Vietnamese managed to regain political autonomy. Then, in 968, a legendary leader named Dinh Bo Linh (*DIN BŌ LIN*), having defeated the other warlords and unified the realm, proclaimed himself Vietnam's first emperor.

Henceforth Vietnam was ruled by native regimes rather than outsiders, but this autonomy did not end Chinese influence. Indeed, as China regained strength under the Song dynasty, Dinh Bo Linh and his heirs found it advisable to recognize Song rulers as overlords and pay them tribute. In response China's rulers largely left Vietnam free to develop its own institutions. But Vietnam's rulers continued to borrow ideas that had proven successful in China, forming a stable state with its capital at Hanoi, developing a Chinese-style bureaucracy, and eventually enduring their own dynastic cycles. They also gradually expanded to the south, incorporating over the next five centuries the various kingdoms making up the region called Champa, whose culture had hitherto been influenced by India. This process eventually brought Southeast Asia's whole eastern coastline under Vietnamese rule (Map 14.7).

How was early Korea influenced by Chinese conquest and connections?

Korea and the Chinese Impact

14.5   **Compare and contrast the experiences of Korea and Vietnam in gaining and maintaining autonomy from China.**

China's influence also affected Korea, the large peninsula extending from the Asian mainland toward Japan (Map 14.8). Like the Vietnamese, Koreans developed a distinctive language and culture, and then came under Chinese rule in the second century B.C.E. Also like the Vietnamese, Koreans adapted Chinese ideas and institutions to fit their local culture. Eventually Koreans, too, regained political autonomy, but for centuries continued to pay tribute to China's emperors.

Early Chinese Influence in Korea

Chinese influence in Korea dates from the third and fourth centuries B.C.E., when refugees from China's Warring States Era migrated to Korea, bringing Chinese farming and writing techniques. Later, in 109–108 B.C.E., Han China's Wudi conquered northern Korea, a few years after conquering the Vietnamese. As in Vietnam, he and his Han successors imposed in Korea their Confucian cultural values and administrative system.

Map 14.8   EARLY KOREA AND ITS KINGDOMS IN THE FOURTH THROUGH TENTH CENTURIES   Korea's culture, commerce, and beliefs were strongly influenced by its connections with China. Observe that, after gaining autonomy from China in the 3rd century, Korea was divided into three rival kingdoms, until first Silla and then Koguryo (later called Koryo) emerged predominant. How was Korea influenced by Chinese connections, and in what ways did its society and culture diverge from China's?

Also as in Vietnam, the Han's collapse in the third century C.E. brought Koreans both autonomy and division into warring states. Eventually, in the disarray of the fourth century C.E., **three kingdoms of Korea** emerged: Silla (*shē-ILL-ah*) in the southeast, Paekche (*PĪK-chā*) in the southwest, and Koguryo (*kō-GOOR-yō*) in the north (Map 14.8). During the next few centuries, as these realms fought each other for supremacy, new waves of refugees arrived from China's Age of Disunity, spreading Buddhist beliefs among the Koreans.

After China was reunified in 589 C.E., both Sui and Tang rulers made repeated efforts to reconquer Korea, only to be rebuffed by Koguryo's resistance. In the 660s, however, Silla joined forces with China to conquer Paekche and Koguryo. Then, having unified Korea with Chinese help, Silla used its united forces to resist full Chinese rule, agreeing instead to pay tribute.

For the next few centuries, Silla ruled Korea as a semiautonomous tributary of China, broadly imitating its society and culture. During this era, Korea, like Vietnam before it, adopted China's writing, imitated its architecture, and sought to replicate its cities and civil service system. Mahayana Buddhism, with monasteries, temples, statues, shrines, and sects similar to those in Tang China, spread across the peninsula. Koreans copied Chinese customs and commodities and even produced ceramics and porcelains superior to China's.

In some respects, however, Korea's administration and society differed from those of China. Government posts in Korea were controlled by local aristocratic families, rather than staffed through civil service exams. Despite the outward appearance of a Confucian civil service, Korea's provinces were mostly run by warlords rather than scholar-officials, and its peasants remained in a status similar to serfdom.

Korean porcelain vase.

The Kingdom of Koryo, 935–1392

In the ninth century, Silla's decline, and that of China's Tang dynasty, gave Paekche and Koguryo a chance to reassert their autonomy. But eventually Wang Kon (*WAHNG-KŌN*), a wealthy merchant who became a military officer, seized control of Koguryo and reunited Korea by conquering Silla in 935 and Paekche in 936. He then shortened his kingdom's name to Koryo (*KOR-yō*), from which comes the name Korea, and established a dynasty that lasted until 1392.

Koryo was even more imitative of China than Silla had been. It set up a new capital at Kaesong (*KĪ-SŌNG*), modeled after China's Chang'an, with a similar gridlike pattern and imperial palace. Koryo established a Confucian bureaucracy with civil service exams, although the old aristocracy still monopolized the major posts. And in the eleventh century, after several invasions by Khitans, Koryo even built its own Great Wall across the northern part of the peninsula.

Like Vietnam, then, Korea blended Chinese ways with its own distinctive culture. In the meantime, across the sea to Korea's east, another East Asian society adopted Chinese ideas, but then diverged from them to become more distinctive from China than Vietnam and Korea.

In what ways did the Kingdom of Koryo blend Chinese customs with Korean culture?

The Emergence of Japan

14.6 Explain how Japan developed a society and culture both similar to and different from China's.

Of all the East Asian peoples, Japan's were among the last to develop a complex culture based on farming. Living on islands more than a hundred miles east of Korea, the early Japanese were largely isolated from outside influence (Map 14.9). With a mild climate, abundant rainfall, scenic mountainous terrain, and ready access to the sea, they lived for centuries on hunting, fishing, and gathering wild food. Rice farming

Map 14.9 JAPAN EMERGES AS AN ISLAND NATION IN THE SIXTH THROUGH TENTH CENTURIES Although influenced by connections with China, Japan developed its own distinctive culture. Nara and Heian (eventually called Kyoto) served as early capitals and homes of Japanese emperors, even as others exercised power in their name. In what ways was Japan affected by its Chinese connections, and in what ways did its society and culture diverge from those of China?

How did Prince Shotoku and his successors encourage Japanese imitation of China?

Horyu-ji Temple, Nara, Japan.

In what ways did Japan distinguish itself from China during the Heian Period?

began by the third century B.C.E., along with the use of bronze and iron. By 300 C.E. the land was dominated by native warrior clans called uji (*OO-JĒ*).

A distinctive religion emerged, based on worship of divine spirits called kami (*KAH-MĒ*), which included not only gods and goddesses of the sun, moon, and earth but also the spirits of ancestors, animals, and natural objects such as rocks, trees, and waterfalls. Worship centered on fertility and purification rites, often performed in a festival atmosphere. Originally nameless, this nature-based Japanese religion was later called **Shinto** (*SHĒN-TŌ*), the "way of the kami."

By 500 C.E. the Yamato (*YAH-MAH-TŌ*) uji, a powerful warrior clan, controlled about two thirds of Japan, thereby making it the ruling dynasty. Tracing their descent from the Shinto sun goddess, Yamato emperors claimed divine status that helped perpetuate their reign. Although others have often ruled in their name, the Yamato heirs have persistently maintained the imperial title, and they still reign today as history's longest enduring dynasty.

Early Borrowing from China

In the mid-sixth century, a new religion came to Japan from China by way of Korea. Buddhism, promoted in Japan by the Soga clan as a compelling new faith, was rejected by other clans as an alien cult, resulting in warfare. In 587 the Soga won and later installed their own Prince Shotoku as regent to the Yamato ruler.

Prince Shotoku, whose exploits are noted at the start of this chapter, directed affairs from 593 until his death in 622. Determined to learn from China's experience and to borrow concepts useful for Japan, he sent several large missions to China for trade and cultural connections. He instituted in Japan a Chinese-style bureaucracy, based on ranks assigned by merit rather than uji status, thus improving the government's effectiveness and strengthening it at the expense of warrior clans. He further promoted Buddhism—building temples, supporting monasteries, and issuing precepts based on Buddhist ideals—including a "Seventeen-Article Constitution" reflective of Buddhist and Chinese Confucian principles.

Thus began an era of borrowing from China. Over the next two centuries, the Japanese adopted China's writing and imitated its literature, poetry, philosophy, art, and architecture. The Fujiwara clan, which came to dominate the Japanese court in mid-600s, copied China's laws, taxes, roads, and civil service. The city of Nara, erected in 710 as Japan's new capital, was modeled on Chang'an, and Japan's Nara Period (710–784) was marked by imitation of Chinese ways.

The Heian Era: Divergence from China

By 794 a new capital, even more imitative of Chang'an than Nara, was constructed at Heian (*HĀ-YAHN*), later called Kyoto (*kē-YŌ-TŌ*), where the emperors would reside for more than a thousand years. During the **Heian Period** (794–1185), Japan gradually stopped imitating China, developing instead a distinctive new culture that blended Japanese and Chinese ways.

Emperor Kammu (*KAH-MOO*), who built the new capital during his reign (781–806), sought to unite his realm religiously by blending Buddhism, imported from China, with Japan's native Shinto beliefs. He promoted various sects that accepted conflicting beliefs as different levels of truth or depicted Shinto as an early revelation of Buddhist beliefs in Japan.

In the ninth century, a new writing system called **kana** (*KAH-NAH*) developed, using simplified Chinese characters to create a phonetic Japanese alphabet. By 1000 C.E., while men in Japan still struggled to write Chinese, which they considered superior, Japanese women, typically denied an education in Chinese, were using kana to produce Japanese classics. The most famous is *The Tale of Genji* (*GEN-jē*), a subtle, sensitive portrayal of Heian court life and the affairs of a fictional prince called Genji. Widely regarded as history's first complete novel, it was composed by a court lady known as Murasaki Shikibu (*moo-RAH-sah-kē SHĒ-kē-boo*), whose published *Diary* also illustrates the richness and complexity of court life in Japan's Heian era (see "Excerpts from *The Tale of Genji*").

Political changes in Heian Japan brought further divergence from China. The powerful Fujiwara clan increasingly dominated the imperial family, first by forcing the emperors to marry Fujiwara women, then by serving as regents for their offspring. As soon as an emperor had a son by his Fujiwara wife, the clan leaders would force that emperor to retire so they could rule as regents for his infant son, the new emperor. But this farce only weakened the government, as other ambitious clans, deprived of influence at court, built power bases in the countryside, while smaller landowners submitted to their protection to avoid taxation.

The Rise of the Warrior Class

By the twelfth century, although the court at Heian continued to claim authority, local warlords with independent estates dominated Japan. Each warlord developed his own

What were the characteristics of Japan's samurai warrior class?

Document 14.2   Excerpts from *The Tale of Genji*

Murasaki Shikibu's classic tale portrays in exquisite detail the lives and loves of an emperor and his court. What insights do these excerpts provide about Japanese culture and court life?

In a certain reign there was a lady not of the first rank whom the emperor loved more than any of the others. The grand ladies with high ambitions thought her a presumptuous upstart, and the lesser ladies were still more resentful. Everything she did offended someone. Probably aware of what was happening, she fell seriously ill . . .

It may have been because of a bond in a former life that she bore the emperor a beautiful son, a jewel beyond compare . . .

With the birth of the son, it became yet clearer that she was the emperor's favorite. The mother of the eldest son began to feel uneasy. If she did not manage carefully, she might see the new son designated crown prince . . .

When the young prince reached the age of three, the resources of the treasury . . . were exhausted to make the ceremonial bestowing of trousers as elaborate as that for the oldest son. Once more there was malicious talk, but the prince himself, as he grew up, was so superior of mien and disposition that few could find it in themselves to dislike him . . .

In summer the boy's mother, feeling vaguely unwell, asked that she be allowed to go home . . . The emperor . . . begged her to stay, and see what course her health might take. It was steadily worse . . .

So, in desolation, he let her go. He passed a sleepless night.

He sent off a messenger and was beside himself with impatience . . . The man arrived to find the house echoing with laments. She had died shortly past midnight . . . The emperor closed himself up in his private apartments. He would have liked to keep the boy with him, but no precedent could be found for having him away from his mother's house through the mourning . . .

The months passed and the young prince returned to the palace. He had grown into a lad of such beauty that he hardly seemed meant for this world . . . When, the following spring, it came time to name a crown prince, the emperor wanted very much to pass over his first son in favor of the younger, who, however, had no influential maternal relatives . . .

Lacking the support of maternal relatives, the boy would be most insecure as a prince . . . As a commoner he could be of great service . . . The emperor therefore encouraged the boy in his studies, at which he was so proficient that it seemed a waste to reduce him to common rank. And yet—as a prince he would arouse the hostility of those who had cause to fear his becoming emperor. Summoning an astrologer . . ., the emperor . . . concluded that the boy should become a commoner with the name Minamoto or Genji.

SOURCE: From *The Tale of Genji*, Vol I and Vol II by Lady Murasaki Shikibu, translated by Edward G. Seidensticker, translation copyright © 1976, copyright renewed 2004 by Edward G. Seidensticker. Used by permission of Alfred A. Knopf, a division of Random House, Inc.

army of warriors, later known as **samurai** (*SAH-MOO-RĪ*), who provided military service to their lords. Peasant labor supported these warriors on lands given them in reward for military service, similar to the manors of medieval Europe (Chapter 9). In time the samurai became Japan's dominant class. Rejecting the urbane Heian society, which they saw as decadent and weak, the samurai adopted an austere rural culture based on courage, honor, discipline, simplicity, and indifference to pain. Supported by foot soldiers and protected by elaborate armor, the samurai fought on horseback, using bows, arrows, and tempered steel swords. Professing total loyalty to their lords, they were trained to value death over dishonor. In a practice called **seppuku** (*SEP-OO-KOO*), also known as hara-kiri, or "belly-cutting," a defeated warrior could restore his honor by slitting his abdomen and slowly killing himself without showing pain.

Portrait of a Buddhist monk from the Kamakura era.

The samurai's rise reduced the peasants to serfdom, forcing them to work the land to support the warrior class. For comfort many peasants turned to Pure Land Buddhism, the Chinese creed that promised its faithful salvation in the Western Paradise. The samurai, meanwhile, embraced Zen, Japan's name for China's Chan Buddhism, perhaps because its stress on meditation, discipline, and simplicity fit their warrior code.

The samurai's rise also undermined the power of the Heian court. In 1185, when the Minamoto (*MĒ-NAH-MŌ-TŌ*) clan defeated the forces controlling Heian in a great naval battle, clan leader Minamoto Yoritomo (*YŌ-RĒ-TŌ-MŌ*) emerged as the country's main warlord. But unlike rebel leaders in such situations in China, he did not seize the throne and end the Yamato dynasty, whose emperors were worshipped as descendants of the gods. Instead, setting a precedent for future conquering warlords, in 1192 he assumed a new post called **shogun** (*SHŌ-GOON*), the commander-in-chief of Japan's armed forces and its real ruler. Thenceforth, while emperors still reigned in Heian (Kyoto) as religious figures, Minamoto Yoritomo and his successors as shogun really ruled Japan from Kamakura (*KAH-MAH-KOO-RAH*), the country's true political center from 1192 until 1333.

Chapter Review

Consequences and Connections

Despite the disasters of the third through sixth centuries, China survived its Age of Disunity and reemerged as Asia's predominant culture for the next seven centuries, profoundly influencing neighboring lands such as Vietnam, Korea, and Japan. From the sixth through thirteenth centuries, under the Sui, Tang, and Song dynasties, China flourished as one of the world's largest and most cosmopolitan societies. Its officials effectively governed an expansive empire, its merchants and manufacturers produced abundant prosperity, and its farmers fed its large population. Its poets, artists, inventors, intellectuals, and religious believers created a culture that was elegant, complex, and technologically sophisticated.

So successful was China that other East Asians followed its example, compelled by Chinese conquest and by commercial and cultural connections. The Vietnamese, Koreans, and Japanese all emulated China's writing, art, architecture, urban structures, Confucian civil service, and Buddhist beliefs, while adapting them to their own cultures. Chinese concepts and connections thus dominated East Asia.

For all its power and wealth, however, China never fully subdued the nomads to its north. The Tang regime held them at bay, but after its fall the Khitans captured China's northern provinces. After failing to defeat them, China's Song dynasty opted instead to pay them tribute. But in the twelfth century the Jurchens, once the Song had helped them conquer the Khitans, overran all of northern China.

The Song survived in the south, as a prosperous society with a rich commercial culture, but its days were numbered. For in the thirteenth century the Mongols, another great wave of invaders from the north, would conquer the Jurchens and then all of China and most of Eurasia as well.

Reviewing Key Concepts

Ask Yourself

1. How and why did Buddhism spread throughout China in its Age of Disunity? Why did Buddhism decline in China by the mid-Song era?

2. What steps did the Sui, Tang, and Song regimes take to bolster China's unity and prosperity? How did they respond to the ongoing threat of the northern nomadic peoples?

3. What were the hallmarks of Chinese society in the Tang and Song eras? How did the peasants' lives differ from those of city-dwellers? How did women's roles and rights differ from men's?

4. Why and how did Vietnam, Korea, and Japan emulate Chinese ideas and institutions? How did they adapt these ideas and institutions to fit their own cultures?

Key Dates and Developments

China		Vietnam and Korea		Japan	
220–589	China's Age of Disunity	111 B.C.E.	Chinese conquer northern Vietnam	by 300	Emergence of uji warrior clans
300–500	Buddhism spreads throughout China	108 B.C.E.	Chinese conquer northern Korea	by 500	Emergence of Yamato clan as Japan's imperial dynasty
581–589	Unification of China by Yang Jian	220–589	Age of Disunity in China, Korea, and Vietnam	500–600	Buddhism spreads to Japan
589–618	Sui dynasty	300s–668	Korea divided into three kingdoms	593–622	Prince Shotoku guides Japan, emulates Chinese culture
618–907	Tang dynasty	668–935	Korea unified under Silla rule		
626–649	Reign of Taizong (Li Shimin)	936–1392	Korea unified under Koryo rule	710–784	Nara era: intensive emulation of China
660–705	Dominance of Wu Zhao (Empress Wu, 690–705)	939	Northern Vietnam gains autonomy from China	794–1185	Heian era: emergence of the samurai
713–756	Reign of Xuanzong	968	Dinh Bo Linh unifies northern Vietnam, becomes emperor	1000–1010	*Tale of Genji*, by Murasaki Shikibu
720–770	Poetry of Li Bai and Du Fu				
755–766	An Lushan revolt	1000–1500	Vietnam expands southward into Champa	1185–1333	Kamakura era: reign of the Minamoto shoguns
907–960	Fall of the Tang and renewed disunity			1192	Minamoto Yoritomo becomes shogun
907–1125	Khitans rule northern borderlands (Liao Empire)				
960–976	China reunified under Zhao Kuangyin (Song Taizu)				
960–1279	Song dynasty				
1069–1085	Wang Anshi reforms				
1127–1206	Jurchens conquer Khitans and rule northern China				

Chapter 15
Nomadic Conquests and Eurasian Connections, 1000–1400

TEMUJIN IS PROCLAIMED GENGHIS KHAN In this 14th-century illustration, Temujin is proclaimed Genghis Khan as his sons (on the right) and supporters look on. Genghis Khan and his successors created a vast empire that connected cultures across Eurasia.

After reading this chapter, you should be able to:

15.1 Describe the cultural and commercial connections created and maintained by Central Asian nomads.

15.2 Discuss the impact of the Seljuk Turks on Southwest Asia.

15.3 Describe the Mongol conquests under Genghis Khan and explain why they were so successful.

15.4 Analyze the connections that the Mongols created between their empire and China, Southwest Asia, Russia, and Central Asia.

15.5 Evaluate the positive and negative effects of the Mongol conquests.

Around 1162, in the harsh Mongolian region northwest of China, the wife of a Mongol chieftain bore him a son named Temujin (*TEH-moo-jēn*). About nine years later, members of a rival tribe poisoned his father, leaving Temujin and his mother without status or support. Raising her son in great hardship, Temujin's mother taught him that he was divinely destined to avenge his father and become a great ruler. Later, when captured by foes and confined in a heavy wooden collar, Temujin overpowered his guard and escaped to a nearby river, hiding there until a friendly tribesman freed him from the collar. This escape further convinced the young Mongol that he was destined for greatness.

Turkic and Mongol Empires

Temujin grew to be a formidable warrior, opportunistic and tenacious in pursuing power. Returning to his tribe, he asserted himself as its leader, vanquished its neighbors, and killed his father's murderers. He won battles and forged alliances with other Mongol tribes, overcoming their fierce independence to unite them into a powerful military machine. Then, proclaimed by them as "Genghis Khan" (*JING-gis KHAHN*)—a title meaning "universal ruler"—he led them on a quest to conquer the world.

Genghis Khan and his followers were part of a wide array of nomadic herders who had long lived in Central Asia. For ages these peoples, most of whom spoke Turkic or Mongolian languages, had lived sparse lives, tending cattle and sheep, moving about in search of grazing grounds, and sometimes raiding or invading settled societies to their east, south, and west.

In the tenth through fourteenth centuries, however, Central Asian nomads made a momentous impact on the wider world. Some took control of northern China, forming empires there. Others, known as Seljuk (*SELL-jook*) Turks, conquered Southwest Asia, embraced Islam, and sparked consequential conflicts with the Christian world. Then the Mongols, led by Genghis Khan and his heirs, overran much of Eurasia, creating the largest land empire the world had ever seen. In time these conquerors adopted many features of societies they conquered, while expanding commerce and helping to spread ideas, technologies, weapons, and diseases. By conquering and connecting the cultures of Eurasia, Central Asian nomads changed the course of world history.

The Nomads of Central Asia

15.1 Describe the cultural and commercial connections created and maintained by Central Asian nomads.

By 1000 C.E., agriculture was the main way of life for most people on the planet. Although it required tedious, time-consuming labor, farming provided much more food, and thus supported far more people, than hunting or herding alone. Agriculture was the economic foundation of the large, complex, settled societies that had arisen in China, India, Persia, Southwest Asia, Europe, and parts of Africa (Map 15.1).

In some areas, however, conditions were unsuitable for farming. These included the northernmost reaches of Eurasia, where it was too cold; the equatorial rain forests of Africa, where it was too wet; and the arid plains and deserts of Africa and Eurasia, where it was too dry. In these regions, where limited food supplies kept populations low, people lived as nomads, moving frequently and surviving by hunting or herding.

The largest region where nomadic life prevailed was the vast Central Asian expanse, extending from Russia's semiarid steppes to the barren Mongolian highlands. Sparsely populated and bleak, battered by harsh winds and brutal winters, Central Asia was both a barrier separating Eurasia's settled societies and the crossroads of the

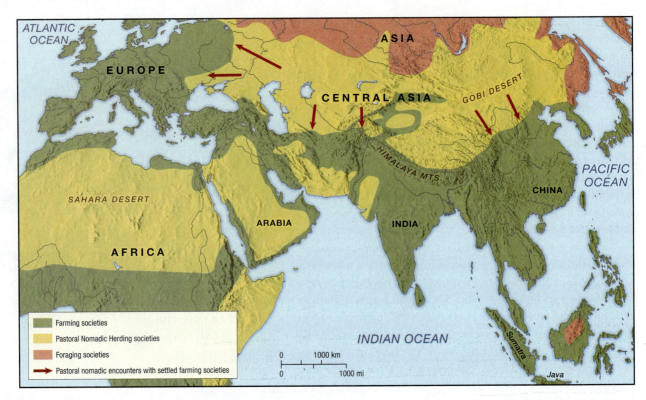

Map 15.1 **AREAS OF FARMING AND HERDING BY 1000 C.E.** By 1000 C.E., settled agricultural societies prevailed where climate and soil supported farming. Observe, however, that in Central Asia, where climate and soil made farming unreliable, people lived as pastoral nomads, occasionally interacting with settled societies to their east, west, and south. How did these connections influence both nomadic and settled farming societies?

Farming societies
Pastoral Nomadic Herding societies
Foraging societies
→ *Pastoral nomadic encounters with settled farming societies*

trade routes connecting them. It thus helped to shape both its nomadic peoples and the commerce and cultures of surrounding societies.

Herding and Horsemanship

Why were horses indispensable to the existence and lifestyle of Central Asian nomads?

Herding was the main way of life for Central Asians. As pastoral nomads—herders who move about in search of fresh grasslands for their herds—they set up camps where they found good grounds for grazing, then moved elsewhere when the forage was depleted. They ate mainly meat, milk, cheese, and butter and clothed themselves with fleeces and hides, supplied by their herds. For protection from the winds and rain, they fashioned large tents called yurts from coarse felt made of matted wool and animal hairs. They even collected the animals' manure, using it as fuel for fires that warmed them and cooked their food.

Some Central Asians raised cattle, many kept goats, and those involved in overland trade used camels, but most Central Asians centered their lives on sheep and horses. Sheep were prized for their meat, milk, and wool, and because they survived better than cattle on the sparse, coarse steppe vegetation. Horses were used for hunting, herding sheep, and pulling carts that carried tents and goods from one campsite to the next. Since mare's milk was preserved by fermenting it into a beverage called kumiss (*KOO-miss*), horses likewise supplied a key source of sustenance.

Horses were also crucial to warfare. **Central Asian nomadic life** meant frequent movement, which often led to clashes with neighboring nomads or settled societies. Especially during famines or droughts, when food and grazing were scarce, mounted nomads fought each other for scarce pasturelands and sometimes raided villages and towns in farming regions. Survival depended on mobility and fighting skill.

A Mongol family outside its tent, or yurt.

Central Asian societies thus were warrior societies. The men lived mostly in the saddle, learning as young boys to eat, sleep, hunt, herd, fight, and raid on horseback. They trained to ride for days without food or rest, to attack in unison, and to fight with fearless abandon. In these endeavors they were ably assisted by their mounts, sturdy steppe ponies bred and trained for discipline and endurance, with long shaggy hair to protect them from wind and cold.

The warriors were greatly aided by their stirrups. Developed by Central Asians in the first or second century C.E., these rings that hung from each side of the saddle secured the feet of the riders, allowing them to stand and maneuver while moving at high speed. They could load and reload their powerful bows and fire arrows in any direction with amazing accuracy while charging or fleeing at full gallop. Large armies from settled societies, vastly outnumbering the nomadic warriors, might chase them out into the open steppes, only to be annihilated by the well-aimed arrows of retreating nomads.

Family and Social Structure

Family and society were structured to meet the needs of nomadic life. Gender roles, social status, governance, and religion all reflected a culture focused on mobility, resourcefulness, and warfare.

Central Asian women played prominent roles, managing camps while the men traveled to hunt, raid, and fight. Women tended the campfires and gathered manure to fuel the flames. They sheared the sheep and goats, and then used the fleeces, along with furs and hides supplied by men from the hunt, to make clothing, mats, rugs, and the large tents called yurts. Women bred the sheep and horses, helped them give birth, milked them, and used the milk to make butter, cheese, and kumiss. And, of course, women bore and nursed the children, caring for and protecting them when the men were gone. Skilled on horseback and adapted to nomadic life, the women could move their whole families and households on short notice. Sometimes women even traveled with the men into combat, attending to their food and supplies.

Marriages, as elsewhere, were arranged by parents, often to enhance family status or political ties. Prominent warriors typically took several wives, frequently maintaining a separate tent household for each. The leading warriors formed a crude nobility, but their status depended more on military prowess than heredity. Status could improve based on bravery in combat or decline in its absence.

Central Asians, like other nomads, organized in clans and tribes small enough to maintain mobility, with no need for complex governance systems. For political and military purposes, however, they sometimes formed larger federations linking many tribes. These federations were typically led by an overlord called the **khan**, who had broad authority but who was expected to consult with a council of tribal leaders and gain its approval for major decisions.

Central Asian spirituality centered for centuries on **shamanism** (*SHAH-mun-izm*), a form of religion in which spiritualists called shamans performed elaborate rituals and induced trances to communicate with spirits, heal the sick, forecast the future, and influence events. Typically consulted by tribal leaders facing major decisions, such as when to do battle or whom to select as khan, shamans played crucial roles in nomadic cultures. Eventually, however, as Central Asians adopted various forms of Buddhism, Christianity, and Islam through contact with settled societies, shamans lost much of their clout.

Connections with Settled Societies

Central Asia was bordered on the east, south, and west by the large, complex, settled societies of China, India, Persia, West Asia, and Europe. With numerous farming villages, thriving towns and cities, intricate social structures, and sophisticated technologies, these wealthy, populous societies tended to see themselves as "civilized" and

How did a persistent nomadic lifestyle impact Central Asian social and family life?

What kinds of cultural and commercial connections were created and maintained by Central Asian nomads?

nomads as crude "barbarians." Settled societies, however, often owed their origins and important attributes to connections with nomads.

CULTURAL AND COMMERCIAL CONNECTIONS   Over the ages, as noted in earlier chapters, **Central Asian nomadic groups** had played pivotal roles in forming, connecting, and challenging settled societies. The Indo-Europeans who migrated to India, the Iranian plateau, Anatolia, and Europe in the second millennium B.C.E. came from Central Asia, imparting and imposing their languages and ways (Map 15.2). So did the Kushans, who ruled northern India from the first to third centuries C.E.; the Xiongnu and other nomads who dominated northern China from the third to sixth centuries C.E.; and the Huns whose attacks on Germans and Romans in the fourth and fifth centuries C.E. foreshadowed the fall of the Western Roman Empire. Central Asians over the centuries had also spread skills such as ironworking and horsemanship, belief systems such as Buddhism, and diseases such as smallpox from one region to another.

Nomadic attitudes toward settled societies were mixed. On one hand, nomads disdained the sedentary lives of settled villagers and townsfolk. Nomads might be poor, and at the mercy of the elements, but they saw themselves as unfettered and free, neither bound to the land and its lord like peasant farmers nor crammed into crowded, fetid cities like urban artisans and merchants. Rugged, vigorous, and violent, Central Asians lived by their horses and herds, with little desire to imitate sedentary neighbors.

On the other hand, to enhance their Spartan lifestyle, the nomads often relied on connections with settled societies. Some nomads bartered with villagers and townsfolk, offering hides, wools, and furs in exchange for such goods as flour, grain, cotton, silk, and ironware. Some nomads even subsisted by facilitating commerce among settled societies, forming and guiding caravans that carried commodities across Central Asia, along the Silk Road and other overland routes.

Other nomads, however, coveting the wealth of the settled societies, repeatedly raided their villages and towns, often abducting their residents for use or sale as slaves. As long as settled societies were united and strong, they could resist the nomads by beating them in battles, buying them off with tribute, and building barriers such as China's Great Wall. But when settled societies were divided and weak, their thriving towns and farmlands made tempting targets for the nomads, especially when drought or famine drove the nomads to seek new sources of sustenance.

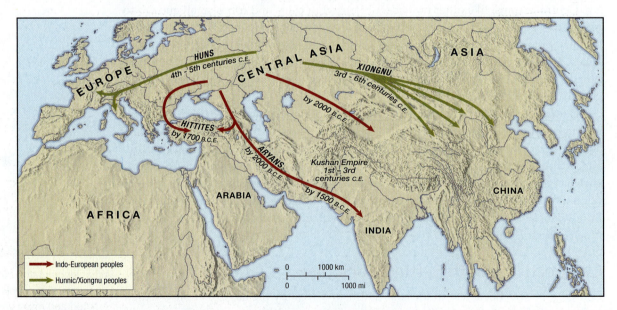

Map 15.2 **KEY CENTRAL ASIAN NOMADIC MOVEMENTS BEFORE 1000 C.E.** Over many centuries, nomadic groups from Central Asia helped forge Eurasian connections. Consider, for example, the historic roles played by the Aryans, Hittites, Kushans, Huns, and Xiongnu. What were the major impacts and connections created by these groups?

THE NOMADS IN NORTHERN CHINA   Nowhere were connections between nomadic and settled societies more consequential than in northern China. Since around 2000 B.C.E., when nomads from Central Asia introduced horse-drawn chariots and bronze weapons to this region, connections with pastoral peoples had played a crucial role in Chinese history (Chapters 4 and 14).

Examples of such connections are numerous. In the third century B.C.E., to protect his realm against nomadic raids, China's First Emperor linked his northern fortresses to create the first Great Wall. In succeeding centuries, many nomads served as merchants and guides along the Silk Road, the great cross-Asian trade route opened by China around 100 B.C.E. Later, in China's Age of Disunity (220–589 C.E.), nomadic groups ruled northern China and supported Buddhism, a religion spread from India to China by Central Asian merchants and nomads.

In the tenth century C.E., as related in Chapter 14, nomadic Mongols from Manchuria called Khitans captured several northern Chinese provinces. In the early 1100s, anxious to oust the Khitans, China's Song dynasty aided other nomads called Jurchens, unwittingly enabling them to conquer northern China and rule it for the next century.

Northern China nonetheless remained a settled society. The Khitans at first tried maintaining tribal ways, but in time they formed a Chinese-style dynasty, the Liao Empire, with a Confucian bureaucracy, civil service exams, and Chinese writing. The Jurchens did likewise, presiding over a populous Chinese realm with a complex economy, cosmopolitan culture, and Confucian administration. In China, as elsewhere, nomads who conquered settled societies tended to embrace their institutions, though often still considered barbarians by the people they ruled.

The Rise and Fall of the Seljuk Turks

15.2 **Discuss the impact of the Seljuk Turks on Southwest Asia.**

While Khitans and Jurchens penetrated northern China, far to the west and south another nomadic expansion unfolded. In the tenth and eleventh centuries, changes in the Central Asian climate, reducing the fragile food supply, may have pushed some tribes to the brink of starvation. Forced to migrate in search of new food sources, they set in motion a series of chain reactions. When one tribe moved into its neighbors' lands, it often drove them into surrounding regions, where they in turn attacked the local peoples. In time some nomadic groups, compelled by such events to combine with others, invaded the cities and farmlands of settled societies.

Driven by such forces, Turkic-speaking tribes from Central Asia infiltrated Islamic southern Asia. One such group, the Ghaznavids from Afghanistan, penetrated northeastern Persia in the mid-tenth century. By the early eleventh century, they moved into northwest India, ravaging and ruling that region (Chapter 12). But then they made a monumental mistake: they let another Turkish group from Central Asia move with its herds into Persia.

The Seljuk Conquests

These newly arriving nomads, who would dominate Southwest Asia for the next few centuries, were the Seljuk Turks. In the decade following 1025, with Ghaznavid consent, they entered northeastern Persia. Led by heirs of their deceased chieftain Seljuk, they had been chased from Central Asia by other Turkish tribes, who found them too belligerent even for the warlike ways of the steppes.

How did the Seljuk Turks manage to conquer and dominate Southwest Asia?

Once in Persia the unruly Seljuks attacked their Ghaznavid hosts, defeating them in 1040 at Dandanqan (*dahn-dahn-KAHN*), a decisive battle that opened southern Asia to waves of Turkish nomads (Map 15.3). The Seljuks then drove westward, plowing through Persia and into Mesopotamia. Having adopted Sunni Islam, they vigorously attacked the region's Shi'ite Muslims. In 1055 the Seljuks captured Baghdad, claiming to free it from Shi'ite warlords, and subjected it to Seljuk rule.

The Seljuk domain was then consolidated and expanded by Sultan Alp Arslan, who reigned from 1063 to 1072. Bent on extinguishing Shi'ism and reuniting the Islamic world under Sunni sway, he planned to attack the Shi'ite Fatimid Caliphate in Egypt. Seeking first to protect his western flank, however, he came into conflict with the Christian Byzantine Empire, whose armies he defeated in 1071 at Manzikert (Chapter 10). This victory sidetracked the Seljuks, who went on to conquer Syria and Palestine but never made it to Egypt. Instead, with Byzantine lands now vulnerable, the Turks flooded westward into Anatolia, a rich farming region that had been for centuries the heart of the Byzantine Empire.

The Great Seljuk Empire

How did Turkish and Persian cultures influence Islamic culture through the Seljuk Turks?

Once in Anatolia, the Seljuks made it a Sunni Muslim Turkish stronghold. They restricted Christianity and promoted Islamic immigration from elsewhere in their empire, granting special rights to those who embraced Islam. Anatolia, which had been a Christian bastion for almost a millennium, was thus transformed into a Muslim land that is today called Turkey.

The Great Seljuk Empire, as the new realm came to be known, was nonetheless centered in Persia. Like others before them, the Seljuks fell in love with Persian culture and adopted many of its features, including its Farsi tongue. Arabic was enshrined in the Qur'an and Muslim worship, but the Seljuk elite spoke Farsi, while commoners spoke a brand of Turkish peppered with Farsi expressions. Under Turkish and Persian influence, Islamic culture thus evolved further from its Arab roots, while Seljuks were transformed from nomadic marauders into settled rulers of a vast cosmopolitan empire.

Hence, rather than ruining Islamic culture, Seljuk rule revitalized it. The Seljuk leaders became proud patrons of literature, commerce, and the arts and crafts, notably including the creation and sale of exquisite fine woven carpets.

The early Seljuk sultans were ably guided by a Persian chief minister, the Nizam al-Mulk (*nē-ZAHM al-MOOLK*), a superb administrator who founded a series of eminent educational institutions and adapted the structures of the long-dead Persian Empire to meet Seljuk needs. A devout Sunni Muslim, the Nizam also guided Seljuk sultan Malik Shah (*mah-LĒK SHAH*), who reigned from 1072 to 1092, into unrelenting warfare against Shi'ism.

This anti-Shi'ite drive met fierce resistance from a radical Shi'ite sect known as "the self-sacrificers." Founded in 1090 by a zealot called "the Old Man of the Mountain," this group terrorized the Islamic world for almost 170 years, slaying numerous Sunni leaders, including the Nizam al-Mulk. According to legend, at a secret mountain fortress its members used hashish (*hah-SHĒSH*), a mild narcotic, to fortify themselves for murder and martyrdom by providing a foretaste of the pleasures of paradise. This sect of Shi'ite killers came to be known in Arabic as hashashin (*hah-SHAH-shēn*), or "hashish users," and hence in the West as the **Assassins**.

Fine woven carpet from Seljuk culture.

The Fragmentation of the Seljuk Realm

Why and how did the Great Seljuk Empire break up into smaller realms?

The assassination of the Nizam al-Mulk in 1092, followed by the death of Malik Shah, sparked a succession crisis that split apart the Seljuk realm. In the west several smaller states emerged, while in the east the Great Seljuk sultans struggled to control what was left of their empire.

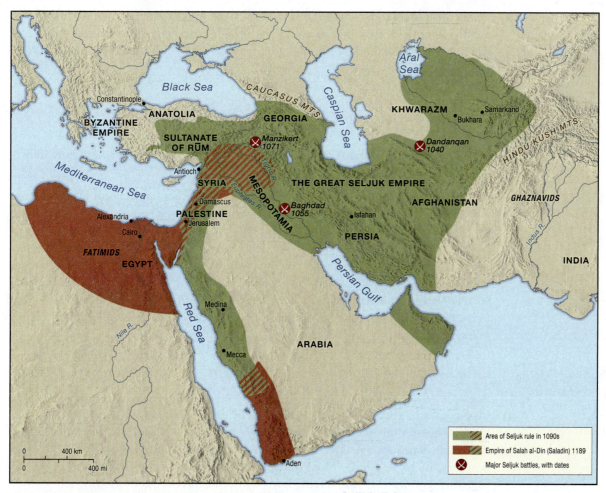

Map 15.3 SOUTHWEST ASIA AND THE SELJUK TURKS, 1040–1189 In the 11th century, the Seljuk Turks, nomadic warriors from Central Asia, created a Great Seljuk Empire, winning key battles at Dandanqan, Baghdad, and Manzikert. Note, however, that this empire began breaking apart after 1092, losing lands to Rūm and Khwarazm, and that a new sultan in Egypt, Salah al-Din, eventually carved out a realm embracing Palestine and Syria. How did the Seljuks help revitalize Islamic culture?

The main successor state in the west was the Sultanate of Rūm (*ROOM*), a breakaway Seljuk regime that controlled much of Anatolia. Since the name Rūm ("Rome") asserted a claim to the Roman heritage, and since the realm of Rūm expanded toward Constantinople, the Byzantine ruler, as Eastern Roman emperor, saw the sultanate as a mortal threat. In desperation he sought aid from the Christian West, appealing to the pope in Rome, who responded by launching a Christian holy war, later called the First Crusade (1096–1099), which defeated Islamic forces in Anatolia, Syria, and Palestine (Chapter 16). But in the next century, the Muslims retook this territory, led not by Seljuks but by Salah al-Din (*sah-LAH al-DĒN*), a gifted Sunni Muslim warrior also called Saladin (*SAH-lah-dēn*). He ended Shi'ite rule in Egypt, served as its sultan for two decades (1173–1193), and drove the Christian crusaders out of Palestine. The Seljuk Sultanate of Rūm endured in Anatolia but lost a key battle in 1202 to Georgia, a realm to its northeast skillfully ruled by a talented woman named Tamar.

The eastern remnant of the Great Seljuk Empire lost power in the 1150s, as its local commanders battled each other for the remains of the realm. In this struggle the commanders of Khwarazm (*khwah-RAZ-um*), a Central Asian region northeast of Persia (Map 15.3), eventually emerged supreme. Known as Khwarazm shahs, they created a large but loose-knit empire that included much of south central Asia and northern

Tamar, ruler of Georgia, 1184–1213.

Persia. Profiting from commerce along the Asian trade routes and an extensive irrigation system that sustained farming on the steppes, Khwarazm endured until 1218, when it was confronted by the Mongols, nomadic warriors whose conquests threatened to engulf all Eurasia.

The Mongol Invasions

15.3 Describe the Mongol conquests under Genghis Khan and explain why they were so successful.

In the thirteenth century, as noted at the start of this chapter, Mongol warriors from northwest of China set out to conquer the world. Genghis Khan and his heirs, leading a coalition of tribes with a combined population of less than 2 million, overran realms from China to Eastern Europe with far richer resources and many times more people. Although **the Mongol conquests** did not cover the whole world, they did encompass much of Eurasia, creating an enormous empire dwarfing all previous realms. In doing so, they forged connections and fostered trade, spreading ideas and technologies that in time enriched and strengthened the settled societies, fortifying them against further nomadic conquests.

The Conquests of Genghis Khan

What was the sequence of Mongol conquests under Genghis Khan?

Beginning in 1206, following a Mongol conference that proclaimed Temujin as Genghis Khan (also spelled "Chinggis Khan"), he and his armies set out for world conquest. First they allied with the Uighur (*WĒ-goor*) Turks (Map 15.4), who later helped the Mongols run their realm. Then they moved against the Xi Xia (*SHĒ shēYAH*) kingdom, northwest of China, ruled by Tibetans call Tanguts (*TAHN-goots*). By 1209 the Mongols conquered Xi Xia, forcing it to pay tribute but not yet destroying it.

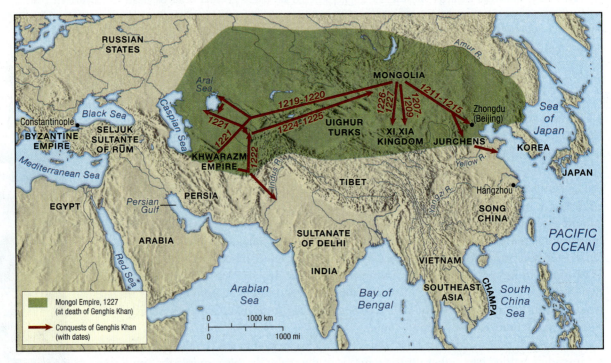

Map 15.4 CONQUESTS OF GENGHIS KHAN, 1206–1227 After Temujin was proclaimed Genghis Khan in 1206, he and his Mongols set out to conquer the world. Notice that his empire eventually extended from the Sea of Japan to the Caspian Sea, incorporating northern China and most of Central Asia. How did these conquests lay the foundations for enhanced Eurasian connections?

The Mongols then moved to their southeast, attacking the Jurchen realm that ruled northern China. From 1211 to 1215, they laid to waste this region, reducing some 90 cities to rubble. In 1215 they attacked the Jurchen capital, a well-fortified metropolis at what is now Beijing, and took it after several months of siege. Then they went on a rampage, plundering its riches, killing its residents, and setting its buildings ablaze. The massacres and fires reportedly lasted a month.

Genghis Khan next directed his efforts far to the west and south. In 1218 he sent emissaries and Muslim merchants to meet the Khwarazm shah, supposedly to seek diplomatic and commercial ties, but also perhaps to scout his realm and find a pretext to invade it. The pretext was provided when one of the shah's governors, with reckless defiance, robbed and massacred the merchants, who were under Mongol protection. Responding with ruthless fury, from 1219 to 1221 the Mongols devastated the Khwarazm Empire, ruining its agriculture by wrecking the irrigation system, pillaging the towns along the trade routes, demolishing Persian cities under Khwarazm rule, and slaughtering the inhabitants. Then, because the Xi Xia kingdom had refused to help him conquer Khwarazm, Genghis Khan returned in 1226 to obliterate it.

Genghis Khan died in 1227, reportedly falling off his horse in battle. By then, however, his Mongols had defeated numerous armies, plundered hundreds of cities and towns, killed millions of people, and created an empire extending from the Sea of Japan to the Caspian Sea (Map 15.4).

Reasons for Mongol Success

The **factors of Mongol success** were numerous, and included their fighting skills and unity, the lack of a united resistance, their use of reconnaissance and terror, their adoption of ideas and techniques from their foes, and their remarkable leadership.

Fighting skills.   The Mongols' skilled horsemanship gave them an immense advantage in mobility, enabling them to strike without warning, capitalize on enemy mistakes, and quickly change direction during battle. With their powerful bows and superb marksmanship they could shoot with deadly precision from several hundred yards away, decimating an opposing force before it could fight back, or fire flaming arrows over the walls of a surrounded city. With their courage and endurance, they could swiftly cover great distances, maintain composure in combat, and almost always outfight and outlast their foes.

Unity and discipline.   Insisting that his generals renounce tribal ties and demanding total loyalty to himself, Genghis Khan centralized his command and instilled iron discipline in his troops. Even when his forces grew to 200,000 and included thousands of Turks and other non-Mongols, they still fought as one and coordinated their actions in combat.

Lack of united resistance.   Animosities among his enemies, and the previous breakup of China and Persia through invasions by other nomads, enabled Genghis Khan to attack his targets one at a time. He was also sometimes aided by his enemies' foes: in northern China, for example, Chinese and Khitans who resented Jurchen rule helped the Mongols end it.

Reconnaissance.   Rarely did the Mongols attack until they had thoroughly scouted their adversaries. From spies, traveling merchants, and tortured captives, Mongol leaders learned about the composition of enemy forces, the layout of cities, and the design of defenses. This knowledge helped them plan their assaults with overpowering effectiveness.

Terror and intimidation.   Almost everywhere, the Mongols' reputation preceded them, complete with reports of merciless invaders, leveled cities, and wholesale slaughter. And the Mongols cleverly fostered this fear, sparing some victims so they could

In order of importance, what were the reasons for Mongol success?

A Mongol archer on horseback.

spread terrifying tales, and using others in battle as human shields. By sowing discord and panic among their foes, while pledging to spare those who offered no resistance and protect those with useful skills—such as engineers, artisans, and merchants—the Mongols even got some to submit without struggle.

Borrowed ideas and techniques. The Mongols ably adopted innovations from the cultures they conquered. From Chinese and Turkish siege engineers, for example, the Mongols learned how to build catapults to heave huge rocks and flaming projectiles over fortress walls, bolstering their assaults on cities and citadels. From their Uighur Turk allies, the Mongols learned to write, adapting Uighur script to express Mongolian words, compile information, maintain records, and communicate over long distances. From Central Asian merchants and Chinese officials, the Mongols learned how to finance and administer an empire. The most eminent such official was Yelü Chucai (*YEH-LOO choo-SĪ*), a Confucian scholar of Khitan heritage who worked for the Mongols and taught them how to govern. In one of history's most astute acts of statecraft, he allegedly convinced them they could make a fortune by exploiting and taxing northern China's cities and farms—rather than destroying them and killing all their people to create new grazing grounds for Mongol herds.

Leadership. A final key factor was their leader himself. Genghis Khan was a masterful military strategist, a talented diplomat, a shrewd opportunist, and a superb leader. Believing himself destined to conquer the world, he inspired his forces to achieve unprecedented feats. Yet he was also a remorseless man who lived to fight and kill and is said to have claimed that a man's greatest joy was to conquer his enemies, plunder their possessions, ride their horses, and ravish their women. History has furnished few other figures so capable and so cruel.

The Mongol Khanates: Conquest, Adaptation, and Conversion

15.4 Analyze the connections that the Mongols created between their empire and China, Southwest Asia, Russia, and Central Asia.

The Mongol conquests did not end with Genghis Khan. After his death, his sons and grandsons continued his campaigns, expanding Mongol rule across Eurasia. In the process they created four great **Mongol khanates**, vast autonomous regions of the Mongol Empire, each ruled by a khan descended from Genghis. These realms included the Khanate of **the Great Khan**, comprising most of East Asia; the Khanate of **the Il-Khans** in Persia and Mesopotamia; the Khanate of **the Golden Horde**, which dominated Russia; and **the Khanate of Jagadai** (*JAH-guh-dī*) in Central Asia (Map 15.5). In adapting their rule to these regions, however, the Mongols were themselves transformed, taking on many ways and ideas of the peoples they ruled.

What connections and resulting effects developed between the Mongols and China?

East Asia: Khubilai Khan and His Mongol-Chinese Empire

The richest and most populous khanate was the one ruled by **the Great Khan**. Chosen by tribal council as Genghis Khan's main successor, he was direct ruler of Mongol East Asia and overlord of the other Mongol realms, whose khans were considered his vassals. As long as the empire remained intact, he was the planet's most powerful person.

Genghis Khan's son Ögödei (*UH-guh-dā*), elected Great Khan in 1229, vastly expanded the whole Mongol realm, sending armies in the 1230s to invade Southwest

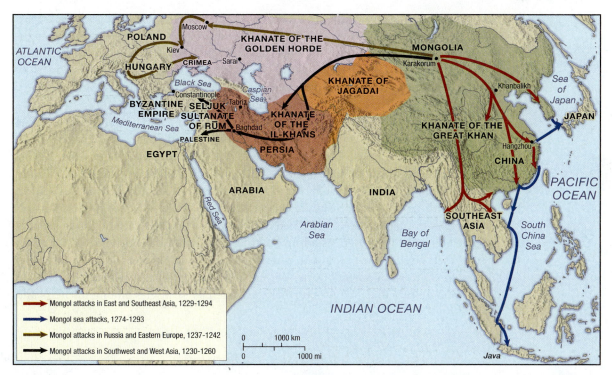

Map 15.5 FOUR MONGOL KHANATES CONNECT EURASIA IN THE 13TH AND 14TH CENTURIES Building on Genghis Khan's conquests, his sons and grandsons conquered Russia, Persia, the rest of China, and much of Islamic West Asia. Notice that they formed four huge khanates connecting much of Eurasia. How did Mongol connections expedite the exchange of goods and knowledge?

Asia and Russia. In East Asia he completed the conquest of North China, routing the last remnants of the Jurchens that survived his father's devastation. Then he planned to move against the Song regime in southern China. But Ögödei died in a drinking binge in 1241, leaving his successors to continue his work.

Ögödei's most eminent successor was his nephew Khubilai (*KOO-bih-lī*) Khan. After leading Mongol armies against the Song regime in the 1250s, this talented leader, ablest of Genghis Khan's grandsons, was chosen Great Khan in 1260. Over the next two decades, he defeated the Song and completed the conquest of China. In 1271 he even claimed the Mandate of Heaven, the divine warrant to rule China, installing himself as its emperor and starting a new dynasty called the Yuan (*yoo-WAHN*). By 1279, when the last Song forces were finally crushed, Khubilai was master of East Asia, ruling as both the Mongol Great Khan and the Emperor of China.

Elsewhere Khubilai was less successful. In 1274 and 1281, he launched against Japan two massive naval invasions, with hundreds of ships, thousands of warriors, and even some gunpowder shells and rockets. But these attacks failed due to Japanese resistance and devastating sea storms the Japanese called **kamikaze** (*KAH-mē-KAH-zē*)—"divine winds" they believed the gods had sent to save Japan. In the 1280s Khubilai sent armies into Southeast Asia, but they were bogged down by the region's dense rain forests, stifling heat and humidity, and deadly tropical diseases. In 1293 he dispatched a seaborne force to attack the island of Java, but this force was decisively repelled.

In China, however, Khubilai reigned supreme. Unlike other Mongols who disdained China's sedentary society, he embraced many Chinese ways. He moved his capital from Mongolia to Khanbalikh (*KAHN-bah-LĒK*), the "city of the Khan," now called Beijing, in northern China. He adopted China's administrative system, adapted

A scene from the Mongol invasion of Japan in 1274.

to urban life, and spared China's cities from ruin if they recognized his rule. He encouraged commerce, promoted use of paper money, repaired and expanded highways, and fostered the formation of merchant corporations. He extended the Grand Canal north to his capital, thus securing transport of grain and goods along an 1100-mile waterway flanked by a paved road. He practiced religious toleration, became a Buddhist, and even had a Christian woman as one of his four main wives.

Khubilai and his heirs were nonetheless deeply resented in China. Many Chinese, regarding their culture as the world's most advanced, saw the Mongol rulers as uncouth barbarians. Chinese Confucians were offended by the Mongols' crude cuisine, their refusal to bathe, and their tolerance for non-Chinese religions such as Christianity and Islam. Confucian men abhorred the high status accorded to Mongol women, including Khubilai's Buddhist wife Chabi, who reportedly exercised great influence. Above all, Confucian scholars resented their own loss of status: although the Mongol regime still employed them as administrators, it reduced their privileges and abandoned their civil service exam placement system, while placing Mongols and other foreigners in most important posts. Within several decades after Khubilai's death in 1294, Mongol rule in China was further weakened by struggles among his heirs and by natural disasters.

Southwest Asia: Mongol Devastation and Muslim Resilience

How did the Mongols affect Southwest Asia, and what accounts for the resilience of Islam there?

In many ways, Islamic Southwest Asia's experience with the Mongols was similar to East Asia's. In both regions, an assault begun by Genghis Khan was resumed and expanded by one of his grandsons. In both regions, the Mongols overcame strong resistance by a wealthy, cosmopolitan society. In both regions, Mongol forces were eventually turned back, but only after carving out an enormous empire. And in both regions, the Mongols adopted beliefs and practices of the peoples they ruled but continued to be seen by these peoples as alien oppressors.

THE MONGOL ASSAULTS ON THE MUSLIM WORLD The Mongol conquest of Southwest Asia started with assaults on Persia. Ravaged during Genghis Khan's attack on Khwarazm in 1219–1221, Persia got a respite when his armies withdrew. In 1230, however, Great Khan Ögödei sent a sizable force there to complete his father's unfinished business. Later, after routing local armies and overrunning Persia, the Mongols dispatched armed forays into Anatolia, defeating the Seljuk Sultanate of Rūm in 1243. But at the time, they lacked sufficient forces to follow up this victory. Nor were they yet ready to invade Mesopotamia, where the Abbasid Caliphs, claiming spiritual leadership of the Islamic world, reigned in the heavily fortified city of Baghdad.

Attackers using a catapult, from Rashid's *History of the World*.

In the 1250s, however, the Mongols resumed their Southwest Asian conquests. While Khubilai led armies against China's Song regime, his brother Hülegü (*hoo-LEH-goo*) assembled a huge force, complete with siege equipment, catapults, and Chinese technicians, to attack Muslim cities and citadels. Hülegü arrived in Persia in 1256 and was joined there by other Mongol forces.

The Mongols first attacked the Assassins, the Shi'ite murder sect, which had numerous fortresses in the rugged mountains south of the Caspian Sea. One by one the Mongols demolished these strongholds. By the end of 1257, the Mongols had killed or captured most of the sect's members, eliminating the cult of killers that had terrorized Sunni Muslim leaders.

But Sunni Muslims had little time to rejoice. Within weeks the Mongols threatened Baghdad, insisting, as their price for sparing the city, that the reigning Abbasid caliph offer them homage and tribute. When the caliph refused to submit, the irate Mongols routed his armies and besieged his city. In February 1258, after holding out for weeks, Baghdad fell to the invaders, appalling the Muslim world. Hülegü let his men plunder the city and had the captured caliph trampled to death by horses. Thus ignobly ended the once-great Abbasid Empire.

The next year, while Hülegü headed homeward with some troops to take part in a Mongol power struggle, the rest of his army moved west into Syria and Palestine. But the Muslim Mamluks who then ruled Egypt, themselves descended from Central Asian Turks, sent a huge force that decisively defeated the Mongols in 1260 in Palestine. Hülegü later returned to Southwest Asia but died in 1265 without regaining the initiative.

THE IL-KHAN CONVERSION AND TRIUMPH OF ISLAM   Hülegü's heirs, a series of Southwest Asian Mongol rulers known as Il-Khans (subordinate khans), focused mainly on ruling their own realm. But the Khanate of **the Il-Khans**, which stretched from eastern Anatolia to India's Indus River (Map 15.5), faced serious problems. In their conquest the Mongols had ravaged the region, destroying its cities and irrigation systems, killing many of its people and wrecking its economy. As their conquests ceased and they lacked new places to plunder, they made things worse by imposing heavy taxes, undermining their own empire and ruining its recovery. The coexistence of Mongol and Islamic law created legal chaos, and a string of short reigns by inept Il-Khans further damaged the regime. So did the fact that the region's people saw their Mongol rulers as alien, barbaric oppressors.

Eventually, however, like earlier rulers of Persia and Mesopotamia, the Mongols were converted by the culture they conquered. Enamored by the splendor of Islamic civilization, they fostered trade, patronized science and scholarship, built cities and schools, and gradually forsook their nomadic ways. Many Mongols became Muslims, including the Il-Khans themselves.

The ablest Il-Khan was Mahmud Ghazan (*MAH-mood gah-ZAHN*), who focused his reign (1295–1304) on rebuilding the region. He adopted Islam, instituted fair taxation, repaired irrigation, and returned abandoned lands to cultivation. Though a Sunni Muslim, he tolerated Shi'ites, who had been harshly persecuted under the Abbasid Caliphate.

Ghazan's prime minister, Rashid al-Din (*rah-SHĒD ahl-DĒN*), was an eminent example of Mongol connections. Born a Jew, he became a Muslim and studied the ideas of places from China to Persia. As a physician familiar with Chinese medicine, he brought Chinese knowledge of human anatomy to the Muslim world, whence it later spread to Europe. As a historian, Rashid worked with Eastern and Western scholars to produce the first great history of the world, a monumental work with lavish illustrations (see catapult drawing on page 296). As an economist and government official, Rashid promoted fiscal and administrative reforms, ably guiding the regime of Il-Khan Mahmud Ghazan.

Unfortunately for the Il-Khans, Ghazan's reign was cut short in 1304 by his death from an illness at age 32. Instead of consolidating his achievements, his successors indulged in the pleasures of their court, letting corrupt officials run the realm. In 1335, when the last of the Il-Khans died without an heir, the empire disintegrated into provinces controlled by ambitious warlords.

The Il-Khan collapse meant the Muslim world had weathered the nomadic onslaught. Both Seljuks and Mongols had brought it death and destruction, but both had also embraced its culture and religion, even providing good governance until their realms declined. Both had actually expanded Muslim horizons, the Seljuks by making Anatolia Islamic and using Persian culture to revitalize Islam, and the Mongols by uniting a Eurasian empire that brought Eastern medicine, scholarship, commerce, and technology to Islamic Southwest Asia.

What were the effects on Russia of the Tatar Yoke?

Russia: Conquest, Tribute, and the Tatar Yoke

Although the Mongol invasion of Russia, like those of China and Southwest Asia, involved the conquest of a vast realm by a grandson of Genghis Khan, Mongol rule in Russia was quite different. For one thing, it was indirect: after ravaging Russia's city-states, the Mongols withdrew, imposed tribute, and made Russian rulers vassals of the Mongol khan. For another thing, Russia's Mongol overlords did not adopt Russian ways. Rejecting Russia's Orthodox Christianity and settled agrarian society, they lived on the steppes, remained pastoral nomads, and embraced Islam. Still, by aiding the rise of Moscow as Russia's dominant city, the Mongol overlords played a key role in Russia's political development.

The onslaught began in late 1237 when Batu Khan (*BAH-too KAHN*), grandson of Genghis and cousin of Khubilai and Hülegü, stunned Northern Russia by attacking in winter, piercing the dense forests by using frozen rivers as highways for his horsemen. That winter his Mongols, whom the Russians called Tatars (*TAH-tarz*), overran Russia's major cities, putting people to the sword and buildings to the torch, spreading terror, death, and devastation. In spring 1238, the Mongols arrived at Novgorod (*NŌV-guh-rud*), a prosperous commercial metropolis, but decided not to attack, partly because the spring thaw made the swampy area unfit for a siege, and partly because the city's merchants quickly agreed to pay tribute. The Mongols had learned that they could profit as parasites, not just as plunderers.

Besides, Batu's main aim was to secure his northern flank for an invasion of Europe. In 1240 he began with an assault on Kiev, former capital of Kievan Rus (Chapter 10), sacking the city and leaving behind fields full of skulls and bones. In 1241 the Mongols moved into Poland and Hungary, where they encountered European knights. Finding arrows useless against the metal armor of these mounted warriors, Batu's marksmen shot the knights' horses out from under them to win major battles. But early the next year, when Batu learned that Great Khan Ögödei had died, he withdrew his forces to the east to influence the choice of a successor.

Europe thus was spared, but not Russia. Batu and his heirs set up a new realm that came to be called the Khanate of **the Golden Horde**. From their capital at Sarai (*sah-RĪ*), amid the steppe pasturelands north of the Caspian Sea, they commanded a domain that extended from North-Central Asia into Eastern Europe (Map 15.5). For

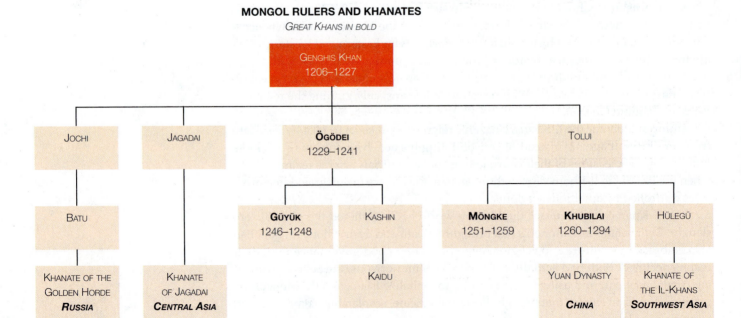

MONGOL RULERS AND KHANATES
GREAT KHANS IN BOLD

the next few centuries, the Mongols dominated Russia, forcing its city-states to furnish tribute, soldiers, and slaves, while playing their princes off against one another. Russians call this era of Mongol domination the **Tatar Yoke**.

Still, the Tatars largely let the Russians run their own affairs as long as their main leader traveled to Sarai and humbly sought the khan's permission to serve as grand prince. At first the khans alternated this office among Russian princes so none would gain too much power. Eventually, however, the khans entrusted it mostly to the rulers of a rising metropolis called Moscow. Henceforth, by doing the khan's bidding and acting as his agents in repressing other Russians, Moscow's rulers usually held the title of grand prince. In time this status would help Moscow become Russia's leading city, and eventually grow powerful enough to challenge Mongol rule.

Central Asia: The Struggle to Maintain the Mongol Heritage

How did the Mongol heritage in Central Asia gradually crumble?

Strife among the Mongols also challenged their empire. Discord stemmed from its size and diversity, which bred conflicts among its regions, and its lack of a clear succession system, sparking power struggles among Genghis Khan's heirs. As early as the 1260s, Batu's successors in the Golden Horde clashed with Hülegü's Il-Khan regime, while Khubilai fought a four-year battle against a younger brother to prevail as Great Khan.

In time the struggles among the Mongols converged in Central Asia, a region Genghis Khan had consigned to his second son, Jagadai. Centered among the other three khanates, **the Khanate of Jagadai** was the empire's hub (Map 15.5). It was also the poorest and least populated khanate, and the one that best maintained the Mongols' nomadic warrior heritage.

War and conquest were part of this heritage, and the empire's expansion had come mainly at the expense of settled societies. But the Khanate of Jagadai, surrounded by the other three khanates, could not expand without attacking other Mongols. At first it saw no need to do so and was content to supply the other realms with horsemen to sustain their assaults.

Eventually, however, after conquering settled societies, the other khanates adopted new customs and beliefs. The Il-Khans embraced Islam, as did the Golden Horde, while Khubilai became a Buddhist, moved his capital from Mongolia to China, and declared himself Chinese emperor. Seeing such changes as a debasement of Genghis Khan's legacy, the Khanate of Jagadai rallied to restore this heritage.

In the 1260s Ögödei's grandson Kaidu (*KĪ-doo*), resentful that his branch of the family had lost in the struggles for succession as Great Khan, took over the Jagadai Khanate, portraying himself as protector of Mongol traditions. He declared that all true Mongols must live in tents on the steppes and not degrade themselves by dwelling in cities and towns. Then, in the 1270s, he assembled an army and attacked the western part of the region ruled by the Great Khan.

Responding swiftly, Great Khan Khubilai sent a strong force to repel the attack. But Kaidu, refusing to admit defeat, stunned the other Mongols in 1277 by invading Mongolia itself. Although Khubilai's armies soon drove back Kaidu's forces, the Great Khan continued his campaigns elsewhere without stopping to finish off Kaidu, whose insurgency thus endured until his death in 1301. A few years later, left without a leader, his followers submitted to Khubilai's successor—but then fought among themselves sporadically for decades. By the 1340s, as a result, the Jagadai Khanate had split into two smaller realms.

The Mongol Empire thus began to unravel, but its impact could not be undone. In conquering much of Eurasia, the Mongols wrought massive ruin, but in ruling it they forged connections that had extensive and enduring consequences.

The Mongol Impact: Connections and Consequences

15.5 Evaluate the positive and negative effects of the Mongol conquests.

The initial impact of the Mongol onslaught was widespread devastation. Across Eurasia hundreds of cities and towns were leveled, thousands of farmlands were ruined, and millions of people were killed. According to contemporary counts, China's population dropped by 40 percent, from around 100 million to about 60 million, while Russia's wealth and talent were disastrously depleted. Southwest Asia was hit especially hard, pillaged first by the Seljuk Turks and then by the Mongols. Many of the region's great cities were destroyed, and its farming took decades to recover from the damage done to irrigation.

In the long run, however, the Mongol era's main impact was increased Eurasian integration. By connecting distant and diverse regions under a common rule, the Mongols promoted trade and travel from one end of Eurasia to the other, vastly enhancing the exchange of goods, ideas, and technologies—as well as the spread of diseases—among Eurasian societies.

Trade and Travel: *The Pax Mongolica*

In what ways did the Pax Mongolica enhance connections among societies and peoples?

Much as Romans had created a Roman Peace, or *Pax Romana*, promoting commercial and cultural exchanges in the early centuries C.E., the Mongols produced a Mongolian Peace, later called **Pax Mongolica** (*PAHX mon-GOL-ih-kuh*), advancing the flow of goods and ideas among Eurasian peoples (Map 15.6).

The *Pax Mongolica* was not just a fortuitous by-product of the Mongol invasions; it resulted from deliberate policies pursued by Mongol rulers. To manage their vast realm, they devised an effective administration, using the Uighur Turks' writing system and employing many Uighurs as civil servants and scribes. To expedite communication, they created a long-distance postal system, with an extensive network of relay stations, staffed by thousands of riders and ponies capable of carrying messages 200 miles a day. To secure interregional travel and commerce, Mongol forces protected trade routes with groups of warriors stationed across Central Asia. To enhance diplomatic relations, Mongol rulers dispatched emissaries to distant realms and welcomed embassies from other lands. They also supplied traveling merchants and dignitaries with an embossed metal seal that served as an early form of passport, to indicate that the bearer's travel was officially approved.

A Mongol "passport"

Aided and protected by such policies, growing numbers of traders and travelers transported goods and knowledge across Eurasia. Merchants conveyed cottons from India; spices from Southeast Asia; timber, furs, and slaves from Russia; silks, porcelains, and teas from China; grapes, wines, and olive oils from Europe; and horses, dates, sugar, and slaves from Muslim domains in Africa and Southwest Asia. Mongol-era travelers also spread knowledge by publishing accounts of their visits to widely varied lands.

One such account was that of Marco Polo, an Italian merchant who claimed to have traveled across Central Asia to China (Map 15.7) and to have worked in Khubilai

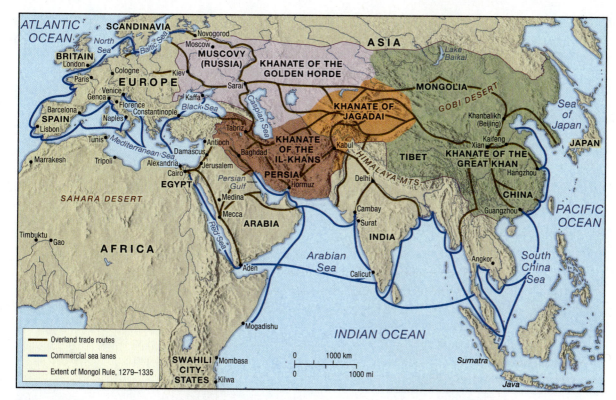

Map 15.6 *PAX MONGOLICA* **ENHANCES CONNECTIONS IN THE 13TH AND 14TH CENTURIES** By connecting much of Eurasia, the Mongols created a *Pax Mongolica* (Mongolian Peace) that enhanced the exchange of goods and knowledge. Note the land and sea routes linking numerous cultures. What goods, ideas, beliefs, and technologies did these connections convey?

Khan's service from 1275 to 1292 (see "Marco Polo on the Mongols"). Later, back in Europe, Polo published *Il milione* (*The Million*), a book describing a vast Chinese empire with huge, prosperous cities, printed books and paper money, flourishing canals and roads, black rocks (coal) used as fuel, great ships in bustling harbors, splendid architecture, and fabulous goods.

At first Marco Polo was dismissed as a liar, and even today some critics contend that his accounts were based not on personal experience but on tales heard from other travelers, amplified by his imagination. But whatever their source, his stories helped inspire in the West a fascination with the East. This fascination, bolstered by accounts of Asian wealth and a growing Western appetite for Eastern goods such as spices, ceramics, textiles, and teas, led later Europeans to embark on epic voyages that would transform the world (Chapter 19).

Another influential travel account was the *Rihlah* ("Travels") of Ibn Battuta (*IB'n bah-TOO-tah*), a Muslim from Morocco who between 1325 and 1355 journeyed some 75,000 miles across the Mongol khanates and beyond. He visited the Mongol Il-Khan, the Golden Horde's center at Sarai, trading towns on the Silk Road, and numerous other settlements in India, Southeast Asia, China, Europe, and Africa. His detailed recollections, dictated after his return, provided his readers, and subsequent historians, with remarkably accurate descriptions of these diverse societies.

Exchanges of Ideas and Technologies

Eager to exploit the talents of their conquered subjects, the Mongols moved people with special skills—such as architects, engineers, miners, metalworkers, and

What ideas and technologies spread across Eurasia in the Mongol era, and how did the *Pax Mongolica* facilitate their spread?

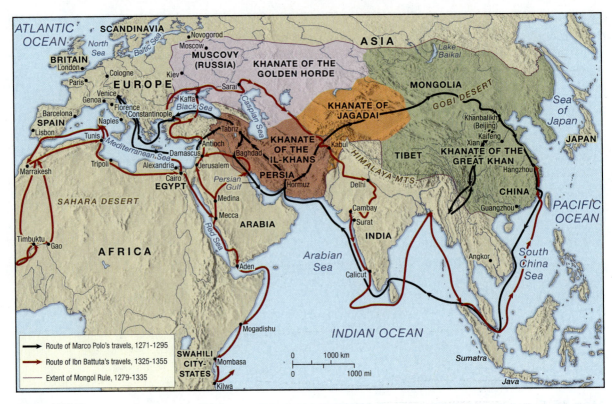

Map 15.7 TRAVELS OF MARCO POLO, 1271–1295, AND IBN BATTUTA, 1325–1355 The *Pax Mongolica* enabled travelers such as Marco Polo (an Italian Christian) and Ibn Battuta (a Moroccan Muslim) to visit many distant lands. Note that Marco Polo reportedly traveled across Eurasia from Italy to China, while Ibn Battuta's travels took him to numerous places in Africa and Eurasia. How did their travel descriptions help inspire others to create new connections?

Document 15.1   Marco Polo on the Mongols

Marco Polo, an Italian merchant who reportedly spent 17 years in the service of the Mongols in China, included in his writings a description of the Mongols, possibly based on accounts he had heard from others. How do these excerpts help to explain the ruggedness and effectiveness of the Mongols as warriors?

The [Mongols] never remain fixed in one location. As winter approaches they move to the plains of a warmer region in order to find sufficient pasturage for their animals. In summer they inhabit cool regions in the mountains where there is water and grass. . . .

It is the women who tend to their commercial concerns, buying and selling, and who tend to all the needs of their husbands and households. The men devote their time totally to hunting, hawking, and warfare. . . . They subsist totally on meat and milk, eating the produce of their hunting. . . . They likewise eat every manner of animal: horses, camels, even dogs, provided they are fat. They drink mare's milk, which they prepare in such a way that it has the qualities and taste of white wine. . . .

Their weapons are bows, iron maces, and in some instances, spears. The bow, however, is the weapon at which they are the most expert, being accustomed to use it in their sports from childhood. They wear armor made from the hides of buffalo and other beasts, fire-dried and thus hard and strong.

They are brave warriors, almost to the point of desperation, placing little value on their lives, and exposing themselves without hesitation to every sort of danger. They are cruel by nature. They are capable of undergoing every manner of privation, and when it is necessary, they can live for a month on the milk of their mares and the wild animals they catch. . . . The men are trained to remain on horseback for two days and two nights without dismounting, sleeping in the saddle while the horse grazes. No people on the earth can surpass them in their ability to endure hardships, and no other people shows greater patience in the face of every sort of deprivation. They are most obedient to their chiefs, and are maintained at small expense. These qualities, which are so essential to a soldier's formation, make them fit to subdue the world, which in fact they have largely done. . . .

When they are setting out on a long expedition, they carry little with them. . . . They subsist for the most part on mare's milk. . . . Should circumstances require speed, they can ride for ten days without lighting a fire or taking a hot meal. During this time they subsist on the blood drawn from their horses, each man opening a vein and drinking the blood. . . .

SOURCE: From Andrea, *Human Record*, 3/e Vol 1 TXT, 3E. © 1998 Wadsworth, a part of Cengage Learning, Inc. Reproduced by permission. www.cengage.com/permissions.

carpenters—all over the empire. Intrigued by the diverse ideas of the peoples they ruled, Mongol rulers also welcomed travel by scholars and religious figures.

Such practices helped disseminate ideas and technologies. Buddhist, Muslim, and Christian communities, for example, emerged in many new places, exposing societies all over Eurasia to their religious ideas. Muslim knowledge about mathematics and astronomy spread eastward to China, where Khubilai Khan employed Persian scholars to help build a new observatory, and westward to Europe, where such knowledge eventually helped inspire a scientific revolution. Chinese expertise in medicine and anatomy was likewise spread westward by traveling scholars and officials, most notably Rashid al-Din. From China also came two enormously influential technologies: printing and gunpowder weaponry.

By the time of the Mongol conquests, the Chinese technique of printing on paper from carved wooden blocks had spread to the Central Asian homeland of the Uighur Turks. Allied with the Mongols, and employed throughout their empire as artisans, scribes, and officials, Uighurs then helped spread printing west across Eurasia. Although printing was initially shunned by Muslims, who deemed that sacred texts must be recopied devoutly by hand, Il-Khan officials in Persia introduced printed paper money in 1294—then withdrew it when people rioted against what they considered worthless paper. In the 1300s, printed playing cards and holy pictures were introduced into Europe, probably by diplomats and clerics who had seen them in Eastern travels during the *Pax Mongolica*. These printed cards and pictures foreshadowed the development in Europe of woodblock artwork and movable-type printing presses during the next century (Chapter 16).

More direct was the Mongol role in proliferating gunpowder weapons. During the Tang era (618–907 C.E.), the Chinese had begun combining saltpeter (potassium nitrate) with sulfur and charcoal to create a substance, later called gunpowder, that burned very quickly or exploded. It proved useful in mining, clearing forests, building canals, and staging fireworks displays. Later, China's warriors also used it in crude arrow weapons and bombs that were thrown or catapulted in battle. In the 1200s such devices helped China to slow—but not stop—the Mongol assault.

The Mongols quickly saw gunpowder's value. While fighting the Jurchens in North China (1211–1215), they learned from Chinese allies how to build catapults and bombs, which later Mongol armies used in their attacks on Islamic Southwest Asia and Japan. By the late 1200s, also with Chinese help, the Mongols learned to cast thick metal firepots and pack them with gunpowder and a big rock or metal ball. Once ignited, the exploding powder propelled the projectile with enough force to smash holes in enemy walls. Thus were born the first cannons.

Gunpowder shells explode overhead during Mongol invasion of Japan in 1274.

Others, too, were capable of copying their foes. Battered by Mongol assaults, Muslims soon learned to make gunpowder weapons, and Europeans, experienced in forging metal pots and church bells, were not far behind. In the 1340s, the English, who had earlier developed gunpowder (either on their own or through knowledge spread by Mongol-era travelers), began using cannons in the Hundred Years War against France (Chapter 16). By the next century, many Eurasian armies had developed handheld firearms.

Although cumbersome and inaccurate, these early cannons and firearms gradually transformed warfare. Initially gunpowder helped nomadic warriors seize the walled cities of settled societies. But guns eventually gave an edge to the settled societies, which had the resources, mines, and artisans to produce them in far greater numbers than the nomads. In time the use of firearms neutralized the nomads' advantages—their horsemanship, courage, and speed—by enabling enemy armies to shoot at them from a distance. The Mongols thus helped spread a technology that aided their undoing.

What were the consequences of the plague pandemic of the fourteenth century, and how did the connections forged by the Mongols contribute to those consequences?

The Plague Pandemic

The Mongols also helped spread a disease that aided their undoing. In the mid-1300s, Eurasia was swept by a pandemic of **bubonic plague**, a deadly contagion typically carried from rodents to humans by fleas. Unaware of how it spread, people then had little protection against this terrible affliction, which brought painful inflammations followed by chills, vomiting, fever, diarrhea, and delirium—often leading to death in three or four days.

The outbreak began in southwest China (Map 15.8), where rats and people had been beset by plague sporadically for centuries. In the 1330s and 1340s, probably aided by traveling Mongol soldiers whose supply wagons harbored infected rats and fleas, the plague spread to other parts of China, where numerous people were already weakened by floods and famines.

Meanwhile, aided by increased caravan traffic promoted by the Mongols, the plague moved westward across Central Asia, spread by fleas that fed on the blood of squirrels, rats, marmots, dogs, and humans. The deadly contagion ravaged caravans and towns along the trade routes, as well as encampments of nomadic herders and Mongol warriors scattered across the steppes.

By 1346, the plague had reached the Black Sea's northern shores, where it afflicted Mongol soldiers besieging the city of Kaffa, a fortified trading port controlled by the Italian republic of Genoa. According to some accounts, in one of history's earliest attempts at biological warfare, Mongols catapulted corpses of plague victims over the town walls into the surrounded city, evidently intending to infect its defenders. Fleeing Genoese ships, apparently harboring infected rats, carried the plague to Egypt and to Europe, where 30 to 60 percent of the people perished in an epidemic called the Black Death (Chapter 16).

The plague pandemic thus ravaged the peoples of Eurasia and northeast Africa, killing millions and leaving a trail of death and devastation. It induced widespread panic, disrupted commerce, and created conditions that contributed to the disintegration of the Mongol Empire.

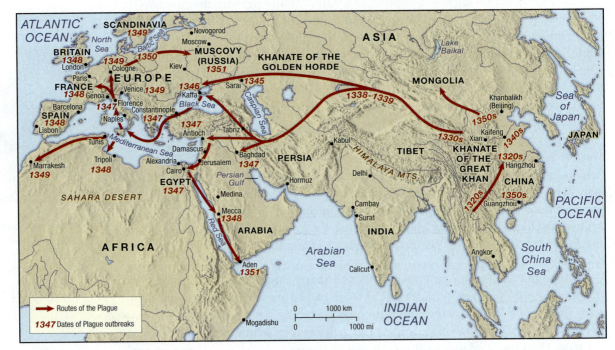

Map 15.8 THE PLAGUE PANDEMIC OF THE 14TH CENTURY Mongol connections also helped to spread disease. Compare this map with Maps 15.6 and 15.7, noting that the plague, having ravaged parts of China, moved west along routes that the Mongols used to connect their Eurasian empire. How did Mongol connections contribute to the plague pandemic? How did plague help end Mongol rule in China?

The End of the Mongol Era

Why did the Mongol Empire collapse in the fourteenth century?

By the 1330s, when the plague pandemic began, the Mongol Empire was already in decline. In Southwest Asia, as we have seen, the Khanate of the Il-Khans dissolved after its last ruler died with no heir in 1335. In Central Asia, the Khanate of Jagadai, torn by internal discord, split into eastern and western khanates during the 1330s and 1340s. In China, Mongol rule was beset by dynastic strife. As Khubilai's descendants vied for power, often by intrigues and assassinations, eight different emperors reigned between 1307 and 1333.

Then catastrophe struck China. In the mid-1330s, deluged by crop-destroying floods, northern China endured a calamitous famine. In the 1340s, before the region recovered, another famine ensued. Faced with widespread starvation, the government strove to repair the dikes and dams, only to have them burst again. Meanwhile, huge amounts of paper money printed to finance the repairs deeply debased the currency. Amid these disasters came the plague, ravaging much of China and intensifying the crisis. By the 1350s, convinced by the disasters that the Mongol dynasty had lost the Mandate of Heaven, many Chinese people joined mass revolts against it.

These disasters and this perception bolstered rebel leaders, especially Zhu Yuan-zhang (*JOO yoo-wahn JAHNG*), a poor peasant orphaned as a youth when his parents died from famine. While other rebels looted the countryside, Zhu amassed an army of supporters. In 1356, as China descended into chaos, he captured Nanjing, one of China's great cities, and made it his capital. During the next decade, he defeated other rebels, gaining control of the entire Yangzi valley. Finally he moved north with his huge army to confront the Mongol emperor, who promptly fled to Mongolia. In 1368 Zhu claimed Heaven's Mandate as the emperor Hongwu (*HONG WOO*) and founded a new dynasty, the Ming (Chapter 21). Mongol rule in China thus came to an end.

The Mongol Empire never recovered from its loss of China. In the late 1300s, a Turkic warrior called Timur (*tē-MOOR*) Lenk tried to reunite the Mongol realm, but his ruinous attacks on other Turks and Mongols instead opened the way for new Islamic empires (Chapter 17) and for Russian independence (Chapter 25). For several centuries surviving Mongol khanates staged sporadic raids on settled societies such as Russia and China. But armed with gunpowder weapons, knowledge of which the Mongols had helped spread, the settled societies with their large armies increasingly kept the mounted steppe warriors at bay. The age of the great nomadic empires was over.

Chapter Review

Consequences and Connections

The nomadic invasions of the tenth through fourteenth centuries devastated Eurasia's settled societies. In a remarkable series of assaults, the nomads of Central Asia, with small populations and simple societies based on herding and horsemanship, ravaged the large armies, fertile farmlands, and cosmopolitan cities of their far more populous and prosperous neighbors. The Khitans, and later the Jurchens, moved into northern China, the cradle of Chinese civilization. The Seljuk Turks overran Southwest Asia, seizing the Islamic and Byzantine heartlands. Then the Mongols, mightiest of the nomads, conquered all of China and much of Eurasia as well.

In the long run, however, the nomadic conquests transformed the nomads and bolstered the settled societies. Over time the victorious nomads adopted many features of the conquered cultures, including governance structures, economic patterns, and religious beliefs. By the time their empires ended, the former nomads had become more settled and cosmopolitan, largely forsaking their tribal and itinerant ways. Furthermore, by forcibly uniting large parts of Eurasia under their rule, the Seljuk Turks and Mongols fostered connections that eventually strengthened settled societies. Indeed, by expediting the growth of east–west commerce and the spread of technologies such as gunpowder and printing, the nomadic conquests eventually enhanced the wealth and power of the Muslim and Christian worlds.

Reviewing Key Concepts

Ask Yourself

1. Why did Central Asians rely mostly on herding and horsemanship rather than farming? How did this reliance affect their societies and governance?

2. How and why were the Seljuk Turks able to conquer and rule Southwest Asia? How were they transformed in the process?

3. What factors account for the Mongols' incredible success? Why were they unable to conquer Japan, Southeast Asia, Egypt, and Europe?

4. Why and how did nomadic conquerors adopt features of the cultures they conquered?

5. What were the main impacts of the *Pax Mongolica*?

6. How did the Mongols compare, in tactics, policies, and impacts, with earlier rulers of multicultural empires, such as Persians, Macedonians, Romans, Muslim Arabs, and Seljuk Turks?

Key Dates and Developments

1025–1040	Seljuk Turks enter Persia
1055	Seljuk Turks conquer Baghdad
1071–1076	Seljuks defeat Byzantines, take Syria and Palestine
1092–1194	Seljuk Empire disintegrates
1114–1127	Jurchens defeat Khitans and conquer northern China
1206	Temujin proclaimed Genghis Khan
1211–1215	Mongols defeat Jurchens and ravage northern China
1219–1221	Mongols conquer Khwarazm and ravage Persia
1237–1241	Mongols invade Russia and Central Europe
1255–1260	Mongols invade Southwest Asia, take Baghdad in 1258
1274, 1281	Japan rebuffs Mongol invasions with help of storms
1275–1292	Marco Polo reportedly resides in China
1279	Khubilai completes conquest of China
1325–1355	Ibn Battuta travels across much of Asia and Africa
1335	Il-Khan regime collapses in southern Asia
1340s	Plague pandemic spreads across Eurasia
1368	Mongols ousted from China; Hongwu begins Ming dynasty
1380–1405	Timur Lenk ravages much of Asia

Chapter 16
The Resurgence of the Christian West, 1050–1530

THE CATHEDRAL AND BAPTISTERY OF FLORENCE In the 11th through 16th centuries, the Christian West experienced a political, economic, and cultural resurgence, as reflected in the splendid architecture of Renaissance Florence.

After reading this chapter, you should be able to:

16.1 Describe the effects on Europe of its conflicts and connections with the Islamic world from the eleventh through thirteenth centuries.

16.2 Discuss the advances made by Europe during the High Middle Ages.

16.3 Explain the causes and effects of the challenges faced by Europe in the fourteenth century.

16.4 Explain how the European Renaissance was enhanced by connections with Muslims, Byzantines, and Asians.

Christian West

Crusade Areas

In 1095 the Byzantine Empire, a shrunken remnant of the once great Roman realm, was in serious trouble. A few decades earlier, the Seljuk Turks had seized its eastern provinces and best farmlands. The Turks had also overrun Syria and Palestine, conquering a region revered as a Holy Land by Christians, Muslims, and Jews. Seeking to shore up his defenses, the Byzantine ruler, as leader of the Christian East, asked the Christian West for help in fighting the Islamic Turks. It proved a fateful request.

Pope Urban II (1088–1099), as head of the Western Church, responded with a grandiose plan to retake the Holy Land for Christianity. At Clermont, France, in late 1095, he called for Christian warriors to drive out the "accursed" Turks. "Wrest that land from the wicked race," he urged, in one account of his speech, "and subject it to yourselves." Inspired by religious zeal, by dreams of wealth and territory, and by a papal promise of "imperishable glory" in the "kingdom of heaven," thousands of European Christians heeded his call.

Thus began the crusades, Christian holy wars directed mainly against Muslims, heralding a resurgence of the Christian West. For centuries, captained by feudal warlords and piloted by predatory Church leaders, Western Christians had lagged behind Muslims in power, wealth, learning, and technology. But in the eleventh century, energized by increasing prosperity and reforming popes, the West began to rebound. The crusades reflected this resurgence and also advanced it by bolstering Western commercial and cultural growth.

Europe's High Middle Ages (1050–1300), coinciding roughly with the crusades, witnessed a flowering of what is now called Western civilization. Then, challenged in the 1300s by famines, plagues, schisms, and wars, the West rebounded again. Enriched by connections with Muslims, it experienced a cultural and technological renaissance, emerging by 1500 as a complex, confident, dynamic, and expansive civilization.

Conflicts and Connections Between Europe and Islam

16.1 Describe the effects on Europe of its conflicts and connections with the Islamic world from the eleventh through thirteenth centuries.

The West's resurgence began in the eleventh century. By then, the Viking and Magyar invasions that plagued Europe in preceding centuries had ceased. Agricultural advances, combined with a warming of the climate, brought increasing prosperity and population growth. The Great Schism of 1054, by cutting off Roman popes from Eastern Christianity, freed them to focus on strengthening their supremacy in the West. And ambitious popes began to institute reforms, curtail corruption, and expand the power and prestige of the Western Church.

Meanwhile, both Muslims and Byzantines had problems. In preceding centuries, the splintering of the Abbasid Empire, and the growth of diverse groups within Islam such as Shi'ites, Sufis, and Almoravids, had undermined Islamic unity. During the 1040s and 1050s, the Seljuk Turks conquered the Muslim heartland, taking Baghdad in 1055 and making the Abbasid caliphs puppets of the Turkish sultan. Although the Seljuks became Muslims, their conquests further fragmented the Muslim world. Then the Seljuks routed the Byzantines in 1071 and went on to conquer Palestine, Syria, and eastern Anatolia, opening the way for expanded encounters between Europe and Islam.

Christians and Muslims in Iberia

As Turks took control in the East, Christians were moving against Muslims in Iberia, the peninsula embracing Portugal and Spain, most of which had been ruled by Muslims since the 700s. In the eleventh century, amid strife among Iberian Muslims, small Christian kingdoms surviving in the north began working for *Reconquista* (*rā-kahn-KĒS-tah*), or Christian reconquest of Iberia (Map 16.1). In 1063 Pope Alexander II (1061–1074) supported their effort by sending in French and Norman soldiers, and he sanctified it by pardoning their sins, setting a precedent for future popes to grant spiritual rewards for Christians who fought Muslims.

Over the next few centuries, forces led by the Spanish Christian kingdoms of Castile (*cass-TĒL*) and Aragon (*AIR-uh-GŌN*) gradually pushed the Muslims back. In 1085, Castile and its allies captured Toledo, an Islamic cultural stronghold in central Iberia. In the northeast, Aragon took several Muslim cities, including Saragossa in 1118. Fearing that Islam might be pushed out of Iberia entirely, Muslims from North Africa intervened, but a united Spanish Christian army defeated them in 1212. Christians took Córdoba in 1236, Valencia in 1238, and Seville in 1248, while Portugal freed itself from Islamic rule by 1250. Although Muslims held Granada in the south until 1492, by the mid-1200s Christians ruled most of Iberia.

Conquests and connections with Muslims in Iberia profited the Christian West. By taking Toledo, long a center of Islamic learning, Christians gained access to its large library of works on science and philosophy, greatly aiding the advance of Western scholarship. Europeans likewise learned how to make paper and forge fine steel swords through contacts with Muslims in Iberia.

Conquests in Iberia also built Western confidence in religious war. Warfare in God's name, often conducted by Muslims, was now conducted by Christian crusaders fighting to take the Holy Land from Muslims.

How did the *Reconquista* benefit Christians politically, intellectually, and technologically?

Map 16.1 CHRISTIANS RECONQUER SPAIN FROM MUSLIMS, 1080–1492
From the 8th through 11th centuries, Muslims ruled much of Spain, building there an impressive Islamic culture. Observe, however, that in the 11th through 15th centuries, Spanish Christian forces steadily defeated and drove out the Muslims. What benefits did Christian Europe gain from its connections with Muslims in Spain?

The Christian Crusades and the Muslim Response

In 1095, as noted in this chapter's introduction, Pope Urban II called for Christian invasion of the Holy Land. Responding to a Byzantine appeal for help, Urban also hoped to bring peace to Europe, ending wars among its peoples by uniting them in a common cause. He wanted to enlarge Christendom through warfare fueled by faith, against the Muslims, who had shown how effective it could be. He aspired to enhance the papacy's power, and perhaps restore its leadership over the Eastern Church (see "Excerpts from Pope Urban II's Speech at Clermont, 1095").

The response to Urban's appeal was dramatic. As he preached his crusade, he was reportedly greeted by shouts of "It is God's will!" Within months, warriors from

Why did the Christians launch their crusades and how did the Muslims respond?

Document 16.1 Excerpts from Pope Urban II's Speech at Clermont, 1095

In 1095, at Clermont in France, Pope Urban II called for a Christian crusade to retake the Holy Land. How did he seek to demonize the Turks and motivate Christians for war?

From the confines of Jerusalem and the city of Constantinople a horrible tale . . . has been brought to our ears, namely, that . . . an accursed race, a race utterly alienated from God, . . . has invaded the lands of those Christians and has depopulated them by the sword, pillage and fire; it has led away a part of the captives into its own country, and a part it has destroyed by cruel tortures; it has either entirely destroyed the churches of God or appropriated them for the rites of its own religion . . . On whom therefore is the labor of avenging these wrongs and of recovering this territory incumbent, if not upon you?

. . . Let the deeds of your ancestors move you and incite your minds to manly achievements . . . Let the holy sepulchre of the Lord our Saviour, which is possessed by unclean nations, especially incite you, and the holy places which are now . . . irreverently polluted with their filthiness . . .

Let none of your possessions detain you, no solicitude for your family affairs, since this land which you inhabit, shut in on all sides by the seas and surrounded by the mountain peaks, is too narrow for your large population; nor does it abound in wealth; and it furnishes scarcely food enough for its cultivators. Hence it is that you murder one another, that you wage war, and that frequently you perish by mutual wounds. Let therefore hatred depart from among you, let your quarrels end, let wars cease, and let all dissensions and controversies slumber. Enter upon the road to the Holy Sepulchre; wrest that land from the wicked race, and subject it to yourselves. That land which as the Scripture says . . . was given by God into the possession of the children of Israel . . . is now held captive by His enemies, and is in subjection to those who do not know God, to the worship of the heathens . . . God has conferred upon you above all nations great glory in arms. Accordingly undertake this journey for the remission of your sins, with the assurance of the imperishable glory of the kingdom of heaven.

When Pope Urban had said these and very many similar things . . ., he so influenced . . . the desires of all who were present that they cried out, "It is the will of God! It is the will of God!"

SOURCE: Robert the Monk, *Historia Hierosolymitana* (Medieval Source book: Urban, IL: Speech at Council of Clermont, 1095).

Italy, France, and Germany assembled and headed for Constantinople, where they converged in 1097 to continue their eastward march.

Thus began the **crusades**, a series of Christian holy wars that lasted off and on for two centuries. Conducted by Western Christians, and directly mainly against Muslims, they also came to include assaults against Jews and even other Christians. Although they ultimately failed to maintain their early aim of enduring Christian control over the Holy Land, they helped to develop connections that enhanced the resurgence of the Christian West.

The First Crusade (1096–1099) was a stunning Christian success. Aided by divisions among Muslims, Christian warriors conquered the lands around the eastern Mediterranean (Map 16.2), creating four "crusader states" and capturing Jerusalem in 1099. But Christians also engaged in butchery and bigotry: unruly "peasant crusaders," aroused against all non-Christians, massacred Jews in Germany, and Christian soldiers pillaging Jerusalem slaughtered defenseless Muslims.

In time, however, the crusaders' conquests and brutal behavior motivated Muslims to combine their efforts and launch retaliatory attacks. By 1144 they amassed a large army and reconquered one of the crusader states. Pope Eugenius III quickly authorized a Second Crusade (1147–1149), led by the German emperor and the king of France. But this time the crusaders lost. After almost battling the Byzantines near Constantinople, they were badly beaten by Islamic Turks in Anatolia, and failed to recover any lost ground.

A few decades later, the West lost even more ground. The brilliant Muslim warrior Salah al-Din, called Saladin in Europe, founded a new dynasty in Egypt in 1173. He conquered Syria and Arabia, uniting them with Egypt into a formidable realm, and then attacked the remaining crusader states. In 1187 his forces took Jerusalem,

Salah al-Din (Saladin).

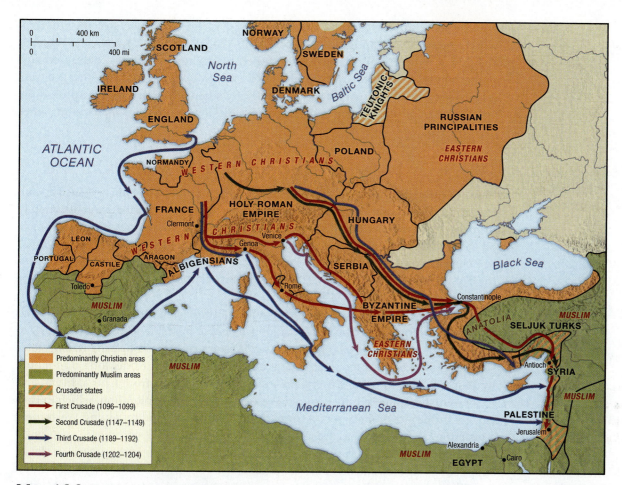

Map 16.2 **CRUSADES CREATE NEW CONFLICTS AND CONNECTIONS, 1095–1300** The crusades involved new conflicts and connections between Christians and Muslims. Note that the First Crusade, in which Christians conquered the Holy Land, was followed by others meant to regain control after Muslim-led counterattacks. How did the crusades enhance connections, and what impacts did these connections have on Western culture and commerce?

refraining on his orders from sacking the Holy City. The First Crusade's work was thus undone, as Muslims again ruled most of the Holy Land.

Europe's three leading rulers—German emperor Frederick Barbarossa (*bar-buh-RŌ-sah*), English king Richard I the Lionheart, and French king Philip II Augustus—now organized a Third Crusade (1189–1192). Planned as a multipronged land and sea assault, it was disastrous for the West. Frederick, in his late sixties, drowned on the way while crossing a river with his armor on. Richard and Philip quarreled constantly, until the latter, citing poor health, returned to France in 1191. Richard soldiered on, and even beat Muslim hero Saladin in several battles, but failed to retake Jerusalem, which remained under Muslim rule.

A decade later, noting weakness and division within the Byzantine Empire, Pope Innocent III (1198–1216) called for a Fourth Crusade (1202–1204), hoping to undo the conquests of Saladin (who had died in 1193) and perhaps to reunite Eastern and Western Christianity. Driven more by greed than faith, however, the Germans, Normans, and Venetians who organized this crusade diverted it against Constantinople. Dismayed at their decision to plunder Christians instead of attacking Muslims, Innocent condemned the crusaders in 1202 but could not control them. In 1204 they sacked the great city, forcing the Byzantine emperor to flee, and replaced his regime with a Western-dominated Latin Empire that lasted until 1261. The Byzantine realm was then restored and endured until 1453, but it never regained its former size or strength.

Later crusades also attacked targets other than Muslims. From 1209 to 1229, crusaders in southern France annihilated Albigensians, radical Christian spiritualists who defied Church teaching by denouncing as evil all aspects of the physical world, including sex and material possessions. In succeeding decades, the Teutonic Knights, a military religious order founded by earlier crusaders, conquered surviving pagan lands near the eastern Baltic Sea (Map 16.2) and invaded Russian regions settled by Eastern Christians. By 1291, when Muslims finally captured the last Christian outpost in the Holy Land, the initial crusading ideals had long since disappeared.

Islamic Impacts on Western Commerce and Culture

In what ways were the Crusades unsuccessful for Europe, and in what ways were they beneficial?

Thus, in terms of their original goals, the crusades ended in failure. Muslim control of the Holy Land, though interrupted by the early crusaders, was ultimately restored. Europe remained divided into feuding states, whose leaders fought each other more than Muslims. The split in Christianity widened, as the crusaders' sack of Constantinople, plundering its cathedrals and great library, intensified bitterness toward the West in the Eastern Church. And brutal assaults against Jews in Europe foretold centuries of anti-Jewish abuse.

But the crusades had unforeseen effects on Europe and the world. They spurred the growth of European credit and banking, as popes and rulers borrowed heavily to finance these costly ventures. They boosted Western commerce, helping Italian states such as Genoa and Venice gain greater access to East–West trade, long dominated by Muslims. By exposing Europeans to textiles and spices from China, India, and Indonesia, this trade in time inspired Western voyages of exploration, which in turn led to Europe's exploitation of Africa and the Americas. And by giving Westerners a taste for cane sugar from West Asia and North Africa, this commerce eventually prompted Europeans to form tropical sugar plantations, worked by African slaves supplied by a brutal, extensive slave trade.

The crusades and *Reconquista* also exposed Europe to the ideas of eminent Muslim scholars. From the writings of mathematician al-Khwarizmi, for example, the West was introduced to algebra, Arabic numerals, and Egyptian astronomy, laying the foundations for the later growth of European science. Through the work of physician and philosopher Ibn Sina, known in the West as Avicenna, Europeans learned about Greek and Indian medicine and ancient Greek philosophy, vastly enhancing Western medicine and scholarship.

New technologies from the Muslim world also enhanced the West's resurgence. Water mills and windmills, which helped farmers drain swamps and grind grain, came to Europe through Islamic Spain. So did production of paper, a key component of inexpensive printed books, later developed in Europe. Navigational innovations, such as the triangular "lateen" sail (which sailors could move from side to side to tack into the wind) and the astrolabe (a device for navigating by sun and stars), were introduced to Europe through contacts with Muslims. So were gunpowder weapons, spread westward from East Asia by Mongols and Turks (Chapter 15). In time such technologies helped European nations become global powers.

Thus, for all their damage, the crusades and *Reconquista* enhanced connections that aided European growth. The Arabic origins of numerous Western words—including *cotton, coffee, sugar, tariff, musket, admiral, algebra,* and *zero*—amply attest to the impact of such connections on European commerce, technology, and science.

The High Middle Ages

16.2 Discuss the advances made by Europe during the High Middle Ages.

The era surrounding the crusades, known in the West as the **High Middle Ages** (roughly 1050 to 1300), brought advances in almost every area of European endeavor.

Agriculture expanded, towns and trade grew, monarchies strengthened, religion thrived, universities emerged, scholarship blossomed, and architecture flourished.

Agricultural Advances

Much of this era's economic growth began with agricultural advances, aided by improvements in climate and technology. Between 1050 and 1200, Europe's climate warmed considerably, creating longer growing seasons and shorter, milder winters. Farmers were able to plant more crops and cultivate more land, often by clearing swamps and forests. Heavy plows made of wood and iron, introduced earlier but widely adopted in the High Middle Ages, enabled farmers to turn over earth instead of just scratching its surface, loosening soil to vastly improve its fertility. The horse collar, a harness placed around animals' shoulders rather than their necks, helped them pull plows and carts with their full body strength. Water mills and windmills helped farmers use natural forces to grind grain and drain swamps.

These innovations were not unique to Europe. For centuries, the Chinese had used heavy plows and water mills, East Asians and North Africans had employed efficient horse harnesses, and Muslims had utilized water mills and windmills. But now interregional connections, enhanced by the crusades and *Reconquista*, helped acquaint Europeans with such devices, which combined with the warming climate to increase the quantity and quality of food. As more food and better diets improved the health of childbearing women and helped more children survive to adulthood, Europe's population grew much larger.

How did interregional connections improve European agriculture?

Water mills in Islamic Syria.

The Growth of Towns and Trade

As the overall population increased, so did the growth of towns, where many people worked as artisans or merchants, supported by the growing food supply. Towns had walls to protect them and marketplaces where artisans and merchants could exchange their goods—such as tools, furnishings, pottery, or clothing—for food brought by local farmers. As more towns emerged, interregional trade increased, and money replaced simple barter.

By expanding European connections with the East and interest in Eastern goods, the crusades and Mongol conquests (Chapter 15) also boosted long-distance commerce. European seaports, led by Genoa and Venice, imported Eastern goods, while banking arose in cities such as Florence to finance commercial ventures. By the thirteenth century, Europe had many urban settlements, ranging from small fortified towns to sizable cities—such as London, Paris, Venice, and Florence—of 50,000 people or more.

In many towns and cities, people in each occupation—such as merchants, carpenters, masons, shoemakers, or weavers—formed **guilds,** associations to promote their commercial and professional interests. Guilds had long flourished in Chinese and Byzantine cities, but in the West they had largely vanished after the fall of Rome. Their reemergence in the High Middle Ages reflected Europe's increasing economic complexity and growing connections with Eastern cultures.

Guilds typically fixed prices, wages, and standards, protecting members from competition and assuring customers of quality. Guilds also provided training, as masters in each craft took on young apprentices, who worked with their masters for several years to learn the trade, then became journeymen who labored for wages, and perhaps eventually masters with their own shops or businesses. Some merchant guilds became so influential that they virtually controlled their towns.

Medieval towns were often unpleasant places. They were typically filled with vermin and waste, which were breeding grounds for disease, and often torn by strife between merchants selling goods from other places and craft guilds trying to protect

How did towns, trade, and guilds contribute to European economic growth?

Medieval walled town.

themselves from such competition. Apprentices were often exploited, and sometimes cruelly abused, by their masters. Women were frequently confined to occupations, such as clothes making and domestic service, that were far less prestigious and profitable than crafts and guilds controlled by men.

The Rise of Royal Authority

How were kings able to enhance their powers at the expense of European nobilities?

As towns grew in power and wealth, they sought freedom from the local warlords who made up the landed nobility. Some towns strove to assert their own autonomy; others allied with kings who, eager to expand their power by reducing that of the nobility, were willing to work with townsfolk against local nobles. The kings issued charters, granting towns the right to form their own governments and law courts. In return, instead of paying dues to the local noble for protection, these towns now paid taxes to the king, helping him hire officials and soldiers so he could rely less on nobles to administer and defend the realm. Under royal protection, towns also often became havens for peasants escaping noble landlords, further undermining the nobles' influence.

Crusades and other wars also motivated monarchs to increase their authority. To organize and finance such complex, costly ventures, kings found it useful to centralize their administrative and tax-collecting system, making their governments more effective, powerful, and wealthy.

Monarchs used different means to centralize their power. In France, King Philip II Augustus (1180–1223) appointed for each province officials called baillis (*bī-YĒ*) to exercise authority and collect taxes in the name of the king. To ensure their loyalty, he made sure that they were paid directly by him and that they had no ties to the provinces they governed. In England, King Henry II (1154–1189) focused on law and order, creating an extensive judicial system run by the central government rather than by local lords, thereby enhancing justice, stability, and royal authority.

Other rulers were hampered by noble opposition. Henry's son King John (1199–1216), having fallen deeply in debt, was forced in 1215 to accept the **Magna Carta**, a "Great Charter" that affirmed nobles' rights, placed the king firmly under the law, and barred him from raising new taxes without their consent. In Germany, Emperor Frederick Barbarossa (1152–1190) had to concede broad political and military autonomy to local princes and nobles in return for their recognition of him as overlord.

The trend of governance in the High Middle Ages was nonetheless toward centralized monarchies. The growth of European populations and economies increased royal treasuries and budgets and mandated more effective central governments, strengthening the authority of the kings.

The Revitalized Roman Church

In what ways was the Roman Church revitalized during the High Middle Ages?

Despite the monarchs' growing power, the Roman Church continued to be Europe's central institution. As Pope Urban II had hoped, his leadership in launching the crusades enabled his successors to act as political overlords as well as spiritual leaders. And since most Western Christians saw the Church as the key to salvation, many donated lands and riches to it to help them get to heaven. Church wealth and power reached a peak under Pope Innocent III (1198–1216), the initiator of the Fourth Crusade. With huge revenues and a powerful bureaucracy, he crushed heresies, meddled freely in politics, arranged royal marriages, and decided disputes among rulers.

New religious orders also revitalized the Church. The Cistercians, founded in 1098 in what is now eastern France, set up monasteries in remote woods and wastelands to avoid worldly corruption. Under Saint Bernard of Clairvaux (*clār-VŌ*) (1090–1153), who promoted the Second Crusade, the Cistercians acquired vast influence; by 1200 they had more than 500 monasteries. The Dominicans, founded in 1215 in southern France by Saint Dominic (1170–1221), took a different approach: rather than withdraw from society as monks, they instead became *friars*, living in the world as beggars and becoming Europe's great preachers and teachers.

Another famous order of friars was founded by the era's most beloved Christian saint. After a dissolute youth as a wealthy merchant's son, Francesco Bernadone (*bār-nah-DŌN-ā*) (1182–1226) had a radical change of heart. He gave up his possessions, dressed in rags, and lived in stark simplicity, ministering to the poor and outcast, and even to animals and birds. His Christ-like compassion attracted many followers, including the future Saint Clare, who started an order of nuns with such strict poverty that they were called "Poor Clares." Francesco himself formed for lay people a secular order devoted to compassion and service. And he got Pope Innocent III to approve what became the Franciscan order: a community of preachers, missionaries, and teachers devoted to the ideals of gentle, faithful Francesco, later revered as Saint Francis of Assisi (*ah-SĒ-zē*).

Yet Church wealth and power also attracted ambitious men who engaged in rampant corruption, and the use of crusaders to fight the Church's foes set a precedent for attacks on other groups. Jews, for example, forbidden to own land in many countries, frequently worked in towns and cities as artisans, bankers, and merchants. Although they contributed greatly to medieval commerce, they were often abused by Christian competitors and neighbors, many of whom believed false rumors (later called "blood libels") that Jewish rituals used the blood of young Christians. Christians who dissented from Church teachings, denounced as heretics by Church leaders, typically faced violent suppression, sowing the seeds for great religious conflicts in the sixteenth century (Chapter 20).

Intellectual and Cultural Developments

Also sown in the High Middle Ages were seeds of scholarship and learning. Confucian academies had long prepared young men in China for civil service, and Muslims had formed learned academies that gathered great scholars in one place. Building on such ideas, medieval Europeans developed the **university**, an educational institution in which scholars from various fields helped students become experts and granted degrees that certified this expertise. A university typically consisted of several colleges, each a sort of educational guild, providing training, setting standards, and accrediting those who mastered their field.

European universities started in various ways. In 1088 some students in Bologna (*buh-LŌN-yah*), an Italian town that had become a center for study of Roman law, formed an association to hire and set standards for teachers. In Paris, around 1170, teachers at the cathedral school formed an instructor's guild and later organized faculties of arts, law, medicine, and theology. Thus began the Universities of Bologna and Paris; others soon arose at Oxford and Cambridge in England, Naples in Italy, and Salamanca (*sah-lah-MAHN-kah*) in Spain (Map 16.3).

Paris became a center of **scholasticism**, a system of study combining Christian faith with ancient Greek philosophy, especially that of Aristotle. Contacts with the Muslim world acquainted Paris scholars with the works of al-Khwarizmi, Ibn Sina, and other such intellectual giants as Ibn Rushd (Averroës), the great Spanish Muslim thinker, and Moses Maimonides (*mī-MAH-nih-dēz*), the noted Jewish philosopher who was Saladin's court physician (Chapter 12). Building on their work, which reconciled Aristotle's pagan philosophy with Muslim and Jewish monotheism, Thomas Aquinas (*uh-KWĪ-nuss*) (1225–1274), a Dominican teacher at the University of Paris, synthesized Aristotle's ideas with Christian theology. Arguing that scholars must use both faith and reason to learn about God and the world, Thomas became medieval Europe's dominant thinker. His writings, especially his monumental summary of theology, the *Summa Theologica* (*SOO-mah thā-uh-LŌ-je-kah*), served for centuries as the main foundation of Western thought.

How did connections between Christians and Muslims contribute to Europe's intellectual and cultural development?

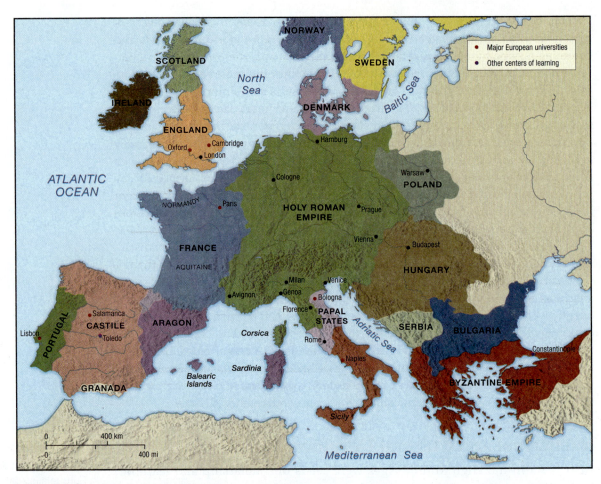

Map 16.3 **EUROPE IN THE HIGH MIDDLE AGES, 1050–1300** Europe's High Middle Ages witnessed the rise of cities, universities, and centralized monarchies. Note that the Holy Roman emperors, whose realm looks impressive on the map, did not fully centralize their power, so the empire was home to many small autonomous states with the emperor as nominal overlord. How did the growth of cities, commerce, learning, and centralized monarchies transform Europe?

Gothic cathedral of Notre Dame in Paris.

As Thomas used reason to reveal God's truth, the French monk Suger (*soo-ZHĀ*) used architecture. As head of a monastery at Saint-Denis (*san-duh-NĒ*) near Paris from 1122 to 1151, Suger constructed a new church, creating an architectural style soon copied throughout Europe. Old-style churches were bulky and dark, their heavy roofs supported by thick stone walls with round arches and small windows. But the new **Gothic architecture** produced soaring churches with pointed arches and towering walls, braced by external support beams called flying buttresses, which freed vast expanses of wall for stained glass windows that bathed church interiors in radiant light. Cities and towns spent fortunes and decades erecting these majestic cathedrals, which embellished and transformed the European landscape.

What was the status of women and marriage in Europe's High Middle Ages?

Exaltation of Women and Marriage

Cathedral construction in the twelfth and thirteenth centuries coincided with a growing devotion to the Virgin Mary, mother of Jesus Christ. Mary emerged as the Church's foremost saint, revered as the mother of God and honored by festivals, prayers, paintings, statues, and shrines. Many Gothic churches, including famous French cathedrals at Paris, Chartres (*SHART*), and Reims (*RĒMZ*), were named Notre Dame (*nō-truh-DAHM*), "Our Lady," in her honor.

The cult of Mary reflected an idealization of women. Among knights a code of chivalry extolled gallantry and loyalty to one's lady as well as one's lord. Male poets and minstrels called troubadours praised women as wondrous beings who inspired men to feats of ardor and courage, while a new literature called "romance" exalted romantic love.

Marriage, too, was exalted, defined by the Church as a sacrament, a vehicle of God's grace, and protected by Church law. Marriage to close relatives was banned, as were divorce and remarriage. Children born outside of marriage were deemed "illegitimate" and barred from entering the priesthood or receiving their parents' inheritance. Women were expected, like the Virgin Mary, to be loyal wives and mothers, devoted to husband and family.

Some women had substantial influence. Wives of nobles often managed their estates, as the men were frequently absent or killed in the course of military duties. And royal women sometimes exercised real power. Melisende of Jerusalem (1105–1161), for example, ruled the Holy Land for several decades as head of its crusader state. And Eleanor of Aquitaine (1122–1204), having gone on crusade as the wife of French king Louis VII, later governed England during the absences of her second husband, King Henry II, and crusading son, Richard the Lionheart.

Such women, however, were exceptions. Lower-class women played important roles—brewing ale, baking bread, making clothes, raising children, caring for the sick, and helping with the planting and harvest—but socially and legally they were subject to men. Women were largely excluded from most guilds and learned professions. And the institutional Church, despite its exaltation of womanhood and marriage, was run by celibate males.

Fourteenth-Century Challenges

16.3 **Explain the causes and effects of the challenges faced by Europe in the fourteenth century.**

By 1300, the medieval West featured thriving commerce, vibrant cities, maturing national monarchies, a powerful Christian Church, and Christian-centered intellectual and social institutions. But in the century that followed, the West was challenged by Church decline, famine, plague, and chronic conflict.

The Avignon Popes

The fourteenth century challenges began with Church decline. As national monarchs grew in power and wealth, they increasingly resisted papal domination. A crisis began in 1294 when France's King Philip IV the Fair (1272–1307), anticipating war against England, imposed heavy taxes on the French clergy. Pope Boniface VIII (1294–1303), forbidding him to do so without papal consent, ordered the priests not to pay. But the king struck back, suspending all shipments of Church revenues to Rome. Faced with this resistance, the pope temporarily backed down.

In 1302, however, Boniface renewed the conflict by issuing an edict declaring that all rulers, indeed all humans, are subject to the pope. Philip retaliated by sending agents to kidnap the pope, shocking all of Europe. The aged and ailing Boniface, although soon freed by supporters, died the next year a broken man.

The Church's crisis nonetheless continued. In 1309 a new pope, pressured by Philip the Fair, moved from Rome to Avignon (*AH-vēn-YŌN*), a papal enclave bordering southern France. Thus began the **Avignon papacy** (1309–1377), also called the Church's Babylonian Captivity (recalling the biblical Jewish exile in Babylon), during which eight popes in succession lived at Avignon rather than Rome. Although not under direct French control, they were clearly under French influence, undermining their credibility and offending most of Europe.

How and why did the Avignon papacy originate?

What were the causes and effects of the plague in Europe in the fourteenth century?

Famine, Plague, and Social Unrest

While thus deprived of effective spiritual leadership, Europeans were hit with horrific disasters. A changing climate, marked by colder weather and heavier rains, wreaked havoc with the food supply, already endangered by population growth. In 1315–1317, floods in the north led to deadly famine in which tens of thousands died, while others ate farm animals and seed crops to survive. Further crop failures in 1333, 1337, and 1345–1347 left the population weak, malnourished, and susceptible to disease.

Then catastrophe struck. In fall 1347, a ship returning to Genoa from Kaffa on the Black Sea landed in Sicily with a deadly cargo. In its hold were rats infested with the plague that had recently ravaged much of Asia (Chapter 15). Carried by fleas from rats to humans (bubonic plague), or spread by coughing of afflicted people (pneumonic plague), the disease devastated Europe from 1347 through 1351. Death toll estimates range from 25 to 45 million people, roughly 30 to 60 percent of Europe's population. This devastating pandemic, which contemporaries called the "great mortality," later came to be known as the **Black Death**. Since victims, who often died in three to five days, were covered with dark swellings called "buboes," the most common form of the disease is now called "bubonic plague."

The cities, filled with people, waste, sewage, and rats, were hit especially hard (Map 16.4). Victims, who gave off vile stench, often were uncared for, as others were reluctant to help for fear of catching the disease. Hoping to save themselves, thousands fled the cities, thus spreading the plague to the countryside.

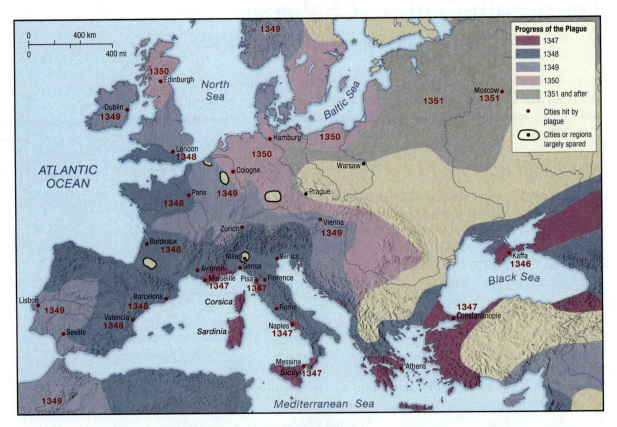

Map 16.4 EUROPE RAVAGED BY PLAGUE PANDEMIC, 1347–1351 Known in Europe as the Black Death, the plague pandemic depopulated cities, disrupted commerce, and traumatized European society. Compare this map with Map 15.8, observing that the plague, having swept west across Eurasia thanks to Mongol connections, spread from the Black Sea port of Kaffa by ship to southern Italy in 1347, then ravaged the rest of Europe in the next few years. What key impacts did the plague pandemic have on European society?

Unaware of what caused the disease, many saw it as divine punishment for sins of Church and society. Some joined groups of flagellants (*FLAJ-uh-luntz*), people who whipped themselves with chains and straps in hopes of gaining God's mercy. Others, assuming their time was short, indulged in the pleasures of food, drink, and sex. Some tried witchcraft or magic; others secluded themselves from human contact (see "Excerpts on the Plague from Boccaccio's *Decameron*").

Even when the plague was gone, its impact remained. Trade was disrupted, as ports turned away ships and towns excluded outsiders. With few workers left to till fields, farms often went untended. Grotesque folk art showed skeletons doing a "Dance of Death," reflecting a general sense of doom.

The shortage of workers forced employers to pay higher wages, leading many landlords to let peasants own some land to keep them from leaving the manor for better pay elsewhere. Some nobles tried passing laws to keep wages down and peasants in place, only to spark rebellion. French peasants, often called "Jacques" (*ZHAHK*) by their lords, went on a rampage called the Jacquerie (*zhah-KRĒ*) in 1358, looting and burning manor houses and killing a number of nobles. The lords responded ruthlessly, slaying some 20,000 rebels. In England, villagers and towns-folk alike joined the 1381 Peasants' Revolt led by a rebel called Wat Tyler, who demanded equality for all, claiming God had not created a privileged class of "gentleman" nobles. "When Adam delved and Eve span," asked the rebels, recalling

---

Document 16.2   Excerpts on the Plague from Boccaccio's *Decameron*

At the start of his **Decameron,** *a collection of tales supposedly told by people who had fled Florence for a nearby villa while plague ravaged the city, Giovanni Boccaccio gives a graphic description of the plague and its impact. What does it reveal about Florence and its people at the time of the plague?*

In the year 1348 . . ., that most beautiful of Italian cities, Florence, was attacked by a deadly plague. It started in the East either through the influence of the heavenly bodies or because God's just anger with our wicked deeds sent it as a punishment to mortal men; and in a few years killed an innumerable quantity of people . . . The symptoms were not the same as in the East, where a gush of blood from the nose was the plain sign of inevitable death; but it began both in men and women with certain swellings in the groin or under the armpit. They grew to the size of a small apple or egg, more or less, and were vulgarly called tumours. In a short space of time these tumours spread . . . all over the body. Soon after this the symptoms changed and black or purple spots appeared on the arms or thighs or any other part of the body . . . These spots were a certain sign of death . . . most people died within about three days . . .

The violence of this disease was such that the sick communicated it to the healthy who came near them . . . To speak to or go near the sick brought infection and a common death . . .

From these . . . occurrences, such fear and fanciful notions took possession of the living so that almost all of them adopted the same cruel policy, which was entirely to avoid the sick and everything belonging to them . . .

Some thought that moderate living and avoidance of all superfluity would preserve them from the epidemic. They formed small communities, living entirely separately from everybody else. They shut themselves up in houses where there were no sick . . . Others thought just the opposite. They thought the cure for the plague was to drink and be merry, to go about singing and amusing themselves . . ., laughing and jesting at what happened. They . . . spent day and night going from tavern to tavern . . .

Others again held a still more cruel opinion . . . They said that the only medicine against the plague stricken was to go right away from them. Men and women, . . . caring about nothing but themselves, abandoned their own city, their own houses, their dwellings, their relatives, their property, and went abroad or at least to the country around Florence . . .

Thus a multitude of sick men and women were left without any care . . . Owing to the lack of attendants for the sick and the violence of the plague, such a multitude of people in the city died day and night that it was stupefying to hear of, let alone to see.

SOURCE: Boccaccio, Giovanni. The Decameron of Giovanni Boccaccio. J.M. Rigg (trans). A.H. Bullen, 1903.

the Bible's first humans, "who was then the gentleman?" Although these and other similar revolts were crushed, the labor shortage improved workers' wages and helped many peasants escape serfdom.

The Great Western Schism

What were the causes and effects of the Great Western Schism?

Compounding Europe's chaos, the Church's crisis intensified. In 1377, aiming to end it, the reigning pope moved back from Avignon to Rome, then died the following year. Intimidated by a Roman mob, the cardinals elected in his place an Italian, Pope Urban VI, who boldly attacked Church abuses. Threatened by his reforms, a number of cardinals, most of them French, later reconvened and declared his election invalid. They chose as pope the French king's cousin, who set himself up at Avignon. But Urban VI in Rome refused to step down, so now there were two competing popes. This **Great Western Schism** (1378–1417) scandalized all Europe, dividing it between backers of Avignon and Rome. Hoping to resolve the crisis, in 1409 a council at Pisa deposed both popes and chose a new one, but the other two defied it, producing a three-way split.

Finally, a Council at Constance (1414–1418) ended the schism by persuading two of the three popes to step down and resume their former status as cardinals. The third, unreconciled, fled to a Mediterranean island, from which he excommunicated the rest of the Christian world. Despite this lonely defiance, a newly chosen pope called Martin V (1417–1431) was able to rule from Rome with general support. But by then the papacy's status had been badly damaged.

Conflict and Fragmentation

How did political conflict weaken fourteenth-century Europe?

Amid these crises, France and England fought a series of conflicts called the Hundred Years War (1337–1453). Aided by their longbows, whose speed of use and accuracy helped overcome French mounted knights, and by their gunpowder cannons, the English won several key battles. By the 1420s, they held large parts of France and seemed on the verge of triumph. But the tide turned in 1429 when the French, who by then had their own gunpowder weapons, were rallied by a teenaged girl named Joan of Arc, who claimed that God had summoned her to drive out the English. Although the English later got hold of Joan and executed her as a heretic, when the war finally ended in 1453 they had lost almost all their possessions in France.

Political conflict also troubled Central Europe. Its nominal overlords, the Holy Roman emperors, failed to centralize power, leaving Germany fragmented into numerous small states while five great families competed for the emperor's role. The Golden Bull, an edict issued in 1356 by Emperor Charles IV, provided some stability by making seven key regional leaders electors who would choose each new emperor by majority vote. But it also confirmed the autonomy of the many local rulers, leaving the empire divided and weak. In 1438 the electors chose as emperor the head of Austria's Habsburg (*HAHPZ-boork*) family, beginning a succession of Habsburg rulers who held the imperial title mostly until 1806. The Habsburgs increased their possessions through strategic marriages but failed to form a centralized German state.

An English longbow, as used in the Hundred Years War.

The European Renaissance

16.4 Explain how the European Renaissance was enhanced by connections with Muslims, Byzantines, and Asians.

In the fourteenth century, with all its challenges, Europeans started a cultural revival called the **Renaissance** ("rebirth"). It began in Italy, where growing commercial wealth amid ruins of Roman grandeur inspired efforts to restore the culture of the classical age. Based initially in Florence, an Italian city-state and wealthy banking center, the Renaissance spread throughout Europe by the sixteenth century, bringing a new vitality to Western culture.

In the Renaissance, as in the High Middle Ages, connections with other cultures were crucial to European renewal. The Renaissance was rooted in Europe's rediscovery of ancient Greek and Roman art and thought, advanced by contacts with Islamic and Byzantine artists and scholars. It was funded largely by wealth acquired through commerce with Eastern cultures and by the banking system that supported such trade. And it was enhanced by technologies such as paper and printing, developed in China and spread westward through the Muslim world.

In the Renaissance, as in the High Middle Ages, religious themes and the Church played a central role. But the Renaissance focused on life in this world rather than life after death.

Roots and Attributes of the Renaissance

Early in the fourteenth century, Florence produced two pivotal figures who helped lay the Renaissance foundations. One was the painter Giotto (*JAW-tō*) (1267–1337), whose portrayals of saints and biblical scenes pioneered **artistic realism**. He created portraits that were lifelike, showing detail, depth, and perspective, overcoming the flatness and stylized rigidity of earlier medieval art. The other was the writer Dante Alighieri (*DAHN-tāah-lig-YĀ-rē*) (1265–1321), whose poetic masterpiece, the *Divine Comedy*, portrayed him as a pilgrim traveling through hell, purgatory (Chapter 20), and heaven. Full of Christian devotion, the work also used biting satire, mocking many popes and rulers by depicting them in hell. Composed in Italian rather than in Latin, it pioneered **vernacular literature**, written in the everyday spoken language of the common people.

A generation later, Florence supplied the two great writers who began the Renaissance. Scorning medieval European culture as Germanic and crude, Francesco Petrarch (*PĀ-trark*) (1304–1374) worked to revive the literature of ancient Rome. He collected ancient Latin texts, wrote letters to famous ancient Romans, composed accounts of their lives, and even penned a Latin epic poem. Yet he also used the vernacular, writing beautiful love sonnets in Italian to a woman named Laura who perished in the plague. Petrarch's contemporary, Giovanni Boccaccio (*bō-KAH-chō*) (1313–1375), likewise wrote in Italian vernacular. Boccaccio is best known for *The Decameron* (*dē-KAM-uh-ron*), a collection of 100 stories told by ten people to amuse themselves while secluded in an estate outside Florence to escape the plague (see "Excerpts on the Plague from Boccaccio's *Decameron*," page 319). Witty, racy, and bawdy, dealing with intrigue, adventure, and sex, the stories are designed to entertain, not enlighten. Boccaccio depicted people as they *were*—charming, crude, and corrupt—not as they *should be*.

Vernacular literature also appeared in the north. In English verse, Geoffrey Chaucer (1340–1400) wrote the *Canterbury Tales*, an assortment of lively, earthy stories told by 30 people from all walks of life traveling together on pilgrimage. In French, Christine de Pisan (*pē-ZAHN*) (1363–1430) wrote biographies, poems, and works about women, challenging her era's gender barriers. Many Latin texts were also translated into French, German, English, and Czech.

Another key feature of Renaissance culture was **humanism**, an outlook emphasizing the value of humans and their activities. Renaissance humanism incorporated *classicism*, *secularism*, and *individualism*. Spurning as Germanic the culture of the Middle Ages, it revered the classical culture of ancient Greece and Rome. Altering the medieval focus on faith and spirituality, it celebrated secular ideals and worldly beauty, even when dealing with religious themes. Rejecting the medieval emphasis on humility and community, it stressed individual pride and achievement.

How did humanism and artistic realism make Renaissance Europe different from medieval Europe?

Crucifix painted by Giotto.

In what ways did Florence and Rome advance the Italian Renaissance?

The Italian Renaissance

In fifteenth-century Italy, the Renaissance flourished. Remains of the ancient Roman world, which surrounded Italians, sustained their desire to revive their region's past glory. The wealth of merchants and city-states, acquired mainly through commerce, enabled them to enhance their prestige by patronizing the arts. And an influx of artists and scholars from the Byzantine Empire, which fell to the Turks in 1453, added to the depth and diversity of Italy's cultural renewal.

Renaissance Italy was politically divided, with the kingdom of Naples in the south, the Papal States (lands ruled by the pope) in the center, and various independent city-states in the north. The leading city-states—Venice, Milan, Genoa, and Florence—were wealthy commercial centers that ruled the lands around them (Map 16.5). Although organized as republics, these city-states were run from behind the scenes by prominent wealthy families. To gain prestige and enhance civic pride, these families promoted art and culture, often competing to outdo each other.

Map 16.5 POLITICAL DIVISIONS IN 15TH-CENTURY ITALY
In the 1400s Italy was distinguished by artistic expression and political disunity. Note Italy's division into city-states, duchies, republics, and kingdoms, with Papal States in the center ruled by the pope. How did commercial connections and cultural competition reinforce the Renaissance?

RENAISSANCE FLORENCE Florence again led the way. For much of the fifteenth century, it was dominated by the Medici (*MED-ih-chē*), a rich banking family that used its fortune to fund paintings, sculptures, palaces, and churches created by the era's great masters. Many wealthy merchants did likewise, while guilds held contests to decide which artists, sculptors, and architects to commission for major projects.

In 1401 a contest was held to decide who would design the bronze doors of the Florence Baptistery (page 307), a chapel used mainly for baptisms. The winner, Lorenzo Ghiberti (*gē-BAR-tē*) (1378–1455), spent decades creating two sets of majestic doors, with panels depicting biblical scenes, sculpted and cast in bronze. The loser, Filippo Brunelleschi (*broo-nuh-LESS-kē*) (1377–1446), gained fame as an architect, designing chapels and cathedrals for the Medici and other Florentines. Models of perspective and symmetry, his works are relatively small, built in the Renaissance spirit on a human scale, unlike the towering medieval Gothic churches built for exaltation of God.

Donatello (*dō-nah-TELL-ō*) (1386–1466), a student and rival of Ghiberti, emerged as the city's leading sculptor. A master of anatomy, Donatello created the West's first major nude statue since Roman times, depicting the Hebrew hero David in bronze. His starkly realistic works also included a monumental sculpture of a mounted warrior, capturing the power and dignity of horse and rider, and a marvelous wooden statue of a gaunt and aging Mary Magdalene, a friend of Jesus believed by some to have been a repentant prostitute.

The standard for Florentine painting was set by Masaccio (*mah-SAH-chō*) (1401–1428), a youthful artist who used perspective, shadows, and light to create a three-dimensional effect, conveying his subjects' personalities through striking stances and expressions. He also mastered the art of **fresco**, or painting on walls when the plaster was still wet so the colors would penetrate it. Later Sandro Botticelli (*bō-tih-CHELL-ē*) (1445–1510), not satisfied merely to depict reality, sought to transcend it by creating beauty, using bright colors, fanciful themes, and sensuous depictions of female anatomy in works such as *Spring* and *Birth of Venus*.

Renaissance Florence also produced outstanding writers. One was Leon Battista Alberti (*al-BAIR-tē*) (1404–1472), whose treatises *On Building* and *On Family* set the

Donatello's sculpture *Mary Magdalene.*

era's standards on architecture and virtue. A multitalented architect, athlete, scholar, sculptor, and statesman, he embodied the ideal of the well-rounded Renaissance man. Another was Niccolo Machiavelli (*MAH-kē-uh-VELL-ē*) (1469–1527), whose classic work, *The Prince*, devised as a ruler's guidebook for unifying Italy, separated politics from ethics. Focusing not on how statesmen *should* act but on how they *do* act, and not on what is *right* but on what *works*, *The Prince* pragmatically advised rulers to use deceit and violence when needed to achieve their goals.

THE HIGH RENAISSANCE   In the early 1500s, envious of Florence's success, ambitious popes such as Julius II (1503–1513) and Leo X (1513–1521) hired prominent artists, architects, and sculptors to help restore Rome as Christendom's greatest city. Thus began the Roman or High Renaissance, an era dominated by three towering talents: Leonardo, Raphael, and Michelangelo.

Leonardo da Vinci (1452–1519) started as a painter in Florence but clashed with the Medici and left in 1482 for Milan, whose rulers gave him greater freedom of expression. There he produced his first masterpiece, *Virgin of the Rocks*, portraying a serene mother and children among plants and boulders. While in Milan he also painted on a convent wall his monumental *Last Supper*, an emotional drama that peers into the apostles' hearts as each reacts to Jesus' disclosure that "one of you will betray me." Leaving Milan in 1499, Leonardo traveled about Italy, spent time in Rome, and then settled in France under royal patronage. In 1503–1506, he created the world's most famous portrait, a beguiling psychological study of *La Gioconda* (*lah jō-KON-dah*), better known today as *Mona Lisa*.

Considered one of history's great artists, Leonardo was also a scientist, sculptor, naturalist, engineer, musician, and inventor. He studied plants, anatomy, optics, mathematics, currents, clouds, and birds' wings, and sketched plans for devices, such as helicopters, submarines, and tanks, whose actual invention lay far in the future. He was a visionary and universal genius.

Raphael (*RAH-fī-EL*) (1483–1520), most beloved of Renaissance painters, was known for his exquisite Madonnas (portraits of the Virgin Mary) and depictions of female beauty. Born in Urbino, he spent time in Florence before 1508, when Pope Julius II brought him to Rome to decorate the papal palace, known as the Vatican because it sits on Vatican Hill. Raphael's *School of Athens*, a huge fresco mural in the Vatican study, is a full expression of the Renaissance spirit. It depicts classical Greek philosophers, some of them painted in the likeness of Renaissance figures, in a setting of harmony and symmetry. In the center are Plato, flanked by theoretical philosophers and pointing upward toward idealism and inspiration, and Aristotle, flanked by logicians and rationalists, with his arm outstretched downward toward realism and moderation.

If Raphael captured the Renaissance spirit, Michelangelo (1475–1564) transcended it. Raised and trained as a sculptor in Florence, he moved to Rome at age 21 and soon caused a sensation with his *Pietà* (*pē-ā-TAH*), a magnificent marble statue of the Virgin Mary cradling the dead body of Jesus. In 1501 he was called back to Florence to create a statue of David, the biblical giant-killer, to symbolize the city's resistance to tyranny. In three years he produced a work of superhuman proportions, a 17-foot likeness of a muscular youth, giant, defiant, and nude.

With singular audacity, in 1508 Pope Julius II summoned the great sculptor to Rome and hired him to paint the ceiling of the Vatican's Sistine Chapel. Lying on his back atop scaffolding near the ceiling, Michelangelo labored four years to produce in fresco a work of colossal genius, an immense set of murals depicting Bible scenes from *Creation* to the *Flood*. In 1536 he added another fresco, the somber and imposing *Last Judgment*, on the chapel's altar wall. In his later years, Michelangelo also served as chief architect for Saint Peter's Basilica in Rome, a monumental edifice whose construction had begun under Pope Julius II.

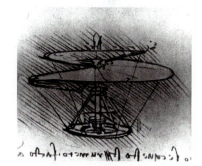

Sketch for a helicopter by Leonardo da Vinci.

Michelangelo's *David*.

Politically, the High Renaissance was a time of tumult in Italy. Trouble began in 1494 when Milan, verging on war against Naples and Florence, asked France for help. Seizing the opportunity, the French invaded and conquered much of Italy, leading the pope to seek assistance from Spain. The next three decades were marked by foreign intervention and internal war, culminating in 1527, when Rome was sacked by foreign forces supposedly sent to help the pope. After this attack the Italian Renaissance subsided. As the Spanish opened the Atlantic, eroding Italy's commercial leadership, and as Protestants challenged Rome's religious primacy (Chapter 20), Italians lost their undisputed leadership of Western fortune, faith, and culture.

The Northern European Renaissance

How did the Northern European Renaissance differ from the Italian?

Northern Europe, meanwhile, had its own Renaissance, which differed from the Italian in several respects. First, it was less classical: northerners studied Greco-Roman classics but did not try to imitate ancient culture. Second, it was less secular: it promoted Christian morals, studied early Church fathers, criticized abuses in Church and society, and abhorred the worldliness of Renaissance popes. Third, it built upon medieval culture rather than rejecting it. Finally, it was less lavish and more practical, partly because northerners had less wealth, and partly because they were offended by Italian extravagance.

FOUNDATIONS OF THE NORTHERN RENAISSANCE   In the 1400s, two men laid the foundations for the Northern Renaissance. One was Jan van Eyck (*YAHN van IK*), the first in a series of superb artists from Flanders, a region (now in Belgium) where commercial towns such as Bruges (*BROOZH*), Ghent, and Antwerp enjoyed prosperity and civic pride like that of northern Italy. Van Eyck (1395–1441) mastered the use of oil paints, which produced vivid colors and dried slowly, giving artists time to paint with precision. He also perfected the realism introduced by Giotto, meticulously portraying the appearances of his subjects. His masterpieces, including the Arnolfini portrait and the Ghent altarpiece, display unsurpassed attention to detail and light.

The other was the German inventor Johannes Gutenberg (*GOO-ten-berg*) (1400–1468), who began a communications revolution. European books had long been hand copied onto costly animal skin parchment, making them expensive and rare. The use of paper and printing from carved wooden blocks, developed initially in China, had spread to Europe in the 1300s by way of the Mongols and Muslims. But this printing process still involved much time and expense, since a whole block had to be carved for each page. In the mid-1400s, however, Gutenberg began using **movable type**, small metal blocks for each letter, arranged in a frame to print one page and then rearranged and reused to print others. Multiple copies of each page were made by inking the type and pressing it on paper, using a **printing press** similar to presses used to crush grapes for wine. The new process vastly increased the number of books and decreased their cost, thus greatly advancing the spread of ideas and knowledge.

NORTHERN WRITERS AND ARTISTS   In the early 1500s, the printing press helped spread the views of some eminent writers. One was Dutch humanist Erasmus (*ih-RAZZ-muss*) (1466–1536), the era's most influential thinker. After leaving the monastery where he spent his younger years, Erasmus lived and wrote in various places, winning universal respect as a man of insight, tolerance, and honesty. Dismayed by the Church's elaborate ritualism and scholasticism's rigid formalism, he promoted instead a simple, humane piety he called the "philosophy of Christ." His works included *Handbook of the Christian Knight* (1503), a guide to moral living in a corrupt society, and *The Praise of Folly* (1509), a stinging satire that ridiculed the hypocrisy of monks, bishops, lawyers, and scholars.

An early printing press.

Another key Northern Renaissance writer was Erasmus's friend Thomas More (1478–1535), an English lawyer, statesman, and humanist. In 1516 More published *Utopia* ("nowhere"), a fictional journey to an imaginary island where people held property in common, worked together for the common good, and avoided poverty and war by using good sense and reason. By thus portraying an ideal society, More implicitly criticized by contrast the violence, corruption, and injustice of the one in which he lived. A man of talent and conviction, he served as Lord Chancellor, England's highest official post, and later died a martyr for refusing to forsake the Roman Church (Chapter 20).

Many northern artists were influenced by van Eyck's realism and use of oil paints, the style and technique of Italian painters, and the development of printing. One was Hans Holbein (*HŌL-bīn*) the Younger (1497–1543), a German portrait painter who worked in Switzerland and England, producing lifelike portrayals of such figures as Erasmus and More. Another was Albrecht Dürer (*DOOR-ur*) (1471–1528), son of a German goldsmith, who became Germany's most innovative artist. Inspired by visits to Italy, he combined Italian techniques of proportion and perspective with a northern talent for detail similar to van Eyck's, creating such paintings as *Adoration of the Magi* and *The Four Apostles*. But Dürer is best known for his woodcuts (carvings on wooden blocks) and engravings (etchings in copper), used to print multiple copies of the same work. Sold as separate prints or used to illustrate books, they made his art available to ordinary people. Although they lacked color, prints such as *The Four Horsemen of the Apocalypse* and *Knight, Death and the Devil* were genuine artistic masterpieces.

The Four Horsemen of the Apocalypse.

Social and Political Effects

The Renaissance was largely an urban phenomenon, affecting mainly the cities, where three distinct social groups emerged. On top were the patricians, wealthy merchants and bankers who dominated urban politics and lived lavishly, hiring artists and architects to exalt their status. In the middle were artisans and shopkeepers, typically guild members, who lived in modest comfort and often had some education. At bottom were paid laborers, who subsisted on irregular wages, and the unemployed, who lived in dire poverty. Cities were cultural centers, but crowded conditions and poor sanitation also made them breeding grounds for filth, squalor, stench, and disease.

In the countryside the Renaissance had less impact. Still, the landed nobles, originally a crude warrior class, began to assume a sense of refined gentility. According to the *Book of the Courtier* (1528), by Baldassare Castiglione (*kah-stēl-YŌ-nā*), the ideal gentleman should be classically educated, widely read, accomplished in arts and music, eloquent in speech, dignified in manner, and graceful in style.

Ladies, too, might exhibit these traits, as education for noble and patrician women became increasingly common. But women were still largely excluded from public affairs and professions. Noblewomen were expected instead to be capable household managers and charming hostesses. And women who worked for wages typically earned far less than men.

Peasants, who still made up about 90 percent of the population, benefited from labor shortages caused by fourteenth-century famines and plagues, and from growing opportunities in cities and towns. Many landlords sought to keep their peasants from leaving the manor by granting them their own land, or by replacing compulsory labor with rent payable in cash. As a result, serfdom declined, especially in Western Europe.

How did the Renaissance affect European social and political life?

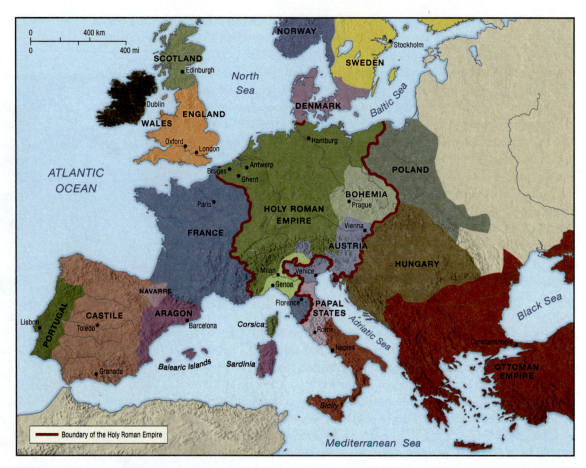

Map 16.6 EUROPE IN THE LATE 15TH CENTURY During the Renaissance, monarchs continued to consolidate their power and their realms. Note that the marriage of the rulers of Castile and Aragon laid the basis for a united Spain. How did commercial connections and centralized monarchies bolster Europe's wealth and power despite its political divisions?

In time, the increased availability of printed books also promoted growing public awareness and literacy among the lower classes.

Politically, the Renaissance advanced the formation of strong national monarchies (Map 16.6), as capable rulers increased their power and the unity of their realms. In France, King Louis XI (1461–1483) imposed heavy taxes on peasants and townsfolk, enlarged the royal army to avoid reliance on nobles, and extended direct control over lands in the north, east, and south. In England, King Henry VII (1485–1509) ended three decades of dynastic strife, enlarged the royal treasury by managing his income frugally, and used his royal council to enforce justice and control unruly nobles. In Central Europe, Emperor Maximilian I of Habsburg (1493–1519), although unable to centralize control of the Holy Roman Empire, vastly expanded his family's domains by arranging astute marriages for himself and his son.

But the biggest success came in Spain, long divided into separate states and ravaged by *Reconquista*. Here the marriage of two monarchs, Isabella of Castile (1474–1504) and Ferdinand of Aragon (1479–1516), linked the two largest realms. To consolidate control and enforce Christian rule, they used the Spanish **Inquisition**, a judicial institution that prosecuted people it identified as heretics—including Jews and Muslims who outwardly converted to Christianity but privately practiced their old faith. In 1492 Isabella and Ferdinand completed the *Reconquista* by conquering Granada, the last Muslim outpost in Spain, and expelled most Jews from their domains. That same year a sea admiral named Columbus, sailing in Isabella's service, embarked on the first in a series of voyages that eventually gave Spain the world's largest empire, made it Europe's greatest power, and altered the course of world history.

Chapter Review

Consequences and Connections

The West's resurgence was partly due to developments in Europe. The warming of its climate, the ingenuity of its farmers and artisans, and the ambition of its merchants and bankers all aided Europe's economic expansion, which helped to fund expensive enterprises. Energetic popes who reformed and revived the Roman Church, and resolute monarchs who turned weak regimes into strong central governments, provided the leadership and stability needed for cultural growth. Talented scholars, artists, architects, and writers splendidly nourished this rebirth. Fourteenth-century challenges disrupted the West's resurgence but did not derail it.

Europe's revitalization, however, also resulted from its connections with Islamic peoples and willingness to learn from them. From the Muslims, Europe borrowed the concept of combining warfare with religious zeal, launching its own Christian holy wars, or crusades. From Islamic scholars, Europe became acquainted with its own Greco-Roman heritage and learned to combine it with Western Christian beliefs. Mongols and Muslims helped Europe learn about gunpowder, paper, and printing, Eastern inventions that boosted Western power and influence. Also through Muslims Europe gained a taste for fine goods from the East and the wealth to be derived from Eastern commerce. These tastes in time inspired Europe's great sea voyages, which aimed at taking control of this trade from the Islamic world.

But Europe's resurgence did not reflect Muslim weakness. Indeed, the Muslim expulsion of Christian crusaders from the Holy Land and Western adaptation of Muslim innovations attested to Islamic preeminence. And, as the next chapter conveys, while Europe was having its Renaissance, Muslims were conquering Constantinople, rebuilding Persia, and subduing the Indian subcontinent, forcibly fashioning three great Islamic empires.

Reviewing Key Concepts

Reconquista, p. 309
Crusades, p. 310
High Middle Ages, p. 312
Guilds, p. 313
University, p. 315
Scholasticism, p. 315

Gothic Architecture, p. 316
Avignon Papacy, p. 317
Black Death, p. 318
Great Western Schism, p. 320
Renaissance, p. 320
Artistic Realism, p. 321

Vernacular Literature, p. 321
Humanism, p. 321
Movable Type, p.324
Printing Press, p. 324

Ask Yourself

1. Why did Pope Urban II initiate the First Crusade? Why were later crusades undertaken? What benefits and damages did Europe derive from the crusades and *Reconquista*?

2. What factors contributed to Europe's political, economic, and cultural development during the High Middle Ages?

3. What challenges tested fourteenth-century Europe, and what were their long-term impacts?

4. What were the main characteristics of the Renaissance? How did the Renaissance differ from the High Middle Ages? How did the Northern European Renaissance differ from the Italian?

5. In what ways did connections with the Muslim world influence Western commerce, culture, learning, and technology during the High Middle Ages and Renaissance?

Key Dates and Developments

1070s	Seljuk Turks defeat Byzantines and conquer Holy Land
1085	Spanish Christians capture Toledo from Muslims
1096–1099	First Crusade
1144	Suger begins first Gothic church at Saint-Denis
1147–1149	Second Crusade
1189–1192	Third Crusade
1202–1204	Fourth Crusade
1267–1273	Thomas Aquinas writes *Summa Theologica*
1309–1377	Popes reside at Avignon
1310–1320	Dante composes the *Divine Comedy*
1337	Hundred Years War begins
1347–1351	Black Death devastates Europe
1348–1353	Boccaccio composes *The Decameron*
1378–1417	Great Western Schism divides Western Church

1430s	Jan van Eyck flourishes in Flanders
1434–1492	Medicis rule Florence: height of Florentine Renaissance
1453	Fall of Constantinople; end of Hundred Years War
1456	Gutenberg publishes Bible printed with movable type
1492	Spanish Christians take Granada; Columbus's first voyage
1503–1506	Leonardo da Vinci creates the *Mona Lisa*
1508	Pope Julius II brings Raphael and Michelangelo to Rome
1513–1516	Machiavelli's *The Prince* and More's *Utopia* published
1527	Sack of Rome by German and Spanish troops

Chapter 17
Culture and Conflict in the Great Islamic Empires, 1071–1707

OTTOMAN COMPASS POINTS A 16th-century Ottoman illustration of the 32 points of the compass. At that time the great Islamic empires still dominated trade routes across the Indian Ocean, but Europeans were challenging them for commercial control.

After reading this chapter, you should be able to:

17.1 Describe the impacts on Asia of the conquests of Timur Lenk.

17.2 Explain the techniques used by the Ottomans to govern their multinational empire.

17.3 Explain how the Safavids used Islam to revive and rebuild the Persian Empire.

17.4 Discuss the challenges faced by Muslim rulers of India under the Mughal Empire.

Mughal
India

Safavid
Persia

The
Ottoman
Empire

The morning of May 29, 1453, dawned overcast and warm on the outskirts of Constantinople, the capital of the Byzantine Empire. Shortly after sunrise, the Ottoman Turkish sultan, Mehmed II, ordered his Muslim troops to storm the city. A large cannon made for the sultan by a Hungarian metallurgist pounded away at the city's thick walls. Shortly before noon a hole was torn in one of the walls, and jubilant attackers piled through the breach into Constantinople. The last Byzantine emperor died in hand-to-hand combat, and by early afternoon Mehmed's forces were in possession of a Christian city that Muslims had sought to conquer for more than eight centuries.

After the battle ended, Mehmed II calmly rode his horse into the Hagia Sophia (*Hā-jē-ah sā-FĪ-ah*), the Church of the Holy Wisdom, and claimed it for Islam as a mosque. According to legend, the Orthodox Christian priests chanting divine services at the time quickly gathered up the sacred objects on the altar and vanished into the marble walls of the church's sanctuary, from which they will return to finish the services when the Muslims are expelled from Constantinople. Oblivious to this possibility, Mehmed surveyed his conquest, gave orders to limit the looting and pillaging, and contemplated the collapse of the last outpost of Christendom in the old Roman East.

All three of the great Islamic empires of the fifteenth through seventeenth centuries—the Ottoman, the Safavid (*SAH-fah-vid*), and the Mughal (*MOO-gull*)—were created through conflict, but they were connected to each other in many ways. Each was established by nomadic Turks from Central Asia. Each dynasty constructed its new empire on the foundations of existing Asian civilizations, adapting its previously nomadic life to the framework of settled agricultural urban societies. Each empire was spiritually and culturally Islamic. And each was influenced profoundly by a Turkish empire that rose and fell with astonishing speed: the empire of Timur Lenk.

The Conquests of Timur Lenk

17.1 Describe the impacts on Asia of the conquests of Timur Lenk.

Timur was born in 1336 into a family of Muslim Turks in Central Asia. His father, a midlevel government official serving the Mongols, claimed descent from Genghis Khan. Timur, who limped from wounds received in battle as a young man, was contemptuously called Timur Lenk, "Timur the Lame," by the Persians he conquered. Europeans corrupted this nickname to Tamerlane (*TAM-ur-lān*). Considering himself a worthy heir to Genghis Khan, Timur set out to conquer Asia and in the process connected several parts of it, although his lack of patience for administration ensured that his empire would not survive him for long.

Timur's Strengths and Good Fortunes

Why was Timur able to conquer so much of Southwest Asia?

Timur followed his father by serving the Mongols, although as a cavalry captain rather than a government official. Charismatic and cruel, he compensated for his limp by turning himself into a master horseman and soon won the allegiance of the Turkish mercenaries with whom he rode. The Mongol leadership of the Jagadai Khanate in Central Asia was torn apart by rival factions, and Timur skillfully allied with one and then the other, pretending to serve each of them while actually serving only himself. By 1360 he had gained control over the lands between the Oxus (*OX-us*) and Jaxartes (*jacks-AR-tēz*) rivers in Central Asia (Map 17.1). Over the next three decades, he mobilized a fearsome force of mounted cavalry in a series of campaigns designed to conquer every region he could reach.

Timur owed his military successes in part to his personal abilities, in part to the quarrels and weaknesses of his enemies, and in part to luck. Some of that good fortune was an ongoing shift in weather patterns that brought ample rains to areas of Central Asia that had previously been arid. New and extensive pasturelands supported the horses and livestock of Turkish nomads who, under Timur's leadership, went from there to conquer large parts of Asia.

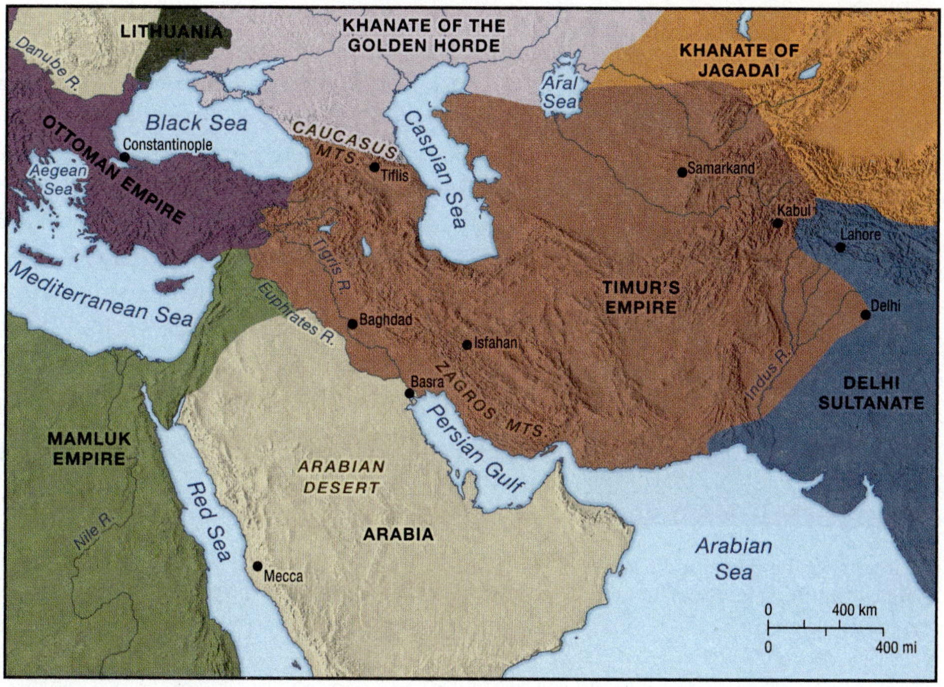

In 1370 Timur established his capital in the Central Asian city of Samarkand (*sah-mur-KAHND*), from which the Mongol Khanate of Jagadai had controlled the region. In 1380 Timur's forces descended upon Persia and ravaged the countryside. They then crossed the Iranian plateau and subdued Baghdad. This conquest took 13 years, largely because Timur himself was, for most of that time, in Central Asia, consolidating his base with decisive victories over the Mongols in their own heartland. By the final decade of the fourteenth century, he was poised to move further.

In 1395 Timur's mounted archers invaded the region of the lower Volga, destroying the Khanate of the Golden Horde within 18 months. The Mongols thereupon surrendered an empire stretching from the Caucasus Mountains northeastward to Siberia. Two years later Timur turned toward India, devastating the Punjab in the west and sacking Delhi. He enslaved numerous Indians to build him a great mosque at Samarkand, leaving behind him desolate cities stalked by hunger and disease. The severed heads of Hindus were piled into immense towers as testimony to his visit, but Indian Muslims fared no better: some were among the 100,000 prisoners he massacred after capturing Delhi. As the fourteenth century drew to a close, Timur marched to the eastern Mediterranean, where he encountered the Ottoman Turks.

Map 17.1   THE EMPIRE OF TIMUR LENK, CA. 1405 The extent of Timur's conquests, undertaken in a time without electronic communication or rapid transit, suggests the difficulty of ruling such vast and varied domains. Compare the location of Timur's empire with the Persian Empire of Cyrus and Darius I (Map 6.3). Then remember that nearly two millennia earlier, Darius had ruled even more extensive lands effectively through satraps. Why didn't Timur institute the sort of efficient administration that characterized the Persian Empire?

Attack on the Ottomans

The Ottomans, successors to the Seljuks in the Balkans, were planning what they hoped would be a decisive assault on the Byzantine Empire. Sultan Bayezid (*BĪ-yeh-zēd*) I, who considered himself heir to the Great Seljuk Empire, had worked for a decade to consolidate the Ottoman realm. Using the Balkans as his base, he hoped to join Europe with Asia by taking Constantinople and western Anatolia. In the process he invaded lands held by Turkish chieftains protected by Timur, and in 1402 Timur routed Bayezid's forces at the battle of Ankara (*AIN-kah-rah*). The sultan himself was captured by Timur and treated with contempt. Timur used Bayezid as a footstool and made Bayezid's favorite wife strip naked to serve midday and evening meals to the

How did Timur's actions inadvertently benefit the Byzantine Empire?

The interior of the chapel at the tomb of Timur Lenk in Samarkand, in present-day Uzbekistan.

Why was Timur unable to consolidate his conquests into a smoothly functioning empire?

conqueror's entourage. Imprisoned in a cage so small that he could not stand, sit, or lie down, Bayezid soon died.

Constantinople was saved from Ottoman assault, but Timur's victory gave no comfort to the Christians. Who or what could stop Timur from turning his attentions on Europe? As it turned out, only his own restless nature. He had taken every acre of land once owned by the Mongols who had ruled him—except China. There the Ming dynasty had claimed the Mandate of Heaven and ousted the Mongol Yuan dynasty in 1368. Timur moved east to prepare his forces for the largest invasion of his career, but while doing so he drank more wine than his 69-year-old constitution could absorb and died of alcohol poisoning in 1405.

Timur as Warrior and Administrator

In many respects, Timur Lenk was an impressive figure. Illiterate but not ignorant, his insatiable curiosity led him to surround himself with scholars with whom he debated questions of religious doctrine, natural science, and history. A skillful chess player, he was in real life a master of both battle and diplomacy, employing every means imaginable to defeat his opponent. His nomadic upbringing provided him with a flexibility of perspective that enabled him to seize the most favorable opportunity. Timur's reputation for ferocity terrified everyone in his path and proved useful in securing his remarkable sequence of victories. Yet Timur presented himself as a unifier who attacked only those disloyal to Islam.

Some of the very qualities that made Timur a magnificent warrior also made him a poor statesman. The tactical flexibility that served him well in battle equipped him poorly for administration. He never cared to rule the lands he conquered, appointing his sons and grandsons as provincial governors while setting forth at once in search of more military glory. His governors were supposed to act only in Timur's name, but because he was almost never in contact with them, they were forced to act on their own. This prevented the creation of durable institutions that might have helped his empire endure.

Timur might have been a builder as well as a destroyer, but his temperament inclined him in other directions. He beautified Samarkand but spent almost no time there, preferring his tents and the back of his horse. His atrocities sealed his reputation. When he died, nothing could hold his lands together. Like a powerful windstorm from the steppes of Central Asia, he leveled everything in his path and then vanished, leaving others to rebuild what he had destroyed.

The Cosmopolitan Ottoman Empire

17.2 **Explain the techniques used by the Ottomans to govern their multinational empire.**

Like the rest of Asia, the Muslim world had been badly battered by the nomadic invasions of the eleventh through fourteenth centuries. The Seljuk Turks, the Mongols, and Timur Lenk had brought war and destruction, but none proved able to hold their huge empires together. Even though they conquered Islam, they were also assimilated by it.

Islam appealed strongly to these nomads. The simplicity of its monotheism, the hope of paradise offered by its five pillars, and the rigor and consistency of its legal code all resonated with tribal peoples oblivious to the complex doctrinal disputes that fascinated Byzantines. Nomads were accustomed to settling quarrels directly, physically, and permanently.

Consequently, although nomadic rule in southern Asia could be exploitative and devastating, it did not destroy Muslim culture. Mahmud of Ghazni's conversion to

Islam could not save the Il-Khan Empire from dissolution in 1335, but it did perpetuate the hold of the Islamic faith. Timur conquered in the name of Islam, not as its enemy. And Mongol advances in Southwest Asia were stopped by Egypt's Muslim Mamluk rulers, who in turn were conquered by invaders from Anatolia known as the Ottoman Turks.

Ottomans and Byzantines

How did the Ottoman and Byzantine empires conflict and connect with one another?

In the late thirteenth century, a Turkic-speaking nomadic group led by a man named Osman (*oz-MAHN*) arrived in Anatolia, fleeing westward from the Mongols. They came as polytheists but were eventually converted to Sunni Islam by the Seljuk Turks, who granted them lands in Anatolia along the Byzantine frontier. These grants placed the Ottoman Turks, so named because they were followers of Osman, in an advantageous position that they were quick to exploit. When the Seljuk state collapsed and the Mongols withdrew, the Ottomans took over as champions of the Muslim cause against the Byzantine Empire.

That once great realm was now in ruins. Even after 1261, when the Byzantines recaptured their capital from the Western crusaders, they were beset by insurrections and civil wars, and they never managed to recover their Balkan provinces of Bulgaria, Serbia, and Macedonia, which the Bulgars had taken. Their glorious capital of Constantinople was in decline, its wealth squandered and its trade with the East having passed into the hands of the Italian commercial republics of Venice and Genoa.

The real winners of the Fourth Crusade were the Turks, who stood by while Christians killed one another. In 1345, Ottoman sultan Orhan was invited across the Dardanelles by a Byzantine faction hoping to gain the imperial throne. Just as the Seljuks had been invited into western Anatolia and never left it, the Ottomans took advantage of Byzantine weakness to construct a network of vassal principalities in the Balkans. When Serbs and Bosnians revolted against Ottoman rule in 1387, Sultan Murad (*MEW-rahd*) I defeated the rebels at the Battle of Kosovo (*KŌ-sō-vō*) in 1389. This outcome provoked the Europeans to mount a multinational anti-Islamic crusade, which the Ottomans defeated seven years later.

These Balkan victories gave the Ottomans a territorial base in Europe and allowed them to consider their strategy for administering the area. Murad was an exceptional ruler who refused to impose Islamic or Ottoman forms of government in the Balkans. He was convinced that new systems must be developed that would take into account local conditions and cultures and permit daily life to continue as it had. With this conviction he laid the foundation of a religiously and ethnically pluralistic society that would create a stable ***Pax Ottomanica***, or "Ottoman Peace," similar in some ways to the *Pax Romana* created centuries earlier by the Roman Empire. Like the Romans, Murad granted citizenship to all foreigners willing to work for his administration.

The primary concern of Murad and his successors was to promote Islam. Several Ottoman officials once told a Byzantine visitor that the westward expansion of the faith had been ordained by Allah, and the Ottomans were the "sword" of that advance. The Byzantine Empire could continue to exist—if its citizens converted to Islam! In reality, of course, the Byzantine realm had been decaying for centuries, so its absorption into the Muslim world would be of far less value than Murad had hoped.

Murad, slain by a Serb at Kosovo in 1389, was succeeded by his son Bayezid I, a proficient warrior and strong leader whose defeat by Timur in 1402 temporarily saved the Byzantine Empire. Once Timur was gone, the Ottomans regrouped. Two successive sultans tried to capture Constantinople and failed. But eventually the Ottomans absorbed Byzantium into their own immense cosmopolitan empire, one that spanned three continents and endured for more than 400 years.

How did Mehmed the Conqueror emphasize the connections between his Ottoman Empire and the Roman and Byzantine empires?

Mehmed II.

Mehmed the Conqueror

The final conqueror of Byzantium was Sultan Mehmed (*MEH-med*) II, who came to the Ottoman throne in 1451, determined to take Constantinople. By May 29, 1453, he had succeeded, as this chapter's opening story describes (see "Mehmed the Conqueror Takes Constantinople, 1453"). Changing the name of the Byzantine capital from Constantinople to Istanbul, he replaced the Christian Byzantine Empire with an Islamic Ottoman realm.

Constantinople's fall threw Western Christendom into despair. Europe was now threatened directly by the Ottomans from the southeast, and the flow of commerce from east to west was completely in Islamic hands. For Mehmed the Conqueror, however, the events of 1453 fulfilled the will of Allah, who had ordained that His sultan rescue the Roman Empire from unbelievers. Mehmed was now both the legitimate Roman emperor and successor to Constantine the Great, and Ottoman *Padishah* (*PAH-dih-sha*), a Persian word meaning "God's deputy on earth" and used by the Ottomans to mean "imperial sovereign." The Byzantine tradition of caesaropapism, in which the same man exercised both political and religious authority, was of great use to Mehmed and his successors.

The ambitious Mehmed sought to make the Byzantine Empire part of an Ottoman Empire and a platform for Islam's conquest of all Europe and Asia. This was a tall order, but Mehmed saw himself as selected by Allah to achieve the worldwide unity of Islam. In addition to capturing Constantinople, his annexation of Serbia and his victory over the White Sheep Confederation in eastern Anatolia and Mesopotamia gave the Ottoman state a huge territorial base.

Document 17.1 Mehmed the Conqueror Takes Constantinople, 1453

Kritovoulos, a Greek, was not present at the siege of Constantinople but soon thereafter visited it and entered the service of Mehmed II, who eventually appointed him governor of the island of Imbros. "He admired the Sultan's military prowess and ability, even while mourning the loss of the City and the downfall of the last vestige of the Byzantine Empire." His description of the conquest of Constantinople is based on the personal testimony of hundreds who took part in it.

Sultan Mehmed, who happened to be fighting quite near by, saw that a palisade and a part of a wall that had been destroyed were now empty of men and deserted by the defenders . . . He shouted out, "Friends, we have the City! We have it! They are already fleeing from us! They can't stand it any longer! The wall is bare of defenders! It needs just a little more effort and the City is taken! Don't weaken, but on with the work with all your might, and be men and I am with you!"

So saying, he led them himself. And they, with a shout on the run and with a fearsome yell, went on ahead of the Sultan, pressing on up to the palisade . . . Now there was a great struggle there and great slaughter among those stationed there . . . There the Emperor Constantine, with all who were with him, fell in gallant combat . . . Then a great slaughter occurred of those who happened to be there . . . men, women, and children, everyone, for there was no quarter given. The soldiers fell on them with anger and great wrath.

For one thing, they were actuated by the hardships of the siege. For another, some foolish people had hurled taunts and curses at them from the battlements all through the siege. Now, in general they killed so as to frighten all the City, and to terrorize and enslave all by the slaughter . . .

After this the Sultan entered the City and looked about to see its great size, its situation, its grandeur and beauty, its teeming population, its loveliness, and the costliness of its churches and public buildings and of the private houses and community houses and those of the officials . . . When he saw what a large number had been killed, and the ruin of the buildings, and the wholesale ruin and destruction of the City, he was filled with compassion and repented not a little at the destruction and plundering. Tears fell from his eyes as he groaned deeply and passionately: "What a city we have given over to plunder and destruction!"

Source: Kritovoulos: *History of Mehmed the Conqueror.* © 1954 Princeton University Press, 1982 renewed PUP Reprinted by permission of Princeton University Press.

The Ottoman State and Society

How did the Ottomans blend diverse traditions into a new governing system?

Having destroyed the last vestige of Imperial Rome, the Ottoman Empire evolved from an Asian-based Turkish political and social system into a multiethnic, intercontinental state. In doing so, it combined previously unrelated administrative methods derived from Turkish, Persian, and Byzantine traditions into a new governing form connecting aspects of three of the dominant cultures of Asia.

THE OTTOMAN GOVERNMENT'S UNIQUE SYNTHESIS   Ottoman government was based on the sultan's exclusive right to rule, a concept drawn from Persian tradition and amplified after 1453 by Byzantine caesaropapism. The sultan was supported in this effort by the four "pillars of empire," a Turkish image taken from the four poles that had traditionally held up the sultan's tent. The first pillar of the government was the **grand vezir** (*veh-ZĒR*), chief minister to the sultan; the second pillar was the judiciary; the third was the treasury; and the fourth consisted of administrators who drew up the sultan's edicts. These pillars existed to enhance the sultan's authority, not to limit it.

But Mehmed II and his successors were not entirely free to rule as they wished. As a Muslim, the sultan was required to conduct himself in accordance with the Shari`ah or Islamic law, based upon the Qur'an, Islamic custom, and the sayings of the first four caliphs. In significant political decisions, he was expected to seek a **fatwa** (*FAHT-wah*), a legal opinion from the highest Islamic legal authority, sanctioning his course of action. Yet seventh-century Islamic law was not always applicable to issues arising in a fifteenth-century Muslim state.

Turkish tradition proved helpful in resolving this problem. The sultan in his role as Padishah enjoyed the right to issue commands and regulations on ordinary governmental matters without interference from the Islamic legal establishment. These state laws, called **kanun** (*kah-NOON*), could be shaped in response to modern issues and problems that the Shari`ah could not have foreseen. Kanun could, for example, be used to authorize the lending of money at interest despite religious objections to the practice. In one form or another, the Turkish principle that state law takes precedence over religious law remained in use for centuries in most Islamic nations.

Ottoman law book.

This practical synthesis of diverse concepts meant that the Ottomans behaved differently from other Islamic states. First, their approach to their enemies was shaped by practical considerations rather than religious zeal. Living side by side with Greeks in the Balkans convinced them of the essential humanity of their opponents and the impracticality of dealing with them harshly. Ottoman willingness to blend governmental traditions enabled them to develop a hybrid system well suited to ruling the assorted cultures and ethnic groups that made up their diverse domain.

Second, the Ottoman system of landholding differed significantly from both Arab and European practice. The nomadic origins of many Islamic societies lived on in the high value placed on land as belonging to the tribe, and the low value placed on individual ownership. European societies, in contrast, placed a high value on individual land ownership, and medieval systems of inheritance encouraged the development of landed nobilities. In Ottoman territory all land belonged to the state. Newly conquered land was distributed by the sultan to his soldiers as a reward. These land grants promoted the growth of a professional standing army. But the lands could not be handed down from father to son; upon a soldier's death, his land reverted to the state. This system prevented the creation of a landed aristocracy that could challenge the sultan. Instead, what evolved was a meritocracy, in which each succeeding generation was rewarded according to the value of its service to the state.

OTTOMAN SOCIETY   The Ottoman state apparatus was thus a unique blend of Turkish, Persian, Byzantine, and Islamic influences. Unique as well was the society on which it rested. The Ottoman ruling class of about 350 people was composed exclusively of slaves belonging to the sultan. Almost all of them were former Christians who converted to Islam. This elite status was nonhereditary; these slaves and their descendants could never become permanent nobility. Promotion was based solely on merit, and demotion was possible in cases of poor performance. Parallel to this ruling class was the corps of **Janissaries** (*JAN-is-sair-ēz*), a 10,000–member infantry, also composed of slaves who were Christian-born converts to Islam and totally dependent on the sultan. Armed with gunpowder weapons, the Ottoman armies were superior to all they encountered until the late seventeenth century.

In Ottoman society, as in Ottoman governance, privilege was based on performance, not ancestry. A household servant might rise to the rank of grand vezir, while a vezir might fall to the status of a blacksmith, all without any loss of dignity. Since all were slaves of the Padishah, all served at his imperial pleasure in whatever post it pleased him to place them. At its height this hybrid arrangement proved remarkably effective, particularly in a multiethnic empire. Ottoman rule did not depend on overwhelming military force to keep conquered peoples in line. Instead, subject peoples might join and move up in Ottoman administration. This possibility minimized internal unrest. The adaptability of these political and social structures helps explain why the Ottoman Empire survived into the twentieth century.

Suleiman the Magnificent

In what ways was Suleiman the Magnificent successful, and in what ways did he fail?

Mehmed the Conqueror lived up to his name, solidifying Ottoman control over Anatolia and moving northwest from Istanbul deeper into Southeastern Europe. The next two sultans, Bayezid II (r. 1481–1512) and Selim (*seh-LĒM*) I "The Grim" (r. 1512–1520), concentrated on warfare in the east and south. Selim ruled for only eight years, but in that time he managed to conquer Syria, Palestine, Egypt, and North Africa, while defeating Persia's new Safavid regime. His conquest of Egypt gave him control of the holy cities of Mecca and Medina, encouraging him to claim the title of caliph, vacant since 1258, thereby completing the transfer of Islamic leadership from Arabs to Turks (Ottoman sultans remained caliphs until 1924). By the end of Selim's reign, the Ottomans ruled about two thirds of the territory of the old Eastern Roman Empire. All that was left for them to conquer was Central and Western Europe.

THE OTTOMAN EMPIRE AS A FORCE IN WORLD AFFAIRS Selim was succeeded in 1520 by his 26-year-old son Suleiman (*SOO-lē-mahn*). Islamic seers, pointing to the sacred number ten, predicted glorious victories for the new ruler: Suleiman was the tenth Ottoman sultan, and he began his reign at the start of the tenth century after Muhammad's move to Medina in 622. Suleiman was also an intellectual, eager to absorb Turkish, Persian, and Byzantine culture and to participate in the European Renaissance's revival of Greek and Roman learning. Suleiman saw himself as a unifier, the leader who could unite East and West under the banner of the Prophet. His 46-year reign extended Ottoman power into Central Europe and across the Mediterranean, terrifying Christian Europe and establishing the Ottoman Empire as a decisive force in international affairs (Map 17.2).

The Ottomans struck first into Hungary, slaughtering Hungarian forces at Mohács in 1526. But Suleiman's resources were inadequate for the permanent governance of a hostile country so far from Istanbul, on the other side of the rugged and treacherous Balkan Peninsula. Selim had been able to control Southwest Asia and North Africa with relative ease, as the inhabitants of those areas had been Muslims for centuries. But Central Europe was intensely Christian and unwilling to submit to Islamic rule. Suleiman burned Budapest and marched his armies home for the winter, leaving Hungary open to the influence of the Austrian Habsburgs. That Catholic royal family immediately began to fortify Central Europe against the Turkish threat.

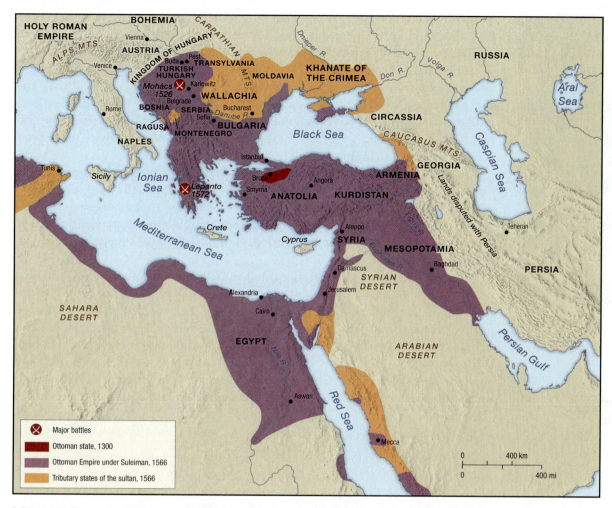

Map 17.2 THE OTTOMAN EMPIRE IN 1566 Comparison with Map 17.1 indicates that the Ottoman Empire at the death of Suleiman the Magnificent was much larger than that of Timur Lenk. Notice that the Ottoman Empire connected parts of three continents and included ethnic groups as diverse as Egyptians, Syrians, Mesopotamians, Turks, Greeks, and Bosnians. What methods did the Ottomans develop to rule such far-flung domains and so many distinct peoples?

Three years later, in May 1529, Suleiman led an immense army to attack Vienna. But the rains were so persistent that summer that the Turks could not bring up their heavy siege artillery over Austria's primitive roads. In October, as winter approached and the cavalry could not feed its horses, Suleiman returned to Istanbul in frustration. In 1532 he tried again, this time failing even to reach Vienna because of poor weather and Hungarian and Croatian resistance. Now, at one of history's turning points, Suleiman concluded that, given distance, weather, terrain, and the hostility of the population, Vienna and Central Europe lay beyond the reach of military conquest launched from Istanbul.

Grudgingly, Suleiman turned his attention toward the East. Over the next three decades, he fought Safavid Persia for possession of Mesopotamia, sent his powerful navy to raid the eastern Mediterranean, and periodically returned west to extend his control farther into Hungary. He continued to play a major role in European affairs, allying with France against the Habsburgs and supporting Protestants against Catholics during the Reformation. Spain's Muslim minority begged him to invade, and if he had done so, that community would have given Spain's Catholic kings an enormous security problem. In 1566, on his seventh campaign into Europe, Suleiman died in his tent, having failed to unify East and West but having succeeded in making the Ottoman Empire a world power.

Suleiman.

What explains the inability of the Ottomans to conquer Europe?

SULEIMAN THE LAWGIVER Despite his constant campaigning, the sultan was often at home; and if to Europeans he was "Suleiman the Magnificent," to his subjects he was "Suleiman the Lawgiver." Like European monarchs, he was not above the law but subject to it, although his exalted status allowed him considerable range of action. Given the centrality of the Shari`ah within Islamic culture, he could not have created a new legal structure, but he did adapt the law to the conditions of his immense multiethnic empire. His subjects lived on three continents and were free to profess non-Islamic faiths, and while not all of them were subject to the Shari`ah, all were accountable under the kanun, which the sultan alone could declare.

Suleiman worked diligently to guarantee that laws would apply equally to all. Corporal punishment was replaced by a system of fines, although forgers and perjurers might still have their right hands cut off. The sultan also strengthened mechanisms for the enforcement of Islamic law, viewing the church–state relationship as one in which two complementary strands reinforced royal authority—a typically caesaropapist perspective.

Was Suleiman the Magnificent an absolute monarch in the sense of having unlimited power? Certainly his authority, dignity, and legal status would justify this description. But Suleiman himself would probably have seen absolutism as a curious contrivance of nonbelievers, of little use to an Islamic sovereign. He was Allah's deputy on earth, the Ottoman Padishah, a ruler for whom the distinction between spiritual and political authority was not a source of tension but of power. Clearly superior, in his own mind, to any monarch in the West, Suleiman would have been unlikely to consider their forms of governance applicable to his lands.

A Faltering Empire

Ottoman fortunes remained favorable for some time after Suleiman's death. Although in 1571 a multinational European navy demolished the Turkish fleet at the Greek strait of Lepanto (*leh-PAHN-tō*), the vessels were quickly rebuilt, and the Turks continued to dominate the eastern Mediterranean. More worrisome in the long run was the takeover of the Indian Ocean spice trade by the Dutch and French in the seventeenth century, costing Istanbul dearly in terms of lost customs duties. That shortfall could not be made up: Ottoman revenues could be expanded only by conquering additional territory, and the empire's failure to advance into Europe meant that its real income would decline during a period of rapid inflation fueled by gold and silver shipments from the Western Hemisphere.

This fiscal challenge might have been addressed by competent leadership, but that was in short supply. Suleiman had been trained as a soldier and provincial governor before becoming sultan, but his successors had no such experience; they were brought up in the harem to protect them from rivals. Bred to luxury and debauchery, they often became alcoholics and drug addicts. The grand vezirs kept the empire running, but since they governed at the sultan's pleasure, one gesture from him could end either a career or a life. With central authority growing weaker, local leaders assumed more and more control, so that the Ottoman Empire was decentralizing just as European governments were concentrating more and more power in their kings.

This placed the Ottomans in danger, and poor decisions compounded the risk to the empire. In 1683, the grand vezir Kara Mustafa (*KAH-rah moo-STAH-fah*) led an immense army to once again besiege Vienna, in an effort to accomplish what Suleiman had already concluded was impossible. The Turks were again defeated, this time by a multinational Christian force led by King Jan III Sobieski (*YAHN sō-B'YEH-skē*) of Poland. Istanbul was forced in 1699 to sign the Peace of Karlowitz, recognizing that Hungary and Transylvania belonged to Austria. For the first time Ottoman expansion had been not only stopped but rolled back. The defeat suggested an uncertain future for the empire, especially as its failure to overcome Christian Europe was paralleled by failures to meet challenges to its leadership within the Islamic world from empires farther east.

Safavid Persia: A Shi'ite State

17.3 Explain how the Safavids used Islam to revive and rebuild the Persian Empire.

Ethnic, linguistic, religious, and geographic diversity characterized the Islamic empires from Istanbul to Delhi. Yet Islam provided a powerful faith-based appeal that helped unify its followers. The five pillars offered each Muslim a framework for living a righteous life. The Qur'an, amplified by the sayings of the Prophet, guided the faithful to a deeper understanding of Allah's will. Islamic law, as developed in the Shari`ah, was interpreted differently in different states but furnished a common code of conduct in civil and criminal matters. Mosques and minarets were found in all Islamic communities, although built in various architectural styles. And while Sunni and Shi'ite observances differed, Islam offered a common tradition that enabled all Muslims to transcend their differences. Nowhere was this more apparent than in Persia.

Shi'ite Islam as a Unifying Force

The Iranian plateau had for centuries endured the ravages of raiders and nomads from Central Asia, but the combination of Genghis Khan and Timur Lenk brought devastation on a scale previously unknown. Invading armies obliterated towns, erecting huge columns of skulls to mark their former sites. The population of Persia declined by 90 percent. Both Genghis and Timur were accompanied by large bands of Turks, who converted to Islam upon arrival in Persia and who eventually rebuilt it once the Mongols moved on to other conquests.

The rebuilders, who called themselves the Safavid movement, were established by a Kurd named Safi al-Din (*SAH-fĕ al-DĒN*), who lived from 1252 to 1334. Claiming descent from the fourth caliph, Ali, and through him from the Prophet Muhammad, Safi founded an order of Turkish Sufi mystics who believed that post-Mongol Persia must be rebuilt on a foundation of purified Islamic devotion and militancy. In opposition to the turmoil and exploitation of Mongol conquest, the Safavid movement preached a positive message of rededication and strength. The order spread across Persia, quickly becoming the most powerful spiritual force in the land.

After Timur Lenk ravaged Persia late in the fourteenth century, many survivors looked to the Safavids as the most cohesive opposition force. When Timur's empire broke up early in the fifteenth century, Safavism turned from preaching to political action. In 1501, forces led by Safi's descendant Ismail (*IS-mah-ĒL*) conquered the Persian city of Tabriz (*tah-BRĒZ*) from the Turkic Confederation of the White Sheep (Map 17.3). Ismail declared himself **shah** (or king) of Persia, a title not used since the defeat of the Sasanian Empire in 651. He also proclaimed Shi'ite Islam the state religion of Persia.

Ismail's 1501 proclamation was highly significant. Persia had been nothing more than a geographic expression, without any independent political identity, since the Arab conquest had reduced it to dependent status. As the Abbasid Caliphate disintegrated, Persia had been torn by the ambitions of warlords and invaders. Now Ismail, by establishing Shi'ism, gave his subjects a new sense of identity and unity that distinguished Persia from its cosmopolitan, Sunni Ottoman neighbor and created what would later be known as the modern state of Iran.

Ismail's accession to the throne was noted immediately in Istanbul. A revived Persian Empire would have been dangerous enough for the Ottomans, but the Safavids were also Shi'ites. Shi'ite Muslims believe that Ali was the legitimate successor to the Prophet and that his murder in 661 constituted a wrong that has never been avenged. Sunni Muslims, the majority in the Islamic world since that time, are in Shi'ite eyes usurpers who have no right to guide the faithful.

Why was Shi'ite Islam so important in Safavid Persia?

A Safavid battle helmet.

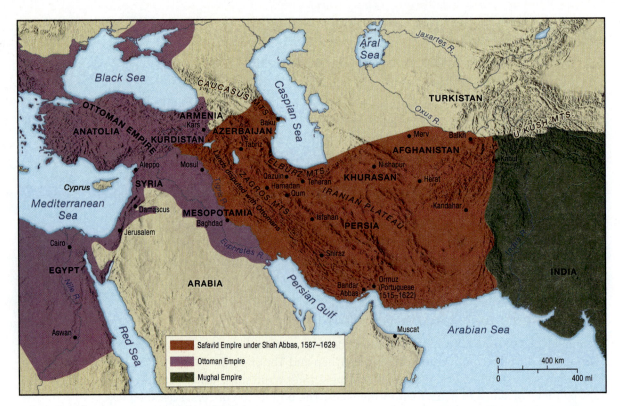

Map 17.3 **THE SAFAVID EMPIRE IN PERSIA, 1600** A shared Islamic faith connected the peoples of Southwest Asia, but differing brands of Islam and other areas of conflict divided them. Notice the geographic location of the Safavid Empire, positioned as a buffer state between the Ottoman Empire (to its west) and the Mughal Empire in India (to its east). The Safavids' adoption of Shi'ite Islam separated Persia from both its Sunni Muslim neighbors, while the natural barriers of the Zagros Mountains and the Hindu Kush discouraged those neighbors from interfering in Safavid affairs. What commercial advantages might this central location have offered the Persians?

Shi'ism divided Persia from its Sunni neighbors east and west. Its rituals underscored that division. Regular commemorations of Sunni persecutions of Shi'ites are important parts of the Shi'ite Muslim calendar, and they intensify with a two-week observance of the murder of Ali's son Hussein by Sunni assassins in 680. Then as now, pilgrims marched tearfully through the streets, whipping themselves and chanting dirges in honor of the martyr.

Developments in Persia were profoundly disturbing to the Sunnis who ruled the Ottoman Empire. They worried that hundreds of thousands of Shi'ites living under Ottoman rule might be sympathetic to the Safavids. In addition, the Safavid dynasty was of Kurdish origin and commanded considerable support in Anatolia. For their part, the Safavids worried about Ottoman intervention, and open warfare broke out when Selim I became Ottoman sultan in 1512. Two years later the Ottomans defeated the Persians and briefly occupied Tabriz but were unable to force the Safavids from power. The animosity between the two Islamic factions deepened. Ismail's successor, Shah Tamasp, considered Tabriz too close to the Ottoman border and moved his capital 300 miles east to Qazvin, beginning a process of making his empire less Turkish and more Persian.

The Safavids defended Persia ably. Tamasp spent most of his reign (1524–1553) repelling invasions by the Ottomans and the Central Asian Uzbeks (*OOZ-becks*), a nomadic people occupying portions of eastern Persia. In all these battles, the Safavids were the smaller but more skillful force. Shah Abbas (*ab-BAHS*), reigning from 1587 to 1629, developed a modern army on the Ottoman model and captured Baghdad. He also allied with the English, who helped his army expel the Portuguese from the

Persian Gulf port of Hormuz (*hōr-MOOZ*) in 1622. Commercial rivalries between European powers enabled Abbas to shrewdly play one against another. By the end of his reign, Safavid Persia was a major regional power whose Sunni rivals, the Ottomans and Mughals, could not reach the Persian heartland without covering forbidding distances.

Shah Abbas was also sensitive to the need for a strong economy. He encouraged the rapid expansion of trade in carpets and tiles, items of exquisite beauty soon prized around the world. Persian silk fetched tremendous profits in Europe, and Vernon Egger points out that silk was almost as important to Safavid revenue as petroleum is to modern Iran. Ottoman hostility obstructed the caravan trade in all these goods, despite the huge profits this obstruction cost the Ottomans. Transferring his capital to the centrally situated city of Isfahan (*ISS-fah-hahn*), Abbas gained freedom from persistent Ottoman raids and rebuilt the city into a commercial center and an architectural wonder. Isfahan's every detail was meticulously planned, from the enormous central square (used for polo matches, festivals, and ceremonies) to the exquisite royal mosque and luxurious summer palace. The shops in the royal bazaar were centrally located for ease of taxation. Isfahan's grandeur and beauty enhanced Safavid legitimacy and celebrated Shi'ite Islam.

The Shah Mosque in Isfahan.

Following the death of Shah Abbas in 1629, Safavid fortunes declined rapidly. He was succeeded by incompetent, pampered rulers who were ill equipped to defend an empire that needed cleverness to survive. While the Ottomans reconquered Baghdad, Afghans and Uzbeks seized large regions of Persian territory in the east, and Russian Cossacks began to press the empire from the north. Persia remained independent not through its own strength, but because the Ottoman and Mughal empires were declining as well.

Regional and Islamic Influence on Family and Gender Roles

How did Persian customs alter Islamic family and gender relations?

In Safavid Persia, as in the Ottoman and Mughal empires, societies were shaped as much by regional customs as by Islamic ideals. In each society, for example, practices affecting family and gender, such as the seclusion of women in the home, were often rooted in regional rather than Islamic traditions.

The Qur'an had established family and gender roles in Islamic Arabia, not only strengthening the patriarchal nature of Arabian society but also enhancing the status of women. Both genders were entitled to human dignity and personal privacy. Women were granted explicit property rights and were protected from impoverishment in case of divorce. These rights and protections had not previously been available to them.

As Islam spread beyond Arabia, however, the status of women was impaired by local customs that often overrode Qur'anic requirements. In Persia, for example, male domination and female seclusion had for centuries been embedded in legal and cultural systems. Marriages were arranged by the fathers or male guardians of the brides-to-be. Brides lived with their husband and his relatives, an arrangement that gave them little security should the marriage fail. Persian men, citing local practice, frequently refused women their rights as Muslims to inherit property left them by previous husbands or other relatives. The Shari'ah allowed women to buy and sell property, but in Persia these actions could be taken only through male agents. Although the Qur'an spelled out certain rights for women, these were limited, and in some cases canceled, by Persian traditional practice.

The seclusion of women and their segregation from public life must be placed in context, however. First, not all women were confined to the home. The seclusion of well-to-do women was a sign that they did not need to work, whereas

Persian women.

poor women usually went about in public with their faces exposed. Second, in traditional family-based Islamic societies, the private sphere was typically much more important than the public. Girls could not be educated *outside* the home in Safavid Persia, but *inside* it they were taught the Qur'an and the sayings of the Prophet, at least in middle- and upper-class families. Most economic activity involved the family, and here women exercised considerable influence away from public view. Men were clearly dominant, but women in the Islamic empires did not define themselves as a separate interest group. They played an indispensable role in family life, in societies in which the family was the center of activity. Finally, there was considerable variation within the great Islamic empires. In the Ottoman Empire, women could conduct business, execute wills, and testify in court, rights unknown to their contemporaries in Europe. In Mughal India, unlike Safavid Persia, women played the primary role in arranging the marriages of their daughters. They were excluded from worship services in mosques but were free to fight in battle; Shah Jahan deployed a contingent of female soldiers, and in the eighteenth century several women commanded military units. Clearly it is difficult to generalize about the roles played by Muslim women.

The Mughal Empire: A Muslim Minority Rules India

17.4 Discuss the challenges faced by Muslim rulers of India under the Mughal Empire.

East of Persia, other Muslims struggled to extend their dominion over India and its Hindu population. In the northern part of the subcontinent, the main Islamic rulers were the Delhi sultans, who had established their regime in 1206. For the next few centuries, while the Mongols overran most of the rest of Asia, these sultans tried to spread their control across India. Although they ultimately failed, the third of the great Islamic empires was eventually constructed on foundations they laid.

The Delhi Sultanate in India

What factors undermined the Delhi Sultanate and opened the door for Mongol invasion?

In the 1220s Genghis Khan complicated the Delhi sultans' situation by chasing Central Asian tribes out of their homelands and into northern India. The reigning sultan, Iletmish (*ill-LET-mish*), prudently refused the refugees' offers of alliance and encouraged them to turn westward into Persia. He thus prevented a Mongol invasion of India. By the time of his death in 1236, Iletmish had consolidated all of northern India under the Delhi Sultanate (Map 17.4).

A sensible and enlightened ruler, Iletmish did what he could to reconcile India's Hindu majority to Islamic rule. He left the Hindu rajahs alone as long as they paid tribute and supported him against the Mongols. He also proved to be a good judge of talent, openly preferring his daughter Radiya (*rah-DĒ-yah*) as his successor because she was clearly more capable than his sons. But when Iletmish died in 1236, her succession was opposed by her brothers and by a group of influential military officers. Radiya battled against this coalition but finally lost in 1240 and died at the hands of Hindus while fleeing Delhi.

Radiya's defeat plunged the Delhi Sultanate into a series of coups and intrigues that ended in 1266 with the assumption of power by the mamluk slave Balban (*bahl-BAHN*), who had been one of the sultanate's most effective generals. He reorganized the army and government in an effort to hold off the persistent Mongols. Balban's death in 1287 was followed within a decade by the rule of Sultan Ala al-Din (*AH-lahal-dēn*), an imaginative, skillful, ruthless leader who expanded the sultanate southward, both to extend its holdings and to raise money and troops required for defense against the Mongols. In 1298 he captured the West Indian state of Gujarat and its vast treasury enriched by the Arabian Sea trade. Then he crossed the Deccan plateau into southern India and managed to occupy the tip of the subcontinent. India, it seemed, had at last been united under Muslim control.

But Ala al-Din's unifying rule did not last. His successors proved capable of organizing victories over the Mongols but not of holding India together. The subcontinent was simply too large and too diverse, linguistically, culturally, and geographically, to be consolidated by groups with considerable talent for warfare but little for administration.

The Delhi Sultanate's authority crumbled rapidly. In 1338, a Sufi sect contributed to the defection of the northeastern state of Bengal from mainstream Muslim rule. In 1347 Muslim nobles formed an independent kingdom on the Deccan plateau. In South India, the Hindu states that Ala al-Din had conquered broke away to form the Vijayanagar (*vē-jā-YAH-nah-gahr*) Empire, and in 1390 Gujarat in West India left as well. These losses weakened Delhi so profoundly that it was unable to resist the catastrophic invasion of Timur Lenk.

Following Timur's atrocities in the late fourteenth century, what remained of Indian unity dissolved. The Delhi Sultanate was reduced to the status of a North Indian principality, and several of its former tributaries now became powerful in their own right. In the fifteenth century, no single state dominated. In 1405 Timur's son established the **Timurid** (*tee-MOOR-id*) dynasty in India, but it lacked the organized military force necessary for effective imperial rule, and northern Indian states generally ignored it.

Further fragmenting the Indian subcontinent was the emergence of a new **Sikh** (*SĒK*) religion in the late fifteenth century. In the Punjab, centuries of conflict between Hindu and Muslim had deeply scarred the population. There a Hindu mystic named Nanak (*NAH-knock*), inspired by a spiritual experience, worked to develop a synthesis of the two antagonistic faiths. Impressed by Islamic monotheism, he accepted the idea of the unity of God; blended it with the Hindu mystical notions of samsara, dharma, and karma; and rejected the Hindu caste system in favor of the Islamic principle of the equality of all believers. Nanak's synthesis, known as Sikhism, still thrives in the Punjab, centered on its holiest site, the Golden Temple at Amritsar (*ahm-RIT-zar*). But his dream of reconciling Hinduism with Islam failed. Rejected by most members of these two opposing creeds, Sikhism became yet another force working against the unity of India.

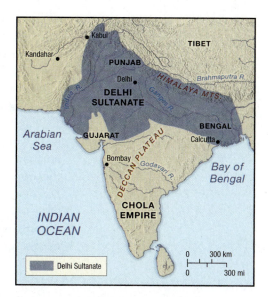

Map 17.4 **THE DELHI SULTANATE IN INDIA, 1236** The Delhi Sultanate was India's best hope for defense against the Mongols. Observe that the sultanate stretched from the banks of the Indus River eastward across the Himalaya Mountains, thereby blocking Mongol penetration of the Indian subcontinent. What factors eventually undermined the regime and opened the door for Mongol invasion?

The Golden Temple.

Babur: Founding the Mughal Empire

India in 1500 was a land in turmoil, divided by religion, culture, and politics. Into this situation stepped the last Timurid, Babur (*BAH-boor*), whose name means "the Panther," a fifth-generation descendant of Timur Lenk and a 13th-generation descendant of Genghis Khan. In 1524 Babur was invited into the Punjab by a faction seeking his help in overthrowing the local sultan. He accepted the invitation and then quickly overran the Punjab and appointed his own officials to rule it. Then on April 21, 1526, Babur's forces faced the spears and elephants of Sultan Ibrahim (*ib-rah-HĒM*) of Delhi at the battle of Panipat (*PAH-nē-paht*). Although his troops were outnumbered two to one, his horsemen were more mobile than the infantry of his opponents, and his cannons blew sizable holes in the elephants. By noon he had won the battle and founded what would be named the Mughal Empire, the greatest Islamic state in Indian history and the most powerful South Asian state in fifteen hundred years (Map 17.5). The Mughals called themselves Gurkani, a Mongolian term for son-in-law; Timur Lenk

How did Babur take advantage of Indian disunity to create the Mughal Empire?

had married two descendants of Genghis Khan. But Arabic- and Persian-speaking Muslims called them al-Mughul, or Mongols, and the name stuck.

Four years later, Babur died. His son Humayun (*hoo-MAH-yoon*) proved to be a useless leader, more interested in casting horoscopes and indulging in opium than in ruling an empire. Babur's Afghan generals were dissatisfied, and one of them, Sher Khan Sur (*SHĒR KAHN SOOR*), challenged the new emperor and defeated him in 1539 and 1540. Sher Khan introduced a unified coinage system and began building what would become the Grand Trunk Road, running from the Khyber Pass east across northern India to Bengal. But Sher Khan died young in 1545, and Humayun seized this opportunity to regain the power that had never much interested him. In 1555, however, after smoking at least one opium pipe too many, Humayun slipped on the steps of his private observatory and fractured his skull. This accident left the Mughal Empire in the hands of his 13-year-old son Akbar (*OCK-bar*), whose name in Arabic means "great." As matters turned out, he deserved the title.

Akbar's Reign of Cultural Accommodation

In what ways was Akbar able to connect the fragmented peoples of India?

Akbar was an active man, a formidable hunter and fighter, but illiterate throughout his life. In addition to his total lack of formal education, he appears to have been an epileptic, suffering from seizures and dramatic mood swings that baffled his courtiers. None of these conditions, however, prevented his becoming one of history's finest rulers.

Akbar could not read, but he could learn from the past. He understood not only that India was huge and incurably pluralistic, but also that no government could endure without the cooperation of the Hindu majority. Accordingly, Akbar initiated a program to reconcile his Islamic regime with the Hindu population. He sent an unmistakable signal by marrying a Hindu princess, who bore him three sons. In 1563 he abolished all taxes levied on Hindus making pilgrimages to shrines and temples. One year later he canceled a tax imposed on non-Muslims. Uncommonly generous, tolerant, and sensible, Akbar was the first Muslim ruler to win significant support from Hindus throughout the subcontinent.

Tolerance and conciliation were not, of course, the only tactics Akbar employed. He also used force to solidify his power. Under Akbar the Mughal Empire tripled in size. Its landmass was one-third that of the Ottoman Empire, but its population of nearly 100 million was four times as large. Yet full integration of southern India proved impossible. Akbar could win battles in the south, but once he returned to the north, southern opposition reversed his achievements.

Akbar controlled a competent bureaucracy that administered the Mughal Empire. He divided his domain into 12 provinces, subdividing each into districts. Each province was ruled by a governor directly accountable to the emperor. Akbar himself selected the highest officials, a majority of whom were Muslims born outside of India, although many were drawn from other religious, ethnic, linguistic, and regional groups (15 percent, for example, were Hindus). In addition to demonstrating tolerance and inclusiveness, this policy brought the best qualified Indians into his service, giving them responsible roles in the Mughal Empire as an alternative to leading rebellions against it.

This bureaucracy also collected taxes. Most Indians were peasants, paying taxes not in money but in produce and livestock. Tax collection was handled at the local level, where revenue agents could assess local agricultural conditions. In years in which the harvest was ruined by insects or bad weather, or in which animals were afflicted by outbreaks of disease, agents were directed to use tax revenues for humanitarian relief. Since the highest ranking tax collectors were Hindus sympathetic to the peasants, the emperor's wishes were unfailingly carried out. Moreover, in legal disputes involving Hindus on both sides, Hindu

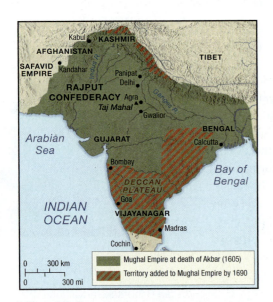

Map 17.5 THE MUGHAL EMPIRE IN INDIA, 1690 Building on the foundations laid by the Delhi Sultanate, the Mughals dominated northern and northwestern India, but the size and topography of the subcontinent prevented them from extending their control further. Note that the central Deccan plateau, a center of resistance to Muslim rule, sealed the Mughals off from southern India's coast until the late 17th century. What weaknesses in Mughal rule made this formidable-looking empire vulnerable to eventual foreign incursions?

rather than Islamic law was used, and the decisions of Hindu courts were final unless the losing party appealed to the throne.

These policies meant that Hindus were better off under Akbar than under any previous Muslim ruler. Indeed, the emperor's tolerance of Hindus began to worry many Muslims. When, after 1581, Akbar put down several revolts in Muslim regions in the north, he increased his popularity among the Hindu majority. Akbar himself practiced Sufi rituals, with additional practices adapted from Hindus, Jains, Sikhs, and Christians. Eventually he developed his own religion, which involved worshipping the sun four times a day. That was too much for most Muslims, who came to view Akbar as an apostate.

Under Mughal rule India's culture became increasingly Persian. Akbar made Farsi the language of administration and Islamic law, offending those who believed that Arabic, the language of worship, should also be the language of state business. Akbar also encouraged the creation of poetry and literature in Farsi, Urdu (*UHR-doo*), and Hindi (*HIN-dē*), rather than insisting on the exclusive use of Arabic or Turkish. In addition, Sufism, the basis of Akbar's ritual observances, was essentially a Persian doctrine, and fashions and etiquette at the Mughal court owed more to Isfahan than to Baghdad or Delhi.

Akbar was not typical of sixteenth-century Islamic rulers. In some ways he resembled an absolute monarch; in others, an enlightened absolutist—one whose absolute rule is tempered by learning and a commitment to the service of his subjects. In his willingness to incorporate aspects of other cultures into a Mughal synthesis, Akbar can justifiably be called modern. But the end of his reign was troubled by a vicious struggle for succession. Akbar's son Salim (*sah-LĒM*) rebelled in 1601, and after four years of turmoil the emperor died, probably a victim of poison. The impatient Salim then became emperor of the most powerful empire in the history of India, and one of the most formidable in the entire world.

The Great Mughals

Salim's reign ushered in the era of the Great Mughals. With much of South Asia unified under their control, there seemed to be no threats to the empire. Salim celebrated his coronation by taking the name Jahangir (*zhah-hahn-GĒR*)—"World Seizer"—and by continuing his father's efforts to create in India a new unified civilization with Islamic, Hindu, and Persian components.

How did the Great Mughals at first build on and then reverse Akbar's tolerant policies?

NUR JAHAN AND SHAH JAHAN: LIGHTING THE WORLD   In 1611 the Persian strand became dominant as Jahangir married a 34-year-old widow from Persia whom he renamed Nur Jahan (*NOOR jah-HAHN*), "Light of the World." She was quick-witted and politically skilled, and since Jahangir possessed neither of these attributes, she quickly became the true sovereign. Through her and her Persian relatives, Safavid style and culture left an enduring mark on India.

Nur Jahan saw to it that her father became Jahangir's chief minister and arranged for the marriage of her niece, Mumtaz Mahal (*MOOM-tahz mah-HAL*), to Shah Jahan ("Emperor of the World"), Jahangir's son by an earlier marriage. She then supported Shah Jahan for the imperial succession. Jahangir, preferring to spend his time drinking wine, making love, and writing Persian poetry, was more than willing to turn military affairs over to his crown prince. By the time Jahangir died in 1627, the Mughal Empire boasted a population nearing 100 million, making it the second largest state in the world after China. Its extensive overland trade routes connected it to the oceangoing networks of Dutch, French, and English to dramatically increase India's exports, especially cotton textiles, indigo, saffron, and sugar. Bengal became a highly productive rice-growing region, resulting in rapid population growth and the swift spread of Islam as the dominant religion there.

The empire's prosperity made Shah Jahan enormously wealthy, enabling him to lavish gifts on his harem of 5000 women and on Mumtaz Mahal, his wife, who bore him 14 children prior to her death in childbirth at the age of 39. Inconsolable, Shah Jahan

The Taj Mahal.

immortalized her with the construction of her magnificent tomb, the Taj Mahal (*TAHZH mah-HAHL*), a masterpiece fusing Persian artistic form with Indian craftsmanship and materials. He also built the Pearl Mosque at Agra (*AH-grah*), a sparkling jewel of white marble and a monument to Muslim rule in northern India. But for all his spendthrift ways, Shah Jahan was not generous to his subjects. Rather than suspend taxation to ease famine and the burden of natural disasters, as Akbar had done, Shah Jahan grudgingly passed out a handful of rupees. This policy prompted recurring revolts on the central Deccan plateau, an area inhospitable to agriculture and a never-ending drain on money and manpower for the Great Mughals. Instead of relief efforts, Shah Jahan sent armies, causing additional resentment.

In the early 1640s, Shah Jahan began construction of a new capital at Delhi, the seventh and last such city to be built on that site, which he immodestly named Shah Jahanabad (see "François Bernier Comments on Conditions in Delhi"). The city was laid out on an immense scale and included two spectacular building complexes, the Red Fort and the Jama Masjid (*JAH-mah mahs-JĒD*) Mosque. All this construction required enormous sums of money, which Shah Jahan obtained by increasing tax rates by 50 percent. Thus, although he left an architectural legacy that dazzles visitors to the present day, he was neither popular nor competent in his own time, and when he fell ill in 1657, his sons saw their opportunity. They intrigued against each other for a year, and in 1658 the winner was the militant Aurangzeb (*ore-RAHNG-zebb*), who ruled for 49 years.

AURANGZEB'S REIGN: REBELLION AND DISUNITY   Aurangzeb's combination of cunning, ruthlessness, piety, and administrative brilliance made him the most formidable of the Great Mughals. Joyless and puritanical, he spent many hours in prayer and ended the extravagant ways of his father. He also ended Akbar's policy of tolerance for non-Muslims, increasing their taxes, denying building permits for temples, and requiring Hindus to pay double taxes for food. Those who protested these harsh measures were trampled by elephants. As taxes increased and starvation threatened, revolts broke out across the empire.

Under Aurangzeb's tyranny, Sikhs in the Punjab transformed their peace-loving faith into an instrument of rebellion and evolved into a militant community, the "army of the pure." All Sikh males were baptized with the surname Singh (*SĬNG*), or "Lion." Sikh men vowed to wear beards and carry sabers for mutual recognition. Easily outnumbering them, Mughal armies held them off, but the Sikhs retained their hatred for Islamic political authority and remained dangerous.

Aurangzeb encountered further opposition from Hindus on the Deccan plateau, where Shivaji Bonsle (*shē-VAH-jēBAHNS-lē*) founded the Hindu **Maratha** (*mah-ruh-TAH*) nationalist movement to resist Mughal rule. Shivaji was a pioneer in **guerrilla warfare**—raids by small bands of warriors aiming to disrupt armies rather than engage them in open battle. Irreconcilable to the Mughal Empire, the Marathas' ferocious Hindu nationalism represented exactly the sort of reaction that Akbar's policy of tolerance and respect had been designed to avoid.

Aurangzeb reacted vigorously, realizing that the different forces arrayed against him were as suspicious of one another as they were of Mughal rule. His armies isolated the Sikhs in the Punjab and plundered the Deccan. By 1700 Aurangzeb had unified India to an extent undreamed of even by Ashoka; the Mughal Empire contained 150 million people and was one of the great powers of the world. But his was a grim victory, costing more than 2 million lives, wasting tremendous sums of money, and despoiling virtually the entire subcontinent. His armies left behind empty cities and devastated farmlands, dooming Central India to famine and disease for years.

Few mourned Aurangzeb when he died in 1707. His ill-conceived policies had created a vast empire while at the same time impoverishing it, and the opposition his brutality had provoked actually strengthened Indian regionalism and disunity. These developments occurred just as India began to notice the danger posed by visitors from Europe.

Document 17.2   François Bernier Comments on Conditions in Delhi

François Bernier, a French traveler in India in the mid-seventeenth century, commented upon the suitability of Indian buildings to the tropical climate.

In treating of the beauty of these towns . . . I have sometimes been astonished to hear the contemptuous manner in which Europeans in the Indies speak of [Delhi] and other places. They complain that the buildings are inferior in beauty to those of the Western world, forgetting that different climates require different styles of architecture; that what is useful and proper at Paris, London, or Amsterdam, would be entirely out of place at Delhi; insomuch that if it were possible for any one of those great capitals to change place with the metropolis of the Indies, it would become necessary to throw down the greater part of the city, and to rebuild it on a totally different plan . . .

The heat is so intense in [Delhi] that no one, not even the King, wears stockings; the only cover for the feet being slippers, while the head is protected by a small turban, of the finest and most delicate materials. The other garments are proportionately light. During the summer season, it is scarcely possible to keep the hand on the wall of an apartment, or the head on a pillow. For more than six successive months, everybody lies in the open air without covering—the common people in the streets, the merchants and persons of condition sometimes in their courts or gardens, and sometimes on their terraces, which are first carefully watered. Now, only suppose the streets of [Paris] transported hither, with their close houses and endless stories; would they be habitable? or would it be possible to sleep in them during the night, when the absence of wind increases the heat almost to suffocation? Suppose one just returned on horseback, half dead with heat and dust, and drenched, as usual, in perspiration; and then imagine the luxury of squeezing up a narrow dark staircase, there to remain almost choked with heat. In the Indies, there is no such troublesome task to perform. You have only to swallow quickly a draught of fresh water, or lemonade; to undress; wash face, hands, and feet, and then immediately drop upon a sofa in some shady place, where one or two servants fan you . . .

SOURCE: From François Bernier, *Travels in the Mogul Empire*, A.D. 1656–1668, translated by Archibald Constable (Delhi: S. Chand, 1968), 240–241.

Chapter Review

Consequences and Connections

From the thirteenth through sixteenth centuries, the Islamic world underwent two profound transformations. In the thirteenth it was devastated and divided by Mongol conquests. In the fourteenth, when it seemed to be recovering from these onslaughts, it was hit by a new wave of invaders led by Timur Lenk. Once again the Islamic world was shattered; once again it was rebuilt.

Those who led this second period of rebuilding—the Ottomans, Safavids, and Mughals—were themselves the descendants of Mongolian and Turkish nomads from Central Asia, and thus relative newcomers to the regions they ruled. With the flexibility of outsiders, they were able to combine cultures, creating hybrid systems that drew from various traditions. Consequently, by the sixteenth century, the realms that their descendants ruled were among the most powerful and prosperous on the planet. But these empires also faced dangers that became apparent in the next century.

One danger came from within. The size, multiethnicity, and religious diversity of their domains bred tensions and conflicts that challenged state and society. Exceptional rulers such as Suleiman and Akbar were able to balance competing interests and treat all subjects fairly, thus maintaining broad support. Other rulers, however, far less talented and tolerant, either sought to impose uniformity by force or withdrew into the pleasures of royal palaces and ignored the needs of their realm. Either way, the results were often mass discontent and sometimes regional revolt.

Another threat came from outside. Europeans, having adopted ideas and technology from the Chinese and Muslims, were searching for new sea routes to connect East and West. This largely commercial quest led them to engage the Muslim world in a long and bitter conflict over commerce. It also brought them in contact with some extraordinary empires that had arisen in the Americas, in total isolation from the rest of the world.

Reviewing Key Concepts

Pax Ottomanica, p. 333
Grand Vezir, p. 335
Fatwa, p. 335
Kanun, p. 335

Janissaries, p. 336
Shah, p. 339
Timurid Dynasty, p. 343
Sikh Religion, p. 343

Maratha, p. 346
Guerilla Warfare, p. 346

Ask Yourself

1. What blended features made Ottoman government and society unique? Why were these features developed?

2. How did the Safavids use Shi'ite Islam as a governing tool in Persia?

3. How did the Mughals manage to rule India despite their status as members of a religious minority?

4. What did Akbar do to reconcile his Islamic regime to the Hindu population?

5. In what ways did each Islamic empire blend Islamic practices with the cultures of the people under its rule? How were social structures, family, and gender roles influenced by this blending?

Key Dates and Developments

1206–1397	The Delhi Sultanate
1360–1405	Conquests of Timur Lenk
1389	Battle of Kosovo; Ottoman rule in the Balkans
1453	Constantinople falls to Mehmed the Conqueror; end of the Byzantine Empire
1501	Shah Ismail proclaims Shi'ism in Safavid Iran
1526	Ottoman victory at Mohács (Hungary) Battle of Panipat; Mughal Empire begins in India
1529	Suleiman fails to take Vienna
1556–1605	Akbar rules Mughal India
1571	Ottoman fleet defeated at Lepanto
1587–1629	Rule of Shah Abbas in Iran
1605–1707	The Great Mughals in India
1683	King Jan III Sobieski defeats Ottomans at Vienna
1699	Peace of Karlowitz

Chapter 18
The Aztec and Inca Empires, 1300–1550

MACHU PICCHU In the 15th century C.E., the Inca Empire constructed this fortress city of Machu Picchu, high in a remote area of the Andes Mountains. The Inca overcame this formidable terrain to create an empire extending for more than 3000 miles north to south.

After reading this chapter, you should be able to:

18.1 Explain how the Great Amerind Empires differed from those of Europe and Asia.

18.2 Describe the main political, economic, and social structures of the Aztec Empire.

18.3 Describe the main political, economic, and social structures of the Inca Empire.

18.4 Discuss the features of the Great Amerind Empires that handicapped them in their conflicts with Europeans.

18.5 Describe the Spanish invasion of the Aztec Empire and account for the Spanish victory.

18.6 Describe the Spanish invasion of the Inca Empire and account for the Spanish victory.

The Inca Empire

The Aztec Empire

Throughout the city, the women arose before dawn. They laid fresh wood on the fires and warmed up a simple meal of tortillas stuffed with beans. Then they awakened their husbands and children for breakfast. The sun was just above the horizon when the men left to work in the fields or started their work at home, making weapons, tools, or goods to be offered for sale. After cleaning the family's dishes and utensils, the women left to sweep the streets and collect the neighborhood's garbage and waste. At midmorning they would carry the refuse to the water's edge, where it would be loaded into canoes and transported to the mainland. Perhaps some of them would pause to talk among themselves, or simply to gaze out over the placid surface of Lake Texcoco toward the mountains in the distance.

These were the women of Tenochtitlán (*teh-nōsh-tit-LAHN*), capital of the Aztec Empire and one of the most unusual cities of the world. Built on a group of islands within a lake in the Valley of Mexico, 8000 feet above sea level, Tenochtitlán was the center of a civilization that by 1500 was less than two centuries old. Its women worked diligently to keep the city clean, a critical task in a tropical metropolis surrounded by fungus-bearing water. They raised the children and maintained the households for their husbands, most of whom worked as farmers or artisans for eight months and devoted the remaining four to military combat on behalf of the empire. As farmers, the Aztecs cultivated a wide variety of nutritious crops; as artisans, they created quetzal feather mosaics of exceptional beauty; as warriors, they constructed a powerful state that awed and intimidated all other Amerinds who knew of its existence. Yet within a generation, the realm in which these Aztecs lived and worked was invaded and conquered, not by other Amerind peoples but by a foreign people from another hemisphere.

The Great Amerind Empires

18.1 Explain how the Great Amerind Empires differed from those of Europe and Asia.

In 1500 C.E., the Amerind civilizations were very new and very isolated. Their newness was due to the relative lateness of the Amerinds' transition from hunting and gathering to agriculture. Before the development of agricultural and urban economies, there had been no need for governments and states with the power to organize labor for public works, such as draining swamps and building walls around cities. All these processes had happened earlier in the river civilizations of Asia and Africa. Also delaying the development of Amerind social organization was the scarcity of large four-footed mammals that could be domesticated for meat and—more important to the economy—for work in pulling plows or heavy loads. These kinds of animals had lived in the Americas before humans arrived, but most had been hunted to extinction shortly thereafter. These and other factors meant that in 1500 early American societies were in earlier stages of development than those inhabiting the Eurasian landmass.

Amerind societies were also isolated compared with Eurasian societies, which had both suffered and benefited from extensive connections among cultures. Economic and technological advantages enjoyed by Europeans in 1500 had been copied or adapted from Persia, Greece, Carthage, Arabia, India, and China—societies that Amerinds did not know existed. European social and governing structures had been influenced by Greece, Rome, the Germanic invasions, and institutionalized Christianity. In contrast, the Aztec and Inca empires had developed in isolation, cut off not only from any knowledge of the older societies of the Eastern Hemisphere but also from each other.

Because of this isolation, Amerinds lacked immunity to Eurasian diseases, familiarity with Eurasian technology, and acquaintance with Eurasian governing structures.

Three Amerind civilizations, however, had evolved more rapidly than others, despite their isolation. They had created class systems that proved capable of technological innovation, including the construction of cities more extensive in scope and more refined in conveniences than most cities in Asia and Europe. The oldest of the three, the Maya culture of what are now Mexico and Guatemala, had achieved substantial complexity before 800. But a combination of undetermined circumstances had first weakened and then destroyed this civilization in the next few centuries. By 1500, millions of Maya lived in primitive conditions in the rain forests, their great cities long abandoned.

The other two cultures had achieved significant cultural complexity only one or two centuries before 1500. In central Mexico, the Aztec people organized themselves around a warrior elite, conquered neighboring tribes through intimidation or force, and built the spectacular city of Tenochtitlán to serve as their capital. Farther south, the Inca people of Peru pieced together an empire stretching thousands of miles from north to south, linked by an intricate network of roads and bridges crossing the Andes Mountains. They assimilated other ethnic groups using techniques like those practiced in earlier millennia by Persia and Rome.

The Aztec and Inca empires each considered itself the greatest on earth, a claim attributable at least in part to its complete lack of knowledge of comparable societies. Eurasian and African societies could learn from each other, but Aztecs and Inca never had that opportunity. Their newness and isolation constituted fatal disadvantages early in the sixteenth century, when European invaders suddenly arrived by sea.

The Aztec Empire

18.2 **Describe the main political, economic, and social structures of the Aztec Empire.**

According to the Aztecs' own creation story, they originated on an island called Aztlán (hence the name *Aztecs*) off the Pacific coast of Mexico but left there in 1111 to search for the land promised them by their most important god, Huitzilopochtli (*hwē-tsē-lō-PŌSH-tlē*), or Southern Hummingbird. By 1325 they had moved onto an island in Lake Texcoco (*tesh-KŌ-kō*), on which Huitzilopochtli told them they would find an eagle perched on a cactus and devouring a snake—the symbol in the center of the modern Mexican flag. The Aztecs, who called themselves Mexica (*mē-SHĒ-kah*), named the valley surrounding Lake Texcoco after themselves, calling it the Valley of Mexico. On the islands in the lake they built Tenochtitlán.

Tenochtitlán: City in the Lake

The Aztecs quickly recognized the advantages of building a city on islands. The lake was full of fish and birds to eat, and Aztecs used its waters to cultivate their crops. Instead of irrigating, they layered mud and lake plants to build large, latticework platforms, called **chinampas** (*chē-NAHM-pahs*), on which they planted their crops. Then they floated the entire structure on the surface of the lake. Nourished by the mud and plant matter, the roots of the crops sucked up the lake water and produced huge quantities of fruits, vegetables, and grains. Chinampas could be strung together to form rectangles of land on the lake, complete with intersecting waterways. With inexhaustible moisture and a tropical climate, conditions that permitted double-cropping, the chinampa system proved capable of sustaining a large population at high levels of nutrition.

What advantages and disadvantages did the Aztecs encounter after building their capital city in a lake?

An Aztec representation of the founding of Tenochtitlán in 1325 C.E.

Building a city in the middle of a lake carried with it two additional benefits. First, cargo could be moved by canoe, within the city on canals and between the city and the mainland. Since Mexico lacked wheeled carts (and the large animals required to pull them), water transport was quicker and less exhausting than packing loads on the backs of people. Second, the location provided valuable strategic protection for an assertive, ambitious people who made enemies easily. The city was connected to the shores by three causeways, each 25 to 30 feet wide, separated at intervals by drawbridges that could be raised to cut off the advance or retreat of hostile forces. To invade Tenochtitlán successfully, an enemy would need to construct a fleet of canoes on the lakeshore. The only other way to penetrate the city was to be invited in.

As a location for a city-state, therefore, Lake Texcoco was an unusual but not irrational choice. Nor were the Aztecs alone in their new surroundings: about a dozen other Amerind towns sprang up along the shoreline, and three of them extended into the lake. By 1500 there were some 50 cities in the Valley of Mexico.

Few cities anywhere in the world could compare with Tenochtitlán. Its center was dominated by a great double temple dedicated to Huitzilopochtli and Tlaloc (*TLAH-lock*), the god of rain. Its many canals were spanned by sturdy bridges. Compared with other cities of the time, it was immaculate: there was good drainage, sewage and garbage were hauled away in barges, and every day a crew of a thousand women swept down and washed public streets. Estimates of its population range from 80,000 to 250,000, but even at 80,000, it would have been one of the largest cities in the world. In 1500, Seville, Spain's most populous city, contained 40,000 people.

Exploitation and Human Sacrifice

How did the cosmic mission theory justify Aztec expansion while providing a mechanism of social control?

Tenochtitlán was the heart of one of the world's most oppressive realms. Following a succession of capable and aggressive leaders, the Aztecs established an empire in 1468 under Motecuzoma I (*mō-teh-koo-ZŌ-mah*), whose name was later corrupted into Spanish as Montezuma. Although lasting only half a century, this empire (Map 18.1) was hated profoundly by all neighboring tribes for its ruthlessness.

Aztec ferocity derived from a **cosmic mission theory** that justified a program of human sacrifice. According to this theory, the sun, source of all heat, light, and life, grows weary during its journey across the heavens. It must be fed a life-giving elixir found only in beating human hearts. For this purpose, human beings were sacrificed on a regular schedule, their hearts torn from their bodies by priests and offered to the sun while still beating. Failure to perform this essential ritual was believed to doom the entire world to perpetual darkness and extinction. Human sacrifice was practiced by other early Amerind cultures, but usually only on important ceremonial occasions or in dire emergencies, such as drought or earthquake. For the Aztecs, human sacrifice was a routine program that allowed elites to legitimize their position.

The cosmic mission theory was, in fact, a political and religious hoax devised by the ruling elite of the Aztec Empire. Warriors and priests both had a stake in it: warriors obtained prisoners of war for the slaughter, while priests sacrificed the victims in the proper manner. Both classes used the theory as a mechanism of social control, employing it to keep commoners subservient to the regime and to terrorize subject peoples. If ordinary Aztecs doubted its validity (and there is no reason to assume that they did), their doubt was never substantial enough to produce revolt. Other tribes were highly skeptical, however, particularly since they were expected to furnish the prisoners of war, but they could do little to alter the situation. This theory also provided a spiritual justification for the perpetual expansion of the Aztec Empire by conquest. Indeed, the Aztecs so terrified neighboring tribes that conquest was not always necessary to secure prisoners of war. The tribes themselves, out of self-preservation, sometimes selected the victims, who were then forced to participate in mock combats staged to make it appear as if they had been captured by Aztec warriors.

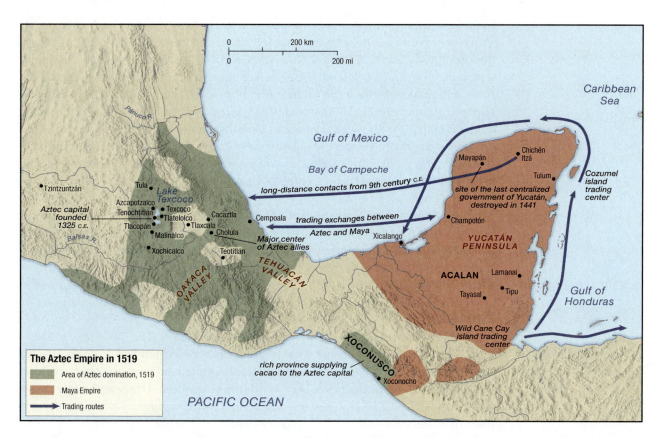

Map 18.1   THE AZTEC EMPIRE IN 1519   Notice the empire's location, west of the old Mayan city-states. The Aztecs were a subgroup of the Chichimec tribe of northern Mexico, and their empire represents an intrusion of the Chichimecs into the fringes of the Mayan homelands. Notice also the existence of connections between central Mexico and the Mayan homelands 300 years before the arrival of the Aztecs, who built trading relationships on preexisting networks. How would the compactness of central Mexico and the Yucatán Peninsula have contributed to contacts between Aztec and Maya?

Society and Culture

The Aztec Empire was founded on blood. But this obsession with human sacrifice did not prevent the Aztecs from developing a carefully stratified society with a standard of living that many throughout the world would have envied.

SOCIAL CLASSES AND GENDER ROLES   At the top of Aztec society was the ruling class, or *Tecuhtli* (*teh-COOT-lē*), drawn from the leading generals, high officials of Tenochtitlán, chiefs of outlying districts, judges in the capital, and priests. This class elected the emperor, a nonhereditary position. The emperor was almost always a distinguished warrior; only once was a priest elected, and even he had been a general, too. Thus, although sons of the Tecuhtli were nobles by right of birth, leadership in the empire was ultimately determined by success in warfare.

The lords of Mexico were wealthy men, but only because of their rank and obligations. Aztec society considered riches to be a result of increasing power and official expenses, not a method of obtaining that power. Priests lived in chilling austerity, and the leading generals and political officials spent money on everything and everyone except themselves. This meritocracy offered the chance for social mobility. Commoners could rise into the Tecuhtli through exceptional skill in combat, while nobles could descend to common status just as readily through incompetence or cowardice. And the empire paid a great deal of attention to the training of both its leaders and its workers: no Mexican child, whatever his or her rank or wealth, was denied an education.

The love of profit for its own sake that the nobles rejected was embraced by the *Pochteca* (*pōsh-TECK-ah*), the merchant caste. Utterly inbred, with marriage restricted

How did Aztec political, economic, and social structures demonstrate the complexity and sophistication of the Aztec Empire?

Human sacrifice.

to those within the caste and with fathers passing businesses on to their sons, the merchants spent their lives on the road selling manufactured goods and luxury items throughout Mexico and Central America. On their journeys they dispensed justice within their own ranks, defended themselves against bandits without the help of warriors, and prayed without the intercession of priests. They sold jewelry, household implements, and elegant mosaics made of quetzal feathers. The Aztec Empire relied on the Pochteca for its material needs and left them alone.

Below the Pochteca were the *Tolteca* (*tōl-TECK-ah*), a caste of artisans practicing trades such as goldsmith, jeweler, and quarryman. Here, too, skills remained within families. This caste had its own chiefs, who represented Tolteca interests within the highest councils of the empire.

Most Mexica were commoners, or *Macehualtin* (*MAH-sā-wahl-tēn*). Full citizens of the Aztec Empire, they enjoyed certain civil rights. Men could own land, send their children to school, share in the spoils of conquest, vote for local chiefs, and if they were intelligent and courageous, rise out of their class to become honored and wealthy. On the other hand, if a *macehual* did nothing to distinguish himself in the first years of his adult life, he was subject to weighty obligations, including communal labor and the payment of taxes (from which nobles were exempt).

At the bottom of the social structure were the *Tlatlacotin* (*TLA-tla-cō-tēn*), or slaves. They were owned by others but were housed, clothed, and fed like ordinary citizens. They could sell their labor in their spare time, accumulate savings, buy land or houses, or even buy slaves for their own service. Marriage between a slave and a free person was permitted, and all children of such unions were born free. Unlike the Atlantic trade that later enslaved Africans, slavery as practiced in the Aztec Empire was based not on race but on bad conduct. Enslavement was a punishment for certain crimes or for chronic indebtedness. It also served as a form of welfare: people who were unsuited by temperament to earning a living, who drank too much, or who were mentally or emotionally unstable could sell themselves into slavery in order to obtain food, clothing, and shelter. Giving up the rights and duties of freedom, they were able to survive.

While men in Aztec society engaged in the governance of the empire and its expansion through battle, women were almost completely confined to domestic roles. The remarkable cleanliness of Tenochtitlán and other Aztec cities was largely women's responsibility. Women also wove the elaborate costumes, cotton armor, and everyday clothing worn throughout central Mexico. Marriage and childbearing were expected and were welcomed with joyful festivities. An unmarried woman was an oddity attributable to some sort of mental or emotional defect. Some women served as physicians and accumulated extensive knowledge of herbal remedies and medical procedures.

LAW, HEALTH, AND DEATH IN AZTEC MEXICO   Governing this complex society was a highly effective legal system. There were no lawyers; judges examined defendants directly and used a wide variety of methods to determine the truth. Judges were drawn from the finest graduates of Aztec schools and took up their posts after years of success as warriors.

In keeping with a society that used the cosmic mission theory as a form of social control, punishment for offenses was harsh. Acts considered serious crimes, such as treason, homicide, espionage, adultery, and homosexuality, were punishable by death, a sentence that was carried out immediately. Minor crimes such as theft were punishable by slavery or mutilation. A judge found to have delivered a false verdict based on bribes or favoritism would be executed. No citizens could take the law into their own hands; nor was there any need to do so, since the administration of justice was so swift and severe. The Aztec Empire wanted to control its people, not rehabilitate them, and it succeeded.

Despite its harshness, Aztec life had its advantages. People bathed several times a week, and Aztec medical practices were advanced for their era. Healers knew how to set broken bones and treat dental cavities. Occasionally they even performed brain surgery. Like their medical counterparts elsewhere, they did not understand the causes of diseases, but they developed effective cures and medicines, many of which are still used in Mexico today.

But no medicine, however effective, could stave off death indefinitely, especially in a society so intent on hurrying it along through war and sacrifice. When the end arrived, all Aztecs understood that it was ordained by fate, part of an unavoidable pattern of birth, death, and afterlife. Warriors who fell in battle were reborn as colorful hummingbirds; women who died in childbirth were transformed into goddesses. The hummingbirds escorted the sun from its rising to its zenith, while the goddesses accompanied it from its zenith to its setting. Farmers who were struck by lightning or drowned (the latter a frequent occurrence in a city built in the midst of a lake) were led by Tlaloc, the god of rain and water, to a paradise of flowers, springs, and gardens. These beliefs mirrored the cycles of nature itself: the sun comes up each morning after passing the night in the Underworld; corn dies in autumn and is reborn in spring; the luxuriant wild plants of Mexico do the same.

For those unfortunates who died an ordinary, undistinguished death, the outlook was grim. Their destination was Mictlan (*MICK-tlahn*), the Underworld, presided over by the god and goddess of the dead. This ghoulish couple ruled a cold, dark realm of dust and bones, seated on thrones surrounded by spiders and owls. The prospect of this afterlife made death in battle welcome rather than something to be feared. Sacrificial victims, whose beating hearts nourished the sun, became one with it and lived forever as part of the source of heat and light that made life on earth possible.

The Aztec goddess Coatlicue.

The Inca Empire

18.3 **Describe the main political, economic, and social structures of the Inca Empire.**

The Inca civilization of western South America developed even later than Aztec society. Covering a much larger range of territory than Aztec Mexico, the Inca Empire extended from what is today northern Ecuador into central Chile, some 3000 miles from north to south. It also differed from the Aztec realm in many other ways since, although these two empires existed at the same time in the same hemisphere, the barriers to travel between them were so great that they developed in isolation from one another.

A Unified Empire

The Inca creation story asserts that the Inca people emerged around the year 1200 from three caves 18 miles southeast of the city of Cuzco (*COOZ-kō*), Peru. Other Amerind peoples lived in the region, including the Huari, the Chanca, and the Chimú. The Inca did not at first challenge any of them, gradually building Cuzco while developing political and social institutions. During this time the Inca were apparently ruled by seven legendary emperors, about whom nothing can be known with certainty. But the eighth ruler, Viracocha (*vē-rah-KŌ-chah*) Inca, laid the foundations of an empire. Between 1400 and 1438, he expanded Inca control over a 25-mile radius from Cuzco, reaching as far south as Lake Titicaca (*tih-tē-KAH-kah*) (Map 18.2).

Viracocha was followed by two remarkable rulers who enlarged the small Inca domain into one of the world's biggest empires. Pachacuti (*pah-chah-COO-tē*), who ruled from 1438 to 1471, gave the realm its official name, **Tahuantin-Suyu** (*tah-wahn-tin SOO-yoo*), the Empire of the Four Quarters. He also made his native language, Quechua (*KEH-chwah*), the language of official business and organized the administrative structure of what was becoming a very large state. By the time of his death in 1471, the Inca ruled all of present-day Peru. Then Topa Inca Yupanqui (*TŌ-pah IN-kah yoo-PAHN-kwē*),

How did the Inca use mitima to create a unified empire?

Map 18.2   THE INCA EMPIRE, 1438–1525 The Inca Empire of Tahuantin-Suyu was carved out of the Andes Mountains between the highlands of Quito and the Atacama Desert. Note the empire's shape, dictated by Andean geography: it was 3000 miles north to south at its longest point, but only 400 miles east to west at its widest. The Aztec Empire enjoyed the advantage of compactness (Map 18.1), while the Inca Empire struggled successfully with geographic disadvantages. How did the Inca overcome those disadvantages?

In what ways did Inca social structure organize an empire with few social classes?

who ruled from 1471 to 1493, extended the empire to the north and south, defeating the Chimú kingdom in Ecuador and conquering the northern half of Chile. Together, given the territory they amassed, he and Pachacuti are ranked with Alexander the Great and Genghis Khan among history's great empire-builders.

The Inca conquered in an unusual way, announcing their attacks in advance and never using force except when persuasion failed. Once defeated, a conquered population was assimilated into the empire through the process of **mitima** (*mē-TĒ-mah*), or resettlement and integration. Within a generation, families resettled in Inca towns had lost their cultural identities and become Inca, a transition made smoother by the complete absence of discrimination against them.

In 1493 a new ruler, Huayna Capac (*HWAH-nah KĀ-pack*), consolidated Inca gains and focused on the administration of the empire. Further territorial advance was blocked—to the east by the dense rain forests of the eastern slopes of the Andes, to the south by the Mapuche (*mah-POO-chā*) Amerinds, warlike and hostile to outsiders. Still, at the beginning of the sixteenth century the Inca Empire, just one hundred years old, encompassed a great expanse of land and a great many peoples, much like ancient Rome and the concurrent Ottoman Empire.

Society and Economy

Inca society contained few distinct social classes. Atop its political pyramid stood the emperor, called the **Sapa** (*SAH-pah*) **Inca**, a man who claimed to rule by divine right because of his direct descent from the sun god, Inti (*ĒN-tē*). He was worshipped as divine during his lifetime; after death he was carefully embalmed and mummified and became a god like his ancestor. Because he claimed divinity, the Sapa Inca was compelled to keep the royal line pure. He could not defile it through marriage to a mortal, so he always chose one of his full sisters as his principal wife. From among her sons, he chose his heir. The practice usually brought the most competent son to power but also set brothers against one another. When the Sapa Inca died suddenly without designating a successor, a brutal power struggle followed.

The Sapa Inca's authority was so great that some of it actually survived him. After death, the emperor's body was embalmed with fragrant resins and dried in the sun in the arid highlands around Cuzco. Then his mummy was enshrined in one of the palaces in which he had lived. Servants attended the mummies of each successive Sapa Inca, deciding when to offer him food and drink, occasionally taking one mummy to visit another or to visit living people in their homes. On great ceremonial occasions, or if the empire faced challenges or dangers, all the mummies would be assembled in the great squares of Cuzco. People would pay them homage, and the ruling Sapa Inca would formally consult them, asking their advice on affairs of state. Thus, the emperors were revered after death as living spirits equal to most of the other gods of the empire.

Below the Sapa Inca, the empire was governed by a two-class nobility, the Inca Caste and the Curacas (*coo-RAH-kahz*). The Inca Caste was composed of blood relatives of the Sapa Inca, usually numbering several hundred people. Curacas were all other governmental officials and their families. Both components of the nobility were exempt from taxes and were supported by produce from government-owned fields tilled by commoners. Sons of the nobility were the only Inca subjects to be educated, in contrast to the Aztec practice of universal education for boys and girls. Since there was no written language, instruction was entirely oral.

Beneath the Sapa Inca and the nobility, all were commoners and all were free; slavery was unheard of in Tahuantin-Suyu. Commoners provided the labor for public works. Since no money existed and payments in kind were unknown, commoners paid taxes through labor service. This duty furnished recruits for the army, laborers in mines and on public works, and messengers who traveled the remarkable system of imperial roads.

Most commoners were farmers, and Inca agriculture was highly advanced, benefiting from centuries of development by earlier societies in the region, and supported by extensive irrigation. Peasants grew a wide variety of crops, most significantly the potato, which they had developed through selective breeding from a hard, unappetizing nut-like root into one of the world's most nutritious foods. Later, after the Spanish conquest of Peru, the potato was taken to Europe, where it became the staple crop of areas such as Ireland and Poland and was eventually grown almost everywhere.

In the Inca Empire, as in Aztec Mexico, most men spent their days farming, while most women, who played exclusively domestic roles, spent their days doing farm chores, housework, and cooking. Married life was the normal state, and the raising of children was considered woman's sacred task. Sexual intercourse before marriage for both genders was relatively common and not frowned upon, although some women selected for highly favored positions at Inca religious shrines remained virginal for life. These virgins wove the elaborate garments worn by Inca idols, swept and beautified the shrines, and were forbidden to speak to men.

A quipu.

Adaptation to the Andes

The Inca ingeniously adapted to their physical environment to keep the empire connected. Their extensive network of roads and bridges allowed them to carry a message from one end of the empire to the other in about 12 days. Since the Sapa Inca ruled from the centrally located capital of Cuzco, he rarely had to wait more than six days for the latest news from outlying areas. The roads were smoothly paved with great blocks of stone and lined with retaining walls. Even in the narrowest mountain passes, a dozen men could walk along them side by side. Across the dizzying gorges formed by swiftly flowing Andean rivers, the Inca threw suspension bridges made of thick fibers and secured at each end by stone pylons. In a kind of postal system, a succession of sure-footed runners traveled these roads and bridges. The messages they carried, in the absence of writing, were composed of a series of knots in cords dangling from a piece of wood called a **quipu** (*KĒ-pooh*).

Physically, the Inca had evolved over the years to meet the demands of their harsh environment. To handle the stress caused by the lack of adequate oxygen at high elevations, their lung capacity was 40 percent greater than that of sea-level dwellers, with much denser capillary beds. Their bodies also contained 25 percent more blood of very high viscosity, with a far greater number of oxygen-carrying red corpuscles. To handle that sort of load, their hearts were enlarged by 40 percent, and their bodies tended to be short and compact, with low centers of gravity. These characteristics are still found today in Andean peoples.

Governance and Religion

Politically, Tahuantin-Suyu was the product of centuries of South American cultural development. Before the Inca became the dominant force in Peruvian life, Peru had experienced a long tradition of centralized political control that made possible extensive public works, road-building, and intervalley irrigation systems. Ceramics and metallurgy were mastered, and commercial relations linked the farthest reaches of the Pacific coast. On this foundation the Inca built new concepts of military organization, colonization, and total state control. Their well-trained ruling class possessed the foresight and skill needed to manage so extensive an empire.

How did the Inca adapt to their challenging environment?

How did Inca governance and religion help unify the empire?

Inca buildings in the former imperial capital of Cuzco. Stones were fit together with such precision that mortar was unnecessary.

The Inca Empire was divided into four provinces (the "four quarters"), each ruled by a governor from the noble Inca Caste. Each significant city was ruled by a lieutenant who reported directly to the provincial governor. Below these leaders were hereditary governing positions filled by Curacas. These local officials, the basic governing personnel of the empire, handled matters such as taxation, public works, minor crimes, complaints, and institutions such as the imperial mass marriage, announced periodically by the Sapa Inca in order to ensure a ready supply of children for the empire. During this ceremony, all single men and women would line up opposite each other, after which the Curacas assigned mates on the basis of physical condition. For obvious reasons, the day before the imperial mass marriage was usually filled with weddings.

Tahuantin-Suyu's division into four provinces somewhat reduced the imperial power of the Sapa Inca. Although his power was theoretically absolute, in practice it was delegated to many governors and local officials.

These men were given considerable latitude in the interpretation and execution of imperial commands, provided that their loyalty was beyond dispute. To guarantee that loyalty, the Sapa Inca occasionally sent from Cuzco a special official known as the *Tocoyricoc* (*tō-COY-rē-cōke*), or "he who sees all." This official was actually an informer charged with reporting on the loyalty and competence of the governor and on the general state of affairs within the province. He was usually a close relative of the Sapa Inca, fearless and incorruptible, and the ever-present possibility of his arrival kept administrators honest.

Inca religion, like Aztec religion, was founded on sun worship. It combined nature worship and magic, all centered on Inti, the sun god. Behind the sun, and indeed behind all things, stood Viracocha, Creator of the Universe, but he was invisible to men and women, while Inti appeared in the heavens every day. The Inca worshipped other deities, too, such as the Storm God. Like ancient Persians and Romans, they tolerated the gods of those they conquered, insisting only on a place of honor for Inti in rites and festivals. Tolerance was essential to the practice of mitima.

Inca gods were believed to be pleased by sacrifice, usually of food, coca leaves (later to become the base for cocaine), and animals. In serious emergencies, such as drought or earthquake, or on important occasions, a pure white llama or a beautiful child might be killed to win the gods' favor. But the Inca never developed any equivalent of the Aztec Empire's "cosmic mission theory" to justify human sacrifice.

Aztec and Inca on the Eve of Invasion

18.4 Discuss the features of the Great Amerind Empires that handicapped them in their conflicts with Europeans.

For all their differences, the Aztec and Inca empires had in common certain institutions that affected their encounters with Europeans. First, authority resided in an emperor whose power was absolute. No assemblies or councils existed to restrict his decisions, and unquestioning obedience to the emperor was demanded. Theoretically the emperor could respond quickly to emergencies, and at the head of an army of dedicated warriors, he would be difficult to defeat. But if either empire were ever defeated, the stress on unquestioning obedience to leaders would make it easier for the conqueror to rule. Unconditional obedience was readily transferable from one set of masters to another.

Second, the youth and isolation of the Aztec and Inca empires handicapped them in the clash of civilizations that began with the European invasions. The invaders came from societies whose extensive intercultural contacts had furnished them with methods, technologies, animals, and immunities unknown in the Americas. It was not a fair contest. The early American civilizations, remarkably rich in their cultural development in comparison with other cultures in the hemisphere, were about to meet their match. No one can say how the Aztec and Inca societies, so highly developed in comparison with other cultures in the Western Hemisphere, might have evolved had Europeans never arrived.

The Invasion and Conquest of Mexico

18.5 **Describe the Spanish invasion of the Aztec Empire and account for the Spanish victory.**

Montezuma II (1502–1520), emperor when the Spanish arrived, was the first priest to rule the Aztec Empire. Thirty-four when elected, he was a valiant warrior as well as a pious man. He was fascinated by magic and omens and by 1519 had come to prefer contemplation and diplomacy to action. These priestly tendencies did not, however, make him gentle: he terrified both his court and the general public and was the most feared ruler in the history of Tenochtitlán. His commitment to consolidating his empire rather than continuing to expand it was grounded not in weakness but in realistic calculation.

Unlike the Inca, the Aztecs had never attempted to integrate conquered peoples into their culture. Their empire was held together by coercion and fear, not by any form of assimilation that might have developed loyalty in the defeated. Therefore, it was not surprising that during the reign of Montezuma II two significant regional powers challenged the supremacy of Tenochtitlán. In the west, the Tarascan (*tah-RAHS-cahn*) Empire united several ethnic groups hostile to Aztec expansion into a small but heavily fortified realm defended by skilled archers. In the east, the **Tlaxcallan** (*tlash-CAHL-lahn*) **Confederacy** knitted together several city-states that spoke Nahuatl (*na-WHA-tl*), the language spoken by the Aztecs and some of their neighbors, into a potent alliance that could have badly injured the Aztec Empire in an all-out war. Cautiously, Montezuma II encircled both sets of enemies as part of a long-range strategy that would yield results in decades rather than years. By 1519 the Aztecs had made substantial progress on both fronts, despite a persistent series of omens that worried their ruling elite and left the emperor perplexed.

The Arrival of the Spaniards

In 1517 disturbing events took place in Mayan territory well east of Tenochtitlán. Bearded men with white skin, riding in what appeared to be mountains floating on the sea, came ashore on the Yucatán Peninsula. More such events took place the following year, accompanied by omens in Tenochtitlán itself. A comet streaked across the sky at midday, temples burned for no apparent reason, and an invisible wailing woman cried out every night. These events were mysterious and unsettling to a people accustomed to searching for messages from the gods. As the Aztecs eventually learned, the strangers in floating mountains were Spaniards in sailing ships following those who had first come to the Caribbean 25 years before, looking for a sea route from Europe to Asia.

The Spaniards who came in 1517, however, were no longer looking for Asia; instead, they were inspired by tales of gold and glory to be found in Mexico itself. Their leader, Hernán Cortés, was an ambitious Spanish lawyer who left Spain to seek his fortune in the Caribbean. In 1519 he accepted a commission from the governor of Cuba to lead an expedition to Mexico to determine the location and strength of a large and reportedly fabulously wealthy empire. He sailed for Mexico with 550 men, including a number of Africans and Cuban Amerinds, and 16 horses.

In the early spring of 1519, as Cortés arrived in Mexico, reports reaching Montezuma became more precise and factual. From the Gulf of Mexico, peasants reported sighting white men catching fish with nets and rods. That summer news

How did the Aztecs react to the arrival of the Spaniards?

Dona Marina and Cortes.

arrived that the strangers were moving inland. Aztec officials met them and spoke with them through a 15-year-old Mayan girl whom the Spaniards had baptized Marina and who spoke both Nahuatl and Spanish. The Spaniards rode on huge animals and carried and dragged long-barreled sticks that could be made to explode, discharging fire and noise. At this point the ruling elite began to consider the possibility that these people, or at least their leaders, might be gods.

Aztec legend stated that Toltec god-king Quetzalcóatl (*kwet-zahl-KŌ-ah-tul*), expelled from Tula (Chapter 5), had vowed to return one day from his eastern exile and reclaim Mexico for himself. He and his forces would appear in boats in the guise of light-skinned men. Given the apparently supernatural capabilities of these strangers' boats, animals, and weapons, the possibility that Quetzalcóatl was returning could not be ruled out. Even if they were mere mortals, their arrival could not be prevented: their boats could land anywhere without warning, and their weapons seemed deadly. Under such unprecedented circumstances, watchful waiting seemed the only sensible course.

The Spaniards insisted on meeting with Montezuma. In response, the emperor sent them more than a hundred porters carrying luxurious gifts normally sacrificed to gods. Included with these presents was Montezuma's order that the Spaniards remain in the east and advance no farther inland. The Aztec emperor was trying either to gain favor with a vengeful god or to deal with powerful invaders in a way that would ensure the survival of Aztec power. In either case, the empire was clearly in danger.

Cortés knew nothing of the legend of Quetzalcóatl, but upon listening to Marina's translations and advice, he realized that Montezuma feared him. He also interpreted the emperor's gifts as an offer of vassalage and therefore a sign of weakness. In Europe, vassalage involved an oath of personal loyalty that gave the lord contractual rights over the actions of the vassal. In Mesoamerica, however, vassalage involved the payment of tribute in return for being left alone. This was a very significant distinction. By interpreting Montezuma's actions in a European context, Cortés seriously underestimated the power of the empire he would encounter. He ignored Montezuma's instructions, accepted the gifts, and pressed on.

Encounter Between Aztecs and Spaniards

What might explain Montezuma's strange behavior toward the Spaniards?

Cortés moved his forces west and concluded alliances with peoples such as the Totonacs (*tō-TŌ-nacks*) and Tlaxcaltecs (*tlocks-CAHL-tecks*), who paid tribute to the Aztec Empire. These Amerinds believed Cortés' promises of liberation from Aztec dominance and sent thousands of warriors to accompany the Spaniards inland. In Tenochtitlán, men were still engaged in the harvest; otherwise, Montezuma would have had hundreds of thousands of warriors ready to defend the empire. Instead, Montezuma arranged for the Spaniards to be escorted into the city, where, without their allies, they would be far more vulnerable.

Nothing had prepared the Spaniards for what they saw on November 8. The road to Tenochtitlán was straight, 11,500 feet above sea level, flanked by two immense active volcanoes; the altitude, solitude, and strangeness of it all began to unnerve the Spaniards. But even this impression paled when compared with the sight of the city itself. Not only was it spectacularly beautiful, it was colossal, with at least 80,000 inhabitants, the capital of an empire of more than a million people. Cortés suddenly realized the magnitude of his miscalculation. He had dismissed as exaggerations Amerind stories of the size and glory of Tenochtitlán, interpreting them in the contexts of his familiarity with Europe and of the modest size of the Mexican towns he had encountered thus far. Now he stood before an Amerind metropolis significantly larger than anything he had imagined, at the head of an army of a few hundred men. The success of his mission and the lives of his men hung by threads.

A 1524 map of Tenochtitlán.

Operating in Cortés' favor, however, was Montezuma's behavior. Meeting the Spaniards face-to-face must have convinced the emperor that they were men, not gods. But even after they entered the capital, in the narrow streets where they could have been trapped, the emperor publicly embraced Cortés and continued to lavish gifts upon him. In the next months, the Aztec military elite pressed for the destruction of the strangers, but Montezuma's subservience prevented any such action. Cortés recognized that he held the advantage, and he soon placed the emperor under a form of house arrest in his own palace.

Montezuma's acceptance of this treatment remains inadequately explained. Some historians assert that he continued to believe that Cortés was divine, but the Spaniards did not behave like servants of a Mexican god. They were horrified at the practice of human sacrifice, especially the Aztec custom of presenting their guests with delicious food liberally sprinkled with human blood. They smashed images of Aztec gods and generally behaved in a manner indicating their disgust with Mexican culture. This was a strange way for gods to behave. Other historians speculate that Montezuma clung to whatever measure of power he could still exercise while hoping that events would turn out in his favor. Had he refused to cooperate with the Spaniards, he would have been taken by force, the imperial elite would have split among potential successors, and the Aztec Empire would be leaderless in its hour of maximum danger. This explanation is more likely than that he considered Cortés to be Quetzalcóatl.

But if Montezuma hoped to preserve his authority by cooperating with the Spaniards, he was soon disappointed. His subservience to Cortés eroded his support among both elites and commoners. It vanished completely in May 1520 when the Aztecs took the offensive at last. They surrounded the Spaniards in central Tenochtitlán, and Cortés proved unable to negotiate his way out of the city. Cortés then ordered Montezuma to direct the Aztecs to stop fighting. Cortés did not realize that the nobility now doubted the emperor's judgment and was prepared to fight the invaders. Montezuma tried anyway but was killed as he attempted to address Aztec forces from the roof of a palace, apparently by a rock thrown by one of his own people.

The End of the Aztec Empire

What impact did smallpox have on Aztec ability to resist the Spaniards?

Denied food and water, under assault from every side, the Spaniards broke out of Tenochtitlán at midnight on June 30, 1520, during a heavy downpour. Some were killed by Aztecs attacking from canoes, but Cortés escaped with most of his men. The Spaniards fought their way through the neighboring hostile regions to Tlaxcaltec lands, which gave them an opportunity to regroup.

Aztec forces did not launch a full-scale attack against the retreating invaders, in part because their armies were not at full strength due to agricultural duties, but primarily because of political instability. During the fighting in Tenochtitlán, the imperial elite replaced Montezuma with his younger brother Cuitlahuac (*quit-LAH-wock*), who had argued from the first that the invaders must be killed. But within three months, Cuitlahuac was dead of smallpox. An infected Spanish soldier carried the disease, and because the peoples of the Western Hemisphere had never been exposed to European diseases and had no immunity to them, this smallpox outbreak killed more than a third of the population of central Mexico in less than a year.

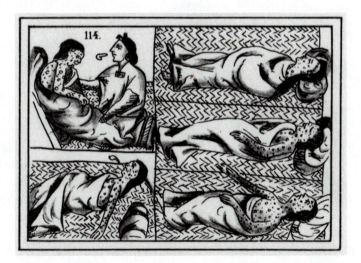

Smallpox victims.

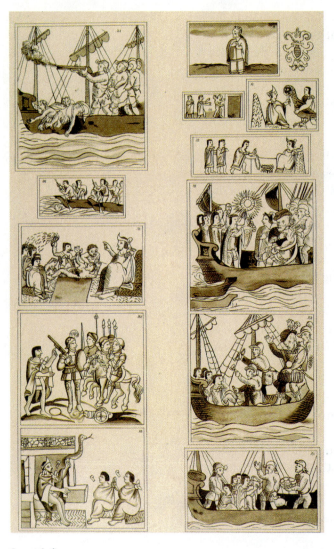

Spanish firepower.

Smallpox is a disease that kills through high fever, dehydration, and debilitation. The dying suffer terribly, and survivors are often disfigured by scarring from pustules. The Aztecs concluded that this unknown plague was either a sign of the wrath of their gods or a punishment sent by the gods of the Spaniards. Certainly, since the strangers did not suffer from the disease (having survived it in childhood, they had immunity), their gods were protecting them. In any case, to the Aztecs the epidemic clearly demonstrated Spanish superiority. It also, of course, killed many warriors and made others unfit for battle.

In February 1521, however, Cuauhtemoc (*kwow-TĀ-mock*), the son of a former emperor, succeeded Cuitlahuac and rallied his forces to attack the Spaniards. The Aztecs fought in closely packed ranks, using archery, spears, and swords with edges of polished obsidian. The Spaniards countered with cannon, muskets, and swords fashioned from Toledo steel. Their metal armor was clearly superior to Aztec armor made of cotton, and their horses terrified Aztec foot soldiers.

Spanish firearms killed 25 Aztecs for every Spaniard killed by the Aztecs, but with more than 100,000 warriors in his armies, Cuauhtemoc's forces could sustain such losses. The Aztecs won a number of engagements and sacrificed captured Spaniards, but in late July Cortés received reinforcements from Cuba. The Aztecs' desperate subjects, now believing that the Spaniards would win, flocked to their ranks by the tens of thousands.

Cuauhtemoc requested peace talks in early August, seeking to learn how much tribute the Spaniards would demand as the price of surrender. But it quickly became apparent that Cortés was interested in total victory, not in turning the Aztecs into vassals of the Spanish Empire. Trapped in the midst of the lake, the Aztecs fought to the end. They finally surrendered the ruins of Tenochtitlán on August 13, 1521. The Spaniards took possession of the city and buried the dead. The most powerful empire in the history of Mesoamerica had been destroyed (see "Two Elegies on the Fall of the City of Tenochtitlán").

Reasons for the Spanish Victory

What factors account for Spain's victory over the Aztec Empire?

Spain's victory in this epic confrontation of European and Mesoamerican civilizations can be explained by several factors, listed from least to most important. First, the Toltec legend of Quetzalcóatl distracted and confused the Aztecs before Cortés entered Tenochtitlán. Second, the Spaniards arrived in early November, when many warriors were busy with the harvest. Third, although each side misinterpreted the actions and motives of the other, Aztec misinterpretations proved the more serious and weakened their resistance. Fourth, Cortés proved a much better leader than the indecisive Montezuma. Fifth, smallpox weakened the Aztec population and nearly eliminated its elite while having no effect on the Spaniards. As it also killed most of the political elite of the Spaniards' native allies, it gave Cortés the opportunity to name loyal commanders in their place. Sixth, Spanish military technology was clearly superior and, together with European tactical insights, gave the invaders a significant, although not decisive, advantage.

Seventh, and overriding them all, was the Aztec policy of enslaving, persecuting, and sacrificing the people they conquered. Had the Aztecs assimilated those they

Document 18.1   Two Elegies on the Fall of the City of Tenochtitlán

Immediately after the fall of Tenochtitlán to the Spaniards, the surviving Aztecs reacted with shock and grief. Both emotions are vividly captured in these excerpts from two elegies, or memorial poems, written by survivors.

FIRST ELEGY

Broken spears lie in the road;
we have torn our hair in our grief.
The houses are roofless now, and their walls
are red with blood.
Worms are swarming in the streets and plazas,
and the walls are splattered with gore.
The water has turned red, as if it were dyed,
and when we drink it,
it has the taste of brine.
We have pounded our hands in despair
against the adobe walls,
for our inheritance, our city, is lost and dead.
The shields of our warriors were its defense,
but they could not save it.

SECOND ELEGY

Our cries of grief rise up
and our tears rain down . . .
The Aztecs are fleeing across the lake;
they are running away like women.
How can we save our homes, my people?
The Aztecs are deserting the city:
the city is in flames, and all
is darkness and destruction.
Weep, my people:
know that with these disasters
we have lost the Mexican nation.
The water has turned bitter,
our food is bitter!
These are the acts of the Giver of Life.

SOURCE: From *The Broken Spears* by Miguel Leon-Portilla Copyright © 1962, 1990 by Miguel Leon-Portilla Expanded and Updated Edition © 1992 by Miguel Leon-Portilla. Reprinted by permission of Beacon Press, Boston.

defeated, Cortés would never have been able to enlist more than 100,000 Amerind warriors as his allies, and without them he could never have conquered the Aztec Empire.

The Invasion and Conquest of Peru

18.6 **Describe the Spanish invasion of the Inca Empire and account for the Spanish victory.**

The fall of Tenochtitlán, a momentous event in Mexico, passed unnoticed in Peru. The Inca, unaware of Mesoamerican civilizations, would have been more surprised by news of the existence of the Aztecs than by their defeat.

Upheavals Among the Inca

Why was the Inca Empire in disarray when the Spanish arrived?

Huayna Capac, who became Sapa Inca in 1493, at first concentrated on consolidating his empire. Then in the early 1520s, he began to extend Inca control into northern Ecuador. While fighting there, he received word that a raiding party of Amerinds had crossed into present-day Bolivia in search of tools and jewelry. Huayna Capac sent a detachment of soldiers to drive the raiders back into what is now northern Argentina and fortify the frontier. He did not know that their war leader was a Portuguese adventurer named Aleixo (*ah-LĀ-shō*) García. Had he known, he would not have understood what the arrival of Europeans signified.

The Sapa Inca continued his campaign in Ecuador. Several months later, in 1526, he received terrifying news: an unknown plague was sweeping through Cuzco, killing strong and weak alike. By forced marches he returned to his capital and soon fell ill himself. The plague, the symptoms of which suggest smallpox, may have been introduced into Tahuantin-Suyu by merchants from Colombia, who had been exposed to Europeans, or by soldiers fighting the raiders from Argentina, who had taken in Europeans like García. Whatever its source, it killed the Sapa Inca and crippled his empire.

Before he died, Huayna Capac had time to consider two matters of supreme importance. First was a series of disturbing reports from the coast. Bearded men were floating southward on the waves, riding in a house of gleaming white. Huayna Capac believed that these visitors, together with the unexplained plague, foretold great trouble for the empire. Second, he changed his mind about which son should succeed him. His principal wife being childless, he had originally designated Huascar (*WHASS-car*), a son by one of his other wives, as his successor. But when the fever overtook him, Huayna Capac selected another son, Ninan Cuyochi (*NĒ-nahn coo-YŌ-chē*). The Sapa Inca soon died, and a few days later Ninan Cuyochi died as well. Huascar now claimed the throne, but the fact that his dying father had passed him over emboldened yet another brother, Atahuallpa (*ah-tah-WHALL-pah*), to contest his right to rule. Huascar seized power in Cuzco, while Atahuallpa did the same in Quito, the empire's second largest city. Tahuantin-Suyu descended into civil war.

Huascar was tactless, willful, and immature, and he alienated so many in Cuzco that the empire's capital gradually lost the will to defend him. Atahuallpa, by contrast, earned the allegiance of the two foremost war chiefs of the realm and conducted himself in battle with dignity and courage. The rugged terrain ensured a long, difficult struggle, but when conflict ended early in 1532 the empire was in the hands of Atahuallpa. One year earlier he had first learned of a landing by Spaniards, who followed the orders of an adventurer named Francisco Pizarro (*pē-ZAH-rō*). Pizarro had set sail from Panama in 1531 with about 180 men to conquer what they had heard was a rich land to the south.

Encounter Between Inca and Spaniards

When Pizarro's forces reached the Inca city of Tumbez, they seized it and learned at once that the Inca Empire had been torn by civil war for four years. The Spaniards, unlike the Inca, understood clearly what smallpox was and knew they had little to fear from it. They also understood that a physically weakened population distracted by internal turmoil was exactly what Cortés had encountered and conquered in Mexico in 1521.

Atahuallpa reacted to the seizure of Tumbez with a mixture of caution and interest. He concluded, incorrectly, that the newcomers were interested in taking sides in the civil war; if so, they might be worth meeting. After he captured Huascar and ended the fighting, he sought information concerning the invaders.

Unlike the Aztecs, the Inca had no Quetzalcóatl legend to distract them, and the fact that several Spaniards had been killed at Tumbez indicated that they were not gods but humans. The Sapa Inca sent an envoy to assess the situation. This man reported that Pizarro had landed with a very small number of men, that his horses were nothing more than large dogs, that his soldiers lacked fighting spirit, and that they could be defeated with two hundred warriors. Now feeling that he could easily rid his domain of these outsiders, Atahuallpa sent them several virgins, escorted by a war chief who promised them silver and gold if they agreed to return home.

In the eyes of the Inca, Pizarro reacted strangely. He accepted the women but declined to leave, marching inland instead. At Tumbez he killed the governor and other high officials, replacing them with Inca who swore loyalty to him. Yet he continually sent messages to Atahuallpa acknowledging the latter's rights as ruler of Tahuantin-Suyu. The Sapa Inca sent word to Pizarro of his recent victory over Huascar

How did the Inca reaction to the invasion differ from the Spanish reaction to the opportunities they encountered?

and pointed out that the visitors were far from home in a foreign and hostile land. Still, the Spaniards continued inland by a route leading to the provincial city of Cajamarca (*kah-yah-MAR-kah*), populated by several thousand Inca and guarded by a large fortress. Pizarro hoped to capture or kill the Sapa Inca and take over the Inca Empire without engaging in a long military campaign like the one Cortés had waged against the Aztecs.

Cajamarca and the End of the Inca Empire

Atahuallpa's attitude and tone differed substantially from Montezuma's approach to Cortés in Mexico. The Sapa Inca was no less confused about the Spaniards' intentions than Montezuma had been, and he held a much lower estimation of their military potential. Still, the Spaniards might be useful as allies in pacifying the areas previously held by Huascar, and their recognition of his authority suggested that they could become his vassals and eventually be assimilated through mitima. In any event, they could not be allowed to march around the countryside unsupervised. Atahuallpa resolved to go to Cajamarca (Map 18.2) and see them for himself.

Atahuallpa arrived ahead of the Spaniards, residing at a compound a short distance from the city. On November 15, 1532, the Spanish entered Cajamarca. The Sapa Inca and his entourage entered the city the following afternoon, as two thousand Inca swept the road before him. Carried on a litter, he was greeted by a single black-robed Spanish priest, who directed him to submit to two men called Jesus Christ and the king of Spain. Declaring that there was only one god in the heavens and that all Inca idols were to be destroyed, the priest presented Atahuallpa with a small black book of Christian devotions. The emperor examined it curiously, but since no one in a culture lacking writing could interpret the symbols on its pages (or even realize that they were intended to be read), he assumed the book was a flimsy idol and threw it on the ground. The priest then retrieved it and fled toward one of the houses surrounding the square, calling out in Spanish.

Atahuallpa instructed his entourage to punish the Spaniards. But musket fire burst forth from the houses, and great numbers of Spaniards, some on horses but most on foot, poured into the square. The perplexed Inca elite stood transfixed until the Spaniards fell upon them with swords and began cutting off their arms and heads. Then the panicked survivors tried to escape, but the Spaniards killed freely, as none of the Inca in the imperial entourage were armed. After the Inca guarding his litter were killed to the last man, Atahuallpa was taken prisoner. Learning what was happening in Cajamarca, thousands of armed Inca warriors outside the city, who could certainly have intervened, fled in terror (see "An Inca Account of the Conquest of Peru").

Having learned from his envoys that the Spaniards lusted for gold and silver, Atahuallpa offered at once to pay a huge ransom for his freedom. Pizarro demanded that two large rooms be completely filled with precious objects, one room with silver and the other with gold. He was soon presented with an amazing treasure: 26,000 pounds of pure silver and 13,420 pounds of 22-carat gold. To make this plunder portable, the Spaniards melted down priceless Inca artworks of great beauty and value, turning them into bars of gold and silver. But Atahuallpa had erred in assuming that he could trust Pizarro. Once the ransom was paid, the Sapa Inca was tried on charges of raising armies to overthrow Spanish rule, murdering his brother Huascar, and marrying his own sister. He was strangled in 1533.

In deciding to kill the Sapa Inca, Pizarro had reasoned treacherously but well. The Inca Caste, after so many years of infighting, was profoundly divided. Civil war, smallpox, and the Cajamarca ambush had killed most of the experienced leaders of the empire. By 1535 the conquest was complete. The Inca Empire offered no significant resistance.

What happened at Cajamarca, and how did the Spaniards capitalize on it?

Document 18.2 An Inca Account of the Conquest of Peru

Diego de Castro Titu Cusi Yupanqui, the son of Manco Inca and the nephew of Atahuallpa, was born in 1530, two years before Pizarro's victory over Atahuallpa at Cajamarca. Titu Cusi became Sapa Inca of the unsubdued state of Vilcabamba in 1560. In 1570, he dictated to a Spanish missionary this account of the conquest.

At the time when the Spaniards first landed in this country of Peru and when they arrived at the city of Cajamarca, my father Manco Inca was residing in the city of Cuzco. There he governed with all the powers that had been bestowed upon him by his father Huayna Capac. He first learned of the Spaniards' arrival from certain messengers who had been sent from there by one of his brothers by the name of Atahuallpa, who was older but a bastard . . . They reported having observed that certain people had arrived in their land, people who were very different from us in custom and dress, and that they appeared to be Viracochas (this is the name that we used to apply to the Creator of All Things). They named the people as such because they differed very much from us in clothing and appearance and because they rode very large sheep with silver feet (by which they meant horseshoes) . . . the Indians saw them alone talking to white cloths as one person would speak to another, which is how they perceived the reading of books and letters . . .

When my uncle [Atahuallpa] was approaching Cajamarca with all of his people, the Spaniards met them at the springs of Conoc, one and a half leagues from Cajamarca . . . After having heard what they had to say, my uncle attended to them and calmly offered one of them our customary drink in a golden cup, but the Spaniard poured it out with his own hands, which offended my uncle very much. Having seen how little they minded his things, my uncle said, "If you disrespect me, I will also disrespect you." He got up angrily and raised a cry as though he wanted to kill the Spaniards. However, the Spaniards were on the lookout and took possession of the four gates of the plaza where they were, which was enclosed on all its sides.

The Indians were thus penned up like sheep in this enclosed plaza, unable to move because there were so many of them. Also, they had no weapons as they had not brought any, being so little concerned about the Spaniards . . . The Spaniards stormed with great fury to the center of the plaza, where the Sapa Inca's seat was placed on an elevated platform . . . After they had taken everything from him, they apprehended him, and because the Indians uttered loud cries, they started killing them with the horses, the swords or guns, like one kills sheep, without anyone being able to resist them. Of more than ten thousand not even two hundred escaped . . .

SOURCE: Titu Cusi Yupanqui, *An Inca Account of the Conquest of Peru*, translated by Ralph Bauer. Copyright © 2005 by the University of Colorado. Reproduced with permission of the University of Colorado Press in the formats Textbook and Other Book via Copyright Clearance Center.

What factors account for Spain's victory over the Inca Empire?

Reasons for the Spanish Victory

Spain's victory in this confrontation can be explained by a number of factors, listed from least to most important. First, the demonstrated success of Spanish weaponry and tactics in Mexico, coupled with Inca ignorance of what had taken place there, gave Spain a decisive advantage at Cajamarca in 1532. Second, as in Mexico, smallpox proved useful, killing the Sapa Inca in 1527 and touching off a civil war over the succession that Pizarro interpreted accurately and exploited skillfully. Third, Atahuallpa underestimated the Spanish, accepting the mistaken reports of his envoy. Fourth, after Cajamarca, the Inca practice of mitima worked to Spain's advantage, as the Inca, assuming the Spaniards would assimilate them as equals, did not resist. Fifth, and most significant, was Pizarro's deception. Pizarro led Atahuallpa to believe he would be freed upon payment of a huge ransom, and so the Sapa Inca did not order his massive armies to attack the invaders. Once the extent of this treachery became obvious, the Spaniards had been heavily reinforced.

In Peru as in Mexico, Spanish greed for gold and silver led bold men to take risks that, in retrospect, seem incredibly dangerous. But the invaders capitalized on every advantage that came their way, destroying the two greatest Amerind empires in the Western Hemisphere. On the ruins of those empires, other Spaniards would build a European empire of their own.

Chapter Review

Consequences and Connections

The civilizations built by the Aztecs and Inca developed in distinctive environments, totally isolated from each other and from the Eastern Hemisphere. Both were based on political hierarchies headed by emperors and dominated by warrior elites, settled economies balanced between agriculture and trade, and polytheistic religions. These two civilizations created large cities, extensive transportation networks, and intricate social structures. Neither had completed its second century of existence when the Spaniards arrived.

Aztec Mexico was clearly the more coercive of the two. Raising human sacrifice to the level of a divine obligation and conducting it with mechanistic efficiency, Tenochtitlán terrified all who lived in central Mexico. Disdainful of other Amerind cultures, the Aztecs sought not to govern but to dominate and exploit them. Many of their vassals welcomed the prospect of Spanish rule. The possibility that the Spanish could be more oppressive than the Aztecs seems not to have occurred to the elites of central Mexico.

Tahuantin-Suyu was no less ruthless in its expansion than Tenochtitlán, but it developed into a militaristic empire that aimed to gain the loyalty of conquered peoples rather than slaughter them. The Inca practice of mitima gave subject peoples a stake in the empire. Human sacrifice, while not unknown, was practiced primarily during emergencies or on important occasions.

When Atahuallpa was captured at Cajamarca, the Spaniards found it easy to rule the general population of the empire. Most Inca appear to have believed that the newcomers would integrate all peoples into their new empire with some degree of equality. Like the Aztecs, however, the Inca interpreted new experiences in terms of old customs and were mistaken regarding the conquerors' intentions. They faced a situation unlike anything they had ever imagined: conquest by aliens from another world.

Reviewing Key Concepts

Chinampas, p. 351
Cosmic Mission Theory, p. 352
Tahuantin-Suyu, p. 355

Mitima, p. 356
Sapa Inca, p. 356

Quipu, p. 357
Tlaxcallan Confederacy, p. 359

Ask Yourself

1. How did the cosmic mission theory shape Aztec society?

2. How did the Inca and Aztec empires differ in their attitudes toward conquered peoples?

3. In the encounters between Europeans and Amerinds, what difference did it make that Amerind civilizations had developed more recently than European civilization?

4. How did Aztec and Inca ignorance of the existence of European civilization handicap them in responding to European invasion?

Key Dates and Developments

ca. 1111	The Aztecs move into central Mexico
ca. 1200	Inca ascendancy begins in the Central Andes
1325	Foundation of Tenochtitlán
1400–1438	Inca expansion under Viracocha Inca
1438–1471	Pachacuti founds Tahuantin-Suyu
1440	Aztecs dominate the Valley of Mexico
1471–1493	Topa Inca expands the Inca Empire
1502–1520	Reign of Montezuma II

1519	Cortés leads an expedition from Cuba to Mexico
1521	Fall of Tenochtitlán
1527	Death of Huayna Capac; civil war in Tahuantin-Suyu
1531	Pizarro leads an expedition from Panama to Peru
1532	Capture of Atahuallpa at Cajamarca

Chapter 19
Global Exploration and Global Empires, 1400–1700

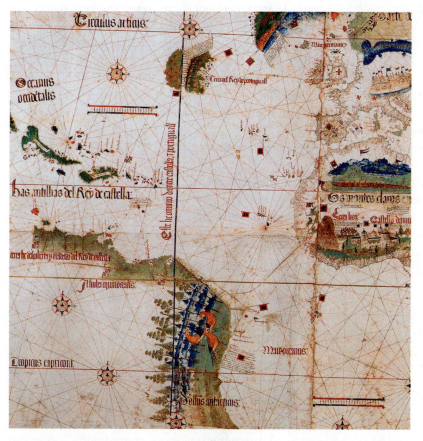

PORTUGUESE CLAIMS IN AFRICA AND BRAZIL A 16th-century map shows Portuguese claims in Africa and Brazil. Few would have predicted that tiny Portugal would lead the way in European exploration of the globe.

After reading this chapter, you should be able to:

19.1 Comment on the similarities and differences between the Iberians and the Mongols.

19.2 Describe the main impacts and connections of the Portuguese sea borne empire.

19.3 Compare and contrast the Spanish and Portuguese empires in the Western Hemisphere.

19.4 Describe the impact on Amerind peoples of the European settlements in North America.

19.5 Explain the advantages and disadvantages of the Columbian Exchange.

The Portuguese
Empire

The Spanish
Empire

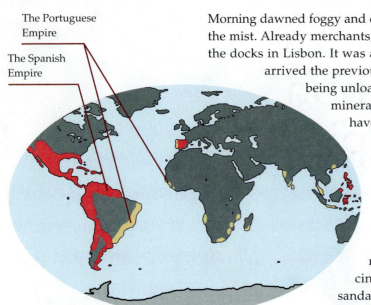

Morning dawned foggy and damp, but by 8 A.M. the Portuguese sun was burning off the mist. Already merchants, artisans, vendors, and shoppers were moving toward the docks in Lisbon. It was a typical day in early September 1600, and a fleet had arrived the previous evening from the Indian Ocean. Now its ships were being unloaded and the docks stacked with exotic plants, animals, minerals, and manufactures. Those who arrived early would have first pick from the cargoes.

Cramming the docks of Lisbon was a staggering variety of commodities from four continents. From Europe itself came wheat, wool, brassware, glass, weapons, tapestries, and clocks. North Africa provided dates, honey, barley, and indigo, as well as ornate metalwork. West Africa contributed gold, ivory, musk, parrots, and slaves. East Africa sent ebony, coral, salt, and hemp. Arriving from India were calico, pepper, ginger, coconut oil, cinnamon, cloves, and nutmeg. Southeast Asia furnished sandalwood, resins, camphor, and saffron. From Macao came porcelains, silks, and medicinal herbs. Finally, Brazil supplied sugar, brazilwood, and monkeys from the Amazon. Lisbon in 1600 was the commercial focus of Europe, a cosmopolitan connector of products and peoples from throughout the world.

Lisbon's prosperity was a relatively recent development. Prior to 1453, world trade focused on the Mediterranean, where Italian city-states like Venice and Genoa competed with Muslim merchants for cargoes and profits. But Mehmed the Conqueror's dramatic victory at Constantinople, which at first appeared to expand Islamic power, actually weakened existing Muslim trade networks. By stimulating Europeans to seek overseas routes to the Indies and the Spice Islands, the fall of Constantinople reoriented European trade, to the eventual benefit of the eager buyers who swarmed over the Lisbon docks in 1600.

The Iberian Impulse

19.1 Comment on the similarities and differences between the Iberians and the Mongols.

Portugal was an unlikely location for a commercial nexus. The Iberian Peninsula, home to Spain and Portugal, sits at the far southwestern edge of the Eurasian landmass, separated from the rest of Europe by the Pyrenees mountains. From the eighth through twelfth centuries, most of Iberia was linked to the Islamic world by Muslim rule. By the mid-1200s, however, fired by the *Reconquista* (Chapter 16), the Christian kingdoms of the North had retaken most of the region. In 1479 the two main Spanish kingdoms, Aragon and Castile, were linked by the marriage and joint rule of their respective monarchs, Ferdinand and Isabella, laying the base for a united Spain. By 1492, when they expelled the Muslims from Granada in the South, this couple ruled most of Iberia—except for the kingdom of Portugal along the Atlantic coast.

By this time Spain and Portugal, far from Europe's centers of commerce and wealth, were embarking on great sea voyages that would soon enlarge European ideas about the geography of the globe. Determined to bypass the Muslims, who controlled the land links and profitable trade with East Asia, both Iberians and Italian city-states searched for an all-water route to India, the Spice Islands, and China, regions that Europeans called collectively the East Indies. The Portuguese, who had been exploring southward along the Atlantic coast of Africa since the early 1400s, finally found a sea route in 1498, arriving in India by way of the Indian Ocean after sailing around Africa. Six years earlier the Spanish had funded an ill-conceived effort to reach East Asia by sailing west across the Atlantic. In the process, and by accident, they discovered what seemed to them a "New World," and they went on to create a western hemispheric empire that rivaled even that of the Mongols in size and significance.

Like Mongols, Iberians had a warrior culture, bred by centuries of *Reconquista*. Like Mongols, they used technologies adopted from other civilizations, such as gunpowder weapons and navigational tools from Asia. Like Mongols, they killed untold thousands through combat, slaughter, and the spread of infectious diseases, gaining wealth and power by exploiting and enslaving millions. And like Mongols, they connected cultures.

Unlike Mongols, however, Iberians zealously imposed their faith on the people they ruled. And unlike Mongols they created new societies that would endure even after their empires were gone.

Portuguese Overseas Exploration

Given the small size and relative poverty of Portugal, it is surprising that this kingdom started the European drive for overseas exploration. But the forces it set in motion had an immense impact.

Like other European nations, Portugal suffered a drastic fourteenth-century population decline from the Black Death and the famines and epidemics associated with it. Depopulation of villages and poorly producing farmland left much of the landed nobility impoverished. Some tried to compensate for their losses by turning to plunder. In 1415 Portuguese raiders captured the Moroccan seaport of Ceuta (*THĀ-oo-tah*), but Portugal's small population and limited resources prevented it from conquering all Morocco in a land war.

The sea offered an alternative route to plunder. Portugal was a nation of farmers and fishermen with a lengthy Atlantic seacoast. Following the conquest of Ceuta, Prince Enrique (*awn-RĒ-kā*), the third son of the king of Portugal and therefore unlikely to inherit the throne, decided to pursue his own interests by organizing maritime expeditions to chart the western coast of Africa. Starting in 1418, these expeditions sought to determine how far south Muslim rule prevailed in Africa and where the Christian faith could be advanced at the expense of Islam (Map 19.1).

The Portuguese also wanted to develop trade relations with African Christians, including the mythical Christian kingdom of Prester John, sought by Europeans since the Crusades. Slowly, Portuguese explorers and traders moved south along Africa's west coast. They covered 1500 miles, reaching as far as present-day Sierra Leone by the time Enrique died in 1460. Later generations called him Prince Henry the Navigator.

The Ottoman seizure of Constantinople had stunned Christian Europe and disrupted its merchants. Muslims were now in control of the eastern Mediterranean, the meeting point of three continents and the focus of world trade for centuries. They took over the traditional land–sea trade routes and raised the fees for safe passage to levels that enriched the Ottoman Sultan and cut deeply into European profits. Their middlemen squeezed European merchants even more by marking up the prices of spices and luxury items as much as 1000 percent. These burdens were enough to convince several Western nations to search for alternative routes to the East Indies.

Henry's expeditions gave Portugal a sizable lead in this search. Its ships reached the equator in 1471 and discovered that, contrary to legend, the ocean there did not boil. They also found that the heat decreased as they sailed farther south. In 1487, Portugal's King João (*ZHWOW*) II dispatched a land expedition across Africa to search for Prester John and for a connection to the Indian Ocean and a sea expedition to search for a route around Africa. The land expedition failed to find Prester John

Why were the Portuguese the first Europeans to carry out overseas exploration?

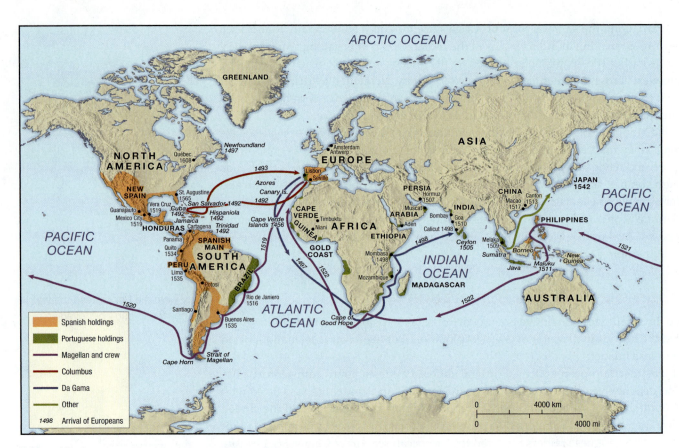

Map 19.1 EUROPEAN GLOBAL EXPLORATION ROUTES, 1415–1522 Note the principal voyages of European exploration, all undertaken for differing reasons. Vasco da Gama's journey to India built on several decades of Portuguese exploration of the western coast of Africa. Columbus's westward expedition was designed to reach first Japan and then the Spice Islands by a route that Columbus believed to be shorter than sailing around Africa. Magellan's circumnavigation of the globe was intended to demonstrate that Columbus could have established a commercially viable connection to Asia had America not been in his way. Why did that conclusion prove incorrect?

but did reach India. The sea voyage, commanded by Bartholomeu Días (*DĒ-ahz*), rounded the Cape of Good Hope at Africa's southern tip and could have gone on to India had not the sailors insisted on returning home. When Días sailed into Lisbon in 1489, he reported that Portugal had found a way to undercut Muslim traders, since cargoes could be shipped by sea for a fraction of the cost by land. Present in Lisbon when Días arrived was a Genoese navigator named Cristóbal Colón, whose proposal for a voyage to find a route to the Indies by sailing westward across the Atlantic had been previously rejected by João II. The Latinized version of this navigator's name was Christopher Columbus.

Columbus's Enterprise of the Indies

How did Columbus's computational errors make it possible for him to land in the Western Hemisphere?

An experienced mariner and cartographer, Columbus knew that the earth was round, and he calculated the distance from Portugal to China at fewer than 5000 miles. He was right about the shape of the earth but wrong about its size. His calculations of one degree of longitude at the equator were off by 15 miles, a mistake that caused him to think that the circumference of the earth was 18,750 miles rather than 25,000. His sources for the size and locations of Asian lands were also inaccurate. But he was able to make a plausible argument that Europeans could reach East Asia by sailing west, across the Atlantic, on voyages that would be shorter and less expensive than going around Africa to the Indies. Moreover, since the journey would be east to west instead of north to south, the winds, currents, and climatic changes encountered along the way would be less troublesome. In 1484 Columbus presented his **Enterprise of the Indies**, a detailed plan for a westward maritime expedition, to João II, and asked for Portuguese financial support.

João referred this request to a committee of experts, who agreed with Columbus that the world is round—a well-known fact by 1484—but considered his estimate of the earth's circumference ridiculously small. This committee, relying in part on the eleventh-century calculations of al-Biruni of Khwarazm, who estimated the radius of the earth at 3930 miles, projected the distance from Portugal to Japan at 13,100 miles, a highly accurate prediction that placed East Asia well beyond the range of any expedition that expected its sailors to carry their own food and drink. Rather than reconsider his estimate, Columbus tried his luck with King Isabella of Castile (although female, Isabella was officially a *king*, and she insisted on being called by that title). She established a similar committee that reported similar findings. Columbus was about to try the Portuguese court again when Días returned to Lisbon in 1489 with good news about the route around Africa. Recognizing that Portugal would pursue that route for trade, Columbus sought support from Venice and Genoa. But these city-states, with established interests in existing routes through the eastern Mediterranean, turned him away.

Still convinced that his calculations were right, Columbus went back to Isabella in 1492 and was rejected again. However, as he was preparing to leave for Paris to try to interest the French, he was called back to Isabella's court. Her finance minister, Luís de Santander (*loo-ĒSSdā sahn-tahn-DARE*), had scolded his sovereign for lack of imagination and offered to finance the Enterprise himself by loaning funds to Isabella. If Columbus were mistaken, Santander argued, he would die on the voyage and a small investment would be lost; but if, against the odds, he turned out to be right, Castile would have a more direct route to the Indies than either Portuguese or Islamic merchants.

Isabella now gave the Enterprise more careful thought. She and her husband Ferdinand, kings of Castile and Aragon, respectively, hoped to instill a militant,

Document 19.1   Columbus Describes His First Encounter with People in the Western Hemisphere, 1492

The Enterprise of the Indies sighted land before dawn on October 12, 1492, and Columbus went ashore after dawn broke. He recorded the events in his own words, including his assumption that his expedition was then very close to Asia.

As I saw that [the native people] were very friendly to us . . . I presented them with some red caps, and strings of beads to wear upon the neck, and many other trifles of small value, wherewith they were much delighted, and became wonderfully attached to us. Afterwards they came swimming to the boats, bringing parrots, balls of cotton thread, javelins and many other things which they exchanged for articles we gave them, such as glass beads, and hawk's bells; which trade was carried on with the utmost good will. But they seemed on the whole to me, to be a very poor people. They all go completely naked, even the women, though I saw but one girl. All whom I saw were young, not above thirty years of age, well made, with fine shapes and faces; their hair short, and coarse like that of a horse's tail, combed toward the forehead, except a small portion which they suffer to hang down behind, and never cut . . . Weapons they have none, nor are acquainted with them, for I showed them swords which they grasped by the blades,

and cut themselves through ignorance. They have no iron, their javelins being without it, and nothing more than sticks, though some have fish-bones or other things at the ends. They are all of a good size and stature, and handsomely formed. I saw some with scars of wounds upon their bodies, and demanded by signs the cause of them; they answered me in the same way, that there came people from the other islands in the neighborhood who intended to make them prisoners, and they defended themselves. I thought then, and still believe, that these were from the continent [of Asia]. It appears to me, that the people are ingenious, and would be good servants; and I am of opinion that they would very readily become Christians, as they appear to have no religion . . . If it please our Lord, I intend at my return to carry home six of them to your Highnesses, that they may learn our language.

SOURCE: Christopher Columbus, *Journal of the First Voyage to America* (New York: A. and C. Boni, 1924), 24–26.

Columbus's first encounter with Indians.

crusading Catholicism in all the Spanish kingdoms and unite them under the rule of their daughter Juana. A new route to the Indies would not only make this unified Spain rich, they reasoned, but also make it possible to convert hundreds of millions of Asians to their faith. Isabella accepted Santander's offer, gave Columbus letters of introduction to the emperor of China, and sent him on his way with three ships, the *Niña*, the *Pinta*, and the *Santa Maria*. Columbus sailed from Palos (*PAH-lōs*), Spain, on August 3, 1492, and made landfall on an island, most likely in the Bahamas, in what is today the Caribbean Sea on October 12 (see "Columbus Describes His First Encounter with People in the Western Hemisphere, 1492"). It was a voyage of fewer than 3000 miles.

Columbus assumed that he had reached islands off the eastern coast of Japan, but the inhabitants did not wear Japanese clothing (indeed, they wore no clothing at all), did not speak Japanese, and did not seem to know anything about Japan. The plant and animal life was unlike anything Asian, and when Columbus returned to Spain in 1493 with samples of what he had found, the general conclusion was that he had landed in an unknown part of the world. Columbus, however, did not agree. He mounted three more expeditions in search of Japan, dying in Spain in 1506 without ever knowing what part of the world he had reached.

Columbus may have been mistaken concerning the nature of the lands he encountered, but Isabella was not. She repaid Santander handsomely and made the discoveries her personal property. Then she appealed to Pope Alexander VI for recognition of Castile's claims to the Indies and its exclusive right to the westward passage. In Christian Europe at that time, such matters were routinely referred to the Vatican. Alexander, a Spaniard, divided the entire world known to Europeans between the two Iberian nations, drawing an imaginary line from pole to pole 450 miles west of the Azores and the Cape Verde Islands (though they are not at the same longitude). Ignoring the rights of the inhabitants whose lands he gave away, he granted everything east of the line to Portugal and everything west to Castile. The Portuguese, who had not yet actually sailed all the way to India, were outraged and threatened war.

Subsequent negotiations between the Portuguese and the Spanish in 1494 resulted in the **Treaty of Tordesillas** (*taur-dā-SĒ-yahss*), an agreement that drew the Line of Demarcation 1675 miles west of the Cape Verde Islands (Map 19.2). Both sides were reasonably dissatisfied but proceeded to claim their halves of the world. The other European powers, not having been consulted, saw no need to comply; nor did Muslims, who paid no attention to the pope. Still, although Europeans did not yet know about South America, the treaty's main effect would be to give most of it to Spain, while leaving to Portugal the large eastern section later known as Brazil.

The Voyage of Magellan

Why did Magellan's voyage reduce the likelihood that Europeans would open commercial connections with Asia by sailing west?

The Spanish followed up on the voyages of Columbus by creating an American empire, first colonizing several Caribbean islands and later conquering the Aztecs in Mexico and the Inca in Peru (Chapter 18). Some, however, continued to believe that profitable trade routes to Asia could be found by sailing westward from Spain.

Thus, while Cortés was conquering Mexico, Ferdinand Magellan (*mah-JEL-lin*), a Portuguese mariner sailing for Spain, was finally accomplishing what Columbus had set out to do. By now it was obvious that the Americas were not part of Asia: in 1497 and 1498 English expeditions had explored the coast of North America, and in 1513 a Spaniard named Balboa saw another great ocean on the western side of the American continents.

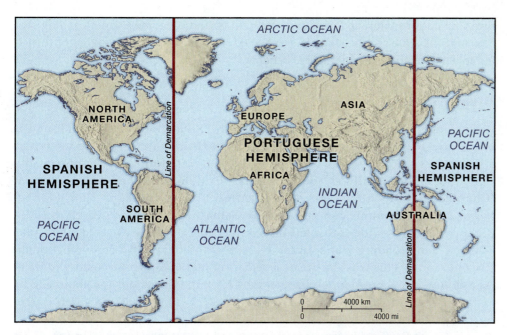

Map 19.2 THE TREATY OF TORDESILLAS AND THE LINE OF DEMARCATION, 1494
Observe that the line drawn by the Treaty of Tordesillas not only divided the Western Hemisphere between Portugal and Spain; it went around the world and bisected the Eastern Hemisphere as well. One can only imagine the reactions of the Japanese and Chinese emperors and the various rulers of India, had they known that their lands had been assigned to two European nations by a treaty of whose very existence they knew nothing. Europe had progressed from exploring the world to dividing it. Why did Europeans believe they had a right to divide the world in this way?

But although ancient Polynesians knew the width of the Pacific, no European yet knew this, and the dream of sailing westward from Europe to reach the riches of Asia lived on.

In pursuit of this dream, Magellan set out from Spain in 1519 with five ships and about 280 men. They headed for South America, where for a year they probed the coast for a passage, finally sailing through what is now called the Straits of Magellan in November 1520. For the next four months, with only three ships left, they crossed the seemingly endless Pacific, eating leather and ship rats once supplies ran out. In March 1521, the near-starving survivors reached the Philippines. They claimed the islands for Spain, but the next month Magellan and many of his men were killed in a conflict with Filipino peoples.

Eventually, in September 1522, one ship with 18 men made it back to Spain, having sailed around the globe. Their voyage had proven that it was indeed possible to reach Asia by sailing west from Europe. But it had also revealed that the trip was three times the distance Columbus had calculated, and that given the distance and dangers involved it was not really worth the trouble.

Magellan's circumnavigation of the globe.

The Portuguese Seaborne Empire

19.2 Describe the main impacts and connections of the Portuguese seaborne empire.

The Portuguese, meanwhile, were finding that using their new sea routes was very much worth *their* trouble. The Treaty of Tordesillas granted half the world to Portugal, and Lisbon set out to make the most of it. Portugal's new oceanic empire rested on firm foundations: knowledge of currents, winds, and coastlines; superb sailing vessels; and first-rate seamanship. The curiosity of Prince Henry the Navigator turned out to have tremendous commercial benefits.

Empire in the Atlantic Ocean

How did Portugal's desire to connect with India lead to its ownership of Brazil?

A generation after Prince Henry's death, King João II authorized the establishment of a fortress and trading post in the Gulf of Guinea in 1482. The next year a Portuguese explorer named Diogo Cão (*COWM*) found the mouth of the Congo River, eventually establishing good relations with the Kongo Kingdom (Chapter 18). Other Portuguese pressed on toward India, as King Manoel (*mahn-WELL*) I commissioned Vasco da Gama to sail around Africa to India (Chapter 23). In 1497 da Gama left Lisbon, reaching the Cape of Good Hope after 93 days, then rounding it and sailing up Africa's east coast and across the Indian Ocean to India. This was the greatest seafaring feat in European history to date. As a follow-up, King Manoel dispatched a 12-ship fleet under the command of Pedro Alvares Cabral (*PĀ-drō AHL-vah-rez kah-BRAHL*) in 1500. Blown off course by a violent storm, Cabral made landfall on an "island" in the western Atlantic, claiming it for Portugal before continuing on to India. It was not an island at all—it was Brazil.

Manoel decided to assess the value of Brazil as an intermediate base for future voyages to India. In 1501 he sent a three-ship expedition to the new land, with Amerigo Vespucci (*ah-MARE-ih-gō vess-POO-chē*) aboard as cartographer and chronicler. In this capacity on a future trip, Amerigo named the entire hemisphere after himself: America. The expedition explored 2000 miles of coastline, leading Manoel to suspect that this was not an island after all. It also brought back samples of a type of brazilwood, a tree whose wood could be used to produce red dye for textiles. This wood gave Brazil its name and Portugal a reason to explore the area further, since it lay too far west to be useful as a way station en route to India. Later, the Portuguese learned that they could make a fortune growing sugar in Brazil, provided they settled it with colonists and African slaves. But for the moment, the Eastern Hemisphere seemed more attractive.

Empire in the Indian and Pacific Oceans

What was Albuquerque's strategy, and how did it help Portugal dominate the Indian Ocean?

The Treaty of Tordesillas, amplified by a papal edict of 1514 forbidding other European powers to interfere with Portuguese possessions, enabled Portugal to avoid European competition in the Eastern Hemisphere for most of the sixteenth century. Its superior gunnery, vessels, and seamanship held off its occasional Asian enemies. But the Portuguese seaborne realm was less an empire than a network of commercial ports and fortifications, designed not for settlement but for trade.

Vasco da Gama's voyage to India opened the Indian Ocean to Portuguese traffic. In 1500, after Cabral bumped into Brazil, one of his ships located Madagascar. The Portuguese established trading posts in India and connected them with their newly founded station at Kilwa in East Africa.

In 1505 the first Portuguese **viceroy**, or vice-king, arrived in India, and beginning in 1510 the second viceroy, Afonso de Albuquerque, began developing the system of fortified posts at strategic locations that guaranteed Portuguese domination of Indian Ocean trade. This entire region already enjoyed dense commercial networks managed by Arab, Chinese, and Indian merchants. Portugal's contribution was to connect these networks to each other.

Albuquerque conquered Goa in 1510 and made it Portugal's headquarters in Asia. During the next five years, his forces took Melaka, Maluku, and Hormuz. Portuguese seamen reached China shortly thereafter, and in 1557 they established a trading post

Document 19.2   Vasco da Gama's Expedition Observes the Spice Trade, 1498

Vasco da Gama's first voyage to India enabled the Portuguese to observe the nature and extent of the spice trade. This excerpt from the journal of one of the sailors charts the course of that commerce. Notice the emphasis placed on the dangers of overland travel, the frequent payment of customs duties, and the enormous income the sultan of the Ottoman Empire derived from those duties. All of these facts led the Portuguese to seek a sea route to the Indies in the first place.

From this country of Calecut, or Alta India, come the spices which are consumed in the East and the West, in Portugal, as in all other countries of the world, as also precious stones of every description. The following spices are to be found in this city of Calecut, being its own produce: much ginger and pepper and cinnamon, although the last is not of so fine a quality as that brought from an island called Ceylon, which is eight days journey from Calecut . . . Cloves are brought to this city from an island called Malacca. The Mecca vessels carry these spices from there to a city in [Arabia] called Jiddah, and from the said island to Jiddah is a voyage of fifty days sailing before the wind, for the vessels of this country cannot tack. At Jiddah they discharge their cargoes, paying customs duties to the Grand Sultan. The merchandise is then transshipped to smaller vessels, which carry it through the Red Sea to a place . . . called Tuuz, where customs duties are paid once

more. From that place the merchants carry the spices on the back of camels . . . to Cairo, a journey occupying ten days. At Cairo duties are paid again. On this road to Cairo they are frequently robbed by thieves, who live in that country, such as the Bedouins and others.

At Cairo, the spices are embarked on the river Nile . . . and descending that river for two days they reach a place called Rosetta, where duties have to be paid once more. There they are placed on camels, and are conveyed in one day to a city called Alexandria, which is a seaport. This city is visited by the galleys of Venice and Genoa, in search of these spices, which yield the Grand Sultan a revenue of 600,000 cruzados in customs duties . . . [about $15 million in 2006 dollars].

SOURCE: *A Journal of the First Voyage of Vasco da Gama, 1497–1499*, translated by Eric Axelson (Cape Town: Stephan Phillips Ltd., 1998), 77–78.

---

at Macao. The Portuguese controlled the Persian Gulf from Hormuz, and their installation at Melaka dominated the passageway from the Indian Ocean to the South China Sea. Fortified Portuguese trading posts were located all along the East African coastline and the seacoasts of India and Ceylon.

Portugal's Commercial Empire in 1600

How did the Portuguese Empire connect Asia, Africa, South America, and Europe?

The Portuguese created their far-flung empire skillfully, employing their navigational expertise to master the seas and sail them at will. They guarded their knowledge jealously, refusing to share it with competitors. They carefully selected important strategic locations that would help them dominate Indian Ocean trade, occupying those locations through a combination of diplomacy and intimidation. Once installed, they protected their positions by negotiating trading rights in contracts that benefited local merchants as well as themselves, giving those merchants a stake in Portuguese success. This strategy enabled a nation with a tiny population of fewer than 2 million people to develop a commercial network spanning the globe.

The Portuguese were responsible for establishing regular oceanic trade across vast spaces: between the Atlantic and Indian oceans, between West Africa and Brazil, between southwestern Europe and West Africa, and between the North and South Atlantic (Map 19.3). These sea routes regularized connections between these regions and enhanced commercial and cultural contacts between societies.

Portuguese vessels carried spices from the Indian Ocean to Europe, and while this was a valuable trade route, Portuguese shipping lanes from one part of Asia to another were even more profitable. The Portuguese sold Chinese silk not only in Europe but also in India, the Maluku Islands, Borneo, Timor, and Hormuz. Cloth from India, spices from the Malukus, minerals from Borneo, and sandalwood from Timor were distributed throughout the Portuguese Empire, as Portuguese ships connected these sites not only to Lisbon but to one another.

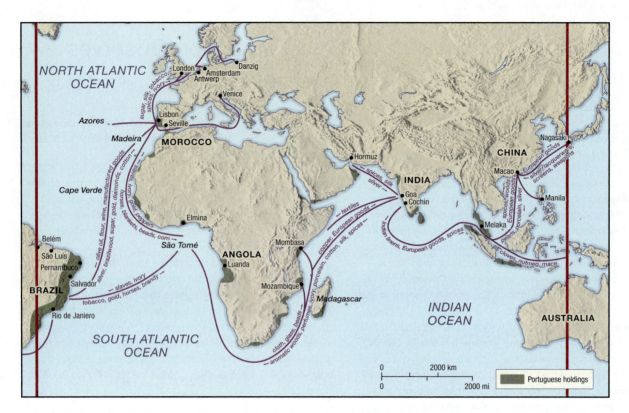

Map 19.3 **THE FLOW OF COMMERCE IN THE PORTUGUESE WORLD, CA. 1600** The Portuguese impulse to expand overseas created commercial connections linking four continents. Note that a bewildering variety of goods, some of which are depicted in the chapter opener, flowed into Lisbon from across the globe. Customs, rituals, languages, clothing, and ideas moved not only to and from Lisbon, but between each of the ports depicted on the map. The result was a vast increase in cosmopolitanism and knowledge from one end of the Portuguese world to the other. Why did this Portuguese challenge worry the Islamic world?

In addition to goods, Portuguese sailors and merchants carried diseases from one region of the world to another. Malaria spread rapidly across the tropics as mosquitoes bred prolifically in the water carried on Portuguese ships. Asians and Africans were generally immune to the most drastic effects of Eurasian diseases, but Brazilian Amerinds were devastated by smallpox, influenza, and measles. More than a century after Cabral reached Brazil, smallpox remained lethal enough to wipe out the entire Amerind population of Sao Luís in northern Brazil in 1621.

In addition to the transmission of germs, goods, and people, the Portuguese spread European culture and practices throughout their empire and scattered bits of information about Asian, African, Amerind, and Brazilian cultures everywhere they went. Building and artistic materials such as rare woods, gems, dyes, and metals were shipped from Asia, Africa, and Brazil to Europe, where they were used in churches, libraries, jewelry, paintings, and furniture. The Portuguese built European-style churches in India and churches with Asian motifs in Brazil. Amerind art was widely sold in Brazil, Angolans purchased colorful Amerind textiles, and Brazilian-inspired furniture graced parlors in Portuguese homes. The Portuguese seaborne empire facilitated widespread transmission of styles and tastes.

This transmission operated in several directions simultaneously. European clothing was introduced in Angola

A modern-day replica of a Portuguese caravel.

and Brazil, with sometimes comical results: top hats were widely worn by foremen of labor gangs in Rio de Janeiro, and for a brief period, Portuguese-style baggy pants were all the rage in Nagasaki. Brazilian tobacco was smoked in Portugal and coveted in Angola, where *arrobas*, bundles of tobacco twisted into ropes and soaked in molasses, became so popular that they were used as currency. West African foods and words entered the culture of eastern Brazil, and African slaves transported to Brazil by the Portuguese became devoted converts to Portuguese Catholicism while retaining rituals and songs from their African religions. The cross-fertilization of cultures produced by the Portuguese seaborne empire was as stimulating, and penetrating, as the connections generated by conflict and conquest among the many great land-based empires of previous centuries.

The Spanish and Portuguese Empires in America

19.3 Compare and contrast the Spanish and Portuguese empires in the Western Hemisphere.

Once the great Amerind empires had fallen to the Spaniards, Spain began consolidating what had become the largest territorial possession in human history. From California to Cape Horn, Spain controlled everything except Portuguese Brazil (Map 19.4). Subduing Mexico proved relatively easy after the conquest of Tenochtitlán. In Peru, however, the Inca found ways to neutralize Spain's mounted cavalry, and although they were unable to expel the invaders, they created an independent Inca kingdom high in the Andes that lasted until 1572. Elsewhere the weaker, less centralized Amerind cultures, including the vestiges of the once-imposing Maya civilization, offered only occasional resistance to their new masters.

At the same time, the Portuguese began recognizing the economic potential of Brazil. Their eastern seaborne empire involved profit-sharing with Muslim traders, but Brazil was entirely theirs, and they used it to profit from the growing European taste for sugar. Unlike Spanish America, with its centralized Amerind societies, Brazil was home to native cultures that lived in the inaccessible interior and had not developed central institutions. These cultures fled from the Portuguese rather than resist them but could not provide the labor required for sugar cultivation. Nor, given their small population, could the Portuguese.

The Amerind Foundation

Spain, in contrast, could construct its empire on the foundations of Amerind societies. Particularly helpful to the Spanish effort was the hierarchical structure of the Aztec and Inca empires. It proved relatively easy for the Spaniards to substitute the king of Spain for the Aztec or Inca emperor at the top of the hierarchy and to expect that the king's orders would be obeyed without hesitation.

Aztec and Inca polytheism also contributed to this submission. Accustomed to a large array of gods, the conquered peoples interpreted their defeat as indicating that their own gods were weaker than those of the Spaniards. It seemed logical to worship the gods who were stronger. The Spaniards, noting this tendency, did nothing to discourage Inca and Aztecs from considering Catholic saints and angels as powerful gods. Mary, the mother of Jesus, actually had a parallel in Aztec religion, in which one female goddess was the mother of all the gods. Through this blending of Christian and Amerind traditions, the defeated societies were encouraged to accept their fate and embrace the new European faith.

How did Iberians build their empires on existing Amerind societies?

Map 19.4   THE IBERIAN EMPIRES IN THE WESTERN HEMISPHERE, 1750 Spain and Portugal, two small countries on the Iberian Peninsula on the southwestern fringe of Europe, constructed enormous empires in the Western Hemisphere. European languages, customs, and products spread throughout these empires, while American, African, and Asian resources, customs, and cultures moved through Iberia into Europe. But notice that large portions of South America—the Amazon Basin, the interior of Brazil, and Patagonia—remained untouched by Europeans. Why?

How did the Iberian need for slave labor connect the Americas to Africa?

Slave Labor

Once Mexico and Peru were pacified, Spaniards began arriving steadily from the mother country, drawn to the Americas by the prospect of wealth in gold and silver or in sugar production. For labor in the mines and fields they expected to use Amerinds, but Amerinds were not easily enslaved for these purposes. First, smallpox and other European diseases to which Amerinds had no acquired immunity killed large numbers of them. Moreover, those who survived had greatly reduced life expectancies, either owing to Spanish cruelty or because they simply found unrelenting labor unendurable in the absence of the religious significance it had had under the Aztec and

Inca empires. Third, many Catholic missionaries to the Americas protested strongly against the enslavement of Amerinds. They argued to the king that Amerinds were people with souls, not draft animals.

The missionaries' genuine concern for the well-being of the Amerinds, however, did not extend to Africans, many of whom were soon imported as slaves. With Amerind workers unavailable, the American colonies needed a labor force accustomed to tropical conditions. There were not enough men in all Iberia to supply this labor force, and if there had been, few could have survived manual labor in tropical climates for very long.

Here the Portuguese took the lead. Having experienced serious labor shortages in Brazil, they imported slaves from trading posts that they had established along the west coast of Africa. Spain followed, and before long Portuguese and Spanish ships carried human cargoes from West Africa, thousands upon thousands of slaves to be sold at auction in the port cities of Central and South America. Iberian America quickly became a mixed society of people of Amerind, European, and African descent who produced a physical and cultural blending unlike anything in the Eastern Hemisphere.

Government and Administration

How were Spanish and Portuguese methods of colonial administration similar to and different from one another?

Governing such diverse and distant empires required new strategies. At first Isabella of Castile, who owned Spanish America outright by virtue of Santander's financing and the Treaty of Tordesillas, simply appointed her chaplain to administer the entire area. When this overworked priest died in 1503, one year after Isabella herself, her husband Ferdinand established a Board of Trade to oversee the increasingly profitable transatlantic commerce. After the final unification of Spain in 1516 under Carlos I (who three years later also became Holy Roman Emperor Charles V), the Americas were governed through councils. Rather than delegate responsibility to a number of ministries or departments (as was done in France and England), authority was assigned in 1524 to a single board, the **Council of the Indies**.

The Council of the Indies supervised every aspect of governance in Spanish America, including legislative, judicial, commercial, financial, military, and religious matters. Meeting in Seville between three and five hours daily, it approved all significant expenditures, decided which Spanish laws should apply unchanged in the New World, drafted revisions for those that required adjustment, and advised the king on everything pertaining to colonial affairs. Formal votes were not unheard of, but usually the Council reached agreement on important matters before submitting its unanimous recommendations to the king for review.

But distance proved to be the most significant difficulty facing those who tried to govern the Western Hemisphere. Sailing from Portugal to Brazil took an average of 70 to 100 days; from Spain to Panama, about 75. Troublesome winds and currents made the return trip even longer. Atlantic crossings were always unpleasant, often dangerous, and occasionally fatal. Ships from the Americas, laden with treasure and exotic goods, were frequently set upon by pirates, although convoys protected by warships eventually reduced this danger. Royal orders and colonial reports took months to cross the Atlantic and were often lost altogether.

The empires thus could not be run from Iberia. Kings and councils might issue laws and edicts, but who would enforce them in America? Clearly agents of unquestionable loyalty were required, men who knew the royal will instinctively, without having to ask questions at every turn. The rulers found such agents in their viceroys, or "vice-kings."

Viceroys were responsible for the execution of the king's orders on virtually every aspect of colonial administration. Until 1717 there were two viceroyalties in Spanish America: New Spain (from California south to Panama, including the Caribbean), and

Peru (from Panama south to Cape Horn). In the eighteenth century, Peru was subdivided into two additional viceroyalties because of its overwhelming size.

Portuguese America developed in a less centralized fashion. King João III in 1534 divided the eastern seaboard into 12 hereditary captaincies, varying in width between 100 and 270 miles and extending indefinitely into the uncharted interior. The proprietors were responsible for the recruitment of settlers and the economic development of their captaincies. The system never worked effectively, and in 1549 João III placed Brazil under the direct administration of a governor-general, whose duties were similar to those of a Spanish-American viceroy. This action accelerated development and attracted thousands of Portuguese settlers to Brazil.

Whether Spanish or Portuguese, these vice-kings were men of talent and expertise, but the principal qualification for the post was loyalty to the king. They had to make decisions in the king's best interests even when the king's orders might be impractical, or irrelevant to conditions in the New World. Under such circumstances, the Spanish viceroy could delay implementation or initiate a reassessment of the situation by invoking the Spanish legal maxim, "I obey but I do not enforce." Portuguese governors-general acted similarly, but without the maxim. A wise monarch would consider such an opinion carefully before overruling his representative.

But the kings of Spain and Portugal were customarily suspicious, and viceroys, like the officials who served under them, were always subject to the **residencia** (*rez-ih-DEHN-sē-ah*). This was a thorough audit of all the appointee's actions during his term of office. It was conducted by a royal bureaucrat sent from the mother country, and it restrained those who might otherwise have been tempted to engage in illegal activity or abuse of power.

All authority came from the king. Neither Spanish nor Portuguese America contained any institution providing representation within the government for ordinary people. Spain itself had such a body, called a *cortés*, but because it was a representative institution that restricted royal power, Spanish kings refused to introduce it into the empire. The only truly representative body in the Spanish Empire was the town council, which maintained roads, policed the streets and markets, and regulated local affairs. But the authority of town councils was limited to the towns themselves. The extensive centralized powers exercised by the Iberian kings over their American empires helped them hold those distant territories for more than three centuries.

The Colonial Church

What roles did the Catholic Church play in the Iberian-American empires?

Iberian expansion was driven not only by a quest for gold and glory, but also by the desire to save the souls of Amerinds, who had never before heard the message of Jesus Christ. That ambitious goal was pursued by the Spanish and Portuguese branches of the Roman Catholic Church.

Ferdinand and Isabella, calling themselves "the Catholic kings," had completed the *Reconquista* by 1492 and had made Catholicism an element of Spanish nationality that helped bring unity to their diverse kingdoms. In America Catholicism would help assimilate conquered peoples into either Spain's or Portugal's colonial order. The pope supported this effort, granting the Iberian monarchs extensive rights over the appointment of bishops, the activities of religious orders, and the organization of all Catholic undertakings in the Western Hemisphere. In return, the kings assumed responsibility for supervising the Church in its evangelical, educational, and charitable efforts overseas.

At first these efforts were directed by the Franciscan, Dominican, and Augustinian religious orders. They concentrated on converting Amerind chiefs, who then saw to it that their people would be baptized. To preach to the newly converted and teach them the elements of the faith, the friars learned dominant Amerind languages and promoted their widening use as a means of centralization.

The Amerinds reacted to conversion in a variety of ways. Some were enthusiastic, eager to worship the new gods who had proven themselves stronger than the old. Others converted for practical reasons, considering it both wise and useful to adopt the belief system of the conquerors. Still others rebelled, like the Inca of the central Andes, who objected to the destruction of their mummies and idols. Considering this destruction to be sacrilegious, bringing natural disasters and diseases, these Inca rebels returned to their ancient beliefs in the 1560s. Their action provoked a stern response from the viceroyalty of Peru, which worked vigorously over the next decade to eliminate the movement.

By 1549 in Brazil and 1572 in Spanish America, priests from the Jesuit order arrived and quickly became influential. Emphasizing similarities between native belief systems and Catholicism, as they did in China, they defended their Amerind followers against many who wished to enslave them. As did the other orders, the Jesuits grew prosperous through their access to native labor. The Church thus became wealthy and earned the resentment of colonial elites. In a land without a banking system, the Church became the principal source of funds for agricultural or commercial investment. It also became the largest property owner in the Western Hemisphere and a powerful manufacturer of pottery, fabrics, and leather goods.

The Plaza de Armas in Cuzco, Peru, displays 16th-century Spanish colonial architectural style.

Education in the colonies was handled exclusively by the Church. It operated all primary and secondary schools, educated Amerinds as part of the conversion process, and founded institutions of higher education such as the Universities of Mexico (Mexico City) and San Marcos (Lima), both established in 1551. In Brazil, however, the Portuguese Church did not establish a university until the nineteenth century. Before that, Brazilians seeking a university degree had to pursue it in Europe.

Religious orders for women expanded during the colonial period and played a major role in social and economic life. Convents attracted Spanish women who wanted to manage their own affairs, obtain a good education, and live lives of piety and service. Some women entered convents in order to escape the burdens imposed by husbands and children, or to lead well-protected lives. Most, however, took their vows seriously and contributed greatly to colonial life. Much more important in Spanish than in Portuguese America, convents owned substantial properties, provided funds for investment, and cultivated literary and artistic pursuits. Through its male and female orders, its strong belief in the importance of its work, and its active involvement with Amerinds, the colonial Church exercised a powerful influence over Iberian America.

Society in the Iberian Empires

What role did race play in the Iberian-American empires?

The people of Spain and Portugal were predominantly white, although a few Iberians were of African descent. But Spanish and Portuguese America contained a great many racial and ethnic groups, and in the Iberian empires a new social order emerged.

THE IBERIAN-AMERICAN SOCIAL HIERARCHY   At the top of the social ladder were white Spaniards and Portuguese, who tended to consider free people of other races as undesirable **mestizos** (*mes-TĒ-zōs*). Mestizos were people of mixed descent, often the result of unions between the invading Iberians—almost all of whom were male—and Amerinds. Children born from Iberian-African unions were termed **mulatto**. Only 5 percent of these unions were marriages, and children born outside of marriage were discriminated against. In Spanish America, whites excluded such people from artisan guilds in the 1540s, from the priesthood in 1555, and from any position carrying with it the possibility of social advancement. Children of mixed race were not, of course, exclusively the product of Iberian-Amerind or Iberian-African unions; Amerinds and Africans interacted as well. The result has been a racial mixture found nowhere else on earth.

As time went on, increasing numbers of Africans were imported to make up for the high death rate among slaves. The Spanish and Portuguese did not encourage slave family formation, as it proved far less expensive to buy and transport Africans than to raise African children to adulthood. Male and female slaves were customarily housed separately. Slaves performed all sorts of physical labor and menial services, ranging from domestic chores and handicrafts to the difficult and life-shortening occupations of miner and field hand.

Iberia had long had slaves, both from Islamic areas and from sub-Saharan Africa, and neither Spaniards nor Portuguese considered black Africans a slave race. For Iberians, enslavement was a matter of social class or wartime misfortune, and it was possible for slaves to purchase their freedom. Still, slavery was a brutal, degrading institution, and even those able to buy their way out of it found their lives severely restricted. Many officials and most Iberians treated all Africans as slaves, even if they were legally free.

Africans, free or unfree, lived on the margins of society in the Iberian empires, as did Amerinds. Africans were subjected to a superficial assimilation, and they hid their culture and customs away from the view of whites. Amerinds converted to Catholicism in large numbers, but most proved less adaptable than Africans to the Iberian colonial way of life. Thus, many Spaniards and Portuguese valued Africans over native peoples as workers.

In their own villages, however, Amerinds maintained independent, largely self-sufficient lifestyles based on their traditional social structures. Spaniards and Portuguese forced Amerinds to work through labor exchanges, in which Amerind villages were compelled to provide a specified number of adults for forced labor for a specified number of days each year. Amerinds adapted themselves to market structures and unwillingly interacted with the Iberian agricultural world. But they played little or no role in colonial town or city life, leaving skilled labor to mestizos and free Africans.

Social class in Iberian America was not based primarily upon skin color, although race was certainly an important factor. Portuguese and Spanish societies were organized according to a European structure of three estates: clergy, nobility, and commoners. The upper levels were reserved for high-ranking bishops and nobles, although Spanish colonial nobles tended to be lower-ranking dignitaries who had earned their ennoblement through military service during or after the Spanish conquests in America. The highest-ranking Spanish nobles had no motivation to go to America, except occasionally as a viceroy or general.

Colonial nobles distinguished themselves from commoners largely by their ownership of great estates. On those lands the nobles built lavish manor houses and presided over large numbers of laborers, servants, and slaves. Most Spaniards in America, of course, were commoners, and they earned their livings as shopkeepers, clerks, overseers, doctors, lawyers, notaries, accountants, merchants, craftsmen, or manual laborers. Some were wealthy, others were poor, but all were European in origin.

Mestizos, excluded from many lines of work, often had to make their living by their wits and skills. By the early 1600s, many had found niches as silversmiths, wheelwrights, tailors, and carpenters, but most worked as servants or unskilled laborers. Free

A Spanish-American family of mixed races. The man is European, the wife is African, and the child is mulatto.

Africans and Amerinds were even less fortunate. Constrained by descent and skin color, they could never move into the commoner class.

Among whites of Iberian descent, one additional distinction was made—between peninsulares (*pehn-ihn-soo-LAH-rāz*) and criollos (crē -YŌ-yōs). **Peninsulares** were white people born in the Iberian Peninsula (hence their name). They monopolized the highest offices in church and state and looked down on **criollos**, white people born in the Western Hemisphere. The names of these groups varied in Portuguese America, but the principle remained the same. The distinction arose with the efforts of Iberian kings to fill the most important positions in their empires with men of social stature whom they knew well. But over time, peninsular status came to be required even for midlevel colonial positions, and eventually the poorest Iberian-born newcomer considered himself the social superior of people whose families had been born and prospered in America for generations. This unfair treatment angered criollos, alienating many who might otherwise have remained loyal to their king but who later gladly joined independence movements.

THE ROLE OF GENDER   Gender distinctions were particularly evident in the Iberian colonial economy. Elite white women usually married, raised large families, and as widows administered the estates of their late husbands. But they could not engage in professional or commercial activity, and those who were frustrated by patriarchal restrictions frequently entered convents in order to gain limited autonomy. Middle- and lower-class white women worked at a wide variety of occupations, including spinning thread, taking in laundry, sewing, peddling goods, selling food, and serving as free domestics in the homes of the elite. Amerind women dominated the town marketplaces as food vendors. Free African women were restricted to domestic service and cooking in inns and marketplaces. Most free women performed some type of paid labor during much of their lives. Survival in Iberian America below the level of the elites was not easy, and women's incomes, however meager, were badly needed.

Amerinds and Europeans in North America

19.4 **Describe the impact on Amerind peoples of the European settlements in North America.**

Before the sixteenth century, the peoples of North America were largely isolated from the rest of the world. Influenced only by occasional trade with Mesoamerican cultures that flourished to their south, the numerous tribes and nations of North American Amerinds developed distinctive cultures, values, beliefs, and institutions, without having to deal with outside interference.

Then, in the sixteenth century, European explorers began to map the continent's coastlines and rivers, looking for gold and a passageway to Asia. In the seventeenth century, having found neither, Europeans started settling in North America, exploiting its resources and farming its lands. In the process, the intruders displaced the Amerinds, whose numbers were already diminished by European diseases.

Coalitions and Contacts

North of Mexico there were no great settled empires like those that existed in the Eastern Hemisphere. Most North Americans lived in village-based societies that rarely included more than a few thousand people, and even the larger nations probably numbered only in the hundreds of thousands. Usually these societies were ruled by powerful kings or chiefs who exercised religious and political authority. They

What was the nature of the Haudenosaunee League of Five Nations?

presided over rituals aiming to establish harmony with the spirits of nature, and over councils made up of prominent warriors and advisors.

Occasionally some societies combined for protection but rarely surrendered their autonomy. In the 1500s, for example, the Haudenosaunee (*HOW-din-ō-SAW-nā*) people of what is now upstate New York organized themselves into a **League of Five Nations**, later called the Iroquois (*EAR-uh-kwoy*) Confederacy. According to oral tradition, a legendary figure called the Peacemaker, along with a mighty chief known as Hiawatha, persuaded regional leaders to end their constant warfare and join together for the common good. But the League, despite an intricate governance system, was more an alliance than a union: each of its five members (Seneca, Cayuga, Onondaga, Oneida, and Mohawk) remained a sovereign nation.

North American Amerinds were politically divided and culturally diverse, but they were not isolated from each other. Using the continent's extensive river systems, they could attack their enemies, travel to distant hunting and fishing grounds, conduct long-distance trade, and maintain a network of contacts with other societies.

Through contacts with Mexico, some North Americans knew that there was a powerful, wealthy empire to their south. They could not know, however, that there existed across the ocean mightier and wealthier empires, whose warriors carried weapons against which the Amerinds had no defense and diseases against which they had no immunity. Unlike Asians, Africans, and Europeans, who constantly feared conquest by more powerful neighbors, North Americans did not anticipate the catastrophe to come.

The Coming of the Europeans

Why did various European states send expeditions to North America?

Not long after the first voyage of Columbus, Europeans looking for a new route to Asia began arriving in North America. In 1497 Italian mariner Giovanni Caboto explored the northeast coast, staking a claim for his English employers, who called him John Cabot. In 1500 Portuguese explorers reached Newfoundland; soon fishermen from Portugal, England, and France were fishing the cod-rich waters off the northeastern banks. They also made contact with coastal Amerinds, who proved willing to trade food and furs for European trinkets and tools.

In the following decades, while the Spanish conquered the Aztecs and built an empire in Mexico, French and English explorers farther north found neither gold nor a climate in which sugar would grow. Lacking such financial incentives, Europeans in the sixteenth century made little effort to colonize the north.

After 1600, however, as the French, Dutch, and English challenged the dominance of Spain, Europeans began to establish permanent settlements in North America. Enchanted by a voyage up the Saint Lawrence River in 1603, French explorer Samuel de Champlain helped start a small colony in Acadia (now Nova Scotia) the next year and founded a settlement at Quebec in 1608. Eventually he established good relations with the region's Huron Amerinds, using French forces and firearms to help them defeat their Iroquois foes. He also helped the Hurons develop a profitable trade in furs. French fur traders followed, as did soldiers who fought the Iroquois, Jesuits who spread Christianity, and explorers who traveled the Great Lakes and the Mississippi River. By century's end the French had claimed these regions as a colony called New France (Map 19.5), based mainly on the fur trade with the Amerinds, most of whom were unaware that their lands were now supposedly subject to someone called the king of France.

Meanwhile other Europeans were arriving. In 1607 about a hundred hearty Englishmen, searching for gold and adventure, founded an outpost called Jamestown (named for King James I)

A 1607 map of the northeast coast of North America, drawn by the French explorer Samuel de Champlain.

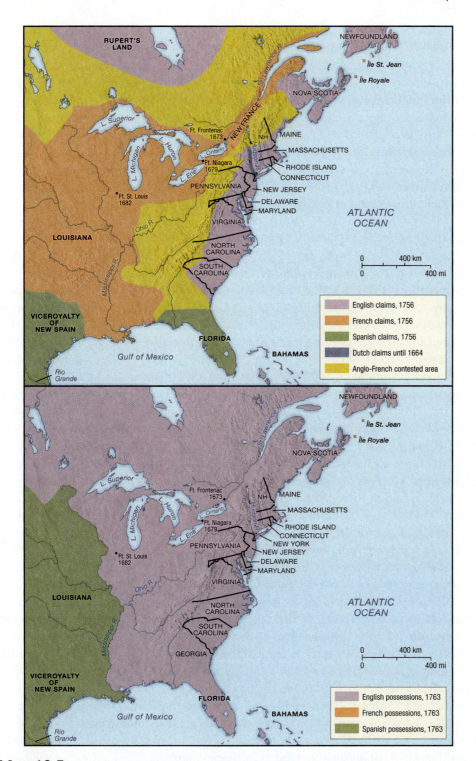

Map 19.5 EUROPEAN EXPLORATION AND COLONIES IN NORTH AMERICA, 1607–1763

European intrusion into North America caused competition for territory, both among European nations and with Amerind peoples. The French, Dutch, and English maneuvered for advantage in what is today the northeastern United States, while the Spaniards amassed massive holdings with minimal opposition from other Europeans. Note that the English colonies of New Hampshire, Massachusetts, Connecticut, Pennsylvania, Virginia, and North Carolina had no western borders; theoretically, each of them claimed land running all the way to the Pacific Ocean. Amerinds adopted a variety of strategies to counter the intrusions, including collaboration, alliance-building, and outright opposition. How did these conflicting European claims and Amerind strategies shape the development of North America?

in a region they knew as Virginia (named for Elizabeth I, the "Virgin Queen"). In 1609 Henry Hudson, sailing for the Dutch, traveled up the great river that now bears his name, seeking a new passage to Asia. He found no such route but did discover a region rich in furs. In the 1620s the Dutch founded the colony of New Netherland, which four decades later was seized by the English and renamed New York. In 1620 about 50 self-styled "Pilgrims" and 50 other English voyagers arrived at a place they named Plymouth, in a region soon called New England. Within a few decades, thousands of other English Puritans, seeking religious freedom, had joined them in forming a Massachusetts Bay Colony. Other English religious groups followed: Catholics created a Maryland colony in the 1630s, and Quakers founded Pennsylvania in the 1680s. By 1700 there was a string of English colonies along the Atlantic coast.

Disease and Demographic Decline

The coming of the Europeans brought disaster to the North American Amerinds. Like their Spanish rivals to the south, the French, Dutch, and English brought deadly diseases to which the Amerinds had no immunity. Europeans also brought agricultural techniques involving large farm animals, metal tools and plows, and crops that required the clearing of huge tracts of forest. With a concept of possession that let individuals claim land parcels as their property and exclude all others, they constantly expanded the amount of land under cultivation. Over time these practices, combined with growing numbers of European immigrants, destroyed the Amerinds' way of life.

At Jamestown, for example, the colonists at first related well to the local Powhatan (*POW-uh-TAHN*) peoples, who provided the newcomers with corn, meat, and fish that helped the colony survive. But as more settlers arrived from England and the Powhatans were ravaged by European diseases, the relationship changed. The peoples clashed, the Amerinds attacked, and the English responded by seizing Powhatan lands. Then, rather than planting food, the colonists grew tobacco, which Amerinds had taught them how to cultivate, and shipped it for sale to England, where smoking became the rage. Within decades the whole region was covered by tobacco plantations, and surviving Amerinds were forced off their lands.

At Plymouth the colony initially survived with the aid of Massasoit (*mass-uh-SŌ-it*), chief of the Wampanoag (*wahm-puh-NŌ-ug*) nation, who in 1621 agreed to help the Pilgrims if they would support his people in battles against tribal foes. Soon, however, clashes occurred between the disease-ravaged Amerinds and growing English communities, which rapidly claimed increasing amounts of land for farms and used firearms when necessary to enforce their claims. In 1675, desperate to save the Wampanoag way of life, Massasoit's son Metacom (*MEH-tuh-kahm*), whom the colonists called King Philip, attacked the Europeans. A brutal war followed, during which the English slaughtered thousands of Amerinds and sold the survivors into slavery. After Metacom was captured and beheaded in 1676, the Plymouth colonists displayed his head on a pole for 25 years. "King Philip's War" effectively ended Amerind resistance, leaving most of New England in European hands.

To the West, the Dutch and English settlers brought tragedy and triumph to the Iroquois Confederacy. On one hand, as elsewhere, the colonists brought disease, such as a smallpox epidemic that killed perhaps half the Iroquois population in the 1630s. On the other hand, the Dutch and English gave the Iroquois firearms to help them fight Hurons and French, enabling the Confederacy to carve out an empire extending from the Hudson River to the Great Lakes.

Similar events occurred elsewhere along the coast. Sometimes Europeans allied with Amerinds to fight common foes, and sometimes Europeans slaughtered Amerinds or drove them off their lands. Sometimes the Amerinds held off the Europeans for awhile, but in the long run their way of life collapsed in the face of European diseases, European weapons, and the spread of European settlement.

How and why did the coming of the Europeans devastate North American Amerinds?

The English Captain John Smith is condemned by a Powhatan chief.

The Columbian Exchange

19.5 Explain the advantages and disadvantages of the Columbian Exchange.

The initial contact between European and American civilizations involved not only conflict and conquest but also connection. Because the two hemispheres had been separated from each other since the submersion of the Bering land bridge more than 10,000 years earlier, many varieties of living things had developed in each hemisphere that were totally unknown in the other. The Eastern Hemisphere had wheat, grapes, horses, cows, sheep, goats, and pigs; the Western Hemisphere had potatoes, tomatoes, maize, cacao, and tobacco. When people from the two hemispheres encountered one another, their connections involved an interchange of crops and animals. In reference to Christopher Columbus, scholars call this process the Columbian Exchange.

Some exchanges of crops improved the quality of life in both hemispheres. The impact was immediately obvious in the Western Hemisphere. Before long wheat and grapes were being grown for the first time in the New World, to make the bread and wine that were central to the European diet and religion. Farm animals brought in by the Iberians provided transport, labor, and food, and they flourished in the Americas.

For the Eastern Hemisphere, corn (maize), potatoes, tomatoes, peanuts, and manioc (*MAN-ē-ok*)—a starchy root plant, now grown widely in Africa and Brazil, also called *cassava* or *tapioca*—proved hardy and rich in nutrients. Eventually becoming staples in Europe, Africa, and Asia, they later helped foster a global population explosion. Other American plants, like cacao (the basis for chocolate) and tobacco, were also sought by people around the world.

Microorganisms were also part of the Columbian Exchange. Syphilis, for example, a debilitating venereal disease that first showed up in southern Europe in the 1490s, was probably introduced by sailors who returned from the Western Hemisphere. But the exchange of diseases proved far more devastating for the Amerinds. Smallpox, measles, and chicken pox, to which most Europeans had been subjected as children and thus developed immunities, ran rampant through unprotected Amerind populations. About 30 percent of children and 90 percent of adults who came down with smallpox died. As a result, Amerind farming was interrupted, social structures shattered, villages depopulated, and entire regions abandoned. Smallpox weakened Aztec and Inca resistance to the Spaniards. All through the Spanish possessions in the Western Hemisphere, smallpox and measles ravaged Amerind communities off and on throughout the sixteenth century.

There are no reliable statistics on pre-1492 Amerind populations, but scholars estimate that the Americas contained between 15 million and 125 million people. In 1600, Spanish estimates indicated a population of one million Amerinds in the viceroyalty of New Spain (Mexico, Central America, and the Caribbean islands). It is clear that European diseases destroyed the overwhelming majority of the Amerind peoples in the greatest demographic catastrophe in history.

African women preparing manioc.

Chapter Review

Consequences and Connections

Tremendous consequences flowed from the Iberian overseas expansion of the fifteenth century. Under different circumstances, China might have discovered a sea route around Africa, or Japanese mariners might have sailed east and found the Pacific coastline of North America. But it was the Europeans whose curiosity and seamanship broadened human geographic knowledge and extended the horizons of the entire world. When they found previously unknown lands, they conquered and exploited them, motivated by a combination of greed and religious faith.

The clash of civilizations in the New World changed forever societies previously isolated from outside influences. Amerind societies largely collapsed in the face of conquest and disease. In their place the Iberians imposed new governance systems, religious beliefs, and social structures. They created a new economy, based on the cultivation of cash crops by imported slave labor. Finally, they transplanted their whole way of life, bringing plants, animals, foods, and diseases common in Europe but hitherto unknown in the Americas.

The political and economic impacts were immense. The Spanish and Portuguese, and later the French, Dutch, and English, were set on a course to become world powers, surpassing the great Asian and Islamic empires. The Atlantic Ocean soon replaced the Indian Ocean and the Mediterranean Sea as the center of world commerce. Eventually, Europe led the world in power and prosperity, in large part due to its exploitation of Africa and the New World.

But the most direct Iberian legacy was the new culture created in the conquered lands. The Spanish and Portuguese empires ended in the early 1800s, but their legacy lives on today. Though modern Latin American societies remain intensely hierarchical, the peoples of these societies, displaying a broad variety of outlooks and customs, celebrate this cultural synthesis as their unique contribution to the human experience.

Reviewing Key Concepts

Ask Yourself

1. Why did Portugal take the lead among European nations in promoting overseas expansion?

2. Why did the Iberian nations enslave Africans and transport them to their empires in the Western Hemisphere?

3. In what ways did the Spanish and Portuguese empires differ from each other? In what ways were they similar?

4. How did the conflicts between Iberian and American civilizations forge connections that changed them all?

Key Dates and Developments

1415	Portugal captures Ceuta from the Muslims
1415–1460	Expeditions financed by Prince Henry the Navigator
1489	Bartholomeu Días rounds the Cape of Good Hope
1492	Christopher Columbus reaches the Caribbean islands
1494	Treaty of Tordesillas divides the world between Portugal and Spain
1498	Vasco da Gama reaches India
1500	Pedro Alvares Cabral lands in Brazil
1516	Carlos I becomes king of Spain
1519–1521	The Cortés expedition overthrows the Aztec Empire
1519–1522	The Magellan expedition circumnavigates the globe
1524	Establishment of the Council of the Indies
1524–1532	Pizarro's three expeditions to Peru
1532	Capture of Atahuallpa at Cajamarca, Peru
1549–1572	The Jesuits arrive in the New World

Glossary

Abbasid Caliphate A succession of caliphs from the Abbasid family that overthrew the Umayyad Caliphate in 750 C.E.

Ahimsa Nonviolence toward all living things, a principle followed by the Jains of India.

Ahura Mazda In Zoroastrianism, the universal god of light who created human beings and gave them free will to choose between right and wrong.

Almoravids Berber followers of a militantly puritanical sect of Islam who believed that in order to conduct successful wars against unbelievers, Muslims must first purify their own souls.

Amerinds Anthropological term for American Indians, used to distinguish them from the Indians of South Asia.

Ancestor worship Veneration of a family's departed relatives and forebears, originally practiced in ancient China.

Andes Mountains The South American portion of a geologic formation running from Cape Horn north through Peru 11,000 miles to the north slope of Alaska and standing as a barrier to cultural connections across the South American continent.

Animism The belief that spirits exist that can either help or harm human beings.

Archaic Period An era in ancient Greece, from 700 to 500 B.C.E., during which city-states matured and population growth resulted in a shortage of farmland, leading Greeks to develop colonies around the Mediterranean world.

Aristocracy Rule by a class of well-born families.

Artistic realism An artistic style pioneered by Giotto, emphasizing detail, depth, and perspective to replace stylized rigidity with lifelike portraits.

Asceticism The practice of extreme self-denial and renunciation of all possessions.

Assassins A Shi'ite sect of killers known as *hashashin*, or "hashish users."

Augustus One who rules with majesty and grandeur; a title Rome conferred on Octavian.

Avesta The sacred text of Zoroastrianism.

Bantu The West African word for "people"; a group of related languages; tribes of West Africans who migrated throughout much of Africa over a number of centuries.

Bishops Christian Church officials presiding over districts known as dioceses.

Bloodletting A Mayan practice that connected the temporal and spiritual worlds and allowed departed spirits to materialize in the body of the bloodletter.

Bubonic plague A deadly contagion typically carried from rodents to humans by fleas.

Caesaropapism The vesting of all spiritual and political authority in a single person in the Byzantine Empire.

Caliph Successor of Muhammad, the Messenger of God.

Caliphate The territory governed by a caliph in the Islamic world.

Capitalism An economic system based on competition among private enterprises.

Castes Exclusive and restrictive hereditary occupational groupings, based on birth and ranked in hierarchical order.

Celibacy Abstinence from marriage and sex.

Chan (Zen) Buddhism A belief system teaching that meditation is the only path to enlightenment and stressing love of nature, simplicity of life, and individual self-discipline.

Chinampas Large latticework platforms of layered mud and lake plants floating on the surface of a Mexican lake and designed for cultivation of crops.

Chosen People The belief that the Jewish people were chosen by the one true God to be His people.

Circle of Equity The Sasanian Persian ruling concept that there can be no monarch without an army, no army without prosperity, no prosperity without justice, and no justice without the monarch.

Civil Service exams Chinese examinations requiring applicants for the state bureaucracy to demonstrate comprehensive knowledge of the Confucian classics.

Civilizations Very large complex societies, or regional groups of complex societies, with widely shared or similar customs, institutions, and beliefs.

Classical Period The era from 500–338 B.C.E., in which classical Greek philosophy, art, and drama flourished.

Code of Manu An early compilation of rules for virtuous conduct in India, probably written down between 200 B.C.E. and 200 C.E., prescribing the dharma for each Hindu caste.

Concubines Women who are not the main wife of a man (commonly a ruler) but are kept by him for sexual purposes.

Confucianism A system of thought in China based on humane conduct and familial respect.

Cosmic mission theory The Aztec theory that the sun must be nourished with an invisible elixir found only in beating human hearts.

Council of the Indies A board established by King Carlos I of Spain in 1524 to supervise every aspect of government in Spanish America.

Covenant A binding agreement between the God of Israel and his chosen people.

Criollos White people of European ancestry born in Spanish America.

Cultural adaptation The process by which hominids used their intellectual and social skills to adjust to their surroundings and improve their chances for survival.

Cultures Unique combinations of customs, beliefs, and practices that distinguish societies from each other.

Cuneiform Wedge-shaped writing developed by the Sumerians.

Daoism A naturalistic Chinese philosophy calling on people to live in harmony with nature.

Democracy Rule by the entire body of citizens.

Dharma The faithful performance of the duties pertaining to one's caste or station in life; such performance determines one's fate in the next life.

Dictator Originating in Rome, a term to characterize a tyrant.

Dowry A bridal endowment of money or property.

Dynastic cycle A four-phase cycle in China during which a dynasty emerges, rules well for a time, then rules poorly and is overthrown by a new dynasty.

Enterprise of the Indies Columbus's detailed plan for a westward maritime expedition to discover a shorter route from Europe to East Asia.

Eunuchs Castrated men who ran the ruler's palace and guarded his concubines.

Farming villages Small settlements of homes in a compact cluster, surrounded by lands on which the villagers raised food.

Fatimid An Egyptian Shi'ite dynasty that broke away from Abbasid rule and established a separate caliphate along the Nile River in 929.

Fatwa A legal opinion from the highest Islamic legal authority.

Five Pillars The basic religious tenets of Islam.

Foot binding A process in which the feet of Chinese girls were tightly wrapped with strips of cloth to make them sexually attractive to men.

Foragers Those who subsist by gathering wild plant foods and hunting wild animals.

Fresco Painting on walls when the plaster was still wet so the colors would penetrate it.

Golden Horde A large Mongol khanate that ruled over Russia and part of Central Asia in the thirteenth and fourteenth centuries.

Gothic architecture A style of European church architecture that produced impressive churches with pointed arches, towering walls, and stained glass windows.

Grand vezir Chief minister to the sultan of the Ottoman Empire.

Great Ice Age An immense stretch of time marked by frigid glacial stages when enormous ice masses called glaciers spread across much of the globe.

Great Khan The main successor of Genghis Khan, direct ruler of all Mongol lands in East Asia and overlord of all other Mongol realms.

Greco-Roman culture A blending of Roman culture with that of the Greeks.

Guerrilla warfare Raids by small roving bands of warriors that aim to disrupt armies rather than defeating them in open battle.

Guilds Associations formed to promote the commercial and professional interests of a particular occupational group, such as merchants, shoemakers, or weavers.

Hellenic The culture developed by Greeks.

Hellenistic The culture resulting from the blending of Greek, Persian, Egyptian, and Indian customs and societies.

Heresy A religious opinion contrary to accepted Christian Church doctrine.

Hieroglyphics Ancient Egyptian writing system based on pictographs.

Hominid A term scientists apply to human beings and their two-legged pre-human predecessors.

Homo sapiens "Wise human," a term designating the species that includes all modern people.

Humanism An outlook emphasizing the value of humans and their activities rather than focusing on faith and spirituality.

Iconoclasm The destruction of religious images known as icons in the Byzantine Empire.

Indo-European A family of languages from India, Iran, and Europe that share many common features.

Inquisition A judicial institution within the Christian Church that prosecuted people it identified as heretics.

Iranian plateau An arid plateau in southwestern Asia, the heartland of the ancient Persian Empire and present-day Iran.

Isma'ilis A branch of Shi'ite Islam claiming direct descent from Isma'il, the last publicly seen imam.

Janissaries Ottoman infantry composed of slaves who were Christian-born converts to Islam and were totally dependent on the sultan.

Jatis Regional subcastes in India, each identified with a certain trade, a specific locale, and often a particular god or goddess.

Jihad In Arabic, a "struggle" or "striving" by Muslims to uphold, defend, or spread their faith.

Kamikaze "Divine winds," storms that sunk Mongol invasion fleets that attacked Japan in 1274 and 1281.

Kana A writing system using simplified Chinese characters to create a phonetic Japanese alphabet.

Kanun State laws used by the Ottoman sultan without restriction from Islamic legal authority.

Karma One's fate or destiny in the next incarnation, as determined by performance of dharma in this life.

Khan A Central Asian regional overlord who exercised broad authority but was expected to consult regularly with a council of tribal leaders and gain its approval for his decisions.

Khanates Vast autonomous regions of the Mongol Empire.

Kinship group An extended family comprising grandparents, parents, siblings, aunts, uncles, cousins, and other relatives.

Knights Armed mounted warriors whose code of conduct entailed strict devotion to their overlords and to the Christian Church.

Legalism A Chinese philosophy advocating strict enforcement of stringent laws by a powerful authoritarian state.

The Lie In Zoroastrianism, a set of false doctrines propagated by Ahriman to lead people astray.

Long count calendar A complex calendar used by the Olmec and Maya peoples to date events according to cycles.

Madrasas Islamic schools.

Magi Persian scholar-priests who guarded Zoroastrian fire temples and compiled Zoroaster's ideas in a sacred text, the Avesta.

Magna Carta The "Great Charter" issued by King John of England in 1215, affirming nobles' rights and placing the king firmly under the law.

Mahabharata The world's longest epic poem, telling of a legendary war between related families in ancient India.

Mandate of Heaven A Chinese ruler's right to rule, provided that he governed justly and humanely.

Manors Large European landed estates owned by nobles and worked by peasant farmers.

Maratha A Hindu nationalist movement founded to resist Mughal rule in India.

Matriarchal Pertaining to a society or system in which women play dominant roles.

Matrilineal Pertaining to a society or system in which children trace their ancestry through their mother's lineage and inheritance descends through the female line.

Medieval Referring to the Middle Ages, the period from the fall of Rome through the fourteenth century in Europe.

Mercantilism A policy designed to create a condition in which a country's trading exports exceeded its imports in value.

Mesoamerica Territory that comprises Mexico and northern Central America.

Mestizos People of mixed descent in Iberian America.

Mitima The Inca practice of integrating conquered peoples through resettlement.

Moksha Liberation from the cycle of death and reincarnation in Hinduism.

Monarchy Rule by one person.

Monasticism A religious movement in which especially devout men and women withdrew from secular society to live in religious communities, where life was characterized by prayer and self-denial.

Monotheism Belief in a single god.

Mosque An Islamic house of worship.

Mount Olympus The highest mountain in the northwest Peloponnesus, believed by ancient Greeks to be the home of the twelve major Greek gods.

Movable type A method of printing using small metal blocks for each letter, arranged in a frame to print one page and then rearranged and reused to print other pages.

Mulatto A person born of a union between an Iberian and an African.

Mummification An elaborate process for preserving the bodies of prominent people after death.

Mystery religions Southwest Asian belief systems that addressed directly the problems of human weakness, divine redemption, and eternal life.

Nation A political community united by its people's sense of common heritage and culture.

Natural law A Roman vision of legal principles applicable to all societies regardless of time or circumstances.

Neanderthals An extinct group of large-brained hominids whose remains were first discovered in 1856 in Germany's Neander Valley.

Neolithic The period between 10,000 and 3,000 B.C.E., during which people developed better tools, domesticated plants and animals, cultivated crops, herded livestock, and established permanent settlements; also known as the New Stone Age.

Nirvana A state of infinite tranquility and peace.

Oligarchy Rule by a select few.

Paleolithic The period of the earliest and longest stage of human cultural development; also known as the Old Stone Age.

Papal primacy The doctrine that the pope has authority over the entire Christian Church.

Pastoral nomads People who raise livestock for subsistence and move occasionally with their herds in search of fresh grazing grounds.

Patriarchal A type of society dominated by males who served as heads of households and as community leaders.

Pax Mongolica The "Mongolian Peace" that advanced the flow of goods and ideas among Eurasian peoples.

Pax Ottomanica "Ottoman peace," the stability, prosperity, and peace that accompanied Ottoman rule.

Pax Romana "Roman peace," a time of stability and prosperity beginning in the reign of Caesar Augustus.

Peninsulares White residents of Spanish America who had been born in Spain.

People of the Book Islamic term for Jews and Christians, peoples who possess their own scriptural texts.

Polis The Greek word for city-state.

Polygyny The practice by which a man took more than one wife.

Polytheistic The practice of worshiping more than one god.

Pope The bishop of Rome, who headed the Christian Church and claimed to be the vicar, or agent, of Christ on earth.

Printing press A machine used to print pages set in movable type.

Purdah The seclusion of married women through their confinement to certain rooms of the house.

Pure Land Buddhism A belief system that claimed that humans could not achieve enlightenment by their own efforts and must rely instead on faith in the Buddha of Infinite Light who ruled the Western Paradise, or "Pure Land."

Quipu A piece of wood with knotted cords dangling from it that served the Inca as a means of sending messages.

Qur'an The holy book of Islam.

Race A concept that divides human beings into categories based on external characteristics, especially skin color.

Ramayana A great Indian epic poem based on Vedic oral traditions.

Reconquista The Christian reconquest of Iberia from the Muslims.

Republic   A flexible form of government by elected representatives.

Residencia   A thorough audit of a Spanish colonial official's conduct during his term of office.

Roman citizenship   A privilege conferred upon all adult males who, by birth or adoption, belonged to one of the three tribes that had founded the city of Rome; later expanded to include foreigners whose allegiance Rome wished to secure.

Samsara   The belief that each being has an eternal spiritual core which is reborn, or "reincarnated," into a new body after the old one dies.

Samurai   An army of Japanese warriors which provided military service to their lords and eventually became Japan's dominant class.

Sapa Inca   The Inca emperor, who claimed to rule by divine right because of his direct descent from Inti, the sun god.

Sati   A practice in India whereby a widow cremated herself on her dead husband's funeral pyre.

Satrapy   One of twenty provinces of the Persian Empire.

Schism   A division of the Christian Church into separate, competing churches.

Scholar gentry   An educated Confucian elite class supported by both official posts and large rural estates.

Scholasticism   A system of study combining Christian faith with ancient Greek philosophy, especially that of Aristotle.

Sea Peoples   Assorted marauders of unknown origins who ravaged eastern Mediterranean lands in the thirteenth and twelfth centuries B.C.E.

Semitic   A language family that includes Arabic, Hebrew, and the languages spoken by ancient Akkadians, Babylonians, and Phoenicians.

Senate   An advisory body composed of the most prestigious statesmen of Rome.

Seppuku   The practice of ritual suicide by which a defeated samurai warrior in Japan could restore his honor.

Serfs   Peasants bound to the manor and under the control of its lord.

Shah   The Persian word for king.

Shamanism   A form of religion in which spiritual leaders called shamans performed elaborate rituals to communicate with spirits, heal the sick, forecast the future, and influence events.

Shari`ah   The holy law of Islam.

Shi'ites   The minority of Muslims, following the "Party of Ali" (*Shi'at Ali*).

Shinto   The "way of the kami," a nature-based Japanese religion.

Shogun   The commander-in-chief of Japan's armed forces and the real ruler of the nation.

Sikh   An Indian belief system that blends and synthesizes Hindu and Islamic elements.

Silk Road   A network of trade routes named for the precious Chinese fabric it conveyed.

Simony   The sale of offices in the Christian Church.

Socratic dialogue   Rigorous questioning and analysis of ethical issues, as practiced by the Greek philosopher Socrates.

States   Territorial entities ruled by a central government.

Struggle of the Orders   A bitterly divisive social contest between patricians and plebeians in the Roman Republic.

Stupa   A massive domed edifice constructed of stone, used as a temple for Buddhist pilgrimage and worship.

Sufism   A mystic strain of Islam that advocates direct union with God through prayer, contemplation, and religious ecstasy.

Sunni   The majority of Muslims, claiming to follow the Sunna, the traditional practices of the Prophet.

Swahili   A language widespread in East Africa; the name of Bantu-Arabic East African culture.

Tahuantin-suyu   "Empire of the Four Quarters," the official name of the Inca Empire.

Tatar yoke   The era of Mongol domination of Russia.

Three Religions   A Vietnamese belief system blending Mahayana Buddhism, Confucianism, and Daoism.

Timurids   Descendants of Timur Lenk who established a dynasty in northern India.

Tlaxcallan Confederacy   An alliance of several city-states opposed to the Aztec Empire.

Treaty of Tordesillas   A 1494 agreement between the Portuguese and Spanish designed to divide the world between them.

Tribes   Large associations of villages, bands, or clans that share a common language and often a common leader.

Tyranny   The illegal seizure of power by someone who had no right to exercise it.

Umayyad Caliphate   A succession of caliphs from the Umayyad family that presided over nine decades of Islamic expansion.

Umma   A purely Islamic community.

University   An educational institution in which scholars from various fields helped students become experts and then granted them degrees to certify their expertise.

Upanishads   Philosophical and religious texts composed by learned writers over many centuries, beginning in late Vedic India.

Varnas   Classes in Aryan Indian society, based on the functions fulfilled by their members.

Vassals   Subordinate warlords who swore allegiance and pledged military service to a higher lord.

Vedic   The culture of Aryan India.

Vernacular literature   Literature written in the everyday language spoken by common people.

Viceroy   "Vice-king," an official responsible for the execution of the monarch's orders in a large subdivision of the empire or realm.

Xiongnu   Warlike Turkish nomads from the Central Asian steppes who threatened China from the north.

Yin and yang   A Chinese principle emphasizing the balancing and blending of natural forces.

Yoga A school of classical Hindu philosophy emphasizing meditation and self-knowledge.

Zen (Chan) Buddhism A belief system teaching that meditation is the only path to enlightenment and stressing love of nature, simplicity of life, and individual self-discipline.

Ziggurats Massive brick towers that ascended upward in a series of tiers, typically topped by shrines that could be used for religious ceremonies.

Zoroastrianism A Persian belief system including the concepts of free will and a Last Judgment.

Credits

Photo Credits

Chapter 1: p. 1, Heritage Image Partnership Ltd/Alamy; p. 3, Howard S. Friedman/Pearson Education; p. 4, Visual Arts Library (London)/The Art Gallery Collection/Alamy; p. 8, Riedmiller/Caro/Alamy; p. 14, Library of Congress, Prints & Photographs Division, [LC-DIG-ppmsca-02937]

Chapter 2: p. 19, Maya Alleruzzo/AP Images; p. 22, INTERFOTO/Fine Arts/Alamy, p. 23, Brian Delft/DK Images, p. 32, Peter Anderson/DK Images; p. 34, N Mrtgh/Shutterstock, p. 35, Lisa/Shutterstock; p. 37, Ashmolean Museum/Mary Evans/The Image Works

Chapter 3: p. 43, Andy Crawford/National Museum, New Delhi/DK Images; p. 46 (t), Larry Burrows/Time & Life Pictures/Getty Images; p. 46 (b), Seal depicting a mythological animal and pictographic symbols, from Mohenjo-Daro, Indus Valley, Pakistan, 3000-1500 BC (stone), Harappan / National Museum of Karachi, Karachi, Pakistan/The Bridgeman Art Library; p. 48, V&A Images, London/Art Resource, NY; p. 52, Richard Ashworth/Robert Harding; p. 60 (t), Scala/Art Resource, NY; p. 60 (c), Werner Forman/HIP/The Image Works; p. 60 (b), Gary Ombler/DK Images

Chapter 4: p. 64, Fotosports Creative/Newscom; p. 67, Eddie Gerald/DK Images; p. 68, akg/Bildarchiv Steffens/Newscom; p. 69, Richard Swiecki/Royal Ontario Museum/Corbis; p. 71, Jian Chen /Stock Connection Blue/Alamy; p. 72, North Wind Picture Archives/Alamy; p. 73, Library of Congress, Prints & Photographs Division [LC-USZ62-44791]; p. 75, Olexiy Voloshyn/Fotolia; p. 77, bjdlzx/E+/Getty Images; p. 81, Hu Weibiao/Panorama/The Image Works; p. 83, Dave King/DK Images

Chapter 5: p. 85, Josemaria Toscano/Shutterstock; p. 87, Phil Degginger/Alamy; p. 90, Gunter Marx/Dorling Kindersley; p. 93, Otis Imboden/National Geographic Creative; p. 95, Danny Lehman/Terra/Corbis; p. 98 (t), Bildarchiv Preussischer Kulturbesitz/Art Resource, NY; p. 98 (b), Mike Peters/Pearson Education; p. 99, Tan Yilmaz/Flickr/Getty Images; p. 103, Werner Forman/HIP/The Image Works

Chapter 6: p. 106, Heritage Image Partnership Ltd/Alamy; p. 112, Eugene Gordon/Pearson Education; p. 114 (t), RIA Novosti/Alamy; p. 114 (b), arazu / Fotolia; p. 119, Soprintendenza alle Antichita della Campania, picture by Raymond V. Schoder/Pearson Education U.S. ELT

Chapter 7: p. 124, Ancient Art & Architecture Collection Ltd/Alamy; p. 127, Antonio Gravante/Fotolia; p. 129, Image copyright © The Metropolitan Museum of Art. Image source: Art Resource, NY; p. 131, Library of Congress Prints and Photographs Division [LC-USZ62-44150]; p. 133 (t), Raymond Schoder/Pearson Education; p. 133 (b), Michael Holford/Pearson Education; p. 136, Gianni Dagli Orti/The Art Archive at Art Resource, NY; p. 138 (t), Pearson Education; p. 138 (b), Pearson Education, p. 143, Image Asset Management Ltd./Alamy

Chapter 8: p. 146, Rough Guides/Dorling Kindersley; p. 152, Museo Provinciale Campano, Capua/Pearson Education; p. 154, Werner Otto/Alamy; p. 155, Library of Congress Prints and Photograph [LC-USZ62-97803]; p. 157, zothen/Fotolia; p. 159, INTERFOTO/Alamy; p. 162 (t), Saint Mammas, 1494 (wall painting), Goul, Philippos (fl.1494)/Church of Timios Stavros (Holy Cross) tou Agiasmati, Platanistasa, Cyprus/Sonia Halliday Photographs/The Bridgeman Art Library; p. 162 (b), Bryan Busovicki/Shutterstock; p. 164, Paolo Cipriani/E+/Getty Images

Chapter 9: p. 166, Nick Fielding/Alamy; p. 170, Historimages Collection/uan Francisco Jiménez Martín/Alamy; p. 171, John Heseltine/Dorling Kindersley; p. 177, Stock Connection/SuperStock; p. 178, J. Bedmar/Iberfoto/The Image Works; p. 180, Werner Forman/Art Resource, NY; p. 183, DeAgostini/Getty Images

Chapter 10: p. 187, Pictures Colour Library/Travel Pictures/Alamy; p. 192, Byzantine School/The Art Gallery Collection/Alamy; p. 194, Dorling Kindersley; p. 197 (t), Michele Burgess/SuperStock; p. 197 (b), St. Michael (tempera on panel), Byzantine, (14th century)/Byzantine Museum, Athens, Greece/The Bridgeman Art Library; p. 198, Iberfoto/SuperStock

Chapter 11: p. 207, Ayazad/Shutterstock; p. 212, Eugene Gordon/Pearson Education; p. 212, Ms 206/1039 The Koran: Two pages decorated with medallions enclosing the lines of verse (vellum), Islamic School, (17th century)/Musee Conde, Chantilly, France/Giraudon/The Bridgeman Art Library; p. 215, Pearson Education, p. 222 (t), Magnus Rew / DK Images; p. 222 (c), Culture Club/Getty Images; p. 222 (b), Culture Club/Getty Images

Chapter 12: p. 225, Andrew Gunners/Digital Vision/Getty Images; p. 229, Dorling Kindersley; p. 230, Heritage Image Partnership Ltd/Alamy; p. 231, Heritage Image Partnership Ltd/Alamy; p. 233, Jon Spaull/Dorling Kindersley; p. 237, Dorling Kindersley; p. 240, Neil McAllister/Alamy

Chapter 13: p. 245, Scala/Art Resource ,NY; p. 245, Ariadne Van Zandbergen/Alamy; p. 246, Sabena Jane Blackbird/Alamy; p. 247, Ancient Art & Architecture Collection Ltd/

Alamy; p. 249 (b), Pearson Education; p. 250, Library of Congress [LC-DIG-ppmsca-04048]; p. 253, Pearson Education; p. 254, Prentice Hall School Division; p. 258, Brian Delft/Dorling Kindersley; p. 260, Vanessa Burger/Images of Africa Photobank/Alamy

Chapter 14: p. 262, Marka/SuperStock; p. 267, Eddie Gerald/Dorling Kindersley; p. 268, Linda Whitwam/Dorling Kindersley; p. 270, British Library/Robana/Hulton Fine Art Collection/Getty Images; p. 274 (t), Nigel Hicks/DK Images; p. 274 (b), Image Republic Inc./Alamy; p. 275 (b), The Metropolitan Museum of Art/Art Resource, NY; p. 275 (t), Dennis Hallinan/Alamy; p. 277 (t), From FAIRBANK. East Asia, 2E. © 1989 Wadsworth, a part of Cengage Learning, Inc. Reproduced by permission. www.cengage.com/permissions; p. 279, Christie's Images/Fine Art/Corbis; p. 280 (b), MJ Photography/Alamy; p. 282, Portrait of Muso Kokushi (1275-1351) Muromachi period (ink, colour and gold on paper), Japanese School (16th century)/Freer Gallery of Art, Smithsonian Institution, USA / Gift of Charles Lang Freer/The Bridgeman Art Library

Chapter 15: p. 284, Ms.Supp.Pers.1113. fol.44v Temujin has himself proclaimed Genghis Khan, his sons Ogodei and Jochi to the right, from a book by Rashid al-Din (ink and gouache on vellum), Persian School, (14th century)/Bibliotheque Nationale, Paris, France/The Bridgeman Art Library; p. 286, Barnabas Kindersley/Dorling Kindersley; p. 290, Tony Souter/Dorling Kindersley; p. 291, Copy of a fresco depicting Queen Thamar (1184-1213) and her father King Grigori III (1156-1184) (colour litho), Georgian School, (12th century) (after)/Bibliotheque des Arts Decoratifs, Paris, France/Archives Charmet/The Bridgeman Art Library; p. 293, Mongol archer on horseback, from seals of the Emperor Ch'ien Lung and others, 15th-16th century (ink & w/c on paper), Chinese School, Ming Dynasty (1368-1644)/Victoria & Albert Museum, London, UK/The Bridgeman Art Library; p. 295 (t), Samurai Takezaki charges Mongol invaders as shells explode overhead during the Mongolian invasions of Japan in 1274, illustration from 'Kokka' magazine, May 1921 (colour litho), Japanese School (13th century) / Bibliotheque des Arts Decoratifs, Paris, France / Archives Charmet / The Bridgeman Art Library; p. 296, The Granger Collection, NYC; p. 300, The Metropolitan Museum of Art / Art Resource,

NY; p. 303, Samurai Takezaki charges Mongol invaders as shells explode overhead during the Mongolian invasions of Japan in 1274, illustration from 'Kokka' magazine, May 1921 (colour litho), Japanese School (13th century) / Bibliotheque des Arts Decoratifs, Paris, France / Archives Charmet / The Bridgeman Art Library

Chapter 16: p. 307, Ian G Dagnall/Alamy; p. 310, Bettmann/CORBIS; p. 313 (t), Alistair Duncan/Dorling Kindersley; p. 313 (b), cynoclub/Shutterstock; p. 316, mpanch/Shutterstock; p. 320, Dorling Kindersley; p. 321, Rough Guides/Dorling Kindersley; p. 322 (b), Dorling Kindersley; p. 323 (t), akg-images/Newscom; p. 323 (b), Vaclav Zilvar/Fotolia; p. 324, Library of Congress Prints and Photographs Division [LC-USZ62-5476]; p. 325, Library of Congress Prints and Photographs Division [LC-USZ62-84269]

Chapter 17: p. 329, BnF, Dist. RMN-Grand Palais/Art Resource, NY; p. 332, Glen Allison/Stockbyte/Getty Images; p. 334, INTERFOTO/Alamy; p. 335, MARKA/Alamy; p. 338, Dorling Kindersley; p. 339, Image copyright © The Metropolitan Museum of Art. Image source: Art Resource, NY; p. 341, Christopher and Sally Gable/Dorling Kindersley; p. 342, LAM Collection/Alamy; p. 343, B.P.S. Walia/Dorling Kindersley; p. 346, Sam DCruz/Shutterstock

Chapter 18: p. 349, Pearson Education; p. 351, INTERFOTO/Alamy; p. 353, Scala/Art Resource, NY; p. 355, John Mitchell/Alamy; p. 357, Andy Crawford/Museum of Archaeology and Anthropology, Cambridge/DK Images; p. 358, James Sawders/Pearson Education; p. 360 (t), Spanish and Aztecs fighting/British Library, London, UK/© British Library Board. All Rights Reserved/The Bridgeman Art Library; p. 360 (b), Newberry Library/SuperStock; p. 361), Peter Dennis/DK Images; p. 362, The Art Archive at Art Resource, NY

Chapter 19: p. 369, Image Asset Management Ltd./Alamy; p. 374, Classic Image/Alamy; p. 375, DDAA/ZOB WENN Photos/Newscom; p. 378, Paul Bernhardt/Dorling Kindersley; p. 383, Shaun Higson b&w/Alamy; p. 384, Spaniard and Mulatta Produce a Morisca, c.1715 (oil on canvas), Juarez, Juan Rodriguez (1675-1728) / Breamore House, Hampshire, UK / The Bridgeman Art Library; p. 386, CORBIS; p. 388, IllustratedHistory/Alamy; p. 389, Archive Farms/Getty Images

Text Credits

Chapter 1: p. 2, maps.com; p. 5, maps.com; p. 6, maps.com; p. 10, maps.com; p. 11, maps.com; p. 17, maps.com

Chapter 2: p. 20, maps.com; p. 26, Hammurabi's Code of Laws. Translated by L. W. King. http://eawc.evansville.edu/anthology/hammurabi.htm; p. 39, Revised Standard Version of the Bible, copyright 1952 (2nd edition, 1971) by the Division of Christian Education of the National Council of the Churches of Christ in the United States of America. Used by permission. All rights reserved; p. 20, maps.com; p. 21, maps.com; p. 24, maps.com; p. 27, maps.com; p. 28, maps.com; p. 29, maps.com; p. 31, maps.com; p. 34, maps.com; p. 36, maps.com; p. 38, maps.com; p. 40, maps.com;

Chapter 3: p. 44, Davis, Nuel Pharr. 1969. Lawrence and Oppenheimer. New York: Simon & Schuster; p. 62, R.C. Dutt, translator (1899), The Ramayana: The Great Hindu Epic, Book I: The Bridal of Sita. http://hinduism.about.com/libray/weekly/extra/bl-ramayana1.htm; p. 44, maps.com; p. 45, maps.com; p. 47, maps.com; p. 53, maps.com; p. 54, maps.com; p. 56, maps.com; p. 58, maps.com

Chapter 4: p. 65, maps.com; p. 66, maps.com; p. 70, maps.com; p. 73, English translation copyright © 1998 by David Hinton from The Analects by Confucius. Reprinted by permission of Counterpoint; p. 74, James Legge, The Life and Teachings of Confucius (London, 1895), 67. p. 75, English translation

Index

Note: Page numbers followed by "f" refer to figures. Page numbers followed by "m" refer to maps.